THE PALACE OF MINOS : A COMPARATIVE ACCOUNT OF THE SUCCESSIVE STAGES OF THE EARLY CRETAN CIVILIZATION AS ILLUSTRATED BY THE DISCOVERIES AT

THE PALACE OF MINOS : A COMPARATIVE ACCOUNT OF THE SUCCESSIVE STAGES OF THE EARLY CRETAN CIVILIZATION AS ILLUSTRATED BY THE DISCOVERIES AT

Evans, Arthur, Sir, 1851-1941 and evans, Joan, 1893-

www.General-Books.net

Publication Data:

Title: The Palace of Minos : a Comparative Account of the Successive Stages of the Early Cretan Civilization as Illustrated by the Discoveries at Knossos
Volume: 1
Author: Evans, Arthur, Sir, 1851-1941 and evans, Joan, 1893-
Reprinted: 2010, General Books, Memphis, Tennessee, USA
Publisher: London : Macmillan
Subjects: Crete (Greece) – Antiquities
Greece – Civilization

THE PALACE OF MINOS : A COMPARATIVE ACCOUNT OF THE SUCCESSIVE STAGES OF...

PREFACE

THE excavations carried out by me from 1900 onwards on the site of Knossos, which brought to light the prehistoric Palace and its dependencies, were provisionally described in my somewhat full and copiously illustrated Reports in the Annual of the British School at Athens. Of the extent of the great building the view opposite, showing its remains from the East, and the Tell on which it stood, will give the best idea. It embraced fully six acres of ground.

But to the excavators, entering on what was then in fact a wholly unexplored world, the true relationships of the vast mass of new materials there brought to light could only be gradually elucidated. The finds in many cases necessarily came out piecemeal, and the lacunas in them were often only filled in after intervals of years. The ground-plan of the Palace itself and its successive stages could only be laboriously traced out by means of the cumulative results of successive campaigns. Every step forward was in the dark. There was no existing building of the class to serve as a guide, and logically consecutive exploration was impossible. It became evident, moreover, that, marvellously rich in materials as was the Palace Site of Knossos, its full story could only be told with constant reference to the supplementary light supplied by the parallel excavations which the discovery of the Palace of Minos' had called forth on other Cretan sites.

It seemed to be highly desirable, therefore, that at least a summary presentment of the results obtained by the excavations at Knossos should be set forth in a systematic fashion, as part of a single story and in close relation to the evidence obtained from these other sources. As a preliminary step, however, to any such undertaking it was necessary to elaborate a system of archaeological classification which should cover the vast field occupied by the prehistoric Cretan civilization. With this object I had already submitted to the Anthropological Section of the British Association, at its Cambridge Meeting in 1904, a preliminary scheme for classifying the successive phases of the prehistoric civilization of Crete, and for which I then ventured to propose the term Minoan. An outline of this scheme, by which this Minoan Civilization was divided into three main Sections

Early, Middle, and Late each with three Sub-Periods, was submitted by me to the Prehellenic Section of the Archaeological Congress at Athens in 1905 of which I was a President.

The proposed classification was favourably received by my colleagues, to several of whom I subsequently had an opportunity of explaining many points in detail on the scene of the excavations at Knossos itself.

Subsequent discoveries made some modifications of the original system desirable, and a sketch of this revised outline of classification was laid by me before the Archaeological Congress at Rome in October, 1912, where the idea of the present work received most welcome encouragement.

In the case of the Palace site of Knossos not only the immense complication of the plan itself, with its upper as well as its lower stories, but the volume and variety of the relics brought to light unrivalled perhaps in any equal area of the Earth's surface ever excavated have demanded for the working up of the material a longer time than was required for the actual excavations. To take a case in point, the painted stucco fragments could only be gradually pieced together as the result of long and laborious efforts. Prof. Droop, for instance, who kindly undertook the investigation of the remains of the Shield Fresco devoted a whole season to its reconstitution, and many weeks again were spent in a necessary revision of this. Mr. Theodore Fyfe, my architect in the earlier campaigns at Knossos, has done most brilliant work in illustrating the decorative designs of the wall-paintings, 2 while Mr. Noel Heaton has brought his expert chemical and technical knowledge to bear on a minute examination and careful analysis of the painted stucco itself. 3 The restoration of the painted stucco reliefs has also been a very lengthy task. In all this work the fine artistic sense and archaeological intuition of Monsieur E. Gillieron has been constantly at my disposal. The elaborate 1 Unfortunately, indeed, owing to the incompetent hands to which the editing of the Comptes rendus of the Congress was entrusted, the abstract supplied by me of the above communication appeared not only in a mutilated but in a wholly misleading form. The order of Periods was inverted, and I was made, for instance, to ascribe the chief masterpieces of Minoan Art to the last epoch of its decadence! I published therefore a corrected version of the proposed scheme, which appeared in 1906 under the title of Essai de classification des tpoues de la civilisation minuenne.

2 See his monograph on the Painted plaster decoration at Knossos Journ. of the Royal lust. of British Architects, vol. x, no. 4 (1902).

3 See Noel Heaton, B. Sc., F. C. S., The Mural Paintings of Knossos Journal of the Royal Society of Arts, Jan. 7, 1910. Minoan Lime Plaster and Fresco Painting, R. I. B. A. Journ., Sept. 1911, and compare his contribution to G. Rodenwaldt, Tiryns, vol. ii, p. 211 seqq.

architectural plans of Mr. Theodore Fyfe and Mr. Christian Doll have been the result of years of expert labour. On Mr. Doll mainly devolved the Atlantean task of raising and re-supporting the sunken elements qf the upper stories, and his practical experience of the anatomy of the building has been of service at every turn. Many drawings for this work have been gradually executed by competent artists like Monsieur E. Gillieron and his son, Mr. Halvor Bagge, and Mr. E. J. Lambert. 1 It will be seen that this process of reconstitution and restoration, carried out after the publication of the provisional Annual Reports, has given many of the most important finds a wholly new value, and a summary illustration of these fresh results will be found in the present work. Among the hitherto unpublished specimens of Knossian antiquities here represented, in addition to frescoes and coloured reliefs, are a whole series of ceramic and other relics, and plans, sections, and details bearing on the successive Minoan phases.

For an account of the actual course of the principal campaigns of excavation in the Palace area itself, which, as already explained, had to follow more or less experimental lines, and also for many minor details, readers may be referred to the above Reports published in the Annual of the British School at Athens from 1900 to 1905 inclusive. The results of the supplementary researches made on this site in the succeeding years, and notably in 1913, have, however, only to a partial extent seen the light, and that in a very abbreviated form. A fuller description of the Little Palace to the West, with a revised Plan, will be found in Vol. II of the present work, and, in addition to the adjacent houses such as the Royal Villa, the very important South House will be for the first time described. A summary account of the neighbouring cemeteries will be also given in a later Section and especially of the Royal Tomb of Isopata and of the important tomb of the Double Axes' more detailed descriptions of which have been already published by me in Arciacologia The object of the present work, as already stated, is, while correcting as far as possible erroneous impressions contained in the original Reports, not only to complete the actual materials, but to co-ordinate and systematize them in such a way as to present the discoveries at Knossos as 1 Coloured Plates in a fuller form will be issued in a separate Atlas.

2 See Archat-ologia, lix (1906), The Prehistoric Tombs of Knossos': I. 1 he Cemetery of Zafer Papoura; II. The Royal Tomb of Isopata: Ixv (1914), I- The Tomb of the Double Axes and associated group at Knossos.

part of a continuous story and as illustrating the course of the Periods into which I have ventured to divide the Minoan Age.

But for the proper setting forth of that story, comparative illustrations from other sources have been constantly necessary. Gaps in the Knossian evidence have thus been filled in, with the kind permission of my friends and colleagues who have excavated other Cretan sites. In the case of the Palace itself I have had constantly in view the parallel edifices explored by the Italian Archaeologists at Phaestos and Hagia Triada, the discoveries in which have been placed so freely at my disposal by their excavators, Professor Federigo Halbherr and Dr. Luigi Pernier. The town sites and their contents brought to light by Mrs. Boyd Hawes at Gourniil and by Prof. R. C. Bosanquet and Prof. R. M. Dawkins and their colleagues at Palaikastro, on behalf of the British School at Athens, as well as that of Zakro excavated by Dr. D. G. Hogarth with its remarkable hoard of Minoan sealings and the interesting researches of Prof. J. L. Myres in the votive sanctuary of Petsofa, have also supplied many valuable comparisons. Miss Edith Hall (Mrs. Dohan) has clone much to elucidate the sepulchral remains and cultural evolution of pre-historic Crete. To the Committee of the British School at Athens and to the Council of the Hellenic Society I am much beholden for their liberal permission to reproduce illustrations of these discoveries from the Annual and Journal. In the course of this work 1 have been constantly indebted to the kindness of the Director of the Candia Museum, Dr. Joseph Hatzidakis, who by his own excavations at Tylissos, Malia, and elsewhere has himself made such important contributions to our knowledge of Minoan times. In all this I have also to associate his colleague Dr. Stephanos Xanthudides, the Ephor General of Cretan Antiquities and fortunate Explorer of the early ossuary tholoi of Messara, and of the-Sepulchral Cave and later Sanctuary at Nirou Khani, N. E. of Knossos.

This fresh material from other sources has been specially helpful as regards the Early Minoan Age. The evidence regarding this, though continuous at Knossos, was more fragmentary in its nature than that relating to the Age of Palaces. Supplementary data of considerable interest have here been forthcoming from the Sepulchral Cave referred to, from the primitive 'tholos' ossuaries excavated by Professor Halbherr and Dr. Xanthudides, and from the early settlement at Vasiliki explored by the American archaeologist, Mr. Richard Seager. The full brilliancy attained by this Early Minoan phase of Cretan civilization was first revealed, however, by Mr. Seager's epoch-making discoveries in a cemetery of that Age in the little island of Mochlos. 1 Part of these excavations I was myself privileged to witness, and, thanks to Mr. Seager's great kindness, I have been enabled to make a large use of his materials in illustrating the Early Minoan Sections of this work.

It must, however, be clearly understood that the site of Knossos is the central theme of the present work. Not only am I able to speak at first hand about this, but the series of objects from that site is, on the whole, more complete than can be found elsewhere. Moreover, the stratigraphic evidence on which my whole system is grounded is here better ascertained and more continuous, going back in fact without a break to remote Neolithic times.

In attempting to set forth the characteristic products of the successive Minoan Periods it will be seen that I have not relied on a single category only, such as ceramic types indispensable as they are in this connexion. I have here clone my best to correlate these with other parallel branches of art so as to present a collective view of contemporary phenomena. Much, indeed, is lost by looking at one class of objects without taking constant count of the side lights thrown by other works of the same epoch. The clay and metal forms of vessels, for instance, are inseparably connected; ceramic designs at Knossos are seen to be largely the reflection of the decoration of the

Palace walls; and the history of the Greater Arts is well illustrated in a compendious form by the types on seals and gems. These latter objects indeed, so abundantly forthcoming from the soil of prehistoric Crete, have proved of special utility in the present work of classification, and in some respects fulfil the same function as coins at a later date. Closely allied, moreover, with the sphragistic category, especially in the Early and Middle Minoan Age, is what many will regard as the most important of Cretan discoveries, the evidence of the successive stages in the evolution of the Art of Writing, beginning with a rude pictography and advancing through a conventionalized hieroglyphic signary to a fully developed linear script, which itself shows an earlier and a later phase.

In the present work it is naturally impossible to give more than a conspectus of the successive forms of script. The earlier part of the subject

The excavations took place in 1908. The final publication was made in 1912 (Explorations in the Island of Mochlos, by Richard B. Seager. Published by the American School of Classical Studies at Athens. Boston and New York, 1912).

has been already dealt with in the first volume of my Scripta Minoa?- and the materials for the fulj publication of the clay documents of the two linear scripts A and B are already in an advanced stage of preparation. The special employment of Class A for religious purposes in the closing phase of the Middle Minoan Age is illustrated below, and some of the most important documents in the developed linear script B, from the Archives of the Later Palace, together with a summary account of its inner economy as illustrated by them, will be given in the concluding part of this work.

I have also felt that the view here presented of the Minoan Age, though based throughout all its earlier outlines on the Cretan discoveries, could not be adequately drawn out without some attempt to set forth its relation to the Mycenaean culture of Mainland Greece, of which, in fact, it supplies in an overwhelming degree the antecedent stages. Among the earlier contents, at least, of the Shaft Graves the finest objects are seen to be actually of Cretan importation and, in the absence of intact royal tombs, at Knossos, those of Mycenae are practically the sole repertory for the Minoan goldsmiths' work of that epoch. The results will surprise many. Few probably have yet realized how absolute is the dependence which these comparisons substantiate. In this work of comparison I am specially grateful for the helpful information supplied me by Dr. G. Karo, Director of the German Institute at Athens, who has made the subject of the Mycenaean relics a special subject of research, and whose friendly offices even the outbreak of the Great War did not interrupt. I am further indebted to his colleagues, Dr. Kurt Miiller and Dr. Gerhart Rodenwaldt, and to the kind facilities accorded by Dr. V. Stais, Director of the Athens

Museum. To Mr. A. J. B. Wace, the Director of the British School, I am also greatly obliged for much help at Athens as well as for the early communication of the results derived from his supplementary investigations at Mycenae.

The opportunity here offered has also been seized to bring into relief many new points of view, and to throw out suggestions regarding the genesis and evolution of various types. The Egyptian relations of prehistoric Crete have been particularly emphasized, and much fresh evidence has been brought forward as to the relations of Minoan civilization with that of the Nile Valley, with other parts of the Aegean world, and even with the further shores of the Ionian Sea and the Western Mediterranean basin.- 1 Oxford, Clarendon Press, 1909.

2 For more general views of the results of excavation in Crete and of the comparative place that they occupy, I need hardly refer to the luminous survey of the late Professor

On Egyptological matters I have received valuable assistance from my Oxford colleague, Mr. F. Ll. Griffith, while Professor Flinders Petrie, the late Dr. L. W. King and Dr. H. R. Hall of the British Museum, and Mr. C. C. Edgar, of the Cairo Museum, have supplied me with much required information.

In cases where the same conclusions may have been put forward by other investigators before the appearance of these pages, I can at least claim that my own views as here expressed have been independently arrived at through a continuous experience of the results of the excavations both at Knossos and on other Cretan sites. The writer has, therefore, some right to be allowed to set down his own conclusions, gradually formed, in the course of years, from a first-hand knowledge of the materials, without seeking to inquire at every turn whether similar opinions may have been already expressed in print in other quarters. Where I have been consciously indebted to the researches or ideas of others, I have, indeed, always endeavoured to express my acknowledgements. I was fortunate in securing the services of Dr. Duncan Mackenzie as my Assistant in the excavations, and my thanks are exceptionally due to him for the continued help that he has rendered to me at every turn in the course of the present work, and for his careful revision of the proofs. His special archaeological knowledge, particularly in the ceramic field, 1 is so widely recognized that it is with great satisfaction that I am able to record that in all main points in my scheme of classification he is in complete agreement with me.

In 1913, in order to decide various important problems regarding the building which remained to be elucidated, I undertook a supplementary campaign of excavation on the Palace site, in the course of which I executed about a hundred fresh soundings beneath the floors.

Difficulties and preoccupations, however, caused by the Great War delayed the publication of this work, the materials for which were already in an advanced state in 1914. Since then, moreover, a vast amount of new R. M. Burrows in The Discoveries in Crete and their bearing on the History of ancient Civilisation, London (John Murray), 1907; to Professor Rend Dussaud's Civilisations prehelleniques dans le bassin de la mer Egee, Paris (Geuthner), 1914; or to the learned series of contributions by Dr. H. R. Hall, of which the last are contained in his History of the Near East (Methuen and Co.), London, 1919.

1 Two monographs on Minoan pottery have been published by Dr. Mackenzie in the Journal of Hellenic Studies, vols. xxiii, pp. 152-205; xxvi, pp. 243-67. See too his comparative studies on the relations of Crete and Melos in Excavations at Phylakopi, pp. 238-72, and on Cretan Palaces and the Aegean Civilization, in B. S. A., XI-XIV.

evidence has accumulated, partly due to the gradual completion of fuller architectural plans of the Palace itself and its contiguous buildings, and to the laborious reconstitution, already referred to, of the frescoes and other remains, partly to the results of fresh excavations, such as those which Mr. Seager and the Cretan Ephors as well as others in Mainland Greece were able to pursue, and all this has had to be assimilated with the data already collected. This further supplementary process, since it was indispensable in order to bring the work up to date, has necessitated the repeated breaking up and remodelling of the large part of this book that was already in print, and the insertion of a whole series of new figures and plates. In order, moreover, to obtain a fuller knowledge of the fresh materials and for the further investigation of certain doubtful points, I commissioned Dr. Mackenzie to visit Crete in the Autumn of 1920, and the valuable information that he was able to obtain for me on the spot is also incorporated in this work.

The present Volume, prefaced by a general sketch of the Course of Minoan Civilization, is devoted to a brief survey of the Neolithic stage and of the Early Minoan phases, followed by an account of the Palace in the Middle Minoan Age. It is hoped that the Second Volume may cover the history of the Later Palace and with it the First and Second Periods of the Late Minoan Age. A Third and supplementary Volume on a smaller scale will include a short history of the site in the concluding Late Minoan part of the Age, together with a tabular view of the Nine Minoan Periods, a general index, and Plans and Sections of the Palace in separate folding sheets and in a more elaborate form than has been yet attempted.

ARTHUR EVANS.

YOULBURY, BERKS., NEAR OXFORD, June i, 1921.

PAGE

Pottery; Light on Dark Decoration; Beginnings of true polychrome technique; Cycladic Elements Pyxides and Marble Idols; Grotesque Vessels; Ivory Seals; Animal figures; Specimens from Ossuary Tholos of Platanos; Cylinders and Conoids; Meander and Labyrinth Pattern Sixth Dynasty Comparisons; Egypto-Libyan Button-seals Source of Cretan double sickle Types; Three-sided Bead-seals; Female potters and draught-player; Imitation of Egyptian draught-board sign (men); Leg Amulets; Burial Urns and Clay Cists Proto-Egyptian and Libyan Comparisons; Approximate dating of E. M. III.

THE MIDDLE MINOAN AGE THE FIRST MIDDLE MINOAN PERIOD (M. M. I) 5. M. M. I: (A) FOUNDATION OF KNOSSIAN PALACE.127 Age of Palaces begins; Traces of earlier foundation at Knossos; M. M. I elements of Palace at Knossos; Wall construction and analysis; Early signs on base blocks of enceinte parallel signary at Phaestos; Relations of Craftsmen's signs to Linear Script; Early Keep with walled pits; Insulae within fortified enceinte; Rounded angles of original W. block; Terracotta water-pipes; M. M. I stage at Phaestos; Early Pillar Basement at Knossos; Oval House, Chamaezi; Rounded angles of Knossian insulae compared: Foundation Walls of Palace; Ossuary Tholoi superseded by Cists; tendency towards individual interment; Clay sarcophagi and jars.

6. M. M. I: (B) THE PEAK SANCTUARY OF KNOSSOS, AND THE TOMB OF ZEUS 151

Cretan Cult of natural features; Specially prominent at beginning of Middle Minoan Age; Rock sanctuaries; Votive objects of Petsofa; Exploration of similar votive stratum on Summit of Juktas; Outer Temenos wall enclosing early settlement; Was it a City of Refuge? Inner shrine and Ash altar; Peak Sanctuary of the Early Palace Traditional Tomb of Zeus'; Gold Signet from Knossos illustrating early Baetylic Cult; Minoan

Magazines and great Pithoi; New stratigraphic evidence; Storage pits and cists; Ceramic types; Mature style of Barbotine decoration, combined with brilliant polychromy; Architectonic influences, and earlier Palace Style; Bull's Head and Ostrich Egg rhytons'; Imitations of Breccia Veining; Royal Pottery Stores Eggshell cups and bowls; Imitation of inlaid metal work; Arcaded fluting on cups at Knossos and Mycenae the Sacral S'; Egg-shell ware copies of vessels in precious metals of Royal Treasury; Originals from Shaft-Graves of Mycenae; Early ceramic imitations of Vapheio' Cups; Thorn-bossed bowl; Fine polychrome vase from Knossos with foliated scrollwork; Imported examples found at Phylakopi; Acme of polychrome decoration about middle of this Period; the M. M. II a Ceramic style.

12. M. M. II: (D) THE LOOM-WEIGHT DEPOSIT: LATER CERAMIC PHASE (b) AND REACTION OF WALL-PAINTING. 248

Basement Chambers N. of Domestic Quarter; Stratified contents; M. M. Ill remains in upper layers; Contents of lower Basements mature M. M. II; Loom-Weight I eposit Evidences of religious connexion; Miniature Shrine and votive vessels; Painted plaster decoration and plaster Cist; Ceramic characteristics of Deposit; The Palm Tree Jar; Lunate frieze on vessel; Imitations of painted plaster pattern; Architectonic origin of bands of disks; Mature polychrome style M. M. II: Stellate flowers with pointed petals; Pottery from latest M. M. II deposits at Phaestos parallel with that from I xom Weight area; Evidences of a contemporary catastrophe; Imported Minoan pottery at Kahun, c., in Egypt represents earlier and later M. M. II styles; Origin of foliate bands from flower chains; the Abydos Vase from Xllth Dynasty Tomb; Chronological conclusions.

PAGE 13. M. M. II: (E) THE HIEROGLYPHIC DEPOSIT: SEALINGS AND SEAL-

STONKS. 271

Advance in naturalistic design also affects glyptic works; Gem-impressions on Clay Sealings from Hieroglyphic Deposit; Attempts at portraiture Effigies attributed to Minoan Dynast and his Son; Naturalistic scenes on other seal-impressions; Types of M. M. II seals; Signets and prism seals with hieroglyphic formulas; Royal bead-seal; Advanced Hieroglyphic Script of Class B; Clay bars, labels, and tablets; Linearized sign groups; Numerals; Independent Evolution of Minoan Hieroglyphic script, aided by Egyptian suggestion; Hieroglyphic signary an epitome of early Cretan culture; Selected signs Saffron, Bee, Olive Spray, and Ship; Silphium-like figures compared with types on coins of Cyrene.

14. M. M. H: (F) EGYPTIAN MONUMENT AND RELATIONS.286

Diorite Egyptian Monument of User found in Palace Twelfth or early Thirteenth Dynasty date; Connected with Nome of Goddess Wazet (Aphroditopolite); Minoan intercourse with Egypt, uninterrupted to c. 1760; Approximate date of close of M. M. II; Cretan craftsmen employed for Pyramids of Illahun and Hawara; Egyptian religious influence on Crete; Sea-communications discovery of submerged pre-Hellenic port of Isle of Pharos; Colossal construction of harbour works; Estimate of Minoan and Egyptian factors in their execution; Port of Pharos visited by Menelaos; Question of Minoan ports of Crete; Considerable submergence on N. Coast; Ancient harbour and port town of Knossos includes Venetian port of Candia; Island of Dia; Minoan port of

Hagia Pelagia; Catastrophe at end of M. M. II synchronous with break-up of Egyptian unity; Perhaps symptomatic of wider movements in E. Mediterranean Basin.

15. M. M. II: (G) THE TOWN MOSAIC 301

Town Mosaic; Circumstances of discovery in M. M. Ill a filling material; Probably heirloom from M. M. II b Sanctuary; Ivory Draughtsmen in same deposit; Fragmentary remains of large Composition; Central feature towers and houses of fortified town; Associated features relating to land and sea; Warriors, ship and negroid figures; Fa9ades of Town Houses; Modern impression four- and six-paned windows; Architectural affinities with Terra-cotta Shrine and M. M. II construction; Sanctuary on Wall; The Warriors and their Arms; Figured representations more archaic than those of faience objects of Temple Repositories; Comparison with Chest of Kypselos; Libyan element in Composition Comparison of negroid heads with Jewel Relief; Plaques in shape of scales with Double Axe marks; Scales, Oriental Convention for rocks; Survivals on later Minoan rhytons' with Siege Scenes; Theme of the beleaguered City and Epic tradition.

THE THIRD MIDDLE MINOAN PERIOD (M. M. Ill) 16. M. M. Ill: (A) THE BEGINNING OF THE NEW ERA. 315

Epoch of Transition; Heralded by great catastrophe at end of M. M. II; Continuity of culture preserved but emergence of new elements; Possible Dynastic change; New linearized Script, Class A; Partial dislocations at Knossos; Close of Period well marked by stratified deposits and great Remodelling; Data from W. and E. wing contrasted; Great filling in on E. slope; Evidences of intermediate M. M. Ill phases; Line of delimitation between M. M. Ill and L. M. I more definite in pottery; Difficulties attending some of the greater naturalistic works such as wall-paintings and reliefs; Such can only be referred to a great Transitional Epoch; Importance of Spiral Fresco Deposit; Magazine of Medallion Pithoi and Corridor of Bays.

PARK 17. M. M. Ill: (B) THE DOMESTIC QUARTER 32-

Dramatic development of the Excavation discovery of Grand Staircase and Residential Quarter in great East Cutting; The Domestic Quarter; Preservation of Upper Stories; Work of Restoration; Halls of Colonnades and Double Axes; Quern's Megaron; Court of Distaffs; Alteration of Drainage System; Service Quarter and Staircase; Room of Stone Bench and Upper Hall of Double Axes; System above Queen's Megaron Bedrooms, Bath-rooms, and I atrines; Treasury of Shrine; The Grand Staircase of five flights, approached from Central Court; Tapering wooden columns their origin in primitive stone pillars; Low column hases; Use of Cypress wood; Evidence of fluted columns; M. M. Ill Construction: Timber framework of walls and windows; Important architectural equations supplied by area of Spiral Fresco; Chronological data structural core of Domestic Quarter M. M. Illrt; Existing superficial features mainly M. M. Ill 6 and Iate Minoan; Iassage East of Domestic Quarter Marbled and labyrinth frescoes; Egyptian Meander as House Plan; The Labyrinth and Minotaur at Knossos.

is. M. M. Ill: (C) NORTH-EAST BORDERS AND BASEMENTS OF M. M. Ill EAST HALL. 360

Northern Branch of Lower E.-W. Corridor; Columnar Lobby and Upper Story block; N. E. Room Submergence of M. M. II Magazines with Great Knobbed Pithoi;

Court of Stone Spout and M. M. Ill Wall; Earlier gypsum facade line of a N. E. Insula, running E.-W.; Presumed Stepway to E. Postern; Corridor North blocked in M. M. 1116 and converted to Magazine; So-called School Room; Enclave including Loom-Weight Basement; Its later M. M. Ill stratification; M. M. Ill Walls superposed here on M. M. II; Important Deposit with Spiral Fresco, Column bases, and painted stucco bas-reliefs of bull-grappling scenes; Comparison of fresco bands with decoration of tank in bull-catching scene on gem; Remains derived from M. M. Ill East Hall above; Drainage system of its Court Vertical ducts, stone drain-heads, and Conduit; Stone spout and blind well choked with M. M. Ill sherds; Substructures showing Plan of great East Hall.

19. M. M. Ill: (D) NORTH QUARTER AND ENTRANCE. 3X5

Continuation North of Upper Terrace Facade; The North-East Portico' through passage to Postern on the East; The Northern Quarter; Destruction due to Vicinity of I ater Town; In M. M. Ill, probably Workmen's Quarter; Signs of improved conditions in L. M. I; Discovery of Inlaid Draught-board; Fallen from Upper Floor connected with L. M. I East Hall, though probably M. M. Ill heirloom; Ivory Draughtsmen from border area; Description of Gaming Board postponed to later Section; The Corridor of the Draught-board and Stepway to Central Court; North-Eastern Hall and connected Store-rooms four-columned. Megaron; N. E. Magazines; North-Eastern Entrance; Its system probably linked with that of Northern Entrance; Built drain running to main Cloaca of N. Entrance; The Northern Entrance Passage: Narrowed in M. M. Ill, with Bastions on either side; M. M. Ill Masonry and Signs; Eastern line of Bastions later removed; Portico above W. Bastions, subsequent to this removal; Sally Port and inner (lateway: Bastion and Tower dominating outer Gateway; Approached by Roadway from West and from Harbour Town the Sea Gate of the Palace; Propylon and Guard-room; Extensive fortification of N. approach; Hall of Eleven Pillars probably Depot, with Loggia above; North Pillar Crypt M. M. Ill a Construction and Signs; Crypt of Columnar Sanctuary: Well of Greek Geometrical Period.

20. M. M. Ill: (E; NORTH-WEST BAILEY AND LUSTRAL AREA. 4 5

N. W. Entrance System scene of initiatory rites; N. W. Bailey and Temenos of Lustral Area: The Lustral Busin; Its Store-house or Treasury: Stratified deposit within Basin; Earlier and Later stages of M. M. Ill represented; Ritual vessels of PAGE

Clay and Stone from Basin; Stone Ewers; Inlaid limestone bowls their painted clay imitations; White-dotted Ware and other contemporary types; Moulded ears of barley on small jug; Pedestallecl Vases; Polychrome imitation of Egyptian Alabastron type; White dotted Ware M. M. Ill a; Discovery in same Deposit of Alabastron lid of Hyksos King, Khyan; Place of Khyan in Hyksos series; Pharaonized Dynast re-unites all Egypt; Predecessor of the Apepis; Chronological materials; Wide range of Khyan's Monuments; Approximate date of close of M. M. Ill a. Khyan's lid evidence of peaceful intercourse rather than of Conquest; Use of Alabastra in connexion with Lustral Basins.

21. M. M. Ill: (F) WEST PALACE REGION, AND DOUBLE AXE CULT. 423

Approach to Central Court from N. W. used by Votaries; Miniature Frescoes from Upper Sanctuary on this side; W. Porch Royal or Official entrance; Porch and Corridor in existing shape Late Minoan; W. Palace Section Tripartite division; Sanctuary and Treasure-house; Pillar Rooms Crypts of Columnar Sanctuaries; Significance of Double Axe Marks; Evidence supplied by S. E. House of M. M. Ill date; Its Pillar Room and Ritual Table; Double Axe sign on pillar and pyramidal base of Axe; Vessels of offering and Sacral Knot of ivory; Sacral Knots in Minoan cult; Minoan Tartan; Early Cave in corner of Pillar Crypt; Pillar with Double Axe sign in Palace of Malia; Discovery of Sanctuary of Niru Khani colossal Double Axe heads; Bases of Double Axes in Knossian Palace; Ritual from Sarcophagus of H. Triada; Evocation of the Dead; Tomb of Double Axes' at Knossos; Columnar sanctuary above Pillar Room at Knossos; Bases of fallen Columns; Fragments of architectural frescoes found beneath later Cists; Fagade of Columnar Sanctuary of Double Axes; Axes inserted in Columns; Comparison from Mycenae; Use of Variegated materials; Frescoes from Shrine above; Double Axe central feature in cult of Minoan Goddess; The Palace regarded as House of the Double Axes'.

22. M. M. Ill: (G) FLOOR-CISTS OR KASELLES OF WESTERN PALACE REGION." 448

Separate enclosure of section of West Magazines; Enclave of the Kaselles or Floor-Cists; Those of the Long Gallery; Remains of precious contents; Some Cists used as Vats; Original Cists; Closed at end of M. M. Ill; Stratigraphic evidence of Cists beneath Stepped Porch; Kaselles' of Eighth Magazine; Superficial recipients, of later construction; M. M. Ill relics in filling beneath these; Traces of later use as Oil Vats; Mostly paved over by close of L. M. I; Three Epochs traceable in West Magazines three Stages in construction of their Entrances.

23. M. M. Ill: (H) THE TEMPLE REPOSITORIES AND ROYAL DRAUGHT-BOARD 463

Treasury Quarter of Palace; Survival of pre-Palace Cult Centre; Superficial Cists of Later Shrine; Discovery of earlier Temple Repositories beneath them; Their Contents; M. M. Ill Pottery; Precious relics below; The Western Repository; Broken Stone Hammers; Remains of Treasure Chests; Gold foil and inlays; Comparison of inlays with Royal Draught-board; Its description; Crystal plaques with Silver and Kyanos backing; Argonauts and Marguerites; Plan and Character of Game; The Citadel; Compared with Greek Polls; Discovery of ivory men compared with Predynastic Egyptian type; Solar symbol on base of one of these; Connected with Minoan Goddess on mould and fresco; Reconstruction of part of Draught-board from Temple Repository; Parallel remains from Fourth Shaft Grave at Mycenae; Small ivory disks with Minoan Craftsmen's marks'; Faience inlays of Mycenae Board of Knossian Palace fabric; Sacral Knots' of faience associated with Board; Deposit of Gaming Boards in Tombs: Egyptian practice; Minoan Boards dedicated to Goddess and a special property of Dead.

PAGM 24. M. M. III: (I) KNOSSIAN FAIKNCK: Tin-: HEADS. 486

Fnience fabrics from IVth Shaft Grave identical with those of Tempk- Ri-positorivs at Knossos: Evidences of early development of native faience in Crete; Its Egyptian origin; Moulds found at Knossos; Analysis of Knossian faience (Re-srarches of Church and Heaton); Method of manufacture; The Palace fabric of Knossos; The faience beads imitations of Egyptian types; History of the 'segmented variety; Diffusion of faience bead types by Minoan Commerce; Occurrence of segmented and other imported forms in S. K. Spain and British Isles; Chronological bearing on Western Bronze Age; General indications of Minoan connexions with West Mediterranean Basin; festoons, apparently of beads and pendants, between Columns of Minoan shrines.

25. M. M. III: (K) THE SNAKE GODDESS AND RELICS OK HER SIIKINE 49,5

Contents of West Temple Repository inscribed tablets, seal-impressions; Bone and ivory relics; Sacrificial element Libation tables; Faience relics from Eastern Repository; Votive bowls and ewer; Rose-leaf Chalice; Fruits and flowers; The Snake Goddess; Her Votary or Double fashionable dress; Lioness crest of Votary; Lions, concomitants of Goddess; Votive robes and girdles of faience; Priestesses as Snake Charmers; Survival of Cult of Snake Goddess Chryselephantine figure from Knossos; Berlin bronze figure with triple coil of snakes Cretan, L. M. I; Later shrines at Gournia and Prinias; Snakes emblem of Chthonic divinity; Snake as domestic genius; Wazet, Snake Goddess of Western Delta; Her papyrus symbol adopted in Crete; Her Uraeus suggests serpent crest of Minoan Goddess; Faience reliefs of Cow and Calf reflect Cult of Isis and Hathor Parallel group of Goat and Kids; Cruciform star symbols of Hathoric Cow, adopted by Minoan Cult; Cross, primitive pictograph of Star; Cruciform symbols on Sealings from VV. Repository Cross as sole type; Cruciform inlay and faience; Marble Cross of Orthodox shape from Repository; Painted sea shells pebbles on floors of Minoan Shrines; Flying fish panel and moulded marine subjects in clay; Compared with Fish Frescoes of Knossos and Phylakopi.

26. M. M. III: (L) MINOAN FRESCO: WALL PAINTINGS AND RELIEFS. 524

Painted Plaster Reliefs imitated in those of faience; Dating of the mural reliefs; The Jewel Relief fragment part of a life-size toilet scene; Probably derived from Columnar Hall above Pillar Crypts; M. M. Ill frescoes on the flat; Scenes of Bull Ring: The Minoan Fresco process; Early Minoan plaster partly structural; Advanced Middle Minoan technique; Stucco layers thinner on Gypsum; Stucco Reliefs; Analysis of material Subterranean Quarry whence obtained; Labyrinth of Gortyna compared; Early Minoan Red facing; Pigments used in later frescoes the Egyptian Blue; True fresco process on wet plaster; Pure caustic lime plaster, a lost Art; Artistic Shorthand of Miniature Frescoes; M. M. Ill Frescoes of S. E. House; The Lily Fresco; Olive sprays; Spikelets of Reeds masterpieces of Naturalistic Art. Parallels from H. Triada; The Cat and Pheasant fresco parallels at Knossos; Free adaptation of Nilotic Scenes; Flying Fish Fresco, Phylakopi work of Knossian School; Dolphin Fresco of Queen's Megaron M. M. Ill; Connexions of Fish Frescoes; Fine fresco designs of female forms by Knossian hand in Melos; The Ladies in Blue; Notched plume decoration on votive arrows; On wings of Sphinxes and Griffins; Combined with asterisk a stellar symbol; Asterisks on stucco face of Sphinx; Notched plume motive on skirts of Goddess; Degenerations of notched plume motive; Its occurrence on hearths at Knossos and Mycenae.

PAGE 27. M. M. Ill: (M) THE PALACE POTTERY STORES. 5.52

Abundant material supplied by Palace deposits; Falling off of ceramic fabric-consequent on Catastrophe of M. M. II; Quick wheel, too, fatal to egg-shell and embossed wares; Symptoms of recovery; Reaction on pottery of revival of Stone

Vase-making; Naturalistic mouldings on Clay vessels; Palatial Store-jars; Influence of naturalistic Wall-paintings; M. M. Ill Pottery Stores and deposits of Palace; S. W. Basement fish-bones in kitchen utensil, inscribed jar; The Temple Repositories imported Melian vessels; Bird on Melian Vases derived from Minoan Griffin; Incised signs on handles, c.; Royal Magazines Medallion pithoi; Pithos with signet impressions; Signets with architectural facades; Store of culinary and other pots knobbed decoration; Probable ritual destination; N. E. Magazines; M. M. Ill layer above Royal Pottery Stores; Area E. of these; The S. E. Insula its sanctuary character and Initiatory Area; Ointment pots from S. E. Lustral Basin; Residential Section of S. E. Insula; Magazine of the Lily Jars Candlestick of Egyptian type; S. E. Bathroom and painted clay Bath; Domestic Shrine; Magazine of False-spouted Jars; Their evolution symptomatic of improved conditions; Quadruple Axe motive; Burial Jar with stellar symbol; Urn burials and clay coffins; Deposit with Ink-inscribed Cups; Forms of M M. Ill Cups; Signs of quick wheel spiral Convolutions and string-cut bases.

28. M. M. Ill: (N) SURVIVALS OF CERAMIC POLYCHROMY AND RISE OF NATURALISM 591

Dated deposits of close of M. M. Ill; Contrasts with M. M. II result of Catastrophe; Monochrome decoration again general; Tortoise-shell rippled ware, anticipation of new style; Survivals of true polychromy; Polychrome Rhyton of Ostrich Egg type with decorative group of Palm-trees; Vessels from Well, Gypsades; Polychrome jars from Repositories; Imitations of conglomerate and breccia; Basin with coloured imitation of granulated rock-work; Minoan wash-basins prototypes of Melian Class; Coiled sprays, M. M. Ill feature on painted sherds from Mycenae Shaft Graves; Shaft Grave sherds paralleled by jars from Temple Repositories; Influence of Naturalistic Wall-painting on pottery; The Lily jars' compared with H. Triada fresco; Vetches, Tulips, and Reeds or Grasses on Vases; Exclusion of Human and Animal figures from pottery contrast with wall-paintings; Fish, however, represented; Reflection of Dolphin Fresco on M. M. Ill jars; Class of small reliefs of marine subjects; Axe plants on M. M. Ill jar; anticipation of late Palace Style; Tangential loops on M. M. Ill Vases link with early 1 M. I decoration.

29. M. M. Ill: (O) THE LINEAR SCRIPT A AND ITS SACRAL USAGE. 612

Hieroglyphic system superseded by advanced Linear Script A; Palace documents of M. M. Ill date; Cups with ink-written Inscriptions from Sanctuary site; Graffiti on Palace pottery of M. M. Ill date; Clay documents of Temple Repositories; Early form of tablets; Tablets from S. E. Insula talent and drachm signs; Business documents with numerals inventories; Clay roundels', inscribed and sealed; Gypsum chip used as trial piece, from Kasella; Lapidary inscriptions of religious character; Inscribed Votive Stone Ladles from Mountain Sanctuaries of Knossos; Clay Votive Ladle from Early Minoan deposit at Knossos; Specimens from votive stations on peak of Juktas and on foot-hill at Trullos; Recurring dedicatory formula on Trullos Ladle associated with Throne and Sceptre Sign; Similar formula on Libation Table from Psychro Cave; On Libation Table and Stone Cup from Palaikastro; Inscribed Votive Tablet of bronze from Psychro Cave; Name of Votary inscribed in characters of Class A parallel phenomenon on Votive Figurine from Tylissos; Ritual interpretation of signs on tablet oaoauyr;; Triple aspect of Cult of Minoan Goddess; Dedicatory formula connected with Cradle,

Temple, and I omb of Cretan Zeus; Official adoption of new Script due to hieratic influences; General knowledge of Art of Writing-Graffiti on Walls; Diffusion of script for commercial purposes to Melos, c.; Earlier anticipations of advanced Linear Script on Seal Stones; Systemati. ation by Central Authority in M. M. Ill; Synopsis of (lass A; Comparisons between Linear and Hieroglyphic sigruiries; Coni ound and barred signs and Numeration; Relations of Linear Classes A and B evidences of overlapping.

30. THE PHAESTOS DISK IN ITS MINOAN RELATIONS. 647

Tablet of Class A found with imprinted Disk at Phaestos; In Cist with M. M. Ill b pottery; Non-Minoan character of Disk; Hieroglyphs stamped by novel method; Order of Sign-Groups on Disk; The Signary small common element with Minoan Scripts; The Manacles'sign; Artistic execution of Signs compared with Minoan; At date of Disk Hieroglyphs superseded by linear signs in Crete; Indications of connexion with S. W. Anatolia; Plumed cap and round shield of later Sea-rovers; Arrow sign on Ship; Anatolian religious element Symbols of Goddess Ma; Pagoda-like building Lykian parallels; Specialized character of signs on Disk; Pictographs not of ancient derivation but drawn from contemporary life; Phonographic elements dual Groups; Preponderant ideography; Simple mnemonic element; Division into Sections terminal dashes; Symmetrical arrangement of two faces; Recurrent sets of sign-groups suggesting refrains; Metrical character of Composition; Record of Sea raid connected with S. W. Region of Asia Minor; Comparison of later Egyptian Sea raids of Lykians and Confederates; Pylon of Medinet Habu; Religious connexion of Disk a Te Deum of Victory; Cretan Philistines among later Sea-Raiders; But Disk not a record of Philistines in Minoan Crete; Non-Minoan accoutrements of warriors on Disk; Keftians true Minoan representatives; Disk a foreshadowing of later ethnic relations; An Evidence of M. M. Ill connexion between Crete and S. V. Anatolia; Unique record.

31. M. M. Ill: (?) SEAL TYPES AND THEIR RELATIONS WITH GREATER ART.-

Change in Signet types no longer present inscriptions; Survivals of hieroglyphic prism seals; Lentoid and amygdaloid bead-seals; Signet rings as those of IVth Shaft Grave impressions of such; Gems of Sphungaras Urns Talismanic Class; Milk Stones; Architectural, pillared and gabled, class Rustic Shrines; Intaglios on Flattened Cylinders'; Plated Steatite example and parallel supplied by rhyton fragment; Fisherman and Skaros' fish; Repository Hoard of Clay Seal-impressions unique chronological value; Contemporary Hoards of Zakro and Hagia Triada; Specimens of Costume and Armour on Sealings of these Hoards; Male types with flowing apron illustrated by votive figurine; The Ritual Cuirass'; Other contemporary finds of Sealings at Knossos; Use of Sieves in Excavation; Religious types from Repository; Horned sheep a nurse of infant God; Architectonic setting; Triple gradation beneath Bull-hunting scenes taken from supports of friezes; Triply graduated supports of Palace Reliefs; Illustrations from Steatite rhytons; Columns between agonistic groups pugilist and column on Sealing; Column equivalent of Grand Stand or Theatre; Fragment of Knossian rhyton; 1 he fallen champion of Boxing Ring; Gladiatorial Scene on Sealing; Wounded champion supported on one arm; Scene of Combatants on Mycenae Signet adapted from agonistic episodes; Ultimate influence of Minoan Theatral episodes on Epic imagery; Episodes of Bull-ring on signets taken over from frescoes and reliefs; Excerpts from Cattle Pieces; Various types of Repository Sealings; Instantaneous impressions of Nature; Prototype of Scylla Sea monster on Mycenae rhyton; Comparisons with Zakro seal-types; Middle Minoan and Early Egyptian Elements.

32. M. M. Ill: (Q) WINGED CREATIONS AND THE FLYING GALLOP 7 01

Middle Minoan Elements of the Zakro Sealings; Fantastic types constant variation to baffle forgers; Fancy thus called into play rapid transformation of types;

Humorous and Demonic creations; Horned Imp on Earlier signet Axe-winged Goblin on Melian pots; Underlying Egyptian motives talismanic Value of Waz symbol; Bats' and Butterflies' wings-winged symbol on M. M. II prism seal; Fantastic forms with birds' wings Creatures of Fancy rather than Religion; Did they become themes of Myth? Mythical accretions to winged figures of Minoan creation; Melian revival; Winged Types appropriate to Age of Daedalos; Winged forms in Crete and Xllth Dynasty Egypt; Prototypes of Griffin Hawk-headed I, ions of Beni-Hasan; Egyptian Seraphim and Cherubim; Early Egyptian Griffins with Hawk's head and Minoan derivations; Minoan Griffins in Flying Gallop; Crested Eagle-headed type; The Egypto-Minoan Griffin Peacock's plumes of Late Minoan forms; Galloping Griffin type traced to M. M. II; The Flying Gallop in Art introduced into Egypt from Crete; Examples on Queen Aah-hotep's Dagger-blade; Flying Gallop on M. M. Ill Sealings and Mycenae blades parallel representations; The Flying Leap on Cretan Seals Recurrence on Hyksos Dagger-hilt; Engraved M. M. II dagger-blade illustrations of Flying Gallop; Fighting Bulls and Boar-hunt; The Boar-hunt in Minoan Art; Converging evidence of Minoan character of Mycenae relics Arms and Goldsmith's Work.

MAPS

East Mediterranean Basin, showing Central Position of Crete. Also Central and Eastern Crete. (Facingp. i.)

PLANS AND SECTIONS

PAGE

IV. M M. II Polychrome Vase and Egyptian Relics from Abydos Tomb.

„ V. Hall of Colonnades. Sketch made previous to Full Excavation of Grand Staircase and before Restoration of Supporting Columns of Balustrade, by Theodore Fyfe.

VI. Queen's Megaron previous to Reconstitution. To Left, Private Staircase; to Right, Inner Section with East Light-Well and Part of South and Fast Colonnade of Hall of Double Axes beyond.

VII. View in Hall of Colonnades showing Window lighting Private Staircase.

VIII. View showing Supporting Blocks of North Column-base of North-East Portico.

„ IX. View of North-West Portico showing High Column-base and Remains of fine Polygonal Paving.

X. Pillar of East Pillar Room, Knossos, incised with Double Axes, Corner of Stone Vat to left.

XL Long Corridor of West Magazines, looking South: Ridge and Peak of Juktas beyond.

THE MINOAN AGE

JfaGNUS An INTEGRO SAECLORUM NASC1TVR OKDO

THK progressive revelations, from 1900 onwards, of a high early rerm civilization on Cretan soil entailed the urgent necessity for devising cenaean a new system and terminology for the Later Prehistoric Age in the

Aegean area. The term Mycenaean no longer sufficed. The great Palaces at Knossos and Phaestos, the smaller but exquisitely appointed building of the same class at Hagia Triada, the town sites of Gournia and Palaikastro, island settlements like Pseira, the archaic mansions of Vasi-liki, the cave sanctuaries of Psychro and Kamares, primitive tholos ossuaries like those of Messara, the early tombs of Mochlos and a further series of discoveries, to which each season adds, have brought forth a mass of materials not only showing us a contemporary culture, parallel with that of Mycenae, in its own home, but carrying the origins of that culture stage beyond stage to an incomparably more remote period. For the first time there has comeinto view a primitive European civilization, the earliest phase of which goes back even beyond the days of the First Dynasty of Egypt.

To this early civilixation of Crete as a whtoie I have proposed and the Useful-suggestion has been generally adopted bj the archaeologists of this and ",.."(, other countries to apply the name Mjnoarp. By the Greeks themselves Mmoan. the memory of the great Age that had preceded their own diffusion throughout the Aegean lands was summed up in the name of Minos.

It is true that very different traditions were connected with that name. On the one side we gain a vision of a beneficent ruler, patron of the arts, founder of palaces, stablisher of civilized dominion. On the other is depicted a tyrant and a destroyer. The grim aspect of the great justiciary Athenian as impressed on the minds of a later generation is already reflected in nns he Homeric epithet oxoo wv. It was, however, reserved for Athenian refuted. hauvinism so to exaggerate the tyrannical side of that early sea-dominion i to convert the Palace of a long series of great rulers into an ogre's den. it the fabulous accounts of the Minotaur and his victims are themselves pressive of a childish wonder at the mighty creations of a civilixation ueyond the ken of the new-comers. The spade of the excavator has indeed clone much to explain and confute them. The ogre's den turns out to be a peaceful abode of priest-kings, in some respects more modern in its equipments than anything produced by classical Greece. The monumental reliefs within its sea-gate visible, it would appear, to a much later date representing bull-catching scenes and, still more, the fresco panels with feats of the bull-ring in which girls as well as youths took part, go far to explain the myth. It may even be that captive children of both sexes were trained to take part in the dangerous circus sports portrayed on the Palace walls.

Minos the destroyer may certainly have existed. That the yoke of the more civilized ruler should at times have weighed heavily on subject peoples is probable enough. But, in the main, the result of recent discovery has been to confirm the more favourable side of Greek tradition.

Minos Until a full interpretation of the inscribed tablets is forthcoming the Law-. r, giver. it must remain impossible to obtain any actual excerpts trom the Laws of Minos', or to ascertain how much of the later legislation of Greece may go back to a far more ancient source. But the minute bureaucratic precision revealed by these clay documents, the official sealings and clocket-ings, their signing and countersigning, are symptoms that speak for themselves of a highly elaborated system of legislation. In view of such evidence the legendary account of Minos, like another Moses or Hammurabi, receiving the law from the hands of the divinity himself on the Sacred Mountain, may well be taken to cover the actual existence of a code associated with the name of one of the old priest-kings of Crete.

Patron of Qf orc lered government we have the proof, and, in a not less striking degree, the evidence of extraordinary achievements in peaceful arts. The Palace traditionally built for Minos by his great craftsman Daedalos has proved to be no baseless fabric of the imagination. The marvellous works brought to light at Knossos and on other sites show moreover that the artistic skill associated with his name fell, if anything, short of the reality. At the same time the multiplicity of technical processes already mastered, the surprising advance in hydraulic and sanitary engineering leaving Egypt far behind bear witness to a considerable measure of attainment in the domain of science. Almost, we are tempted to believe in Talos the mechanical man, or that a Cretan headland was the scene of the first experirnent in aviation the fatal flight of Ikaros!

Greek That the word Minoan was used bv the Greeks themselves in an Minoas. i j II ethnic or dynastic as well as a personal sense is shown by the constantly recurring term Minoa applied to traditional settlements from prehistoric Crete. In the neighbourhood of Gaza, the cult of the Cretan Zeus' lived on into late classical times. The name attaches itself to towns, islands, and promontories not only in Crete itself but throughout the Aegean world. In Delos we find the Minoid Nymphs'. On the mainland of

Greece itself the islet that guards the port of Megara, and a headland of Laconia, bear this appellation. It recurs in Corcyra. In Sicily, where of rt-cent years a series of finds have come to light illustrative of a late offshoot of the Minoan civilization, the Minoan Herakleia bears witness to its abiding tradition. For it was said that Daedalos sought refuge on Sicilian shores, and that Minos himself, following with an ill-fated expedition, found a grave and sepulchral shrine near this Westernmost Minoa.

The dynastic use of the word Minos may perhaps be compared with Dynastic that of Pharaoh, originally signifying him of the great house (Per-o), and "Minos'. Minoan may thus be fairly paralleled with Pharaonic as a term for the dynastic civilization of Egypt. It seems certain that we must recognize in Divine Minos the bearer of a divine title. He is of divine parentage and himself the progenitor of divine beings. Son of Zeus by Europa, herself, perhaps, an Earth-Goddess, 1 wedded to Pasiphae, the all-illuminating, father of Ariadne the Most Holy Minos, in the last two relationships at least, was coupled with alternative forms of the Mother Goddess of pre-Hellenic Crete.

But this divine element in Minos has a special significance in view Divine of a series of analogies supplied by the great religious centres of the K? ng of geograph-ically connected Anatolian regions. In these sanctuaries the priest Anatol a-not only represented the God, wore his dress, and wielded his authority, but often also bore his name. A most conspicuous instance of this is found in the case of Attis- or Atys, whose chief-priest, the Archigallus, regularly took the same name. 3 At Pessinus he was a priest-king. The divine nature of primitive kingship is of course almost universal. 4 It is well illustrated indeed in the case of Egypt, whose Pharaohs took the titles of the Great God, the golden Horus, Son of the Sun-god (Ra), at times, Son of the Moon (Aah), or engendered of Thoth, and so forth.

In Egypt, indeed, the royal and the priestly authority were kept somewhat apart, and the Temple overshadowed the Palace. In the Anatolian centres the royal and the sacerdotal abode was one and the same, and the 1 See Farnell, Cults of the Greek States, ii, Ramsay refers to this practice in his recent p. 479. paper on The Shrine of the (lod Men 2 Kretschmer, Einleitiing in die Geschichte Askaenos at the Pisidian Antioch. (Abstract Jcr xriectischcn Sprache, p. 195, points out that in Journ. of Hellenic Studies, xxxii, 1912, Attis and the Great Mother with whom he is pp. xlix. l.) See also his Sketches in the Religious associated belong to the pre-Phrygian ele-Antiquities of Asia Minor; B. School Annual, ment, in other words to the old Anatolian xviii. 37, c.

element akin to the Cretan. I need only here refer to Frszer's imturu 3 The authorities are collected by Dr. Frazer, on the Early History of Kingship, p. 128 Adonis, Attis, Osiris, pp. 182-4. Sir V. M. seqq.

THE PALACK OF MINOS, ETC.

Knossian Palace was also a Sanctuary. It is these last conditions that seem to have most nearly corresponded with those of Minoan Crete. The cumulative results of the exploration of the great building at Knossos have served more and more to bring out the fact that it was interpenetrated with religious ele- ments. The constant appearance of the sacred double axe or labrys as a sign on its blocks, outnumberingall the other marks on the Palace walls put together, and recurring on stucco and painted pottery, on seals, and in concrete shape on the altar of a shrine, is itself of special significance in connexion with the surviving traditions of the Labyrinth on this spot and the closely related Carian cult. The wall-paintings themselves have (in" almost all cases, a religious connexion direct or indirect. It is now clear that a large part of the West

Wing of the Palace was little more than a conglomeration of small shrines, of pillared crypts designed for ritual use, and corresponding halls above. 1

Room of The best preserved existing chamber, moreover, of this Quarter, the Room designed f tne Throne, teems with religious suggestion. With its elaborately carved for,. cathedral seat in the centre and stone benches round, the sacral griffins

Religious.

Func- guarding on one side the entrance to an inner shrine, on the other the throne itself, and, opposite, approached by steps, its mysterious basin, it might well evoke the idea of a. kind of consistory or chapter-house. A singularly dramatic touch, from the moment of final catastrophe, was here, indeed, supplied by the alabastra standing on the floor, beside the overturned oil-jar for their filling, with a view, we may infer, to some ceremony of anointing.- It is impossible to withhold the conclusion that the Room of the Throne at Knossos was designed for religious functions.

The salient features in its arrangement (Fig. 1), in fact, suggest an interest- ing comparison with a ritual chamber recently discovered in one of the kindred

Com- Anatolian sanctuaries. This is the Hall of Initiation excavated by the with Hall British explorers 3 in the sanctuary of Men Askaenos and a Mother Goddess, of Men, described as Demeter, near the Pisidian Antioch. The throne itself, the stone benches round, and the tank on the opposite side to the throne, find all their close analogies, and are arranged in the same relative positions. In the

Galatian Sanctuary we see, on a larger scale it is true, a chamber with a throne in this case near, not actually against, the back wall to the right of the entrance, while, opposite it on the left side on entering the chamber, 1 See my paper on The Restored Shrine on in connexion with the N. I. ustral Basin.

Central Court of the Palace at Knossos' (Journ. See p. 419, below, Fig. 304 b.

of R. Inst. of British Architects, 1911, p. 289 3 Miss Itf M. Hardie (Mrs. Hasluck Mr.

seqq.). For the! Room of the Throne see W. M. Calder, and Sir W. M. Ramsay. See

Vol.11. J. H. S., 1912, p. in seqq., and 13. S. A., xviii - So, too, the Alabastron of Khyan stood (1911, 1912), p. 37 seqq.

is an oblong tank. 1 Here, too, along the back wall runs a rock-cut bench or divan, and the chamber was approached by an ante-room or prouaos.

Cult arrangements are often handed down almost unaltered through The long peri- ods of years, and the striking analogies here presented afford pries?- a real presumption for believing that the much earlier Room of the Throne K "K S-at Knossos and its adjoining tank were devised for similar rites of initiation and purification. Like him who presided over these Anatolian rites, a Minoan priestling may have sat upon the throne at Knossos, the adopted

GRIFFIN FACING THRONE

A.—I INNER SHRINE

CENTRAL AREA OF PAVEMENT COVERED WITH PAINTED STUCCO

FIG. 1. PI. AV OF ROOM OF THK THRONF, AT KNOSSOS. Scale, i cm.= i m area. Son on earth of the Great Mother of its island mysteries. Such a personage, indeed, we may actually recognize in the Palace relief of a figure wearing a plumed lily crown and leading, we may believe, the sacral Griffin. 1 It is probable, indeed, that in Crete the kingly aspect was more to the fore than in the religious centres of Asia Minor. But both the actual evidence from the Palace site and the divine associations attributed to Minos lead to the conclusion that here, too, each successive dynast was a priest for ever after the order of Melchizedech and made like unto' the Son of God

The names both of Minos and of Knossos, together with others bound up with the religion of the spot, connect themselves with those Asiamc regions where priest-kings most thrived. The termination in-ws, qm foreign to Greek nomenclature, is characteristic of a whole class of personal 1 See the plan given by Sir V. M. Ramsay, Minor. . 5. A., xviii, p. 4, Fig. i. Sketches n the Rtligma Annuities of Asia See Vol. II, frontispiece (PI. I)

THE PALACE OF MINOS, ETC.

Anatolian names of the Carians and their kin. 1 The name Kvws is thrice connected t ie Korykian Cave and Temple of the priestly dynasts of Olbe in Cilicia. 2 Tcixws the bronze-man of Minos and fabled guardian of Crete bears a name of the same family. The name of MLVO; itself recurs as an element in Minassos, a Pisidian town, 3 whose later bishops may well have perpetuated a much earlier religious tradition. The name of Daedalos is found again in that of the town of Daedala (TO. Aaisaxa) on the borders of Caria and Lykia, where was his reputed tomb.

The most ancient features in the Cretan religion find, in fact, their

Religious closest analogies on the Anatolian side, where was another Ida and another Dikte. There too we recognize under manifold appellations the same Great Mother with a male satellite who may stand to her in various relationships a tradition which survived in Crete, in Rhea and the infant Zeus. There too we see the same cymbal-clashing Corybantic train with names like Panamoros, showing how deeply rooted was this idea in the old Asianic stock. In both areas attendant animals, as different in their nature as lions and doves, are attributed to the Goddess. Finally, the most sacred emblem of the aniconic cult of Crete, the double axe, is equally on the Anatolian side a central object of cult, and its Lydian name labrys has suggested a key not only to the title of the Carian Zeus, Labraundos, but to that of the Labyrinth, 4 here identified with the palace sanctuary of Knossos. Throughout a wide Anatolian region very early religious traditions were taken over by peoples of more than one stock. It is also evident that more than one of the linguistic elements, which in that region often overlie one another, has left its mark in the early place-names of Crete. The Phrygian element, though it may be relatively late, clearly has its place in the island.

How far there was a true ethnic relationship between Crete and the neighbouring Anatolian regions is not so well ascertained. The evidence of 1 Pick, Vorgriechische Ortsnamen (1905), 3 Its site, still known as Minasun, was dis-pp. 26, 27; Kretschmer, Einleitung in die covered by Prof. Sterrett. It is also known Geschichte der griechis-chen Sprache, p. 357. from coins with the alliance inscription Among names of this class are Carian Stwws, MINAZZEHN KAI KONANEHN OMO-KKuto'ticos

(Lykian Exatoxras, Akatamna NOIA. For the comparison with Mi? cf. Lykaoninn Kav G, Cilician Kvis, Mws, Fick, op. at., p. 27.

IU.7s, c. Kretschmer, op. at., p. 104 and A. Fick, 2 E. L. Hicks, Inscriptions from Western op. at., p. 6 seqq. Arkwright, on the other Cilicia (J. H. S., xii), pp. 230, 231, 254, 255. hand (Lycian and Phrygian Names, J. H. S., The name occurs both on a tomb near the 1918, p. 45 seqq.) does not admit the-nd-nth Korykian Cave and on a stone of the N. anta equation. Conway, B. S. A., viii. p. 154 seqq, of the temple above it. There would even while accepting the equation, regards the seem to have been an Anatolian Knossos.-nth names in Crete and the Peloponnese as (Cf. Ramsay,. . S., 1912, p. jyo. 1! Phrygo-Cretan.

early racial type supplied by such sources as the Hittite reliefs of Gods Karly and princes points to the widespread existence in Eastern and Central deranceol Asia Minor of a race still represented by the modern Armenians and pro- Iir h, y-nouncedly brachycephalic. 1 Corroborative materials of early date from South- Asia West Asia Minor, where Hittite monuments fail us, are still for the most part to seek. The modern population of Lykia and adjacent islands, according to Dr. von Luschan's observations, 2 presents two distinct elements, hypsibrachy-cephalic and dolichocephalic, but what seem to be the oldest representatives of the indigenous stock belong to the former high, short-headed class, of Armenoid affinities The long heads', on the other hand, come into prominence in the maritime tracts, and comprise a considerable section of the Greek-speaking population. That dolichocephalic types, closely parallel to those of Minoan Crete, early existed on the Western shores of Asia Minor is shown by their occurrence in the Third Settlement at Hissarlik. 4 In Crete skulls of the Neolithic Age are still wanting. From the earliest Minoan Age onwards, however, the evidence is continuous, and tends But of to show that, though from the beginning of it a brachycephalic element ce phais In existed in the island, whether the earliest or not is uncertain, over half the Crete-skulls were dolichocephalic and about a third mesocephalic. 5 Towards the close of the Minoan Age the proportion of brachycephals, due probably to the 1 See especially Dr. Felix von Luschan's s Boyd Dawkins, B. School Annual, vii, observations, summarized in his Huxley Lecture pp. 150-5; W. L. H. Duckworth, ib., ix, for 1911, on The Early Inhabitants of Asia pp. 340-55; C. H. Hawes, ib., xi, pp. 296,

Minor (Anthr. Inst. Journ., xli). Dr. von 297; Burrows, Discoveries in Crete, pp. 166,

Luschan there shows that the type formerly 167; Mosso Esairsioni net Mediterranto termed by him Armenoid practically coin- (1907), pp. 275, 276. Sergi's examination of cides with the Hittite. This type, as he had three skulls from the Sub-Minoan Cemetery already pointed out in 1902, (ib. p. 242), is at Krganos (American Journ. of Archaeology, v, the basis of the later Jewish and so-called 1901, pp. 315-18), shows a survival of simi-

Semitic type as distinguished from the pure lar tendencies. They were either dolicho-

Arab. cephalic or mesocephalic. These results have 1)ie Tachtadschy tincl andere Ueberreste now been confirmed by the comprehensive der alten Bevolkerung Lykiens' (Archiv filr measurements of Von Luschan, Beitrage zur

Anthropologie, f., 1891, p. 31 seqq). The Anthropologievonkreta(Z? r-.; MW f, single old Lykian skull examined by Dr. Heft 3. 1913, p. 307 seqt).). The percentages Luschan from a grave at Limyra (op. ,, for the Middle Minoan skulls, for instance, are: p. 43 seqq.) resembles the Tachtadji type. Duckworth 65-3 dolichocephals, 26-15 rneso- 3 Such as the Tachtadji or Mahometan cephals, 8-55 brachycephals: von Luschan 58-8 wood-cutters and the Bektashi sectaries. dolichocephals, 35-3 mesocephals, 5-9 brachy- 4 See Prof. Boyd Dawkins, ft. School cephals. The results obtained by von Luschan Annual, vii. pp. 152, 153. and Hawes with regard to the modem Cretans also show a remarkable correspondence.

THE PALACE OF MINOS, ETC.

intrusion of Alpine Man from the North, shows a tendency to increase. To-day the long-headed type is in the minority.

These craniometrical results as well as other bodily measurements may be taken to imply that in Minoan times a large part of the population belonged to the somewhat long-heacled Mediterranean Race. A typical representative of this Mediterranean Race has indeed been recognized in the Cupbearer of the Knossian wall-painting 1 with his dark eyes, ruddy brown complexion, black wavy hair, and short compact frame. 2 The head of this figure is shown in Fig. 2, c, while d reproduces that of the dancing lady fresco from the Queen's Megaron.

Arme- noict

Type of

Early

Cretan

Dynast.

FIG. 2., b. PORTRAIT HEADS ASSOCIATED ON M. M. II SEALING (J). c. FROM CUP-BEARER FRESCO. d. FROM DANCING LADY FRESCO.

The fine-cut nose tilted forward at the point hich distinguishes the figures of the Late Minoan wall-paintings, such as c and d, has generally a straight bridge. But at other times it is decidedly aquiline, and this characteristic is well marked in the design which must be regarded as the first Minoan attempt at distinct portraiture. This is seen on a sealing, otherwise impressed by a signet bearing a hieroglyphic formula of frequent occurrence, in which I have ventured to recognize an official title of a hereditary nature since it recurs with varying personal badges on a series of prism-seals of successive periods. 3 Beside this, is the impression of a head of an adult male personage, with waved hair falling in a lock behind and a decidedly aquiline

Cretan and Albanian types. The waving hair gives it a high appearance. But it is unsafe to draw too exact craniometrical deductions from this, in part, conventionalized wall-painting.

"Scripta Minoa, i, pp. 271, 272 (Figs. 124, 125), and see p. 266, Table XXII 1 See Vol. II.

2 In my first account of the Cupbearer fresco (Knossos, Report, 1900, pp. 15, 16; B. S. A., vi; Monthly Review, March, 1901, p. 124) I had described the head as high and brachycephalic. and compared certain existing nose (Fig. 2, r). On another sealing the head of the same personage is coupled with that of a very young boy, presumably his son, and a portrait of a child would hardly have been executed except

in the case of one of royal blood (Fig.-, (. Then; is then a very strong presumption that the adult head portrayed is the actual likeness of a Minoan priest-king, whose personal badge, as we learn from a contemporary prism-seal with the hieroglyphic title in a fuller form, was a seated cat, 1 suggestive of Egyptian relations. The profile before us dating from the Second Middle Minoan Period certainly suggests that at any rate the earlier priest-kings themselves belonged to a ruling caste of the old Anatolian type, to which the name Armenoid may be given. On the other hand the Late Minoan profiles c and d suggest the intrusion of a new dynastic element of Mediterranean stock.

A consciousness of the essential foreignness of Minos to the Greeks comes out in a passage of the Iliad where he is made the son of the daughter (Europa) of Phoenix,:1 a version which nearly approaches the truth if we may regard the term toivices or red-men 4 as having been first suggested by the ruddy brown race of the Cretan frescoes. An ethnic relationship, moreover, is implied in the tradition that Minos was brother of Sarpedon, who stands for the Lykian race, which at any rate was not Hittite.

If there were any real historic warrant lor the existence of more w. istheie than one king of the name of Minos it would serve to corroborate the dynastic use of the term. The idea is mainly based on the genealogy of which Diodoros is the principal source, 5 a statement in Plutarch's Tkesau, ami earlier and later entries in the Parian Chronicle, in which the name of a Minos is mentioned at two different epochs. 7 But the accounts by no means tall). According to the tradition followed by Diodoros there were two kings of the name, the first the grandfather of the second. This would give an interval between the two of about ninety years. In the Chronicle it is over a century and a half. The whole genealogy, moreover, is involved in mythical elements. 8

A too obvious intention of this interpolation of a second Minos is 1 See below, p. 277, Fig. 207, a op. tit., Chandler's restoration of the first entry p. 270, Fig. 121, a. (Marmora Oxoniensia, p. 21, 1. 41), A J OY - For a somewhat exaggerated example see MINttz OJ TTP ntOZ E BA ZIAEYZE the Armenian type from Aintab, illustrated by KPHTHZ, still seems preferable to TT PO- von I. uschan, Anthr. lust. Jmirn., xli (1911), TEPOZ, c., substituted by Boeckh, as Flach

PI. XXV. 3 II. xiv. 321. (Chronicon Pariuin, p. 6) points out, invito 4 Cf. Kick, Iorgriffhische Ortsiiamen, pp. 123, lapide.

,24. Hoeck's criticism of Minos I and Minos

Diod. iv. 60. Pint. Ties. 18. II (Area, ii, p. 50 seqq.) still holds gcwd.

THE PALACE OF MINOS, ETC.

Dorian adoption of Minos.

Epony-

Myths.

Achaean Legend.

supplied by the desire to secure a lower rung for the ladder of ascent by means of which the new Dorian line of rulers might be brought into immediate relation with the representative name of the older indigenous dynasty. By the new-comers, Achaean as well as Dorian, the old hierarchical tradition attaching to the name of Minos was invoked as a sanction for their own claims. He was at the same time made more real by being brought down to the age immediately preceding the Trojan War. The adoption of Minos' itself finds an almost exact parallel in the adoption of Agamemnon not only by the Achaeans but by the later Spartan kings. 1

According to Diodoros' account 2 the Dorian eponymus Doros, after his arrival irr Crete, weds the daughter of Kres' and becomes the father of Asterios. Asterios in turn takes to wife Europa, who had already, by Zeus, given birth to Minos, Rhadamanthys, and Sarpedon. Minos I marries Itone, daughter of Lyktios (eponymus of Lyktos, later the great Dorian centre), and begets the namegiver of the neighbouring Lykastos. Lykastos' is father by Ida of Minos II, who in turn is made the establisher of the first thalassocracy among the Hellenes. The whole genealogy is pure myth of the eponymic kind, which may have a certain value in. so far as it reflects the blending of the indigenous elements of Crete with the Greek new-comers, but which had the obvious aim of first, in a way, annexing the Minos I and thus leading up to a second who could be described as of Dorian birth.

In the more usual legend, which is in fact incorporated in that given by Diodoros, we hear only of one Minos. In the Iliad he belongs to the second generation before the Trojan War. He is there the father of Deukalion, who impersonates the Hellenic stock in the oldest sense of the word, and through him the grandfather of the Achaean leader Idomeneus, lord of Knossos, whose name itself seems to point to early settlement in the land round Ida. The dominion of Idomeneus, according to the catalogue of ships, included, besides Knossos, Gortyna, Lyktos, Miletos, Lykastos, Phaestos, and Rhytion, 4 and thus embraced the whole of Central Crete. That it represents in part at least an ethnographic break is indicated by one significant fact. The sister city of Carian Halikarnassos, the Cretan Karnessos," is 1 Such is the implied claim of the Spartan 2 The account of Diodoros, iv. 60, is, as envoy in his answer to Gelon of Syracuse when Hoeck points out (Kreta, ii, pp. 27, 53), largely he proposed to take command of the allied derived through an Attic medium.

3 xiii. 449-51, and cf. Od. xix. 178 seqq. 1 . ii. 645 seqq.

' The older name of Lyktos was Ka r rrrd-iroxts (Hesychios, s. v.: cf. Pick, Vorgriechische Ortsnamen (1905), p. 29.

Greeks: fj. flj. vuiv U7rapaipjrr ai VTTO (Herod, vii. 159).

6 IIcaoirisi; Aya-

TIJV re xai now Lyktos, later the great Dorian centre. This early account of Achaean domination in the island (which does not exclude the participation of other Hellenic elements such as the Dorian) seems to give us a real glimpse of the historic conditions in Crete at the beginning of the Iron Age. But when we go back from Idomeneus, through Deukalion of hoary tradition, to the generation beyond him we find ourselves in a very different atmosphere. The sister of Deukalion is Ariadne, his mother Pasiphae, and his father, Minos, is the direct emanation of the divinity. In other words e find ourselves again caught up in the celestial cycle of the old Cretan religion. 1 If there be any value attaching to the early dates supplied by the larian Parian Chronicle, or that of Eusebius, the first historical appearance. of a king i c e. bearing the name of Minos is projected within the last brilliant age of the pre-Hellenic civilization of Crete. The year given by the Parian 1 Sir William Ridgeway, in his paper entitled Minos the Destroyer rather than the Creator of the so-called Minoan culture of Cnossus (Proc. Brit. Acad., 1909-10, p. 98 seqq.), sets forth some original views on these matters. Holding by the tradition of two kings of the name of Minos, he regards Minos II as Achaean on the strength of the genealogy given in the Iliad. Idomeneus was an Achaean, but, if he was such, his father Deucalion and his grandfather Minos must have been Achaeans (p. 94). This was certainly the inference desired by the logographer. Minos II having been dealt with in this somewhat summary fashion, Minos I has his turn. That his brother Rhadamanthys is twice spoken of in the Iliad as avk (iv. 564; vii. 523) might not by itself be sufficiently convincing, since such a descriptive touch would be a natural move in the process of adoption. It was necessary therefore to resort to what can only be described as les grands moyens. The fabled relationship with Phoenix seems to be the chief basis for the statement (p. 125) that Minos I passed into Crete from Palestine at the close of the fifteenth century B. c. He was one of 'the tall fair-haired Achaean invaders who, we are asked to believe, had made their way to Syria from the North across the Dardanelles, like the later Gauls, and through Asia Minor (p. 126). Swooping down from

Canaan to Crete, this Achaean leader with the un-Hellenic name deals a fatal blow to Minoan civilization.

Not only here are chronological conditions ignored but the historic course of events is actually reversed. In the fifteenth century B. C., the sea-paths round the East Mediterranean angle were already, perhaps via Cyprus, bringing (retan wares to the ports of Canaan, and painted sherds of the later Palace style of Knossos begin to appear in the deposits of its Tells. (K. g. at Gezer, Maca-lister, vol. ii, p. 155, Fig. 318 part of an alabastron with 8-shaped shields and stars; L. M. 1 b from the Second Semitic stratum.) In the superimposed Canaanite stratum imported Aegean pottery of the Tell-euAmarna class abounds. But the stage of armed occupation to which the formation of Philistia was due was not reached till a still later date, and the Philistine pottery of native fabric showing a matt-paint Metope style (Mackenzie. Ain Stems, If. Y. Y. Annual. 1912-1913, p. 32) is found in the superimposed stratum. It is possible that Achaean or Dorian swarms took part in the Philistine movement, following in the wake of earlier Cretan pioneers. But a current of invasion, from Palestine to Crete, at the close of the fifteenth century B. c., is excluded by the elementary facts of East Mediterranean history.

Marble answers to 1462-1 ii. c. 1 It is well within the limits of the last Palace Period at Knossos. A Mainland Mycenaean reaction becomes, indeed, perceptible shortly after that date, but there was certainly no room either for Achaeans or Dorians in the island. In view, indeed, of the essential continuity of the concluding phase of Minoan culture 2 it is highly improbable that Greek elements had any foothold in the island even at the later date, 1294-3, in which the name of Minos again occurs in the Chronicle 3-this time in connexion with Theseus.

This endeavour to annex Minos and to thrust back Achaean or Dorian Inter- dominion in Crete into the glorious clays of Minoan history is indeed in the only part and parcel of a process of which many other traces are perceptible. Odyssey. striking illustration of this process is supplied by an interpolation in the Odyssey only recently exposed by Professor Beloclv but which, when once attention has been called to it, must command general recognition. This is nothing less than the famous passage 5 which has so long supplied the charter for the pre-Homeric occupation of Crete by

Achaeans, Dorians, and divine Pelasgians' in company with the old inhabitants. The poet is speaking of the traditional populousness of the island, so well brought home to us by the crowded scenes of the Knossian frescoes: tttretyaecrtot, ecu f. vvi Knvra. Troa es"

TTCTI 8 evl Kifoo-ds, ju. eyaa. T7 Trdxi? ev a re evvewpos ysacrixeue AIDS yu. eyctx. of oapicrtT?.

1 he interpolator regardless of the order of composition or even of the most obvious grammatical requirements has broken into the sentence Ninety Cities and among them Knosos to insert a brief summary of the later ethnography of the island including an allusion to the three Dorian tribes!

If we may accept the view that the name of Minos, in its origin that of a divinity or deified hero, was borne, like that of Attis, by a succession of priest-kings, it goes far to explain the generalized use in which we already find the word Minoan in classical times. 0 In the present connexion the use of this term to designate the early civilization of Crete has much to 1 This is the date given by F. Jacoby, "Od. xix. 175-7: Chronicon Pariuw (1904), p. 6. J. Flach, AA, SofxAwvyxSo-o-a tyxtvv?

Chron. Par., p. 6, makes it 1423-2. Iv 8 'Ereovp s xeyax ropes, tv k K S
St-c Yol TT
Awpiees T Ty xuK 9, Slot Tf Iltauo-yot.
Jacoby,,, p. tit., p. 8 (Flach, op. tit., c Already in CW. xvii. 523, where the'stranger is described as Kprjrtj vaittaw, oft Mivwos yevos
Ausonia, iv (T 9 Tox evmv, the race of Minos' seems to be equivalent to the old Cretan stock in this generic-sense.

recommend it. To make use of Minos' like Pharaoh or Caesar avoids, Minoan 1 at any rate, the prejudgement of ethnographic qviestions that may occasionally jovnos arise in relation to the dominant element. It dispenses, moreover, with the sian-use of the term Knossian", which might well seem too local and restricted. 1

That intrusive ingredients may have made their way into Crete from time to time is probable enough. It has been suggested below that at the intrusive very dawn of Minoan history offshoots of the pre-dynastic Egyptian population may have found their way hither from the Delta. Towards the close of the Early Minoan Age, again, there are signs of a considerable infusion from the Northern direction, evidenced by the appearance of many types of Cycladic objects. The different kinds of sepulture found co-existing in the Late Minoan cemetery of Zafer Papoura, near Knossos, moreover, certainly point to family traditions drawn from heterogeneous sources. But, from whatever quarter exotic elements may have been drawn, it is clear that the Hutessen-native stock was strong enough to assimilate them. The culture as a whole 0 fminoan is cast in he same mould and shows an essential unity. There may doubtless have been more than one dynasty in the course of that long story. Setbacks there certainly were, partial or local destructions, as the centre of power shifted from Knossos to Phaestos or from Phaestos again to Knossos. But, as is shown at Knossos by the later cemetery, and at Hagia Triada by the flourishing history of its later settlement, even the destruction of the great palaces brought with it no real break. From the close of the Neolithic Age to the transitional epoch when iron was coming into use throughout a space Neolithic of time extending, at a moderate estimate, over two thousand years the yoiid course of the Minoan civilization is singularly continuous and homogeneous. M"" n.

The term Minoan as used for the present purpose embraces the Copper and Bronze Ages of Crete but does not include that more primitive stage of culture represented by the Later Stone Age. At Knossos vast remains of this underlie the Palace and its immediate forerunners and form, in fact, the Tell on which they stand. These Neolithic strata, going clown in places over The-Tel 26 feet below the later remains, and representing at a reasonable calculation os an antiquity of some ten thousand years, illustrate in a continuous course the evolution of the successive phases of that culture and admit already of some 1 Sir William Ridgeway, op. tit., p. 126, adds word Knossian. But I have consistently used as a more imperative reason for rejecting the the more general term Minoan. The most name " Minoan" that, as it is now being used misleading of all designations at least for all by Dr. Evans and his followers, it deliberately the early stages of the culture is the German assumes that all the Bronze Age culture of the kretisch-mykenisch. Mycenae only comes in Aegean radiates from Cnossus'. This might at a comparatively late date. have been a just criticism against the use of the

THE PALACE OE MINOS, ETC.

Neolithic connexions with Anatolia.

Relations of Anatolian culture to Early Minoan.

Necessary reserves.

rough classification. We have here the rucle foundation on which the whole of the elegant fabric of the Minoan civilization ultimately rests, and, though the material is as yet imperfectly explored, a summary survey of the salient features of this more primitive prehistoric stage has been included in this work. 1

Early points of contact are there indicated not only with Greece and the Aegean world but in a special degree with Anatolia. Parallel forms of certain primitive types of crouching or squatting clay images the prototypes, we may believe, of later forms of a Mother Goddess seem to have been common to'both regions, and the range of these figures is now shown to extend to the Middle Euphrates, while kindred groups may be traced through the Semitic lands, and even beyond the Caspian. 2 The habit of using stone maces also finds analogies over a wide East Mediterranean area. On the whole the Neolithic culture of Crete (representative of the Aegean Islands in general) may be regarded as an insular offshoot of an extensive Anatolian province, but at the same time as displaying certain formative sympathies with Thessaly and other parts of mainland Greece.

That there were already some inter-relations between this culture and the outside world is shown by the fact that the obsidian of Melos in its worked or unworked state was finding its way not only to Crete but to the Nile Valley in Neolithic times. With it came probably the Naxian emery, so important for every kind of lapidary work.

But, as a whole, down to the end of the Later Stone Age, Crete forms part of an inert mass of indefinite extension, with little to distinguish it from the mean level of primitive culture in other parts of the Aegean and Anatolian world, or indeed throughout a large European area.

Such links with any higher civilization as may have existed we should naturally have sought in the East Mediterranean region, the more so as we have seen that the old underlying element in Crete had remote Anatolian connexions. These relations should at no period of Cretan history be left out of sight. As regards Early Minoan times, however, caution is necessary against being led astray by later conditions. The days of the Royal Road through Central Asia Minor were not yet, and the Hittite sculptures on Mount Sipylps, which attest the breaking through of the indigenous inland Power to the mouth of the Hermos, belong rather to the close of the Minoan Age. That by the middle of the Third Millennium before our era the Cap-padocian uplands had become the centre of a primitive Hittite civilization may be admitted. To judge, however, from existing data, the distinctively Hittite culture left little mark on the South-Western region of Asia Minor. 1 See p. 32 seqq. " See below, p. 49.

The earliest evidence of a direct importation from the Oriental world is Ois-supplied by a cylinder 1 of the First Babylonian Dynasty found in a deposit"

belonging to the mature earlier phase (a) of the First Middle Minoan Period. " la ". The inscribed clay tablets, which now appear, also attest an influence from that side.

That throughout its course Minoan civilization continued to absorb Asiatic . iii i TI l-. I-inents elements from the Asiatic side is, on the face of it, probable enough. I his in Minoan process was, in fact, the continuation of an early drift and infiltration, going (back to the most primitive times, and to which probably the first acquaintance with metals was due. The cult of the Double Axe was, as we have seen, common to both areas, and there is a strong presumption that its original home is to be sought in that direction. Votive axes of terra-cotta, both double and single, were brought to light moreover during M. de Sarzec's excavations at the early Chaldaean site of Tello. 2 The stone mace has the same wide easterly range. We have even a hint that the favourite bull-grappling sports of Minoan Crete, with their acrobatic features, had their counterparts in Cappadocia as early as 2400 n. c. 3 The Early Minoan ivory seals in the shape of animals and the conoid types have also a wide Oriental distribution, and the 'signet form that survives into Middle Minoan times show a parallelism with certain Hittite seals. A few Cretan hieroglyphs also suggest Hittite comparisons.

Taking the data at our disposal as a whole there is little evidence oriental of direct relations with the Easternmost Mediterranean shores before the fl " cn ces close of the Middle Minoan Age. The Early Babylonian cylinder may? J ft indeed be regarded as an incipient symptom of such relations, and the Minoan fashion of flounced costumes may have owed its first suggestion to models from that side. Early in Late Minoan times a regular commercial intercourse was established with Cyprus and the neighbouring coastlands of North Syria and Cilicia, which was the prelude to actual colonization, eventually resulting in a distinct Cypro-Minoan School of Art. From the 1 See below, pp. 197-8, Fig. 14. having a structure on his back suggesting the - L. Heuzey, Decouvertes en Chaldee par seat or throne of a deity. In front of the

Ernest de Sarzec, livraison, PI. 45, 5, 6. bull is the figure of a man who ha fallen face on 3 A sealed clay envelope from Cappadocia the ground, feet in the air. He is falling on (Pinches, Liverpool Annals of. rchaeology and his left arm, the right being stretched out back

Anthropology, i, p. 76 seqq., No. 23) bears the wards. Farther to the right is a man stand- impression of a cylinder in the indigenous style, ing on his head and with his hands on I and dating, according to Professor Sayce, t. ground to support himself. The figures 2400 n. c., described as follows (p. 77): On to have been acrobatic in nature. See below, the extreme right is a horned bull kneeling and p. 190.

THE PALACE OF MINOS. ETC.

Reflex Action from Cyprus and N. Syria. Religious Influences.

Late Operation of Oriental Influences in Crete or Asia Minor.

Anatolia and Crete on a parat close of

Neolithic.

Whence came new impulse?

Intensive

Pre-

Dynastic

Egyptian influence on Crete.

First Late Minoan Period onwards we trace the reflex of all this in many signs of Syrian influences. The clay tablets that form the vehicle of script continuously reflect Oriental models. That religious influences from Semitic sources were also beginning to operate is by no means improbable. Who shall say how early the old Chaldaean tradition of the legislator receiving the law from the God of the Mountain was implanted in Crete, as it had been in Israel? Of great significance, moreover, is the appearance in Cretan signets belonging to the closing part of the First Late Minoan Period of priestly figures, wearing long robes of oriental fashion, and bearing ceremonial axes of a typically Syrian form. It is clear, too, that chariots and thoroughbred horses together with their accoutrements reached the Minoan and Mycenaean princes from the same side. In the last Late Minoan Period, moreover, there occur bronze figurines of a male divinity with a peaked headpiece which stand in a close relation to similar types from North Syria and the Hittite regions. In all this, account must be taken of the intermediary activities of the Keftiu people of the Egyptian Monuments.

But it must be clearly realized that the waves of higher civilizing influences that ultimately reached Crete through Syria and Cyprus from a more distant Mesopotamian source only affected Minoan culture at a time when it had already reached a comparatively advanced stage. Neither were they able to penetrate as yet with effective results through the mountain ranges of the interior of Asia Minor.

It cannot be gainsaid, indeed, that, as far as can be gathered from the evidence before us, the civilization of the Eastern Aegean shores at the close of the Neolithic Age stood on no higher level than that of Crete. It could not give more than it possessed, and we must seek on another side for the quickening spirit which about this time begins to permeate and transform the rude island culture.

In what direction then are we to look for this very early influence, thanks to which, in the course of a few generations, the Cretans had outstripped all their neighbours of the Aegean basin and evolved the high early civilization to which the term Minoan is properly applied?

That the main impulse came from the Egyptian side can no longer now be doubted. Cumulative evidence, drawn from various sides, to which attention will be called in the succeeding Sections, shows that this influence was already making itself felt in Crete in the Age that preceded the First Dynast)-. Not only does it appear, for instance, that stone vases of Pre-dynastic fabric were actually reaching the island, but a whole series of Early Minoan forms can be traced to prototypes in use by the Old Race of Egypt. In both cusrs again we find the same aesthetic selection of materials distinguished by their polychromy, so that the beautifully coloured vases of Mochlos find their best analogy in those of the prehistoric tombs of Naqada rather than in those of the Early Dynastic Age. Certain types of small images, the subjects and forms of seals, and the game of draughts, go back to the same early Nilotic source. That a maritime connexion between Crete and the Nile Valley began already in very early times will surprise no one who recalls the important part played by both rowing-galleys and sailing vessels in the figured representations of the late Pre-dynastic Period in Egypt, 1 and the Old Race had already a Mediterranean outlet at the Canopic mouth of the Nile. 2 Models of Kucilityof boats, found in both Early Minoan and Cycladic graves, show that the islanders " " r l l themselves were already filled with the sea-faring spirit. 3 How comparatively course, easy, indeed, under favourable circumstances, is the passage of the Libyan Sea is shown by the fact that the sponge-fishing craft that touch on the east coast of Crete, manned at times with a crew of less than a dozen men, ply their industry as far as Benghazi. The Etesian winds of summer and accompanying current greatly aid this transit.

The proto-Egyptian element in Early Minoan Crete is, in fact, so Wasthere clearly defined and is so intensive in its nature as almost to suggest some- t tle-thing more than such a connexion as might have been brought about by ment- primitive commerce. It may well, indeed, be asked whether, in the time of stress and change that marked the triumph of the dynastic element in the Ntr Valley, some part of the older population then driven out may not have made an actual settlement on the soil of Crete.

Further waves of influence from the same side succeeded, in part due, influence it would seem, to some continued relations with members of the older indi- um jer genous stock of the Delta coasts, 4 but now, in a progressive degree, to contact J witli the dynastic element in Egypt. Exquisite carinated bowls of diorite and other hard materials such as were executed for the Pharaohs of the Fourth and immediately succeeding dynasties found their way to the site of Knossos' where they were imitated by the indigenous lapidaries and potters. In the darker period of Egyptian history that intervenes between the Sixth and 1 See Petrie, Naqada and Ballas, pp. 48, 49 4 The Haau (afterwards Haunebii) or Fen-and Pis. LXVI, LXVII, and J. Capart, Les men of the Egyptians. Cf. Newberry, lot. at., debuts de Fart en gypte, p. 116, Fig. 83, and and H. R. Hall, Oldest Civilization in Greece, p. 192, Fig. 141 pp. 158, 159; The Ancient History of the Near

See below p. 291, and P. Newberry, Liv. East, p. 35. Annals, c., I, p. 17 seqq. See below, p. 85.

3 See below, pp. 118, 120, Figs. 87, 7 a, 89,6.

Eleventh Dynasty this transmarine influence, as illustrated by the button-seals' and leg amulets, takes again a character perhaps best described as Egypto-Under Libyan1 In the great days of the Middle Kingdom the purer Egyptian Kingdom element once more asserts itself, and countless Nilotic models, among which the lotus and papyrus are very distinguishable, are henceforward assimilated by Minoan art. The most striking record of this connexion is the diorite monument of User, found in the Central Court of the Knossian Palace in a stratum belonging to the Second Middle Minoan Period. 2 On the other hand, the counterpart of the evidence from Cretan soil is seen in the beautiful polychrome pottery of Middle Minoan fabric found at Kahun, Abydos, and elsewhere, in association with remains of the Twelfth and the early part of the Thirteenth Dynasty. 3

An astonishing series of discoveries recently made beneath the present sea-level off the former island of Pharos, at Alexandria, may place the relations of Ancient Egypt with the Minoan world in a wholly new light. The moles and wharves and capacious basins have now been traced out of a vast pre-Hellenic harbour, which rivals the Pyramids in its colossal construction. 4 Hyksos That the intercourse with the Nile Valley was not broken off during the

Knossos. period of the Hyksos dominion is shown by the occurrence again on the Palace site of Knossos, in a deposit belonging to the earlier part of the Third Middle Minoan Period of the alabastron lid of King Khian. Increased It was, however, during the early part of the Late Minoan Age in Crete and of the New Empire in Egypt that these inter-relations were most manifold under j n their complexion. The correspondence of Egyptian and Minoan technique pire. in metal-work is often such that it is difficult to say on which side was the borrowing. Types, too, are fused. The Egyptian griffin takes Minoan wings. Late The reproduction of Nile scenes by Minoan artists is at times so accurate and detailed as to convey the impression that guilds of Cretan craftsmen were course actually working at this time on Egyptian soil. The abundance there of im-Egypt. ported L. M. I vessels fits in, too, with a personal contact of another kind between the Minoan world and the Nile Valley evidenced by the Egyptian representations of the People of the Isles of the Sea and their offerings. In the latest Minoan epoch, when Crete itself had become largely isolated through the decay of its sea-power, the commercial relations with the Nile Valley for the most part passed into the hands of the Cypriote and Mycenaean branch, but 1 See below, p. 123. 3 See below, p. 267, Figs. 198, c, 199, a.

2 See below, p. 288, Fig. 220. Theassocia- These discoveries are due to M. Gaston lions of the stratum in which this monument lay Jondet, Engineer in Chief of Kgyptian Ports are now thoroughly established (loc. cit. p. 287). and Lighthouses. See below, p. 292 seqq.

this does not affect the main phenomenon with which we have to do. This is the highly important historic fact, brought more clearly into relief with every fresh discovery, that for some two thousand years the Minoan civilization of Crete was in practically uninterrupted relations with that of Egypt.

The material evidence of interpenetration with Egyptian elements General cannot of course always give a clue to the more intangible influences that may have been brought to bear in the domain of ideas in Cretan religion to Egypt .-11-I- of Minoan for instance, in law and government, or even in literary tradition. That Culture, the elaborate systems of Minoan writing were of independent evolution is certain, but there are good reasons, for instance, to suspect the stimulus of Egyptian suggestion in the rise of the Cretan hieroglyphic signary, and a few individual signs seem to have been actually borrowed. 1 The wearing of amulets iof Egyptian form, such as the leg-shaped pendants, shows a certain community in popular superstition. The use of the Egyptian sistrum for the ritual dance of the Hagia Triada vase is a very suggestive symptom, and the adoption of a type of double-spouted libation vessel Religious associated, as it appears, with a primitive cult of Set and Horus, 2 may ne xions. point to a very ancient religious connexion. In Late Minoan times the evidences of a real religious syncretism accumulate witness the constant recurrence of sphinxes and griffins and the adoption of the Egyptian was and a id-i symbols, or of Hathoric emblems like the cow suckling her calf. Ta-urt, the Hippopotamus Goddess, becomes the prototype of Minoan Genii.

When it is realized how many elements drawn from the Minoan world lived on in that of Hellas 3 the full import of this very ancient indebtedness to Egypt at once becomes apparent. Egyptian influences, hitherto reckoned as rather a secondary incident among late classical experiences, are now seen to lie about the very cradle of our civilization.

But the essential character of this influence must not be misunderstood. Advan-As regards Egypt, Minoan Crete did not find itself in the position in which ulir Palestine and Phoenicia, having only land frontiers, stood towards the great Position, border Powers of the Nile and of the Euphrates. With the sea between, it could always keep the foreign civilization at arm's length. Its enterprising inhabitants continually absorbed and assimilated Egyptian forms and ideas, developing them on independent lines. They took what they wanted, nothing more, and were neither artistically nor politically enslaved.

Something has already been said of the old underlying connexion 1 See Scripta Minna, i, pp. 197-8. See my Address on The Minoan and 2 See below, p. 80. Mycenaean elements in Hellenic Life .f. S., x ii (1912), p. 277 seqq. C 2

THE PALACE OF MINOS, ETC.

Cycladic Intercourse.

Troadic Connexions.

Minoan Influence on Melos.

Western Relations with Anatolia, which was in fact an inheritance from late geological times when Crete formed its South-Western foreland. The actual land bridge, it is true, had long been broken through, though the island stepping stones remained, Rhodes bulking large among them. But across the open Aegean basin that lies north of Crete, and over which the Etesian winds blow steadily throughout the summer days, direct intercourse had early begun with the Cyclades and still further lying coasts and islands. From a remote Neolithic Period the obsidian from Melos had found its way across this basin.

Intimate relations between Crete and the Cyclades are a well-marked feature of the Early Minoan Age. At the time of its most characteristic development we see Crete, the Aegean islands, and, North-Eastwards still, the First Settlement of Troy interfused with similar elements. The early silver trade from the Troadic side, about which more will be said, seems to have played a leading part in this diffusion. But of actual work in precious metals the most brilliant manifestation is to be found on Cretan soil. How poor is the jewellery of Hissarlik or the Cycladic graves compared with the exquisite fabrics of Mochlos! Per contra, towards the close of the Early Minoan Age, a current of influence makes itself perceptible from the Central Aegean, bearing with it more primitive ingredients. Typical marble idols of Cycladic fabric and material appear in Cretan deposits, and the clay pyxides' or round-liclded boxes, derived from the same quarter, present a form of ceramic decoration, consisting of incised and punctuated patterns with chalky inlay, which in Crete is but sparsely found beyond the close of the Middle Neolithic. The spiral system, with widely ramifying Northern connexions, now enters Crete from the same direction. On the other hand, the abundance of Middle Minoan polychrome sherds at Phylakopi shows an ever-increasing preponderance of Cretan influence, which by the close of the Middle Minoan Age completely dominates Melian culture. Symptoms of this are the use of the advanced Linear script, A, 1 and the employment of Knossian artists to paint the panels of the Palace walls. 2 Indirectly, at least, a connexion may be said to have subsisted between Crete and mainland Greece from the Early Neolithic Age onwards. The same primitive commerce in obsidian, that linked it with Melos and the Central Aegean, had wide ramifications that extended not only to the Greek mainland but to Italy and what was then the Far West beyond. Certain correspondences in types that occur in the Neolithic products both of Crete and the Aegean area such, for instance, as the steatopygous images may have been due to a common heritage of great antiquity and indeed reappear 1 See below, p. 561. 2 See below, p. 542.

THE MINOAN AGE on the Egyptian as well as the Anatolian side. Hut the spread of similar products along continuous lines west of the Ionian, and even of the Tyrrhene Sea is not an accidental phenomenon, being everywhere coincident with the Aegea course of the old obsidian routes. Pottery that belongs to the same context Inter- . course as the Neolithic ware of Crete has been found in South Italy, Sicily, Sardinia, with Italy. the intermediate island of Pianosa, and the Ligurian Caves. 1 So, too, the only Italian sites on which Neolithic clay images have been found lie on this line, in Sicily and Liguria.- In the Second and Third Early Minoan Periods and the early part of the Middle Minoan Age, when Cretan civilization already occupied a com- 1 M;. 3. BONE OBJECT FROM SIKEL CEMETERY OF CASTEI. I. UCCIO, NEAR SYRACUSE (e.).

mantling position in the Central Aegean basin, the evidence of this Western in- tercourse becomes even more conclusive, and it is a fair conclusion that the Troadic silver trade may have found an extension, partly perhaps through Minoan agency, to the Tyrrhene shores. Among the E. M. Ill relics of the Tholos ossuary of Kumasa in Central Crete were found silver and copper daggers of elongated triangular shape with a strong mid-rib:! which present a close conformity with daggers 4 of the Chalcolithic period in Italy and Sicily. It is in M. M. I that the most striking proof of actual import from the Aegean Early side is afforded by some tubular bone objects, probably handles, with globules Relations in relief and incised ornamentation, found in tombs and cave-dwellings of the First Sikel Period 5 and identical in character with examples from the third 1 See T. E. Feet, Tie Stone and Bronze.;. v Italy and Sicily, p. 135 seqq., and pp. 284, 285.

- In The Sepulchral Deposit of Hagios Onu-phrios near Phaeslos in its relation to primitive Cretan and Aegean Culture (Appended to Cretan Piciographs, c., Quaritch,

1893) I had already called attention to the parallelism presented by the clay figures of the Finalese Caves (Liguria) and of Villafrati, near Palermo, to Aegean forms; and cf. my Pre- historic interments of the Balzi Rossi Caves i nd their relation to the Neolithic Cave-burials of the Finalese (Anthr. Inst. Journ., 893, pp. 303-5).

3 A. Mosso, Escursioni nel Mediterraneo, p. 216, Fig. 120; and Le armi piii antiche di rame e di lronzo, pp. 490, 491, Fig. 8. (Excavations of Dr. Xanthudides.) See below, p. 100.

4 Peet, op. cit., p. 258, Fig. 136, and p. 260, Fig. 142, and cf. pp. 282, 283.

"Orsi, Bull. Paletn., 1892, pp. 7, 8; Au-sonia i (1907), pp. 5, 6; Grotta Lazzaro.

THE PALACE OF MINOS, ETC.

Troadic Silver Trade. Minoan and

Minyan imitations of Troadic Types.

spirali-form decoration of Maltese Sanctuaries.

Minoan Influence in Iberic West.

stratum of the Second City of Troy. 1 Among the decorative designs are reticulated bead patterns of Middle Kingdom Egyptian type, 2 accompanied by curving tendrils and what seem to be stellate flowers on short stalks, suggesting sympathy with Minoan motives (Fig. 3). It seems clear that the Troad was betimes the emporium through which silver, from the rich deposits of its own back-country, was diffused throughout the Aegean world. Silver vessels of Troadic types and their fine ceramic imitations appear in Crete at the very beginning of the Middle Minoan Age, and some Minyan types of Mainland Greece attest the same influence.

In the same Early Metal Age cemetery of Castelluccio, near Syracuse, that produced a series of the bone handles, there came to light two door-slabs of tombs presenting spiraliform designs, and a still more fully developed system of interlocked spiral decoration is seen on the Megalithic sanctuaries of the Maltese islands notably in the newly discovered Temples' of Hal-Saflieni and Hal-Tarxien. 3 These are locally of late Neolithic, or perhaps Chalcolithic, date, but their horned spiraliform decoration shows a curious parallelism with certain decorative motives of the finest M. M. II polychrome ware. 4

To the great epoch of Minoan expansion (to be distinguished from later, more purely Mycenaean, waves in the same direction) must be traced the engrafting of certain rapier-like sword types and of vessels with reed designs of pre-Mycenaean tradition on Sicilian soil. Still further to the West the same influence makes itself perceptible in Eastern Spain. 0 Some bronze figures of Minoan type seem to have been actually imported, and the fine bulls' heads found in Majorca, with long urus-like horns, on which at times the sacred doves are perched, point to a Minoan school. 7 The sacral horns of Minoan cult themselves recur.

It was certainly in pursuit of very solid commercial objects that

Minoan or other Aegean merchants pushed forward into the West Medi- 1 Schlie-mann, Ilios, p. 514, No. 983, Troja, with the Predynastic Egyptian class and point to p. 116, No. 41; Troja u. Ilion, i, p. 392, Fig. 376 (A. G6tze)c. See also Petersen in Rom. Mitth., 1898, pp. 164-6. The stage of evolution evidenced by the dagger types of this stratum shows affinities with that of M. M. I Crete.

Compare the Griffin's collar from Beni-Hasan, p. 710, Fig 533, below.

3 For Hal-Tarxien see Prof. T. Zammit, Archaeologia, 2, xvii (i9(6 p. 127 seqq. and 2, xviii (1917), p. 263 seqq. Compare my observations,Vw. Soc. Ants,, vol. xxviii, pp. 251, 252. The steatopygous figures betray an affinity

Libyan intermediaries. The Megalithic constructions themselves, as Albert Mayr has remarked (Die vorgeschichtlichen Denkmaler von Malta, p. 719), point the same way. For the Aegean comparisons see, too, my Myc. Tree and Pillar Cull (1901), pp. 100, 101.

See below, p. 261 and Figs. 194 k, 1;.".

5 Prehistoric Tombs of Knossos, p. 108.

"P. Paris, Essai stir Iart et Findustrie de r Espagne primitive (Paris, 1903-4) and Arch. Anz., 1906. Cf. Serif to. Minoa, i, p. 96 seqq.

7 P. Paris, op. ., i, pp. 157, 158.

terranean basin. The increase in tin alloy in the copper implements in use Trade in in the Aegean area from the close of the Early Minoan Age onwards points ijp; i a r " L. at least to one objective. In connexion with the early tin trade attention will be called below to the diffusion among the Early Bronze Age remains not only in Spain, but in the British islands, of a segmented type of faience bead, the fabric of which had been taken over by the Minoans from Egypt. 1 Of another result of these Western relations we have direct evidence in the import into Crete, from the close of the Early Minoan Age onwards, of the kind of volcanic glass known as liparite and peculiar to the Aeolian Islands. Lumps of this material were found in the Palace at Knossos and, as has already been mentioned above, liparite bowls were cut by native lapidaries, following diorite models of the Fourth or succeeding Dynasties, while these, in turn, were imitated in painted clay early in the Middle Minoan Period. The manufacture of liparite vessels was still in vogue in Crete in the early part of the Late Minoan Age.

Aegean influences, in their origin, at least, due to the early trade in Relations the native obsidian, were operating, as we have seen, in Mainland Greece a j n an d already in Neolithic times and are traceable in many directions during Greece, the early Ages of metal. The evidence, however, of distinctively Cretan ingredients in the Mainland culture does not become clear till the Middle Minoan Age. Even then the materials are still very few.- It is only Scanty among the sherds connected with the Minoan settlements at Tiryns and Mj l noan Mycenae that specimens occur which must be regarded as offshoots of the jjjj! M. M. Ill ceramic style. The general dearth of such material in the; reece. preceding Periods only heightens the effect of the wholesale invasion of Main- Hut land Greece by Minoan forms at the close of the Middle and beginning of the sa e in" va. Late Minoan Age. This was no gradual change, led up to by successive stages, but a sudden revolution involving the idea of actual conquest and widespread Forms settlement. It implies a real break in local conditions, and the dominant J element that now comes into view represents an incomparably higher stage of civilization than anything that had existed before on the Helladic side.

Some of the new features, indeed, now introduced show points ol divergence from Cretan forms so far as they are at present known to us. One remarkable phenomenon that now meets us is that the Megaron at Mycenae, which as we now know goes back at least to the borders of the 1 See below, p. 491. below p. 166, and Fig. 117 f) Steatite vases - A matt-painted globular jug from Elateia of Cretan M. M. I fabric occurred on the Aspis in lhocis, probably of Cycladic origin. shows the site at Argos. See Bulletin de Corresfondanee influence of the M. M. I butterfly motive (see Hellenitne, 1906, p 38, Fig. 68.

THK PALACE OF MINOS, ETC.

Trojan tradition of Me-garon at Mycenae.

Mycenaean Culture essentially Minoan.

Crete Cradle of European Civilization.

Middle Minoan Age, 1 does not represent the apsidal type then in vogue in Mainland Greece, including the site of Tiryns itself. 2 Rather it seems to be an adaptation of the traditional Trojan form which here rises into view in an organically Minoizecl aspect. The Court in front, moreover, with its bordering Corridor, answering to the same palatial system, is constructively-treated after die manner of a Cretan light area. Where had this complete fusion been effected with the Anatolian type?

The whole framework of the civilization that now rises into view at Tiryns and Mycenae, Thebes and Orchomenos is still Minoan. The inner spirit of Minoan society is still reflected; its ideas of. life and death, its sports and pastimes, its sepulchral rites and religious cult. Among the countless objects of art such as those found in the Shaft Graves at Mycenae, the Tholos' tombs of Vapheio and Volo, or in the earlier of the rock-cut chambers, the finest are actually of Cretan importation, while the rest are local reproductions of fabrics in the current Cretan style. Even where arrangements vary, every detail of the decoration is purely Minoan. Mycenaean culture in its later phase no doubt chose a course of its own, and, largely independent as it then was of its original Cretan direction, took a more markedly provincial form, parallel to the Third Late Minoan stage in Crete. But in its earlier manifestations it was not only moulded on that of the most brilliant period of Cretan civilization but was continually dominated from that side. The genesis of Mycenaean arts must be sought on Cretan soil, and two-thirds of the long course of Minoan civilization lay already behind them.

In other words, this comparatively small island, left on one side to-day by all the main lines of Mediterranean intercourse, was at once the starting-point and the earliest stage in the highway of European civilization. The early relations of Minoan Crete, both on the Egyptian and Aegean sides, glanced at in the foregoing pages, sufficiently illustrate the advantages that it 1 The frescoes belonging to the Megaron in its original form recently discovered by Dr. Rodenwaldt are of the earliest Miniature style probably M. M. Ill b. Agonistic scenes of the Minoan class are represented, and a fragment (found earlier) shows women looking on from the windows of a shrine of the Double Axe Cult (see below, p. 444, Fig. 320).

- K. M tiller, Ath. Mitih. 1913, p. 86; G. Karo, Fiihrer durch die Rtdnen von Tiryns, p. 7. The apsidal type of house recurs in the same Middle Helladic stratum at Korako near Corinth (American excavations), at Olympia and Orchomenos, while at Thermos in Aetolia it persists to a date contemporary with L. M. I. (For the material see Vol. II.) The simple oblong Megaron type with the fixed hearth makes its first appearance at Corinth and Orchomenos in strata contemporary with the Late Mycenaean Palaces. The evidence of its existence in Middle Helladic times is still to seek. Nor is there any link of connexion forthcoming with the older Thessalian class.

drew from its geographical conditions. Kprjri m you? m, ztvoa ivl ofaom ir6irp: cemr. il the central position of Crete in the East Mediterranean basin at once strikes the j n "J.; 1 " eye. 2 A half-way house between three continents, pointing East and West and Mediter-barring both the Aegean and the Libyan Seas, this mid-sea land had sufficient territorial extension to permit the growth of a distinct and independent national life. Insular, but not isolated, it was thus able to develop a civilization of its own on native lines and to accept suggestions from the Egyptian or the Asiatic side without itself being dominated by foreign conventionalism. Primitive navigation, first reared perhaps in the land-locked harbours of the smaller Aegean islands, was early enlisted in the Minoan service. Long ages before the birth of Venice, Crete had espoused the everlasting sea, and the first naval dominion in Mediterranean waters was wielded by Minoan Knossos.

The Egyptian relations, as above indicated, supply a certain measure for the duration of the Minoan civilization. It has been already suggested that the very pronounced Pre-dynastic element in Early Minoan culture may "-uides. connect itself with some actual exodus of part of the older race of Nile-dwellers, due to the pressure of Menes' conquest. Taking the accession of the First Dynasty as a rough chronological guide to the beginning of the Minoan Age, and accepting provisionally Meyer's upper dating, we arrive at 3400 H. c. by a century or more.:! The lowest term of anything that can be called pure Minoan culture can hardly be brought clown much below 1 200 H. c.

For this considerable space of time, extending over some two thousand two hundred years, the division here adopted into three main Sections, Triple the Early, Middle, and Late Minoan, each in turn with three Periods of its own, will not be thought too minute. It allows, in fact, for each Period an average duration of nearly two centuries and a half, the earlier Periods being naturally the longer. This triple division, indeed, whether we regard the course of the Minoan civilization as a whole or its threefold stages, is in its very essence logical and scientific. In every characteristic phase of culture we note in fact the period of rise, maturity, and decay. Even within the limits of many of these Periods, moreover, the process of evolution visible has established such distinct ceramic phases that it has been found convenient to divide them into two sections a and b.

The three main phases of Minoan history roughly correspond with those of the Early, the Middle, and the earlier part of the New Kingdom in Egypt, dence with 1 Homer, Odyssey, xix. 172. the pure E. M. I style could hardly have been
See Folding Plate facing p. i reached much before the close of the Fourth
A transitional Sub-Neolithic stage has Millennium B. C. See p. 70, below.
however to be allowed for and the evolution of
The Early The Early Minoan Age, the beginning of which indeed seems to overlap to a certain extent the close of the Pre-dynastic Age in Egypt, supplies, in its middle Period (E. M. II), evidence of inter-relations with the Egypt of the Fourth, Fifth, and Sixth Dynasties. Certain features that characterize its concluding Period (E. M. Ill), on the other hand, betray a contact with the quasi-Libyan elements that came to the fore in the Nile Valley during the troubled times that follow on to the Sixth Dynasty.

This Early Minoan Age, the beginnings of which are taken to include a phase of somewhat gradual transition, to which the name Sub-Neolithic may be given, must have extended over a relatively considerable space of time. The date of the accession of Menes, approximately fixed at 3400 B. c., has been taken above as supplying a rough terminus a qiw for the beginning of this Age, while its lower limits would be about 2100 B. c.

This is an Age of gradual up-growth and of vigorous youth. The primitive culture of Crete now assumes its distinctive features. It works out its independence of the surrounding elements of wider geographical range from which it grew, and takes up a commanding position in the Aegean world. The great hypogaea at Knossos already foreshadow palatial arrangements.

Among its most characteristic products are the elegant stone vessels of choice and brilliantly variegated materials. The fabric of painted pottery with geometrical designs, first dark on light then light on dark, also makes considerable progress. Goldsmith's work attains a high degree of delicacy and perfection and, in this branch, as well as in the reliefs and engravings on soft stone and ivory, natural forms are at times successfully imitated. The seals show a gradual advance in pictographic expression.

Middle The Middle Minoan Age covers the Period of the Middle Kingdom Minoan in Egypt including that of the Hyksos domination. Its first Period seems largely to coincide with that of the Eleventh Dynasty, overlapping, however, the first part of the Twelfth. Its acme, the Second Middle Minoan Period, is marked by a growing intimacy of relations with the Egypt of the Twelfth and Thirteenth Dynasty, while, in a stratum belonging to the concluding M. M. Ill Period, occurred the alabastron lid of the Hyksos king Khyan. The chronological limits of this Age lie roughly between 2100 and 1580 B. c.

This is pre-eminently the Age of Palaces. The foundation of the great buildings at Knossos and Phaestos goes back to the close of M. M. I., or to shortly after 2000 B. C. The hierarchical position of the priest-kings was now consolidated. A true Early Palace Style had evolved itself by the end of M. M. II an epoch marked on both sites by a great catastrophe.

It was followed in M. M. Ill, however, by a monumental rebuilding and a Mainland splendid revival, leading up to the first era of expansion in Mainland Greece,? richly illustrated by the earliest elements in the Shaft Graves of Mycenae.

This is the Age of brilliant polychromy in ceramic decoration, and of the earliest wall-paintings. I n its latest phase it is marked by an extraordinary development of naturalism in design. But what especially distinguishes this middle stage of Minoan culture is the final evolution of the Art of Writing from the mere pictography of the earlier Periods. By M. M. I we already see the full evolution of a hieroglyphic style. In M. M. Ill, Class A of the Linear series has already taken its rise. To the same Period belongs the Phaestos Disk, but the characters differ from the Cretan and may best be ascribed to some related element in S. W. Asia Minor.

The Late Minoan Age corresponds with the Eighteenth and Nineteenth The Late Dynasties in Egypt, at most including the early part of the Twentieth. Its A First and Second Periods would cover the reigns from Aahmes to Amen-hotep III. The beginning of the Mainland L. M. III stage is already illustrated by the earlier sherds of the rubbish heaps' of Tell-el-Amarna of the time of Akhenaten and his immediate successors 1 (c. 1370-1350 B. C.). By the thirteenth century Minoan and Mycenaean art was in full decadence, and it is difficult to believe that anything that can be described as ptfte Minoan culture is to be found in Crete later than the early part of Rameses 111's reign.

Thus the time limits with which we have to deal for the Late Minoan Age lie approximately between 1580 and 1200 n. c.

The early part of this epoch, including the transitional phase which The preserved the fine naturalistic style of M. M. Ill, is the Golden Age ot Xge of Crete, followed, after a level interval, by a gradual decline. The settlement Cretc already begun in M. M. Ill of large tracts of mainland Greece is now continued, and the new Mycenaean culture is thus firmly planted on those shores. But the generation that witnessed this consummation saw also the final overthrow of the Palace at Phaestos, and the brilliant sole dominion of remodelled Knossos that followed on this event was itself, after no long interval, cut short. The overthrow of the great Palace took place at Expan-the close of the succeeding L. M. II Period, the result, according to the inter- fowwm. pretation suggested below, of an internal uprising, apparently of submerged elements. It looks as if the Mainland enterprise had been too exhausting. The centre of gravity of Minoan culture shifted now to the Mycenaean side.

1 J'fl-f-, lnarna, V. XXVII 52, 28, c., as the L. M. Ill a Mainland phase. Most, how-well as in part of an alabastron, isrc. in the B. M. ever, show distinctly later associations. wv see the I, M. I tradition characteristic of

Finally, some hostile intrusion from the North, which is naturally to be connected with the first Greek invasions, drove away the indigenous settlers who had partially reoccupiecl or rebuilt the ruined sites at Knossos and elsewhere, and put an end to the last recuperative efforts of Minoan Crete.

The culture of the succeeding Age when iron was coming into general use, though still largely permeated with indigenous elements, is best described as

Sub-Minoan, and lies beyond the immediate scope of the present work.

Artistic The brilliant naturalism of the grand Transitional Epoch that links reached the Middle with the Late Minoan Age reaches its acme in the high reliefs in L. M. I. O f painted stucco at Knossos, in the frescoes of Hagia Triada and such works as the harvester vase. The Court atmosphere at Knossos developed a greater formalism in art, well illustrated by the ceramic designs in

Palace the later Palace Style. Such remains, however, as the Room of the

L. M 6 II. Throne which dates from the latter epoch, show the refinement in civilized surroundings then attained. So too Class B of the linear script, now in vogue, and confined as far as is known to Knossos, represents the highest development of the Minoan system of writing. But the rococo spirit now visible, and which, already in L. M. I, manifests itself in the artificial groups of the Court ladies of the Miniature frescoes, was a harbinger of the gradual decline that marks the course of the last Minoan Period.

graphical e classification of the Minoan culture into nine successive Periods base of does not rest on merely theoretical deductions as to the evolution and suc- present. r T.

Classifica- cession oi types. In the case ot the excavations at Knossos a constant endeavour has been made to apply geological methods, so that the sequence here adopted rests on a mass of stratigraphical evidence. In such evidence.

Methods, as indeed in that afforded by geological strata, the succession of deposits in individual cases presents lacunae which have to be filled up from data supplied by other sections. Only, moreover, by considerable experience has it been possible to guard against certain subtle causes of error, such as, for instance, the total removal of a floor belonging to one construction and its substitution by another on the same level. In order to revise the evidence, largely with a view to the present study, three months of the year

Supple- 1913 were devoted by me, as already mentioned, to supplementary excava-

Tests f t ons on the Palace site, in the course of which about ninety explorations were made beneath the floors at various spots. The result has been, while correcting some individual errors in previous Reports, to corroborate the results already obtained as to the general classification of the successive Periods.

A good section resulting from the excavation of a part of the West

Court of the Knossian Palace is given in Fig. 4. It shows how great Section a relative depth is occupied by the Neolithic deposit, though in a neighbour- "vc ing pit it was even greater. The three Early Minoan Periods were represented C urt at by distinct layers. Above these was a definite flooring, and at this point occurred one of the lacunae in the evidence referred to above. The First Middle Minoan Period was not represented, the floor having probably been in continuous use. In a contiguous area, however, this gap is fully supplied. Otherwise the succession of the Minoan Periods is here complete up to the pavement of the Court, laid down in L. M. I. Above this point the deposit was of a more unstratified nature, containing remains of the L. M. II and L. M. Ill Periods.

The evidence supplied by the stratification of the successive cultural deposits at Knossos is more complete than that on any other Cretan site. Its general results, however, have been corroborated by the careful researches of fellow explorers on other Cretan sites, though special allowances have in these cases to be made for local conditions. Thus in great residential centres Palatial like Knossos or Phaestos changes in fashion had a tendency to set in somewhat a j, ead of earlier than in more remote provincial localities and to attain a more characteristic development. In the East of Crete the First Middle Minoan style shows a tendency to persist, while, on the other hand the mature class of polychrome ware in what may be called the earlier Palace Style becomes decidedly sparser away from the great centres. At Palaikastro, for instance, there was a tendency, as Mr. Dawkins has observed, for the older M. M. I traditions to survive to the borders of M. M. III. So, too, the later Palace Style of L. M. II is the special product of Knossos, and its place elsewhere is not infrequently taken by somewhat degenerate versions of L. M. I types. These considerations must always be borne in mind, but the best standard of classification is clearly to be sought on the site which supplies the most complete succession of links in the long chain of evolution.

To take one important centre like Knossos as the norm for such a strati- Hcst ficatory classification of the Minoan Periods is advisable for another reason, Regarded as a whole, the successive human strata on a given site show in each case a certain uniformity wherever struck. Knossian

This is notably the case at Knossos, where we repeatedly find floor levels exposed in various parts of the site which exhibit a parallel series ot ceramic or other remains. Such uniformity of deposit must be taken to mark a wide-spread change or catastrophe at the epoch to which it belongs, and recurring

Arbitrary Element in Strati-graphical Divisions.

Transition without real break.

3 o THE PALACE OF MINOS, ETC.

strata of this kind may be reasonably regarded as so many landmarks of successive historic stages.

When, ao-ain, a stratum containing ceramic or other remains of the same epoch is found to be of widespread occurrence on two or more important sites it may be taken as an indication of some general catastrophe, affecting, probably, the whole of Minoan Crete. The most striking instance of this is the evidence supplied by a well-marked deposit at Knossos and Phaestos characterized by an abundance of M. M. 11 pottery in the same advanced stage and pointing to a more or less contemporary destruction.

All such stratigraphical demarcations are of their nature somewhat arbitrary and any idea of Minoan civilization as divided into so many distinct compartments must be dismissed from the minds of students. All is, in fact, transition. What has been said above must again be repeated. From the earliest Minoan stage to the latest there is no real break such as might be naturally explained by conquest from abroad. Crude foreign elements, indeed, appear at intervals, but they are rapidly absorbed and assimilated. There are checks, it is true, and intervals of comparative stagnation, but though its pace occasionally varies, the course of evolution is still continuous One form merges into another by imperceptible gradations and vhere, as is the case with a large part of the material, an object is derived from an unstratified deposit it is at times difficult, in default of direct evidence, to decide on which side of a more or less artificial dividing line it should be placed. On such individual questions opinions must constantly differ. But the classification of the Minoan Age into its Early, Middle, and Late stages, and the corresponding division of each into three Periods, finds its justification both in logic and utility.

THE EGYPTIAN CHRONOLOGICAL SYSTEM ADOPTED IN THIS WORK

WITH regard to Egyptian chronology I have thought it best to take that of ogy Dr. Eduard Meyer (Aegyptische Chronologic, 1904; Nachtrdgc, 1908) as at least adopted a provisional standard. I am well aware of the objections of many Egyptologists against bringing down the date of the Twelfth Dynasty so low as 2000-1788 B. c. which

Standard, follows from the acceptance of 1876-1872 B. C. as the Sothic dating for the seventh year of Senusert III (Borchardt, Aegypt. Zeitschrift, xxxvii, p. 99 seqq.). Dr. H. R.

Hall in his recently published Ancient History of the Near East observes (p. 23) that it seems impossible to force all the kings of the Thirteenth-Seventeenth Dynasties into so small a space as 250 years, cut down their reigns as we may.

Meyer's system, nevertheless, has received a powerful corroboration from the recent researches of Monsieur Raymond V Veill l who, after an elaborate examination K. Veill of the evidence, considers it possible to reduce the interval between the Twelfth and the Eighteenth Dynasty to about 210 years, the period required by the Sothic dating. It tween must be remembered that a fixed Sothic date in the other direction is supplied by the. r "j e!! h, Calendar of the Ebers Papyrus, from which it follows that the ninth year of Amen- teenth hotep I was 332 years later (within 3 years) than the seventh year of Senusert III. Dynasty. The date of the accession of Aahmes, the first king of the Eighteenth Dynasty, thus works out approximately at 1580 K. c. 2

On the other hand Prof. Flinders Petrie's severely logical proposal (Researches in Petrie's Sinai, Hyo6, pp. 163-85, ch. xii, and Historical Studies, 1911, pp. 10-23) to solve the. hl sh dat dimculty by pushing back Senusert Ilia whole Sothic Cycle of 1461 years and thus patible raising his date to 3300 B. C. seems to me to be quite incompatible with the Cretan witn evidence. The recent discovery of a cylinder of the First Babylonian dynasty in evidence, association with Cretan scarabs imitating early Twelfth Dynasty types also supplies a valuable chronological equation quite inconsistent with this higher dating.

The characteristic polychrome wares of the Second Middle Minoan Period have M. M. II been shown by Professor Petrie's discoveries at Kahun and by the tomb found by c Professor Garstang at Abydos where they were accompanied by cylinder-seals of w j t h Senusert III and Amenemhat III (see below, p. 268 seqq.) to be contemporary with Twel (the Twelfth Dynasty. It further appears that these wares overlapped the Thirteenth. Thir-

But between the well-defined Knossian stratum containing pottery of the Middle teenth Minoan polychrome style and the Late Minoan deposits of ascertained connexions as fj es. going back to the beginning of the Eighteenth Dynasty, or approximately 1580 li. c., Qnly M. there are only remains of a single phase of culture, the Third Middle Minoan. This M. lllbe-Age of transition is itself marked by successive phases, but it seems unreasonable and K! " to extend it over more than four or five generations. teenth

This rough estimate would bring the close of M. M. II and, with it, of the early part of the Thirteenth Dynasty to a date approaching 1700 D. c. Such an approximate term agrees, in fact, very well with Meyer's dating for the Twelfth Dynasty. When the alternative to this is to raise the Sothic dating by 1461 years, and to attribute therefore a duration of something like a millennium and a half to the Third Middle Minoan Period, it can hardly be doubted on which side the greater probability lies.

For the earlier dynasties I have taken the higher margin allowed by Dr. Meyer.

1 Monuments et histoire de la p riode com- (Classical Revieu, xiv, 1900, p. 148; cf. Hall, prise entre la fin de la XII 6 Dynastic et ia loc. tit.) makes the seventh year of Senusert restauration The"baine Journ. Asiatiqiie, Rec. either 1978 or 1945 B. C., that is from about des Memoires 794-77. 70 to somewhat over too years earlier than 2 The independent calculation of T. Nicklin the date given by Borchardt and Meyer.

1. THE NEOLITHIC STAGE IN CRETE

Minoan Culture in Crete evolved out of Neolithic; Caves and Rock-Shelters; But and Ben divellings; Deep Section at Knossos; Evidences of High Antiquity; Lower,

Middle, and Upper Neolilhic; Typical products of Middle Neolithic phase; Inlaid pottery; Steatopygous Clay Images; Ancestors of Stone types; Evolution of extended Figures; Aegean and Anatolian families related wide Oriental range; Prototypes of Mother Goddess; Stone Implements; Chrysocolla stud; Primitive Commerce.

Minoan THE Minoan culture of Crete as defined in the present work has outgrowth its starting-point in the transitional Age during which the use of stone lithic. for implements and weapons was beginning to be supplemented by that of copper. But this Chalcolithic phase, more specially referred to in the succeeding Section as Early Minoan I, was itself to a large extent the out- growth of the Later Stone or Neolithic Age that had preceded it. It is, indeed, in many of its aspects still Sub-Neolithic, nor can any true idea be gained of the rise of Minoan civilization without some realization of this ruder antecedent stage, though the full materials for the study are still to seek.

Materials Neolithic remains, however, are numerous and scattered over a large for Neo- p ar(; o f Crete, including objects derived from caves, rock-shelters, isolated phase houses, and settlements. A cave, the earlier contents of which belong to this adequate. Period, was explored by Professor Bosanquet at Skalaes near Praesos in

But re- An extensive Neolithic station at Magasa near Palaikastro has been described by Professor Dawkins, 2 which abounded in stone implements, the celts spread in being in many cases of the thick stumpy kind usual in Aegean deposits. In connexion with this station was a rock-shelter and by it the remains of a house, consisting of a single course of undressed limestone blocks and interesting as showing a fairly rectangular outline. It is of the but and ben dwellings, kind, with a small entrance chamber and a larger one within 1 Inside it, 1 B. S. A. viii, p. 235. with some mixed finds on the adjoining plateau

P. S. A. xi, p. 260 seqq., and PI. VIII. w hi c h he calls Campignian, meaning by 3 Dawkins, op. cit., p. 263, Fig. 2; cf this ill-chosen name proto-Neolithic. But

Mackenzie, B. S. A., xiv, p. 360 seqq. and SO me of these, e. g. the obsidian borers, p. 368. The excavated house-floors found by resemble those from Magasa, others, like the

Monsieur I Franchet at Trypiti, E. of Candia cores and corresponding flakes, belong to (Rev. Anthropologique, 1914, p. 294 seqq., and the Bronze Age of Crete and Melos (cf.

Nouv. Arch, des Missions sdentifiques, t. xx. Phylakopi, PI. XXXVIII. 19-28). Bosanquet, f. i. 1917), contained no evidence of date, and . H. S. xxxviii, pp. 203, 204, has shown the belong to a type still in use in Crete and the amenability of M. Franchet's conclusions re-

Aegean islands. M. Franchet connects them garding these remains.

NEOLITHIC STACK: THE TKLL OF KNOSSOS

ORIGINAL SURFACE OF GROUND 4 =-r L T T-.-

F-. ffe . ' PWEMENT OF 1 WEST COURT INOANS STRATUM

STRATUM BELONGING TO EARLY MIHOAH j, LEVEL, EARLY MlnOAN I

LDIIIHICvvyl

Fin. 4. SECTION 01 Uisi COURT AT KNOSSOS. J

THE PALACE OF MINOS, ETC.

Palace Site of Knossos a. Neolithic Tell.

Section under West Court.

Chronological Speculations.

besides some potsherds, were found nineteen stone axes and obsidian points with an obtuse base analogous to the class of flint Neolithic borers. Such worked obsidian flakes were common on the site, and show that there was already a commercial connexion with Melos. The pottery found was of a fairly advanced Neolithic fabric.

Neolithic debris have occurred beneath the Minoan buildings at Knossos, Phaestos, and other Cretan sites. At Phaestos the Neolithic deposits beneath the Palace seem to have been considerable 1 though their depth is as yet not ascertained. But the mass of Neolithic material underlying the Palace site at Knossos far exceeds in depth and volume that of any known European locality. The Hill of Kephala is, in fact, a Tell resembling the great mounds of Chaldaea, Palestine, or Egypt, made up by layer after layer of earlier settlements going back in this case to remote prehistoric times. Some idea of the relative depth of this Neolithic deposit may be gathered from the West Court Section, given in Fig. 4. 2 It will be seen that whereas the Minoan and all later strata taken together occupy 5-33 metres, 3 or about 19 feet of the section, the Neolithic deposit extends below this for a depth of 6-43 metres, or about 23! feet in a neighbouring pit 8 metres, or 26 feet to the virgin rock.

The best fixed datum here as regards the Minoan strata is afforded by the pavement of the West Court which belongs to the close of the Middle Minoan Age, in other words to a date approximating to 1600 B. C. 4 The beginning of the Early Minoan Age has been tentatively set down above as 3400 n. c. which gives an interval of 1,800 years for 2-82 metres of deposit. If we might assume an equal rate of accumulation for the 8 metres of Neolithic deposit we should require for it a space of over 5,100 years. It maj be objected that the wattle and daub constructions of Neolithic times might favour a higher rate of accumulation, and that some allowance should be made on this score. It must still be remembered, however, that down to 1 See A. Mosso, Ceramica neolitica di Phaestos, Man. Ant., xix (1908), p. 141 seqq. But the deposits examined by him were mixed Neolithic and Early Minoan. This fact vitiates his conclusions as to the depth of the Neolithic stratum.

B. School Annual, x (1904), p. 19, Fig. 7, and see p. 18 seqq. The pottery of this Section was examined by Dr. Mackenzie.

The lowest of these strata, however, 33 centimetres in thickness, is best described as Sub-Neolithic.

4 In some chronological speculations set forth by me in 1904 on the basis of this section (. School Annual, x, p. 25), I took the present surface of the ground as a datum, which is less satisfactory. I also used Lepsius' dating of the First Egyptian Dynasty 3892 B. c. as a provisional basis for the beginning of E. M. I, which entails a higher dating for the Neolithic Age

NEOLITHIC STAGE: THE TELL OF KNOSSOS 35 the latest Minoan Age, besides hewn stone, rubble materials, unburnt bricks, Vastanti-and, in the case of smaller dwellings such as we have to deal with in this area, roofs of reeds and clay were still largely in use. Very considerable accumula- Neolithic tions must therefore still be taken into account, and the population on the ment. Tell itself was probably denser than in more primitive times. It is doubtful therefore if any deduction be necessary, but even taking off 10 per cent, from the sum of years arrived at above for the duration of the Neolithic settlement on the site of Knossos, it would yet amount to about 4,600 years Its beginnings would go back to 8000 B. C. and it would thus have a total antiquity approaching 10,000 years. Such speculations, however, can have only a relative value.

Unfortunately, although the amount of miscellaneous Neolithic materials nifls-brought out by the Knossos excavations has been considerable, the exact ay V" data have hitherto been mainly forthcoming from two or three exploratory (-"i ifi-pits. The reason of this is the fact that in a large part of the Palace area a good deal of the Neolithic deposit was partly levelled away when the building was constructed for the Central Court and surrounding structures. On the Eastern slope again there has been a good deal of denudation. It has been only possible to obtain comparative observations of the contents of metre-levels where the excavation of the Neolithic deposit was carried clown to the virgin soil, which in the Palace area could only exceptionally be the case. But Earliest the information supplied by the test-pits where it has been possible to sound ofkuossos the full extent of the deposit is very consistent in its results, and by the aid of " d this a great deal of the scattered material can be placed in its proper context.

It is clear that the Neolithic settlement of Knossos does not itself by any means represent the earliest stage of that culture. In the lowest stratum the implements are ground and polished and the pottery is generally of a fairly advanced quality with a good burnished surface.

Setting aside what maybe called the Proto-Neolithic element which is Lower. here absent, the Later Stone Age deposits of Knossos illustrate three dle principal stages of evolution. The strata may thus as a whole be divided Upper. into the Lower, Middle, and Upper Neolithic of Knossos. 1

The Lower Neolithic comprises approximately the first two and a half 1 The results of Dr. Mackenzie's careful north of the Central Court. The deposit here examination of the Neolithic pottery from the reaches in places a thickness of 7 metres above test-pit in the West Court are given by the virgin rock. The specimens from succes-him in his paper on the Pottery of Knossos sive half-metre levels are kept separate. They (J. H. S., xxiii, 1903, p. 158 seqq.). The are preserved in the Reference Museum general results have been corroborated by my formed on the site. recent cuttings into the Neolithic strata to the

THE PALACE OF MINOS, ETC.

Lower Neolithic of Knossos.

Middle Neolithic: Incised Ware.

White (and red) Inlays.

Surviving Tradition: Outside Crete.

Rippled Ware.

metres above the soft virgin rock. 1 The pottery in this layer, as throughout the Neolithic phase, is hand-made and of imperfectly sifted clay, though the surface is already more or less burnished. The vessels are generally wide-mouthed with a flattening at bottom. The pottery is distinguished from that of the stratum above by its brownish surface as contrasted with the blacker tint of a good deal of the

Middle Neolithic. The main negative distinction of this early class, however, is the comparative absence of incised ware.

The practice of incised decoration (see Fig. 8 below) is the special characteristic of the Middle Neolithic phase which, if we take this feature as a guide, may be said to begin by a very gradual transition in the second half of the third metre. In this and the following metre of deposit the actual amount of incised fragments is still however rare, amounting only to from two to three per cent. 2 Up to the fifth metre the ornament is still produced by simple incision, but, about this level, the new process of filling in the incised or punctuated patterns with a white chalky material first makes its appearance. 3 In rare cases, moreover, a ferruginous red material is used in place of this. The occurrence of this white and red pigment in incised geometric decoration coupled with the black ground characteristic of this Neolithic stage naturally suggests that we have here the prototype of the early polychrome class of painted pottery which first makes its appearance at the close of the Early Minoan Age. But as a matter of fact this Neolithic tradition was in Crete itself interrupted by a long interval of time. The connexion probably exists, but it is supplied by the more conservative tradition of the Central Aegean islanders, and punctuated and incised patterns with white inlaying material re-entered Crete in the wake of strong Cycladic influences about the close of the Early Minoan Age. 4 These patterns were taken over at the beginning of the Middle Minoan Period on the early polychrome vessels with similar geometrical designs.

Together with this inlaid decoration, the more uniform black ground of the pottery, and the brighter burnishing, a new feature now makes itself apparent. This is the rippling of the surface of the- vessel (Fig. 5), 1 Taking the West Court test-pit as the standard. The deposit in that under the Third West Magazine was originally deeper. As pointed out by Dr. Mackenzie (pp. at., p. 161) the formation of deposit was more rapid and accordingly greater in quantity, especially in the best Neolithic Period, at the centre of the Knossos hill than towards the periphery.

8 Mackenzie, op. a., p. 159.

3 In the fifth metre of the test-pit of the Third Magazine, out of 524 fragments 18 happened to be incised and of these almost all showed the incisions filled with a kind of white chalk (Mackenzie, loc. fit.) I called attention to this curious phenomenon in . School Annual, x, p. 23; cf. p. 115 below.

NEOLITHIC STAGE: THE TELL OF KNOSSOS 37 probably by means of a blunt bone instrument, from the rim downwards. On the vessel being afterwards polished the greatest possible amount of glitter was thus obtained.

The remains of vessels from the Neolithic stratum were, as a rule, too fragmentary for restoration. A few more perfectly preserved examples, mainly illustrating its Middle phase, are, however, given in Fig. (, but some of the commonest types of which we have evidence, such as the open bowls with slightly flattened base and the clay ladles, are not there represented. On the other hand, Fig. 0, 2, 9 with the fully developed handles and the fragment of the bowl with the bridged spout (8) the forerunner of a long Minoan series may belong to the latest Neolithic stage.

The miniature cup-like forms (Nos. 4, 5, 6, 7) and the small cylindrical vessel (10) recall an interesting discover) made by Professor Mosso in a Neolithic deposit at Phaestos. 1 In this, together with a clay female image of the squatting class described below, 2 were remains of shallow clay bowls, too small for ordinary use, one with two holes for suspension, and amongst pectuncultis shells found with them, a specimen artificially flattened below. It seems probable that these objects had served a votive purpose in connexion with the little image, and the religious character of the deposit was confirmed by the association with the other relics of a large lump of magnetic iron; a mineral apparently not native to Crete. 3 In later times, as will be shown below, sea-shells formed a regular part of the equipment of Minoan shrines. 4

More or less rectangular clay 'trays' with partitions (n, a, b, c are typical products of the Middle Neolithic Age. Sometimes, as their fragments show, they were provided with short legs. Some characteristic examples of these fabrics, as illustrated mainly by its most flourishing phase in the Illustrative Types ofvessels.

Votive Objects.

Votive Neolithic Deposit at Ihaes-tos.

FIG. 5. Riii'i. KD WARE (NKOLITHIC) (f.).

1 Mon. Ant., xix, 1908, p. 151 seqq. 1il,. 12, 6 a, and Fig. 13, 3, and cf. p. 47.
See Mosso, op. ., pp. 153, 154. and note, i. See below, p. 517 seqq.

THE PALACE OF MINOS. ETC.

Evolution of Handles.

Upper Neolithic.

Beginnings of painted Decoration.

Sub-Neolithic Phase.

prolonged Middle Neolithic Period will be found in the accompanying Figures.

Typical Neolithic handles will be seen in Fig. 7. The wishing bone type, Nos. i, 3, 5, 6, may have been derived from the use of a forked withy or osier sprig with its two flexible ends tied round a wooden bowl. We find it, indeed, in an atrophied form on certain Early Minoan chalices that retain in their decoration a reminiscence of the wood-work graining. 1 This type of handle finds parallels and derivatives in Cyprus, the Troad, and Northern Greece. 2 The apex of the fork where it leaves its undivided stem forms the handle In 8-14 we trace the evolution of the broad vertical handle from a mere perforated knob (8 a, 8 b, 9). On the other hand, Figs. 7, n and 8, n below show that by the period of the incised wares the fully developed strap handle was already in existence.

The Upper Neolithic phase merges rapidly into what may be called the Sub-Neolithic and must be regarded as of short duration. It is a period of decadence from the point of view of the old Neolithic technique and of transition to new methods.

Thus, as we approach the seventh metre, the incised and rippled decoration of the flourishing Neolithic epoch shows a tendency to die out and soon practically disappears. By the time the seventh metre is reached the hand-burnished ware that is still found is quite plain, in this respect resembling that of the lowest stratum. On the other hand, the majority of sherds show the beginnings of a new method of painted decoration by means of an at first almost lustreless black glaze slip. This is of a darkish colour, and there are at times faint traces of white geometric patterns in imitation of the inlaid chalk decoration of the preceding Neolithic period. 3 Finally, as the borders of what may best be termed the Sub-Neolithic phase are reached, the interior of the pottery is no longer of the traditional grey tone, but takes a paler and, at times, a ruddier tint, showing that the processes of baking were now more advanced, and heralding the advent of the potter's oven. The Sub-Neolithic fabrics that succeed merge in turn, by an imperceptible transition, into those of the First Early Minoan Period, with which for convenience sake they are here grouped. There is no real break between the latest Stone Age of Crete and the Chalcolithic phase or earliest Age of Metals.

See below, pp. 59, 60, and Fig. 19.

2 Interesting parallels to this class of handle may be found in the Early Metal Age wares of Thessaly (Wace and Thompson, Prehistoric Thessaly, pp. 185, 186, Fig. 134; Lianokladhi Stratum III: with Minyan ware) and of Macedonia (H. Schmidt, Keramik der makedonischen Tumuli. Z. f. Eihn., 1905, p. 98). Varieties of the allied form of handle with a mere perforation (Fig. 7, 7) occur both in Thessaly and Macedonia and in the earliest stratum of Troy (H. Schmidt, op. cif., p. 99).

IMC,. 6. NEOLITHIC POTTERY, KNOSSOS (-.).

THE PALACE OF MINOS, ETC.

FIG. 7. NEOLITHIC HANDLES, KNOSSOS. 1-7. WISHING HONK TYPE AND DERIVATIONS. 8-H. EVOLUTION OF VERTICAL HANDLE FROM PER-FORATED Kxon (-.).

NEOLITHIC ST.; E: THK TELL OF KNOSSOS 41 1 ic. 8. MIDDLE NE-OLITHIC INCISED AND PUNCTUATED DECORATION. WITH CHALK INLAY, KNOSSOS (f.).

Till Neolithic graves are discovered it will be impossible to give anything like a complete series of ceramic forms. Here it is impossible to give more than a very summary idea of this Cretan Neolithic culture. Inlaidde- In Fig. 8 are given some examples of the incised and punctuated in- coration. j a j c j c i ecorat j on o f the Middle Neolithic style. The patterns are mostly of a simple geometrical class, some of them, like the chequer motive, 4,- of obviously textile origin. But specimens like those reproduced in Fig. 9 Plant show early attempts to imitate plant forms. Fig. 9, a, b apparently represents branches. Such delineations have a special interest in view of the important place occupied by plant motives in later Minoan times. In these rude beginnings we may see a remote anticipation of the perfection of naturalistic design that produced the saffron-flowers and lilies.

the exquisitely drawn grasses and fern-like foliage that illustrate the acme of Minoan art.

Clay spools and other small indeterminate objects shown on Fig. 10 also at times bear similar incised or punctuated decoration. Nos. 2, b, and 3 a, b, c, d seem to be spools for winding FIG. 9. INCISKD PLANT MOTIVES.,,. T,,-. r"

thread, No. i (a, o) may be part ot a handle. The sub-oval object No. 4 (a, b, c on the other hand, almost looks c. like a small clay 'tablet, and on side, b, a figure appears resembling the mountain sign of the later hieroglyphic script. There seems no reason, however, to attach importance to such analogies. Even had such a clay nodule come to light in a Neolithic deposit nearer the old Chaldaean border, chronological discrepancies would surely have been fatal to any attempt to regard it as a primitive imitation of an inscribed tablet.

Whorls The lay s P ndle whorls (Fig. 10, 5-9), which occur in great abundance.

are either plain or merely distinguished by lines or notches. None of the more elaborately decorated class characteristic of the early strata of Hissarlik are here found. The Hissarlik finds, indeed, are of distinctly later date.

Bone im- Bone implements abound in the Neolithic deposit and many of these, plements.,.

such as the shuttles and needles, have to do with weaving and textile industries. Some of the pointed instruments found may have been used for making the incised and punctuated decoration on the pottery. Others with a broad flat edge may have served for smoothing the surface. Punches, perhaps for leather, and scoops are also frequent.

NEOLITHIC STAGE: THE TELL OE KNOSSOS 4,

FIG. 10. CI. AY SPOOLS, WHORLS, c., MIDDLE NEOLITHIC, KNOSSOS (r.).

Of special interest are the small clay figures in the round many of them with the characteristic incised decoration representing animals, birds. and human forms. Fig. 11, i a, b, c is a bird with slightly opening wings and apparently a fan-shaped tail, suggesting a dove. Considering how intimately

THE PALACE OF MINOS. ETC.

FIG. 11. CI. AY BIRDS AND ANIMALS, MIDDLE NEOLITHIC, KNOSSOS (.)

Birds and the cult of the Dove is associated in subsequent Periods with the Minoan Goddess, this figure may well have stood in some religious connexion. The little clay ox, 4 a, 6, evidently the indigenous short-horned variety the Bos Creticus of Boyd Dawkins also recalls the abundance of such figures in Minoan votive deposits. No. 3 is probably the head of a goat, and 5 that

NEOLITHIC STAGE: THE TELL OF KNOSSOS 45 of a hound. More uncertain is the prot me 2 a, 6, which appears to have belonged to the rim of a vessel.

Some fragmentary remains of male figures have been found, and the Human rude rectangular image, Fig. 12, 5 seems to be of this sex, but the bulk of the clay figures in human shape are female. They are of two main types. One is flat and broad, Fig. 12, i a, b, f, and seems to be ot rare occurrence. The Steato-other, Fig. 12, 2. 3, 6 ancl Fig. 13, i A, B below, is much more frequent and late Kwnaie Neolithic specimens occur of green steatite. This type is short and stumpy lma s es-and shows an extraordinary development of the rump, which is often even more prominent than that of modern Bushman women. This exaggeration, however, may be partly due to very widespread primitive notions as to the adipose character of feminine beauty. Such figurines are found throughout a large part of the Mediterranean and Aegean basin and South-Eastern Europe, and have an undefined extension still farther East. Striking examples are supplied by the prehistoric Egyptian clay figures of this class from Naqada and the monstrously obese seated Their images of clay ancl stone found in the Megalithic sanctuaries of Malta, bution. Steatopygous figurines recur in a series of Neolithic stations extending from Thessaly l and Bosnia to Thrace, and north of the Danube to Roumania, Southern Russia, and the Polish Caves. 3 Obese female figures in stone and in a squatting attitude, of sub-Neolithic date, occur in Mainland Greece. But, as we shall see, the nearest parallel to the present series comes from the

Anatolian side. It may be that some distant connexion will ultimately be established between this Neolithic family and the still earlier images of the Aurignacian Age with the organs of maternity so prominently shown, of which the Venus of Brassempouy, and that of Willendorf in Lower Austria, stand as classical examples.

The Neolithic Cretan images of this class seem to belong to two main Two main T. i i i L Neolithic varieties. In the one case the figure appears squatting with the legs bent types, under the body (cf. Figs. 12, 2, 13, 3). In the other (Fig. 13, i, 5), we may recognize a sitting attitude, with knees up and both feet drawn together in front. The squatting attitude, which is a simple modification of the other, finds 1 Tsuntas, Ilpo'io-ropicai Aicpotroatw, c. PI. Urgeschichte der bildenden Kunst in Europa 32; Wace and Thompson, Preh. Thessaly, (1898), see esp. p. 206 seqq., and Pis. III-V, 232 seqq. and passim. But many of these and my own independent study, Hagios Onu- clay figures seem to be later than the Aegean phrios Deposit, c.: Suppl. to Cretan Picto-

Neolithic. graphs, c, Quaritch, 1895, p. 124 seqq.

3 For a general view of the distribution of G. Ossowsky, Fouilles de la Caverne de these primitive idols', see S. Reinach, La Sculp- Wierzchowska-Gbrna (Antigua, 1887, p. 32 tureen Europe avant les influences grteo-romaines seqq., and PI. VIII, 4). (Anthropologie, 1894 and 1895), M. Hoernes,

NEOLITHIC STAGE: THE TELL OE KNOSSOS 47 an interesting analogy in the case of an early black clay figure with incised Seated decoration from Adalia, the ancient Attalia, on the Pamphylian coast. 1 In ciay the front view of this figure, reproduced in Eig. 13, 17, the two feet, one of them ema e slightly obliterated, are seen meeting in front and implying thus a squatting posture. This point of similarity to the Cretan type is, moreover, enhanced by the position of the arms and hands which are laid over the breasts. It is evident, indeed, that the Adalia figurine is of a more advanced fabric. 2 In this case the head with its delineation of the hair and features shows marked points of approximation to the well known owl-faced images of Hissarlik, arguing also an approximation in date.

In the case of the Knossian figurines, the head is generally broken off, and where preserved is a mere protuberance as in Fig. 12, i and 4. In the succeeding Period, as we shall see, features begin to appear.

There can be little doubt that the other type of image of flatter mould Broad, with the rounded body below and cruciform upper section (Eig. 13, 2) has variety. the same origin as the steatopygous class and was also intended to indicate a crouched or sitting attitude. In this case, however, the steatopygy is rendered, as so often in similar cases, by means of the expanded contour. The two side sections in the lower part of this figure seem to answer to the shortened legs of the crouching type, as seen in Fig. 13, i. This is further brought out by the existence of a sub-Neolithic marble type, sketched in Fig. 13, 5, in which the same attitude is suggested.

It is, in fact, in relation to the later widely disseminated family of stone Clay types that these crouchingneolithicfigureshavethe greatest interest. A glance Crouched at the diagrammatic Fig. 13 will at once brint; home these affiliations. The "yp 5 Ancestors two marble figurines from Amorgos, Nos. 10 and n, the first of which of Stone betrays a certain parallelism with the Cretan sub-Neolithic form, 5, show that the well-known fiddle-shaped forms of the Cyclades 3 go back to Neolithic 1 J. L. Myres,.4 6. Inst. Journ., xxx(i9oo) vanced fabric, see T. E. Peet, I niv. of Liverpool p. 251 seqq., and Pl. XIV. The back view Annals of Archaeology and Anthropology, vol. ii, of the image presents the peculiarity of showing, p. 145 seqq., and Pis. XXVI, XXVII.

on its left flank, the sole of a foot. This may " I pointed out the value of the clay Neolithic be regarded as a reduplicated representation image (Fig. 12, i = 13, j), as supplying the proto- of the foot seen in the front on this side, type of the fiddle-shaped forms, in a com-

Professor Myres, however, thinks that the munication to the Anthropological Section of partial obliteration of the right foot in front the British Association (see Man, 1902, No.

was done intentionally, and the sole put in 146). It confirmed a conjecture already made behind on the other flank as a substitute. by Prof. J. L. Myres, loc. cit., that the violin- 2 For other specimens of idols from near shaped type of marble figure, may very likely Adaliaofwell-cookedyellowishclayandmoread- represent a squatting type.

THE PALACE OF MINOS, ETC.

NEOLITHIC STAGE: THE TELL OE KNOSSOS 49 prototypes in clay of this class, the existence of which may eventually be Clay ascertained in other parts of the Aegean area. Very remarkable squat- Type" 1"

ting figures of alabaster, preserving in their front aspect a curious parallel to Ancestors these Cycladic fiddle-shaped types, have been recently discovered in Bronze shaped

Age Kurgans' of the Caucasus (Fig. 13, n 6), 1 No. n is to be regarded as a truncated offshoot of the same family. This last-mentioned type, moreover, is also included in the Trojan group (Nos. 13, 14, 15) where, however, we find a tendency (No. 15) to reproduce the owl-shaped features of the Adalia figurine (No. 17). The heavily formed limestone idol (No. 16) from the site of Sykeon (Sarilar) 2 carries these parallels into Galatia.

Interesting, too, is the recent discovery of a limestone figurine of kindred Mesopotype (No. 18), at Serrin on the Mesopotamian bank of the Middle Euphrates. 3 mian The idol itself, with its eyed physiognomy, fits on to the Anatolian Idol. group and suggests derivation from a squatting type parallel with that from Adalia. Stone figures of a closely related form extend, however, as far afield as the South-Eastern shores of the Caspian. A specimen executed in a flesh-coloured stone with the breasts clearly modelled (Fig. 13, 19) in fact occurred in the rich early treasure found in 1841 in a mound near Asterabad, 4 together with a copper spear-head of a Sumerian type that goes back at least to the middle of the Third Millennium B. C.

In view of these phenomena, there can be little doubt of the original prevalence of the squatting or seated type throughout this wide Aegean and West Asiatic region. The female clay images from the Neolithic deposit at Knossos, of which remains of at least a score have now been found, are all of this kind, and the single example of a flatter form (Fig. 13, 2) is itself only a transitional version of the same class.

1 N. I. Veselovsky, Izvjestiya Imp. Arch, as Middle Hittite, i. e. not earlier than

Komm., Petrograd, 1910, pp. 3, 4, and Pis. I, r. 1750 B. C. Unfortunately, however, the II. From Kuban. evidence as to the tomb-group is by no means
"J. W. Crowfoot, Explorations in Galatia clear.
as Halyin. . H. S., xix (1899), p. 34, Archaeoiogia, xxx (1844), p. 248 seqq., Fig. i. Pl. XVI, 5. The spear-head (Fig. 10) with its
The objects are now in the Ashmolean characteristic tang, represents the same general
Museum, and have been published by Mr. type as that attributed to King Sharru-Gi of
C. L. r oo ey(Z. iv. Anh. ofarca., v, Pl. XXIV). Kish (f. 2 700?). Heuzey, Die. en Chalde"e,
They were said to have formed part of an Pl. V, ter, N. i; cf. King, Sumer and Acfad., interment and to have been found in company p. 229, Fig. 58. Rostovtzeff, The Sumerian with two bronze implements, a tanged dagger Treasure of Astrabad. Journal of Egyptian and an elongated flat celt marked with Archaeology, Vol. VI, p. 4 seqq. twelve dots and classified by Mr. Woolley I E

THE PALACE OF MINOS, ETC.
Evolution of Extended Types of Stone Figures.
Clay
Prototypes of Extended Stone Figures.
Transitional Forms.

Yet, as ve shall see, in the succeeding Age both in Anatolia and Crete, and notably in the Cyclades, more or less extended figures become the prevalent type. How is this divergence from the Neolithic prototypes such as we see them at Knossos to be explained?

Unquestionably, full-length clay types of adipose female figurines appear in the Neolithic strata of mainland Greece, as for instance at Sesklo. 1 But we have to bear in mind that the Neolithic phase in Thessaly and other mainland regions considerably overlaps the Early Metal Age of the Aegean. Moreover, it is wholly unreasonable to suppose that Neolithic types from that side could have exercised a formative influence in Lycia and Pamphylia, where, as we shall see, extended figures parallel with the Aegean class make their appearance at a time contemporary with the Early Minoan.

The influence of early extended types to the North or East need not be excluded, but the actual genesis of these Aegean types may be traced in such intermediate forms as that shown in Fig. 13, 4. This is clearly related to the crouched or seated figures (Fig. 13, i A, i B), but the legs from the knee down are better indicated. From this to the stone idols' with legs of stumpy dimensions it is only a step. As a matter of fact, moreover, it will be found that, even in the more advanced Cycladic specimens of the extended class, traces of a more contracted posture are often visible.

The transition from the seated to the more or less extended posture of the stone examples is illustrated by Nos. 6-9, 20 of Fig. 13. Two of these female images were recently discovered near Iflatun Bunar on the borders of Lycia and Pamphylia. 2 No. 6, of limestone, presenting an exceptionally adipose contour, shows the legs rounded off in front and truncated below in the profile view. No. 7, of serpentine, is marked by a greater flattening out of the body, its steatopygous character being indicated by the greater widening of the flanks. This feature is carried still further in an analogous type, No. 3, found near Gortyna. 3 It consists of black and red breccia of a kind much used by the Cretan lapidaries of the Early Minoan Age, viov KOL

Tsuntas, Al npourropucai Axpoiroacis Atxr;-Xov, PI. 32, and p. 283 seqq. The resemblance between Fig. 1 2, 2,?, and 6, and the limestone figure from Iflatun Bunar (Fig. 13, 6) is striking. For other examples of steatopygous clay figurines of Neolithic date in a more or less extended position, see Wace and Thompson, Prehistoric Tiessafy, p. 1 23, Fig. 7 1 , p. 126, Fig. 75 , p. 127, Fig 76 (Tsangli), p. 147, Fig. 91 b (Tsani Maghula).

2 These were obtained by Mr. H. A. Ormerod at a site called Chukur Kend in 1911, and were presented by him to the Ashmolean Museum. See B. S. A, xix, p. 48, Fig. i.

3 This figure was obtained by me in 1896 but I could not discover the exact deposit in which it had lain. The head, which seems to have been of stumpy dimensions, is partly broken away.

NEOLITHIC STAGE: THE TELL OF KNOSSOS 51 to the First Period of which the figure may approximately be ascribed. The marble figure from Knossos, No. 9, is one of a class representing a somewhat featureless offshoot of the preceding type.

The above evidence points to the existence already in the Neolithic Helaied Age, both on the Aegean and Anatolian side, of related families of squatting ancpAna-or seated female figures formed of clay and of obese or steatopygous pro- I? 1 1?. t portions. The appearance of one of the stone offshoots of this family as far East as the Middle Euphrates is a phenomenon of the greatest interest in connexion with the diffusion of a parallel group of female figures through a wide Semitic region to the ancient Sumeria and even to the seats of the Anau culture in Southern Turkestan, 1 though from an early date, the Semitic The types took on a specially sensuous character. In the latter case the earliest-j-"

evidence points to an extended posture, but as no data are forthcoming as Mother .,,,,,,. i. i. Goddess, primitive as those of Neolithic Crete this impression may be eventually modified. Among the earliest known examples of this oriental class are the clay figures, identified with the Babylonian Mother Goddess, found at Nippur and dated about 2700 B. c. 2 These suggest the nude figures that make their appearance on early Chaldaean cylinders and stand in a possible connexion with the legend of the Goddess Ishtar, who, to procure the Waters of Life for her wounded Thammuz, descended, mother-naked, to the Nether World.

That the later Syrian or Cypriote types of the oriental Mother Western Goddess' may have eventually reacted on the Aegean and Anatolian Anal g es-province is highly probable. But there is no question of the early Neolithic forms of Mainland Greece and the Balkan regions having been affected from that quarter, and the same is true of such Early Minoan stone types as the yide above. We have to do with parallel phenomena, the operation of which is t jn UO us traceable throughout a geographically continuous region extending from the f x p e a ns " Aegean, and the Adriatic, to the Persian Gulf and even beyond the Caspian, lei Forms.

To what cause was ultimately due the sympathy in ideas that gave birth to these parallel families of prehistoric images throughout this vast conter- 1 Pumpelly, Explorations in Eastern Tur- images are the predecessors of a long series, kestan (Second

Mission), vol. i, PI. 46, Figs, repeated under an increasingly sensuous as-9-17. The clay figures found in the Kurgans pect. Neo-Babylonian examples were found of Anau are of a fairly advanced sensuous by Koldewey in the Temple of Borsippa. character. They are associated with painted These nude figures are in any case con-sherds parallel with those of the Second Period nected with Istar's double, the Goddess Sala of Elam. (Nikolsky, Rev. Arch,, 1891, p. 41, and cf.

2 Hilprecht, Explorations in Bible Lands, Dr. G. Contenau, La Deesse nue baby-loniennc I 9 3 P- 342 and Plate opposite. With these (1914)1 P- 115 seqq.).

was a male figure, identified with Bel. These

THE PALACE OF MINOS, ETC.

Neolithic Prototypes of Minoan Mother Goddess.

Survival of Primitive Type.

Correspondence of Archaeological and

Linguistic Con- minous area, remains an enigma. Was it possibly a remote inher-itance from Late Palaeolithic times? In any case it can hardly be a mere coincidence that all these various provinces of ancient culture the Aegean, the Anatolian, the Syr-ian, Cypriote, Mesopotamian, and Elamite where the habitprevailed of forming these Mother idols, whether extended or seated, were the later scenes of the cult, under varying names and attributes, of a series of Great Goddesses who often combined the ideas of motherhood and virginity. In Crete itself it is impossible to dissociate these primitive images from those that appear in the shrines and sanctuaries of the Great Minoan Goddess.

Some of these indeed are fashionably robed, in accordance with the exigencies of a civilized and somewhat superfine age. Others, however, still stand out in all their archaic crudity and nakedness. Thus a rude female image from the Shrine of the Double Axes at Knossos (Fig. 14, a, 6) half-seated, in a manner that points to a slightly extended derivative of the crouched type (Fig. 13, A) not only reproduces the traditional gesture of the arms upon the breasts, but is decorated by means of incisions bearing traces of chalky inlay itself a survival of the Neolithic practice.

Enough will have been said to show the special value of the clay figures from the Stone Age deposits of Knossos in determining the place of the Cretan Neolithic culture. These figures, for which a far higher antiquity may be claimed than for the most ancient clay images of Nippur,

FIG. 14. IMAGE FROM SHRINE OF DOUBLE AXES, KNOSSOS (L. M. Ill) (c).

THE PALACE OE MINOS, ETC.

Neolithic Stone Implements in Crete.

Range of

Stone

Maces.

Chryso- colla stud.

and which precede in date the class of stone figures, are seen to have collateral relationships far to the East of the Aegean.

At the same time, the indications thus supplied of conformity in custom and belief entirely coincide with the linguistic evidence which brings what seems to have been the predominant element in the aboriginal population of Crete into near relationship with the Carians and their kin.

Similar affinities are also shown by certain forms of stone implements. Typical examples of Neolithic implements from the site of Knossos are given in Fig. 15 a. 1 The stones principally used are greenstone, serpentine, diorite, jadeite, and especially for the smaller implements, such as chisels or adzes (Fig. 15 a, 4, 5), haematite. Obsidian was used for knives and arrowheads, and the abundance of cores of this material shows that it was worked on the spot. The celts' are of two main types. One (No. i) is thick and heavy, with the butt end much roughened to facilitate hafting. The other (Nos. 2, 3) is shorter and broader. The most distinctive of the stone implements, however, are the maces (Nos. 6, 7, 8), generally found in a broken condition. In some cases the early biconical form of boring is well-marked (No. 6) and contrasts with the tubular drilling of later Minoan times. The finding of stone maces among the Neolithic implements is of special interest as a link of connexion with the Anatolian side. Stone maces, which in Greece proper make their appearance about the beginning of the Age of Metals, 2 seem to have had a much earlier history on the side of Asia Minor. Their use was also characteristic of early Chaldaea, and they recur in prehistoric and proto-dynastic Egypt.

The stone maces seem to be more characteristic of the later Neolithic phase in Crete, 3 and it is possible that in this case the usage may have gradually infiltrated from the Asianic side.

A discovery made in 1913 at a depth of 5-75 metres beneath the northern border of the Central Court at Knossos shows that the taste for brilliant and exceptional materials so characteristic of Early Minoan times was already rife among the Neolithic inhabitants. Here, in close association with a serpentine celt and with black hand-polished pottery, some of it inlaid, 1 The materials of the specimens on Fig. 5a are as follows: i. greenstone; 2, 3. serpentine; 4, 5. haematite; 6. black and white breccia; 7. black stone with white quartzite veins; 8.

greenstone.

I SUntas, A Ilpo'io-TOpicai Axpotroaeis AIXTJ-viou KOI 2cwAov, pp. 322, 323.

3 Stone maces continued in use during the Early Metal Age in Crete, the later examples being characterized by their straight perforation, due to the use of the tubular drill. That they continued at least in occasional use in Crete down to Late Minoan times is shown by the occurrence of a fine, faceted specimen in the Mace-bearer's tomb at Isopata. See Tomb of the Double Axes,-f., Quarhch, 1914, p. 18, Fig- S-

NEOLITHIC STAGE: THE TELL OF KNOSSOS 55 was found what appears to have been a large stud of a brilliant greenish blue colour, somewhat mottled (Fig. 15 b). The appearance of the stone at first suggested the employment of callais, a kind of turquoise used for beads and pendants by the Late Stone and Early Metal Age population of Western Europe. The material, however, in this case proved to be a copper silicate, 1 or chrysocolla, and may have been derived from some Cretan locality. A fragment belonging to the Last Palace Period, of what appears to have been an imitation of an anodon shell, seems in fact to be of the same material.

Fir,. 15i. CHRYSOCOLLA STUD FROM MIDDLE NEOLITHIC DEPOSIT, KNOSSOS.

(2 and 3 are restored.)

The very extended relations of the Neolithic Aegean culture are well illustrated by the ramifications of the early trade routes. In Professor Petrie's opinion, the emery used by the inhabitants of the Nile Valley for cutting and polishing their stone beads and other objects in the Late Prehistoric Period 2 was brought from the Aegean region. The obsidian of Melos had already found its way into Egypt in even more remote prehistoric times, and Crete was a natural stage in the course of the whole of this commerce. Melian obsidian seems also to have already found its way into Italy. But the drift of primitive commerce had a wider range. A still more striking illustration of the remote derivation of ornamental objects of Mediterranean usage in Neolithic times is seen in the occurrence among the. Stone Age deposits in a Ligurian Cave and, in an early Fondo di Capanna of the Reggiano, of shells like the Mitra olcacea 4 and Meleagrina margaritifera or mother-of-pearl shell," whose nearest habitat is at present the Persian Gulf and Indian Ocean.

P. Strobel, Bull. Jatetn., iii (1877), p. 56. The fragment found in a Kondo di Capanna at Rivaltella seems to have been used as a polisher. Issel and Strobel regard these discoveries as evidence that the early inhabitants who possessed these reiics had emigrated from the Eastern Mediterranean regions. Hut the drift of early commerce may be thought a sufficient explanation.

Evidences of
Karly Neolithic intercourse in Mediterranean.
Emery and
Obsidian Trade.
Shell Commerce.

1 Professor Bowman, of the Mineralogical Department of the Oxford University Museum, kindly examined the specimen.

2 e. g. at Naqada where blocks of emery were found (Petrie, Naqada and fialas, p. 45).

3 See T. E. Peet, The Stone and Jlronze Ages in Italy, p. 150.

4 A. Issel, Bull. Jaletn., xiii (1887), pp. 173, 174. Five specimens were found in the A rone Candida Cave.

THE EARLY MINOAN AGE
Transi-
Aspectsof E. M. I.
Sub-
Neolithic
Phase.

Potter's 2. EARLY MINOAN I; WITH SUB-NEOLITHIC (E. M. I)

Sub-Neolithic phase; Incipient use of potter s oven olive Deposit at Mocklos; Clay Horns of Consecration; Pedestalled bowls; Sepulchral Cave of Pyrgos, N. E. of Knossos; Tall Chalices- atrophied Wishing-bone handles; Burnished decoration imitations of ivoodivork graining; Comparisons with Arkalokhori Chalice E. M. Ill; Pedestalled bowls and suspension pots; Trojan and Cycladic parallels; Early painted ware; Incipient use of lustrous paint; Further evolution of figurines; Egyptian Stone Vases of Pre-dynastic and Proto-dynastic types found at Knossos; Was there a Settlement from

Nile Valley? Copper implements known Chalco- lit hie phase; Egyplo-Libyan seal types monstrous forms Evolution of Minotaur; Rectangular Houses; Ossuary tioloi; Chronological clues supplied by Egyptian evidence.

THE earliest stage of what is here defined as the Minoan culture of Crete is seen in a stratum which at Knossos and elsewhere is immediately super-posed on the Neolithic. The phase here illustrated is of a broadly transi-tional nature and must be taken to cover a considerable interval of time. Provisionally, at least, it has been found convenient to include within it the

Sub-Neolithic phase, which in many of its products is hardly distincniish- able trom the Upper JNeohthic. On the other hand, it will be seen that its more advanced stage corresponds with the First Settlement at Troy. Now, too, we also obtain distinct evidence of connexions with the Nile Valley in late prehistoric times and of an intensive pre-dynastic influence.

The principal finds of the better preserved pottery of the present Period are from the caves and rock-shelters, at various sites, used both for dwellings and interments, and the earlier objects from the ossuary tholoi of Messara. The votive deposit of Mochlos will be described below, and a new and very important source is the Sepulchral Cave of Pyrgos, at Nirou Khani, N. E. of Knossos.

ie P otter y i s hand-made, generally with a reddish core produced by the greater amount of firing due to the incipient use of the potter's oven. During the early part of this Period many Neolithic ceramic types survive; the polish of these, however, is inferior to the best Neolithic.

In Fig. 16 are given a series of clay objects brought to light by Mr- Seager T in an early stratum beneath Tomb V of E. M. II or E. M. Ill I am indebted to Mr. Seager for the all hand-made and of coarse fabric. No in- photograph of these objects. The vessels cised ware occurred. Parts of a painted vase found were of red and black clay, sometimes of the early geometrical, dark on light style burnished, more often not. The vases were were found.

dale at Mochlos, and which is almost certainly to be regarded as a votive deposit. 1 The pottery here found must be referred to a comparatively early stage of the present Period and is best described as Sub-Neolithic. At Voti the same time the discovery in the shallow bowl of Fig. 1C, d, of a fragment iepositat of copper, perhaps part of a knife, shows that the use of metal was already be-ginning. The First Early Minoan Period may be described as Chalcolithic. In addition to heaps of plain pots and cups, usual in the votive deposits of Minoan Crete, there was here found a red clay object with a horned projection rising at each end, Fig. 16, c, of quite exceptional interest from the religious point of view. There is great probability in Mr. Seager's view that we have

Fid. 1C). POTTKRY FROM EARLY VOTIVE DEPOSIT, MOCHI. OS ( ).

in this horned object the precursor of the Horns of Consecration, generally formed of clay with a plaster coating, that mark the later Minoan sane- of clay. tuaries. 3 In the succeeding Period the miniature votive form of the sacred Double Axe. their principal cult object, was already in existence. The ritual elements of Minoan cult can thus be traced back to the borders of the Neolithic Age.

Clay ladles with handles of varying lengths abundant at Knossos among Ladies the Neolithic forms are well represented in this deposit (Fig. 16, a, 6); these K. M. I ladles, however, are of reddish clay often covered with a red wash. Another Neolithic type, the plain handleless cup of hemispherical form, is also common (Fig. 16,), as well as others with a flat bottom (,). I he 1 Seager, Mochlos, pp. 92, 93, and Fig. 48, Nos. 29-42.- Op. tit., p. 93. See Vol. II.

and Cups.

cups now, however, begin to present a pedestal (Fig. 17) and thus supply the prototypes of a long series of Minoan cups belonging to the four succeeding Periods. In the same way Fig. 16, d, showing a kind of pan or shallow bowl on a cylindrical stem, like the later fruit stands' of the Middle Minoan Age. Fig. 16, e shows one of the clay rings for the support of round-bottomed pots. Later on these coalesce with the bottom of the vessel and supply its base.

A very interesting type common to this Sub-Neolithic stratum at Knossos consists of a bowl-shaped receptacle supported on a hollow base in the form of a truncated cone (Fig. 17). These vessels, which have a black

FIG. 17. SUB-NEOLITHIC PEDESTALLED BOWLS, KNOSSOS (Restored) (f)-

FIG. 18 i, 2,3. E. M. VESSELS FROM CAYI 0) MIAMI-.

The Sub-Neolithic Pedes-talled Howls. Parallels from Abydos (Dyn. 1).

hand-polished surface, present the closest parallelism with certain pots indistinguishable in colour, burnish, and general appearance found with the First Dynasty remains at Abydos. 1 The clay of these is not Cretan, but it is possible that the resemblance indicates an approximate contemporaneity.

Shallow basins on hollow stems expanding below are also found. These seem to be the prototypes of the frtiit-stands' so prevalent in the early part of the Middle Minoan Age. In one of these belonging to the votive deposit of Mochlos was found a piece of copper. 3

The carinated two-handled bowl (Fig. 18, i) from the cave of Miamu, explored by Professor Taramelli, 4 is of special interest from its early Troadic affinities. The square-mouthed pot of the 'two-storied class (Fig. 18, 2) from the same cave suggests, on the other hand, comparisons with similar types 1 Petrie, Abydos II, p. 24; cf. Knossos, 113, 137; 65. 7, 8, 23; 67 and 68. Report (1904), pp. 23, 24, and Fig. 8, A. 3 Seager, op. tit., p. 93.

Cf. for Spain A. H. et I. Siret, Les Premiers 4 American Journal of Archaeology, i (1897),

Ages du Metal, Planche 20. 99, 103, 106; 55. p. 287 seqq. Cf. pp. 302, 303, Figs. 13, 14, 5- found in the Neolithic deposits of Ligurian Grottoes. 1 In Fig. 18, 3 is shown a suspension vessel with incised decoration. E-like marks are incised on another fragment: they are of decorative origin, and not signs of a script.

At Pyrgos, on a headland about seven miles N. E. of Knossos. Sepul-recent blasting operations on the new Coast road revealed an extensive cav of

Cave containing hundreds of interments covering the whole of the Early: Minoan Age and of great importance from the evidence it supplies of the N. K. of survival of Neolithic traditions. 2 Close to this, at a spot known as Nirou Khani, there had also been discovered a Sanctuary building of Late Minoan date replete with cult objects connected with the worship of the Double Axe. 3

Among the most characteristic vessels brought to light were tall (chalices (Fig. 19, A, H) clearly evolved from the Sub-Neolithic pedestalled burnished bowls or goblets illustrated above in Fig. 17, and of the same reddish t- T section, due to the baking, but which from their finer fabric and shapelier form may be referred to the most advanced phase of the present Period. Fragmentary specimens of similar chalices had also occurred in Early Minoan I deposits of the site of Knossos, 4 and it will be seen that the black burnished decoration that they present on the dull, dark grey surface slip is itself an inheritance from Late Neolithic times. A curious feature of B is the horned rudimentary prominence with a vertical perforation apparently the degeneration of a wishing-bone handle. On the other hand Atrophied the rim of A is crinkled in a manner very suggestive of imitations of metal boi g' vases. The fine texture also suggests metallic influences, which towards the handle. close of this Period may certainly be taken into account.

The decoration, in both cases divided into panels and zones, is, as will J be seen, very elaborate, but its interest centres in the elongated curvilinear wood-motives of the upper zone of A. A comparison with the imitations of wood- gra i n j n g. work graining in painted plaster, both Minoan and Egyptian, can leave little doubt as to the source of these decorative motives, and this conclusion is con- so " firmed by their reappearance, with a clearer definition of the knots and concen- Arkalo-tric rings, on the inner margin of a vessel found in an E. M. 1 1 1 association in chalice the Cave of Arkalokhori, near Lyktos 5 (Fig. 19 B), of similar, but even finer 1 e. g. Arturo Issel, Liguria Geologita e Excavated by Dr. Xanthudides. see below, Preistorica (Atlas, PI. XXVIII, 13). p. 436, Fig. 313, p. 437.

2 The remains have been explored by the 4 Other specimens occurred in the lowest Ephor General, Dr. S. Xanthudides (now pub- stratum at Vasiliki. Seager, Exeat's, at Vasiliki, lished, Apx. Aea. T. 1918, p. 136 seqq.), thanks 1904, p. 6, Fig. 2; Goitrnia, PI. XII. 12 and to whose kindness I am able to reproduce the p. 50. Mr. Seager now agrees with me in specimens in Fig. 19. The latest painted referring this stratum to E. M. I.

sherds here found are E. M. Ill and clay J. Hatidakis, B. S. A, xix, p. 35 seo. q- and cofrins begin to appear. Fig. 3. Some M. M. I a pottery was also found.

THE PALACE OF MINOS, ETC.

Evolution of E. M. chalices from wooden bowls.

Revival of incised and punctuated Yare:, Collared vessels.

Suspension pots.

Trojan and

Cycladic Parallels.

texture, with the same dull grey surface and burnished decoration, and also showing at the side of the bowl a rudimentary prominence, still further atrophied. Other Pyrgos chalices with two loop handles supply both in form and technique curious comparisons with the Lianokladi Goblet type of the later, Minyan ware.

The reaction of the graining of wooden material on Minoan ceramic decoration is itself intelligible to any one who realizes what a large part wooden vessels play, even to-day, in the forest-grown regions of South-Eastern Europe, amongst which in prehistoric times Crete must certainly have taken its place. An example of the influence of wood graining on L. M. I vase-painting is given in Fig. 19, G, from Zakro. Cross currents of metallic influences must be admitted, but it looks as if these elegant Early Minoan chalices had been ultimately derived from simple wooden bowls with forked withy handles. As the base on which the bowl was set became an integral part of the vessel the handle gradually shrank away.

There is at this time a considerable revival of the incised and punctuated decoration, but without the chalky filling so characteristic of the Middle Neolithic phase. Many vessels so ornamented are provided with well-made upright collars, as Fig. 20 from Knossos and Fig. 21 found with the late E. M. I painted jug, Fig. 26, at Gournia. Fig. 22, from the lowest stratum at Vasiliki, 1 which, like others of this well-marked fabric e. g. Figs. 20, 21 is of finely levigated clay, grey throughout, shows a very close incised decoration; the completion of the lower part of this must be regarded as uncertain. It is provided both with looped horizontal and doubly perforated vertical handles. A remarkable round-bottomed bottle with incised ornament from the Pyrgos Cave is given in Fig. 19, c.

The class of vessels with handles for suspension is of frequent occurrence at this time, and these seem to have survived in use during the early part of the ensuing Period. They are of various shapes, generally with a more or less rounded bottom, and are provided either with vertically perforated ledge handles or small loops. They often show a neat collar fitted with a cap-like cover having perforated ears answering to the handles. A good example of this on a small scale is shown in Fig. 23 from the H agios Onuphrios deposit, probably derived from a primitive tholos' ossuary, and Fig. 24 illustrates a form with a higher cap and collar, from the rock-shelter of Hagios Nikolaos near Palaikastro, where several primitive vessels of this and other types were brought to light. 2 These suspension pots with caps (. loiirma, Pl. XII. 13, described by Seager, dance of sherds of the typical grey ware. ib., p.5o. This stratum, now recognized as E. M. 2 M. Niebuhr Tod, Excavations at Palai-I(seenote4, p.59), wascharacterizedbyanabun- kastro,. S. A., x, p. 341, and Figs, i and 2.

Flg. 21. ROCK-SHELTER, GOURNIA. (f

FIG. 20. E. M. I INCISED POT; GREY WARE, KNOSSOS ( ).

FIG. 23. SUSPENSION POT, HAGIOS ONUPHRIOS (-).

FIG. 22. LOWEST STRATUM, VASILIK! (f.).

THE PALACE OF MINOS, ETC.

are closely allied to a family of suspension vessels found in Early Cycladic graves and in the first stratum of Troy. 1

Vertically It is of interest to note that the perforations for suspension in this class of vessels are always vertical. The perforated ledges of the pure Neolithic ware, on the other hand, are always horizontally bored. By a gradual enlargement of the hole this latter type developed into broad loops, large enough to be held by the fingers, and so into ordinary upright handles. The

Pierced Handles.

mfrz

FIG. 25. E. M. I PAINTED JUG, HAGIOS ONUPHRIOS (f).

FIG. 2G. E. M. I PAINTED JUG, ROCK-SHELTER, GOURNIA (4 1).

vertically perforated ledges of the present E. M. I class in their turn supply the prototypes of a long series of horizontally set handles.

It has been pointed out by Dr. Mackenzie 2 that the painted fragments,- found on the site of Knossos in the stratum that merges into the latest coration. Neolithic show already in an incipient form the leading characteristics of the

Light on Dark and Dark on

Light 1 B. S. A., iii, pp. 44-5. Figs. 10-15 (Melos) I E0. A PX. 1898, PI. IX, i-s(Paros); Troja und Ilion, I, p. 248, Figs. 109, iro, in.

- The Pottery of Knossos (J. H. S., xxiii, IC J 3. PP- if4, 165).

EARLY MINOAN I (WITH SUB-NEOLITHIC) two main classes of later Minoan wares. In one series we see an imitation of the black hand-polished ware of the Later Stone Age. A black glaze slip is in this case spread over the surface of the clay, and at times bands of lustreless cream-white, apparently the old chalk medium, appear on this. In the other series the buff ground of the clay is left exposed, and dark glaze bands are painted on this. This represents the first appearance of the true glaze technique in the Aegean World. 1 The inner texture of the vessels is no longer the peaty grey of the Neolithic wares, but brick red. The finer fragments when dropped, give a clink like that of Mycenaean ware.

The class of painted ware presenting dark or deep reddish brown geometrical ornaments on a buff ground comes into prominence towards the close of this Period, and supplies the precursors of the earliest phase of the E. M. 11 ceramic style. This dark on buff style, after an interval of comparative latency in the succeeding era, once more emerges into greater prominence at the beginning of the First Middle Minoan Period, and under superior conditions of fabric and glaze finally triumphs in the characteristic ceramic class of the Late Minoan Age.

FIG. 27. E. M. I PAINTED POT, HAGIAPHOTIA(-) It is often difficult to distinguish the E. M. I products of the above class from those of the succeeding Period. It will be convenient, however, to include in the present class certain painted vessels of the gourd type with a high beak and round bottom, 2 the last feature being a usual characteristic of the more primitive wares. Such a vessel from the earl) deposit of Hagios Onuphrios, near Phaestos, 3 is given in Fig. 25. A similar vessel (Fig. 26) 4 with globular body but a flat base, from an early rock-shelter burial at Gournia, presents hatched decoration in reddish brown paint, forming two out-curving triangles or wings. A special interest attaches to this class of pattern, since the butterfly or double-axe motives of the succeeding Periods are evidently derived from it.

1 Cf. Mackenzie, loc. cit. (Franchet, he. at., formerly grouped this class with E. M. II. p. 207, treats this as his own discovery). 3 Pictographs, c., p. 114, Fig. 106.

1 Mr. Seager agrees with me in the con- 4 Gournia, PI. A. 3. venience of this classification though he had

E. M. I Geometrical Class of Brown on Buff.

Butterfly and Double-Axe Motives.

THE PALACE OF MINOS, ETC.

Incipient use of Lustrous Paint or Urfir-

Stone Derivatives of Neolithic Clay Figurines.

Later Figures with more Detailed Features.

Appearance of Early Egyptian Forms of Stone Vases.

Other Evidences of Early Connexion with Nile Valley.

Fig. 27, 1 found in a rock-shelter at Hagia Photia, has a base as well as collar, but it follows the archaic tradition in its suspension handles. The upper part shows a deep ferruginous red lattice pattern on a pale ground. The above vessels illustrate the incipient use of lustrous paint or Urfir-niss, henceforward an abiding characteristic of theminoan fabrics. 2 In this Period we see a growing tendency to make figurines of hard stone instead of clay, or occasionally steatite. Some of these simply reproduce the earlier class of squatting female figures of very adipose form. 3 Others represent the broader and flatter clay type which also goes back to Neolithic times and which leads up to the violin-shaped earlier Cyclaclic class (Fig. 13, io). 4 At the same time, a more upright class of stone figures seems to have originated from versions of the seated class by a gradual process of extension the legs at first being little more than stumps. It would also appear that at this time more attention was paid to the features of the head, which in the Neolithic class is often a mere protuberance. This later tendency is illustrated by the head of a figure from Central Crete (Fig. 13, 20) executed in a fine-grained alabaster, the delicate striations of which give it the appearance of fossil ivory. The slight curve of this figurine as seen in profile is very characteristic; the hips are very broad, like the contemporary example in breccia from Gortyna (Fig. 13, 8).

The primitive connexion with the Nile Valley, to which reference has already been made, is illustrated by the appearance in Crete principally at Knossos of a whole series of Egyptian stone vessels of forms and materials in vogue not only during the first four dynasties, but in the Late Prehistoric or Pre-dynastic Period that preceded them. 5

That there existed some special bond of community between the early Cretan culture and that of an indigenous Nilotic element of great antiquity is established by a series of phenomena in different departments of Art, but all leading back to the same conclusion. In dealing with the seal-types of the succeeding Early Minoan Periods it will be shown that many of the most characteristic designs, such as the composite and monstrous shape to which that of the Minotaur itself owes its origin, go back to Pre-dynastic types.

1 Gournia, p. 56, Fig. 38, 3. Height 13 cm. With this painted vessel was found a globular pot of grey clay with shallow scoring, provided with four small suspension handles (ib., Fig. 38, 4 2 See above, p. 63, note i.

3 For the evolution of these see the Table, Fig. 13, p. 48 above.

1 The Cycladic type Fig. 13, n represents a later stage.

' Attention has been called to some of these discoveries in my account of the Sepul-chral Deposit of Hagios Onuphrios'(Supplement to Cretan Pictographs, c. Quaritch. 1895, p. 117 seqq.).

EARLY MINOAN I (WITH SUB-NEOLITHIC)

We shall also see that there occurred in the early Cretan ossuaries figures recalling those of Naqada and other Late Prehistoric cemeteries in Egypt.

A remarkable illustration of an imported vessel of very early Egyptian Pre-fabric must be recognized in a syenite bowl found in 1900, during the first ex- Egyptian ploration of the Palace site at Knossos, on the borders of the Neolithic and Sub-Neolithic clay deposit inside the South Propylaeum l (Figs. 28 and 31). found at It has a flat collar, not undercut, and ledge handles without perforation.

This type of vessel is characteristic of the Late Pre-dynastic Period. During the early dynasties, as may be seen by the contents of cemeteries such as Tarkhan, the vast majority of the larger stone vessels were open bowls, and though, as Prof. Flinders Petrie informs me, bowls with the flat collar survived to the Second Dynasty, they were generally of rough fabric

FIG. 28. PRE-DYNASTIC EGYPTIAN BOWL OK SYENITE FROM KNOSSOS and at times without ledge handles. After the Second Dynasty they disappear.

In Fig. 29 an Egyptian porphyry bowl of the same class 2 belonging to the Late Prehistoric Period is shown for comparison, and in Fig. 30 another, also of porphyry, of higher build.

The same tradition is illustrated by a large bowl of hornblende Early porphyry found in an unstratified deposit to the North of the Palace site at Knossos in 1910 (Fig. 32). It shows the same general form, with the Porphyry flat collar, not undercut as the syenite specimen (Fig. 31), but it had been Knossos. unfortunately much rolled and is partly broken away at the sides. It does not seem to have had any ledge handles and finds its closest parallels therefore in Egyptian types of Second Dynasty date.

In the prehistoric Egyptian type, Fig. 30, we must unquestionably seek the pro- totype of an Early Minoan vessel in an indigenous material con- 1 Knossos Report, 1903, p. 98, Fig. 67 7, b. perforated. Reproduced with Prof. Flinders 2 From the Petrie Collection, University Petrie's kind permission. It is of black and College. The ledge handles are only partially white porphyry: width across handles 15-5 cm.

THE PALACE OF MINOS. ETC.

Tradition of Pre-Dynastic Stone Vessels in Crete.

How is it to be ex plained:

Suggested Settlement of Prehistoric Egyptian Elements.

sisting of brown serpentine, found near Elunda in East Crete, the site of the ancient Olous l (Fig. 33). It presents the same flat collar, and its well-marked base is itself a Pre-dynastic characteristic. 2 Later derivative forms of the same prototype occurred in the Mochlos tombs 3 (Fig. 34).

A smaller upright form of stone pot (Fig. 36), of which examples were found in tombs of the Second Early Minoan Period, 4 may be regarded as a lineal descendant of one of the commonest shapes of stone vessel found in the Late Pre-dynastic or Prehistoric cemeteries of Egypt, such as Naqada (Fig. 35). In this case intermediate Early Dynastic links are wanting.

It may well be asked to what special conjunction of circumstances was due this abiding tradition of proto-Egyptian forms in Early Minoan Crete. Can it be adequately explained by such intercourse as, for example, the obsidian trade may have already brought about in pre-dynastic times between Crete and the Nile Valley? Are we to consider these early trade relations sufficient in themselves to account for what seems to have been the wholesale importation into the island, at this remote period, of Egyptian products, afterwards to be copied by indigenous craftsmen? It may be allowed that this early intercourse was a contributory cause of the phenomena with which we have to deal, but it can hardly supply more than a partial explanation. The data before us suggest some more active agency. Can it be that the internal movements which brought into prominence the later, Dynastic element in Egypt drove part of the aboriginal population of the Nile mouths, already schooled in the rudiments of navigation, to take refuge on the further shore of the Libyan Sea? Remarkable as this latter conclusion would be, the balance of existing evidence might seem to incline in its favour.

It looks as if about the beginning of the Dynastic Period some partial interruption took place in this early intercourse between Egypt and Crete. On the whole, the models followed by the Cretan lapidaries go back, as we have seen, to those of the earlier Egypto-Libyan class. From at least the Fourth Dynasty, however, direct relations between the dominant Egyptian caste and Minoan Crete are continuously traceable.

As might be expected, it is at Knossos again, the traditional head- 1 See my Sepulchral Deposit of H. Onu- But it is one of the most characteristic features phrios: supplement to Cretan Pictography c.; Quaritch, 1895, p. 118, Fig. 112.

2 Freiherr von Hissing, Der Antheil der iigyptischen Kunst am Kunstleben der Volker (Munich, 1912), p. 36, lays stress on the fact that the definition of the base does not appear on Egyptian stone vases till the Sixth Dynasty.

of the late Pre-dynastic class with which we are here concerned.

3 Mochlos, p. 48, iv. 6 (Fig. 18 and PI. II). See below, p. 88.

4 Of grey steatite. Ibid., p. 25, ii. j (Fig. 7 and PI. II). See below, p. 91.

PRE-DYNASTIC EGYPTIAN VASES OF PORPHYRY; FOUND IN EGYPT.

l; i."!. PRE-DYNASTIC EGYPTIAN ivKMTK BOWL FROM KNOSSOS (f f.).

FIG. 32. HORNBLENDE AND PORPHYRY BOWL (SECOND DYN. EGYP-TIAN) FROM KNOSSOS (f).

I IAN VESSEL, SERPENTINE: ELUNDA(C.).

1. CRETAN STONE VESSEL, Mocm. os (-J-.).

FIG. 35. PREHISTORIC EGYPTIAN. FIG. 36. E. M. II,

HleRAKONPOLIS (f.). MOCHLOS (".).

THE PALACE OF MINOS, ETC.

quarters of Minoan civilization, that this new connexion becomes most perceptible.

Know- Copper was known at this Period. A fragment, apparently of a small

Cofpefin knife of this metal, occurred in an E. M. I vase, 1 and the somewhat stylized

Steatite whorls" withrude Picto-graphs.

FIG. 37. THREE-SIDED STEATITE SEAL, KALOCHORIO, CRETE (f c).

Chalco- form of some of the triangular daggers of the E. M. II Period (see below, Phase Fig- 70) points to the anterior existence of simpler types of this weapon.

Otherwise, as is abundantly shown by the Sub-Neolithic strata at Knossos, there was a considerable survival of the use of stone implements, notably small celts and obsidian knives. The culture, as already said, is Chalcolithic.

As to many classes of objects, the existence of which may be eventually traced back to this Period, suc fr as ornani ents of gold or silver, the evidence is still defective. It is clear that certain very primi- tive types of seals with rude linear pictographs and signs must be assigned to the First Early Minoan

Period, if only for the reason that more developed types of the same class are associated with remains of the succeeding epoch. The seals in question are mostly in the form of cones or conoids and irregular three-sided bead-seals of large calibre, associated with pictographs of the rudest linear class. Their material is the native steatite (Fig. 37). 2 We here see the first elementary stages of the graphic art that was eventually to lead to the highly developed systems of Minoan writing.

It is a noteworthy fact that on some of these early seal-stones convoluted and monstrous forms begin to appear which attest the influence of a class of types very frequent on a series of cylinder- and prism-seals of black steatite 1 See above, p. 57, Fig. 16, d. from Kalochorio, east of Ca. a.(Scripta Minoa, 2 Fig. 37 is a rude three-sided seal of steatite i, p. 116, Fig. 48).

FIG. 38A. STEATITE WHORL, H AGIOS ONU-PHRIOS (f).

KARLY MINOAN 1 (WITH SUB-NEOLITHIC) belonging to the late Prehistoric Period in Egypt. On face b of the three-sided seal (Fig. 37) we see a figure having the legs of a man but with the upper part of the body bent back and terminating fantastically. A whorl of green steatite from the early deposit of Hagios Onuphrios near Phaestos (Fig. 38A) 1 shows a curious horned figure apparently with human legs a rude anticipation of the Minotaur. In the same way contorted human figures, Minotaurs, and composite animals are among characteristic designs on the prehistoric Egyptian seals, amongst which a perforated prism, from Karnak (Fig. 38 u), 2 supplies a prototype for the same Cretan form. The influence of these on Minoan glyptic types reveals itself in many ways. 3 On face c for instance of the Karnak prism a bull-headed human figure is clearly discernible.

Fantastic Types derived from Early Egyptian Cylinders and Prism-Seals. Rude Minotaurs.

FIG. 38 B. PRISM SEAL IN BLACK STEATITE FROM KARNAK: c SHOWS A HUMAN FIGURE WITH BULLS HEAD. A TWO-HEADED GOAT APPEARS ON d.

Once more we are led back to a contact between Crete and the Nile Remoter Valley more ancient than the earliest historic dynasty. But the ultimate fl uences connexion of these types leads us even beyond this. As in the case of the lo y cylinder form of seal itself, with which they are specially associated, and of Culture, many other elements of Early Nilotic culture, the true source may have to be eventually sought much further afield. The fantastic semi-human types from which the Minotaur sprang themselves suggest the monstrous creations that attach themselves to the legends of Gilgamesh and Ea-bani. So, too, the two-headed composite animals might be taken to be the derivative modifications of the crossed bulls and lions seen up-reared on the Chaldaean cylinders.

1 The other side of the whorl is engraved with signs of a curiously alphabetic character. (See Scripta Afinoa, i, p. 118, Fig. 526.)

J Scripta Mitioa, p. 123, Fig. 58.

3 See my Further Discoveries of Cretan, c. Script, 1898, p. 369. (Mycenaean is used for Minoan.) Cf. Scripta Minoa, i. p. 122 seqq.

Effects of Was there some intermediate source? These composite figures may at

Tech- least be regarded as the creations of a similar cylinder technique, nique. The remains brought to light in the lowest stratum of the Town site at amjuiar Mochlos show that rectangular stone houses were already in use at this time, stone As already noted, indeed, the square plan itself goes back in Crete to a remote ine. M, I. Neolithic Period. On the other hand, from the fact that certain E. M. I types Ossuary occur in the primitive ossuaries of the Messara district, built in the shape of and tholoi, we may also infer the existence of round huts or wigwams. These

Hu"s d tholoi have small entrances and consist of a domical construction of clay and rubble, strengthened with a stone facing inside and out. Cave- The more usual places of sepulture during this Period seem to have been caves, like that of Pyrgos, and rock-shelters.

Transi- From the transitional character of the E. M. I Period, which is here taken

Character to mc 1 uc 1 e tne Sub-Neolithic phase, it must be regarded as having occupied and a very considerable interval of time. It contains, indeed, the elements mate of an eventual subdivision. Reasons have already been given for sup-Szyot P osm g at it overlapped at least the later part of the Pre-dynastic Period;. M. i in Egypt. On the other hand, as will be shown in the succeeding Section, various pieces of evidence tend to connect the Second Early Minoan phase of culture with the period of Egyptian history covered by the Fourth, Fifth, and Sixth Dynasties. The accession of Sneferu, the first king of the Fourth Dynasty, according to Dr. Eduard Meyer's reckoning took place about 2800 B. C. Menes is dated by him 3315 B. C. As, ex hypothesi, moreover, the First Early Minoan Period, or at least its Sub-Neolithic stage, overlaps the close of the Pre-dynastic Age, it may be carried back on this chronological basis to about 3400 B. c. If we thus include in it the somewhat ill-defined but certainly lengthy transitional phase that succeeds the pure Neolithic, its total duration may be roughly reckoned from the latter date to about 2800 B. C. It would however be unsafe to place the full development of the E. M. I style much before the close of the Fourth Millennium before our era.

Acme of Early Minoan Culture; Early buildings of Vasilik); Painted Plaster on Walla; Primitive Tkoloi; House Tombs' of Moclilos; Pottery with dark on light decoration; Vessels from E. J f. I House-floors, Knossos; Origin ofbutterfly ornament; Clay Boats and Tables of Offering; Prototypes of classical Kernoi; Mottled Ware; Comparisons with Early Egyptian spouted vessels; Cynocepliali on Ivory Seals; Idols' of ft olo-Egyptian foi i; Faience Boiul and Beads; Influence of Fourth to Sixth Dynasty Stone Vases; Carinated Bowls; Stone Vases from Mochlos; Relief of Dog; Cylinders and Seals of Clay and Ivory; Goldsmith's ivork; Flowers and Foliage; Eye bandages' Embryo Death Masks anticipations of Mycenae; Copper Arms and Implements; Votive Double Axes; Dove pendants; Chronological limits.

THIS is the epoch at which the Early Minoan culture of Crete attains E. M. II: its most brilliant development. Our knowledge of the extraordinary advance Early in various branches of art achieved during this Period is mainly due to? Mr. Seager's explorations of the early tombs of the Islet of Mochlos in Eastern Crete. Within this Period are also comprised most of the earlier

FIG. 39. PLAN OK E. M. II BUILDINGS AT VASILIK! (SEAGER): HOUSE ON THE HILL TOP.

elements of the primitive tholoi of Hagia Triada, and Messara. Remains of an E. M. II house to the south of the Palace at Knossos, underlying M. M. I walls, came to light in 1908, the floors of which produced an abundance of pottery, including the characteristic mottled ware (see Fig. 40). Two successive plans of buildings found by Mr. Seager at Vasiliki,

THE PALACE OE MINOS, ETC.

Elaborate E. M. II Buildings at Vasi-liki.

Timber framework.

Painted Stucco on Walls

Tholos' Ossuaries.

House Tombs'.

Huts.

answering to the earlier and later phases of this Period, show that stone buildings existed of rectangular design and elaborate arrangement, which seem to have been two or three stories high. The later of these plans is shown in Fig. 39. l Large sun-dried bricks were used in the upper part of the walls, which were also framed vertically and horizontally with wooden beams, their inner and outer framework being linked by cross pieces. We have here an anticipation of the later Palace construction.

A remarkable feature of these buildings is that the walls were coated with rough lime plaster, showing a fine surface wash of deep red, 2 the direct forerunner of the later fresco paintings. This coarse stucco covering, of great hardness, owing to the formation of silicates, fulfilled a constructive function byjarotecting the sun-dried bricks or rough rubble of the walls.

Apart from the occasional use of natural caves and of artificial holes in the rock for sepulture, two main classes of ossuary tombs were now prevalent, the primitive tholoi and the built chamber or cist tombs. The tholoi present a low incurving circuit wall above which, as already noted, was originally a domed structure of clay and rubble. They represent, in fact, circular hut dwellings. Besides cists, generally of upright slabs like the Cycladic, the principal built tombs at Mochlos were of rectangular construction formed of roughly squared stones with doorways originally blocked by slabs. They were found open above, but there was evidence that both these and the cists had been originally roofed with reeds and clay. These chamber tombs were, in fact, miniature stone houses.

The best example at Mochlos is supplied by the original plan of Tomb VI belonging to the earliest phase of E. M. II (Fig. 73, p. 102). It consisted of an entrance room communicating at the back, through a door opening to the right, with an inner chamber. 3 This back room is here placed beside the other, the rocky steep behind probably making this location more convenient. The essence of the arrangement is the familiar but and ben system, which, as we have seen, goes back in Crete to Neolithic times.

1 From Seager, Excavations at Vasiliki, by the blocking of the door leading to the 1906 (Transactions Dept. of Archaeology, Univ. inner compartment and by the building of of Pennsylvania, ii, 1907, p. 112, Fig. i). a low wall across the entrance room. In 2 Noel Heaton, I Iinoan Lime Plaster and Fresco Painting (Journ. of R. Inst. of Brit, Architects, xviii, p. 698). Similar remains of the deepred-faced plaster with a very smooth surface occurred in Early Minoan deposits at Knossos.

Fig. 73, placed at the end of this section, both this blocking and the annexed Tomb V are removed.

4 See above, p. 32. Also Mackenzie, Cretan Palaces IV, B. S A., xiv, pp! 362-5, 368-74, 3 Cf. Seager, Explorations in the Island of and compare with the Mochlos House Tomb Mochlos, p. 41, Fig. 15. The internal arrange- the Early Minoan Ossuary at Kastri, loc. tit., ment was modified in the E. M. Ill Period p. 363, Fig. 5, and p. 365.

THE PALACE OF MINOS, ETC.

Painted Geometrical Decoration on Pottery.

Simple but and ben huts, moreover, constructed with roughly hewn stone blocks are associated with contemporary Cycladic remains. 1 This tomb-plan in fact supplies a typical example of the simpler form of rectangular hut still in use in Crete at the beginning of the Early Minoan Age. The house of the dead is here a reduced model of the house of the living.

A Sub-Neolithic tradition is still perceptible on some of the early pottery of this Period, notably a class of fine grey ware. Apart from this, the first ceramic phase of the E. M. II culture is chiefly characterized by-painted vessels showing a geometrical decoration of a darker hue on a pale

Dark on

Light

Styles.

E. M. II Domestic Ware from House-floors, Knossos.

FIG. 41. E. M. II PAINTED BOWL

FROM MOCHLOS.

FIG. 42. JUG FROM MOCHLOS.

buff ground. These vessels represent the continuation of a class which, as we have seen, was already coming into prominence among the later ceramic fabrics of the preceding E. M. I Period. 2 A similar kind of painted ware is found in contemporary Cycladic deposits, as for instance in the tombs of Syros. Many vessels and fragments representing the ordinary domestic types of this E. M. II class were found on some house-floors of that date that came to light at Knossos on the Southern slope of the Palace site bordering the S. Corridor (Fig. 40). Amongst these were high-beaked jugs, bowl-shaped ewers with prominent spouts emerging from their sides, open bowls, some with triple excrescences on their lower periphery, and numerous cups with low pedestals which fit on to an E. M. I type. The surface of the cups and bowls in many cases showed signs of having been pared with a knife, a technique which is still more emphasized in the succeeding 1 he. cit., p. 364

See above, pp. 62, 63, Figs. 25, 2(1, 27.

E. M. Ill and M. M. I Periods. There were also specimens of the mottled decoration illustrated below (Fig. 4(3).

On the more developed types of this class the geometrical decoration Hatched becomes more elaborate, hatched triangles in varied combinations being a con-. jyurr-spicuous feature (Figs. 41, 42). The butterfly ornament pairs of these tl y ()r i-with the apex meeting survives into the First Middle Minoan Period.

Among the monochrome vessels of this Period, one from Hellenika, near Palaikas-tro, is remarkable as being in the shape of a boat with a Clay high prow and tail-like rudder. This type, significative of maritime enterprise, recalls Cycladic examples of the same kind. What appears to be a clay boat with a high prow at both ends, belonging to this or the succeeding Period, was found in a house at Mochlos.

An interesting form of clay vessel also makes its first appearance during this Period, which seems to be the prototype of the typical Minoan Pedes- kernoi. These vessels, of dark burnished ware, are either round or p al oval in outline, and consist of a flat-bottomed pan supported on a pedestal. They seem, as will be seen from the restored examples, Fig. 43, a, 6, to be due to the coalescing of what must have been originally three separate elements: (i) the pan-like receptacle; (2) the flat table; (3) the pedestal. So far as the two last elements are concerned, this evolution presents a curious parallelism with the Early Dynastic Egyptian Tables of Parallel Offering 3; in that case the round flat table and the pedestal are found Kg yp, j an in their separate as well as their united phase (Fig. 45), and a shallow stone T f a nff S bowl was often placed on the table. This parallelism finds a further striking ing. illustration in the vessels grouped on a similar stand, Fig. 43, c, from the early tholos ossuary of Kumasa 6 (E. M. II-III). The triple group of pots with their archaic perforated handles here clearly indicates a ritual destination, and anticipates in another form the triple cups of the Diktaean Libation Table.

But this Early Minoan type itself stands at the head of a whole linoar family of later kernoi," a class of vessels specially devoted to the cult of Rhea, who herself represents the tradition of the Great Minoan Goddess.

1 Reproduced from Seager, Mochlos, p. 36. 5 Xanthudides, B, S. A., xii, p. 11, Fig. i. Fig. 41 is from Tomb II, Fig. 42 from Tomb I. Prof. Bosanquet has already instanced a

The simpler type, 6, is from E. H. Hall, parallel form of vessel from Phylakopi, consist-

Sphoungaras, p. 49, Fig. 22, F. a is from Seager, ing of three pots supported by a hollow stem,

Mochlos, p. 71, Fig. 40. Others occurred at a forerunner of the kernos type (B. S. A., iii,

Pyrgos. 54 seqq.). For the later xipvai from Eleusis 3 These are of both alabaster and clay. and elsewhere see O. Rubensohn, Mitth. d. k. d.

4 Alabaster Table of Offerings from El Kab. Arch. Ins., 1898, p. 271 seqq., and PI. XIII.

THE PA LACK OF MINOS, ETC.

FIG. 43. a. TABLE AND PAN, MOCHLOS ( ). F IG. 43. c K. ERNOS, KUMASA( ): E. M. II-III.

FIG. 43. b. TABLE AND PAN, SPHUNGARAS (J).

5(ctio n of G reek f rno: (cttdm-aj Cm.)

FIG. 44.

FIG. 45. EGYPTIAN OFFERING TABLE OF ALABASTER (if.), IVTH DY-NASTY, EL KAB.

EARLY M1NOAN II

THE PALACE OF MINOS, ETC.
Mottled or
Vasiliki Ware.

To the last, moreover, a reminiscence of the original table of support of early Egyptian derivation survived in the contour of this class of vessel. 1

The second phase of E. M. II pottery is distinguished by the predominance of an entirely new and beautiful class: the mottled ware, first known as a distinct category through Mr. Seager's excavations in the early building at Vasiliki. It begins already in the first period of the building, which goes back to the Sub-Neolithic Age, runs parallel with the geometric dark on light wares in the next architectural stage, and in the third stage, answering to the latter part of E. M. II, entirely supersedes it. Only a small survival of this style is found in the last stage of the building corresponding with E. M. III. The clay is fine and hard, and the pots are so deftly turned as almost to appear to be wheel-made. 2 They seem to have attained their shapely form by being placed on small disks of wood or stone, which were then turned by hand. The surface of this mottled ware shows a body colour of red, shading to orange, variegated often in distinct patterns with lighter bands and patches of black merging into bronze. Some idea of the effect, without the colouring, may be gained from the sherds and vessels reproduced in Fig. 46. 3 The brilliant hues and variegated appearance were produced in the process of firing.

In its general aspect this method of decoration finds more or less contemporary Mediterranean analogies of very widespread distribution, from the red-faced Copper Age ware of Cyprus to that of the Early Metal Age explored by the brothers Siret in South-East Spain. Of special interest, however, is the parallelism presented by the typical red-faced ware of prehistoric Egypt, the interior and rims of which were coloured a lustrous black. This comparison has, moreover, an additional value from the fact that this style survived on the Egyptian borders among the remains of the old indigenous stock and was, in fact, reintroduced into the Nile Valley at a considerably later date by the aboriginal population to whom the pan-graves are ascribed. The correspondence extends even to details. At Sphungaras, where numerous specimens of this class of ware occurred, the inside of the vessel presented a uniform black hue, which extended evenly over the rim, as if these vases, like the black-topped ware from Egypt, 1 Compare the Greek kernos', Fig. 44, from H. Nikolaos (Lato pros Kamara), Xanthudides, op. tit., pp. 16-18, and Figs. 4, 5. This vessel, though in the form of a pedestalled bowl below, shows the 'square-cut rim of the earlier table. The lamp, a characteristic feature of the later kernos' type, was perhaps anticipated by the central recipient often seen in the Minoan class.

J They are, in fact, so described in Gournia, p. 50.

Cf. Seager, Excavations at Vasiliki, 1904 (Transactions,., I9O5), Pl. XXXIV; Gournia, Pl. B. C and D from Palaikastro are in the Ashmolean Museum.

EARLY MINOAN II had been placed upside down in a bed of coals'. 1 The same process was at times followed in Cyprus.

In the above cases we have to do with the application of this method to Greater primitive hand polished wares. In the Vasiliki class we see it largely adapted oxydation to the early glaze technique. 2 The root cause in producing this effect of surface seems, however, to be that suggested by Professor Flinders Petrie:! in the case of the Egyptian black-topped pottery, namely, the greater or less direct exposure of the vessel to the hot air of a kiln, which preserves the red oxide of the surface material. It is clear, however, that the Minoan potters

FIG. 47. METALLIC TYPES OF E. M. II VESSELS FROM SPHUNGARAS (r.).

possessed a method of reserving certain parts of the vessel from direct Patterns .,-.,. i produced contact with the furnace air in such a way as to produce a variety of simple by patterns or other definite effects. 4 Thus several of the specimens given in Fig. 46 present an appearance, recalling the pebbly section of conglom- this tech- erate stone, such as is imitated at times on Middle Minoan painted vases. In 1 Edith H. Hall (now Mrs. Dohan), Excavations in Eastern Crete: Sffumngaras, pp. 48, 49- 2 See Seager, Excavations at Iasiliki, 1904,. ri, note. The old method, however, survived at Vasiliki and elsewhere, and a large part of the surface of the vessels is often simply hand-polished. The cup (Fig. 46, D) is an instance in point, the black bands appearing on the red-faced and hand-polished clay.

1 Naqada and Ballas, p. 37. Prof. Petrie adds, it is precisely the same question of hue and composition as on Greek vases, where the black may become red wherever a draught of air impinged upon it.

No satisfactory explanation has yet been given of the manner in which these patterns were produced. Franchet, A T ouv. Arch, des Missions, c., XXV, pp. 19, 20, regards this system as the beginning of true colour technique, and even proceeds to bring the E. M. II mottled vases of Vasiliki into direct connexion with painted vases of advanced M. M. I types from the same site. He described this as the invention of black colour and of polychrome decoration. 1 iscrepancies in date, however, do not affect M. Franchet, who consistently ignores the stratigraphic results of his predecessors in Cretan research and substitutes for the Minoan Periods a crude classification of his own, based on the Bronze Age of provincial France.

THE. PALACE OF MINOS, ETC.

Imitations of Copper Vessels.

the spouted vessel from Gournia, Fig. 4, u, 1 the body of the bowl shows distinct patterns consisting of cruciform figures between horse-shoes. This vessel, moreover, supplies a very interesting example of the combination of the two contemporary styles, its spout being decorated with a usual geometrical motive, black on a creamy ground. On the high-beaked jug, Fig. 46, A, we see a kind of oval pattern repeated at intervals.

Ware of this class also derives a special interest from the occurrence for the first time of certain forms clearly dependent on metal prototypes. The jug, Fig. 47, a, from Sphungaras shows not only the carinated outline of some copper original, but the riveting together of its upper plates is indicated

Comparisons with Early Dynastic Spouted Vessels.

FIG. 48. EARLY DYNASTIC EGYPTIAN COPPER VESSELS, a. ABYDOS (f). b. MAHASNA.

by the rows of impressed dots at intervals, evidently reminiscent of the studs or nail heads. The rigid pedestal and angular recipient of the goblet, Fig. 47, c, and the stiff outlines of the cup (S) are also suggestive of metallic influence. Of still greater "interest in their associations are the spouted ewers such as Fig. 46, B, with their prominent curving spouts.

A feature of many of these spouted vessels, examples of which exist in stone as well as in clay, is the relatively small hole by which the spout communicates with the interior. This peculiarity suggests some curious points of comparison with a class of Egyptian vessels of copper, clay,

FIG 49. DOUBLK SPOUTED EGYPTIAN VESSELS: a. PRE-!)YNASTIC (LIMESTONE) l FOURTH DYNASTY (ALABASTER) i.).

FIG. 50. DOUBLE SI-OUTED CRETAN JUG (STEATITE FROM GOURNIX (J t.).

THE PALACE OF MINOS, ETC.

Double Spouted Egyptian Vessels.

Double Spouted Cretan Type.

Egyptian Form for Dual Libations.

and alabaster or aragonite, belonging to the early dynasties. These Egyptian forms of which the copper type seems to be the original are also distinguished by their prominent spouts into which the liquid passed by a similar small hole in the wall of the vessel (Fig. 48, a). With these are often associated in proto-dynastic graves copper cups and bowls of a type (Fig. 48, b) suggestive of a long Minoan series, with and without handles.

The presumption that this early class of Egyptian ewer exercised an influence on certain forms of Early Minoan vases is, moreover, carried still further by another not infrequent feature. Many of the Egyptian ewers show the curious peculiarity of a double outlet. Sometimes the spout is divided by a partition running down its centre, each channel being provided with a separate hole (see Fig. 49, (5). 1 At other times this dual arrangement takes the form of a pair of spouts set side by side, as exemplified by two copper ewers from the Tomb of Khasekhemui of the First Dynasty.- That this was, in fact, the earlier variety of double spout is seen from its occurrence in the case of a limestone bowl from a Late Pre-dynastic grave at Naqada, Fig. 49, a. 3 It is, therefore, a highly significant fact that a similar form of double spout should recur in a class of bridge-spouted vessels which are the modified descendants of the Early Minoan spouted jugs above described. 4 The steatite jug from Gournia, Fig. 50, representing a variety of this class, is provided with a double spout practically identical with that exemplified by the specimen from Naqada. The Gournia vessel, though itself probably not later than the beginning of the Middle Minoan Age, thus perpetuates a very early tradition of which more primitive examples may eventually come to light on Cretan soil.

The peculiar arrangement common to both the above types of a double outlet and channel dividing what was poured from the vessel into two streams could serve no practical end and must surely have been due to some religious motive. Prof. Flinders Petrie has suggested with reference to the early Egyptian ewers with double spouts found in the tomb of King Khasekhemui of the First Dynasty, 5 that the motive for so strange a form 1 Fig. 49, b is an alabaster (aragonite) vessel of Fourth Dynasty date from El Kab (Ashmolean Museum). A copper ewer with divided spout of the same date from Mahasna is in the Cairo Museum. (Fr. von Bissing, Metallgefasse, c., 3436.) 2 Petrie, Royal Tombs, ii, p. 26; PI. IX, 13,14.

3 Petrie Collection, University College.

4 See my observations, Prehistoric Tombs of Knossos (Quaritch, 1906), p. 149, where the connexion with the Egyptian copper ewers was first pointed out.

r Royal Tombs, ii, p. 27.

EARLY MINOAN II may be seen perhaps in the coequal worship of Set and Horus in this reign; the simultaneous offering of libation to both Gods could be secured by this double spout.

Is it conceivable that such a system in the case of a parallel class of vessels originated independently in Crete and Egypt? In Egypt we see that the idea seems to attach itself to the still earlier use of double spouts, common in the Prehistoric Age.

In view of such correspondences it is difficult not to admit the influence of these spouted ewers of proto-dynastic Egypt on Minoan vessels. The addition of a handle is itself, moreover, a concession to insular custom which finds a parallel in other cases where Egyptian utensils were copied. We see the same addition made to a form of long-spouted libation vessels, otherwise closely akin to the usual Egyptian type, reproduced in the Cretan hieroglyphic signary. 1

Many other small objects associated with the remains of this Period point to early connexions with Egypt and the further shores of the Libyan Sea. Ivory seals such as one from a M. M. II tomb at Mochlos present the device of two cynocephali 2 (Fig. 51). The use of ivory itself is a strong indication of trade relations with Egypt. 3 A silver cylinder with a very wide perforation found at Mochlos answers in type to an Early Dynastic Egyptian class. In the primitive tholos ossuaries such as that of Hagia Triada, moreover, were found indigenous idols' or human figures 4 belonging to this or the ensuing Period which curiously recall the prehistoric types from Naqada and other cemeteries, and reproduce the domed head and pointed chin of the early inhabitants of the Nile Valley.

Perhaps to Set and Horus.

FIG. 51. IVORY SIGNET SEAL FROM MOCHLOS ((.).

Ivory Seal with Cynocephali.

Idols' of Proto-Egyptian Type.

1 Scripta Minoa, i, p. 197, No. 40, and see below, Fig. 212, b.

2 Seager, op. cit., p. 24, ii. 42 (Fig. n), from Tomb II, containing the richest deposit of gold jewels. Only one object from this tomb (op, cit., Clay Jug, p. 24, II. b) could be brought down as late as the beginning of the E. M. Ill Period. Another ivory seal with a similar device occurred, however, in an E. M. Ill stratum of the Town site at Mochlos. The types, therefore, probably belong to the borders of the two Periods.

3 There is no kind of evidence 01 any direct relations with Cyprus or the Syrian coasts till the Middle Minoan Age, and if, as Dr. von Bissing supposes, the ivory came from that quarter it must have reached Crete via Egypt.

4 F. Halbherr, Memorie del R. Istituto Lorn-bardo, xxi (1905), p. 251, and PI. XI, Fig. 27. Similar types occurred in the tholos of Kumasa: cf. H. R. Hall, Aegean Archaeology, PI. XIV, 4.

THE PALACE OE MINOS, ETC.

Comparative examples from both groups are sketched in Fig. 52. These male figurines entirely diverge in type from the traditional forms inherited in Crete from Neolithic times. Rude schist idols however, more or less pointed below, occurred, with Cycladic types, in the Sepulchral Cave of Pyrgos.

PRE-DYNASTIC EGYPT NAQADA.

FIG. 52. PRIMITIVE THOLOS, HAGIA TRIADA (ALABASTER, MARBLE AND STEATITE).

Allusion will be made in the next Section to the amulets in the form of human legs from the same primitive ossuary, which fit on to an Egyptian or

Egypto-Libyan class characteristic of the troubled period that follows on the Sixth Dynasty. In this, as in the case of the small human figures, we see an

Dynastic indebtedness on the Minoan side of something more than a formal nature, Egyptian and which belongs, in fact, to the domain of popular religion. The t j on double-spouted ewers, for some dual rite of libation, suggest influences of the same kind, and it is a highly significant fact that the instrument used for the ceremonial dance of the harvesters on the vase from Hagia 1 The Naqada specimens are mostly in the Petrie, Naqada, pp. 45, 46, and Pl. LIX.

Ashmolean Museum. Fig. a is of vegetable A good general view of the early Egyptian paste; b, c, and d are of schist and ivory. The figures is given in J. Capart, Les Debuts de Part specimens from Hagia Triada are of steatite en Egyptc, p. 78 and p. 150 seqq. and alabaster. For the Naqada figurines see

Triacla, belonging to a much later date, 1 should not only be a sistrum an instrument of purely Egyptian association but a sistrum of a distinctly archaic form.

Amongst other instances of undoubted indebtedness to Egypt Faience is the occurrence of objects of glazed paste in native faience c. O f a p a l e bluish green colour, resembling that in use during tne earl Y dynasties of Egypt. In Tomb VI at Mochlos, in a purely MOCHLOS. E. M. II medium, in addition to beads of this material there came to light a much decayed faience bowl. 3 Among the beads, a pear-shaped form (Fig. 53) 4 answers to a common Egyptian type which Prof. Flinders Petrie ingeniously derives from the cone-shell beads of the Prehistoric Age. 5

The earlier wave of influence that reached Crete across the Libyan Sea Fourth to had, as we have seen, carried in its wake elements belonging to the Late Dynasty Pre-dynastic Period and to a less extent of the two earliest dynasties, To this there now succeeds another wave representative of the middle phase of the Early Kingdom and including the period from the Fourth to the Sixth Dynasty.

The Palace site of Knossos has brought forth cumulative evidence both of the actual import and of the prolonged imitation of a class of shallow bowls, generally executed in hard materials, and characterized by an angular or carinated contour. Diorite bowls of this kind, of exquisite fabric, were Car!, 1 nated found in the tomb of Sneferu (Snofru), c. 2840-2820 H. c. (Figs. 54 and 55, a), Howls of and are a representative product of the Fourth Dynasty. A fragment of a typical example in alabaster has also been found in the recently explored temple of King Sahure 6 of the Fifth Dynasty, c. 2673-2661 B. c., and though similar evidence regarding the Sixth Dynasty is not as yet forthcoming, we may assume that such carinated bowls continued to be executed throughout the brilliant central phase of the Early Kingdom in Egypt.

Fragments of two shallow bowls in diorite with this distinctive carinated contour were found on the Palace site at Knossos. 7 It will be seen from 1 L. M. I. See Vol. II. The cone-shells themselves, or a variety 2 For the Minoan faience see especially with a higher spire, were reproduced in corne-p. 486 below. Its fabric continued in Crete lian and lapis lazuli at the time of the Twelfth from E. M. II to the last Palace Period, Dynasty.

L. M. II. 6 L. Borchardt, Grabdenkmal des Sahure, 3 Mochlos, p. 54, vi. 22. Band I, p. 116, Fig. 152. From the temple 4 Somewhat enlarged. From a sketch made of the King at Abusir.

by me at Mochlos at the time of the excava- 7 A. J. E., Knossos Report, 1902, p. 122 tion. seqq. (B. S. A., viii).

THE PALACE OF MINOS, ETC.

FIG. 54. DIORITE BOWL FROM TOMB OF KING SNEFERU (FOURTH DYN.) (f.)   a.   SECTION OF DIORITE BOWL FROM TOMB OF KING SNEFERU (FOURTH DYN.) b. RESTORED SECTION DIORITE BOWL, KNOSSOS.

c. RESTORED SECTION LIPARITE BOWL, KNOSSOS. FIG. 55.

Fig. 55, b that the form is practically identical with that of a vessel of the same material from the tomb of Sneferu.

It is not unreasonable to suppose that vessels like the above, not only of very hard material but of great beauty, may have been handed down as heirlooms to a considerably later date. That these fine models were reproduced by Cretan vase-makers as late as the beginning of the Middle Minoan Age is made probable by another highly interesting discovery on the Palace site at Knossos. This is a fragment of a very similar bowl with Similar vessel of a highly carinated outline (Fig. 55, c), executed in liparite, a form of obsi- i. jparite. dian or volcanic glass which seems to have been confined to the Aeolian islands. A large unworkecl lump of this was actually found in the Palace l and, in spite of the hardness of the stone, the early bowl may itself have

FIG. 56. PORPHYRY Bowi. SHOWING EGYPTIAN TRADITION. ROYAL TOMB, ISOPATA (J).

been of Knossian fabric, since there is no evidence that the Egyptians used this material. From the beginning of the Palace Period (M. M. I) it had a considerable vogue in Crete. Apart from actual remains of liparite vessels, Ceramic the proof of this is supplied by a class of dark faced ware with white 0 flipa-spots, evidently copied from this stone, and including actual imitations of rlte carinated bowls of the present class. 2 The ceramic copies referred to seem themselves to belong mainly to M. M. II and III. On the other hand, masterpieces of the lapidary's art in liparite still occur at the beginning of the Late Minoan Age, witness a beautiful vessel in the form of a doium shell from the Palace of Hagia Triada now in the Museum of Candia.

1 See above, p. 23. It was found in a in height, and has been illustrated by Mosso, M. M. II stratum beneath the chamber con- Le Origini dela Civilta Mediterranea, p. 285, taining the Miniature Frescoes. It is 43 cm. Fig. 180. See below, p. 178, Fig. 127

THE PALACE OF MINOS, ETC.

Cari-BOW? of influence on Cretan

Lapidaries.
indi-genous
Evolu- tion.

A derivative of one of the early carinated Egyptian bowls must be seen in a fine exam P le (Fi g- 5G) executed in a deep green and black porphyry with white crystals the lapis Lacedaevionins found in the Royal Tomb at Isopata. 1 It had been provided with a pair of holes, vertically bored, on either side, apparently for the insertion of metal handles, but these perforations had been filled in with similar stone at a later elate. It seems, therefore, to have been itself an heirloom, though its material points toadate not earlier than M. M. III. Large stores of this Spartan basalt were found in the Domestic Quarter of Knossos, and served as the raw material of the Palace lapidaries.

It has been shown that the tradition of these carinated Egyptian bowls in diorite and other hard materials was preserved intact by the Minoan lapidaries to the early part of the Middle Minoan Age, and that they were imitated by them in materials as hard and fine as those of the prototypes. But the Egyptian prototypes themselves go back to a distinctly earlier epoch and there is an overwhelming presumption that the date of the first introduction of these vessels into Crete corresponds with the Period during which their fabric was rife in Egypt 2 the Middle Period, namely, of the Early Kingdom. In other words, they probably belong to the Fourth, and are not later than the Fifth or, at most, the Sixth Dynasty.

Of the indebtedness of the Cretan lapidaries to Nilotic models, not only throughout the above Period but at a still earlier date, there can no l n g er be any reasonable doubt. Without such an apprenticeship, indeed, h ow; s Jt possible to conceive that the insular workmen could have attained such a mastery in their craft as to enable them to produce the beautiful series of original forms of vessels executed in native materials revealed to us by Mr. Seager's explorations of the Early Minoan tombs of Mochlos? The ultimate derivation of these types, in a large number of instances, from Nilotic prototypes, can hardly be contested. Yet in the rich array of stone vases here found, as seen already in the tombs of E. M. II date, the shapes as well as the materials have already assumed an indigenous character. They are once, or even twice, removed from the Proto-dynastic or Pre-dynastic 1 Prehistoric Tombs of Knossos, p. 146, and PI. XCVIII, s. i (Archaeologia, lix).

1 Fr. von Bissing, indeed, Der Anteil der iigyptischen Kunst am Kunstleben der Volker, Munich, 1912, p. 36, cites certain instances of the revival of archaic forms of stone vases referred to in his catalogue of those in the Cairo Museum (Stcingefassc, Einleitung, c., pp. iv, xvi, xxxiii, xlv). But he cannot cite a single instance of revival in the same hard materials (diorite, syenite, c.) of Early Dynastic shapes.

As to the alternative thesis, according to which the manufactures of one Age were exported in another, it is not too much to say that, if such a supposition is to prevail, Arch-aeology as a science is at an end.

THE PALACE OF MINOS, ETC.
Stone
Vases from
Mochlos.

models, and, where more direct reproduction is traceable, we see the reflection of Sixth Dynasty originals. 1 It is during the Second Early Minoan Period that the fabric of stone vases reaches its acme in Minoan Crete. Although these vases are all hand-made they are very finely contoured, and the materials are chosen with true artistic instinct the research of gaily huecl and variegated stones

VI-l

XXl3

FIG. 58. CRETAN STONE VASES, MOCHLOS, E. M. II (f.).

showing once more a curious correspondence with the practice of Pre-dynastic Egypt. Among these are brilliantly coloured breccias, veined marbles, opaque and translucent green steatite, and various forms of alabaster. With the exception of a few marble forms of Cycladic importation the materials seem to have been purely indigenous.

How rich in these fabrics was the Early Minoan Cemetery of Mochlos, is best shown by Fig. 57, illustrating the contents of Tomb II, belonging to the E. M. II Period. 2 1 See below, p. 92.

lid: imitation ot black burnished ware (ht.

From a photograph kindly given me by 6cm., diam. 10-5). b. clay jug, traces of white

Mr. Seager. This was the richest tomb opened. The only E. M. Ill object in this tomb seems to have been the clay jug, II b, found at a slightly higher level than the bulk of the deposit, which was E. M. II. II a. grey paint on black ground (E. M. Ill), c. small breccia bowl. d. small bowl, opaque green steatite, e. vase and cover: same material as d. f. grey and white marble cup. g. bowl, same material. . cup of translucent green steatite.

marble bowl with holes in rim for tying on . spouted bowl, coarse white limestone, three

EARLY MINOAN II

Other examples of vases of this Period from the same Cemetery are E. M. u given with the Tomb numbers in Fig. 58. 1 Of these V i and VI 2 are com- Vessels, posed of a local variety of alabaster, brilliantly veined and shading from Mochlos-orange to pink and white. XIX 2 is remarkable from its elegance of form, while the veined marble vase, XXI 3, has walls as thin as a china tea-cup.

It has already been pointed out that the extraordinary perfection now attained can only be explained on the assumption that a considerable advance in the lapidary art had been already attained in the First Early Minoan Period. The evidence ad- Early duced above of the actual importation of vessels f n g rt y u p. tl: of Late Pre-clynastic or Proto-dynastic fabric, and of such characteristic Egyptian materials as syenite and diorite, confirms this conclusion.

The shape of the E. M. 11 stone vases, for the most part, illustrates the evolution of such prototypes on indigenous Cretan lines. It is often possible, however, to trace the influence of prototypes not later than the Fourth Dynasty. A small bowl, for instance, of opaque green steatite from

Tomb 11 at Mochlos, 2 still presents the characteristic flat collar of the Early Egyptian stone bowls, such as the syenite example. Fig. 31 above, but of narrower dimensions. It has, moreover, four ledge handles instead of two, and these of a slightly incurved shape. The exotic model has here been adapted by the Minoan craftsmen on original lines. In the case of Fig. 58, X and Fig. 57, , showing two ledge handles, the early Egyptian suggestion is not less manifest. The handles in this case follow the usual Cretan fashion in having the perforations for suspension

FIG. 59. STONE VASE, MOCHLOS, E. M. II (r).

knob handles. . vase of dark grey steatite of early Egyptian derivation, k. small pot, translucent green steatite. . clay saucer, dark on light geometrical ornament, see Fig. 41 above, m. bowl, clear yellow alabaster, n. bowl, translucent steatite, o. pot of alabaster. . small jug, translucent green steatite, q. grey and white marble bowl on foot (ht. 7-3 cm., diam. 14-8 cm.), r. clay jug; E. M. II ware. 1 From facsimiles presented by Mr. Seager to the Ashmolean Museum. The Roman numerals refer to the numbers of the Tombs. V i alabaster brilliantly veined, handles re- stored (height 9-8, diam. 11-4 cm.): walls only partly hollowed out: Early E. M. II fabric. VI i grey and white marble (ht. 6 cm., diam. 7-5). VI 2 alabaster (ht. 12 cm., diam. 10-5). VI 3 grey and white marble. XIX 2 dark grey steatite (ht. 9 cm., diam. 5) XXI 3 grey and white veined marble. X apparently serpentine.

2 Seager, op. cit., Fig. 7, II d., and Pl. II, II d. Ht. 4-5 cm., diam. 6-4 cm. With the exception of one clay jug (II) the contents of this tomb seem to be of the E. M. II Period.

Reaction of Clay Forms.

92 THE PALACE OF MINOS, ETC.

vertical instead of horizontal. A dark grey steatite pot (Fig. 59), also from Tomb II at Mochlos, 1 shows an analogous form, but its ledge handles are not perforated. Except that in the Egyptian case the ledge handles are perforated horizontally, this pot is obviously a derivative of a class already numerously represented in the early cemeteries, like Naqada and Hierakonpolis belonging to a Pre-dynastic medium and illustrated by the example shown, Fig. 35 above. 2

The deviations from Egyptian models and the purely original types among the Cretan stone vases must be regarded as largely due to the

FIG. 60. MARBLE VESSEL, MOCHLOS.

FIG. 61. SIXTH DYNASTY EGYPTIAN VASES (r.).

influence of indigenous clay vessels. The vertical instead of horizontal perforation of the ledge handles above noticed is an example of this. The perforation in the edge of certain bowls (cf. Fig. 57, a), in order to be able to fasten the lid, is another instance. A breccia copy 3 occurred of the characteristic cap-like cover common to Crete, the Cyclades, and the Troad at the beginning of the Early Minoan Age. 4 So, too, a marble replica, was found of the clay bowls with the prominent spout (Fig. 58, VI i).

It seems reasonable to assume that in such cases as those cited above 1 Seager, op. cif., p. 25, Fig. 7, and Pl. II, (op. at., Fig. 46, XXI. 6). 11 j- 2 Serpentine: Hierakonpolis. See above, p. 61, Fig. 23.

It was found in Tomb XXI at Mochlos Op. tit., Pl. V, VI i, p. 52, Fig. 22.

where early Egyptian forms of stone vases were reproduced in a modified Copies of form by the Cretan lapidaries, the Minoan copies were of somewhat later Dyaatty elate than their prototypes. Where, however, the imitation is of a literal s f tone kind, it may be taken to afford a strong presumption of contemporaneity. Examples of this latter class are supplied by a vase of grey and white marble from Mochlos (Fig. (50), and by another stone vessel of the same kind found by Dr. Xanthudides in a primitive ossuary at Portl in the Messara district,- both of which are literal reproductions of a characteristic Sixth Dynasty type. Three Egyptian examples are shown in Fig. 61. That to the left is of diorite, a stone clearly imitated by the Mochlos specimen, Fig. 60. The central vase is specially important since it bears an inscription of the time of Pepy I (Mery-ra) s which approximately fixes its date to 2486 B. C.

That a considerable advance towards the naturalistic rendering of steatite animal forms was already achieved by the Minoan lapidaries is shown by Relief a remarkable lid of green steatite from Tomb I at Mochlos, the contents of ofd s-which seem to belong almost exclusively to the Second Early Minoan Age. 4 This lid presents a handle in relief carved in the form of a couchant dog, of jackal lineage (Fig. 62). As Mr. Seager remarks, in any Cretan village one can see dozens of crop-eared clogs of the same peculiar long-legged and emaciated type which served the Minoan artist as his model for this handle some 4,000 years ago.

How far engraved designs on seals had advanced by this date on naturalistic lines it is difficult to say. Unfortunately, most of the evidence regarding Early Minoan glyptic art is derived from the great Tholos ossuaries, where it is impossible to distinguish objects of one Period from those of another. It is therefore advisable provisionally to assign the seals showing the highest artistic development to the succeeding E. M. Ill Period.

1 Op. tit., p. 80, M. 3, and Pl. II. ii. 115, G.). The vase is from the Petrie In the Candia Museum. Collection, University College, London, and 1 The inscription, which bears the cartouche is 14-3 cm. high. This photograph is due to of Mery-ra (Mry-R"), refers to the first occa- the kindness of Prof. Flinders Petrie. sion of the Sed-festival. A Sed-festival oc- 4 Definite evidence of this is supplied by curred in Pepy I's eighteenth year, which, if we the painted jug with dark on light decora-take the beginning of his reign as approxi- lion consisting of hatched triangles (above, mately 2504 B. C., would fix its date as 2486 B. C. Fig. 42). Seager, Momos, p. 20, i b, and p. 36, This festival is referred to in an inscription at Fig. 13, i b. The pedestalled dish, i a, has also Hammamat (Petrie, History of Egypt to Six- E. M. I associations. tccntk Dynasty, p. 93; Lepsius, Denkmaler.

THE PALACE OF MINOS, ETC.

tions.

Cylinder Among the typical forms of seal which were in vogue during the w! th S Side P resent Period are cylinders perforated at the side and engraved at the Perfora- extremities a purely indigenous type unknown either to Egypt or Babylonia. Specimens exist in steatite, ivory, and clay. A somewhat broken example from Tomb XVIII at Mochlos 1 is given in Fig. 63. It is of green translucent steatite, and probably belongs to the E. M. II elements of that tomb. Of the same date is a remarkable ivory cylinder from Tomb VI 2

FIG. 62. GREEN STEATITE LID FROM MOCHLOS ( ).

xviii.

FIG. 63. CYLINDER SEAL OF GREEN STEATITE, MOCHLOS ( ).

FIG. 64. IVORY, MOCHLOS (f c.

E. M. II Seals.

engraved above and below with decorative designs, in one case a kind of plait-work figure, in the other, combinations of triquetras. The curved ivory seal, Fig. 64, from Tomb 11, 3 is interesting as showing for the first time in a pure E. M. II medium the motive of interlocked coils, which seems to lead up to the returning spirals of the succeeding Age.

In the ivory seal representing the two apes, Fig. 51 above, has been shown another type of this Period with a bottle-shaped body and perforated excrescence above. This will be seen to stand at the head of a somewhat large family of Cretan seals of what I have termed the 1 Seager, Mochlos, p. 70, Fig. 39.

"Op. fit., p. 54, Fig. 24, and p. 108. This cylinder is pierced vertically with four small holes and horizontally with three.

3 Op. cit., p. 34, Fig. 12, II, 41. The seal had been broken at an early period, and was found riveted together by a bronze peg.

'signet type. Many perforated cones and conoids also probably go back to this Period.

Other ivory seals are known in the shape of birds' heads, the hole for suspension passing from the top through the beak. Specimens were found in an E. M. II deposit at Sphungaras in Eastern Crete (Fig. 65), and similarly shaped seals occurred in the primitive tholos of Kumasa.

To the limits of this Period must be also carried back the finer class of compact three-sided bead seals of steatite with designs more fully and pictorially executed than the Primitive Linear Class.

The materials of the seals are still soft, such as soapstone and ivory.

FIG. 65. IVORY SEAL, SPHUNGARAS (f).

FIG. 60. GOLD BRACELET, MOCHLOS ( ).

The use of hard stone for glyptic purposes seems to have been as yet unknown. But beads were already made of cornelian, amethyst, and crystal." The perfection already attained by the Minoan goldsmiths was perhaps the most surprising revelation produced by the Mochlos discoveries. Characteristic examples of their work will be seen in Figs. 66-68. Some of the gold chains brought to light are of almost microscopic fineness, and may vie for instance with the most refined fabrics of the Alexandrian goldsmiths of the Ptolemaic Age Several forms of ornament, such as the diadems or gold bands, the pins, pendants, and bracelets, present points of affinity with types from contemporary Cycladic tombs, where, however, the precious metal used was silver. 4 Others, again, recur in the Second

Excel-

Go! d-, Work.

1 Edith H. Hall, Excavations in Eastern Crete: Sphoungaras (Philadelphia, 1912), pp. 52, 53, and Fig. 25, A.

In Scripta Minoa, p. 130, I was inclined to bring down the first appearance of this class of prism-seal to the E. M. Ill Period. I have since learnt of the authenticated discovery of a bead-seal of this class in a pure E. M. II deposit.

3 Beads of these materials occurred in a necklace from Tomb XIX (E. M. II) at Mochlos (Seager, op. fit., p. 72 and Fig. 41). See Fig. 67.

4 A silver diadem from Siphnos (Tsuntas -, 1899, PI. X, I, p. 123), with the XXI. 14

FIG. 67. JEWELLERY FROM MOCHLOS TOMBS (E. M. II). (ALL c., EXCEPT No. 11.5 WHICH is c.)

Tlin

FIG. 68. GOLD LILIES FROM MYCENAEAN THOLOS TOMBS, a, b, DIMINI, c, VOLO.

Settlement of Troy. The characteristic bracelet, Fig. (56, is paralleled by a silver example from an early Cycladic tomb in Siphnos, and the same plait-work band recurs on a gold arm-ring from the so-called Treasure of Priam at Hissarlik. 1

Where, however, the Minoan goldsmiths of this Period greatly excelled Golden all other craftsmen of the Aegean shores was in their admirable repro- and" 0 ductions of flowers and foliage. They seem to have specially delighted in such Folia g e-subjects. Among the finds from the Mochlos tombs notably Nos. II and XIX, the original contents of which showed a pure E. M. II element-occurred a whole series of objects of this class gold pins terminating in marguerites, lilies, or crocuses, roses of gold-foil, and many-petalled flowers like the scabious shamrock and other leaves, and pendant sprays of olive (Figs. 67, 69).

These floral and foliate forms present a curious anticipation of the moulded faience objects of the same class, belonging to the close of the Middle Minoan Age, from the Temple Repositories at Knossos. But of even greater importance, as illustrating the continuity of Minoan tradition in Mycenaean art, is the recurrence of similar stellate flowers and pointed leaves among the gold ornaments brought to light by Schliemann in the Myce-Shaft Graves. A still more direct perpetuation of this floral style in jewellery 5." is seen, however, in the elegant gold-foil lilies from the Mycenaean tholos vivals-tombs at Dimini and Volo 2 (Fig. 68).

Several of the gold bands or diadems' from the Mochlos tombs Gold also present obvious points of resemblance with those from the Shaft Graves w j t h " at Mycenae. In this case, however, two of these gold bands exhibit?" a peculiar feature, suggestive of a special religious usage. This is the appearance of two incised outlines of human eyes (Fig. 67, II. 5), clearly indicating that they were intended to serve as a kind of bandage over the eyes of the dead person. They are, in fact, embryo death-masks, and it Embryo is worth while observing that similar eye-bandages of thin gold plate, supple-Masks, mented by plates for the mouth, are a usual feature on ancient Bolivian Bolivian mummies. 3 As Early Minoan funeral accessories they are of the greatest outlines of a dog and bird pricked out on it, with M. M. I. It doubtless, however, contained presents a close analogy with a gold band with some earlier relics. It belongs to the Third similar animal forms from Mochlos (Seager, Period of the Second City. op. fit., p. 27, and Fig. 9, II, 4) Kuruniotes, Ef. Ap., 1906, pp. 232, 233, 1 Troja und Ilion, i, p. 358, Fig. 296, c. The Figs. 8, 9.

date of the actual deposit of the Treasure Mr. E. Thurlow Leeds, F. S. A., of the judging from certain dagger types (IKos, p. 476, Ashmolean Museum, is my informant. Figs. 801-3) and other indications corresponds

THE PALACE OF MINOS, ETC.

interest as presenting the ancestral form from which the sepulchral masks of Mycenae were evolved.

Anticipa- The death-mask, in primitive conception, may either be used to protect the

Mycenae dead from the malign influence of evil spirits, or to shield the living from direct death- overlooking bv the dead.

masks.

(I)-

FIG. 69. GOLD JEWELS OF FLORAL AND FOLIATE TYPES FROM E. M. II TOMBS, MOCHLOS; SEAGER (TOMB NUMBERS GIVEN) (f).

It can hardly be doubted that in these more rudimentary bandages we have the actual prototypes of the gold death-masks of the Mycenae Shaft Graves. These, it is true, cover the whole face, as is usual in such cases. A smaller gold plate, hitherto unpublished, from Grave V, 1 however, only 1 See Vol. II.

EARLY MINOAN II sliows traces of the eyes and nose, while on another found in the Late Minoan tomb of Muliana in East Crete, 1 the nose alone is indicated. In these cases we may fairly trace a reminiscence of the pre-existent usage of a mere gold bandage like the present. In Minoan Cyprus we find only mouth-plates.

It is a symptom of the comparative wealth of Crete in the Early

XIX. 33

XIX. 29

XIX. 28 11.46 11.45 11.44 11.43

FIG. 70. COPPER WEAPONS AND INSTRUMENTS FROM MOCHLOS (E. M. II) (r.).

Minoan Age that gold objects are more plentifully forthcoming from these tombs than silver, so frequent in contemporary Cycladic deposits. A cup and finger-ring of the latter metal were, however, found at Mochlos and two silver daggers, to be mentioned below, occurred at Kumasa.

Triangular copper daggers now appear, often with an incurved base (Fig. 70. II. 45). As pointed out above, this can hardly be the most primitive type, and we must presuppose the existence of copper daggers of the simpler triangular form in the preceding E. M. I Period. Among 1 Xanthudides, E. Ap., 1904, p. 49, Fig. 12. H 2

THE PALACE OF MINOS, ETC.

silvcr these triangular dagger-forms that can with great probability be ascribed to and tne 1 ow er limits of the present Period, that reproduced in Fig. 71 1 has an

Daggers, exceptional interest. It is one of a pair of silver daggers found with a copper specimen of the same type 2 in a primitive tholos' ossuary of

Kumasa by Dr. Xanthudicles. It has rivet holes about its upper margin and is characterized by a sharp and well-marked median rib, which in itself must be regarded as a somewhat advanced feature. The silver material recalls the

FIG. 71. SILVER DAGGER FROM THOLOS OSSUARY, KUMASA ( ).

PIG. 72. COPPER TWO-PRONGED SPEARHEAD, H. ONUPHRIOS DEPOSIT (f).

blade-like silver ingots of Hissarlik and, like these, it. may have served as a form of primitive currency. Copper daggers representing a somewhat elongated outgrowth of the present example, though with less prominent ribs, are found in Cycladic graves 3 contemporary with E. M. 111. But what is specially interesting is the fact that a practically identical dagger-blade of copper has been found in a sepulchral cave belonging to the Chalcolithic Age of Central 1 Mosso, Le armi piii antiche di rame e di bronzo (Memorie della R. Accad. dei Lincei, 1908, p 491, Fig. 8).

! R. Dussaud, Les civilisations prfhelleniques, c., 1914, p. 41, Fig. 22.

8 Tsuntas, Kvcxa8 ca (Ec. Ap., 1898),

PI. XII, 8. The forms of the associated marble images and other objects suggest an advanced Early Cycladic phase. Unfortunately, however, tomb-groups are not distinguished. A somewhat shorter specimen without any definite rib is given, together with its handle, by Diimmler, Italy, near Volterra. 1 It is worth noting as a further indication of primitive Similar commerce that in the same cave burial were found conical tin buttons- of blade a form widely disseminated through the Celtic and Iberian West.

It is not so clear whether the curious two-pronged spearhead of copper (Fig. 72) found in the Sepulchral Deposit of H. Onuphrios: i belongs to this P ron s ed or the succeeding Period. Its associations, if we may judge from later heads. parallels, are also of a very suggestive kind. It recalls the two-pointed spears of Lycaonia, the two-pronged bronze implements of the Carian mercenaries found at Tell-Nebesheh, and the symbolic forked weapons of Babylonia. 4

A very characteristic type of copper implement, of repeated occurrence in Copper the Mochlos Tombs, consists of a blade with expanding edge with a tang at the upper end fitting into the handle (Fig. 70, XIX. 29, I.). In two cases Twee-remains of ivory handles were found. 6 This refinement, and the fact that they generally occurred in company with depilatory or other tweezers (see Fig. 70), makes it probable that these cutters played some part in the intricacies of the Minoan toilet. 0 Of the tweezers, both forms occur in contemporary Early Cycladic tombs. 7 It is noteworthy that the thick variety is identical with an early dynastic Egyptian type. Egyptian fashions would thus seem to have affected the Minoan toilet from an early Period. At a later date we shall see bronze mirrors introduced from the same source.

A form of perforated adze-axe of copper, well represented at the Adze-beginning of the Middle Minoan Age (see below, p. 194, Fig. 141, c), can also be traced back to this Period., In Tomb II at Mochlos, in a purely E. M. II medium, was found Votive a small votive axe of copper (Fig. 70, II. 46), and two others of lead. Axes! As in the case of the Horns of Consecration from the E. M. I votive deposit described above, 8 we have here an interesting testimony to the antiquity of Minoan cult objects. The place of the Double Axe in Cretan religion is fully illustrated by Late Minoan and Mycenaean remains.

Restevorgriechischerbevolkerungaufdencycla- ment to Cretan Pictographs, c.), p. 136, den (Ath. Mitth., 1886), p. 16, Beilage I, 6. It Fig. 139.

was found in a cist-grave in Amorgos with Petrie, Tunis, Pt. II, PI. iii, and pp. 20, advanced Early Cycladic objects, including a 21. They were found in tombs dating from pyxis with very fine spiraliform decoration. the 8th to the 5th century B. C.

1 In the ossuary grotto of Monte Bradoni. In Tomb I at Mochlos; op. ., Fig 44, Colini, ftiil. di Paetn., xxv (1899), PI. IV. 3, I. . Another specimen, with remains of an and pp. 301, 302. ivory handle, occurred at H. Nikolaos.

Cf. Peet, The Stone and Bronze Ages in Seager, ib., p. 21.

Italy, p. 196. These buttons have two con- 7 E. Ax- 1898, PI. XII, 4 (Amorgos); verging perforations below for attachment. 1899, PI. X, 40, 41, 42 (Syros).

8 See my H. Onuphrios Deposit (Supple- Seep. 57, Fig. 16, t.

D ve In this connexion may be mentioned an interesting indication of dants: a sympathy between the popular religion of Crete and the Cyclades at Raite" ls Ep c h- In Tomb IV at Mochlos was found a chalcedony dove, vertically pierced for suspension as an amulet, and resembling similar dove pendants of stone found in Early Cycladic tombs. 1 We are thus led to infer that the later Minoan Dove cult goes back to a primitive religious stratum with a wide Aegean extension.

A series of phenomena, indeed, bears witness to the amount of common elements in the culture of Crete and the other Aegean lands, including the Anatolian littoral. This, no doubt, was largely the outcome of very ancient affinities, but the correspondence in small details of ornament and design also points to a close continued intercourse.

Chrono- It has been shown that the Egyptian associations of the beginning of limits of the Early Minoan Age point rather to the Late Pre-dynastic Period or, at E. M. II. most; to the time O f the ear li es t dynasties. Much of this very ancient tradition unquestionably lived on into the Second Early Minoan Period. It may even have been kept alive by some surviving remains of the older pre-dynastic element in the Delta or, as has been suggested above, by colonial representatives on Cretan soil. On the other hand, as already demonstrated, we now begin to come in contact with elements well illustrated by certain forms of imported and imitative stone vases which bring us down to the Fourth, Fifth, and Sixth Dynasties. The E. M. II Period must, on the whole, be regarded as roughly contemporary with these. This would represent an interval of time extending from about 2800 to 2400 before our Era.

FIG. 73. PLAN OF HOUSE TOMB, MOCHLOS TOMB IV, SHOWING BUT AND BEN PLAN. (THE LEFT WALL ALSO SERVED FOR TOMB V.) 2 1 Mochlos, Fig. 20, IV, 7; E. A PX., 1898, PI. VIII, 16, 17, 23.

2 See p. 72 above.

4- EARLY MINOAN III (E. M. III)

Partial Set-back; Characteristic E. M. Ill Features; Cycladic Connexions; Egypto-Libyan Influences substituted for Purer Dynastic; Great Circular Hypogaea at Knossos One excavated under S. Porch of Palace; Bee-hive vault and staircase, tunnelled in rock; Probably subterranean S. entrance of an earlier Palace; E. M. Ill Pottery; Light on Dark Decoration; Beginnings of true polychrome technique; Cycladic Elements Pyxides and Marble Idols'; Grotesque Vessels; Ivory Seals; Animal figures; Specimens from Ossuary tlwlos of Platanos; Cylinders and Conoids; Meander and Labyrinth Pattern Sixth Dynasty Comparisons; Egypto-Libyan Button-seals Source of Cretan double sickle Types; Three-sided Bead-seals; Female potters and draught-player; Imitation of Egyptian draught-board Sign (men) Leg Amulets; Burial Urns and Clay Cists Proto-Egyptian and Libyan Comparisons Approximate dating of E. M. III.

THE culture of the last of the Early Minoan Periods does not give the Partial same brilliant impression as the immediately preceding Age. The richer " tombs at Mochlos are E. M. II. At Vasiliki 'the architecture markedly deteriorates. The house-walls of this Period are very poor and built of small stones'. 1 The naturalistic spirit in art, however, survives in certain ceramic works and finds a continuous development in engravings on seals.

Cycladic connexions, bringing with them the spiral system, now attained Cycladic a maximum. On the other hand, owing to the troubled state of Egypt nexions. between the Sixth and Eleventh Dynasties, the stimulating influences that had previously operated from that side were now in abeyance. Such influence as there was well illustrated in the case of the button-seals was of a semi-barbaric kind. To this source, best perhaps described as Egypto-Libyan, Egypto-can be traced the double sickle pattern which makes its appearance on a j, fl series of Cretan seals. The meander, a glyptic motive at that time popular ence:. T, V Bution- m Egypt, also makes its way in various forms to Crete, to become in time Seals'.

the progenitor of regular labyrinth designs, an example of which decorated Ieander the Palace walls at Knossos.

The Domestic and Sepulchral construction seems to have continued on the same lines as those of the preceding Period. Both the ossuary tholos and built tombs, such as those of Mochlos, were still in use.

It is now, however, that for the first time we have to do with monumental works of a wholly new class in connexion with the later Palace site of Hypo-

Knossos. These are in the shape of great hypogaea, the scale of which Knossos.
THE PALACE OF MINOS, ETC.
Early filling of one excavated under S. Porch ofpalace.
Bee-hive Chamber and staircase cut out of rock.
Difficulty of exploration.

suggests that some earlier forerunner of the Palace may have existed before the levelling away of the summit of the Tell, to make room for the construction of its Central Court and Western Section.

The hypogaeum actually excavated had been filled in to support the foundations of the South Porch of the Palace, which descended into it to a depth of 3-30 metres, and the filling material itself seems to have been supplied from the results of the levelling process on the hill-top above. Its ceramic contents belonged intensively to the earliest M. M. I. phase 1 and the character of the sherds corresponded with those found about the foundations of the Palace, though in this case there was little or no trace of incipient polychromy. Some Early Minoan fragments and even a few Neolithic also occurred, but these were a vanishing quantity.

The hypogaeum was executed in the soft rock, here of a ferruginous tint, and presented a circular plan nearly 100 feet in circumference at its widest point. The floor itself was about 15 metres below the later surface level, but it has to be borne in mind that the slope of the hill had been here cut into to form the terrace on which the South Corridor and adjoining Porch were set, so that the original level of the surface must have been at least a metre higher, making the height of the vault about 16 metres.

The chamber curved gradually over above, so that the whole would have formed a great bee-hive vault as shown in Fig. 74. Towards the base the diameter slightly contracted again so that the section must have been somewhat bottle-shaped. The descent into the interior was effected by means of a winding staircase tunnelled in the rock, with a low parapet, of which a portion was preserved, to protect it at the intervals where it was open at the side. It is obvious, moreover, as shown by Mr. Doll in his Section, Fig. 74, that these openings, like the course of the staircase itself must, for the stability of the whole vault have been arched over. These arched openings would have admitted air and also light when the vault was illumined. The staircase must have been approached and entered above by a passage-way or short tunnel like the doorway of a tomb.

Owing to the treacherous nature of the rock and the great depth of the floor of the hypogaeum, its exploration was the most difficult task in the whole history of the excavation on the site of Knossos. Excavation from above, almost directly under the foundations of the South Porch, proved too dangerous, and in order to approach the base of the chamber a cleft 1 These included numerous pedestalled cups There were also fragments of hole-mouthed with bands either in matt white on a dark slip pots with ridged decoration in the new bar-or in a dark glaze medium on the clay surface, botine style.

PALACE Of KVOSSOS- faRLY HYPOCAEUM
SOUTH PORCH
SCOT I ON THffo STEPS N 2627
OAUltff Of Mtfir. Stf AT I 00 ASOVf fioOf -OSS 7
SECTION THROSTAIRCASE
KCYPia,
SHOWIHC gmnain MLAJION
JO SOUTH POUCH a
SOUTH CORRIDOR
SECTION A. A
FIG. 74. PLAN AND SECTIONS OF EARLY HYPOGAEUM BENEATH SOUTH PORCH OF PALACE, KNOSSOS; PROBABLY SUBTERRANEAN SOUTHERN ENTRANCE OF EARLIER BUILDING.
THE PALACE OF MINOS, ETC.
Second hypo- gaeum beneath corner of
Palace.
For what purpose were they executed?
S. Hypo- gaeum probably guarded entrance.
Idea of a Store Pit.

resembling that of a railway cutting had first to be opened out from the Southern foot of the hill, at a cost of great labour. Even then it was only possible to explore a small part of the actual floor of the hypogaeum.

There are indications that a similar hypogaeum had been filled in at the same time as the other, at the South Eastern Corner of the Palace. Here the great basement slabs have partly sunk below their original level and on one side part of the circular cutting in the rock has become exposed.

What purpose did these great underground vaults serve? That the hypogaeum explored could have been a cistern seems to be excluded by its proximity to the slope of the hill and by the fact that no trace of any coating of impervious cement was found in the interior. The suggestion that it was in fact an underground pit for the extraction of material used for pottery is hardly by itself sufficient. The potter's clay was doubtless a useful byproduct, but the apparent symmetry of the work and the carefully planned winding staircase surely points to some more permanent purpose. The staircase itself, in combination with the great bee-hive chamber, suggests analogies with the spiral staircases enclosed in the walls of the Nuraghe of Sardinia or of the Brochs of Scotland, but in these cases we have to do with construction above the ground.

Being near the Southern steep of the hill, immediately under the later Southern Entrance of the Palace, and on the natural line of approach from the point where the torrent below was traditionally bridged over, a strong probability arises that there was also an entrance on the ground floor. In that case we would here have to do with a circular vaulted guard house, recalling that of the Megalopolis gate at Messend, combined with the inner stairway. That no trace however of such a lower entrance or sally-port was struck by the actual course of the excavations may be explained by the fact that it would have run somewhat to the West, as indicated on the Plan.

The idea of a tomb is excluded, though the mistaken belief that the beehive vaults of Mycenae were treasure houses (drjo-avpoc) might be thought to supply an alternative solution. The practice of excavating pits, more or less domed over above as store-houses is indeed widespread. As receptacles for corn they are common in Syria and they recur, perhaps owing to Arab agency, in Southern Italy. 1 They are found to-day in the island of Cos 2, and else- 1 Foggia, originally Fodia, derives its name from such store-pits. Their position is marked by stone posts, giving the site the appearance of a cemetery.

2 Dr. Mackenzie informs me that he has seen exceptionally large examples at Antimachia in Cos excavated in the chalk rock.

where in the Archipelago. But in all such cases access was obtained by means of a pit from above.

The existence of two hypogaea, apparently both on the same large scale, on what was later the Palace border may certainly be regarded as an indication that, as suggested above, they stood in relation to some Early Minoan predecessor of the great Palace.

The later elements of the primitive ossuaries of the tholos' type, both at Hagia Triada and in the Messara district, belong to this time. There are some reasons for supposing, however, that those constructed at this epoch were of lesser dimensions, like the small Ossuary found at Hagia Triada (Fig. 75). 1 . Wissw fc.

- s syg.

Perhaps in connexion with the earlier Palace.

Ossuary tholoi and House Tombs.

FIG. 75. SECTION OF SMALLER OSSUARY THOLOS AND SEPULCHRAL ANNEXES AT

HAGIA TRIADA.

This had unfortunately been almost entirely cleared out and used as a repository for L. M. Ill sarcophagi (larnakes). The epoch of its disuse is marked, however, as in the case of the larger tholos, by a M. M. I annexe consisting of the ossuary cists characteristic of that Period. These cists themselves fit on to the earlier type of house tomb so well illustrated in East Crete and which at Mochlos continued in use during the present Period. The houses of the Fourth Period of the settlement at Vasilikl produced characteristic E. M. Ill ceramic remains. Similar pottery occurred in great abundance in the north trench at Gournia, and was found in a stratified deposit at Palaikastro, immediately below a layer representing the First Middle Minoan phase. 2 Definite evidence of the relative chronological 1 R. Paribeni, Man. Ant., 1904, p. 691, R. M. Dawkins, B. S. A., x, pp. 198, 199, Fig. 7. Fig. 2; xi, pp. 269, 271, Fig. 5, a, b, c.

THE PALACE OF MINOS, ETC.

Knossian evidence.

E. M. III Pottery.

Partial Survival of Dark on Light Geometrical Ware.

Characteristic Style Light on Dark.

position of the handiwork of this Period was also obtained in the later tombs at Mochlos. At Knossos, the latest pottery on the floors of the Early Minoan houses, found to the South of the Palace, belonged to this Period, and its closing phase may include the earlier elements in a transitional deposit known as the Vat Room Deposit found beneath the early Palace floor to the north of the E. Pillar Room. 1

The exaggerated types of vessel with abnormally long spouts still continued in use in this Period, though towards its close the beaks show a tendency to become less prominent and gradually approach the more sober proportions of the Middle Minoan Age.

In the earlier stage of the E. M. Ill ceramic fabrics, the old dark on light geometrical class and the mottled ware still survive. This latter becomes gradually extinct, but the geometrical class with the buff ground seems never to have entirely died out. At Knossos, at any rate, it partially survived to the borders of the First Middle Minoan Period, in the early part of which it re-emerges into prominence, together with some of its characteristic patterns, notably the butterflies' or double axes'.

But the characteristic ceramic product of the Third Early Minoan Period was a new style of painted ware showing a light decoration on a dark ground (Fig. 76). This ware, though represented at Knossos and elsewhere in Central Crete, is specially abundant in the East of the island, where its deposits are in places so thick as to point to its production having extended over a considerable interval of time. 2 It may well be that the evolution of the new, Middle Minoan, style had effected itself more rapidly in the great palatial centres of Crete, at Knossos and Phaestos, than in the eastern extremity of the island, and that there had been a certain overlapping of the two styles.

Some characteristic forms of the light on dark E. M. Ill pottery are given in Fig. 76. Many types of the preceding Period will be seen to survive, including the jugs with prominent side-spouts ending in an elongated open channel. Good specimens of this class occurred at Knossos in the upper deposit of the Early Minoan house floors. Towards the close of the Period, 1 A. J. E., Knossos, Report (1903), pp. 94, 95 (?. S. A., ix). See below, pp. 165-171.

2 Mr. Seager remarks (Mochlos, p. 9) that besides the evolution visible in style and forms a long duration for this Period is suggested by the enormous quantity of light on dark geometric ware that is found on early sites on and near the Peninsula of Hierapetra. The first large deposit was found in 1904 at Gournia, where a great heap of these sherds had been piled up just outside the town limits. This heap was composed of thousands of fragments of light on dark geometrical ware and must represent accumulations of a long term of years.

however, spouts show a general tendency to abbreviation, the open channel, too, becomes more truncated, and, pari passii with this, the tubular part

FIG. 76. E. M. Ill WARE FROM MOCHLOS, c. ( ).

of the spout becomes shorter. By the beginning of the first Middle Minoan Period this tubular section shows a tendency to disappear entirely and the abbreviated open part of the spout is simply bridged over by the rim 1 One from Mochlos (pp. fit., Fig. 50, 92) with hatched incisions on its shoulders is regarded by Seager as transitional, E. M. Ill to M. M. I. A type of vessel with side-handles (derived from the early perforated ledge-handles of E. M. I) is still found in the early part of M. M. I which shows the survival of a similar type of spout (cf. p. 144, Fig. 105, below). A similar vase is illustrated by Miss E. H. Hall (Excavations in Eastern Crete: Sphoitiigaras, p. 55, Fig. 28, yjand cp. p. 56. Owing to the fact that it presented traces of circles of red paint she assigns it to M. M. I, but adds on other grounds it might well be called Early Minoan II.

THE PALACE OF MINOS, ETC.

of the vessel. Often indeed the open spout starts directly from the shoulder of the bowl as is already the case with some Early Minoan types of vessel.

FIG. 77. (a), CONOID IVORY SEAL FROM EARLY THOLOS OSSUARY, HAGIA TRIADA: ( ) SIDE-SPOUTED JUG FROM KAMARES CAVE (c.).

COLOURS RED STRIPES

WITH WM IT E BORDERS ON DARK GLAZE

GROUND

FIG. 78. SIDE-SPOUTED JUG FROM KNOSSOS, E. M. Ill, SHOWING BE-GINNINGS OF POLYCHROME DECORATION (c.).

In Fig. 77, b is shown a jug of this class from the Excavations of the British School in the Kamares Cave 1 which illustrates the curtailment of the tubular part of the spout in the latter part of E. M. III. The vase itself is

1 R. M. Dawkins, The Excavations of the Kamares Cave in Crete, B. S. A., xix, Pl. iv, top, and p. 13. The spout is completed in the drawing from which Fig. 77, b was taken. Mr. Dawkins rightly classes this vessel with E. M. III.

noteworthy from the character of the spiraliform pattern that it presents which closely corresponds with that of a contemporary conoid seal of ivory from the early tholos ossuary at Hagia Triada, here placed beside it for comparison, Fig. 77, a.

The side-spouted vessel, Fig. 78, which as its form shows including the well-marked collar belongs to the same stage of evolution as the preceding, has a special importance as illustrating the beginnings of the true polychrome technique. It came to light some years since, South West of the Palace site at Knossos and its coloured decoration agrees very closely incipient with that of a small two-handled jar from the

Deposit of Hagios Onuphrios 3 m on near Phaestos, found with marble figures in the Third Early Cycladic style. Knossian In both cases we see bands of a dark Indian red, bordered with dull white, on a black-brown glaze ground. The white pigment itself on this Knossian vessel and on others of the same small group is of the somewhat dingy cream colour usual on E. M. Ill pottery and does not present the clear tint of the new white that came into vogue at the beginning of the M. M. I Period. On the other hand the matt Indian red colour that is here seen beside it makes its appearance for the first time 4, and the increased lustre of the dark glaze slip itself, in spite of the somewhat gritty texture of the clay, is also noteworthy. It shows in places a metallic sheen. The exceptional features in the polychromy of this vessel, taken in connexion with the simplicity of the decoration and the morphological characteristics which link it with the earlier tradition, give sufficient warrant for placing this specimen together with the Hagios Onuphrios jar within at least the lower borders ofe. M. III.

The patterns on the ordinary E. M. Ill light on dark ware some E. M. ill typical examples of which are given in Fig. 76 present, in addition to Patterns: the simple geometrical forms of the class with the light ground, certain new Jx igl? ton features. Curvilinear and spiraliform motives now for the first time appear, and an interesting example has been already given in Fig. 77 of the 1 F. Halbherr, Mem. del R. 1st. Lombardo, form in the Vat Room Deposit belonging xxi, Pl. X, Figs. 25, 26. to the earliest M. M. I phase (see p. 167, 3 This vessel was acquired by me before the Fig. 118 a (6, n) below).

Excavation of the Palace, and at a time when Cf. Mackenzie. The Middle Minoan Pot- it was impossible to define its position in the tery of Knossos (J. H. S., xxvi, p. 245). The

Minoan ceramic series. orange tints, as Dr. Mackenzie observes, came

Hagios Onuphrios Deposit, c., p. 115, in later and, so far as the present instance goes,

Fig. 105. The form of this jar with its two are not found before M. M. I. side handles survives in a distinctly developed interaction of the scrolls on signets and vases. Among typical patterns are spirals, often linked by ribbon-like connexions expanding into an elongated lozenge-shaped form. Disks connected in the same way are frequent. Some are filled with a lattice work of hatched lines, some contain a cruciform pattern or have their margins intersected by segments of circles. Festoons are of frequent occurrence, and a twisted cord or cable pattern which at times breaks up into a succession of SS. Some typical specimens are given in Fig. 79. l Figs. 80, a, b, show a series of illustrative fragments of this ware from the North Trench at Gournia 2 and Palaikastro. Fig. 80, i anticipates t ie l ater rosette, 2, the asterisk and spiral, so much affected on L. M. I vase decoration. Together with these geometrical designs may be noted some very rude attempts to delineate animal forms. Several painted sherds from the same deposit at Gournia bear summary sketches' of goats showing the head and the whole or part of the body filled in with cross-hatching. The small fragment Fig. 80 a, 8 shows part of the

FIG. 79. TYPICAL E. M. Ill head and the fore-legs of the animal. 3 CERAMIC PATTERNS (E. H. HALL).,.

Curvilinear motives already begin to

Spirali- appear on seals of the preceding Period, witness the cylinder, Fig. 64, d,
Patterns. w t 1 nter l c ked curves. But the first generalization of the spiral system
in Crete, and its application not only to signets and other objects of soft stone but to
ceramic decoration, is a characteristic phenomenon of E. M. III.

There can be little doubt that its introduction into Minoan Crete was due to Cycladic
influences, which at this epoch reach their maximum. We see the system already highly
developed on Early Cycladic pyxides such as the well-known example from Melos
with a representation of a hut. An example of a steatite pyxis with linked spiral
ornament found in Crete, and representing either an importation from a Cycladic
source or an indigenous copy, is given in Fig. 81, a. It is closed with a lid, on which
the same ornament appears. 4 A steatite button from the Hagios Onuphrios Deposit 5
1 Fig. 79 is from Edith H. Hall, The Decora- 3 Others are reproduced by Miss Hall
(op. tive Art of Crete in the Bronze Age, p. 7, Fig. 6 fit., p. 9, Fig. 8).

(cf. Transactions Dept. of Arch., Univ. of From the Naue Collection. Cf. the
similar

Pennsylvania, i, Pt. Ill, Pis. XXVI-XXXIII. claypyxisfromsyra,. A PX.,1899, Pl.
VIII.

2 From Boyd Hawes, Gournia, y. 57, Fig. 42 'Cretan Pictographs, c. (J. H. S.,
xiv), (E. H. Hall). p. 59j Fig. so.

repeats in a ruder form a type much better represented by an object of the E. M. lll
same kind found at Kouphonisi. 1 A quadruple spiraliform design is also taken f 0 m
Decora- tion.

FIG. 80 a. E. M. Ill PAINTED SHERDS FROM NORTH TRENCH AT GOURNIA
(t.).

FIG. 80. E. M. Ill SHERDS, (i) GOURNIA, (2) PALAIKASTRO.

FIG. 81. STEATITE PYXIS AND RING FROM CRETE WITH SPIRALIFORM
PATTERNS ( ).

over into the round flat bezel of steatite rings (see Fig. 81, b, otherwise resembling
ivory examples from the ossuary tholoi.

The simple coil as a decorative unit appears early in Egypt and elsewhere. On
prehistoric painted vases from Egypt it represents an imitation 1 Diimmler, Reste
vorgriechischer Bevolke-rung auf den Cydaden (Ath. Mitlh., 1886), p. 16, Beilage I,
i, p. 25.

1 Boyd Hawes, Gournti, PI. XII, 34. Dawkins, B. S. A., x, p. 199, Fig. z.

THE PALACE OF MINOS, ETC.

North Aegean Origin of Spiral System.

Thraco-Pontic Neolithic Province.

of the round pebbles of their prototypes in conglomerate. But there is no evidence
of the employment by the early Egyptians of any fully developed system of spiraliform
ornament. The scarabs with running spiral borders, formerly, on account of the names
that some of them present, assigned to the Fourth and succeeding Dynasties, are now
shown not to go back earlier than the beginning of the Middle Kingdom. 1 The sources
of the Aegean spiral decoration must therefore be sought elsewhere than in Egypt,
2 and may be said to have shifted North. In that direction we are confronted with

the developed spiral system seen on the pottery of the Neolithic station of Butmir in Bosnia and by that of a vast

FIG. 82. CLAY PYXIS (6) AND LID OF ANOTHER (a). SEPULCHRAL CAVE, PYRGOS, NIROU KHANI, N. E. OF KNOSSOS (i).

Neolithic province extending from Thessaly and Thrace to Roumania and Southern Russia. The evidence tends to show that it was already rooted on the North Aegean shores and the Cyclades before it reached Minoan Crete.

Among the Arkalokhori remains also occurred clay boxes or pyxides, a class of vessels that now appears in Crete and is very characteristic of contemporary Cycladic deposits. A specimen of one of these and the lid of another of unquestionably E. M. Ill fabric are given in Fig. 82, from the Sepulchral Cave of Pyrgos, N. E. of Knossos. Like others of this class, these show the persistence of the old Sub-Neolithic technique, with their well-baked reddish internal texture and dark brown burnished surface.

1 The earliest given by Petrie in his Scarabs then prevalent as to the date of certain scarab and Cylinders with Names (1917, Pl. XI, are types. The influence of Middle Empire scarab of the Xlth Dynasty.

types with spiraliform decoration on M. M. I 1 In Cretan Pictographs, c., p. 59, I had and II seals is, however, clear. See below, looked to Egypt for the source of the spiral p. 200 seqq. motive in Crete, owing to the erroneous ideas

Such vessels bear an incised and often punctuated decoration also very reminiscent of primitive tradition.

These vessels resemble a primitive class of which many illustrations belonging to the Neolithic Age in Crete have been given above, and which shows a great persistence in the Copper Age pottery of Cyprus and a wide

Anatolian region. It now reappears in Crete, apparently from a Cycladic source. The extent to which it was once more popularized in the island is seen from the fact that certain dotted designs of the polychrome vases belonging to the earliest phase of the M. M. I style are directly taken from ,. these chalk-filled patterns. The comparative examples put together in Fig. 125 below

E v"J supply sufficient evidence of this.

Further indications of the strong stream j- of Cycladic influence that had set in at this time will be seen in the imported vases and r- " other objects of Parian marble. The most , characteristic of these imports are the marble idols' or human figures of a typical Early Cycladic class. 1 These, as will be seen from Fig. 83, differ from the traditional Cretan types, such as those given in Fig. 13 above. Neither have they anything in common with what may be called the Egypto-Libyan group, shown in Fig. 52.

A remarkable ceramic feature of this Period is the appearance of vessels grotesquely moulded in human or animal form. In Tomb XIII at Mochlos was a vase (Fig. 84) in the shape of a female figure holding her breasts. The vessel shows a yellowish white decoration on a dark ground. The figure wears a kind of turban, and from the similarity of the attitude may well be identified with the matronly figures represented by the early clay idols. It seems probable, indeed, that in this case as in others we see before us a primitive Mother Goddess. 2

A curious vessel in the shape of a- young bird opening its mouth for food (Fig. 85), found by Dr. Xanthudides in an early tholos ossuary of 1 Dr. Karo has noticed, as an evidence of the comparative value attaching to these figures of imported material in Crete that in almost all Imported Cycladic Idols'.

FIG. 83. CYCLADIC MARBLE IDOL
FOUND IN SltEIA, CRETE (f).
Grotesquely Moulded Vessels.
Comic
Bird
Vase.

cases they bear evidence of having been mended. 2 Mr. Seager, Mochlos, p. 64, also takes this view.

THE PALACE OF MINOS, ETC.
FIG. 84. VASE IN SHAPE OF FEMALE FIGURE; MOCHLOS (SEAGER) (f).
FIG. 85. VASE IN SHAPE OF YOUNG BIRD, KUMASA (XANTHUDIDES) (-J (.).

Kumasa may also be referred to this Period. It is of comic appearance, and strikes quite a new note in Minoan art. A striking comparison is supplied by a grotesque four-footed bird-vase with open beak, of local Neolithic fabric, from Kodjadermen in N. E. Bulgaria. 1 It also recalls certain Trojan skin types.

Further progress on the path of natural representations is noticeable in some of the signets of this Period, which are still of soft materials such as ivory and steatite. Prominent among these are the seals, mostly of ivory, though at times of steatite, in the shape of birds or animals, or the heads of such, carved in the round, with transverse or slanting perforations and flat bases showing engraved designs. This type no doubt goes back into the E. M. 11 Period, 2 but the fine examples of these recently found by Dr. Xanthudides in the tholos tombs of Messara seem to have been mainly associated a with E. M. Ill pottery.

FIG. 86. IVORY SEAL FROM THOLOS OSSUARY, Another type, appa- ll ESSARA; DOVE AND YOUNG (f). rently a dove sheltering its young with its wings, is seen in Fig. 8G. a Though the surface in this case is a good deal worn, the design conveys the impression of great natural sympathy in the treatment of the subject. The material is ivory, and it has a horizontal perforation through the sides and a vertical one at the back of the neck. The central pattern engraved on the base consists of four linked spirals a motive, as we have seen, very characteristic of this Period. Among more or less contemporary relics from the Deposit of Hagios Onuphrios 4 was a steatite seal also in the form of a bird with a cross

Naturalism in signet designs: animal forms.
Dove sheltering its young.

1 Jahrb. d. k. d. Inst., 1915, Anzeiger, p. 219, Fig. 2.
5 See above, p. 95, Fig. 65.
Found by Dr. Xanthudides in a tholos ossuary of Messara. Thanks to his courtesy this and the seals shown in Fig. 87 are here for the first time reproduced.
4 See my Supplement to Cretan Pictographi, c. (Quaritch, 1895), p. 108 and Fig. 82.

V. i m m,- r. VS J7

FIG. 87. IVORY SEALS FROM LARGER THOLOS OSSUARY, PLATANOS, MESSARA. ( ) perforation and engraved below with a rude animal figure. This signet presents a curious parallelism with a black steatite example said to have been found in the Hauran. 1

A series of ivory seals from the larger ossuary tholos of Platanos, ivory recently explored by Dr. Xanthudides 2 are reproduced in Figs. 87 and 88, a.

Nos. i, 2, 3, represent respectively a squatting ape, a couchant ox, and Tholos of a boar's head. The absence of a tail in the first might suggest the Barbary Ape, but the omission is possibly an accident of the engraving. On the other hand the baboon-like figures on Fig. 88, a, with their handlike forepaws, are clearly taken from the Egyptian cynocephalus in his usual adorant attitude.

These comparisons perhaps indicate an African source for the ivory found so abundantly in these South Cretan ossuaries. As in the case of the bird signets, however, the forms of these find their closest parallels on the Syrianc. Asiatic side. Stone signets in the shape of couched oxen, sheep, and other animals, with similar cross perforations and engraved figures below, are found sporadically over a wide tract of country extending from North Syria to Babylonia, and even, apparently, beyond the Persian borders. 3 The conoids, Fig. 77, a, above, and Fig. 90, have much the same range and are diffused besides along a more westerly zone from Cappadocia to the Troad.

More distinctive in their character are the Early Minoan cylinders, which, in place of the longitudinal perforations common to both the Oriental and the Early Dynastic Egyptian class, are bored through at the side somewhat near the circumference. An E. M. II steatite specimen has already been illustrated in Fig. 63, p. 94 above. 4 A striking point of divergence from the usual cylinder type lies in the fact that these Minoan cylinders Minoan have their engraved designs on the top and bottom, in place of the circumference, as is the universal rule elsewhere. The use of the flat surfaces for sealing involved the lateral method of perforation, and at the same time, in order to secure a larger field, these cylinders are for the most part broad in comparison with their height. Their sides are generally incurved.

1 Op. tit., Figs. 82, 83, and p. 108. ibexes below. Specimens without the trans-
! The objects are drawn from casts kindly versal perforation, one with a rude figured supplied me by Dr. Xanthudides. representation below, were found by M. de

A white marble specimen in the form of Sarzec at Tello (Decouvertes en Chaldre, vol. i, a couchant animal, apparently an ox, from Pl. XXXVI. n, 13, and p. 323).

Beyrout, with uncertain globular engraving 4 A clay cylinder of this type from the Hagios below, is in the Ashmolean Collection; another Onuphrios Deposit has already been illus- in the form of a sheep was obtained from trated by me, Cretan Pictographs, c., p. 107,

Persia. It presents an engraved design of two Fig. 81.

THE PALACE OF MINOS, ETC.

Impressions of ivory cylinders of this class from the larger tholos at Platanos are illustrated in Fig. 87, 4, 5, 6 1 animals.

FIG. 88. IVORY SEALS: a, END OF CYLINDER FROM PLATANOS; b, FRAGMENT FROM

THOLOS, HAGIA TRIADA.

It will be seen that, among the motives of this series of seals, successive figures of the same animal are frequent, such as the lions and spiders on Fig. 87, 4. Such processional subjects are themselves reminiscent of a similar decorative feature in proto-dynastic Egyptian Art. On Fig. 87,6, which l ma snows a lion i n Pursuit of another animal, there appears a rude human figures of figure. In Fig. 88, a may be detected the adorant cynocephalus, and the palmette of the border which recurs in 87, 9 certainly approaches the Egyptian tree-symbol. Scorpions also a feature of the early dynastic cylinders are of frequent occurrence, and the linked pair on another ivory seal from Platanos, Fig. 87, 10, fits on to the Vlth-XIth Dynasty scheme illustrated below in

Fig. 9 2. The walking figures of dogs on a fragment of an ivory seal from the early tholos of Hagia Triada, Fig. 88, b, are very naturally rendered. 2

The ship on the three-sided ivory seal, Fig. 87, 7, coupled with fish and a t-like sign, throws an interesting light on the maritime enterprise of the Period, to which the ivory material of so many of these seals and the foreign connexions of some of their forms bear further witness. Another contem-

FIG. 89.

THREE-SIDED BEAD-SEAL OK STEATITE, EAST CENTRAL CRETE (-).

Ships on Signets.

1 A specimen from the early tholos at Hagia Triada is given in Scripta Minoa, i, p. 120, Fig- 53 2 Halbherr, Memorie del r. 1st. Lomb., xxi (1905), PI. XI, Fig. 25.

porary illustration of ships will be seen on the three-sided steatite bead seal from East Central Crete reproduced in Fig. 89, b. They have the same high prows with triple forked terminations and similar rigging and upright stern. The three crouched human figures of f answer to a type which survives into Late Minoan times and may perhaps be taken to represent rowers.

Among the characteristic forms of seals at this time are massive Typical signet rings with a large round bezel like that with quadruple spiral ornament seals, shown in Fig. 81, b, low flat cylinders of the type described, 1 and pear or bottle-shaped signets, 2 generally of dark steatite, which seem to be the outgrowths of the type illustrated by the ivory example, Fig. 51 above. No imitations of the Egyptian scarab form are as yet found.

a FIG. 90.

IVORY SEALS SHOWING MEANDER, FROM OSSUARY THOI. OS OK HAGIA TRIADA (HALBHERR). (- ".)

The perforated conoid type is often associated with meander motives 3 Mean (Fig. 90, a, b, c), which have a special interest in a Cretan connexion as supplying the ultimate source of the labyrinth in art such as we see it developed in a fresco of the Knossian Palace belonging to the last Middle Minoan Period.

At times, as in Fig. 90, c, these patterns are of a more or less curvilinear character, and it seems possible that the more elaborate forms may have originated from the squaring of spiraliform designs a process which has often taken place in decorative art under textile influences. So, too, we see the key-pattern of early Greek art standing in a derivative relation to the Mycenaean 1 Cf. Scripla Minoa, i, p. 1 20, Fig. 53. that some of these conoids belong to the pre- 2 Ib., p. 121, Fig. 54. ceding E. M. II Period, and, with them, some s Halbherr, op. cit., Pl. X. It is possible of the meander types.

THE PALACE OF MINOS, ETC.

Meander Types on Egyptian Seals.

True Labyrinth.

On which side was the Indebtedness?

spiral borders. 1 In this case, however, the process may have been due to the first introduction of spiraliform patterns amongst craftsmen used to the angular system not in textile motives alone but in other branches of decoration.

A suggestive point in connexion with the E. M. Ill meander patterns is the parallel appearance about the same time of similar designs on a series of seal types found in Egypt and dating from the Sixth and immediately succeeding Dynasties 2. At times these designs are fairly elaborate. On a steatite plaque acquired by Prof. Flinders Petrie at Memphis (Fig. 91), 3 two facing figures of men with their knees drawn up, in the linear style of this Period, are seen above a true labyrinth. On completing the corner of this, it appears that there were five false turns to be avoided before reaching the centre. 4

These Nilotic seals exhibiting the meander patterns are of greyish white steatite, and of various forms, including oblong plaques like the above, flat-faced seals of semi-oval outline and button-shaped signets. They belong to a class which, though partly reproducing Egyptian types, is only half Egyptian in the dynastic sense of the word, and which seems to have been due to an element of the population in the Delta or its borders that had maintained many of the traditions of the prehistoric inhabitants of the Nile Valley.

The meander pattern comes in suddenly on the Egypto-Libyan seals of the present class about the time of the Sixth Dynasty, and is paralleled by the more or less contemporary appearance of similar key motives on the Cretan seals.

There was no antecedent spiraliform stage in Egypt such as we find on the Aegean side that might, as suggested above, have contributed to the evolution of these meander patterns. Nor is there any known source either in the Nile Valley or on the Asiatic side from which they could have been 1 Cf. Petrie, Egyptian Decorative Art,

FIG. 91. STEATITE PLAQUE FROM MEMPHIS (PETRIE).

In ceramic decoration such meander patterns appear as early as the Fourth Dynasty, e. g. bowl of Sneferus' time. De Morgan, Origines de FEgypte, Pl. XI.

8 Memphis, iii, Pl. XXVI, 2. See too p. 359, Fig. 259, b.

Op. fit., pp. 15, 16. Petrie observes that the human figures are completely in the style of the button-seals which belong to the Sixth to Eighth Dynasties'. He compares the square labyrinth with classical Cretan types. The other side of the plaque is engraved vertically with five double-lined columns having twenty-two horizontal strokes between each.

introduced ready-made. At the same time the Egyptian hieroglyphic series Key exhibits key and meander patterns of simple forms, in the one case y- "00 (iner, indicative of irrigated land, in the other CD (ia,), representing Egyptian a simplified form of the fuller pictographic plan of a Palace court. The glyphs. latter connexion is important in its relation to the labyrinth in art. 1 A Palace

The appearance of these meander patterns on Early Minoan seals must be taken in connexion with other motives on seals of an Egypto-Libyan class which during this Period exercised a direct influence on the glyptic repertory of Crete. This reaction of what seems to have been the older element in Egypt on Early Minoan culture is indeed continually manifesting itself.

Among the constantly recurring motives of these Egypto-Libyan influ-seals of the Period which begins with the Sixth and continues to the

Eleventh Dynasty are the opposed, confronted, or reversed figures of men 2 Libyan and animals. Several of these designs find their reflection on Cretan seals Seals. indeed, an early example may be seen in the monkeys back to back on the ivory signet, Fig. 51 above, which, from the associated objects, has been placed within the limits of the E. M. II Period. Among the types that now Reversed appear on a very characteristic class of- these Egypto-Libyan seals is a design consisting of two lions in reversed positions. The lions here are clearly of Egyptian derivation but in a barbaric setting, and this type of button-seal, which is found already at the close of the Sixth Dynasty, is of exceptional importance as supplying the prototype of a whole series of motives that appear about this time on Minoan seal-stones.

It will be seen from the Fig. 92, B, C 3 that the reversed lions coalesce Becomes in such a way as to give the main outlines of a mere pattern, resembling a double sickle, which in turn influences the types on a long succession of Cretan bead-seals (Fig. 92, D, E, F and Fig. 93 B,). Most of these seals, which are of steatite, belong to the perforated three-sided class, but at times the button type is itself taken over.

The above chronological evidence also supplies a clue to the approximate date of a very characteristic class of three- and four-sided bead-seals exhibiting subjects of a pictographic character (Fig. 93 A, n). 4 This conventionalized type of prism-seal dates back to E. M. II 5 but the bulk of these 1 See belov, p. 358. seqq): Further Discoveries, c. (J. . S., xvii, 2 See for example the confronted men on p. 331 seqq.). Scorpions, spiders, fishes, the labyrinth-seal, Pig. 91, above. hunted goats, ostrich-like birds, and revolving 3 Compare Scripta Minoa, i, p. 128, Fig. 65. disks recur.

4 See Scripta Minoa, i, p. 130 seqq., and 5 See above, p. 95, with note 2. Cretan Pictographs, c. (J. H. S., xiv, p. 337

THE PALACE OF MINOS ETC.

seals may be referred to the present time. They mark their owners' Potters' vocation and often present amuletic signs. Subjects relating to the potter's craft are frequent on these. In Fig. 93 A, a i, a diminutive man is moulding

Seals.

BUTTON-SEAL OSSUARA OF HAIA. TR. IADA

FIG. 93A. THREE-SIDED BEAD-SEALS. a, STEATITE: f, BROWN STEATITE (FACE 2, Two POTS IN VEN, 3- CRUCIFORM PATTERN): d, YELLOW STEATITE (FACE 2, BULLS HEAD; 3, Two FORI PARTS OF DogS)- ALL FROM KASTELI PEDEADA, S. E. OF KNOSSOS (f).

a large jar with handles above and below the earliest record of a Cretan pithos, though a parallel Cycladic type is known. In d 2 a pot is apparently being taken out of an oven. The table-like object on Fig. 93 A, a 2 with its s y witHji Rp; i. fp)is

FIG. 92. TABLE SHOWING DERIVATION OF CRETAN DOUBLE SICKLE TYPES FROM REVERSED LION TYPES OF EGYPTO-LIBYAN BUTTON-SEALS (4) square divisions leads us to a remarkable series of comparisons. It is in fact a Minoan draught-board and in the triangular object beneath the hand of the Draught seated personage we must recognize a conical draughtsman. 1

FIG. 93 B. THREE-SIDED STEATITE BEAD-SEALS FROM CENTRAL CRETE: a, SPECIMI

SHOWING END; b, c, d ANOTHER EXAMPLE (b ILLUSTRATES THE DOU-BLE SICKLE) (I).

The design on the six-faced ivory signet from the early tholos of H. Triada (Fig. 93 c, 2) leads us a step further. It is a Minoan adaptation of the Egyptian draught-board sign men (b, c) as it appears already on proto-dynastic cylinders (Fig. 93 c, b 3), and the draughtsmen here show the characteristic knobbed head. The long-robed women of Fig. 93 A, b i, adoring a rayed solar symbol, already wear the peaked collars or cowls that survived as a Middle Minoan fashion. The similarly clad figure on c i is a female potter. d i recalls the crocodiles of the cylinders.

A type of perforated amulet of steatite, in FIG. 93 c. a, DRAUGHT-BOARD r,

AND PIECES ON E. M. Ill IVORY the shape of a human leg, belonging to the later SIGNET (FRACTURE RESTORED). e l eme nts of the ossuary tholoi, takes us in the same direction as the double sickle on the bead-seals. Similar pendants occur in Egyptian graves belonging to the Sixth Dynasty and immediately succeeding Period. 4 They were invariably attached as amulets to the anklets of the dead, arm-shaped pendants being suspended from the wrists.

This contact with primitive Nilotic elements also gives a suggestive interest to the appearance of clay burial cists and jars, both lidded, containing

Adaptation of Egyptian Draughtboard Sign.

b, c, EARLV TYPES OF EGYPTIAN DRAUGHT-BOARD SIGN (men. e, f, EGYPTIAN PIECES.

Amulets: Parallels from Egypt.

1 Inverted conical draughtsmen above a board are seen on an Early Dynastic Egyptian cylinder (Petrie, Scarabs and Cylinders with Names, PI. II, 49, and cf. PI. IV, 98).

! Halbherr, Rendiconti, c., 1906, p. 33, Fig. C. But the subject remained enigmatic.

3 b from sealing of Narmer, Petrie, Royal Tombs, II, 93 (cf. Mena); c. from cartouche of Queen Hatasu (for comparison).

4 e. g. at Mahasna. J. Garstang, Afamsna, PI. XXXIX and p. 30.

Burial Urns and Clay

Cists;

THE PALACE OF MINOS, ETC.

Prehistoric Egyptian and sons.

Approximate Dating of E. M. III.

contracted skeletons. The clay cist or larnax has a very long history in Crete and specimens with rounded angles have now been found associated with Early Minoan pottery in the Sepulchral Cave of Pyrgos above referred to, North-east of Knossos. 1 Those of the E. M. Ill Period still show rounded corners and burial jars occur of oval form which may be described as miniature cists. Both burial cists and jars occurred in the Pachyammos cemetery (see Fig. 94). 2 The vessels were simply buried in the sand. They were closely packed together and range from E. M. Ill to the close of M. M. III. In the case of the jars especially the bodies had evidently been tightly trussed before the rigor mortis had set in. It seems

FIG. 94. E. M. Ill BURIAL CIST AND JAR: PACHYAMMOS, EAST CRETE, (i 1-) possible indeed that the ancient Cretans, like the Libyan tribe of the Nasamones, described by Herodotos, had forced the dying to take a sitting posture. 3 Clay burial cists, some of oval form, and pots placed bottom upwards, with contracted skeletons, are characteristic of prehistoric Egyptian tombs. 4 Have we not here the source of a long Minoan line?

It will be seen that the Egyptian or Egypto-Libyan connexions, of which we have so many evidences during the Third Early Minoan Period, point to the troubled time that intervenes between the Sixth and the Eleventh Dynasties. According to the system here adopted the approximate elate of this Minoan Period would lie between 2400 and 2100 B. C., slightly overlapping the Eleventh Dynasty.

1 See above, p. 59, and p. 150.

2 Seager, The Cemetery of Pachyammos, Crete, pp. 9-13, 28, Pl. XII.

Herod., lib. IV, 190; cf. E. H. Hall (Mrs. Dohan), Sphonngaras, p. 62.

4 e. g. De Morgan, Origines de FEgypte, pp. i37 38, Figs. 467, 468 (Kawamil: the cist

Fig. 468 resembles Pachyammos types but with holes in its sides instead of handles for the attachment of the lid). For the clay burial cists see too Petrie, Quibell, and Spurrell, Naqada and Ballas, Pl. Ill, Ayrton and Loat, El Mahasna, Pl. VII. 38.

THE MIDDLE MINOAN AGE

MIDDLE MINOAN I 5. M. M. I: (A) FOUNDATION OF KNOSSIAN PALACE.

Age of Palaces begins; Traces of earlier foundation at Knossos; M. M. I elements of Palace at Knossos; Wall construction and analysis; Early signs on base blocks of enceinte parallel signary at Phaestos; Relations of Crafts-metis signs to Linear Script; Early Keep with walled pits; Insulac wit Inn fortified enceinte; Rounded angles of original W. block; Terra-cotta water-pipes; M. M. I stage at Phacstos; Early Pillar Basement at Knossos; Oval House, Chamaezi; Rounded angles of Knossian insiilae compared; Foundation Walls of Palace; Ossuary tholoi superseded by Cists; tendency towards individual interment; Clay sarcophagi and jars.

THE Age which now succeeds is par excellence the Age of Palaces, marked Age of by the foundation of the great Minoan buildings, and from this time onwards Knossos may be said to set the pace for the insular civilization.

It will be shown that the foundation of the Palace itself on this site Traces of in its earliest form, as recovered for us by the recent excavations, did not itself take place till the latter part of the present Period. But coming U on at (events had already cast their shadows before them. That some local predecessor of the great building had covered at least a part of the site before the close of the Early Minoan Age is rendered probable, as has been already pointed out by the discovery of the spacious vault of the hypogaeum beneath the South Porch which seems to form part of the subterranean entrance of an earlier building at the same point. Store-vessels representing the incipient stage of M. M. I were found beneath the floors of the West Magazines and relics from the treasury of an earlier shrine were brought to light beneath the Central Palace sanctuary. 1 It is probable indeed that the original laying out of the early Keep or Tower, now ascertained to have existed by the Northern Entrance, maybe of the same proto-Palatial age.

As a trustworthy means of obtaining a chronological guide, a system of Wall wall analysis' has proved effective. This consists of the examination of Anal y sis-the ceramic fragments, often very minute, contained in the interior of the

THE PALACE OF MINOS, ETC.

walls and under the base blocks above their foundations, in positions which seemed to exclude the possibility of later disturbance.

The researches into the wall cavities were facilitated by a curious feature in the construction of the West wall itself. The interior of the wall was filled with rubble masonry about a metre thick and the outer and inner

FIG. 95. VIEW SHOWING INTERIOR OK W. WALL, KNOSSOS, WITH PART OK THE RUBBLE FILLING REMOVED. MORTISES KOR WOODEN CROSS-BARS ARE VISIBLE.

orthostatic gypsum slabs were originally locked together by means of wooden bars, dovetailed into the mortises which are visible on either side. 1 (Fig. 95.) The first tests of this kind were made in 1905 at three different points in the rubble filling between the orthostats of the best preserved, southern section of the West wall (see Fig. 95), from the Third to the Tenth Magazine. 2 The results were concordant, indeed, but not altogether free 1 Knossos, Report, 1901 (B. S. A., vii), pp. 3, 2 See Knossos, Report, 1905 (B. S. A.,), 4 and Fig. i. p. 2O se qq The fragments were examined by

Dr. Mackenzie and myself.

M. M. I: FOUNDATION OF KNOSSIAN PALACE 129 from elements of doubt. The evidence seemed to point to the existence of an original structure dating from the close of the First Middle Minoan Period, and to a subsequent remodelling of the fa ade in the course of M. M. III. 1

These analyses were perforce confined to the part of the West wall Results of above the base slabs of the orthostats. But the section North of this, where vv Wali the upright gypsum blocks were wanting, offered an opportunity of testing the c-contents of the actual wall foundations beneath the base slabs. The undisturbed material found beneath these, at a point behind the Twelfth Magazine, gave a different result from the foregoing. There were absolutely no fragments belonging to M. M. III. The latest sherds here brought to light belonged to an early stage of the First Middle Minoan Period. 2 Corroborative of this, moreover, was another interesting test. It will be seen from the view outside the West Porch, given in Fig. 90, 3 that, about three metres West of the existing South section of the facade, a line of large slabs runs parallel with it, curving round towards the East side of the Porch. But these slabs, which (after a slight setback, such as is usual in the Palace walls) follow the more Northern line of the facade, may with great probability be taken to represent its original continuation southwards, and to be the base slabs, embedded in a tough Earlier clay stratum, of a Western facade-line along this section. Immediately "vaii" under the second of these slabs from the North end were found, besides a mass of Neolithic and Early Minoan sherds, a score illustrating the earlier M. M. I phase, but nothing later. 4 All this points to the conclusion that the 1 The fragments found that could be defi- led me in the original Report (op. tit., p. 21) nitely classified were practically divided into to draw the too sweeping conclusion that 'the two groups, M. M. I and M. M. Ill, the former construction of the West wall belongs to the much preponderating. In Test Pit i, made in close of the Middle Minoan Age. In view the filling between the orthostats, from their of the further wall analyses referred to below, existing top to the base block on which they this conclusion must be greatly modified, rested (55 centimetres), the fragments as The following is the analysis of 319classified analysed by Dr. Mackenzie were M. M. I, 315; fragments from the interstices of the foundation

M. M. II, none; M. M. Ill, 81; unclassed, wall of rough stones beneath the base slabs at 171; L. M. I, obviouslyintrusive, i. In Test this point: Neolithic, 52; Sub-Neolithic or

Pit 3, where the depth of the rubble deposit E. M. I, 42; Early Minoan in general, 127; was greater (1-05 m.), my own analysis was: M. M. I, 98.

M. M. I, 50; Late M. M. I, 5; M. M. Ill, 25; See too the Sketch Plan, Fig. 152, below.

unclassed, 28; L. M. I, i. Five fragments Of the sherds examined, 20 were M. M. I.

here brought to light, at first set down as late The others (in the first half-metre) were: E. M. M. M. I, seem to be best described as in general, 146; and Neolithic, 460. M. M. I l. The presence of M. M. Ill sherds I K

M. M. I: FOUNDATION OF KNOSSIAN PALACE 131 original wall on the side of the West Court dates from the mature M. M. I IVriod. Probably, not long after that date, the original line of the fa? ade was thrown back along its southern section. This in turn was remodelled early in M. M. III.

Sibsci iient researches beneath the massive base blocks of the original North wall of the Palace outside the North-East Entrance showed that there too the latest sherds were early M. M. I.

In 1910 a series of similar tests were made along the base blocks of Tests in another massive wall-line apparently the innermost enceinte on the East v-iu ofe Slope. 1 As was also the case with the North wall, huge blocks- were here turned over in the process, so that the element in the interstices within was

FK;. 97. MASSIVE BASK BLOCK Vr S. E. CORNER OK EARI. Y V. i. i. LINE,

S, INCISED WITH LARGE SlgN.

absolutely pure. These researches again showed a uniform composition of the interior element, no sherds later than. early M. M. I coming to light, and the great bulk being either Neolithic or Early Minoan. 3 Tests made in the original southern wall-line (see below, p. 208, Fig. 154) produced identical results, and, as shown above, the latest sherds found in the great hypogaeum beneath the South Porch were also early M. M. I.

l Immediately East of the area where the stones beneath two of these large blocks, by myself and Dr. Mackenzie, may be given as examples: (i) Neolithic, 322; Early Minoan, 137; M. M. I, 7. (2) Neolithic, 320; E. M. in; M. M. I, 25. Only one or two examples of polychrome sherds were found in the course large piiivi were found, and half-way between the Stone-spout area and the East Bastion, and again farther South, a little East of the light-well of the Hall of the Double Axes.

- One of these blocks was 1-96 metres long by 1-20 broad, and 0-55 cm. thick.

The results of the examination of the sherds in the interstices of the foundation of these tests, and these of an early class with powdery scarlet pigment.

THE PALACE OF MINOS, ETC.

Large Signs on Early-Base Blocks.

The base blocks of these enceinte walls, the date of which is thus ascertained, were characterized by incised signs, many of them of abnormally large proportions. One of the largest of these, consisting of a combination of the double l fork and trident signs, at the South-East Palace Angle, is shown in Fig. 97. Its width is 80 cm. (31! inches), its height 42 cm. (i6 inches), and the cutting is 25 cm. wide andii5 deep. Such a sign as this far transcends an ordinary mason's mark, and may well be credited with some definite meaning.

On a roughly squared base block near the North-West angle of the

FIG. 98. INCISED DESIGN ON BASE BLOCK FOUND NEAR NORTH-WEST ANGLE OF PALACE.

Palace, which seems to belong to the same class, there occurred indeed a quite monumental incision (Fig. 98). Linked The remaining part of the design, which is somewhat group and broken off on its left margin, is about a metre wide. The rude picto-graphic figures.

left section seems to represent a linked group of signs including the + and H, such as occur on some early seal– stones. The right portion, on the other hand, suggests a rude human l Another very large example is supplied necting bar, was 72 cm., or about three-quarters by a deep-cut, dumb-bell-like sign. No. 9 of of a metre, wide! Fig. 99, consisting of two rings joined by a con-

M. M. I: FOUNDATION OF KNOSSIAN PALACE 133 figure with one hand upraised and an object behind, which somewhat recalls the primitive seated and be-wigged figures (see inset, p. 132) on a well-known class of Early Dynastic cylinders. The influence of these on primitive Minoan design has been already noted. l An Early Minoan tradition is visible in every feature of this elaborate design, and it might be thought perhaps that it was derived from a building still earlier than the first Palace of which we have the existing constructions. But the rough hewn stone on which it is incised is indistinguishable from other base blocks of the present series.

The signs are always incised on the upper or lower surfaces of the slabs, often left very rough, and they could not have been intended to be visible to the eye. Even those at present conspicuous on the face of the limestone masonry of the Palace were themselves doubtless hidden from view by their painted stucco coating of varying thickness. The incised marks in fact must be taken in relation to the material itself and to their disposition at the time of construction. At times, as in the case of stamps on Chaldaean bricks, they may have had a consecrating value.

The signs on these base blocks of the early enceinte and terrace walls Earlier must be recognized, from the position in which they are found and the signs, on character of the work itself, as belonging to the Age which saw the founda- tion of the Palace. They are accordingly grouped together here in the M. M. I.

Table, Fig. 99. Those of extraordinary dimensions, indeed, such as Fig. 97, found on certain base blocks, belong to an archaic category, and considerable labour must have been, expended in cutting out designs sometimes three- quarters of a metre in length and deeply incised. But, apart from these exceptional examples, the signs of this earlier class are on the whole larger and more deeply cut than those of the succeeding Periods. It is, moreover, Corre- interesting to find that two-thirds of the Knossian types of this group are d e practically identical with signs on the blocks of the earlier Palace at Phaestos. 2 wi h mark

These comparisons will be found noted in the Table. Palace at

There are some thirty-three such marks on the base blocks of the Early Palace at Knossos, several of these appearing in variant forms, some of them, as will be seen, of a more or less compound character. and occasionally they appear in groups. Out of the root-forms of these early signs of which we have the evidence, about two-thirds are common to both Knossos and Phaestos, and many of the numerous compound varieties which occur are 1 See above, pp. 68, 69, and cf. Scrip ta Minoa,- For the Phaestos marks see Pernier, Jlon.

i, p. 1 24. The inset is from Petrie, Scarabs and Ant., xii (1902), p. 87 seqq., and cf. xiv (1904),

Cylinders with Names (PI. II. 43), the position p. 431 seqq. reversed for better comparison.

also identical. The systems of combination and tokens of differentiation, such as the spurs of 201, and 22 b or the A above 23 c and 24 c, largely correspond in the two groups, and it seems not unreasonable to infer that a good deal of the work on the two sites may have been executed by the same guilds of workmen.

Crafts- These marks' on the early Palace blocks form only one in a series of categories of craftsmen's signs found on objects of various materials, such compared as bone and ivory or faience. Though such marks or signs can harcllv with

Linear in themselves be described as actual characters of a system of writing, cnpt a certain underlying community may at the same time be detected in their evolution. Their general aspect is itself alphabetiform. Several forms on the basement blocks referred to correspond with those of the primitive pictographic signs of Cretan seals. Over half of them, moreover, are practically identical in form with linear types of the developed Minoan Scripts A or B. These, ideo- at least, must have had a conventional ideographic meaning associated with

Element, them, and the same is true of the craftsmen's signs in general. Detailed researches into the application of such signs to parts of the building at

Knossos show in fact that they were used with a certain method in reference

Religious to their distribution. There can be little question, moreover, that a series tion. of these, amongst which the double axe is of most frequent occurrence, had a religious signification and were employed consistently in certain regions which had a specially sacral connexion. This, however, refers to the super- structures, where the

Double Axe sign greatly outnumbers the others. 2 On the base blocks this sign can claim no such predominance.

M. M. I We see then that at the beginning of the M. M. I Period a more or

Knossos 6: ess sc l uare area on the site of Knossos had already been enclosed with a massive enceinte of walls. Moreover, the evidence supplied by the filling in of the great hypogaeum or subterranean entrance vault referred to in the preceding Section tends to show that it is to this Period that must be referred the levelling away of the hill-top for the formation of the Central

Central Court. The last ceramic relics found with the earth thus dumped clown into the cavity of this vault, which was filled in to support the founda- tions of the South Porch of the Palace, prove to belong to the earliest phase of M. M. I.

These researches into the early enceinte walls are so fundamental in character, so decisive in their results, and of such chronological importance 1 For a comparative study of these and other Scripta Minoa.

craftsmen's signs "of the two Palaces I must See below, pp. 218, 425 and p. 449, Fig. refer to my forthcoming second volume of 322.

that it has been thought well to refer to them here in some detail, the more so since no adequate account of them has as yet been set forth.

They have now been amplified and confirmed by a curious discovery made in the course of the exploratory campaign carried out in 1913. The area flanking the north-west side of the Central Court and the adjoining part of the West wall of the Northern Entrance Passage had been known for some Deep years l to include a group of deep walled pits sometimes called dungeons', for which, indeed, they may well have served (Fig. 100). These descend to

Discovery a depth of nearly twenty-five feet, but had evidently been filled up at a very rounding early date, and later Palace lines drawn without reference to them.

In making a supplementary examination beneath the floor of the small chamber containing a knobbed pithos, which was supposed to overlie the area of one of these (No. V), I found that it really lay above and on the margin of a massive wall of rubble masonry, going down seven metres to the level of the floor of the walled pits, and built up against a cutting in the Neolithic deposit. This wall was now followed out externally by means of deep cuttings and of tunnels under the later structures, and proved to be Early the containing foundation wall of a more or less square keep or tower, within Tower. which were enclosed the deep walled cells. Like them, it descended about seven metres below the surface level of the Central Court, and it was on;. ill sides built up against the Neolithic cliff, here artificially cut out (see Plan, Fig. 101).

The upper wall of this structure seems to have been composed of massive limestone slabs, the lower courses of which were partially preserved on the

North side, 2 and to a slight extent on the West, where they stepped up.

Early A noteworthy feature of the foundation wall was that its corners were mostly rounded off, though those of the masonry above, in the single place where they had been well preserved, were angular. The date of this building was fixed by an examination of the small pottery fragments from inner crevices of its substructures, portions of the rubble masonry being

Keep: removed for this purpose. The result of this analysis was to show that
M! M. I. iere too tlie latest elements belonged to an early phase of M. M. I. 3 It thus
appears that not long after the very beginning of the Middle 1 See Knossos, Report,
1903 (B. S. A., ix), Neolithic, 74; Sub-Neolithic and E. M. I, pp. 22 seqq. 7 6; E. M.
II and III, 37; M. M. I, 32. No 1 The early sign: i occurred on two slabs, polychrome.
(2): Neolithic, 16; Sub-Neolithic

The results of two tests, at upper and lower and E. M. I, 17; E. M. II and III, 8; levels
respectively, were as follows. The frag- M. M. I, 10. The building may therefore
ments capable of classification were (i): possibly go back to M. M. I a.

FIG. 100. DEEP WALLED CELL OF EARLY KEEP, KNOSSOS.

Minoan Age a massive stone Keep or Tower, with deep walled cells within, was
erected on this spot. Its outer dimensions were not very

NORTHERN
ENTRANCE
PASSAGE t i
CENTRAL COURT
SCALE. OF METRES
SCALE OF FEET

FIG. 101.   PLAN OK EARLY KEEP, SHOWING DEEP WALLED CELLS
WITHIN.

large, some 20 metres E.-W. by 15 N.-S,,-and it seems to have been completely
isolated. 1 It shows, however, the same orientation as that of 1 The deep trenches and
tunnels executed West sides, and parts of the North and East, outside the foundation
walls on the South and make this conclusion almost certain.

the Palace, its South wall corresponding with tin- border-line of the Central Court,
which must already have been levrllcd at this time. The East wall, moreover, follows
the line of the later West wall of the Northern Entrance Passage. It formed therefore
an integral part of the earliest Palace plan.

Two remarkable features in the plan of the West Win;; of the Central Knossian
Palace had long suggested to me the conclusion that the Central v. vinj,-area of this
had also originally formed an isolated block. Immediately North of the Ante-room of
the Room of the Throne the gypsum orthostats of the early inner line of wall traceable
on this side curve inwards in a westerly direction, without any apparent reference to
the later plan of the building, and suggest the original continuation of a boundary
wall running in this direction,- and excluding the N. W. Quarter (see Fig. 102). This
inward curve of the original orthostatic wall, moreover, finds a curious counterpart
in the curving course of the base slabs opposite the West Porch, which, as already
pointed out, mark an earlier line of the West facade at this point (see Fig. 0(5). 1 lere
we seem to trace the first stage of the southern wall belonging to the same isolated
block, which would have contained the area of the Magazines and Pillar Rooms, and
that later occupied by the Room of the Throne.

It may further be remarked that the original gypsum wall-line of this Defensive
insula facing the Central Court resembled in its general character the t er ior outer
wall-line of similar construction that formed the Southern boundary of the Palace,
bordering the South Corridor, and the continuation of which may fagade be traced

along an upper terrace of the East Slope. In other words, the central section of the Palace facing the Central Court was not in its original Court. conception an interior line at all. It did not give free and almost continuous communication with the Court by means of porticoes and broad stepped approaches as did the later fa ade on this side, built out some three metres East of the original line. Rather, it takes on a somewhat defensive aspect as part and parcel of a self-contained structural unit.

The curved outline of the angles of this insula supplies an interesting point of comparison with the oval building of M. M. I date at Chamaezi in Eastern Crete, described below, 3 and we may, as there suggested, trace the reaction of other rounded types of primitive Cretan and Cycladic buildings.

From what has been said above it is clear that the area of the Palace Massive site at Knossos was laid out in the course of the First Middle Minoan Enceinte.

1 See my A'tiassos, Report, 1904 (B. S. A., turn further on, following the East wall, per- x, p. 26 seqq., 6 The Earlier West Facade haps, of the Long Gallery so as to include the of the Central Court, and Pl. I, A, B). N. W. angle of the region of the Magazines.

Tliis wall may well have taken a northern 3 See p. 147 and Plan, Fig. 108.

M. M. I: FOUNDATION OF KNOSSIAN PALACE 141

Period, and fenced round with enceinte walls which, on the North and East sides, at any rate, were of the most massive construction. The hill-top had been already levelled to make room for the Central Court, and the main lines of orientation laid down. But the buildings within the enceinte and Jnsulae round the Central Court seem to have been largely distributed in isolated Enceinte, blocks. The methodical character of this distribution into insulae is best brought out by the diagrammatic Plan of the Palace given below at the beginning of 9. Amongst these this early Keep or Tower occupied a prominent place, dominating the Northern Entrance Passage and Sea-Gate, as it existed in its original form.

Both in the massive walls and in this tower-like structure we see the Signs of obvious design of fortification, which, indeed, clung to the Northern Entrance to Kortifica-the last. Open and exposed to attack as seem to have been the great Palaces " on-both at Knossos and Phaestos in their later phases, we can hardly avoid the conclusion that defensive considerations entered largely into their original plans. This, indeed, is made probable by contemporary analogy, not only as supplied by early Cycladic strongholds, but in Crete itself and the very neighbourhood of Knossos. The Cyclopean walls of roughly horizontal structure that surround the settlement about the peak sanctuary of Juktas, 2 described below, belong, as their ceramic associations show, to the First Middle Minoan Period, and are therefore contemporary with the early walls of Knossos. Both at Juktas and in the Palace plan we see not only bastions at intervals but the frequent short returns so characteristic of the West fa ade of Knossos. These Minoan traditions of fortification will be seen to have an important bearing on certain features that recur at Tiryns and elsewhere. 3

Among the earliest elementsof the Knossian Palace is the system of water- Water-conveyance, by means of terra-cotta pipes. These, with their collars and ciay X stop-ridges, are of admirable construction, and the tapering form of each section P 1 5 of gave the water a shooting motion well adapted to prevent the accumulation

Construc-of sediment. These pipes (see Plans and Sections, Fig. 104) show an advance l on nearly all modern systems of earthenware pipes, the sections of which are parallel tubes. Those by the area of the Stone Drain-head (Fig. 103) are comparatively near the surface and layed to a fall North. Those of the South Slope, on the other hand, run, over three metres deep, beneath the foundations of the South Porch, and show an upward slope of I in 18-90 metres. 4 If 1 See p. 203, Fig. 152. were made by my architect, Mr. Christian C. T.

- See below, p. 155, Fig. 113 a. Doll, by whom the Plans and Sections shown in 3 See Vol. II. Fig. 104 were made. To these is due the deter-

THE PALACE OF MINOS, ETC.

this upward slope formed part of the original arrangement, it might be taken as evidence that the Minoan engineers, at the close of the Third Millennium iu:., made a practical application of the fact that water finds its own level. From the position, however, in which this section of piping was found, above the filling of the Hypogaeum, the evidence falls short of certainty. Later Re- That the inner arrangements of the Palace area were radically modified

"f paiace S at some time between the date of the M. M. I structures and a Interior mature phase of M. M. 11 is well shown by the evidence forthcoming from the original Keep. The walled pits were here filled up, and new walls with foundations in some cases going very deep down were drawn across them, in places at right angles to the original foundations, and prolonged beyond their boundaries. At a level a little below that of the Central Court new floors were laid down, and in the case of one of these, belonging to a small room to the West of this area, a chronological terminus ad quetn is obtainable. On this floor, composed of somewhat rough stones, was the base of a knobbed pithos presenting a late example of a class well represented in the Early Magazines of the East

Slope. With this were cups and other ceramic fragments belonging to a mature phase of M. M. II (see Section, p. 235, Fig. 177 below).

It would therefore appear that the structures to which this floor belonged date from the early part of derneath the S. Porch. As it here passes over smaller than the others. Their faucets have lips the earth filling of the Hypogaeum the possibility 9f a slight sinking must be kept in view. But, if that was the case, the whole sank equally, for the clay cement of the joints was not broken. It will be seen that the course of the pipe is somewhat curved. Mr. Doll observes that the pipes of the Eastern area are in every way

FIG. 103. CLAY WATER. PIPES: NEAR AREA OF STONE DRAIN-HEAD.

02 cm. thick, and their spigots, instead of tapering with the general taper of the pipes, were wave-surfaced outside for the grip of the cement or clay. Some, at any rate, of those on the South Slope have handles, which are wanting in the case of the others.

M. M. I: FOUNDATION OF KNOSS1AX PALACE 143

THE PALACE OF MINOS, ETC.

that Period. It is to this epoch then that we must refer the first great remodelling- of the interior arrangements of the Knossian enceinte, which linked up and unified what appear to have been a succession of separate blocks ranged round the Central Court.

Full Evo- The full evolution of the Palace as weknow it was thus achieved, but as this Knossian consummation is most conveniently connected with the beginning of the Second Middle Minoan phase it is better to deal with this and the great sister building at Phaestos in their comparative aspects in the succeeding Section. It seems not improbable that the Palace at Phaestos may have passed through a similar stage in which it consisted of a conglomeration of separate units round a central area, the whole protected by a more or less square enclosure of boundary

Palace, Work of M. M. II

FIG. 105. M. M. I VESSELS FROM STRATUM BELOW EARLY MAGAZINES AT PHAESTOS ((-.).

M. M. I walls. That elements of the building, the extent of which is as yet imperfectly in Palace ascertained, belong to the First Middle Minoan Period is clear from the Phaestos ev ence supplied by the Early Magazines beneath the later light-well of the Propylaea. The latest ceramic relics found in these Early Magazines, which mark the date when they were filled in for the new constructions, are certain cups of a characteristic type which constantly recurs in association with advanced M. M. II fabrics, and which, both at Phaestos and Knossos, mark a very wide catastrophe at that epoch. But among the remains in a stratum dating from the time that immediately preceded the construction of the Early Magazines themselves were found vessels of types characteristic of the earliest M. M. I phase 1 (Fig. 105). They represent in fact the same ceramic stage as that found immediately beneath the foundation slabs of the Palace at Knossos. The spouted type on the right is in itself an inheritance from E. M. III. 2 The two Palaces, in fact, seem to have been founded 1 This interesting observation regarding the was kindly supplied me by Dr. Pernier. stratum in which the M. M. I pottery was found 2 See above, pp. 109-111.

THE PALACE OF MINOS, ETC.

M. M. I Basement with Monolithic Pillars at Knossos.

Early Pillar Room. Perhaps Crypt of Sanctuary.

at the same epoch at a mature stage, that is, of the M. M. I phase and in man)- respects repeat each other's history.

Among the best preserved structures of the hill of Knossos which must be referred to the beginning of this Period, and even preceded the foundation of the Palace as we know it, is a deep basement chamber with two monolithic pillars excavated in the S. E. angle of the Palace area (Fig. 106). Whether or not this structure formed an annexe of a larger building, 1 it is interesting as supplying the earliest example of the Pillar Rooms that play such an important part in Minoan buildings, and which, in many cases, certainly served a religious purpose as the crypts

Dove Vase.

FIG. 107. POLYCHROME VESSEL IN FORM OK DOVE FROM M. M. I BASEMENT (f f).

of columnar sanctuaries above. 2 The chronological place of this early Pillar Room is shown by the ceramic relics found on its earliest floor level. These belong exclusively to the initial stage of M. M. I, and afford good illustrations of the earlier phases of polychromy. 3 A remarkable vessel here found in the shape of a dove, 4 with white and red colouring on a black glaze, may well have had a ritual use (Fig. 107).

The stone houses of this Period, as is shown by the remains of such beneath the West Court pavement at Knossos, and to the North of the Palace site, are, like those of the preceding Early Minoan Periods, normally 1 It lies outside the area of the existing Palace, and its orientation is somewhat divergent.

2 See vol. ii and cf. A. J. E., Pillar Rooms, c. p. 63 seqq. (Archaeologia, 1914).

s See below, p. 172, and Mackenzie,.. H. S., xxvi, pp. 244-8, Pis. VII, IX.

4 . H. S., 1901, p. 79, Fig. i.

M. M. I: FOUNDATION OF KNOSSIAN PALACE 147 of rectangular construction. An exception to this rule is, however, supplied M. M. I.

by a house excavated on a height at Chamaezi, in the Siteia Province, by Dr. Xanthudides. 1 The top of a lofty knoll had been here levelled in Minoan times to make room for a building which, following the lines House of of the site itself, was of elliptical outline (Fig. 108). Its date is fixed by chamaei1- the vases and other objects found on its floors, which were characteristic products of the M. M. I culture. 2

This house is of exceptional interest, not only from its oval outline, but Oval as affording a good early example of the Minoan system of lighting the INNER COURT LIGHT-WELL)

VOTIVE CLAY FIOURCS

BRONZE AXES. lie.

FIG. 108. OVAL HOUSE, CHAMAEZI (M. M. I).

interior by means of light-wells, here represented by a single rectangular court of small dimensions in the centre of the building (12). In Room 4, moreover, was found the earliest example of a movable hearth in the form of a flat clay disk hollowed in the centre, while ashes that had probably belonged to it lay near.

Dr. Noack has put forward an ingenious theory that the house of Dr. Chamaezi, with its oval outline, squared inner chambers, and small oblong Theory, central court, supplies an example of an aboriginal type of rounded building out of which the elaborate rectangular plan of the Cretan Palaces was (. APX-, i9 6 p- 117 se qq- 1 Cf. B. S. A., xiv, pp. 417-18.

Traces of Rounded

Knossos.

THE PALACE OF MINOS, ETC.

evolved. 1 It is impossible, however, to accept this view. The Palace as a whole presents a square plan, and it is now clear that the rectangular type of dwelling-house was dominant in Crete from Neolithic times onwards. As a matter of fact, the original Palace plan at Knossos belongs, as already shown, to the same epoch as the Chamaezi house, though its arrangement had not yet attained complete organic unity.

At the same time it cannot be denied that the constituent units of the Palace present traces of curved construction. The orthostatic wall bordering on the Central Court at Knossos and which, ex hypothesi,

FIG. 109. FOUNDATION WALLS AT NORTH-WEST CORNER OF PALACE, KNOSSOS.

originally belonged to a separate insula of the building, has, as shown "in Fig. 102, above, a curved termination at its North end, and this seems to have corresponded with a rounded corner traceable in the foundation slabs to the South-West The foundation walls of the Keep, moreover, had rounded turns, though the walls above seem to have had rectangular corners.

It is interesting to note a similar phenomenon in Cycladic fortress and house construction of the same period, as, for instance, at Paros and Syros. 2 1 F. Noack, Ovalhaus und Palast in Areta, 2 Tsuntas, Kvicxcuw (E. Apx- 1898.168 1908, p. 54 seqq. Cf. Mackenzie, Cretan seqq. and Figs. 9, 10), 1899, pp. 115-17, Fig. Palaces, iv, B. S. A., xiv, p. 415. 32; and cf. Noack, op. tit., pp. 53, 54.

M. M. 1: FOUNDATION OF KNOSSIAN PALACE 149

On the other hand, no evidence is at present forthcoming of the well- Absence denned mainland form, such as that of the pre-Mycenaean settlements at psidal Orchomenos, Olympia, Tiryns, and elsewhere showing an apse-like con- Type f struction at one end of otherwise rectangular houses. iand.

One interesting feature of the early wall construction at Knossos is Founda- - i i r 11 11 tion Walls that on the North side of the site, where the ground fell away and the beneath subsoil was less stable, the great base-slabs, described above, were supported. on a well-constructed walling of smaller blocks. A good example of this Knossos. foundation work which was exposed in the course of excavation near the North-West Corner is shown in Fig. 10!). The blocks were bedded on thick layers of clay mortar so as to ensure their fairly even setting in horizontal layers, and it will be seen that their arrangement is roughly isodomic. Some of the large base-slabs above are seen projecting from the foundation wall to the right of the Figure.

The tombs of this Period, so far as is known, were ossuary cists, Tholos' which superseded the great tholos chambers. Thus, the great tholos ar jg" of Haeia Triada mentioned above 1 seems about this time to have fallen SU P"

seded by into disuse, but certain cell-like annexes 2 contained, together with the cist bones, quantities of M. M. I pottery, including numerous vases in the characteristic barbotine style.:! The same seems to have been the case with the much smaller 'tholos', remains of which were discovered by Dr. Paribeni 4 in another part of the site. 5 Here the original contents of the chamber itself had been almost entirely cleared out, but outside it, in a sepulchral annexe recalling that of the other ossuary, the contents were of a uniform M. M. I character. The pottery, the characteristic forms of the stone vases notably the bird's-nest type and the bronze implements and other relics here found must all be referred to the present Period.

The ossuary type of interment seems to have been general at this time Other and to have taken various forms. At Hagia Triada we see ossuary Q V S cists annexed to the old tholos, now disused. At Palaikastro there arles-occurred ossuaries in the form of square buildings divided into long narrow compartments. 0 At Gournia, moreover, were found rectangular house 1 pp. 71, 83. 4 R. 1aribeni, Ricerche net Sepolcreto di

See Halbherr, Mtmorie del r. Istituto Haghia Triada (Afon. Ant., xiv, 1904, p. 677 Lombardo, Syc., vol. xxi (1905), p. 250, and seqq.). See above, p. 107, Fig. 75. PI. IX, Fig. 20. 5 Op. a., p. 691, Fig. 7.

3 Op. tit., PI. VII, Fig. 16. See below, Bosanquet, B. S. A., viii, pp. 291, 292, p. 179. Figs. 5, 6.

THE PALACE OF MINOS, ETC.

Tendency tombs, shaped like small dwelling-houses with doors complete, but choked individual with human bones in disorder, and described by their excavator as veritable burial. charnel houses'. 1 Separate skeletons were also buried in a contracted

FIG. 110. PAINTED CLAY CHEST OR M. M. I, PACHYAMMOS (c.).

LARNAX: Indi- posture, as described above, both in jars 2 and in lidded clay chests like t iat s own m Fig. HO. 3 There is, in fact, at this epoch a general tendency to substitute for the great common bone houses, used by comparatively large communities, smaller family cists and even individual receptacles.

1 Boyd Hawes, Gournia, p. 56.

See p. 126.

From the cemetery discovered by Mr.

Seager on the sea-shore at Pachyammos near Gournia. Some of these, as already shown, pp. 125, 126, go back within the limits of E. M. III.

6. M. M. I: (B) THE PEAK SANCTUARY OF KNOSSOS, AND THE OF ZEUS.

Cretan Cult of natural features; Specially prominent at beginning of Middle Minoan Age; Rock sanctuaries; Votive objects of Pet sofa; Exploration of similar votive stratum on Summit of Juktas; Outer Temenos wall enclosing early settlement; Was it a City of Refuge? Inner shrine and Ash altar; Peak Sanctuary of the Early Palace Traditional Tomb of Zens'; Gold Signet from Knossos illustrating early Baetylic Cult; Minoan Beth-el; Mother Goddess and youthful Satellite; Anatolian parallels; Minoan signet showing mourning scene at tomb of young warrior God Cretan Zeus; Baetylic obelisk on Knossian ring illustration of Tomb of Zeus'; Cave sanctuaries of Psychro (Diktaion Antron) and Kamares; That of Knossos recognized in the great Cave of Skotei no.

VERY interesting evidence has come to light which shows how large a part the worship of certain natural features such as mountain-peaks, caves, and rock-shelters played in the Cretan religion at the beginning of the Middle Minoan Age. This it will be seen has a direct bearing on the Early Palace Cult of Knossos, and indeed illustrates its whole religious history.

The M. M. I Period is distinguished by the prominence assumed by Votive a special kind of sanctuary containing votive figurines of terra-cotta and other objects, and connected with such natural features. Already in 1894 a small votive station of this class had come to my notice under an overhanging conglomerate rock just below the remains of an early akropolis at Upper Zakro in East Crete. 1 Similar votive figurines were found in an annexe to the oval house of Chamaezi described above. But a more con- Petsofa. spicuous example, situated on a rock-terrace a few feet below the limestone peak of Petsofa, above Palaikastro, was explored by Prof. J. L. Myres in 1903.-Here, within terrace walls enclosing what seems to have been a later sanctuary Votive chamber with plaster benches, were found masses of votive terra-cottas 1 Votive terra-cottas, partly excavated by me legs and horns. Some of these were copied here, partly obtained from a neighbouring and published by Dr. Mariani in Man. Ant., vi peasant, are in the Ashmolean Collection. (1895), p. 182, Fig. 17; p. 176, Fig. 5.

They consist of a female figure with a Medici" The Sanctuary Site of Petsofh, B. S. A., collar like those of Petsofa, and remains of ix, p. 356seqq. The excavation was completed male figures, goats, oxen, and their separate by Mr. C. T. Currelly. Sanctuaries.

M. M. I: PEAK SANCTUARY: THK TumI!! ZEUS 153 . Ill) including human figures and their parts, animals such as oxen and their horns (an), goats, rams, swine, dogs, tortoises, hedgehogs, mere vermin, like stoats or weasels (tt), and birds, apparently doves (66). There were also many miniature vessels (y), what seems to have been a rude representation of a tree (2) resembling those of Cypriote sanctuaries, 1 and small clay balls (s, f) compared by Professor Myres to the Buddhist prayer-pellets.

The male and female figures throw a unique light on the Minoan niustra-costume of this Period. The male figures are nude except for their girdle j j 0 and foot-gear, and often bear a short dagger, apparently with a flat tang Costume. inserted into the handle. 2 Sometimes they wear a small disk-like cap, and in one case the two ends of a plaid hang down from the shoulders. The men are coloured red and the women white, according to the convention, common to Egypt, adhered to throughout Minoan times. The women wear a skirt and girdle and a bodice open at the breast and rising into a Medici collar behind, a feature already noted on E. M. Ill seals and which survived into M. M. II. On their heads is a hat expanding in front (b, d, e). The votive objects included separate parts of the human Prophy-body heads, arms, legs, and even the body itself cloven from crown to fork showing that they were in many cases offered up for the healing or averting of disease. Coupled with the representations of vermin, such prophylactic Philistine figures curiously recall the golden emerods and mice made as trespass offerings by the Philistines themselves, in part at least, of Cretan origin. com-

How late the religious associations of such votive stations as that of Petsofa went on in Crete itself is shown by the traditions that have clung to the legendary site of the Tomb of Zeus, on Mount Juktas, a few Tomb of miles SSVV. of the site of Knossos, and the most prominent feature of the landscape.

The persistent traditions that have placed here the burial place and monument of the Cretan Zeus have themselves a special interest. It was Cretan their adherence to the unorthodox aspect of primitive religion involved in unortho-the idea of a mortal Zeus that earned for the Cretans Kallimachos' " epithet d of liars', adopted by St. Paul. The reputed inscription of the tomb, 1 Myres, of. cit., p. 379. r. Prof. Myres sees a kind of over-skirt with the

The type of dagger-blade seems to be that square end of an apron below. given in Fig. 142, c below. 4 i Sam. vi. 4, 5, and cf. Myres, op. til., 3 Fig. 1 1 1, a, is taken from Myres's reconsti- p. 382, note 2, and Scripta Afinoa, i, p. 79. tuted female figure (np. ., PI. VIII). For the 5 Hymn i, v. 8, 9: collar or cowl on E. M. Ill seals see above, Kpijtcsdeiircvo-Tar" Kalyaptatot, oa. va, rtio p. 94, Fig.!)3 A, 6 I, C1. It recurs On the KprjTK lt(Krt)vavro- av ou 0ar, ia-a-l

TOV Aios ratios J, may itself cover some lingering reminiscence of the hereditary divinity attaching to the name and office of the Knossian Priest-Kings, and perhaps of the ultimate identity of Minos with the Cretan Zeus 2 a very different conception from the Greek Sky-God.

The The tradition, attested by a series of classical and Christian writers, 3
Tomb of surv j ve d to late Byzantine times. In the eleventh century Michael Psellos
4

Mt. Juk- speaks of the legend as still living, and relates that the Cretans pointed to
Christian a cairn or heap of stones as covering the Tomb of Zeus. This well
Tradition, describes t ne ruinous remains on Mount Juktas, to which the name
Mv-fjjia

TOV Zid has clung to the present day among the country people. 5 The sepulchre
of the Mortal God of that earlier religion has itself, indeed, been replaced a little
farther along the ridge by a chapel dedicated to Christ the

Lord (AvOevr 7s Xpicrros). 6 There is a pilgrimage here on the feast of the
Discovery j n 1909 I undertook a preliminary excavation of the structures visible

Sane- on the peak of Juktas, 8 already twice visited by me. This resulted in the
orfndge discovery of a shrine and a votive station of the same kind as that of Petsofa.

of Juktas. These remains lie, at a height of about 2,300 feet, on the more Northerly
summit of the long ridge of Juktas, which, though somewhat lower than one

South of it, is that which strikes the eye at Knossos itself. It dominates, in fact, the
whole Central Court of the Palace. Here, it is natural to suppose, was the sacred peak
of the Mother Goddess who presided over the Palace

Sanctuary itself the prototype, we may believe, of the lion-guarded pinnacle of
rock on which she appears on the sealings of her central shrine, adored 1 Schol. in
Callimachum, Hymn, i. of the Southern face, reproduced in Fig. 113.

2 See the Introduction to this work, p. 2. Curiously enough he makes no mention
of The passages relating to the Tomb of the structures on the summit.

Zeus are collected by Meursius, Creta (Am- 4 Avaywyi; as TOV Tavraxov.

stelodami, 1675), p. 80. I may refer to what Dr. Hatzidakis, the Director of the
Cretan I have said on the matter in my Myc. Tree and Museum, is my authority for
this. The variant

Pillar Cult, 1901 (f. H. S., xxi), pp. 23, 24. Mijjta TOV Aia is also current.

The site was visited by Pashley (Travels in 6 The Mountain above the Cave of
Psychro

Crete, 1837, i. 212 seqq.), who observed foun- (the Lyktian birth-cave of Zeus)
and a part of dations of massive walls and a hollow within the Eastern Dikta also bear
this name. Each still visible and apparently the result of an is a Mountain of the Lord
(Aphendi Vouno, excavation in search of treasure. He also A. E., Academy, June 20,
1896, p. 513).

noted the Cyclopean wall below (p. 220 and The feast of the Transfiguration is on
p. 210, vignette). The latter was fully described August 6. It is to be noted that the
Church by Dr. A. Taramelli, Ricerche archeologiche contains a Chapel of the Panagia.

cretesi (Man. Ant., ix, 1899), p. 70 seqq., s In this work I had the valuable
assistance who gives a sketch plan and section and of Dr. D. Mackenzie. Only a
summary notice (p. 71, Fig. 74) a good example of a part of these discoveries has as
yet appeared.

Fig. 112. RIDGE OF Mr. JUKTAS FROM NEAR SHE OF TYLISSOS, SHOW-
ING PROFILE OF ZEUS.

lie. 113 a. CYCLOPEAN WALL OF TEMENOS OF JUKTAS (M. M. I). (TER-RACE OF MINOAN SANCTUARY VISIBLE BEHIND.)

FIG. 1136. SKETCH PLAN OF PART OF RIDGE OF JUKTAS, SHOWING TEME-NOS AND SHRINE.

by a youthful male satellite and within which her cult might naturally be associated with that of her divine son.

This summit of the mountain, connected with that to the South by a narrow neck, consists of a more or less oval headland, about a hundred metres in length, strewn as elsewhere with limestone boulders and crowned by a rock cut platform on which are the ancient constructions (see Sketch Plan, Fig. 113). Separated from these by only a few metres is the edge of the precipitous Western steep of Juktas, descending sheer some 2,000 feet. The view on this side is extraordinarily spacious. embracing the rich champaign of Candia backed by the long snow-clad range of Ida, while seawards, beyond the sacred Isle of Dia, may be discerned in clear weather the high cliffs of Melos. The conical outline of the northern extremity of Juktas itself, as seen from the sea, is a valuable landmark for the port of Candia, as it must once have been for the ancient haven of Knossos itself. Its broadside view, on the other hand, as seen from the West, presents a very different The pro- aspect, and it is interesting to recall, in connexion with the later form of its Mountain religious traditions, that, the long ridge of the mountain rising in successive peaks has given rise to a widespread belief in the island that it reproduces the profile of the native Zeus. Its outline, indeed, seen from this side, as in the view taken near the site of Tylissos given in Fig. 112, looking across the undulating lowlands of Malevizi, may suggest to the least imaginative eye the head of the God turned skyward, as if pillowed on his holy rock and wrapped in eternal slumber. 1

Temenos The peak sanctuary itself is enclosed at a varying distance, which on its ing shrine east s i c e i s about roo metres, by a massive temenos wall of huge blocks cio d ean y " m stly rough hewn in an oblong shape and in some places consisting Wall. of nine courses and rising to a height of about 5 metres. This Cyclopean construction (Fig. 113 a) is slightly battered externally and presents its a series of angles and bastions. In its treneral character it recalls .-., O O da te the early walls of Phylakopi in Melos, of St. Andreas in Siphnos, and of Chalandriane in Syros, 2 while its approximate date is established by the fact that in the inner interstices between the blocks some of which were removed for the purpose of investigation there occurred typical M. M. I a sherds. Its erection was therefore contemporary with the epoch that immediately preceded the foundations of the early Palace as we know it.

1 A good view of the profile of Juktas as Andreas with their successive bastions, see seen from somewhat nearer the sea is given by Tsuntas, Ej! Apx-, 1899, p. 127 seqq. He Mr. A. Trevor-Battye, Camping in Crete, 1913. considered that this system of fortification was See pp. 183, 184, and Figure. of Mainland origin. For Phylakopi see D. Mac- 2 For the walls of Chalandriane and St. kenzie, Excavations at Phylakopi, p. 256.

M. M. I: PEAK SANCTUARY: THE TOMB OF ZEUS 157

The wall runs across the neck of the ridge North and South of the Sanctuary, and follows close to the edge of the precipice itself. Approaching Remains this Temenos by the winding mountain path that leads from the site of incnt

Knossos, an opening is seen in the northern wall line, marking what was within probably the main entrance in ancient times. The rocky steep within the circuit wall is abundantly strewn with Minoan sherds, many of them M. M. I, which indicate a considerable habitation of this area. Remains of lar-e pithoi, indeed, point to something more than temporary settlement, though intermittent occupation by great pilgrim crowds at festival times may account for many of the relics found. It seems possible, moreover, that

B 2 " CONJECTURAL M GAZH.

Scat

FIG. 114. SKETCH PLAN OK EARLY SANCTUARY ON Mr. JUKTAS.

owing to the sanctity of the spot it may have served as a place of asylum, in other words, as a kind of City of Refuge.

The remains of the actual shrine and votive station on the peak itself J' h, e,.8 i; eat ., Ashlaltar belong to two periods. 1 he earliest stage in the local cult is represented andlater by a grey ash stratum reaching to the bare surface of the rock and filling its crevices, the ceramic contents of which were M. M. I and II. Above this was a reddish stratum of burnt earth containing sherds of the M. M. Ill Period, and surrounding the foundations of a rectangular building of ashlar blocks with outer terrace walls of rougher construction. The building seems to have been entered by an ascending corridor or stepway A A on its South face, but the interior portion on this side had been much disturbed,

THE PALACE OF MINOS, ETC.

Domestic

A Casa Santa.

A Votive Station.

and owing, it would appear, to the work of native treasure hunters, a large hollow had been excavated in the floor of the entrance room and into the sacral deposits beneath this. Much of the structure itself has no doubt also found its way down the neighbouring steep to the West. For these reasons it was difficult to follow its outlines in detail, but the restored Plan, so far as it was possible to recover it, is indicated in the sketch, Fig. 114. It supplies an interesting parallel to the later shrine at Petsofa.

The entrance chamber B i was flanked on its Eastern side by what seems to have been a magazine (B 2), and fragments of plaster facing were found still attached to its inner walls. An inner room C was entered by a doorway of which some traces were still visible, and in this area were considerable remains of a white-faced cement pavement.

Thus in Late Minoan days, to which these constructions belonged, the central feature of the upper sanctuary seems to have reproduced the arrangement of a small house of the early Cretan and Aegean but and ben type, about 16 x 10 metres in its exterior dimensions. The inner shrine had thus a purely domestic aspect. It was a little house of shelter and refection for the Goddess on her mountain top, a Casa Santa, like that miraculously transported from Bethlehem to Loreto.

There must clearly have been some means of access along the West flank of the building from the entrance passage A to what seems to have been an outer yard or temenos of more or less triangular form, which was supported by rough terrace walls on the immediately adjoining rocky slope to North and East. This would have been the hypaethral part of the Sanctuary, well adapted for the exposure of a pillar form of the divinity. It seems probable, moreover, that this small temenos may have been entered on the North-West by a portal of its own. The existence of such an annexe to the shrine itself is, indeed, clearly indicated by an interesting glyptic representation to be described below.

The reddish deposit of burnt earth that lay about the foundations of the shrine contained sherds of the M. M. Ill Period, and below this, reaching to the bare surface of the rock, was the grey ash stratum already mentioned. This great ash altar, answering to that of Petsofa, contained similar votive relics, including male and female human figures of clay, together with those of animals, such as oxen and goats, and also separate limbs l both human and animal, part of a vessel with wild goats in relief like one from the l An arm showed a perforation, apparently numerous. Some M. M. I pottery of thebar-for suspension. In one case two human legs botine class here occurred, were joined together. Clay horns of oxen were

M. M. I: PEAK SANCTUARY: THK TOMB OF ZEUS 159

Cave of Psychro, and prayer pellets' like those of Petsofa. The votive deposit continued into the red M. M. Ill stratum above. Goats and oxen here occurred of larger build, and, inter alia, clay locks of human hair, the raised arms of an adorant, and curious flat, shell-like coils. But the most Votive interesting find was a votive limestone ladle of a kind of which other specimens had been found on the steep below, with traces of an inscription in Class A of the Linear Script. Moreover, on the height of Trullos, a foothill of Juktas, in a contemporary votive deposit, a similar ladle has come to light with a fuller inscription in the same form of script, l inscribed with a dedicatory formula containing several elements of that engraved on the Libation Table of the Dictaean Cave of Lyktian tradition. 11

The votive cult attaching itself to the Holy Sepulchre of the The Cretan Zeus is thus seen to have been shared by the legendary scene of first n his Nativity, the cave where the she-goat suckled him. In the same way "j. the sanctuary of Petsofa overlooks the site of his later Dictaean Temple. Cult. It is safe to assume that here, as elsewhere in the pre-Hellenic Age, the female form of the divinity took precedence of her son or satellite. In the case of Juktas, indeed, the peak sanctuary of Knossos, there is a curious indication that this was so. In the Central Palace shrine was found a series of L. M. II signet impressions exhibiting the Minoan Mother Goddess, Lady of the Double Axe, standing on a rocky peak between her guardian lions and receiving the adoration of a votary perhaps himself a Priest-King. 3 A gold signet-ring from the site of Knossos, Fig. 115, may be even taken to foreshadow the Tomb of Zeus. 4

This remarkable 5 signet, of the usual Minoan form with the besil at Gold right angles to the hoop, was obtained by me on the occasion of my first Rm visit to the site in 1894, and though it unquestionably belongs to the date of the later Palace, throws such a unique light on its early baetylic cult that it scene of ,.,, Haetylic seems best to reproduce it in this place. Cult.

We see here an obelisk, in front of a hypaethral sanctuary enclosed in walls of isodomic masonry, above which rise the branches of a group of 1 An account of these inscribed ladles' and 3 See A. J. E., Knossos, Report, 1901, p. 28 their connexions is given below, p. 623 seqq. seqq., and p. 29, Fig. 9. Only the staff of the

For the Trullos ladle see Xanthudides, E. object that she holds is visible. It may well

A-PX-, 1909, P- 179 seqq. Cf. below, p. 625, have been the Sacred Double Axe. Fig. 462. 4 See Vol. II.

For a further demonstration of the view I published this signet in my Mycenaean that the Cave of I'sychro represents the Lyktian Tree and Pillar-Cult, p. 72 seqq. (. H. S.,

Aikratbv avrpov I must refer to my forthcoming xxi, p. 170 seqq.). Second Volume of Serif ta Minoa.

THE PALACE OF MINOS, ETC.

Mother

Goddess

Young

Warrior

God.

trees with triply divided leaves like those of fig-trees. Descending in front of the obelisk is what appears to be a young male God holding out the shaft of a weapon, and with his tresses flying out on either side l in the manner in which motion through the air is usually indicated in Minoan art. In front of him is a taller figure, who may be identified with the Minoan Mother Goddess, with hands raised in an attitude, for which so many early Babylonian analogies exist, of prayer or incantation, and expressive of the means by which she is bringing down the warrior youth, whether her paramour or her actual son, in front of his sacred pillar. She stands on a stone terrace and behind her are rocks and vegetation indicative of a mountainous locality. Through the portal of the sanctuary itself is seen a lower pillar of dual

A Minoan Beth-el.

FIG. 115. GOLD SIGNET RING FROM KNOSSOS, SHOWING SCENE OF BAETYLIC WORSHIP (LATE MINOAN). (f) formation set up within the enclosure, which, in view of Cypriote analogies, may be recognized as the female baetylic pillar, or at least one in which the female element preponderated.

We have here a unique illustration of the primitive baetylic cult of Crete, in which the aniconic image serves as the actual habitation of the divinity and into which, or upon or beside which, he may at any time be brought down by appropriate ritual. The obelisk in fact is literally God's house, as in the case of the Beth-el set up by Jacob. In a small terra-cotta shrine found in the Palace belonging to the M. M. II Period we see this spiritual possession indicated by the doves perched on the capitals of the columns, or in other cases they descend on the human figure itself.

l In my original account, Myc. Tree and Pillar Ionian Shamash, I had erroneously interpreted Cult, p. 74, owing to the analogy of the Baby- these as rays shooting out from the shoulders.

MM. I: PEAK SANCTUARY: THE TOMB OF ZEUS 161

A later age seems to have regarded these baetylic pillars as actual tombs of divinities. Thus the sanctuary of Paphos was said to have contained the Grave of Aphrodite and of her young male favourite, Kinyras. So, too, in the holy grove of Amathus was pointed out the tomb of Apollo, as, at Amyklae, that of his beloved Hyakinthos. In this connexion we have constantly to bear in mind the essential fact that the primitive Cretan religion must itself be regarded as an offshoot of that of a wide Anatolian region. The steatopygous images that occur already in the Cretan Neolithic strata 1 fit on to an Oriental series, and in their later developments are to be clearly identified with a Mother Goddess 2 whose cult, under many names and adopted by many peoples, extends far beyond the Euphrates. But, side by side with the Great Mother, there also recurs throughout all this vast area

Baetylic
Pillar regarded as Tomb
Divinity.
Wide range of cult of Mother Goddess and
Youthful Satellite.

FIG. 116. MOURNING SCENK FOR DIVINE YOUTHFUL HERO ON GOLD SICNET RING (LATE MINOAN, MYCENAE) (J).

a youthful satellite, variously regarded as the consort, son, or paramour of the Goddess, mortal though ever resurgent, and there is every probability the Cretan Zeus, the Child of Rhea, who represents this element in the later tradition in the island, may be traced back to its earliest religious stratum.

One of the functions of the Great Mother, the Mater dolorosa of antiquity, The is to mourn her ever young but ever mortal consort, and it requires no great stretch of imagination to recognize such a scene of lamentation on " a another gold signet (Fig. 11(5). 3 Here we see a figure of the Goddess or her attendant, bowed down, in a mourning attitude, over a kind of miniature temenos, within which stands a small baetylic pillar with a diminutive Minoan shield, seen in profile, hanging beside it. 4 To the right of this a similar figure, perhaps the Goddess repeated, is about to receive refection 1 See above, p. 46, Fig. 12. Myc. Tree and Pillar-Cult, pp. 79, 80.

2 See above, p. 51. For the festoon between the pillars see below, p. 494.

THE PALACE OF MINOS, ETC.

Tombstone of young God: the
Cretan Zeus.
Obelisk on
Knossian Signet anticipation of later Tomb of Zens.
Cave Sanctuaries: Psychro.

from the fruit of a tree, which springs from another representation of a small hypaethral sanctuary containing a similar baetylic pillar, its boughs being pulled down for her by a youthful male attendant. 1 Here there can be little doubt that the mourning scene refers to a Minoan equivalent for Attis or Kinyras, Adonis or Thammuz, but imaged here as a youthful warrior God, in other words the Cretan Zeus.

The baetylic pillar is, in fact, here regarded actually as the grave-stone. It is clear, indeed, that the ideas of the aniconic image and the sepulchral monument must have had a natural tendency to coalesce the tombstone itself in primitive belief being the actual tenement of the departed spirit. In the case of the obelisk on the signet from the site of Knossos we may venture to recognize a baetylic monument of the early religion that actually existed in the neighbourhood of the Palace, and which, renewed perhaps at a later date, survived in later tradition as the Tomb of Zeus'. The mountainous locality in which the scene is placed supplies an additional warrant for identifying the site with the peak sanctuary of Juktas.

It would seem that two distinct phases in the character of the cult are here traceable. It is only in the later stage that we see a formal shrine and habitation erected for the divinity, supplemented doubtless by an aniconic pillar form. There are, indeed, some traces of earlier walls, perhaps belonging to a more primitive enclosure, but the comparatively wide distribution of the sacral ash stratum on the rock surface, which extends South and East beyond the later house of the Goddess, may be taken to point to a more direct form of nature worship. It looks as if, according to the earlier religious practice, the rocky peak itself, which stood forth as representative of the sanctity of the whole mountain, was the primary object of the cult, and received the offerings directly, as the indwelling place of the Godhead. Here the summit was chosen as the object of cult; in other cases it might be a rock shelter like that of Petsofa or Zakro, while there can be no doubt of the prevailing veneration in which caves were held, representing as they did a visible access to the under-world and often provided with natural Bethels' in the shape of their stalagmitic pillars.

It is evident that the votive cult of the cave sanctuaries of Crete also assumed a special importance from this Period onwards, and in these cases the offerings were often of greater intrinsic value. It is probable that a certain proportion of the bronze figures and votive weapons 2 found 1 On a parallel representation from a gold symbolic of the dead warrior, signet ring found in the Vapheio tomb (see op. " e. g. Hogarth, The Dictaean Cave(B. S. A., tit., p. 78, Fig. 52) a smaller mourning figure is vi), p. 110, Fig. 42 (dagger-blades in the upper seen to right prostrate on a large Minoan shield, and lower row).

M. M. I: PEAK SANCTUARY: THE TOMB OF ZEUS 163 in the great cave at Psychro (here identified with the Diklaion Antron of Lyktian tradition) is of Middle Minoan date, as unquestionably some of the pottery, 1 though a much larger proportion is Late Minoan.

Of well-defined M. M. I date was much of the pottery deposited Kamares. in the Cave of Kamares 2 which opens, some 6,000 feet up, on the Southern steep of Ida, above Phaestos. Here in fact was found the series of Votive vases that first brought into notice the polychrome class of Minoan Kamares. ware and thus gave it the name, till lately in general use, of Kamares pottery. The greater knowledge now acquired, however, of the varying Kamarcs 1 phases of this polychrome style and the proofs of its co-existence with other ceramic types bearing monochrome designs, have made it increasingly difficult to employ the term Kamares' with sufficient precision.

The Cave of Kamares, which overlooks the Akropolis of Phaestos, was Sacred evidently the sacred cave of its inhabitants. That of Knossos itself is Knossos: probably to be sought on the limestone plateau of Skoteino, about three skoteino: hours' journey East of the Palace site and approached by an upland route. p OS j ni, This cavern, which is on a far vaster scale than the others mentioned and scale-gives the whole locality the appropriate name of the Dark, yawns beneath the brink of a rugged hollow of the plateau. The rock face above and around the cavern mouth is deeply stained through natural agencies with bands and patches of black and orange red, curiously suggestive of Middle Minoan polychromy. Within, it opens into a spacious vault with broken stalagmitic columns, recalling on a colossal scale a ruined temple. Galleries wind above and descend to depths beyond, and the torch-written inscriptions that they bear show that the cave was visited by early Venetian travellers as one of the marvels of Crete. The peasants of the Minoan neighbouring village of the same name have reported the discovery here at s t "a m different times of bronze figures, doubtless of the usual votive class, nor " was the usual Cretan legend wanting of a golden boy with diamond eyes. cave. In the course of a very summary exploration, rendered difficult by the masses of ddbris and great blocks fallen from above, it was possible to establish the fact that the cave contains an abundance of Middle Minoan sherds, going back to the beginning of the Palace Period. The general character of the remains, in fact, as at Kamares, was earlier than that of Psychro. Its thorough excavation, in any case a considerable undertaking, might throw new light on the early votive cult of Knossos.

1 Op. fit., p. 101, Fig. 27. in 1913 by the British School at Athens, under - The exploration of tliis cave was completed Mr. 1)awkins's direction.

n irotratsaki fit iajmVTHa M 2

Beginnings of M. Af. I phase precede foundation of Palace; Earlier Centres of Culture in E. Crete; Great advance in Arts and Crafts at Knossos at close of E. M, III.; Evidences of a local predecessor of Palace; Series of early M. M. I deposits beneath Palace floors; Deposit under Room of Stone Vats; Us varied contents clay sealings with hieroglyphs of Class A, egg-shell ware, advanced lapidaries' work, faience and inlays; Fore-arm of figurine analogies with later Temple Repositories; Abiding sanctity of area; Other contemporary deposits belonging to M. AI. a; Votive clay 'sheep-bells; Growing poly chromy, on pottery, shown in M. M. 7b; Early geometric patterns; Influence of stone vases on ceramic polychromy; Barbotine ornament; Moulded and naturalistic decoration; Animal figures; Flowers and Foliage; Shells; Deposit beneath W. Court; Rhy tons' in form of bulls, wifh acrobats; Burial jars and chests.

Begin- IT will be seen from what has been already said that the foundation of M. M. I the Palace of Knossos, as we know it, does not correspond in date with the Period beginning of the First Middle Minoan Period as here fixed. It is an precedes fpunda- important symptom of a new order of things, but not the beginning of that Palace. new order. Converging lines of evidence, to which attention has been already called, point, indeed, to the conclusion that there was already in existence at this epoch a local predecessor of the Great Palace.

It is clear that a new style, representative of the First Middle Minoan Period, was attaining maturity by the time when the new building was constructed. The sherds extracted from the original wall foundations and immediately beneath them, and the latest found in the filling of the great hypogaeum beneath the South Porch, all represent what on many grounds must be regarded as the first phase of this new style. For the ordinary ware, the characteristic light on dark decoration of the last Early Minoan Period has already given place to a revival of the dark on light. This dark brown on pale buff technique is, in fact, a survival of the style in vogue in the Second Early Minoan Period, and which at Knossos, to judge from the E. M. Ill house-floors, was never really set aside. On the other hand, the light on dark method, though also well represented on the house-floors in question, was never so popular here as it was throughout. the Easl end of the island, where indeed its use may have somewhat overlapped the beginning of the Middle Minoan Age.

Earlier The variety of curvilinear patterns on this East Cretan class of light

Minoan on c ar k decoration, the superior fineness of the mottled ware of Vasiliki.

and, still more, the exquisite work of the jewellers and lapidaries of Mochlos, culture in lend colour to the view that in the Early Minoan Age the chief seats of the indigenous arts and crafts should be largely sought in Eastern Crete. But already in E. M. II I the ivory seals of the Central district show a considerable Great artistic development. At Knossos, moreover, side by side with the some- f n Arts 6 what plain light on dark ware, with its simple geometrical patterns, we see and, . r?.-. Crafts at ceramic art advancing on quite new lines from the beginning of the present Knossos Period. This advance is further marked by the appearance of elaborate J; j OS mosaic work, by lapidaries craft applied to crystalline stones, by the fabric of vessels of egg-shell fineness, and by the increasing use of ceramic polychromy, incipient traces of which we have already noted on the latest class of E. M. Ill vases. To this must be added the first appearance of the conventionalized hieroglyphic script in its earliest form (Class A).

All these new departures in ceramic and other arts are illustrated by the remains representing the latest cultural stratum that underlies the early constructions of the Palace as we know it.

It has been already noted with regard to the spacious hypogaeum or Evi-entrance vault discovered beneath the later Palace enceinte, that it clearly stands in relation to some earlier building of the kind, which probably P r e-owed its removal to the planing away of the original hill-top in order to supply O f Palace the emplacement of palatial constructions on a larger scale. That, already by the beginning of the Middle Minoan Age, an earlier residence of Minoan Priest-Kings had crowned the hill of Knossos is made further probable by the discovery of a rich and varied deposit of this date beneath the existing Palace floor and on the borders of what was in later times the Central Palace shrine.

This discovery was made beneath the pavement at the entrance of the Hre-early Magazine that opens immediately North of the East Pillar Room (see Deposit

Plan, Fig. 121) known as the Room of the Stone Vats, from the cavities,, u perhaps for wooden receptacles, seen in its side slabs. This slabbing itself of Stone goes back to the earliest period of the existing Palace, and was laid direct on the Neolithic clay, an upper stratum of which had been levelled away for the new constructions throughout this part of the building.

The deposit itself occurred in a small pit going down about a metre deeper into the Neolithic layer than the pavement level. Limited as it is in extent, it gives a very comprehensive insight into the culture that existed at Knossos in the epoch that immediately preceded the laying out of the existing Palace. 1 1 For a detailed account of many of the Report, 1903 (H. S. A., ix), pp 94-8, and cf. objects found in this Deposit see Knossos, Figs. 65, 66.

PALACE OF MINOS, ETC.

Transitional E. M.1II-M. M. I pottery in Vat Room Deposit: Cycladic pyxides'.

The pottery here brought to light presents certain archaic aspects, and it is possible, indeed, that it contains some objects that fit in best with the latest phase of E. M. III. Typologically at least, the pyxides', or lidded clay boxes, remains of which were here found, Fig. 118 b, belong to a class which was in vogue in the Cyclades in the Period corresponding with the last Early Minoan. The incised and punctuated decoration seen on these specimens in some cases as Fig. 118 b, 3 show a chalky inlay, which in Crete had already died out in sub-Neolithic times. Similar types are

FIG. 117. M. M. la JUGS WITH BUTTERFLY PATTERNS, a, b, KNOSSOS, c, MATT PAINT IMITATION, DRACHMANI, PHOKIS.

characteristic of a whole group of pottery belonging to this Third Early Cycladic class. In the case of certain pyxides', as in that of certain idols of Parian marble found in Crete, we must recognize, as already pointed out, 1 Jugs with actual imports from the Central Aegean. When we turn to the other pattern fabrics in this deposit an exceptional effect is produced by the pots covered with a thick hand-burnished wash of a dark reddish-brown colour, on which are displayed hatched medallions and butterfly patterns in the new clear white (see Fig. 118 a, i, 2). On the other hand, a series of short-beaked liutter- jugs found here with dark brown decoration on a pale buff slip are among the most abundant of the earlier M. M. I products (Fig. 118 a, 3, 5, 9, 21, and Fig. 117, a, 6, though the tradition both of their colouring and of the butterfly or double axe patterns that they often exhibit goes far back into the Early Minoan Age. This type of jug has a special interest, since a more globular imitation in matt paint with similar butterflies' 1 See above, p. 115, Fig. 83.

fly Decoration of Jugs.

PALACE OF MINOS, ETC.

Early M. M. I pottery from Vat Room Deposit.

Eggshell Yare.

(Fig. 117, c) was found in a contemporary deposit near Drachmani in Phokis in company with Minyan and Helladic ware. 1 Though itself, probably, of Cycladic fabric, it is interesting as showing the indirect influence at this time of Minoan ceramic types on those of Mainland Greece.

The group of vessels from the Vat Room Deposit, shown in Fig. 118 a, will be found to supply a very good type series for the initial ceramic phase of the M. M. I Period. The paring of the surface of the cups, a procedure taken over from the preceding Age, is well illustrated by this group. It was sometimes, as is seen in 20, repeated in a series of diagonal strokes. The open bowl 18 shows a series of curved furrows, probably produced by the thumb while the vessel was slowly revolved on a disk; 12 is the top of a lamp, covered with a thick red wash slightly burnished. Its pedestal was missing, but it belongs to a class that attained a considerable vogue in Middle Minoan times. Certain plain, red-faced jars, 4, 19 and 6,-n, the former with an envelope-like sign incised, are of special importance as supplying the direct forerunners of the two principal types of jar found in the neighbouring Temple Repositories, belonging to the last Middle Minoan Period. This will be seen to be only one of a series of comparisons that bring out the curious parallelism between the two deposits.

Among the more exquisite fabrics from this deposit are several that already represent in its full development the egg-shell ware in which the polychrome masterpieces of the early phase of M. M. II were to be afterwards executed. Among these are some very fine band-handled cups (Fig. 118 a, 8 and Fig. 120) with narrow streaks of the new white on a dark glaze slip. Altogether characteristic of the new polychromy, moreover, were the remains of pedestalled cups, of which a specimen is given in Fig. 118 a, 7 and Fig. 120, with four white and two scarlet bands ascending spirally from the stem. Here, the deep Indian red that appears already in E. M. Ill is superseded by a much more brilliant vermilion pigment. Of great interest, too, is a miniature form of tumbler (Fig. 110, a) found here and in a contemporary pre- Palace deposit beneath 1 G Soteriades,.

FIG. 119. a, MOTTLED EGG-SHELL WARE TUMBLER; b, CRYSTAL CORE; c, d, FRAGMENTS or CLAY SEALINGS: FROM VAT ROOM DEPOSIT.

1908, p. 87, Fig. I3, and Aev. es Etudes Grees xxv 11 p. 259, Fig. 6. and cf. Wa ce and Thompson, xxv (191, p,-, h. Tiessay, p. 204, Fig.,40.

M. M. I: CERAMIC PHASH. s the flour of the First Magazine. 1 The surface of these shows a survival of the red and black mottled technique of the preceding Age, but the tenuity of fabric, already noted in some of its wares, is here even surpassed, at least as regards the average thickness of the walls, which does not exceed a single millimetre.

The Minoan egg-shell ware, of which such brilliant polychrome examples are forthcoming during the early part of the succeeding M. M. II Period,

Fie. 120. OBJKCTS IN VARIOUS MATKRIAI. S i ROM VAT ROOM DEPOSIT (M. M. I).

had in fact already attained its tie plus ultra of fineness at Knossos by the very opening of the Middle Minoan Age. In sympathy with this, moreover, as is shown by the remains of a vase of marble-like material which also occurred in the Vat Room Deposit (Fig. 120), a similar tenuity of fabric was 1 Knossos, Report, 1901 (B. S. A., vii), p. 48. native formaore was quite unable to piece These tumblers' were found in a much broken them together, condition and so thin were their walls that our

PALACE OF MINOS, ETC.

Relics found in Vat Room Deposit.

Crystal Core.

Faience Beads and Inlays.

Shell Mosaic: perhaps Draughtboard.

Forearm of Figurine.

Vat Room Deposit derived also now achieved in lapidary work. As will be seen below, from the characteristic forms of certain egg-shell vessels, a main inspiration of this fabric may have been the imitation of metal-work. But, as will be demonstrated in a later Section of this work, 1 in the succeeding Middle Minoan epoch, imported ostrich eggs actually formed the body of a type of libation vases, which by the early part of M. M. II were imitated in clay and supplied the prototype of a long line of Minoan rhytons'.

A great variety of objects were found in the Vat Room Deposit in addition to the pottery (see Fig. 120). Among these was an obsidian block, containing nests of crystals, and several flakes of that material, pieces of gold plating, thicker than the mere foil found with later remains, and of copper (much oxidized) on which the gold had probably, in part at least, been overlaid. Amongst stone vessels were remains of a cup and of a bridge-spouted bowl of coarse alabaster, part of a finely-made cup of dark grey limestone with white horizontal veins, and the fragments of the marble-like vessel already referred to, the marvellously thin fabric of which resembled egg shell. A tapering cylinder, of thimble-like shape, cut out of rock crystal (Fig. 119, b, which also occurred, was apparently a core produced by boring, and, as in other similar cases, broken off by the lapidary in the process of hollowing out a vessel of that material. There was also a great variety of beads in the native faience, some very minute, some bugles, and others globular with a large perforation (see Fig. 120). The small beads were of a deep cobalt blue, but the larger presented the pale green tone of the Sixth Dynasty Egyptian tradition. Remains also occurred of inlays of the same faience and of very fine texture, but most of the plaques that here came to light were of white shell. As roughly indicated by the arrangement in Fig. 120 the larger plaques seem to have surrounded medallions with quatrefoils that may have been filled with some other substance. They possibly belonged to a draught-board, a fore-runner of the magnificent example described below. There were also curving pieces from some foliate design.

Of special significance was the discovery in this Deposit of the forearm of a small figurine (Fig. 120). It was apparently of moulded material, 2 which seems to have been some kind of vitreous paste with a pale surface, and the arm may well have belonged to a predecessor of the Snake Goddess.

From this discovery and the choice character of many of the relics found in the Deposit we are justified in concluding that we have here part of the contents of a Treasury belonging to the sanctuary of a building that 1 See Vol. II.

: The fore part ot this is truncated a curious way as if there had been some kind of articulation.

M. M. I: CERAMIC PI I ASKS had preceded the existing Palace on this spot. The associated jars, as already pointed out, illustrate an earlier stage of those found so abundantly in the later Temple Repositories, and the occurrence here of remains of inscribed clay sealings of the hieroglyphic class A (see Fig. 119, f, (f) afford another significant parallel. 1 It is, moreover, of great interest that these relics of an earlier shrine should have been brought to light in the area actually adjoining the chamber where the later Temple Repositories were dis-

OlERCYlnC

TEMPLE

EP05ITORIF5

DEPOSIT Of SEALS WITH GODPE55 5MRikt froniki-li-quary of Earlier Palace.

H iero- glyphic Sealings.

Abiding Sanctity of this Region.

FIG. 121. PART OK PLAN OK WKST QUARTER OK PALACE SHOWING POSITION OF VAT ROOM DEPOSIT.

covered 2 (see Fig. 121). We may reasonably conclude that the special sanctity that clung to this part of the site throughout the whole course of the Palace history was inherited from an earlier building. This special sanctity in fact survived into the Late Minoan Palace, after an epoch of ruin and destruction, the smaller and more superficial cists here found (Fig. 1 21), preserving the tradition of the earlier Temple Repositories, then covered in.

1 Unfortunately these were very fragmentary, border of a circular seal impression here found

A broad arrow sign characteristic of the hiero- as well as another piece with grain-like objects glyphic class A was however discernible on one were also typical of the sealings of the epoch. (-co Fig. 119,), and a part of the ladder 5 See below, p. 463.

Contem- Remains altogether parallel with the Vat Room Deposit and, like it, porary.

Deposits representing the cultural stage of the earlier occupants oi the site, in the fof epoch immediately preceding the foundation of the Palace, came to light at v. Maga-various other points. The construction of the Second West Magazine had shaved off the top of a tall jar l decorated in the early polychrome style on which a yellow pigment already appears. It contained, together with a small high spouted vase with brown on buff geometrical decoration, a clay brazier and banded cups of early M. M. I style, a core and flakes of obsidian and a piece of pumice-stone, another evidence of contemporary connexion with

Melos. A contemporary jar, likewise cut off at the rim, was found in a similar way resting on an earlier level beneath the floor of the First

Magazine, 2 and within this, together with other smaller vessels, occurred remains of a series of exquisitely thin mottled ware tumblers, like Fig. 119, a, which absolutely equate the group with the Vat Room Deposit. Both the above deposits were contained in small pits excavated in the superficial

Neolithic stratum on which the floors of the later Magazines were laid. They were both practically equidistant about i- metres from the line of the later West wall, and it is possible, therefore, that Magazines of an earlier building may have here preceded those of the existing structure.

Contents A more copious supply of contemporary vessels was obtained from the

House y floor of a house that seems to have been levelled away at the time of the floor. construction of the West Court of the Palace. 3 Specimens of the pottery from this floor are shown in Fig. 122, including the jug, Fig. 122, i, and Fig. 123, a, which may be taken as the best example of M. M. I polychromy in its earliest phase. Here, outlined in deep Indian red or madder borders, which perpetuate the earlier tradition, are seen double-axe-like figures, with their interior dotted clear white on a black ground and their edges involved in the curves of a bright orange-red band. The pedestalled bowl, No. 12, with brown on buff decoration, presents a form of very old inheritance and finds Cycladic parallels.

Stratum same early M. M. I ceramic phase which may conveniently be of Base-defined as M. M. I a belongs the pottery from the earliest stratum found in

Mono- the basement of the Monolithic Pillars, 4 together with the clove vase. 5 The

Pillars. ee K nossos Report, 1900 (. S. A., vi), pp. 16-18. Fora coloured reproduction of the p. 21. The jar was found i-50 m. from the polychrome jug see ib, Pl. I. In the adjoining

West end of the Magazine. area North was the M. M. I b deposit, pp. 186- 2 1-65 m. from the West end of themagazine. 188 below.

See Knossos, Report, 1907 (B. S. A., vii), p. 48. Fig. 100, p. 145, above. Specimens of the 3 It lay on the North side of the Court about pottery from this deposit are given by Macken-6m. West of the small altar base. For the zie, H. S., xxvi (1906), Plates VII and IX. deposit see Knossos, Report, 1905 (B. S. A., xi), Fig. 107, p. 146, above.

M. M. I: CERAMIC PHASES latter vessel affords another good example of the early polychrome style, and with it were found many sherds of the same class, mostly with simple geometrical decoration, white, orange, and vermilion on the black glaze

FIG. 122. M. M. I VASES FROM FLOOR OF HOUSK UNDER LATER WEST COURT, KNOSSOS.

ground, occasionally, however, on a pale buff or deep red glaze wash. At times, too, the triangular spaces left by the patterns are covered with white dots like those within the axe-like figures on the polychrome jug, Fig. 123, a. Here, too, occurred the fragment with ibex heads and a beetle, reproduced

PALACE OF MINOS, ETC.

M. M. I: CERAMIC PHASES in Fig. lIW below, 1 as an illustration of the beginnings of naturalism in ceramic design. The plainer cups and small vessels from this deposit show an absolute correspondence with those from the pit beneath the floor of the Room of the Stone Vats. In the same context must be placed a large hoard of pottery from an early well- found in the small area immediately west of the Court of the Stone Spout, and which descended to a depth of 22 metres (82 feet). Here were found specimens of cups with their surface raised in irregular ridges, illustrated below in connexion with the characteristic barbotine or prickly ware that conies in at this epoch. Here, too, occurred numerous specimens of a class of clay objects very characteristic of M. M. I deposits (Fig. 124). They were known to our workmen as 'sheep-bells', to which, indeed, they presented much resemblance. They have a loop handle at top, and on either side a horn-like projection, while their upper part is also provided with two small perforations through which a string may have been drawn for the suspension of a clapper. It seems probable that they were, in fact, votive bells, 3 to be hung up in shrines or on the boughs of sacred trees, where they would be tinkled by the breeze, as were later the bronze bells at Dodona and elsewhere.

FIG. 124. VOTIVE CI. AV SHEEI–BKI. L, M. M. I

VKI. I., Kxossos ( ).

With these other parallel finds may also be grouped the pottery from an early M. M. I house floor, found in the North quarter of the Minoan town of Knossos. 4 All these deposits bear the stamp of absolute contemporaneity. They all present a certain archaic aspect as compared with the succeeding phase of Middle Minoan ware, and it is to be noted that in the case of the simpler vessels there is a greater tendency towards the old dark on light style. The occurrence of this well-marked stratum throughout the whole Knossian site may certainly be regarded as the result of a widespread local destruction, possibly even a methodical demolition, which immediately preceded the construction of the Palace as now known to us.

In this early group of deposits we have already noted the incipient Incipient appearance of ceramic polychromy, which in the later phase of M. M. I and p the succeeding M. M. II Period was to attain such prominence. Some chromy.

1 See p. 183. this theory does not explain the perforations.

Sec Mackenzie, The Pottery of KHOSSOS, Not unfrequently they are double, and in one

J. H. 5., xxiii (1903), p. 167, Fig. i. case a bull's head appears between the bells'.

3 Dr. Hatzidakis, TYAio-o-os MmovKif, p. 229, 1 See too, Mackenzie, Middle Minoan Pottery has suggested that they were votive robes, but of Knossos, J. H. S., xxvi (1906). PI. X.

PALACE OF MINOS, ETC.

examples of this, as applied to the glaze technique, have already been assigned to the closing phase of E. M. III. To about the end of the earlier M. M. I class may be assigned the vessel from Gournia, Fig. 133,-, 1-4- INCISED AND PUNCTUATED WARE WITH WHITE FILLING.

5-8 POLYCHROME IMITATIONS (M. M. I.)

FIG. 125. INCISED AND INLAID GEOMETRICAL PATTERNS COMPARED WITH EARLY POLYCHROME (- (.).

with its geometrically arranged red and white foliage, and Fig. 123, b, representing the base of a fruit stand, a common type of this Period.

In a sense, as we have seen, polychrome decoration goes back in Crete to the days of the punctuated and incised Neolithic ware, the inlaying material of which was occasionally, though rarely, a ferruginous red as well as a chalky white. As has been shown above, this inlaid decoration had died out before the beginning of the Early Minoan Age, and the objects of this class, such as the pyxis' lid, Fig. 1183, 3, above, and the further specimens from the Vat Room Deposit, Fig. 125, 2 and 3, seem to have been due to influences coming from other Aegean regions where the older style had survived.

It is nevertheless a signi- influence ficant fact that on some of the; f e o arly examnlesof the polychrome style metric 3. Patterns in vase painting, which must, on M. M. I from the typological point of ' ome view at least, be regarded as Pottery. early in the series, it is associated with the chevrons, punctuated vandyking, and chequer-

FIG. 126. BIRDS NEST TYPE OF BRECCIA: patterns representing the old M. M. I (MOCHLOS) (H-). Neolithic tradition. This is clearly brought out in Fig. 125 where No. i represents the pure Neolithic style and 2 and 3 specimens from the Vat Room Deposit of early M. M. I date, while Nos. 5 to 9 are fragments of M. M. I vessels with similar designs in bright red, orange, and white on a black glaze ground.

The problems raised by these correspondences are difficult to solve. Central Aegean influences, such as are illustrated by the pyxides, can hardly suffice to explain the phenomena with which we have to deal. It seems possible that the Neolithic geometric style accompanied by incipient polychromy on a dark ground had maintained itself on some class of domestic utensils in perishable materials, such as skins, gourds, or vessels of wood, and that in this way the intermediate links have been lost.

Apart from this, there can be little doubt that a main impulse at work influence in the striking development of polychrome designs on pottery that charac- vesseit terizes the present Period is to be found in the brilliant and variegated on Po v- r chrome materials of the stone vases already in vogue in the preceding Early Decora-Minoan Era. Although, in the course of the Middle Minoan Age, the use of these variegated materials for stone vessels was to a great extent superseded by dark steatite and coarse alabaster, brilliant specimens of stone vessels, especially of the bird's-nest type, were still in vogue at the beginning of the present Period. Fig. 126 gives an example of a bird s-nest vase of red and white veined breccia with a dark ground, from a M. M. I Breccia.

1 Nos.? and 6 are from the early M. M. I Cf. . H. S., xxvi, Pl. VII, 3, 4; B. S.-., xix, stratum of the Monolithic Basement at Knossos. Pl. V, i.

interment at Mochlos. 1 In Fig. 127, a from Knossos is shown the cover of a similar vase cut out of the same stone. Examples given in this Figure, clearly demonstrate that the decoration on some of the polychrome vessels of this and the succeeding M. M. II Period is due to the attempt to imitate the natural combinations on such stone vessels. The bizarre IM. of LIPARITE M. M. II

BRECCIA COVER I

POLYCHROME IMITATION t.

LIPARITE (EGYPTIAN FORM OF VESSEL

POLYCHROME IMITATION OF CONGLOMERATE M. M. II.

POLYCHROME IMITATION M. M. I.

FIG. 127. CERAMIC IMITATIONS OF STONE VASES (BRECCIA, CON-GLOMERATE, AND LIPARITE) (j c.

red veining of Fig. 127,, c, d, is taken from some such breccia models as that shown for comparison. The white border which accompanies the veins of the breccia constantly recurs on the pottery and will be Liparite. found to have a long ceramic history. So, too, bowls of imported liparite with a highly carinated contour, a fragment of one of which is shown in Fig. 127, e, z explain both the contour and white-spotted decoration on 1 Seager, Mochlos, p. 38, Tomb III a (Fig. 46 and Pl. IX).

2 From Knossos. In the Candia Museum.

For the origin of this form of stone vessels from Egyptian prototypes see above, p. 85 seqq. and Fig. 55.

M. M. I: CERAMIC PHASES a plain black ground of a class of M. M. vessels of which many fragments Conglo-have come to light (Fig. 127,). 1 On the other hand, the cup (g) repro- merate-duces the round variegated pebbles of some fine form of conglomerate.

A typical product of this time is the barbotine or prickle decoration. Bar. Simple examples of this occur in the M. M. I a deposits, but it attained its botine highest development in the latter part of this Period and the early part of tion. the next. The introduction of the quick potter's wheel, however, later on in M. M. I I seems to have been rapidly fatal to it. This decoration was produced by roughening the walls of the vessel. These are sometimes worked up into a thorny surface resembling that of certain forms of crustacean, like a common Mediterranean crab or the shell of a sea urchin, and such natural objects doubtless supplied suggestions for it. Numerous specimens of this ware were found in the ossuary cells annexed to the primitive tho-los at Hagia Triada (Fig. 129, 6, c, d). The jug, Fig. 128, from a house South of the Palace site at Knossos, 2 is a good specimen of the advanced M. M. I b class, and reproduces the two small side handles which form one of its characteristic features, together with I the finely toothed lips. The clay is coarse and yellow, and the glaze on the body of the vase a dull brown-black. The barbotine work is here washed with a creamy white, and the laced pattern within its intervals combines reddish brown, vermilion, and white colouring-. Double festoons in white are suspended from the This specimen is probably of M. M. II For a coloured illustration of this jug see date. Both the form and decoration survived Hogarth and Welch, J. H. S., xxi (1901),

FIG. 128. POLYCHROME VASE WITH BARUOTINE DECORATION, KNOS-SOS (M. M. I b) (J c.).

to M. M. III.

r8o THE PALACE OF MINOS, ETC.

bright red band round the middle of the pot, an interesting anticipation of a form of decoration frequent in Late Minoan times. This vessel derives a special chronological importance from the close parallelism that it presents with a jug, exhibiting similar barbotine and painted decoration, including the festoons, found at Phaestos 1 on the floor of a small house, in company with polychrome cups of the most typical M. M. I b class, and parallel with those from the floor deposit beneath the West Court illustrated below. 2 Sometimes the surface is raised into sharp ridges or thorn-like bosses, and on cups of this Period from Knossos an exaggerated effect is occasionally produced resembling rock-work (Fig. 129, a). 3. This barbotine decoration as combined with advanced polychromy seems to have attained its greatest development about the close of this Period and beginning of M. M. II, and typical examples are given below in Coloured Plate I. 4 Somewhat later, an exquisite development of it is seen in bowls like Suppl. Pl. Ill, a with red bosses resembling the thorns of a rose-bush.

Bowls An interesting class of bowls now appears, chiefly represented by finds Miniature from Palaikastro, but of which fragmentary examples have been found inctVV- at Knossos and elsewhere, showing various small figures and miniature sels: vessels modelled in their interior. In Fig. 130, a and c we see single figures, in the first case of a flying dove on a slender pedestal, 5 in the second of an ox. 6 In b the whole of the interior is covered with miniature

Oxen, c. oxen, rank behind rank, to the number of nearly 200, with the figure of a herdsman, upright in the centre." Numerous Egyptian parallels are to be found for these bowls with animal figures. Sometimes the whole inner surface is covered with small vases such as cups and funnel-shaped vessels resembling miniature examples found in the Sanctuary of Petsofa (see

Fig. Ill, y, above). There can be no doubt that bowls of this class were made for votive purposes. The usage itself continued into M. M. II. 8

Naturalism is carried still further in some painted designs on the flat. A widely distributed class of spouted jugs presents a succession of swimming 1 Pernier, Man. Ant., xii, Pl. VIII, 6 and Hogarth and Welch,. H. S., xxi, Pl. VII, a, b. p. 20. On the same house floor was found 3 J. H. S., xxiii, p. 167, Fig. i, 5.

a fragment of painted stucco showing white Opposite p. 231.

dots on a black ground, like contemporary 5 From the Bone-enclosure, Palaikastro; ceramic imitations of liparite. This seems to Bosanquet, B. S. A., viii, p. 294.

be the earliest definitely dated example of wall- 6 Dawkins, B, S. A., ix, p. 302, 5 a.

painting other than monochrome. 7 Bosanquet, loc. cit.

2 See p. 187, Figs. 135, 136. Coloured " A fragment of a small M. M. II bowl from illustrations of polychrome cups of the class Knossos shows in the interior miniature vases represented in the floor deposit are given by of this funnel-shaped type.

M. M. I: CERAMIC PHASES IMC;. 129. M. M. I b VESSELS WITH ROCK-WORK (a, KNOSSOS) AND BARBOTINE DECORATION (li, c, d, HAGIA TRI-ADA) (:).

FIG. 130. M. M. I Bowus CONTAINING SMALL FIGURES, PALAIKASTRO (Jr.).

THE PALACE OF MINOS, ETC.

Naturalistic Designs on M. M. I Vases: Fish, Heron, Wild Goats, Water-Beetle.

fish (Fig. 131, a). 1 On the interior of the bottom of a bowl from Knossos (Fig. 131,), unfortunately very imperfectly preserved, fish with red markings are seen swimming on its dark glaze ground amidst curved red objects, spotted white, and perhaps representing sponge or coral, as on the later marine frescoes. In the centre of the bowl, which obviously had a votive character, was a miniature raised basin. The lower part of a white fish appears on the outside of the bowl showing that the design was repeated on the exterior. The outside also bears characteristic traces of paring.

FIG. 131. M. M. I PAINTED VESSELS SHOWING SWIMMING FISHES: a, JUG, VASILIKI; , BOWL, KNOSSOS (RESTORED) (f f.).

Flowers

Foliage.

Representations of birds and animals, very exceptional in Minoan art, also now occur. 2 A fragment from Gournia 3 in the early dark on light technique exhibits a long-legged crested bird, apparently a heron (Fig. 132, 6). Another from the earliest stratum of the Monolithic Pillar Room at Knossos 4 (M. M. I a) bears the heads of three Cretan wild goats and, on a larger scale, a water-beetle, very accurately delineated (Fig. 132, a).

We also note a growing tendency, more fully developed in the ensuing Periods, to make a decorative use of flowers and foliage. A very charac- 1 Cf. Seager, Excavs. at Vasiliki (Pein. Trans., vol. ii, Pt. 2).

2 See below, p. 605.

3 Boyd Hawes, Gournia, p. 38, PI. VI, n.

4 See Mackenzie, J. H. S., x. xvi, p. 247.

M. M. I: CERAMIC PHASES

FIG. 133. M. M. I POLYCHROME POTTERY WITH FLOWERS AND FO-LIAGE: n, l, t,, Kxossos e, PALAIKASTRO ( ); c, HAGIA PHOTIA (c.); g, GOURNES; h, VASILIKI (.).

(I);

M. M. I: CERAMIC PHASES teristic feature of the mature early M. M. I a phase of this Period is a succession of palmette-like sprays alternately matt reel and white on the black glaze, well illustrated in Fig. 1315. In c from a Cave burial at Hagia Photia "they are reduced to a geometrical type. On the highly decorative fruit-stand from Palaikastro, e, a similar motive forms part of the petals of quatrefoil flowers. To the succeeding M. M. I b phase must be ascribed the spouted

FIG. 134. M. M. I a POLYCHROME CUPS (AND b f.).

vase ( ) presenting alternate pairs of red and white crocus-flowers arranged Begin-in chains' a motive that survives into the succeeding Period. Natumlis-

The whorl-shell motives that now appear, and of which examples from l ing.

l Nos. a, l, d, f, are from Knossos. The jug, g, is from the votive pit by the ossuary cells at Gournes, N. E. of Knossos (Hatzidakis, A A. i-., 1918, Pl. Ill, 13. See below, p. 198,11.5). h is from Vasiliki (Seager, Trans. Dept. Arch. Univ. Pa., vol. ii, 1907, Pl. XXXII, and p. 125).

For the Palaikastro fruit-stand see B. S. A., ix, p. 308, Fig. 8. On the fragment b, berries, alternately red (only partly visible) and white, appear on stalks.

THE PALACE OF MINOS, ETC.

Whorl-shell Motive.

Typical M. M. la Decoration.

Chronological Landmark.

Deposit on House-floor beneath W. Court.

Palaikastro are given in Fig. 134, a, b, 1 are later on absorbed in the general scheme of spiraliform decoration. The pedestalled cup (Fig. 134, c) from the same site shows a more elaborate design than the early polychrome example, Fig. 118 a, 7 above, from the pre-Palace deposit beneath the Vat Room floor, but, like the other specimens given in Fig. 134, it should still probably be referred to the mature stage of the earlier M. M. I a class. As in the case of the E. M. II mottled cups, Fig. 46, D, E, above, its base is hollowed out like the kick of a bottle. With this are placed two polychrome vessels from Vasiliki which have a special chronological value. One of these is a cup, Fig. 134, d, with orange and white decoration on a dark ground, the zigzagging pattern on the upper border of which presents a decided parallelism with that which runs round the interior of the bowl of the Palaikastro fruit-stand (Fig. 133, e). The other (e) shows vermilion and white patterns on the black glaze, including repetitions of the swastika symbol, which is frequent on contemporary pottery from this site. These two vessels are from House B at Vasiliki which, as Mr. Seager has shown, 2 belongs to an earlier epoch than House A. Its ceramic contents are equated with those of a series of M. M. I a deposits, including the most advanced types from the Vat Room at Knossos, the fruit stand (Fig. 133, e) and the Cups, 134, a, 6, c, from Palaikastro and the Gournes vessels (cf. Fig. 133,), and what is of the greatest consequence, the latest pottery from the smaller tholos at Platanos which was associated with the Babylonian cylinder, dated above to c. 2100 B. C.

The jar with the flower chains on the other hand was found in House A of Vasiliki the pottery of which defines the most advanced stage of M. M. I b.

At Knossos, the foundation of the Great Palace, as we know it, supplies the dividing line between the earlier and later phases of the M. M. I style. As, however, in the Palace itself, the course of existence was continuous, and the pavements remained at the same level till well on in M. M. II, and in the West Quarter even to M. M. Ill, floor deposits representing pottery of this later M. M. I class have not come to light there. For much we have therefore to depend on the evidence of scattered sherds, but the floor of a small house brought to light a metre and a half beneath the later West-Court pavement 3 has done much to supply the lacuna in certain lines.

Dawkins, B. S. A., ix, p. 305, Fig. 4. i, 2. p. 14. This chamber was immediately con- 2 Report of Excavations at Vasiliki (Penn. tiguous on its S. side to that containing the Trans., vol. ii, Pt. 2), PI. XXXI, Figs, i, 2, M. M. I a deposit shown in Fig. 122, p. 173 and p. 128. above. The pottery here found was at first 3 See Knossos, Keport, 1904 (B. S. A., x) called M. M. II.

FIG. 135. FLOOR OF CHAMBER BELOW WEST COURT, SHOWING M. M. I b POTTERY.

FIG. 136. M. M. I b POLYCHROME WARE FROM CHAMBER BELOW WEST COURT.

THE PALACE OF MINOS, ETC.

A sketch of this floor and its contents, in the state in which they were uncovered, is given in Fig. 135, and a selection of some of the vessels

FIG. 137. RHYTONS IN FORM OF BULLS WITH ACROBATIC FIGURES: MF. SSARA (i.).

in Fig. 136. These include cups and bowls belonging to the more advanced polychrome class of this Period (M. M. I 6). Among them k shows a breccia veining, but the carinated contour and lustrous glaze in this and 1 See Knossos, Report, 1905, p. 14, Fig. 8, and p. 16. The sketch is by Mr. H. Bagge.

other cases reflect originals in metal-work. In this connexion p and o afford good examples of the egg-shell ware of this epoch, illustrating its combination with polychrome decoration on a black-glazed ground which was to attain such perfection in the succeeding Period. The three-handled hand-burnished jar n has very archaic relationships, and the pan 66 is interesting as showing the parallel striations on its base produced by cutting it off by means of a string from the disk, on which it had been shaped. 1 The clay object aa with brown striped decoration on a light ground is important as showing the survival of the votive sheep-bell type so frequent in M. M. I a.

During the later ceramic phase of M. M. I we see the dark glaze ground becoming finer in character, and both the barbotine and polychrome decoration often combined attain a more subtle development. Very good specimens of this style occurred in the cist-like annexes of the ossuary tholoi at M. M. I b Hagia Triada 2 and elsewhere, and in the Kamares Cave. 3 Among the finest chrome examples may be cited the jug from a house South of the Palace site at st x le-Knossos illustrated in Fig. 128 above. 4 Some of the characteristic hole-mouthed bridge-spouted jugs of this later M. M. I phase are wheel-made.

Ritual libation vessels resembling the classical rhytons' now for the Bull's first time appear in the shape of bulls, with a large aperture in the upper part of the neck and a smaller orifice in the lips for pouring out the contents. These vessels are the predecessors of a more varied Minoan class in which only the head of an animal is represented. Of still greater Rhytons interest is the appearance of a type of similar vessels showing small figures of men clinging to the bull's horns or engaged in what seem to be acrobatic per- with, formances over his head (Fig. 137). s It cannot be doubted that we Figures, have in these an allusion to the sports of the bull-ring so prominent 1 The importance of these parallel striations pp. 38-40), who was unaware of Mr. Dawkins' was first noticed by Dawkins (Extavs. at observations made fourteen years previously.

Palaikastro, B. S. A., ix (1903), pp. 301-3). Paribeni, Man. Ant., xiv, PI. 42, 2, 3, and 4,

Mr. Dawkins there suggests that the clay was and above, Fig. 129, b. c, d.

separated from the slow wheel by means of a 3 Dawkins, B. S. A., xix, Plates IV (below), 'straight cutting instrument. The use of VI, VII; and p. 16, Fig. 3.

string for this purpose seems, however, to be For a coloured illustration of this jug, see better reconciliable with the appearance of Hogarth and Welch, J. H. S., xxi (1901), these striations. From the latter part of PI. VI i.

M. M. II the striations are curved and more or From the ossuary tholoi discovered by less concentric (cf. Dawkins, J. H. S., xxiii Dr. Xanthudides at Kumasa and Porti in (I 9 3) P- 2 49 Fg- 2. and see p. 590, Messara. It is owing to the special courtesy

Fig. 434, b, below), and point to the cutting off of of the finder that I am able to reproduce these the vessel from the clay left on the wheel when vessels here. Fig. 137rf(p. 190) is from Mosso, in rapid motion. See too Franchet (of. at,, Scavi di Creta, p. 184, Fig. 95.

THE PALACE OF MINOS, ETC.

Minoan

Circus

Sports.

in the Late Minoan Age. These sports, in which girls as well as youths were trained to take part, and of which the tales of the Minotaur and the Athenian children may be in part a later echo, were clearly of a very acrobatic kind. They are essentially circus performances, to be distinguished from the feats of Minoan cowboys in grappling wild bulls. Perilous they must undoubtedly have been, but they were far removed from the mere exposure

Hittite Parallel.

FIG. 137 d. HEAD OF BULL RHYTON GRAPPLED BY MEN (f).

of captives to wild bulls, such as we see depicted on a Pre-dynastic Egyptian palette. It has already been noticed: that these Knossian sports find an apparent parallel on a Cappadocian cylinder dating from about 2400 B. c., and therefore probably distinctly earlier than the beginning of the M. M. I Period. That these performances should appear in connexion with a type of vessel the ritual destination of which is undoubted z is itself a highly suggestive circumstance. The later circus-shows of the same kind, as seen in the wall-paintings, also seem to have had religious associations, and to have been held in honour of the Great Minoan Goddess.

1 See above, p. 15, note 3.

2 See Section in Vol. II dealing with Minoan rhytons'.

8. M. M. I: (D) METAL-WORK, SEALS, AND FOREIGN RELATIONS.

Silver vessels and clay imitations; Kant liar os type points to Trojan source; Influence of Early Troadic silver trade; Clay imitations of bronze amphoras; Bronze iveapons and implements; Hieroglyphic Script, Class A; Seals and sealings; Hemi-cylinder of Ivory with Betrothal Scene; Babylonian cylinder from Platanos; Ishtar the Interceder and Syrian Adad; Chronological indications supplied by discovery; Imitation and adaptation of Early Twelfth Dynasty Scarab types; Appearance of Hip-popotamus Goddess later source of beneficent Minoan Genii; Decorative seal types of Egyptian derivation; Influence of Egyptian ceiling patterns; Conclusions as to chronological limits of M. M. I.

OWING to the defective character of the sepulchral evidence, objects in metal-work, especially in the precious metals, are as yet but sparsely forthcoming. Silver vessels already appear in the latter part of the E. M. Age Silver as well as in the contemporary Cycladic deposits. Although, however, types of vessels in precious metals have not come to light in the Middle Minoan Palaces at Knossos and Phaestos, the reflection of such metallic originals is seen in a whole series of ceramic forms belonging to M. M. I and II. Happily, both an original silver vase and elegant imitative types in painted clay were found in a House Tomb ossuary of this Period at Gournia influence Fig. 139, a, b, c). 1 The M. M. I b deposit beneath the West Court at or Knossos was specially rich in such imitative forms showing carinated out- types lines and a lustrous metallic glaze. The thinness of the walls is also characteristic and the egg-shell ware itself seems to have been due to the desire to rival the fineness of metal-work.

The special interest of this silver kantharos type lies in the derivative relation in which it stands to still earlier Trojan forms that themselves go back to the simple two-handled horn (see Fig. 138). This connexion makes it probable that the appearance of these types in Crete was itself a result of 1 Boyd Hawes, Gournia, Pl. C, Figs. I and 3, and cf. 2. Cf. Seager, Excavations at Iasiiik't, 1906, Pl. XXXI, 2. 8 See above, p. 187, Fig. 136-

FIG. 138. TWO-HANDLED HORNS (, c, d, e) AND KANTHAROS TYPE TROY II. V (i).

FIG. 139. SILVER VASE (a) AND CERAMIC IMITATIONS OF METAL FORMS (l, c, d).

a, , f, GOURNIA, d, PSEIRA

M. M. I: METAL-WORK, SEALS, FOREIGN RELATIONS 193 the Troadic silver trade. The great wealth of the Hissarlik site in silver Diffusion vessels and the silver bars found there are explained by the fact that the Types" neighbouring ranges were rich in argentiferous ore and that many remains! jl om. of ancient surface mining occur. 1 That this commerce affected the ceramic Source-types both of the Aegean world and of Mainland Greece through many channels is shown at a somewhat later date by the diffusion of the Minyan class of ware.

The common use of silver plate in the island at this epoch is also well illustrated by a large painted clay bowl from Pseira (Fig. 139,), 2 with three handles, which reproduces the features of the silver prototype even to the rivet-studs and the alternating sheen and shade of the metallic original. As already observed, it is to the existence of these ceramic copies that we owe the best evidence of the wealth of the Minoan lords in precious metals in the palmy days of the Middle Minoan Age.

The imitation of Egyptian copper vessels imitation had, as we have seen, already begun in the vessels Second Period of the Early Minoan Age, and in the next Period indigenous types of the kind were also reproduced. On the floors of House A at Vasiliki, in company with pottery of the M. M. I b class, Mr. Seager discovered a peculiar class of fine ware the surface of which presented an iridescent effect and in which we may recognize a local Minoan attempt to imitate a metallic sheen. Here was found the two-handled amphora, Fig. 140, 3 with slightly pinched-in mouth, which is clearly a very direct imitation of a copper original, the effect, indeed, enhanced by its iridescent surface, is so successful that at first glance it might easily be mistaken for a vessel of bronze. This copper amphora type, or, rather, a simpler stage of it, has left its impress in a coarser form on a common type of plain M. M. I

Flg. 140. Cl. AY IMITATION OF

COPPER AMPHORA, M. M. I b, VASIUKI, CRETE.

1 See especially Prof. W. Gowland, F. R. S., Archaeologia, 2nd ser., xix, 1920, pp. 138-41. Professor Gowland calls attention to the considerable deposits of argentiferous galena in the mountain districts N. E. of Mt. Ida and in the Olympus range. Some of the ancient workings have been re-opened, notably the mine of 1 i

Balia, at the present time the most important in Asia Minor for lead and silver.

! R. B. Seager, Excavations in the Island of Pseira (Univ. Pennsylvania Trans. Ill), p. 20,

Fig- 5-

R. B. Seager, Excavations at Vasilikt in 1906 (Ib. II),. pp. 125, 126.

THE PALACE OF MINOS, ETC.

jars. 1 The common M. M. Ill amphoras with their mouths slightly pinchec as in Fig. 403, c, also belong to the same tradition. Among the Mainland Minyan forms of Piperis, 2 moreover, contemporary with the Cretan M. M. I phase, we find imitations of a similar amphora type.

Some satisfactory materials as to the forms of M. M. I bronze implements were forthcoming from an exterior compartment of the early house

FIG. 141. BRONZE WEAPONS AND IMPLEMENTS FROM CHAMAEZI (M. M. I) (f c.).

M. M. I at Chamaezi, adjoining that containing the figurines, and which must fm "e- certainly be referred to this Period. 3 Among the implements and weapons ments found here (Fig. 141) was a long chisel, a, a spearhead or dagger with a long Weapons, perforated flat tang, b, two double axes of somewhat square cut, and an adze-axe, c. Again, from the annexe of the smaller ossuary tholos' at 1 e. g. certain clay amphoraforms of the Vat Room Deposit (cf. Fig. 118 a, 4 and 19). These represent a simpler stage with a more or less round mouth. They are also earlier in date than Fig. 140.

- V. G. Childe, On the date and origin of Minyan Ware (J. H. S., xxxv, p. 197, Fig. i, and p. 203), who notes that the amphorae are not the least Trojan in form. The metal prototype may therefore have come from Crete.

Dr. Xanthudides (E. Apx-, 1906, p. 120 seqq.) at first regarded them as of later date, though he admitted the early associations of the spear or dagger with the flat perforated tang. The Mochlos finds show that the double axe itself goes back to the

E. M. II Period. There is evidence, moreover, that the adze-axe (dfira-inov) is also already associated with E. M. II remains. Fig. 142, a, and the broad-tanged dagger, l, show a certain parallelism with Trojan forms belonging to the third stratum of the Second City.

M. M. I: METAL-WORK, SEALS, FOREIGN RELATIONS 195

Hagia Triada 1 were obtained a series of bronze daggers (Fig. 142) among which the tanged types with the slightly flanged square shoulders are of exceptional interest as the direct progenitors of the square-shouldered swords, and their horned successors belonging to the early part of the Late Minoan and Mycenaean Age. These weapons were found together with fine polychrome vases, ranging from late M. M. I to about the middle of M. M. II. It seems probable therefore that the flanged type, being the more advanced, should be referred to M. M. II a.

It appears from Professor Mosso's analysis 2 of some daggers of types similar to the above that they in some cases contained over 9 per cent, of

Dagger Prototypes (M. M. I) of Later Minoan Hronie Swords.

Tin Alloy inm. M. I Daggers.

FIG. 142 a-d, BRONZE DAGGERS FROM ANNEXE OF SMALLER THOLOS AT HAGIA

TRIADA (M. M. I) (-.).

tin. On the other hand, an analysis made by him of part of a blade found with Kamares Vases' from the first Palace at Phaestos showed 89-5 copper and 3-146 tin.

It is characteristic of this Period and of the progress in methodical Hiero-organization that, in place of the more or less advanced pictography already scnpt C of attained by the close of the preceding Age we are now confronted with class A-a regular hieroglyphic system of writing. Class A of this, in which the signs are still of a somewhat rude and archaic form, is the special product of M. M. I. The materials are chiefly found on steatite bead-seals, of the same three- or four-sided shape as those presenting the antecedent class of picto- 1 R. Paribeni, Man. Ant., xiv, PI. 44, Figs. p. 718, Fig. 541, a, b, below. 6-1 1, cf. pp. 704, 705. Compare the remark-! Lt origini delta civilta able engraved dagger-blade from Lasethi, p. 234 seqq.

mediterranea

THE PALACE OF MINOS, ETC.

graphic signs, but somewhat elongated (Fig. 143). 1 Some seal impressions are also known, including Fig. 144, found together with the dove vase, Fig. 107 above, 2 and other early M. M. I types on the original floor of the early Pillar Basement to the South-East of the Palace site at Knossos. 3 The fragments from the Vat-Room deposit belong to the same class. These are of special synchronistic value since they show that this advance in the Art of Writing had been already achieved before the foundation of the Palace as we know it.

Continued use of Ivory Seals.

Hemi-Cylinders.

bed FIG. 143. FACES OF THREE-SIDED STEATITE BEAD-SEALS SHOWING HIEROGLYPHS OF CLASS A. (f)

FIG. 144. CLAY SF. ALING WITH SIGN-GROUP OF CLASS A. EARLY PILLAR BASEMENT, KNOSSOS. (f)

The Early Minoan usage of ivory seals still continued in vogue during the early part, at least, of the present Period. Among forms now found the hemi-cylincler is of special interest as fitting on. like the E. M. Ill button-seals', to a characteristic Egypto-Libyan class of the Sixth to Tenth Dynasty Period. The specimen Fig. 145 belongs in style to the latest stage of sphragistic art represented in the tholos ossuaries. It is moreover noteworthy as presenting a nude male figure with a dagger at his waist, corre- 1 Scripta Minoa,. (a) p. j 49) p. x a See p. 145, Fig. 106. (6) p. 150, P. 5 a; (c, if), ib., P. 6, a, It, Scripta Minoa, i, p.

See p. 146. Knossos 229, from near

M. M. I: METAL-WORK, SEALS, FOREIGN RELATIONS 197 spending in type with the Petsofa figures of early M. M. I date. Facing this figure, on the convex side of the half-cylinder, is that apparently of his bride, with long flowing tresses, flounced from the shoulders downwards, while below is a dog and four beaked ewers of metallic aspect such as occur in groups on some of the most primitive of the hieroglyphic prism seals. On the flat side is an archer followed by a dog, shooting an arrow at an ibex in a wooded country, indicated by a tree.

The girl's dress here is simpler than the usual Babylonian garb as worn by the Goddess Ishtar, for in that case the upper part is folded over like that of the Greek chiton. It is, however, of great interest as being foreign to any known example of Minoan female attire. Was it perhaps a special bridal robe? The maiden herself is depicted as grasping the man's hand as if the pair were plighting their troth. The dress shows a certain analogy with the flounced garments such as appear towards the close of the Middle Minoan Age, but these are merely skirts, extending from the waist downwards. On the other hand, there is no resemblance between this dress and the gowns with bell-shaped skirts and which leave the bosom bare, such as are repeated in the case of the figurines of Petsofa and other contemporary deposits. The flounces in this case, falling from the shoulders, certainly suggest a Syrian influence. The characteristic Minoan flounced skirt that makes its appearance later on may itself have owed its evolution to the same suggestion.

That direct Oriental influence was now at work is made evident by a new and remarkable discovery. In his recent excavation of a smaller ossuary at Platanos near Gortyna, Dr. Xanthudides brought to light a Babylonian haematite cylinder of fine workmanship. The design on this cylinder, which through his courtesy I am able to reproduce in Fig. 146,

Betrothal scene: a hint of Syrian influence on dress.

FIG. 145. IVORV HALF CYLINDER (FOUND IN THE VICINITY OF KNOSSOS).

Babylonian Cylinder from Platanos.

THE PALACE OF MINOS, ETC.

Mother Goddess, Ishtar, the inter-ceder.

The Amo-rite God.

Chronological conclu- is of special importance, since its place in Babylonian art is now fairly ascertained. The female figure dressed in the cawac s, consisting of zones of striped folds, is Ishtar, as the equivalent of the Sumerian Mother Goddess Innini, and who first appears in this praying attitude in the Dynasty of Ur (c. 2474-2357).

1 She mediates for humanity with all the Gods, 2 and is found on seals interceding to various deities on behalf of their owners. But the male divinity, here saluted by the Goddess, is of later introduction on the seals. This God with the short garment reaching to the knees, who holds a mace to his side, is entirely foreign to Sumer and Akkad, and, though sporadically of somewhat earlier intrusion, first becomes frequent on seals in the time of Hammurabi.:! He has been identified with the Western Adad of the Palestinian region, closely connected with the Hebrew Jahveh. As Amurru, the Amorite God, he naturally came to the fore under the Amorite First Dynasty of Babylonia, the beginnings of which have been now astronomically fixed at 2225 B. C. 4 The date of Hammurabi's accession has on this basis been fixed at 2123 B. C.

The cylinder itself must be regarded as an early example of its class, and its fresh condition tends to show that it had not been FIG. long in circulation. This evidence which points to a date round about 2000 B. c. throws new chronological light on the First Middle Minoan Period. The cylinder was associated with pottery of the mature M. M. I a class 5 and thus approximately corresponds in date with the foundation of the Knossian Palace. This result gains additional 1 Thureau-Dangin, La Chronologic de la A good example of this God (otherwise 6. BABYLONIAN CYLINDER OF HAEMATITE: PLATANOS.

Dynastic de Larsa (Rev. dassyriologie, xv. i (1918)). Professor Sayce, to whom I owe much information on this subject, prefers c. 2500 B. C. for the beginning of this Dynasty.

"See on this Dr. S. Langdon, Tammuz and Ishtar (Oxford, 1914), pp. no, in, c.

s Hayes Ward, Seal Cylinders of Western Asia, p. 176, observes that it is rare for this figure to appear before the time of Hammurabi, frequent as it is after that period. I do not remember to have seen it on any case tablets of the time of the kings of Ur and of Gudea.

Ramman Martu), adored by Shala, is given, op. fit., p. 77, Fig. 207; cf., too, p. 178 seqq., Figs. 480, 481.

4 Kugler, Sternkunde und Sterndienst in Babel (Miinster, 1912), II. Theil, i. Heft.

5 The pottery was examined for me in the Candia Museum by Dr. Mackenzie. It represents the same mature M. M. I a phase as the vases from the ossuary cells of Gournes (J. Hatzidakis, Apx- Aear., 1918, p. 45 seqq., and PL 3).

M. M. I: METAL-WORK, SEALS. FOREIGN RELATIONS 199 importance from the discovery in the same tholos ossuary at Platanos of Minoan imitations of Egyptian scarab types of an early Twelfth Dynasty class.

In the votive deposit of the Cave of Psychro, answering to the Diktaion Amethyst Antron of the Lyktian tradition, was found an amethyst scarab (Fig. 147) xnth recognized by Egyptologists as a typical Twelfth Dynasty fabric. Amethyst, Dyna, y h Egyptian scarabs of this type generally bear the inscription on a gold plate Cretan applied to their lower surface. In this case, however, the face of the stone g iyp, s. itself has been engraved by a native hand with a group of Minoan Twelfth hieroglyphs, consisting of the solar disk with curved rays between two vases with high spouts. 2 From the fact that this vase-sign belongs to the engraved more archaic class (A), 3 it seems probable that this inscription comes within Minoan at least the lower limits of the present Period, though the engraving of seals p of formed of the crystalline stones does not seem to have been usual in Crete Class A. till the succeeding M. M. II Period. But, as we know from the Vat Room

FIG. 14". TWKI. KTH DYNASTY SCARAD (AMKTHYST) ENGRAVED WITH MINOAN HIEROGLYPHS OF CLASS A. (f)

Deposit, rock crystal had been already successfully attacked for the manufacture of vases at the very beginning of M. M. I, and beads of cornelian and other hard materials date well back into the Early Minoan Age.

Indigenous imitations of Egyptian scarabs in soft stone or ivory Cretan certainly begin before the close of the present Period. Several examples 0 were found in the smaller tholos of Platanos, where the later associated and ivory. pottery is described as M. M. I. Of these the white steatite scarab (Fig. 148) is of special interest, since it unquestionably represents a Minoan Appear-copy of a standing figure of the Hippopotamus Goddess Ta-urt or Thueris Hrtppo-a frequent subject of early scarabs, 4 and who also appears on still earlier j cylinders. 5 She has one hand raised in the adorant attitude, while the other Ta-urt. no doubt in the original scheme rested on the hilt of her characteristic knife- 1 Scripta Minoa, i, Table XII, No. 107. in the scarab impression from Kahun (Petrie, 1 Ib., No. 47 Illahun, Kahun, and Gurob, PI. IX, 39). Op. (it., PI. I, p. 5 b. 5 e. g. Petrie, Scarabs and Cylinders with

A good Twelfth Dynasty example is seen Names, PI. VI, No. 140.

THE PALACE OF MINOS, ETC.

Ta-urt source of later Minoan Genii.

Imitations of Xllth Dynasty scarab types.

like instrument. Behind is an uncertain animal form, and in front spiraliform scrolls.

The appearance already at this epoch of a Minoan version of the Hippopotamus Goddess derives a special interest from the fact that several centuries later, in the early part, that is, of the Late Minoan Age, we recognize the same divinity in a fully assimilated form, taking its place as a beneficent Minoan Genius. The race of Minoan Genii, so well exemplified by a series of later gems, though partially metamorphosed and generally provided with a lion's face and claws, still retains unquestionable evidence of its origin in the figure of Ta-urt and exhibits her characteristic mane. Moreover, as will be shown in a later Section, something of her beneficent nature has entered into the spiritual being of these later Genii, who appear as bearers of the quarries of the chase, waterers of thirst) palms, bringers of rain by means of magically sympathetic libations. It was always difficult to understand how such fully equipped demonic personifications could have sprung suddenly to life. We now see that the Ta-urt type had been already imaged by Minoan artists generations earlier, and had thus been able to root itself in the popular imagination.

Another Minoan scarab, of similar white steatite (Fig. 149) from the same tholos ossuary, is engraved with a spiraliform pattern clearly imitated from a design of a class found on a common type of Twelfth Dynasty scarab, in which case the spiral coils are at times seen to terminate in the talismanic nefer sign, often reduced as on the Cretan example to the stem and loop, without the cross-piece. In other cases such spiraliform scrolls are connected with the ankh or life sign, a reminiscence of which again is to be seen in the circle and T-cross set horizontally in the lower part of the design in Fig.

149. In some characteristic Egyptian scarab types of the Twelfth Dynasty (Fig. 150, a, b decorative scrolls also connect themselves with the waz or sacred papyrus stem. This, again, we see taken over in the Minoan button seal (Fig. 150, e). It will be seen that this sacral symbol

FIG. 148. WHITE STEATITE SCARAB FROM SMALLER THOLOS OF PLA-TANOS WITH FIGURE IMITATED FROM THE EGYPTIAN GODDESS, TA-URT. (f)

FIG 149.

WHITE STEATITE PLATANOS. (f)

M. M. I: METAL-WORK, SEALS, FOREIGN RELATIONS 201 continued to influence Cretan signets to the close of the Middle Minoan Age. 1 The pattern on the Cretan prism-seal f represents a secondary stage of the Egyptian motive, c. On d, on the other hand, the curved canopy of the scarabs attaches itself to the broad arrow of the Minoan hieroglyphic signary.

The waz motive and its Minoan adaptations illustrated by the above Influence seal types have a special interest in connexion with a remarkable piece symbol.

EGYPTIAN SCARABS XIItH DYNASTY

EARLY CRETAN SEAL-STONES FIG. 150. EGYPTIAN SCARAB-TYPES COMPARED WITH THOSE OK MINOAN SEALS.

of painted plaster, illustrated below, 2 which supplies an unique record of the original fresco decoration of the M. M. II Palace.

A clay sealing (Fig. 151),;1 presenting two impressions of what was apparently an ivory signet, found, in a M. M. I association, N. E. of the room of the Stone Drain-head 4 at Knossos, clearly stands in connexion with similar ceiling designs going back to the earliest Period of the Palace. The diagonally connected double coils here seen with their cruciform flowers and terminal palmettes of Egyptian character 5 are enclosed in a border of 1 See below, p. 705, Fig. 528. See Coloured Plate I, k t p. 231.

5 This motive already occurs on the E. M. Ill ivory seals, e. g. p. 118, Fig. 87, 5 above,

See too Knvssos, Report, 1903, p. 23, Fig. 10. and may be an adaptation of the Egyptian 4 Formerly known as the Olive Press'.

Room of the tree sign, which was also used as a decorative motive.

THE PALACE OF MINOS, ETC.

similar coils. This design, indeed, may be taken to indicate that ceiling patterns representing the Orchomenos type in a somewhat more primitive form already existed in what may have been an earlier Palace of M. M. I a date.

Conclu- The sequence in which the present Period stands to the last Early tochrono-Minoan would carry its beginnings well up into the Eleventh Dynasty, or to logical Limits of

FIG. 151. CLAY SEALING FROM M. M. I a DEPOSIT, KNOSSOS. (c. f) c. 2100 B. c. On the other hand, the appearance of the scarab type of seal-stone, particularly of that shown in Fig. 147 above, which is executed in hard stone, points to a time when Twelfth Dynasty influence was already beginning to make itself felt. We may conclude that the mature style of M. M. I a already somewhat overlapped the Twelfth Dynasty of Egypt which begins about 2oco B. C. The latest phase of this Period may extend to about 1900 B. C., shortly after which date, as we shall see, imported M. M. II a pottery begins to appear at Kahun.

LATER
SOUTH-WEST
QUARTER
THE SECOND MIDDLE MINOAN PERIOD 9. M. M. II: (A) CONSOLIDATION OF KNOSSIAN PALACE.

Earlier Palace Plan consolidated; Its Regional arrangement survival of original lusu-lac; Great Cutting on E. slope; Architectural parallels between Knossos and Phaestos; Roman and later Comparisons; Raised Causeways; Ortliostatic Walls; Kaldciim and Mosaiko paving; High Column bases; Use of variegated materials; Early Palace types of Porch; N. W. Portico and Entrance syslem; Lnstral Basin and Initiatory Area; Scene of ptirificatory rites for those entering Building; Early Shrines example at Phaestos; Miniature Tcrra-cotta Shrine front Loom Weight Basement at Knossos; Columns with perched doves sign of Divine Possession; Doves perched on Votaries at Knossos and Mycenae; Portable Seat for Divinity or Priest; Early use of palanquins.

WE have seen that the foundation of the Palace at Knossos dates from a time when the remains of the earlier phase (a) of the M. M. I style was already stratified, or to shortly after 2000 B. C., the elate of the beginning of the XI Ith Dynasty of Egypt. By the close of M. M. I 5the Knossian Palace as we M. M. I know it seems to have been already laid out, including its enceinte and en- p ces" 1 trances and the general disposition of its several quarters round the Central Court. But, though from the beginning we have to deal with a unitary plan, Aggrega-the component parts at first largely existed as separate blocks or islands, which, L,"," as is best shown in the annexed diagrammatic Plan, Fig. 152, 1 are clearly traceable through all later changes and have greatly facilitated its methodical description. The Corridors may originally have often been open gangways between these insulae, some of which, like the N. W. Bailey, had a separate Regional circumvallation. The N. E. quarter, indeed, had a gypsum fa9ade, running t nge " from W. to E., 2 and the curving corner of the fasade oi the W f. Central block has been already described. 3 The S. E. Insula is equally well delimited.

Very early in the Palace history, however, a process of organic fusion set in. The early Keep, itself originally a conspicuous island, was absorbed by supplementary M. 11 constructions and its original lines over- Unifying ridden. It is best to place this final consolidation of the building early in; n M. M. its Second Middle Minoan phase.

The system thus evolved seems to have conformed in most of its main lines with that which persisted into Late Minoan times. There were, however, some noteworthy modifications. The existing West Porch is a M. M. Ill construction. The three first Magazines of the old arrangement 1 Executed in accordance with my system 2 See below, p. 364, Fig. 264. by Mr. Theodore Fyfe, F. R. I. B. A. See above, p. 139 and Fig. 102.

(A, 13, c on Plan) were later abolished. The facade of the West Wing on a section of the Central Court was slightly moved forward, and the whole Throne Room system is the work of the latest Palace epoch.

When ve come to the Domestic Quarter on the East slope of the hill we shall see that, though its exterior wall-lines, the position of its Grand Staircase, and its drainage system persisted, the M. M. II arrangement of its interior seems to have been largely superseded. 1 It would seem that the succession of narrow terraces, rendered necessary by the steep slope of the hill on the East side, was soon found to be incompatible with the more grandiose ideas of the Minoan builders. They wanted a broader platform for their constructions, and to secure this a great rectangular Cutting was made into the Neolithic strata on this side. Within this the lower halls of the Domestic Quarter and the deep basements

Great adjoining them to the North were now built. An original upper fa9ade-line E U siope. n f gyp sum which abuts on the South light-area of the Queen's Megaron, was cut short at that point by this excavation, and the whole of this upper terrace-line was removed between that point and the S. E. angle of the basement at present known as the Room of the Stone Drain-heads. The continuation of the foundations of this old inner wall-line appears, however, beneath the East wall of that room. Beyond this, again, the line took a slight bend East, and at this point by the N. E. Portico described below part of the original gypsum fa9ade again emerges into view. An early doorway communicating with the Portico is also visible.

There is every reason to believe that the supporting walls of the great Cutting, together with the South wall of the South light-area of the Queen's Megaron and the massive interior wall that follows the course of the lower East-West Corridor, as well as its continuation North towards the Court of the Stone Spout, belong to the early part of this epoch. The walling of the South light-area of the Queen's Megaron, incised with large examples of

M. M. II the branch sign, supplies a typical specimen of contemporary light-area masonry (Fig. 153). 2 Between the courses is a clay bedding, about a centi-

Feauires metre thick, an early feature, and above is a flat parapet, which recurs in TWO in a similar terrace-wall E. of the Northern Entrance.

It-will be seen that the great Cutting is divided into a broader section, in which were laid out the principal halls of the Domestic Quarter, and a narrower zone including a rectangular M. M. II structure with deep basements, in which, as will be shown, most valuable relics of this Period were 1 M. M. II door-jambs, for instance, appear 2 The stepping back of the wall above beneath the S. wall of the Lair. ensures a better incidence of light.

FIG. 153. WALL OF S. LIGHT-AREA OF QUEENS MEGARON, KNOSSOS; M. M. II a.

discovered. This block formed part of a separate enclosure, the E. Central Enclave of the Plan. It was of massive build, and eventually supplied the substructure for the East end of what seems to have been a great Palace hall above.

The flat strip bordering this Enclave on the East was occupied during the greater part of this Period by a series of Magazines containing large pithoi of the knobbed class and standing in connexion with the still existing group a little North. Early, apparently, in the succeeding Period, however, this arrangement gave way to a finer system. A Northern branch of the Lower East-West Corridor that now comes into existence was made to follow the outer wall-line of the Enclave above described, to a fine rectangular chamber, opening on the Court of the Stone Spout. Both this chamber and the Court overlie M. M. II pithoi.

Both at Knossos and at Phaestos certain main features in the arrangements at once strike the eye. 1

Careful In both Palaces we see a more or less rectangular structure of vast extent that of Knossos covering, with its Courts, over six acres the whole grouped Palace round an oblong paved area. The lines in both cases are at right angles to one another, and the whole design divides itself into zones and rectangular units. Both buildings, moreove-r, were carefully oriented, the major axis in either case running from North to South. With this, too, in the better preserved Roman plan of Knossos, corresponded the main lines of access by which the Central italic l f Court was approached through the Sea Gate and Northern Entrance Passage parisons n one direction, and by the South Porch in the other 2 an arrangement anticipating the cardo of the Roman Castrum. To a certain extent, moreover, we have the equivalent of the decumanus maior. About the middle of the Central Court, both on its Western and its Eastern side, opened two main gangways. That to the West takes indeed a tortuous passage to the Western Entrance. But that to the East, by which access was obtained to the Grand Staircase, led through it, by the East-West Corridor beyond, to what seems to have been the Water-Gate of the Palace, 3 above the Kaeratos stream.

1 See too my observations, Bird's-Eye View on the West. Pernier, Rendiconti dei Lined, xvi of the Palace of Knossos, Journ. R. I. B. A., 1902, (1907), p. 261 and Fig. A; cf. Noack, Ovalhaits, pp. 104, 105. c., p. 8, and see below p. 214, Fig. 160 and

Pernier, Rapporto preliminare, c., Man. note 2.

Ant. fxii, 1902, p. 59, suggested that the prin- 3 Remains of structures seen on the slope cipal entrance to the Phaestos Palace was on here South-East of the Light-Area of the Hall of the South Side. This part of the area, how- the Double Axes, seem to have belonged to ever, had been denuded away. A later dis- a bastion with stepped descent resembling the covery showed an entrance on a lower level to East Bastion farther North on this side. S. W., with a columnar portico analogous to that In the middle of the Northern boundary of the Central Court at Phaestos is seen the opening of the Northern Avenue of approach on that side. 1 Opposite this was, originally, its main entrance passage.

Too much must not be made of the Roman parallels, or those of the still Keserva-earlier folk of the Terremare, that may suggest themselves in these geometrical arrangements. Certain divergences in the Italic schemes are at once perceptible, as for instance, in the position of the Praetorium and in the exclusion of the Forum, as at Pompeii, Timgad, or Silchester, from the crossing-lines of traffic. 2 In the root conception of the Cretan Palaces we have rather to do with a natural method of laying out new foundations and settlements, Parallels independently adopted in many countries and in very different ages. Four partite"" quarters grouped round a central square was essentially the plan followed 1lan-by Frederick Stupor Mundi and our Edward I in their new civic foundations from the Sicilian Terranova to Winchelsea and Flint.

The individual insulae here grouped round the Central Court may in some cases have originally represented separate house plans. Of this we see clear traces in the S. E. Insula and in the later Throne Room system.

In both Palaces the early features of the West Court and its confines show remarkable points of agreement. The platform to the North at corre-Phaestos, approached by a raised causeway and broad lines of steps d,! " in (Suppl. PL II), answers on a larger scale to the later Theatral Area at Plans at the head of the ancient road of approach to the Knossian Palace, mainly used, a nd perhaps, for ceremonial receptions. 3

Both at Knossos and Phaestos there were found, on the borders of Walled these outer Courts and areas, beneath the Late Minoan pavements, circular pj ts. walled pits containing quantities of potsherds, fragments of movable hearths of clay and stucco, and other broken objects. These walled pits, which date back to the earliest days of the Palaces, seem to have been 1 See Man. Ant., xiv, Pis. XXVII, XXXI, 2. had been already explored outside its North 3 See the late Professor Haverfield's sum-wall at this point) was found to contain pottery, mary of the evidence in Ancient Town-planning the last elements of which were M. M. II.

(Oxford, 1913). I that at Phaestos, as in the undisturbed 3 In its present form the construction of the part of the walled pit to the North-West of the

Theatral Area at Knossos seems to be L. M. I, Theatral Area at Knossos, the latest sherds were but there was an earlier paved construction of the M. M. II Period. In the round walled below it. A terminus a quo for the date of the pit known to the natives as kouloura- paved square in front was obtained by a test beneath the later pavement of the West Court excavation carried out in 1913 beneath the of Knossos, the last elements were M. M. III.

floor of its North-West angle. The seg- It seems probable that these receptacles were ment of a circular walled pit (part of which cleared out at intervals.

THE PALACE OF MINOS, ETC.

FIG. 154. SECTION OF OUTER AND INNER WALL-LINE OF SOUTH FRONT OF PALACE AT Kxosso,

SHOWING TO RIGHT P. XRT OF REMAINS OF CENTRAL GYPSUM PAVING OF VERANDAH.

specially constructed for the reception of rubbish, and throw an interesting sidelight on the methodical measures taken for the maintenance of cleanliness and order.

The West Court of both Palaces is traversed by the raised causeways,

M. M. II: CONSOLIDATION OF KNOSSIAN PALACE 209 just referred to (Suppl. Pis. I, II), which, in the Southward direction, led Raised Causeways.

towards an entrance porch supported by a central column (see below, Figs. 158, 150).

A further point of correspondence is supplied by the fact that the lower course of the wall that flanks the West Court in both cases is constructed of the same upright or orthostatic blocks, at Knossos of gypsum, at Phaestos of limestone showing traces of a coating of red coloured plaster. The later line of the West wall at Knossos (Figs. 95 and 90) l with its gypsum orthostats appears, from the analysis of the sherds found within it, to have been built at the close of M. M. I or the very beginning of M. M. II.

The outer wall-lines of the Southern front at Knossos, which are themselves an early element of the Palace, present some peculiar features. There was here a decided slope, and, West of the Southern Entrance Porch. I?. ol J 1 ble

Wall-line which, as we have seen, overlay the still earlier Hypogaeum was a double of s. line of exterior walling (see Fig. 154). The outermost line, showing the usual orthostatic arrangement of gypsum blocks on a limestone plinth, rose at a lower level and thus served as a massive terrace wall for what appears to have been an open verandah between it and the inner wall-line, along the centre of which ran a causeway of gypsum paving. The inner wall-line, of the same construction as the other, was itself guarded by the high outer terrace wall, and it was found convenient to have narrow openings in it for access to a series of magazines. This double line of walling, with the remains of the central line of pavement between, is shown in Fig. 154.

A massive timber framework was from the first associated with the good masonry of the Middle Minoan Age, an inheritance from the Early Minoan biuldings.-of which the remains at Vasiliki supply the best example. 2 In place, Stone however, of the wooden doorposts supported on gypsum bases, so generally in jambs, use in the ensuing Age, the earlier builders often cut ledges and reveals for the framework of the door in superposed limestone or gypsum blocks such as will be seen in the door-jambs of the Long Corridor of the W. Magazines (Suppl. PI. XI). These jambs, many of them incised with the double axe mark, are of the same date as the neighbouring fa9ade and the gypsum pillars of the two crypts. 3

A characteristic early feature at Knossos was the paving of both Courts and interior spaces with thick limestone slabs of uneven shape and the under side of which was often very irregular. From a certain resemblance to the 1 Many M. M. I sherds occurred, but no For the distribution of the double axe sign M. M. II. in this Sanctuary Quarter see below, p. 449,

See above, p. 71. Fig- 322.

THE PALACE OF MINOS, ETC.

Kalde-rim Paving.

paved Turkish roads, this class of pavement became known to the Cretan workmen as kalderim. It occurred below the M. M. Ill level at many points throughout the East Quarter, and M. M. II store jars were found resting upon it in the East Magazines and the Room of the Knobbed Pitlios'.

FIG. 155. REMAINS OF MOSAIKO PAVEMENT BELOW LATER GYPSUM SLABBING.

QUEENS MEGARON, KNOSSOS.

Traces at times were found of the painted plaster that filled the interstices.

The result of test excavations made in 1913 at various points in the Queen's Megaron and Bath Room and in the adjoining light-wells was to show that at about thirty-five centimetres beneath the later floor level 1 there had existed, throughout a large part of that area, a paved kalderim of this class. Intermediate, moreover, between this and the gypsum slabbing 1 In the Bath Room the depth was somewhat greater, c. 50 cm. of the later floor, a pure and overlying M. M. 1 1 deposit 1 4 cm. thick, was found a finer polygonal pavement of a new type (Fig. 155), which seems to have come in about the close of this Period. This class of pavement consisted of smooth polygonal slabs of iron-stained limestone locally known as almond-stone or duvysaxotTtrpa, and so closely grained as almost to resemble the texture of a lithographic block. Its interstices were filled with white or red plaster, and the brilliant effect of this veined polygonal arrangement led our Mosaiko' Cretan workmen to describe it as mosaiko. Good examples of it recurred in the Magazine of the Medallion Pithoi, described below, and much fragmentary remains of this class of pavement came to light in the North-West Portico (Fig. 161 and Suppl. Pl. IX). The interval between this and the kalderim (14 cm.) was occupied by a pure M. M. II deposit.

From the last phase of the M. M. Ill Period, (6), onwards, gypsum or Varie-plain limestone was almost exclusively employed for the bases of columns, Materials which were themselves reduced to a very slight elevation, often rising only fcolumn 3 Hases in 5 cm. above the pavement level. In the earlier Periods, however, there was Early a much greater use of coloured materials such as variegated breccia and conglomerate, veined marble and limestone, serpentine, or porphyry the materials employed often recalling those of the early stone vases.

These polychrome column bases of the Early Palace were decidedly Higher higher than the later class. One at Phaestos, of black limestone with y " quartzite veins, was as much as half a metre in height as compared with p l x-a diameter of 70 cm. 2 Others belonging to the original building on that site Column approach these dimensions, 3 and an example of variegated limestone still existing in situ in the North-West Portico at Knossos which apparently goes back in its original form to M. M. II is of the same high shape, though its upper surface has been somewhat broken away (see Fig. 161, and Suppl. Pl. IX). The foundation slab of another column base is seen in a line with it, and bordering these are the remains of a polygonal Mosaiko' pavement.

The use of such comparatively high column bases of variegated materials Survival survived both at Knossos and at Phaestos into the earlier phase of M. M. III. nto sf Two bases of this class were found in the area of the Spiral Fresco', the 1 See pp. 320, 321, Figs. 233, 234. diminutive peristyle.

2 Those, for instance, abutting on the great A column base of the earlier Palace at light-well at Phaestos, above the Early Maga- Phaestos is seen in situ on a higher level, zines. The South-Eastern House at Knossos, a little East of the old West Portico, worked the original features of which may belong to into the later pavement of Corridor 7 Its the M. M. Ill Period, shows good examples of diameter is 83 cm., and the material is deep rich variegated bases on a small scale in its red with crystalline veins.

THE PALACE OF MINOS, ETC.

Re-used Examples.

early M. M. Ill date of which is well ascertained (Fig. 156). It has been suggested below that though probably of earlier origin these were immediately derived from a M. M. Ill a East Hall. Their top diameter was 58 cm. and their height 34 cm., and they were cut out of the black breccia with orange red and white veins from the quarries of the Kakon Oros, the promontory that overlooks the site of the sea-town of Knossos on the East. Another column base identical in its material and original dimensions came to light in situ on the stylobate of the neighbouring North-East Portico' or Loggia, ascribed below to the same epoch 1 (Fig. 2(58 and Suppl. Pl. VIII). It is noteworthy, however, that in this case a ledge is visible on its upper

FIG. 156. EARLY COLUMN BASE OF BRECCIA FROM SPIRAL FRESCO AREA.

FIG. 157. COLUMN BASE OF LEDGED TYPE FROM E. BORDER OF EAST PORTICO.

circumference, showing that it had been readapted to fit a somewhat smaller wooden shaft than that for which it had been originally designed.

It is not improbable that all three of these bases may, as in other cases, have been taken over from an earlier Palace construction, since we know that the Spiral Fresco area was occupied by an important M. M. II Sanctuary.

A specimen has been placed here in Fig. 156, as in any case representing an

Disuse of Early Palace type. The great hardness of the material explains the tendency, c. noteworthy also at Phaestos, 2 to re-use such bases. When, however, in the

Base at c osni g M. M. Ill phase and the Late Minoan Age the effect produced by

Close of painted stucco imitation was thought adequate for decorative materials, such M. M. III.

1 See p. 370.

1 A series of broken or recut column bases irom the earlier Palace are seen at Phaestos by the Central Court.

hard stone column bases were completely discarded in favour of the easily worked limestone and gypsum.

In connexion with the partial survival of such variegated column bases t m-into M. M. Ill, it is of interest to note that at Mycenae, the original Minoan column elements of which seem to go back to the penultimate epoch of M. M. Ill, the fashion of breccia column bases was still in vogue. The nearest approach Early to this material, the local conglomerate, was used for the great bases still 0 fmy-visible, some in the foundations of the Greek Temple on the Acropolis renae-height, and others on the slope below. 1 But at Mycenae the fashion, thus begun, was persistent both for bases and threshold slabs to the latest days of the Palace.

On the borders 01 the same Palace region at Knossos that contained the breccia column bases of the form shown in Fig. 15j there occurred two specimens of the variant type, Fig. 157, with a somewhat irregular ledge below. They were finely executed in a softer black material with white veins, and the upper part of their circumference above the ledge is brilliantly polished. That sketched in the figure, the larger of the two, occurred in a stratum underlying a M. M. Ill b floor. 2 We have here, perhaps, a somewhat later type that had come into vogue by the beginning of M. M. III. It is possible, indeed, to trace its later evolution in the fine gypsum examples with their lower ledge found in the Room of the Column Bases', and which had clearly belonged to the upper Columnar Hall of the Central Palace Sanctuary on that side. These are referred below 3 to M. M. 111.

The high column bases, above described, formed polychrome feet for Survival the wooden shafts above, and it is interesting to note that, as is shown by "hrome the Knossian frescoes depicting columnar shrines of the Third Middle Feet of Minoan Period 4 and the early part of the Late Minoan Age, this feature in Wall was reproduced in the painted stucco decoration of the wooden shafts, which appear with a dark zone at their base.

1 The dimensions of these, as ascertained in its upper diameter and rises c. 23 cm. above for me by Dr. Mackenzie, are about i m. in the pavement.

their upper diameter and 1-20 m. below. Their 2 It was found just East of the North-East height is c. 42 cm. The great Mycenae bases Portico' referred to above, 30 cm. beneath are slightly cushioned out round their a floor with M. M. IIIJ tripod pots, and almost circumference. The large column-base at directly above a filled-in well, containing the entrance of the Propylaeum at Phaestos M. M. I a pottery. A smaller column base of (which is slightly oval) has an upper diameter the same type and material came to light N. of of 1-45 x 1-35 m. Another, of black material the area of the Stone Drain-heads'.

shot with quaruite veins, in the Columnar Hall See p. 442, Fig. 318.

N. E. of the Magazines at Phaestos, is 1-16 m. See below, p. 443, Fig. 319.

THE PALACE OF MINOS, ETC.

The imitation blocks of variegated marbles seen below such shafts on the same wall-paintings suggest, moreover, that the walls themselves were at one time partly coated with plaques of decorative materials.

Porches and porticoes are among the salient features of the early Middle Palace Minoan Palaces. The West Porch of Phaestos and another similar porch types of porch. on a lower terrace S. W. of the Palace, 1 supply the typical plan and un-

Early Palace i-n S JrpD E

Central fine gypsum ln porch, polygonal lime-stone pavement

For Porter of itemed

FIG. 160. PORCH (ON PHAESTOS.

SOUTH-V LOWKR LE f O- Mouth of jar in sunken part of pavement of porch

FIG. 158. WEST PORCH OF KNOSSOS. FIG. 159. WEST PORCH, PHAESTOS.

questionably belong to the earliest epoch of that Palace (see Figs. 159, 160). W. Porch The West Porch of Knossos, which is the best existing example of this class of structure on that Site, seems to owe its present form to the great Restoration of M. M. III. The comparison of its ground-plan with those of the two early Phaestian porches 2 given in Figs. 159, 160 shows, however, that the arrangement answers to that of the Early Palace system.

at Knossos compared with Phaestian Examples.

1 Pernier, Rendicontidel Lincei, 1907, p. 261 and Fig. A.

a Fig. 159 shows the West Porch at Phaestos, opening on the W. Court, as fully excavated (details from notes made by me in 1913). In this case there seem to have been two small lodges. Fig. 160 is the porch lower down the steep, to the South-West of the Palace, more recently discovered by Dr. Pernier (Rendiconti, c., 1907, p. 261 and Fig. A; and cf. Noack, Ovalhaus itid Palast in Crefa, pp. 6, 7).

We see here repeated the square portico with central column, approached across the adjoining Court by raised causeways and leading on the left to an entrance passage with central slabbing in this case the noble Corridor, the processional decoration of which belongs to the history of Late Minoan times. At the back of the porch in this case there appear the limestone jambs of two stately portals, one opening on the Corridor, while that to the right gives access to a convenient lodge. This lodge was evidently the seat of some high official guardian or Major domus' of the Palace.

The existing remains lead to the conclusion that the fine Corridor Access to of the Procession to which the West Porch gave entrance affords access to "lace: the interior of the Western Quarter by means of a second section at right from w.

Iorch. angles to the first, which led along the top of the Southern terrace of the building and finally debouched on the Propylaeum on this side. Thence an ascending ramp led to a broad flight of steps supported on the right by a bastion, the foundations of which seem to be early, and thence gave access to a series of upper halls. How far this arrangement was anticipated in the Early Palace it is difficult to say, but much of the substructures of this region unquestionably go back to the earliest days of the Palace.

The remains of the South Porch at Knossos show a simpler scheme, s.-Porch and the irregularities that it displays may be partly accounted for by the fact that it was built over the filling of the great circular Hypogaeum described above. Here we have a small room without a column; a warder's lodge of exiguous dimensions faced its entrance, and the interior passage opened on the left. This abutted on the South Corridor and seems to have ascended by an open ramp to the Central Court, as indicated on the Plan given in Fig. 152.

Of more importance was a portico and entrance West of the Northern N. V. Entrance Passage, and included in a projecting quarter of the Palace on that. c n side. This quarter to which the name of North-West Bailey is here given, trance; though separated from the main body of the building by a terrace wall, Bailey, runs directly from East to West. That it was included in the original Palace enceinte is shown, however, by the occurrence at intervals along both its Western and Northern borders of remains of characteristic masonry that elsewhere supports the base-slabs of the Early Palace walls, and of which a specimen underlying its N. W. angle is given in Fig. 109 above. 1 It is clear that a roadway corresponding in direction to the main line of the paved Way in Late Minoan days followed the Northern boundary 1 See pp. 148, 149.

THE PALACE OF MINOS, ETC.

N. V. Portico: Early Features.

Inner Ramp.

of this Bailey, and thus gave access by a stepped ascent between the inner and outer wall of a kind of outer Ward (see Plan, Fig. 152 above) to this North-West Portico. It forms a somewhat narrow lobby 7 by 4! metres with a bi-columnar opening on its East side facing a small light-area. The base of one of the columns, of a fine grey limestone with light and dark striations, is still in situ, and the foundation block of the other was brought to light about 2 metres to the North of it (see Fig. 1(51 and Suppl. PI. IX). Both the light-area and the covered part of the Portico showed the much fractured remains of a polygonal pavement of the mosaiko

FIG. 161. NORTH-WEST PORCH AND ENTRANCE AT KNOSSOS; ALSO SHOWING HACK OF BASTION A or NORTHERN ENTRANCE PASSAGE.

class characteristic of M. M. II, consisting of the finely grained almond stone with its bright orange-red laminations.

Opening on the light-area at its S. end by a single door was what may have been a small Guard-Room, while the covered part of the Portico led in that direction to a double doorway giving access to what from the drain-head beneath the inner part of its threshold l and the ashlar masonry visible on either side was an open ascending corridor. This ramp must have wound up round the area occupied by the early Keep to the interior of the West Wing of the Palace, as shown on the Plan, Fig. 152. It is possible that the Portico was entered on its North side by a similar double doorway.

1 The continuation of this drain was traced beneath the later Bastion A of the N. Entrance Passage.

FORE-HALL OF INITIATORY AREA In its West wall there was probably a single doorway, immediately to the right on entering, corresponding with another of which one jamb exists at its further end. These two doorways gave access to the Ante-Room of what is described below as the Initiatory Area, and would have been convenient respectively for the entrance and exit of votaries making their round. The Portico itself (see Plan, Fig. 102) forms a perfect square, and the fact that the S., W., and N. lines of this correspond with walls of early Palace date, as well as the character of its pavement and column-bases, point to an original arrangement of M. M. 11 date. At the beginning of M. M. Ill the back oi Bastion A of the N. Entrance Passage was superposed on its earlier E. boundary wall, and it is possible that other features such as the Southern line of doorways may in their existing form belong to that date.

In the latter part of the Third Middle Minoan Period and at the time when the neighbouring Lustral Basin was submerged and built over, the main doorways of the N. W. Entrance were blocked by a massive wall immediately behind them (see Fig. 161).

This N. W. Entrance system cannot be considered without reference to a remarkable feature of this part of the site, the sunken area, namely, with its descending flights of steps and columnar balustrades. This is the most conspicuous example of a class of construction which is of continual recurrence in the Minoan Palaces and of which the tank by the Room of the Throne at Knossos affords a late example. The striking parallelism between the latter and the reserved area, in that case provided with water-pipes and basin, at the back of the Hall of Initiation in the Sanctuary of Men Askaenos, has already been pointed out. 1 There can, as will be shown, be little doubt that these bath-like sunken areas of the Minoan Palaces fulfilled a ritual function, and they may perhaps be best described as lustral basins'. The large basin of this class, the walled enclosure of 1 See above, pp. 4, 5.

Access to Initia-toryarea 1.

Original Elements, M. M. II.

FIG. 162. PLAN OF NORTH-WEST PORTICO.

Later Blocking of N. W. Entrance.

Relation of N. W. Entrance to neighbouring Lustral Hasin.

THE PALACE OF MINOS, ETC.

Purificatory Station.

Altar Bases.

The Pillar Crypts and Double Axe Cult.

Early Shrine at Phaestos.

which flanked the North Piazza on the West, had been evidently remodelled at the beginning of the Third Middle Minoan Period, and a full illustration of it, together with a description of its contents, is therefore reserved for Sections dealing with that epoch. 1 But the small, inner masonry of its walls, with its distinct interstices filled with clay mortar, bears an early character, as does also the form of the column bases, and the main lines of this structure, like the outer walls in which they are contained, must probably be included among the original features of the building, and this view is corroborated by the similar sunken area to the S. E. of the West Porch at Phaestos, which certainly belongs to the Early Palace there. These sunken areas, indeed, in both cases seem to have formed part of purificatory stations for those who visited the buildings with a religious object. That at Knossos defines the special character of the North-West Entrance.

Two altar bases, marking the special sanctity of the Western Palace region, are visible in the Court that flanks its outer wall, itself repeatedly marked with the Double Axe symbol. The two Pillar Crypts of its Middle Section bear a distinctively religious character. The Eastern Pillar is reproduced in Suppl. Pl. X, with part of a stone vat visible behind it. From the character of the incised marks and other indications these Pillars must clearly be reckoned among the structures of the earlier Palace. It will be shown that these square gypsum pillars, on which the Double Axe symbol is continually repeated, 3 were themselves objects for offerings, and at the same time gave support to the columns of an upper sanctuary devoted to the central Palace cult. The shallow stone vats beside the Eastern pillar stood, as in other cases, in connexion with ritual oblations. In view, however, of the fuller evidence as to this cult forthcoming in the last Middle Minoan phase and in the early part of the Late Minoan Age, it has been thought better to reserve this subject for a later Section. 2 In the South-East House, which goes back to M. M. Ill, the pyramidal socket of the sacral weapon was found in sitti, before the pillar of its Crypt.

The Palace of Phaestos has supplied a well-preserved example of an 1 See below, p. 405 seqq.

2 See below, p. 4 3 seqq. For the double axe marks in this Palace region see p. 449, Fig. 322.

FIG. 1G3.

PLAN OF SACELLUM, PHAESTOS.

VN. NUIlpAVEMEIfr

SECTION A-B actual shrine of this Period with its fittings complete. On the borders of the West Court, there came to light a small sanctuary (Fig. 1 i:5) consisting of three alined cells, 1 built out into the Court itself in front of the Palace facade and of a rectangular chamber within, access to which was obtained through an opening in the line of the fa9ade wall. This chamber (Figs. 104, H5) 2 wasprovided on three sides with low benches, at the end of the innermost of which opened a little niche containing amongst other articles stone pounders, as if for the preparation of barley for sacral use. In position within this little inner sacellum were various objects of cult, including a remarkable table of offerings 3 of clay with Tables o stamped designs of oxen and S- 1 shaped figures. On the floor of this inner room, amongst other relics, wasa blue steatite libation bowl decorated with rosettes and tangential loops. Clay clay lamps also occurred, some with bases and others of a rough simple fabric. An interesting find was a Triton or Conch-shell, used as a ritual horn, and of which terra-cotta imitations were associated with the miniature Knossian shrine described below. Among the painted pottery found were vessels of a diminutive size analogous to a votive class found at Knossos in the Loom-Weight area, 4 and a large hole-

FIGS. 164, 165. SECTION AND PLAN OF INNER SANCTUARY OF EARLY SHRINE, PHAESTOS.

Ritual 1 L. Pernier, Man.., xii, pp 33, 34: xiv, p. 405 seqq. The cells, however, were not symmetrical as in the case of the ater shrines. They contained tables of offering and other cult vessels and burnt bones of animals. This part of the Sanctuary was at first described as an altar.

1 Man. Ant., xiv, p. 407, Fig. 38.

1 Op. cit., PI. XXXVI.

4 See below, p. 255, Fig. 191.

mouthed and bridge-spouted jar in shape and decorative style parallel with specimens found in the same area, 1 and representing the ceramic fashion

M. M. 11 b in vogue at the time of the final catastrophe of the Early Palace. The stratigraphic evidence derived from the Basements of the Loom Weights, which is of first importance for the history of the closing phase of the present Period, will be found illustrated below in its ceramic and other aspects. One very interesting discovery here made 2 has, however, a special pertinence in the present connexion since it gives a clear insight into Miniature the salient features of a Knossian sanctuary of this Period and its appur- J tenances. This consists of the remains of a miniature pillar shrine and shrine, altars, together with a portable seat, in painted terra-cotta (Fig. 106). The exterior of the structures here represented shows painted imitation of chequer-work masonry recalling that of the Shrine in the Miniature Fresco 3 and vertical and horizontal lines of disks which may be regarded as reproducing the painted stucco imitation of the ends of round beams and cross-bars, of constructive use. The original surface of the terracotta, which shades off from buff to pale brick red, had been coloured black, white, and red, according to the regular polychrome tradition of the contemporary pottery. We see window slits resembling some of those of the faience 4 house inlays, to be described in the succeeding Section, but placed together here in groups of three or four instead of two. The altars and shrines, as is usually the case in later Minoan examples, were surmounted by a succession of sacral horns'. In Fig. 1(56, u, is shown a base which seems to have served as an altar, of a very typical Minoan and Mycenaean form Altar and with incurving sides, such for instance as is seen with sacral horns above and trees behind on a lentoid intaglio from the Idaean Cave 4 with a votary before it blowing a triton or conch-shell (Fig. 167). It is interesting to Conch-observe that amongst the remains of the present sanctuary were found " fragments of miniature triton-shells of painted terra-cotta with red and white pets, bands, pointing to the same ritual use (Fig. 168). In the early Sacellum at Phaestos, as already noted, a specimen of a conch-shell trumpet itself came to light and another occurred in a little shrine to the S. E. of the Knossian Palace. 5 1 See below, p. 255. Fig. 22). A similar base constantly recurs as 2 A'tiossos, Report, 1902, pp. 28-32. a support for heraldic pairs of sacred animals s See Vol. II. lions and griffins and is seen within the door-4 The gem from the Idaean Cave is a crystal way of a shrine on a Zakro sealing (see below, lentoid (Myc. Tree and Pillar Cult, p. 43; p. 308, Fig. 227, c.). Mariani,

Antichita Cretesi, Man. Ant., vi, p. 178, See below, p. 580. Fig. 12: Furtwangler, Ant. Gemrn., iii, p. 47,

THE PALACE OF MINOS, ETC.
Columns with Seated Doves.
Pillars of the House.
Cult of
Dove
Goddess.
Baetylic Trinity.

But of all these remains the highest religious interest attaches to a terra-cotta group belonging to some religious structure on a larger scale than the others. It consists of three columns on a common base, supporting in each case, above their square capital, the round ends of a pair of beams on which a dove is perched (Fig. 16(j, F). The square capital itself and the beam ends above it must here be regarded as the equivalent, in an epitomized shape, of the roof beams and entablature of a building. In other words, they are the Pillars of the House, and the doves settled above them are the outward and visible sign of the divine presence and protection. A clay sealing with a similar device of a dove perched above roof-beams resting on a column, itself set on an altar base as in the Lions' Gate scheme, has now come to

FIG. 167. CRYSTAL LENTOID, IDAEAN CAVE. ( )

FIG. 168. TERRA-COTTA VOTIVE CONCH-SHELL TRUMPETS FROM SHRINE.

(f) light at Mycenae 2 a singular illustration of the Minoan source of its cult.

The doves also coloured according to the polychrome scheme with white and powdery red spots on a black ground illustrate the antiquity of the Minoan cult of the Dove Goddess. The dove vase of the M. M. I Period has been interpreted above as a ritual vessel. 3 Dove amulets already existed in Early Minoan times, and the miniature dove with white inlays, from the Middle Neolithic stratum of Knossos, tends to show that the dove cult itself, otherwise so widespread among the primitive population of the East Mediterranean basin, goes back to a very much more remote age.

Of the columns themselves, each one may be regarded as a separate religious entity, since in place of a common entablature the superstructure 1 In all, fragments of seven columns of different sizes were found, besides the group.

2 From a well excavated by Mr. Wace in 1920 (to be published in the H. S. A.). The column in this case had animal supporters, apparently goats. The associated objects (a bull's head rhyton, c.) point to a date more or less contemporary with the close of the Palace period at Knossos. 3 See p. 146, Fig. 107.

(. oddess or

M. M. II: CONSOLIDATION OF KNOSSIAN PALACE 223 is in each case separately rendered by a kind of architectural shorthand. This trinity of baetylic pillars (which has many parallels in Semitic cult) itself recalls the triple arrangement seen in the case of the Temple Fresco at Knossos and of several Late Minoan and Mycenaean shrines. The triple gold shrines of Mycenae are also coupled with seated doves.

The seated birds, as already observed, symbolize in this and other cases Birds as the descent of the divinity into the possessed object. At times, as in D " n " f the above instances, it is the baetylic pillar or the cell that enshrines it. The Posses-celebrated scene on the sarcophagus of Hagia Triada shows raven-like birds brought clown by ritual strains and libations on to the sacred Double Axes, which are thus charged as it were with the divinity. The doves on the gold chalice from Mycenae and of Nestor's Cup repeat the same idea.

But it was not only the cult object itself that could be thus sanctified by the Asso-descending emblem of spiritual indwelling. In the case of the gold plates with from the Third Shaft Grave at Mycenae the doves are seen not only perched on the Shrine but on the head and fluttering from the shoulders of a nude 1Hestess. female personage (Fig. 10J)). 2 So too the central clay image from the late Shrine of the Double Axes' (L. M. Ill 6) at Knossos 3 shows the dove settled on her head. In these cases we have either images of the Dove Goddess herself, reinforced by what may have been her older zoomorphic form, or of a priestess, deified by the descent of the dove spirit. 4

The extent to which primitive Minoan religious conceptions were Alighting fa-miliar to the Semitic mind is here again illustrated by the striking parallel Baptism of the baptism in Jordan and the picture drawn by the Evangelists of the Holy Spirit descending in bodily shape like a dove and lighting on Jesus. 5 What has to be borne in mind in all these connexions is that it is not only the inanimate or aniconic object, such as the pillar or the sacred weapon, that may become, through due ritual, the temporary dwelling-place of the divinity, but that the spiritual Being may enter into the actual worshipper or votary in 1 See below, p. 440 and Fig. 317. shape. Another faience figure from the

Schuchhardt, Schliemann's Excavations, Temple Repository shows the animal form pp. 198, 199, Figs. 181, 183. Schuchhardt of her divinity on her head, in the shape of assigns the gold shrine to Grave III together a seated lioness. It may be an actual votary with the female figure. Schliemann, Mycenae, or priestess, whose possession is thus indi- p. 267, had included the templein Grave IV. cated. In other cases the lions or lionesses while attributing the figure to Grave III. rest their forepaws against the divine or deified 3 Knossos, Report, 1902, p. 98 and Fig. 56. figure. (Cf. lentoid intaglio from Franks 4 In the case of the Snake Goddess' (see Collection, Myc. Tree and Pillar Cult, p. 67, below, p. 500), the zoomorphic form of the Fig. 45.)

THE PALACE OF MINOS, ETC.

Other Signs of Possession.

Portable Seat of Terracotta.

Minoan Palanquins.

Restoration of Fresco Design.

Use of Palanquins in Minoan Crete.

M. M. I Ox-wagon Vessel.

human form, who for the time becomes a God, just as the baptized Christian becomes alter Christus. This possession is often marked by soothsaying and ecstatic dances, and an orgiastic dance on a Late Minoan signet, to be described below, finds its pictorial explanation in the descent of the Goddess. Musical strains such as those of the lyre or the conch-shell or the sistrum of Egyptian cult were a means of invocation.

These highly interesting terra-cotta models illustrating the religious structures and ideas of the M. M. II Period are supplemented by an object the scale of which answers to the same series as the group of columns in the form of a portable seat (Fig. 166, c). 1 Within it are some remains of the lower part and attachments of a figure. It is evident that we have here a palanquin either for a divinity or for his earthly representative, the Priest-King, recalling the sedia gestatoria still used by the Papa-Re at Rome.

What appears to be an illustration of a subject of this kind is supplied by some fragments, probably belonging to a single panel of wall-painting, found in a basement near the South Propylaeum at Knossos, known as the Room of the Clay Signet. 2 These fragments, which apparently belong to the last period of the Palace, have suggested a restoration of a complete scene, showing two pairs of ceremonial bearers within the shafts of a kind of palanquin containing a seated figure. 3

The portable seat itself is of wider interest as showing the probable means of transport made use of by the Minoan lords in the earlier period of Cretan history, when horse-drawn chariots were as yet unknown, and which, as we see, for ceremonial purposes survived their introduction. Both the earlier, raised causeways and the narrow line of paving that runs West from the Theatral Area seem to have been designed for the porterage of such palanquins. That before the close of the preceding Period however some form of ox-wagon had come into use may be inferred from the remarkable discovery made at Palai-kastro of a cart-like vessel with disks for wheels. It is in the M. M. I polychrome style, showing an angular fret pattern and triglyphs on its upright sides.

1 In Knossos, Report, 1902, p. 31, Figs. 15, a Knossos, Report, 1901, pp. 19, 20. a, b, this object is incompletely restored, 3 See Vol. II and Knossian Atlas, I. without the poles behind.

FIG. 169. DOVES PERCHED AND FLUTTERING ABOVE GOLD FEMALE FIGURE; THIRD SHAFT GRAVE, MYCENAE.

Drainage System in Knosnan Palace; Stone Drains of Northern Entrance; Tributary systems of Northern and North- Western Insulae; Drainage system of Domestic Quarter complete circuit; Tributary system of North-Eastern Palace Region; Shafts for roof drainage, access and ventilation; Later changes; Latrine of Domestic Quarter modern arrangements; Upper story drainage system.

THE beautiful construction of the terra-cotta water-pipes belonging to Drainage the original elements of the building has already been described. 1 Another y stem at

Knossos; admirable feature in the early Palaces was the method of dealing with Slonc the accumulated volume of the surface waters by means of capacious stone and ducts lined with cement. At Knossos both on the North and East sides are I)ucts-well-preserved remains of widely ramifying systems in which a part is played both by descending shafts and by well-constructed stone drains, large enough to admit the passage of a man.

The most capacious example of these great built drains or Cloacae is afforded by that which ran down the Northern Entrance Passage and took the overflow waters of a good deal of the Central Court and its borders. A small section of this outside the Northern Entrance and flanking the exterior Portico on this side is shown in Fig. 170, where some roof slabs were missing. Northern So spacious was this main drain that it was possible to explore it for some affl " distance beyond the Palace boundary to the North-East, beneath a neighbouring field. Just above the section shown, the Cloaca is entered by a smaller stone-built affluent descending from the N. E. postern, and thus serving what seems to have been a distinct Northern insula of the Palace (see Plan, Fig. 286). So too on the West side of the Northern Entrance Passage, upon the platform above, another small built drain starts from the inner border of the Southern Entrance of the N. W. Portico and runs thence beneath the back walls of the later Bastions A and B, on its way to join the main Northern channel. 2 A stone-built affluent of this channel, on the N. W. border of the Central Court, stood beyond, in connexion with a sink or latrine, and was joined by two tributary conduits taking the overflow from a small early cistern on the West side of the Court. 3 This cistern was brought to light in 1913, three metres in front of the original frontage line on that side, and may have drawn its supply from a verandah roof.

1 p. 141 seqq and Figs. 103, 104. 3 See note i, p. 230, and Plan, Fig. 152,
Above p. 217, Fig. 162, and below, Fig. 286. above.

THE PALACE OF MINOS, ETC.

Each individual quarter or insula of the Palace seems in fact to have had a drainage system of its own, standing in a tributary relation to the great main channels.

An important system, of which many remains have been preserved, was that of the Domestic Quarter and its borders.

FIG. 170. VIEW SHOWING PART OF STONE DRAIN UNCOVERED, BELOW N. ENTRANCE, KNOSSOS.

Drainage of Domestic Quarter.

The general arrangements of its original drainage l are shown by Mr. Doll's Plans and Sections, Fig. 171. a, 6, c. The main conduit formed a complete circuit consisting of a Northern and a Southern branch, which both descended from a water-shed in what was later the S. E. corner of the Hall of the Colonnades. The channel, moreover, that resulted from the con- 1 We shall see (Vol. II) that in Late Minoan times a radical change took place in a part of this system.

COURT
OF lo DISTAFFS
FIG. 1
PLUM Of UPflr FLOOR HOWH
CORRIDOR TO y-
QUEERS MEGARON
ON UPfth H. QOR
SCHL:
FIG. 1
CHAMBER ii-oas IM i-oo aowc lllilil I I 1 f I 1 1 1 Htrmtt
PLAN AND SECTION OK S. V. PART OF DRAINAGE SYSTEM AS REMOD-
ELLED EARLY IN M. M. III. (CHRISTIAN C. T. DOLL.)

THE PALACE OF MINOS, ETC.

Shafts for
Roof
Drainage.
Access and Ventilation.
Stone Drains and Latrines.

Latrine of Domestic Quarter.

fluence of these two sections of the system received a further affluent just below the point of junction from another large stone conduit which served the Eastern border of the Domestic Quarter and the area North of it. The Southern arm of the system also shows an inlet connected with the later light-well of the Queen's Megaron and which may have originally served an earlier Court in this area.

The shafts in this Quarter were undoubtedly constructed with a view to the roof drainage of this region. Of these the smaller shaft c belongs to the original system, but it results from the careful structural analysis carried out by Mr. Doll in recent years that the block of masonry containing the shafts A and B was a later addition. It is now clear, indeed, that the masonry, with its piers enclosed in a solid wooden framework, is characteristic of the early part of M. M. Ill, as illustrated by so many constructions of the Domestic Quarter. One or other of these shafts may have been used to secure access and ventilation, and both A and u stand in relation with small latrines on the upper story. A still more elaborate latrine was constructed on the ground floor, which also seems to have formed part of these supplementary works, though it is described below for convenience sake in the present connexion. The stone channels themselves, ventilated by air-shafts and made accessible by manholes, were so roomy, that, in the course of their excavation, my Cretan workmen spent whole days in them without inconvenience. It would thus have been easy to clean them out when necessary. At the same time their use in connexion with latrines would hardly have been tolerable unless they were pretty constantly flushed. Between September and April the recurring, and at times torrential, rainfall would have produced this result.

The plan of the latrine on the ground floor is remarkable (see Fig. 172) On the face of the gypsum slab to the right is a groove for a small wooden post, which may be regarded as having served for the support of a seat about 57 cm. above the floor. Outside the doorway of the latrine is a flag sloped towards a semicircular hole, forming a sink, and from this opens a small duct leading to the main drain. The aperture leading to the main drain, partly masked by a curious projection, 2 deviates from the centre of the seat, thus basin or receptacle for the excreta. Judging 1 See Knossos, Report, 1902, pp. 85-7.

2 Capt. T. H. M. Clarke, M. B., D. S. O., R. A. M. C., who acted as medical adviser to the High Commissioner in Crete, observes of this projection: It has been suggested that it may have been used for the attachment of a balance flap to shut off the escape of sewer gas; perhaps it was employed as a support for an earthenware by the shape of the cavity, this basin would have been vertical in front and sloping at the back, or in other words it would resemble in shape the " wash-out" closet of the present day, in which a certain amount of water is kept in the basin by a ridge, over which the excreta are carried by a flush of water (Prehistoric

SLAB JUNK. TO CENTRE.

SECTION ,1 METK

FIG. 172.

PLAN I,. N AND SECTION OF LATRINE. (THEODORE FVFE.)

THE PALACE OF MINOS, ETC.

leaving room on the right for some vessel used for flushing the basin. As an anticipation of scientific methods of sanitation, the system of which ve have here the record has been attained by few nations even at the present day.

System of Evidence pointing to an elaborate system of drainage of roofs and upper u PP er story Courts by means of descending ducts or pipes in connexion with the drainage, basement conduits has come to light in various parts of the building. 1 At the East angle of the later Throne Room system the remains of such an exterior pipe of plaster were actually found communicating with a similar plaster duct running above the Late Minoan pavement. 2

Of special interest, however, in relation to the methods of discharging surface waters from upper light areas and roof terraces were the remains brought to light in the North-Eastern region bordering the Domestic Quarter. We have here a complete system of drain-heads which, as will be shown below, 3 were by means of vertical ducts brought into connexion with the light court of what seems to have been a great East Hall belonging to the close of the M. M. Ill Period.

Sanitation in Crete (r. Medical Jourti., 1903,

P-59 1 Thus in the Basement of the Jewel Fresco a section of a large built drain was found running N. beneath a wall which must have belonged to the original interior drainage of this part of the building. It was choked with pottery M. M. I-III. Early drains have already been referred to, p. 225, as connected with the roof line of a verandah along the original facade of the Palace on the section later broken through by the Antechamber of the Throne Room. Here was a cement-lined cistern or settling tank, about a cubic metre in capacity, from which two overflow conduits led in slightly divergent directions to an affluent of the great

North drain (see Fig. 152) running along the front of the N. V. Section of the Central Court. The conduits were square in section, one of terra-cotta (30 cm. deep x 12 broad), the other of limestone (8 cm. deep x 16 broad). They lay 80 cm. below the surface and contained M. M. II b. pottery, as also ihe cistern. The affluent of the main N. drain referred to, which was of built construction like it, stood in connexion with a lateral closet showing a circular aperture in its pavement.

1 The very friable remains of this superficial duct were unfortunately destroyed by careless visitors to the site.

3 See below, p. 379seqq., Figs. 275, 270.

PLATE I

Jn. M. M. II: (C) ROYAL POTTERY STORES; ACME OK POLYCHROME FABRICS

Magazines and great Pithoi; New slratigraphic evidence; Storage and cists; Ceramic types; Matttre style of liarbotine decoration, combined with brilliant polychromy; Architectonic influences, and earlier Jalace Style; Hull's Head and Ostrich Egg rhyions; Imitations of Breccia Veining: Royal Pottery Stores Egg-shell cups and bowls; Imitation of inlaid metal work; Arcadedfluting on cups at Knossos and Mycenae the Sacrals'; Eggshell ware copies of vessels in precious metals of Royal Treasury; Originals from Shaft-Graves of Mycenae; Early ceramic imitations of Vapheio' Cups; Thorn-bossed bowl; Fine polychrome vase from Knossos with folia ted scrollwork;

Imported examples found at Phylakopi; Acme of polychrome decoration about middle of this Period; The M. M. II a Ceramic style.

A FURTHER point of correspondence between the two Palaces in addition to those enumerated above is supplied by the Early Magazines, of which in either case examples occurred with the original store jars or pithoi resting on their floors. At Phaestos, Magazines belonging to the original Palace were found both bordering the West Court and beneath the light-well of the later Pi opylaeum (see Plan. Fig. 173). 1 In the latter case several of the jars showed polychrome designs (Fig. 170).

On the other hand, in the Magazines bordering on the West Court at Phaestos, in the East Magazines, and elsewhere at Knossos, there were found huge pithoi. showing a monochrome 'trickle ornament on the plain clay. The sides of these bore a moulded rope decoration (Figs. 174. 3 175) an imitative survival of liarly Magazines with Great Store Jars.

Painted rithoi at Phaestos.

Knobbed rithoi.

FIG. 173. EARLY MAGAZINES HKNEATH LIGHT COURT OF LATER PROPY-LAHA, IHAKSTOS.

1 Pernier, JMon. Ant., xiv, p. 415, Fig. 42. 1 Pernier, op. fit., p. 451 seqq., Pl. 34, d.

THE PALACE OF MINOS, ETC.

Rope

Moulding.

Trickle Ornament.

Storage of Oil.

the actual rope cradles, such as would have been used in the transport of these great jars. In the interspaces of this rope moulding were large knobs and numerous handles, arranged in zones. The trickle ornament which varied the natural surface of the clay in these was itself no doubt suggested by the natural stains produced by the trickling down the sides of the liquid contents of such jars. There can be little doubt, indeed, that they were mainly used for the storage of oil, which, to judge by the space devoted to these pithoi in the Palace Magazines, must have been a principal source of wealth to the Minoan princes, and may have been early exported to Egypt. The oleaginous nature of their contents can indeed be gathered from the excessive combustion with which in some cases they were associated, and the carbonized infiltrations with which not only the pavements but the immediately underlying strata were affected. 1

At Knossos, according to the Early Palace

Great Pithoi of Knossos.

FIG. 174. BOSSED Pithos (M. M. II), PHAESTOS. (HEIGHT 1-28 M.) arrangement, a considerable area on the North-East slope was occupied by a series of Magazines devoted to the storage of these knobbed oil jars (see Plan, Fig. 152).

The great size of these pithoi will be gathered from the view given of reconstituted specimens in Fig. 175. The supplementary explorations in connexion with these Magazines, conducted in 1913, show that they extended over a neighbouring area named from the stone spout in the later (M. M. Ill), light court wall there visible, and the spaces immediately South of it. A terminus ad quern for the dating of the oil jars themselves was, moreover, supplied by a conclusive piece of evidence. The base of one of these great pithoi was found in situ, with part of its circumference actually beneath the

This was notably the case in the Magazine the Corridor of the Bays (seep. 320, Fig. 233, the Medallion Pithoi immediately East of and Fig. 278).

THE PALACE OF MINOS, ETC.

Pittot at Knossos M. M. I I

Knobbed base of a wall of good masonry belonging to a hall of the early part of the Third Middle Minoan Period. Moreover, on the same kalderim pavement, of the Early Palace class, on which the pithoi stood, were found fragments of polychrome vases of the mature M. M. II style. So. too, in the area of the Early Keep, the lower part of a similar store jar was found in situ, the upper part of which, as became apparent in the course of the recent re-investigation of this area, had been cut off by a M. M. Ill floor 1 (see Section, Fig. 177).

In this case again the pitjws, which was bossed rather than knobbed, rested on a typical kalderim pavement, laid on the top of the outer foundation wall of the early Keep, belonging, as has been shown, to the early part of the M. M. I Period. With the Store jar was found a typical M. M. II cup showing a white band on the black glazed ground (see Fig. 177). This pithos, like most of its class, was decorated with the trickle ornament and its low bosses were

Fir,. 176.

PAINTED Pithos, PHAESTOS. (HEKIHT 1-08 M.) 1 The section originally given, Knossos, Report, 1903 (B. S. A., ix), p. 26, Fig. 13, was vitiated by two radical misconceptions. A test made below the kalderim pavement on which the base of the knobbed pithos rested struck the interstice between the foundation wall of the Keep and the face of the cutting into the Neolithic. This conveyed the wrong impression (suggested by the analogy of the neigh- bouring areas) that the pavement covered the filling of another walled pit. On the other hand, while the clay and plaster pavement of the floor above was well preserved near the North wall of the chamber, it was not realized that the greater part of its central area had been broken in, and M. M. Ill pottery had thus in places intruded into the interspace cm which the pithos stood. This was, therefore, also surrounded with impressed circles–direct forerunners of the medallions' of the M. M. Ill class.

. Surface level.

- t f Istf Minoan floor in i scfotnng area . 73?"- Stucco and csy r)i A' t ir-""y. "x-f-f li xv ' "? cement foor

M-i.,. Vt. y. f. ss-f "" Q;- r.1 M. M. I1 broken through -f-l-; t T:."-.

c ia.– X.

M. fill Srrarum with knobbed Pithos resfiny on pavec floor rd cup.

fthe centra parf of this area had been disturbed fhrouoh breaking in of

M J fi. Ill floor-

M M. IIpovemenr of., aroe irreouar slabs

"! l f ml

Foundation wall of ear keep M. M. I aoina down 7metres

J + 4-4- IMG. 177. M. M. II FLOOR WITH BASE OF KNOBBED Pithos AND M. M. Ill FLOOR SUPERPOSED (AREA or KEEP, KNOSSOS).

The jars found in the Early Magazines beneath the light court of r r at the Propylaeum at Phaestos of which a specimen is shown in Fig. 176, chrome

Store-ascribed to the M. M. Ill Period. My supple- room) with M. M. Ill vases in situ upon it. jars at mentary researches of 1913, which led here to Below this, moreover, beside the pithos, the the discovery of the containing foundation wall typical M. M. II cup, mentioned above, was of the Keep, also brought to light a part of the found, upper floor (near the South-East corner of the phaestos- are of a different class. They are smaller and bear designs in brownish-red with white borders on a buff ground, representing the mature M. M. II polychrome style. The knobbed from the West Magazines at Phaestos were also associated with mature M. M. II polychrome pottery. 1

While the great store-jars certainly served for the most part to contain oil, the storage of solid possessions such as grain or other produce, or of more precious objects, seems to have been mainly effected, at least in the earlier

Age of the Palaces, by means of pits or repositories beneath the floors.

Pits for The deep-walled cells of the early Keep, described above, though they beneath very probably served as dungeons, may also be regarded as typical,

Floors. on a ar g er SC ale, of the methods of storage in vogue at this time.

In some cases, as that of the deposit beneath the Vat-Room floor at Knossos and that of the Third Magazine, mere pits, excavated in the Neolithic clay, with at most a plaster facing, were used as receptacles. Within the

North-East angle of the wall of the Phaestian Palace appeared a series of receptacles in the shape of rectangular walled cavities, in one case divided into smaller cists by cross partitions of red clay and plaster. 2 Some of the pottery found within them goes back to the earlier part of the Middle Minoan

Age, but, as at Knossos, the cist-partitions seem to be a M. M. Ill addition. 3

Later The part played by the underground receptacles, to which the name of selles'. kaselles has been given, in the Palace construction at Knossos is well known. There is evidence that the numerous examples of these which largely underlie the system of the West Magazines and adjoining Corridor took their present form in the Third Middle Minoan Period, 4 though some form of pits for storage was doubtless already in existence in the preceding

M. M. n Palace Period. There seems to be a considerable probability that the simpler

Cists. type of cist seen in the more Western of the two Repositories, in which were found the fittings of the Snake Goddess's shrine, with its walls of massive masonry, represents. a tradition going back to the present Period. 6 That many of these sunken cists were used for the deposit of precious objects is clear, and, as we shall see, in the kaselles of the more advanced class elaborate precautions were taken to preserve their contents from damp.

1 Halbherr, Mem, R. 1st. Zwz., xxi, pp. 253, in one of these pits, associated with objects of 254. See above, p. 232, Fig. 174. the latter class, that the celebrated Phaestos 2 Pernier, Ausonia, iii, 1909, p. 255 seqq. Disk and a clay tablet of the

Linear Class A 5 They also contained a more superficial were found (Pernier, loc. tit., and see below, deposit, including pottery and other objects p. 648). that had fallen into them, apparently from See below, p. 448 seqq. a chamber above, at the time of the final 5 See below, p. 467. catastrophe in this part of the Palace. It was

Although much of the earlier fabric both at Knossos and Phaestos has Splen-been effaced or obscured by later stages of construction, it is clear that by the Second Middle Minoan Period great Palatial centres existed on both sites, marked by a degree of splendour and of civilized refinement such as had never been attained before in any Aegean land. The unity and order thus evolved must have manifested themselves on the Palace walls in.

in Poly-"

a hundred decorative details now lost, but of which we see a reflection in the chrome fine polychrome designs on the contemporary pottery. Thus there now arises p"

what may fitly be called the Earlier Palace Style presenting decorative Palacc motives to a great extent architectonic in their origin.

It was natural, indeed, that the acme of this ceramic art should have M. M. I I

Poly- been the special product of these residential centres of the Priest-Kings. The chrome remains of this in its most brilliant aspect, as seen in the exquisite egg-shell ware, are best represented at Knossos, though fine examples were also brought to light at Phaestos. On the other hand, in the more outlying districts, such as Palaikastro at the extreme East of the island, it is less well illustrated, and there is a tendency for the preceding M. M. I style to persist and to merge gradually into the concluding Middle Minoan phase.

Various decorative elements more or less isolated in the preceding Age Fusion of are now welded together into an organic whole. Compare, for instance, the!; j e r m ents butterfly or Double Axe motive of Fie. 1:5, a, simply surrounded by into ,-,.,. Organic undulating bands, with its complete incorporation into the design on the cup whole. shown in Fig. 181 below. The polychromy itself becomes less crude and often displays delicate nuances of tint. The white appears of a beautiful creamy tone, the red has a touch of orange or terra-cotta, while the crimson emerges with a cherry tint recalling that of a rich red wine. l The black has sometimes a purple tone, and a brilliant metallic lustre is often given.

Among M. M. II types now occur rhytons or libation vases in the B U "S form of heads of bulls, instead of the whole body as was usual in the Rhy-preceding Age. Fragments of these have been found in the M. M. II deposits of Knossos, the light patches, such as those about the eye, picked out with a brilliant white glaze resembling enamel.

In a later Section, devoted to this special class of vessels, it will be also Ostrich shown that a remarkable class of rhytons', the body of which was formed T yp e. of an ostrich's egg, goes back at Knossos to the date of the finest ceramic polychromy of the M. M. II Period. The ostrich egg type, which survived in egg-shell and faience under its original form among the early elements of the Shaft Graves at Mycenae, stands at the head of a whole family of such 1 Mackenzie, The Pottery of Knossos, fc., p. 172.

THE PALACE OF MINOS, ETC.

Imitations of Breccia Veining.

vessels, and is itself a striking proof of early relations with the further shores of the Libyan Sea.

The M. M. I ceramic tradition is maintained and developed in several directions. In cups like Fig. 178 we can still trace the imitation of the brilliant veins of breccia and marble vases that is so closely bound up with the origin of the polychrome style on pottery. Among the examples given in Fig. 127 above of such imitative decoration, d, with white-spotted brown veins on a buff ground, and probably also c, with white-edged red veins on a black ground, belong to this Period. The bizarre striation of these is directly taken over from the stone originals, and the white edging by which the veining is

FIG. 178. RESTORED PART OF EGG-SHELL CUP, KNOSSOS, WITH IMITA-TION BRECCIA VEINING.

FIG. 179. SPOUTED VASE FROM KAMARES CAVE WITH PAINTED IMI-TATION OF CONGLOMERATE. ( ) often accompanied is, as already pointed out, based on a natural characteristic of the native breccia. This natural bordering was, moreover, taken over in a generalized way on to many M. M. II polychrome designs, especially those on a buff ground. 2

A remarkable bridge-spouted bowl, brought to light by the recent excavations of the British School in the Kamares Cave (Fig. 179 3), seems to represent some kind of conglomerate varied by what look like sections of fossil sponges or madrepores. This must, however, be placed amongst the latest fabrics of this Period (M. M. II ti).

Many cups and bowls representing the early phase of M. M. 1 1 exhibit a light ground throughout, on which appears a bizarre polychrome decora- 1 Compare, too, Fig 442, p. 602 below.

2 Cf. the Phaestian jar, Fig. 176 above.

3 R. M. Daw-kins, B. S. A., xix, PI. XII, below, and cf. p. 23.

tion 1 of this stone-ware class. Some very beautiful egg-shell cups of which fragments were found in the Royal Pottery Stores at Knossos, described below, show this veining in dark-brown on the stippled, light ground with the usual white borders, as suggested by the stone formation (Fig. 178).

The fine reproduction of the carinated contour and spotted decoration of an early liparite bowl shown in Fig. I27,", above may also be referred to this Period.

The barbotine or prickle ware, the rise of which has been noted under M. M. I, seems to have attained its highest development in combination with a brilliant polychromy about the beginningof the present Period. A group of representative examples in this mature style is given in Coloured Plate I, though it may oftenbe difficult to say of individual specimens on which side of the border line between the First and Second Middle Minoan Periods they should be placed. The pedestal of a fruit-stand from the Basement of the Monolithic Pillars at Knossos (a) is interesting as illustrating the evolution of the arcade pattern which plays an important role in M. M. II ceramic design from Outings, in this case horizontally arranged. The curious triangular object on this pedestal recurs on the elegant hole-mouthed vase from the Kamares Cave (fy where it is supposed by Mr. Dawkins to represent a murex shell. The side of a pyxis found outside the small tholos at Hagia Triada,: i here partly completed, is remarkable for its decorative treatment of successive coloured bands.

An outgrowth of the barbotine style may be traced in the thorn-like excrescences of a beautiful type of two-handled bowl or tazza Imitation
Liparite.
li. irbo-tine" Ware combined with
Advanced Polychromy.
FIG. 180. VASE WITH BEETLES IN RELIEF ( ).
Thorned Bowls'.
1 See above, p. 178, Fig. 127, d, and cf. Dr. Mackenzie, f. ff. S., xxvi, p. 254, and Pl. VIII (Coloured Figures).
2 Dawkins,. S. A., xix, Pl. IX and p. 20.
3 R. Paribeni, Mon. Ant., xiv, p. 699. Pl. XLII, 3.
THE PALACE OF MINOS, ETC.
Reliefs of Cockchafers and Shells.
The Royal Pottery Stores.
Strati-graphic Evidence.
with crinkled rim (see Suppl. Pl. Ill, a). 1 In their naturalistic form and ruddy hue these exactly resemble the thorns of a rose-bush. A tendency is also now perceptible to place small reliefs of animate objects on the outer margins of vessels. A curious instance of this is shown in the goblet, Fig. 180, where a living presentment of a cockchafer is set in each of the spaces between the three handles. This vessel, which has a dark glazed ground, was found, together with the finest egg-shell ware in the Royal Pottery Stores', at Knossos. Sea shells also occasionally appear in a similar position on vessels of this Period, such as the cockle and the Murex or Triton. It will be seen that these marine reliefs were further developed in the succeeding Period on clay, faience, and stone vases.

But the crowning revelation of the excellence attained by the Minoan potters and vase-painters by the middle of the present Period was the discovery of what may be fitly described as the Royal Pottery Stores to the North-East of the Palace site at Knossos. The ceramic fabrics here found, in their fine egg-shell-like texture, in their harmonious colouring and its delicate combination with subdued relief, are hardly rivalled by the potter's work in any time or country. It has been well said that for the decorative feeling in colour effect one has to go to another technique belonging to a much later time, that namely of old Venetian glass. From the refined elegance of the contents of these store-rooms it can hardly be doubted that the fabrics here found were destined for the table of the Knossian Priest-Kings.

The relatively early place of these exquisite egg-shell fabrics in the M. M. II series is thoroughly established by the stratigraphic evidence. 2 In the area in which they were found, enclosed within early rubble walling, at about 1-25 m. below the surface, there came to light, lying on their sides, plain M. M. Ill jars, some showing drip ornament of a class well represented in the N. E. Magazines belonging to that Period. Below this was a layer of wood-ashes packed with painted sherds similar to the pottery found in the adjoining Basement of the Loom Weights, and which, as will be shown below, belong to the concluding M. M. 11 phase, (6). Beneath was a pale clayey stratum 20 cm. thick with similar sherds, and underlying this again was another deposit of wood ashes 45 cm. thick, the result of some earlier local conflagration, embedded in which was the egg-shell ware in the shape of cups and bowls, and 1 For a coloured illustration of this see Knossos, Report, 1903 (B. S. A., ix, p. 19, and Pl. II. 2). It was found, about 3.20 metres down, in the area immediately E. of the Room of the Stone Drain-heads.

2 Cf. Knossos, Report, 1902, p. 118; but the terminology there employed is necessarily antiquated.

PLATE II

EGG-SHELL WARE OF POLYCHROME STYLE (M. M. II a) remains of peclestalled goblets. This deposit rested on a stamped clay floor. Further concordant elements for the comparative place of these remains is supplied by the circumstance that these Pottery Stores were cut into by the Magazines containing the knobbed pithoi, which seem themselves to synchronize with the earliest constructions of the Domestic Quarter.

It has been already shown that marvellously thin cups of egg-shell Egg-shell ware in the old traditional mottled style were already turned out in the early-part of the preceding Period, and even by the close of E. M. III. But these

FIG. 181. POLYCHROME CUP OF EGG-SHELL WARE, KNOSSOS. (-) products of the M. M. II potter's art applied to the new glaze technique, and often combined with the most brilliant polychromy and delicate repousse work, stand on a much higher plane.

Among the cups from the Royal Pottery Stores Fig. 181 is one of the The most beautiful. It is light and spontaneous as a bubble, and the design Liiy"cup. below the calix of a water-lily as it floats on the surface of a pool is in keeping with the lightsomeness of form. This floral motive may well have been suggested by a lotus vase of Egypt, but the treatment is more delicate, and the subdued delicacy of the embossed relief enhances the effect of the design. The outer leaves of the calix are here black with a central vein of red, the 1 See above, p. 169. I R

THE PALACE OF MINOS, ETC.

Egg-shell

Ware

Cups.

Influence of Metal Types.

inner petals white, and the outer leaves of the corolla are outlined against a bright red background. The Double Axe motive parti-coloured, white and scarlet is repeated in the elaborate frieze round the upper border.

A group of three cups from this Deposit is given in Coloured Plate II. Admirable in the harmony of its design and hues is No. i, on which coiled shell-like sprays, creamy white and crimson-veined, are linked with rosettes, reserved in the lustrous black ground. A similar colour effect recurs in 2 of the same Plate, while 3 is specially distinguished by its rich metallic sheen.

This last feature is in harmony with the growing influence of metal types, especially of silver, on ceramic forms, already noted under the M. M. I Period. 1 Among the remains of vases of the egg-shell class some present Imitations of Silver Vessels.

FIG. 182. a, b. STAMPED WARE, WITH METALLIC LUSTRE: ROYAL POTTERY STORKS, KNOSSOS. (f). c. HIEROGLYPHIC CACHET OF FABRIC, PALAIKASTRO.

a lustre hardly distinguishable from that of old plate, and on such examples painted decoration is often replaced by stamped or embossed patterns such as might well have been impressed on thin plates of metal (Fig. 1S2, a, b. Two cup-handles of plain examples of this ware from Palaikastro actually present the potter's cachet in hieroglyphic characters (Fig. 182, c). 2 Such fabrics curiously recall the metallic forms and lustre of the class of Italo-Greek tazzis and other vessels which reproduce the silver plate in vogue at the Court of Dionysios of Syracuse, and which often exhibit in their bowls actual casts of his magnificent medallions'. with the signature, still discernible, of the great engraver Euainetos. 3 Imitations in clay of crinkled silver vessels of the M. M. I Period have been given above (Fig. 139, p. 192), and a good instance of similar metallic 1 See above, p. 191. For metallic imitations mission, in Scripta Minoa, i, p. 157, P. 43.

from Phaestos see Pernier, Man. Ant., xii, s See my Syracusan Medallions and their 1902, pp. 113, 114. Engravers, p. 113 seqq.

Published, with the Excavators' kind per- influences is supplied by the under side of a bowl of a tall fruit dish, of which part of the pedestal was also found, belonging to the latter part of the present Period. 1 It is covered below with a creamy whitewash apparently suggested by the sheen of its silver model (Suppl. Pl. Ill, 6).

The prototypes in precious metals are reflected in other ways in the imita-painted decoration. A fine example of this is seen in the cup, Fig. 183 a, a, 2 t I l " d of where the delicate fluting of the original is reproduced in orange yellow on Metal the dark ground in a manner that seems to represent gold inlay. 3 A bronze dagger-blade with designs of a boar hunt and fighting bulls, illustrated in a later Section of this volume, 4 carries back the beginnings at least of the splendid art of the Mycenae blades to this epoch. 5 In connexion, moreover, with some of the most typical cups in precious Arcaded metal found in the Shaft Graves at Mycenae the imitative goblets like the above, with arcade ornament derived from metal fluting, have a peculiar value. In Fig. 183 a, 4, showing a clay copy of cups like the gold examples below from Mycenae we have the record of fluting arched both above and below like that of 5 from the Fourth Shaft Grave, coupled with a foliate band equivalent to that which strengthens the middle zone of 8. The Sacral s lustrous dark olive-tinted glaze of this goblet is relieved with matt white, yellow, and deep crimson decoration, 6 a conspicuous feature in which is the SS motive, alternately red and yellow, repeated between the double arcading both on the outer zones of the goblet and round the interior of its rim. This symbol is repeated on a clay table of offerings from Phaestos accompanied by figures of oxen and it is reduplicated beside a bucranium on a hieroglyphic seal. Its sacral significance is clear, and its appearance round the cup oddly recalls the reiteration of the jewelled SS on the high Order of much later sovereign Pontiffs the collar of the Santo Spirito.

In Fig. 183 a, i, is shown a section, restored in the drawing from frag- Egg-shell ments of another cup from the Royal Stores, of an egg-shell ware bowl quite cop s of as fine as its metallic prototype. The exterior effect of its delicately fluted Vessels " walls is emphasized by matt white and red decoration on a lustrous dark Metals of ground, and the arches of the lower row are surmounted by fleur-de-lis Treasury.

1 It was found in a well on the right side heads. See coloured reproduction, Knossos, of the Vlissia brook, S. W. of the Palace site at Report, 1903 (B. S. A., ix), Pl. II. i.

Knossos, in company with the little polychrome For the interior pattern see Fig. 194, c.

jug presenting the lily sprays, J. . S., xxi, 4 See below, p. 718, and Fig. 541, a, b.

. So, and below, Fig. 196. D See below, p. 715 and Fig. 538.

5 Found with the thorn-bossed tazza, Supp. 6 For a fuller description of the details of this

Pl. Ill, a. East of the Room of the Stone Drain- cup, see Mackenzie,.".-S 1., xxiii, p. 177.

THE PALACE OF MINOS, ETC.

finials of curiously Gothic aspect. 1 Alongside is shown the incave interior effect of the double arcading. This goblet itself points to a repousse original in metal-work with inlaid ornamentation.

The existence of these polychrome clay vessels reproducing the typical shape, the fluted and arcaded decoration, and even the varied inlays of an existing class in precious metals that formed part of the treasure of the Priest-Kings of Knossos in the great days of the early Palace, is itself a fact of far-reaching importance. All fine examples of such vessels, moreover, of

FIG. 184. CUPS SHOWING LIGHT ON DARK AND DARK ON LIGHT DEC-ORATION: ROYAL

POTTERY STORES.

which remains have been found, were from this site, and no trace of this arcaded class has been found elsewhere.

At Knossos, indeed, neither the Palace Treasury itself nor royal tombs have come to light to supply the originals. But types at any rate closely parallel to what these must have been, as well as others that represent their immediate outgrowth in metal-work, have been preserved for us among the precious vessels of the Shaft. Graves at Mycenae. One or other, indeed, of tne S goblets there brought to light, may well have found an earlier resting-M rav na f P ace n l e Knossian Treasury. The cup 5 (Fig. 183 a), for instance, with its doubly arched flutings, occurred in the Fourth Shaft Grave in a Minoan 1 Another polychrome fragment, Fig. 183,3, presents a simple arcading with a fleur-de-lis starting from the sides of the pillars.

Originals Shaft association which itself carries it back well within the limits of M. M. III. The gold cup 7, found in Grave V, and 8, from the Second Grave, reflect architectonic influences such as are already visible in the Knossian types I and 4. The pillars here even show separate blocks and the angular arches of 8 might recall the Carlovingian arcading of Lorsch or its Saxon equivalent at Deerhurst. 1 The fragment of the silver cup 6 with its double-headed arches answers to a decorative type copied in Knossian stone vessels of the beginning of the Late Minoan Age. 2 but already seen in the half rosettes of painted friezes going back to M. M. III.

It further appears that vessels with handles of the characteristic type of those of the Vapheio gold cups were already finely imitated in clay at Knossos by the close of this Period or the early part of M, M. 111. A fragmentary specimen of a handle and part of a rim of a goblet with a lustrous brown glaze: is given in Fig. 183 6, I, and with it, for comparison, the silver beaker from Mycenae with gold and niello inlays, which may have approximated to it in form. Specimens in metal of the Vapheio type of cup, as we shall see, were known in M. M. Ill Crete.

In Fig. 184 a, 6, we see illustrated on Cups themselves of Vapheio shape the dark on light as well as the light on dark tradition. 4 At the same time it is clear that the curved or kidney-shaped pattern, white and brown respectively on a and the white blotches on b, were repeated in each case by means of the same stamp. Sometimes, as in Fig. 185, showing part of the base of a cup, 3 the type repeated is very regular, in this case resembling a capital C, but here, too, the mechanical character of the 1 Architectural parallels of Minoan date are analogy with those on a class of M. M. Ill ii Architectonic influences.

Karly ceramic imitation of Vessels with Handles of Vapheio type at Knossos.

FIG. 185. PART OK BASE OF CUP WITH PRINTED PATTERN.

Printed Patterns.

however wanting, if we except the rough analogy of the Tirynthian Galleries (L. M. III).

- Metal bowls and ewers with a simple kind of fluting are also seen in the hands of the Keftian Chieftains on the Early XVIIIth Dynasty Monuments. For a fluted bronze jug from Dendereh which perhaps stands in this relation, see Petrie, Dendereh.

The ridges round the collar present some limestone bowls (see below, p. 413, Figs. 297, 4 See Mackenzie, The Pottery of Knossos (J. H. S., xxiii), pp. 176, 177. The interior of l is flaked dark on light.

5 This fragment (from the Kouloura) seems to be of somewhat later date than Fig. 184, a. The string-marks on its base clearly indicate the quick wheel (see p. 259).

vo-V

FIG. 186. M. M. II POLYCHROME WARE OF MATURE CLASS a, WITH FOLIATED SCROLLS. a, g, KNOSSOS; KAMARES CAVE; b, e, d, e, IMPORTED SPECIMENS OF KNOSSIAN FABRIC,

PHVLAKOPI.

PLATE III reproduction is made evident by the recurrent thickening at the ends of the curves. It is possible that these C-shaped prints were produced by a half section of cane. The white blotches of Fig. 184, 6, look as if they had been dabbed on by a small sponge at the end of a stick.

Another good illustration of the simultaneous usage of the light on dark Light on and dark on light technique is afforded by the elegant crinkled bowl, Suppl. darkon d PI. Ill, a, found with the fragments of the arcaded goblet, Fig. 183 a, 2,! i ht-with which, indeed, the arched decoration of its inner border shows considerable affinity. Its crinkled sides, with their lustrous black ground and white festoons are further distinguished by deep-red prickly bosses, imitating the thorns of a briar rose. In contrast to this polychrome effect, however, the interior part of the bowl shows the buff ground flaked with dark glaze. This vessel belongs to the acme of the M. M. II style and to an epoch contemporary with the fine egg-shell ware.

On the clay floor of a small cellar belonging to the North-West Spouted Building at Knossos, 1 in company with characteristic vessels, the style of Etabontt which points to the earlier phase of M. M. II, came to light the highly Scr "" decorative spouted vase shown in Coloured Plate III and Fig. 186, a. This is the most elaborate specimen of M. M. polychrome ceramic design yet known. The front and back display a variety of scroll-work and curving sprays, while the central motive of the sides is a kind of fleur-de-lis. The design is laid on in creamy white, orange, and crimson on a lustrous black ground. The decorative scrolls may be compared with those on the contemporary prism seal, Fig. 207, a, below.

Details of the scroll-work on this vessel agree in a remarkable manner Corres-with decorative features on some of the earliest imported fragments found at,"f cr Phylakopi in Melos, which have for this reason been set together with it in Decora-Fig. 18(. 2 In some cases, as b, the correspondence is so remarkable as to imported involve the conclusion that the group of vases here represented from the shvrds' at Melian site was of Knossian Palace fabric. The whole group, including the Phyla-jar from Knossos, must be regarded as belonging approximately to the same Acme of epoch as the fine egg-shell cups, and as illustrating the acme of the earlier M. M. II polychrome class, which may be distinguished from the later series Sty e-as M. M. II a.

1 See Knossos, Report, 1903, p. 118, Fig. 73, 1hylakopi, pp. 149, 150, Figs. 128, 130, 133. and p. 119, Fig. 74, and cf. Vol. II. Among With these has also been grouped the bowl,, the vessels here found was a jar with drip from the Kaniares Cave, showing a schematied ornament, and several characteristic cups. figure of a sepia, with asterisks and foliation in 2 For Fig. 180, b, c, d, e, see C. C. Edgar, this particular style appended to its tentacles.

12. M. M. II: (D) THE LOOM-WEIGHT DEPOSIT: LATER CERAMIC-PHASE (6) AND REACTION OF WALL-PAINTING.

Basement Chambers N. of Domestic Quarter; Stratified contents; M. M. Ill remains in upper layers; Contents of loiver Basements mature M. M. II; Loom- Weight Deposit Evidences of religious connexion; Miniature Shrine and votive vessels; Painted plaster decoration and plaster Cist; Ceramic characteristics of Deposit; The Palm Treejar; Lunate frieze on vessel; Imitations of painted plasterpattern; Architectonic origin of bands of disks; M attire polychrome style M. M. II b; Stellate flowers with pointed petals; Pottery from latest M. M. II deposits at Phaestos parallel with that from Loom-Weight. area; Evidences of a contemporary catastrophe; Imported Minoaii, pottery at Kalnm, c., in Egypt represents earlier and later M. M. II styles Origin of foliate bands from flower chains; The Abydos Vase from Xllth Dynasty Tomb; Chronological conclusions.

The THE best materials for the concluding phase of M. M. II ceramic art Weight were supplied at Knossos by the contents of some deep basements on the Base- Eastern slope, forming that architectural enclave to the North of the merits.

Domestic Quarter to which reference has been made above. 1 The principal part of this area derives its name from the loom-weights that here came to light in such abundance (See Plan and Section, Fig. 187 a, Fig. 187 b.

The discovery has been already noted of fine painted vessels and of the miniature terra-cotta shrine in these basements, and it will be seen that there is every reason to believe that one or more of the chambers above them and from which most of these relics were derived bore a sanctuary character. Later on, in the M. M. Ill Period, these structures, reinforced and intersected by new and massive walls became the basis of what seems to have been a great East Hall of the Palace on a higher level. The outer walls of this later building followed the old lines; one of them, however, divides the original Basement of the Loom-Weights into two sections (see Plan, Fig. 187 a). The level of the basement floors of this new building, which consisted of plaster, was 2-20 metres above the earlier pavement, and was separated from the uppermost deposit containing M. M. II relics by some 70 centimetres of filling earth. Above the M. M. Ill basement floor, in the section N. of the partition wall referred to, was a deposit derived from the Hall above, containing remains of a spiral fresco, 1 painted stucco reliefs, and column bases, which represent the earlier M. M. Ill phase. Above this again was a layer of filling materials about a metre thick, overlying which was a clay floor upon which stood tripod pots belonging to the close of this Period. 2

The original basements themselves consisted of a main chamber occupying most of the East side, together with a smaller compartment North of it, and three spaces on the West. Throughout the whole of this area was a well-defined stratum belonging to the close of M. M. II, 3 and certainly affording the best collective evidence of its matures! aspect to be found either at Knossos or elsewhere. As already noted, the miniature Discovery terra-cotta shrine 4 was found in this stratum. The faience tablets, moreover, ott; reproducing the house-fronts and towers of a contemporary town, the scattered Shrine remains of which occurred, under less definite stratigraphic conditions, Mosaic, in the filling earth of the N. E. compartment, stand, architecturally, in such close relation to the shrine that they too must be grouped with the M. M. II contents of these basements.

At a common depth of about 5 metres, 5 floors appeared throughout Relics .-ii-i belonging the greater part of this area, 8 coated with hard cement presenting a yellowish to M. M. white surface. 7 In the N. W. chamber were two ledges rather than steps " e " t a " d plastered over in a similar way, behind which a large patch of similar plaster Upper about a metre high clung to the S. wall of this basement. In the larger chamber, specially named after the loom-weights, was a dais, plastered like the floor and raised 19 cm. above it, which ran under the foundations of the 1 See below, p. 370. The fresco began companied by dumping of older materials had 1-70 m. below the datum level and continued occurred. In the North-West corner of this to 2-20 m. down. area also came to light the M. M. I seal im- ! This floor was 70 cm. below the datum pression, Fig. 151, above, and two bowls, level one imitating inlaid work in precious metals, : 1 In 1913 I had a new opportunity of going Fig. 183 a, 2, the other presenting the remark- through the pottery found in two sections of the able thorn-bossed decoration, Suppl. PI. Ill, a,

Western basement, which had been arranged both of which must be referred to the mature according to floor-levels and half-metre depths M. M II a Period.

in the Reference Museum formed in the 4 See above, p. 221 seqq., and Fig. 166.

Palace (B 114,115. In both sections M. M. II Reckoning from a triangular datum block remains, parallel with those E. of the dividing in the wall that divides the W. and E. sections wall, became general at about 4-20 from the of these structures, datum block. In the N. part of the area, 6 See below, Section, Fig. 187 b.

bordering the foundations of the old Upper In the small N. basement the cement was

Terrace Facade, considerable disturbance ac- red-faced.

oouaod isv3-Hiaon do TIVM dcXHdhOO 1S3M 1SV3 d3MOl :.;: k-.:.

-". FILLING.".; . I. M U I BULL S 7." TWO I: BRECfc? A

P1RAL., FRESC6.-. COLUMN BASES

METRES 5 ABOVE, INCLUDING THE AREA OF THE SPIRAL FRESCO.

M. M. Ill partition wall, widening out at its S. end to 2-05 m. Masses of pottery were found immediately above this, for which it had obviously served as a stand, and the underlying fragments between it and the floor of the room were of the same general character. 1

Taken as a whole, the relics found in the Loom-Weight Basement, though, as the associated pottery showed, deposited at the same date, were

FIG. 188, a, b.

FRAGMENTS OF PAINTED PLASTER DADOES, M. M. II b; FROM LOOM-WEIGHT BASEMENT.

divided into two classes, one belonging to the basement floors themselves, and the other derived from an upper floor that had fallen in.

Remains of the decoration of the upper chamber came to light in the Remains shape of fallen fragments of two painted plaster dadoes (Fig. 188, a, 6) the Wall only known examples belonging to this Period, and exhibiting a colour scheme Decora-different from that of the later Palace. Thus a shows three horizontal zones above guided as in later examples by impressed string lines coloured 1 Beneath this floor the latest elements were pieces of painted plaster presenting a pinkish

M. M. I a. Deeper down was Early Minoan, overlying Neolithic deposit. This came out as the result of a supplementary excavation carried out for me by Dr. Mackenzie in 1920.

See Fyfe, Painted Plaster Decoration at Knossos (R. I. B. A. Jouni.,. 4), p. 109, Figs, i, 2. The pattern in the lower zone of Fig. 2 is here interpreted, however, as a series of crescents. In the N. V. corner of this basement above the floor-level were also found two large surface, and evidently derived from the upper field of the wall above. Dr. Mackenzie notes of these fragments that they were backed by a terracotta coloured cement, containing pounded potsherds and small pebbles, 4 to 5 centimetres thick. Over this was a layer of white, fairly fine plaster half a centimetre thick, faced in turn by a layer of fine white cement about cm., covered with an ochreous wash, presenting the pinkish surface.

THE PALACE OF MINOS, ETC.

a greyish black, white and red, from which descend wavy bands alternating yellow, grey-black, white, pale bluish grey, and Venetian red. The pattern may be taken to be an early attempt to imitate the veins of some variegated rocks. In 6, which repeats the same hues, we see a succession of lunate bands corresponding with those on the large contemporary jar (Fig. 192, a) from the same area. 1

From the same upper chamber was also derived a miniature vase of pale blue faience with a foot, collar, and thimble-like receptacle of gold plate (Fig. 189 a), which may have contained some perfume as precious

FIG. 189 a. VASE OF GOLD AND FAIENCE.

FIG. 189 b. SMALL CLAY PAN WITH CARBONIZED CONTENTS OVER-LAID BY GOLD SPRAY.

Miniature Votive Vases of Faience Pottery and Offertory Bowl.

as attar of roses. Miniature vessels of painted clay, diminutive copies of larger pots, also occurred throughout this deposit (Fig. 191, sides). These belong to a votive class, and find their nearest parallels in the small offertory cups and vases which occurred in the little Sacellum of the early Palace at Phaestos, 2 together with libation tables and painted pottery of a late M. M. II style, corresponding with that of this Knossian stratum.

A similar offertory element is represented by a small open bowl of plain clay and of a characteristic type containing some carbonized substance 3 overlaid with very elegant fern-like sprays of thin gold plate and wire (Fig. 189 K). That part of this area served a sanctuary purpose is, however, 1 See below, p. 256.

"L. Pernier, Palazzo di Phaestos (Mem. Ant., v, p. 488 seqq., Figs. 93-5, and cf. p. 405 seqq.).

3 Its contents suggest a comparison with the little heaps of carbonized material probably-representing food-offerings found beneath clay cups arranged in rows in the pillar sanctuary of a house excavated by Mr. Hogarth on the hill of Gypsades (B. S. A., VI, PI. VI. i, 2).

best shown by the little terra-cotta shrine and its accessories which from the position in which the remains were discovered must have originally found a place on the upper floor of this M. M. II structure. 1 That this chamber of Sane-belonged to the women's apartments may be inferred by the large stores of loom-weights that it had contained. Over four hundred of these had been Terra-precipitated below from its floor-level and were found above the relics shrine, belonging to the basement proper. These are pear-shaped in outline and m tl s flatter than the oval Late Minoan type. It may be mentioned that looms The with pendant weights supply a recurring sign of the Linear Script A. vv! h In the S. E. corner of the larger basement remains of a plaster chest p a j nte d came to light in position, the outer surface of which was coloured red with Master vertical white and yellow bands at intervals, recalling the style of the dadoes above. On the floor of this basement, together with a certain number of miniature vases, were also found the two large spouted jars illustrated in Figs. 191 and 192.

Upon the plaster dais, and immediately below the foundations of a wall of M. M. Ill date, came to light the remains of the stately jar, Fig. 190, 3 the most remarkable of the vessels found in this Area. It is of exceptionally bulging shape, 4 and in its complete state presented on each face a group of three palm-trees, the central higher than the other two. These are executed in a matt creamy white, with outlines and details of a rosy terra-cotta tint, and stand out boldly against the black lustrous ground. The trees rise from a slightly undulating ground of the same creamy white, and, though the foliage is symmetrically balanced, the sprays and buds of the inflorescence (c) are naturally rendered. The whole effect is palatial and calls up the background of some great fresco design the animal accompaniments, however, being tabooed, as usual, by the Minoan vase-painter. On gem-types of the succeeding age we see both wild goats and lions associated with palm-trees. On a contemporary lentoid, however, three palms on a rocky knoll appear by 1 See p. 221. The fragments were found fragments of one side were taken to England a good deal scattered, some S. and some N. by a British Officer (at a time when the local of the North wall of the larger basement, and Cretan administration withheld even duplicate above the pavement-level. The same was true specimens from the excavators). I have now of the remains of the gold and faience vase. been enabled to place in the Candia Museum 2 See Mackenzie, The Pottery of Anossos a skilful reconstruction of the vessel by (J. H. S., xxiii), pp. 177, 178. The height of Mr. G. H. Young.

the jar with the spiral ornament (Fig. 192, a) Its greatest diameter is 43 cm. as against was 58-5 centimetres. That of the other a height of 54-5 cm. The width of the mouth (Fig. 191) was 49 cm. is 31-5 cm. s Only half of the jar was discovered. The

THE PALACE OE MINOS, ETC.

themselves as on the jar. 1 What is specially interesting to note is that this grand ceramic type of the three palm-trees survived on. vases of the later

FIG. 190. a, JAR WITH TRIPLE GROUPS OF PALM-TREKS, FROM LOOM-WEIGHT BASEMENT; , HANDLE OK JAR; c t INFLORESCENCE OF CENTRAL PALM.

Palace Style to the closing phajse at least of the First Late Minoan Period, since it reappears, in a conventionally decorative form, on one of the 1 p. 275, Fig. 204, d, below. Palm-trees near Knossos and in other districts of the seem to have been introduced into Crete by the island, but their fruit is of small account. Minoans. They still grow wild in the glens amphoras from the Kakovatos tombs. 1 The handles too (6), with their breastplate-like figures, find their adaptations in Late Minoan types.

Ceramic A group of vessels from the Loom-Weight Basement is given in Fig. 191.

eristics' Though, as will be seen, the smaller specimens show a certain tendency ? towards a monochrome decoration of plain lustreless white on the black

Poly- glazed ground, the pottery here found as illustrated by the more important chromy pieces represents a still flourishing polychrome tradition. These vessels in flourish- fact afford excellent examples of the ceramic style in vogue at the close of

M. M. II. They were buried in the position in which they were found by the great ruin that marks that epoch.

As will be shown below, an important chronological guide towards the earlier M. M. II b phase is afforded by a polychrome vase of the hole-mouthed type found in a Twelfth Dynasty tomb at Abydos. 2 The bands of eyed disks that appear on this pot are very characteristic of the present class, though they are accompanied on some of the Loom-Weight vessels with certain decorative details that point to a slightly later date 1

Very characteristic among these later elements are the more attenuated foliate bands seen on the jar (Fig. 191), still accompanied with the disk ornament, in this case orange with red madder eyes. The foliate decoration here seen and continually repeated on the fragments from this deposit has a special interest from the fact that it answers to the style of foliage that characterizes the saffron and lily designs on the two small vases figured below, 4 in which for the first time polychrome is associated with natural designs.

In these naturalistic designs of flowers and foliage, as in the jar with the three palm-trees, we may reasonably detect the reflection of a pictorial style taken from the Palace wall-paintings. But we also now observe in the mature products of M. M. II ceramic design the growing influence of decorative

The models of an architectonic class. Of this earlier Palace style a remark-

Palace a e exam p e s afforded by the fine jar from the floor of the Loom-Weight style. Basement, Fig. 192, a. Here, in the double bands of lunate decoration we recognize a direct imitation of the pattern seen on the contemporary plaster dado, Fig. 188, b above. The crescents on the vase are alternately creamy white and bright red, the latter with a crimson disk. The white spiral frieze of this vase also clearly goes back to dado decoration.

1 See Volume II, and cf. K. Mtiller, Ath. by wild goats.

Mitth., xxxiv (1909), Pl. XXII, 2. The triple 2 See below, pp. 269, 270.

palm group also recurs on a L. M. Ill gold 3 See below, p. 258, and cf. p. 268, Fig. 199.

mouth bandage" from Knkomi (Britishexcavs. See below, p. 264, Figs. 196, 19". Cyprus, Pl. VII, 518) in this case accompanied 1!. TYPICAL MATURE M. M. II POLYCHROME VASKS ILLISTRATIX.; EARLIKR", PAI. i STYLE: a, Kxossos; A-g, IHAKSTOS. a (J), b (-.), r (i), rf (i), (i),(i), (.,)-

Disk On the other hand, the zones of disks such as are seen on the fellow

Motives vessel, Fig. 191 (in this case creamy white with crimson eyes), which appear tural on the dark ground, have in their origin an actual structural significance. The disks in fact are derived from those that in the painted stucco fa ades of the Minoan buildings represent in a decorative fashion round beam ends which rest upon the architrave in the underlying wooden framework. An intermediate link was moreover afforded for the vase painter by the existence of coloured terra-cotta models, like the Miniature Shrine found in this area, in which the rows of disks are seen on a reduced scale in their true architectonic relation, as they also appear on the later wall-paintings of the miniature class. They recur again on the contemporary faience plaques, described below, representing house fronts. These bands of disks, which so appropriately mark the effect of Palatial models on the mature M. M. II b, ceramic style, and are indeed one of its special cachets, play, as will be seen, an important part in the decoration of the Abydos vase described below, 1 which has for us such a high chronological importance.

The fine contemporary jar, Fig. 192, b, from Phaestos, 2 belonging to an advanced stage of M. M. II, shows a further variation of the lunate pattern of a combined with an elaborate decorative design consisting of linked spirals, between the divergent scrolls of which are floral excrescences with pointed petals. These flowers are themselves derivatives of the Egyptian lotus, and the spiraliform combination in which they are here seen represents the adaptation of a class of ceiling pattern well known in Twelfth Dynasty

Ceiling Egypt. Something has already been said of the assimilation of such w j t h ceiling-types in the Minoan Palaces, and examples derived from the later

Lotus Palace at Knossos illustrate spiraliform combinations both with lotus and papyrus. A more individual feature in the Phaestos'design, of great beauty, is to be seen in the sprays of stellate flowers thrown across the spaces between the divergent bands of the spirals.

Other specimens of vases, of contemporary fabric, from Phaestos are given in Fig. 192, on one of which, e, we may trace the effect of whorl-shell models in this case perhaps the Dolium or Triton in the evolution of certain spiraliform patterns.

Corre- The correspondence presented by the ceramic remains of a series enceof of stratified deposits with those which at Knossos have been best preserved

Loom- in the Loom-Weight Basements is one of the many evidences of a parallel catastrophe that befell both Palaces at the close of the present Period.

1 See p. 267.

2 Pernier, Mon. Ant., xiv, p. 457. From a test-pit in Area 5.

at Phaes-tos.

M. M. II: LOOM-WEIGHT DEPOSIT (CERAMIC PHASE 6) 259

Among the ceramic remains at Phaestos may be mentioned not only the Weight contents of the little Sacellum already cited, but the later pottery found in with'that the walled rubbish pit beneath the earlier level of the West Court, the oflatc vessels found beneath the pavement in the region of the later Magazines and Deposits others that came to light in the early Magazines beneath the light-court of the Propylaeum. Apart from the better-known specimens, the fragmentary remains from these deposits on the site of Phaestos show many minute points of agreement with the parallel Knossian strata, 1 including the diffusion on both sites of similar forms of small cups, some with dull white bands on a dark glazed ground, and others of plain clay with pared exterior walls, which must both be regarded as very typical of this epoch.

It is a significant circumstance that in the whole of the Loom-Weight area no specimens of the fine egg-shell ware came to light. Other divergencies in style and fabric, some of them pointing in a later direction, are now perceptible. The bizarre veined ornamentation, an inheritance of the older stone-work tradition, is no longer in vogue. The fluted and impressed imitations of metal work, well represented in the earlier M. M. II phase, are heavier and have lost their sheen.

In the case of the medium-sized vessels, the potter's wheel was now in Late general use, and their bases often bear the concentric markings caused by the string that cut them from their clay base while in rapid revolution. 8 These are clearly shown, for instance, on the base of the polychrome vase tvith the crocus sprays, Fig. 197 below. A late characteristic, particularly observable in the case of the miniature vases (see Fig. 191), is that the handles of these instead of being organically moulded on to the body of the vessel, as in the finer class of the smaller M. M. II fabrics, are manifestly applied to the surface and betray their attachments in the same way as the handles of M. M. III cups. 3 Finally, in spite of the large survival of the fine polychrome tradition, there is now perceptible a certain tendency towards a simple dull white decoration on a dark ground. This monochrome style, which anticipates the usual M. M. Ill ceramic fashion, is well illustrated by the most typical class of late M. M. II cups with a white band beneath their rims, already referred 1 This observation is the result of a close bases of these miniature vessels do not, however, examination of the Phaestos remains during bear traces of the curved concentric striation of repeated visits to the site. the later quick wheel fabrics, such as already 8 See below, p. 590, Fig. 434, b. appear before the close of M. M. II (see below,

Cf. R. M. Dawkins, B. S. A., ix, p. 303, p. 264). They were cut off from the clay by where the careful welding of the lower end of a straight instrument, according to the earlier the handle into the side of the cup is shown to practice. Their exceptionally small size made distinguish the earlier from the later class. The the conditions in this case abnormal.

THE PALACE OF MINOS, ETC.

Light and dark panelled decoration.

Survival of typical M. M. II form of jar to close of M. M. III to, and by the miniature vases here found, on which this plain white decoration was almost universal. 1 The concluding Middle Minoan style is here already foreshadowed.

The remarkable jar, Fig. 193, from the early Sanctuary at Phaestos with its alternating panels of light and dark has a special interest from the link of connexion it supplies both in its form and its decorative ground-plan with a type of jar found in the Temple Repositories at Knossos and belonging to a mature stage of M. M. III. 2 There, too, we see the same general contour and pinched-in mouth, derived, as pointed out above, from a metallic prototype, and the same succession of vertical bands alternately light and dark with no sign of polychromy. On the other hand, the colour scheme of the Phaestos vessel is of the most subtle and elaborate kind. The same elongated cable band that is seen in white running up the foliated stems of the light panels reappears in red on the tangential bands of the dark fields, while flowers and buds of the same scarlet hue are suspended in the interspaces. The F IG. 193. POLYCHROME JAR FROM PHAESTOS. (:.) decorative scheme is fundamentally the same as that of the ceiling pattern seen on Fig. 192, b, and stands in the same relationship.

The survival of this form of vessel to the close of the last Middle Minoan Period, at times in company with the panelled decoration, and, in one case at least, 3 associated with a floral design showing a survival of polychromy on a wholly dark ground, affords striking evidence of the continuity of the Minoan potter's art. It is however an unquestionable fact 1 The ring round the neck of the small of the small one-handled jug above it. oenochoe to the right of Fig. 191, is, however, 2 See below, p. 557, Fig. 404, b. tinted with vermilion. Cf. too the marbling 3 See below, Coloured Plate VII, a.

that both at Knossos and Phaestos the closing phase of M. M. II was separated from the succeeding epoch by a widespread catastrophe.

In Fig. 194 are collected a series of decorative designs illustrating both the earlier (a) and, in its lower half, the later ceramic phase (6) of M. M. II. 1 In d, with its fluted arches and Gothic finials, we have already recognized a reflection of the repousse decoration of contemporary goblets in precious metals.

The cloisonne disk, a, from the diadem ascribed to Senusert ll's daughter, 2 is here included, since the cruciform arrangement of open lilies and intervening buds suggests the source of ceramic designs like b.

The segmental medallion h recurs on the polychrome vase, described below, from Abyclos, belonging to the later phase of this Period. Its pattern formed by four inter-secting circles already appears in light on dark technique in E. M. Ill, 3 together with a variety showing three segments. The pattern certainly shows a great resemblance to that of a well-known Egyptian class of faience plaques and painted decoration, sometimes vith a floral centre, and in the present case the asterisk ornament in the middle of the disk makes the correspondence unmistakable. 4 Such inlays, as we have seen, already appear in the early Vat Room Deposit (M. M. I a).

The development of a motive on a vase from the Kamares Cave given in Fig. 194, , once more suggests a ceiling pattern of a palatial type. We have seen that the red disks between the sprouts are a regular ornamental feature of this epoch, taken over on to the foliate designs from architectonic zones with reminiscences of beam-ends. In other words this pattern is at home in Minoan Crete. But this result is of the greatest interest in view of the striking analogy here presented with the horned ornamentation (also reflected on the pottery 6) of the stone bases and ceilings of the l b is on a M. M. II polychrome figurine Discovered by Professor Flinders Petrie (Melos: Myres, B. S. A., ix, p. 369, Fig. i); (cf. A. M. Lythgoe, Treasure of Lahun, is on a M. M. II b jug (Phylakopi, p. 149, Bull, of the Metropolitan Museum of Ari, Pt. ii,

Fig. 126). Il is interesting as supplying the Dec. 1919, Fig. 6). Senusert II reigned c. 1906- prototype of the Sun-flower on later vases 1887 B. C.

of Melian fabric (op. at., p. 138, Fig. no). See above, p. 113, Fig. 80 A i.

j, with the segmental medallion repeated (cf. Petrie, Egyptian Decorative Art, p. 48,

Fig. 198, it), is from the Kamares Cave as also Fig. 88 (from Prisse, Art, i. 84).

the original bowl from which k is here 5 Prof. T. Zammit, C. M. G., 2nd Report of developed. The other patterns are from Hal Tarxien Excavations (Archaeologia, 1917,

Knossos. Although in most cases, the evidence p. 280, Fig. 13). For the comparison made was derived from fragments, all the restorations recently by Dr. Einar Lexow (Bergens of patterns on Fig. 194 are fully warranted. Museums Aarbok, H)i8-i), Hist.-Antikv. rxkke

FIG. 194. M. M. II POLYCHROME CERAMIC PATTERNS (a EGYPTIAN CLOISONNE DISK, Xllxn DYN.) a f, M. M. II a; g I, M. M. II b; k, CEILING PATTERN DEVELOPED FROM VASE.

latest phase of the Maltese Megalithic Sanctuaries. Such correspondence as that between Fig. 194 k and the incised decoration of the bowl, Fig. 1!.", implies direct relationship.

The architectonic influences visible in the vase decoration of this Period, due to generations of Palace life, were opposed to the more naturalistic impulses of which we find the ceramic traces already in M. M. I. In so far as what may be called the earlier Palace Style was concerned this is self-evident. But it would be a mistake to suppose that the progress of naturalism in design was altogether checked during the brilliant days of the M. M. 11 Palace. The reliefs of shells and beetles on pottery have been already noticed. In a considerably stylized shape, sea-creatures, flowers and foliage still play an appreciable part in vase painting. A naturally rendered crocus chain is already seen in the latest M. M. I phase, and this flower again occurs, on a fine M. M. 11 polychrome bowl from Palaikastro. The natural inflorescence on otherwise conventionally rendered palm-trees has already been noted, and the restored design,

Fig. 194, g, shows flowering olive sprays, the leaves of which are alternately red and white. This variation in the hue of the olive-leaves, noticeable at certain seasons, is constantly reproduced in the wall-paintings where this subject appears the alternating tints there being ruddy brown and olive green. A fragmentary specimen. Fig. 389, below, also presents flowering olive sprays, here with a succession of red, white, and black leaves a very close parallel to the vase design. Two of the fine polychrome jars that illustrate the latest ceramic phase

Naturalist tradition in

M. M. II Vase painting: much stylized.

Palm-trees.

FIG. 195.

INCISED BOWL, HAL TARXIEN, MALTA.

Sprays resembling Fresco Examples.

tir.) between the Maltese horned scrolls and the veined motive on a M. M. Ha cup, see above p. 22. and cf. p. 601 below. (The cup was curiously mis-described by Lexow, p. 13, as of E. M. Ill date, c. 2200 B. C.). In Myc. Tree and I illar Cult, 1901, p. 101, I had alre. idy called attention to the probable influence of Mycenaean (i. e. Minoan) reflections of Egyptian ceiling patterns on the decoration of the Maltese monuments.

1 e. g. Fig. 133, h.

1 Dawkins, B. S. A., x, p. air. The bowl presents a pattern of large white rosettes with a red centre on the black ground connected by bands of orange yellow and with the interspaces filled by crocuses in white. A bowl of fine egg-shell ware like that of Knossos was found in association with this.

THE PALACE OF MINOS, ETC.

of the Early Palace at Phaestos show floral sprays thrown, as it were, into the intervals of the scroll ornament. 1 In the one case we see scarlet buds and blossoms, in the other stellate flowers on red stalks. The small globular jug from a well South-West of the site at Knossos, Fig. 19(, presents a floral design of more definite character. We see here white lilies, with bright red anthers, their leafy stalks being also indicated in white, which recalls the horizontal foliated bands on some of the vessels from the Loom-Weight deposit. This feature recurs on the remarkable hole-

FIG. 196. POLYCHROME JUG WITH LILY SPRAYS, KNOSSOS. ( )

FIG. 197. M. M. II POLYCHROME VESSEL WITH SAFFRON-FLOWERS, KAMARES CAVE. ( )

Saffron- mouthed vase, Fig. 197, found during the recent excavations of the British on M. M. School in the Kamares Cave, 2 presenting delineations of crocus-flowers in a remarkably natural manner. The petals here are white on a lustrous II Vase from

Kamares. black ground, while the pistils and stamens are picked out with red.

This vessel, as Mr. Dawkins has pointed out, is from the potter's point of view of somewhat decadent fabric and was turned on the quick wheel. The band of red disks beneath the design is, like the foliated 1 See above, Figs. 192, 193.

2 R. M. Dawkins, The Excavation of the Kamares Cam in Crete (B. S. A., xix), Pl. X, and pp. 21, 22. Mr. Dawkins points out that the class to which this vessel belongs shows the advanced technique of the quick wheel with strong wheel marks. The

Knossian evidence, however, shows that this stage had already been reached before the close of M. M. II.

sprays which it repeats, a feature shared by typical polychrome vessels of the M. M. 1 1 b phase.

This vase has a special importance in the strong suggestion that Com-it affords as to the dependence of such naturalistic floral designs of the pottery of this epoch on contemporary wall-paintings. The curved outlines from which the plants spring are themselves taken over from the irregular foreground of rocks and hillocks that characterize Minoan landscape pieces. It will be seen at once that both in its subject and in the delineation of the flowers themselves this vessel affords a new standpoint for comparison Saflvon-with the earliest of the Knossian wall-paintings that survives in anything like a complete form that, namely, representing the Saffron-gatherer. 1

The subject of this fresco (Plate IV), 2 a youthful figure, naked except for with a girdle, gathering saffron-flowers, and setting them into bowls in a rocky field, has probably a religious association. The saffron crocus, like the lily, was The a special attribute of the Great Minoan Goddess, who may have been held to preside over what, as we know from the evidence of a series of clay tablets, must have been a flourishing Cretan industry. The saffron gardens of Crete have existed indeed down to modern times, and a record of others is preserved in local names. The figure itself with its grey blue body colour differs from the convention observed by the later school of Minoan wall-painting. It seems nearer to the female convention as regards its hue than the deep Venetian red that marks male figures, and it is possible, therefore, that it indicates a vouner girl rather than a boy. Certain details of the design ,,..,,. Points of such as the festoons of white dots are in sympathy with the ceramic decoration of the First Middle Minoan Period. The bowls here represented show a black ground with white spots and a band of red and belong to the Fresco polychrome class, while the rocks with their, alternate veins of black and f" 0 n"

vermilion red and their white outline recall certain ceramic imitations of Ceramic Decora-breccia of the early part of the Middle Minoan Age. Altogether, both the tion.

1 The fragment of the Saffron-gatherer of Middle Minoan date. There was a well-fresco was found on a floor level about the marked M. M. II stratum throughout this area.

centre of the area originally included in the The fresco probably belonged to a Hall of that

Early Keep. See Knossos, Report, 1900 Period on the upper floor. B. S. A., vi), p. 45, where its Kamares Plate IV is based on the restored drawing character was already noted. It was later, of the fresco fragments by M. Gillievon. The therefore, than the early part of M. M. I. head and outstretched arm are his restora-

Othenvise its provenance supplies some sug- tions. The group of crocus-flowers in the gestion as to its chronological position. A large upper right-hand corner belongs apparently to black steatite bowl found on the outskirts of a companion panel of this wall-painting, though this area has an archaic aspect and is probably it is here included with the other fragments.

THE PALACE OF MINOS, ETC.

Probable Date, M. M. II.

Import of Minoan Polychrome Yare under Twelfth Dynasty.

Minoan Polychrome Sherds at Kahun.

circumstances of its finding and the approach in style of the crocus-flowers to those seen on the polychrome bowl illustrated in Fig. 197 above make it preferable to regard this fresco as coining within the limits of M. M. II. It must be regarded as the only example of a figured wall-painting surviving from the Early Palace walls.

There is clear evidence that during the most brilliant period of the Middle Kingdom in Egypt a country which, owing to natural causes, was poor in ceramic wares the beautiful polychrome fabrics of contemporary Crete were beginning to come into favour. They were perhaps first introduced by Minoan traders and craftsmen employed on the great royal works. A contingent of these seems to have formed part of the settlement at Kahun in the Fayum, called into being by the erection of Senusert II's pyramid on the neighbouring site of Illahun. That large numbers of foreign workmen were collected here appears from the fact that according to Petrie's observations the greater part of the weights and two of the three measures found are foreign weights and measures of Phoenicia and Asia Minor. 1 It is, therefore, not surprising that in the rubbish heaps of this Twelfth Dynasty town, together with Syrian pottery, there occurred other polychrome sherds, several with a fine glaze, to which Professor Flinders Petrie with prescient instinct gave the name of Aegean. 2 The discovery, soon after this, of similar pottery in the Kamares Cave proved its Cretan source. 3

Among the painted fragments from Kahun illustrated by Professor Petrie, part of a hole-mouthed vessel with a textile pattern 4 in creamy white on the black ground recalls the early specimen of this class of decoration given in Fig. 125, 9, p. 176 above, and represents an archaic tradition going back to Neolithic times, though the technique of the vase is characteristically M. M. II. A fragmentary bowl with light brown ground, crinkled rim, and impressed cruciform ornaments, 5 and another with a dark ground and patterns consisting of lines and dotted circles, are also best grouped with M. M. II a. On the other hand, the pointed petals seen on Fig. 198, c, from 1 Petrie,. H. 5., xi (1890), pp. 275, 276, PI. XIV; Kahun, c., p. 42; Illahun, Kahun, and Gurob, 1891, p. 9, and PI. I, Figs. 3-8, 10-15.

2 . H. S., xi, PI. XIV, 5, 6, 7, 8, 10. (In the British Museum.) Similar imported sherds were found on the neighbouring Site of Harageh.

J. L. My res, Prehistoric Pottery from Kaniarais (Prof. Soc. Ants., xv, 1895, p. 351 seqq., and Pis. I-IV), and Dr. Lucio Mariani (Man. Antichi, vi, 1895, p. 332 seqq., and Pis. IX-XI). Myres noted the resemblance to the Kahun sherds.

4 Petrie, Illahun, Kahun,:., PI. I, 14, and J. H. S., xi, PI. XIV, 5 5 Petrie, Illahun, Kahun, f., PI. I, 8, and . . S., xi, PI. XIV, 10. The impressed ornaments are madder-red rimmed with white. For the cruciform pattern in light, cf. Mackenzie, H. S., xxvi, PI. VIII, 4, n.

the side of another hole-mouthed vase from this site belong to a floral type charac-teristic of a very mature stage of M. M. II, when they seem to supersede the earlier type with rounded ends. Similar sprays on a fragment belonging to the close of the M. M. II Period at Knossos are shown on Fig. 15)8,); they are accompanied by the typical red disks. A good parallel is also supplied by a complete flower on a jug, Fig.

198, A, dating from the time of the last catastrophe of the earlier Palace at Phaestos. Fig. 198, B,

Flg. 198. 1OTTERV SHOWING POINTED PETALS OK LATEST M. M. II PHASE FROM K 1U N (c)

AND CRETAN SITES (A, B, D).

reproduces a similar type with curving leaves from the Kamares Cave, 1 diagrammatically completed in Fig. 194, j and the central disk in this case with its segmental pattern, taken over as we have seen from inlaid work, recurs on the vase from Abydos described below. Painted sherds decorated with flowers showing the same pointed petals occur at Phylakopi 2 among the last imported remains of this Period. 3

The evidence from Kahun received a remarkable corroboration in Professor Garstang's discovery of the remains of one of the familiar bridge- 1 J. L. Myres, op. fit., PI. IV, 27. They are thus placed by Dr. Mackenzie.

8 Phylakopi, p. 149, Fig. 126.

THE PALACE OF MINOS, ETC.

Evidence of Abydos Tomb, containing

M. M. II Polychrome Vase.

spouted Minoan vases of this class in a virgin tomb at Abydos, 1 accompanied by glazed steatite cylinders bearing the names of Sesostris (Senusert) III and Amenemhat III, the latter of whom, according to Meyer's chronology, reigned from about 1849 to 1801 i?. c. 2

A view of this vase is given in Fig. 199, a, and it is also shown in company with other relics found in this tomb in Suppl. PI, IV. The form and dimensions of the vessel agree with typical hole-mouthed and bridge-spouted vases of the M. M. II class. The same correspondence, moreover,

FIG. 199. ABYDOS VASE (TO L.) COMPARED WITH OTHER M. M. II POLYCHROME TYPES.

is seen in every detail of the decoration. The beam end bands with alternating disks of red and white and the stellate flowers recur on a series of polychrome vessels from the M. M. II Palace floors of Knossos and Phaestos. The segmental medallions resemble the type given in Fig. 194, h above, which itself represents the persistence of an inlay pattern that already appears in E. M. III. 3 The vase is shown in its original form as restored from the existing fragments. 4 For comparison there is placed with it in Fig. 199, e, a M. M. II polychrome vase from Knossos of the same hole- 1 J. Garstang, Note on a Vase of Minoan Fabric from Abydos (Univ. Liverpool Annals of Archaeology, c., 1913, p. 107 seqq.): The contents of the tomb were noticeably free from intrusive features and uniformly characteristic of the funeral arts of the Xllth Dynasty (p. 108). According to Professor Garstang, Every object found within the tomb, to a number of more than a hundred, was of Xllth Dynasty character (p. no). The

Minoan Vase and most of the Egyptian relics from the tomb are now in the Ashmolean Museum, Oxford (see Suppl. PI. IV).

2 Aegypiische Chronologic, p. 57.

8 See above, p. 113, Fig. 80 b. i.

1 It is reproduced as set up in the Ashmolean Museum by Mr. VV. H. Young. It was published by me in the Ashmolean Museum Report for 1907, where its M. M. II character was first pointed out.

mouthed type, adorned with bands showing a similar succession of coloured disks, and a cup and fragment with stellate flowers, b, c, the petals of which are in this case rounded as on the Abydos example.

The angular foliation of the middle band of the hole-mouthed vase from Knossos, Fig. 199, e, 1 is a very characteristic feature of this epoch. As will be seen from the comparative examples given in Fig. 200 it is in fact an outgrowth of a simple flower chain, such as children make of daisies. As a motive of jewellery such chains are of frequent occurrence in Late Minoan times, derived no doubt from a much earlier tradition (see inset, a). 3 It is a remarkable fact, moreover, that a common decorative motive on L. M. Ill pottery is clearly copied from this later chain-work in precious metal (inset b) It would seem, BJ- indeed, by no means improbable that the appearance of this motive on pottery was due to the actual overlaying of vessels with flower chains cut out of gold foil. A polychrome design of such a chain (Fig. 200, a), conventionally rendered in alternating red and white flowers, already occurs on a M. M. I a vase, and recurs in a more natural shape in the crocus bands of a jar of the close of that Period. The relation of the M. M. 11 types b and c of the Figure is clearly seen. On the other hand, by the close of M. M. 11 the foliation, as illustrated by the specimen, d, from a large jar of the Loom-Weight Basement, had taken on a more attenuated and naturalistic shape under the influence of ceramic plant designs such as the lily and crocus illustrated above, which themselves are the reflection of similar designs that now appear on the Palace walls. On a paler lilac brown ground, with inferior glaze, this attenuated foliation survived on M. M. Ill pottery (Fig. 200, e), and is even traceable in certain sprays that occur on pottery of the beginning of L. M. I. It is noteworthy in this connexion that the poly- 1 Restored from fragments found in the area V. of the Loom-Weight Basement.

2 Fig. 200, a, is from a sherd belonging to a M. M. I a deposit, S. E. of the Palace site at Knossos b is from the Koulouraor walled rubbish pit. (is taken from the hole-mouthed vase, Fig. 199. c, above, d appears on one of the large jars of the Loom-Weight Basement (see above, p. 255, Fig. 191). e is from a M. M.

Ill a goblet found in the Kamares Cave (Dawkins, B. S. A., xix, PI. XII, i). The cup, Fig. 199, d, from the Loom-Weight Area shows a simple survival of the angular type of foliation, Fig. 200, b, f.

Cf. Prth. Tombs of Anossos, p. 76, Fig. 85.

4 Furtwangler u. Loeschcke, Afyk. Iasfti, PI. XIX, 139, and cf. PI. X, 60, and XXXVII, 380, c.

THE PALACE OF MINOS, ETC.

chrome vase, Fig. 199, e, most nearly equated with the Abydos specimen, shows the intermediate form, Fig. 200, c.

The evidence supplied by the Egyptian cylinders points to the close of the nineteenth century B. C., for the date of the imported Cretan vessel found in the Abydos tomb and the parallel example from Knossos, belonging it would appear to the earlier part of M. M. 11 6, may be regarded as of

Twelfth and Early,

Thir- lower.

teenth Dynasty Associations.

FIG. 200. EVOLUTION OF FLOWER-CHAIN PATTERN ON VASES INTO FOLIATE BANDS. (a, M. M. I; 6, c, MATURE M. M. II; d, CLOSE OF M. M. II; e, M. M. Ill a.) approximately contemporary fabric, which does not represent quite the latest phase of M. M. II b.

The great epoch of Kahun carries the chronological limit somewhat As indicated by the hieratic papyri there discovered, it extends from the reign of Amenemhat III to those of Ra-sekhem-khu-taui and Sekhem-ka-ra, the first kings of the Thirteenth Dynasty, or, approximately, from 1849 to 1765 B. C. The general trend of the evidence, indeed, leads to the conclusion that the latest M. M. II phase may be brought down to a date approaching the close of the Eighteenth Century B. C.

AND SEAL-STONES.

Advance in naturalistic design also affects glyptic works; Gem-impressions on Clay Seaings from Hieroglyphic Deposit; Attempts at portraiture Effigies attributed to Mi-noun Dynast and his Son; Naturalistic scenes on other seal-impressions; Types of M. M- II seals; Signets and prism seals i itli hieroglyphic formulas; Royal bead-seal; Advanced Hieroglyphic Script of Class); Clay bars, labels, and tablets; Linearized sign groups; Numerals; Independent Evolution of Minoan Hieroglyphic script, aided by Egyptian suggestion; Hieroglyphic signary an epitome of early Cretan culture; Selected signs Saffron, Bee, Olive Spray, and Ship; Silplrium-like figures compared with types on coins of Cyrene.

STEATITE and ivory representations ofliving objects in intaglio or small relief had been already executed with considerable skill by the close of the Early Minoan Age. Early in M. M. I, moreover, we have evidence that the Minoan lapidaries were beginning to attack hard materials such as rock Hard crystal and, apparently, liparite for the production of vases, and the Egyptian j " Twelfth Dynasty scarab of amethyst engraved below by a Cretan craftsman attacked, with characters of the Minoan hieroglyphic Class A has been included above within the lower limits of that Period. 2 But the general use of hard materials for signets and the growing freedom of treatment mark a real advance.

Two signet impressions on clay sealings from the Hieroglyphic Deposit Ior-at Knossos, representing respectively the heads of a man and of a very slg? young boy, even show considerable achievement in the direction of portraiture " ts (Fig. 201, a, b). A Impressions of both these heads appear on one sealing, and bynast on another (Fig. 206) the man's head, here impressed without the other, is j" nt associated with the stamp of a hieroglyphic formula consisting of the, leg, Son. and gate combination, which recurs, apparently as an official title of an hereditary nature, on seal-stones of both the earlier and later hieroglyphic class. It has even been possible with the aid of this and parallel formulas to compose a kind of Family Tree of Middle Minoan titles and personal badges. 4 On Fig. 207, a, we see this formula on what may be reasonably 1 See p. 170, above. 4 See Serif ta Minoa i, p. 266, Fig. 119 and 2 See p. 199. p. 268, seqq.

3 See, too, above, p. 8, Fig. 2.

THE PALACE OE MINOS, ETC.

supposed to be a royal signet. The features on the sealings are sharply characterized and the elder personage (a), with his high brach) cephalic head and aquiline nose seems, as already observed, to represent the old Anatolian strain of Minoan Crete. 1 It is hardly too much to conclude that we have here an attempt to reproduce the actual lineaments of a Minoan Priest-King and his infant son, who on other grounds may be roughly regarded as the contemporaries of the Twelfth or early Thirteenth Dynasty of Egypt.

These interesting types occurred in a hoard of clay sealings, bars, and labels impressed or inscribed with inscriptions of the advanced hiero-

FIG. 201. PORTRAIT HEADS ON SEALINGS: HIEROGLYPHIC DEPOSIT, KNOSSOS

The Hieroglyphic Deposit.

glyphic Class B, found in an elongated chamber behind the steps of the Long Gallery of the Magazines at Knossos. It is known as the Hieroglyphic Deposit and undoubtedly had been covered over at the time of the great catastrophe at the close of the M. M. II Period. On some of the sealings of this hoard types occurred that show an extraordinarily picturesque development in this branch of art (Fig. 202). 2 We see a hart besidg a water-brook with rugged peaks beyond (a), a fish and sepia stranded, as if by a retiring wave, in a rocky pool (6), and what looks like a sea-grotto, possibly with 1 See Introductory Chapter (The Minoan Age), pp. 6-9.

2 I was so impressed with the very advanced style of. some of these gem-impressions that when writing the first volume of my Scripta Minoa I was still inclined to bring down part of this Deposit within the upper limits of the M. M. Ill Period (see pp. 22, 23, and 143).

But the balance of probability seems to be in favour of assigning it to the latest M. M. II phase. In the stratified group of M. M. Ill deposits referred to in the next Section there is no trace of hieroglyphic inscriptions or sealings and the inscribed documents connected with them are consistently of the Linear Class A.

animal forms above (f). 1 This delight in rocky scenery, equally visible in the Natura-Saffron-gatherer fresco, continued to be a characteristic of Minoan art in the In succeeding M. M. Ill Period. In d we recognize a Cretan wild-goat, while Engrav-e shows an interesting design of an infant beneath a horned sheep or moufflon, suggestive of some variant version of the nurture of the Cretan Zeus'. Above is a spear- or oar-like object. The reticulated work seen here in the background is simply a decorative feature common on gems of this Period and which often occurs in connexion with hieroglyphic signs (see Fig. 207, e, g, and h i).

FIG. 202. GEM IMPRESSIONS ON CLAY SEAUNGS FROM HIEROGLYPHIC DEPOSIT,

KNOSSOS: M. M. b. (f)

As has been already observed, a great chancre in the material of seal- Harder.-i,-i-i Stones stones is visible at this epoch. In place of soft materials like steatite and now ivory, hard stones such as cornelian, amethyst, rock crystal, and jasper are now Used-successfully attacked, though steatite seals are still occasionally found.

The impressions on the clay sealings from the Hieroglyphic Deposit Forms of themselves give a clue to the forms of many of these M. M. II seals. Some of seals and the finest were evidently taken from perforated lentoids of a type already (known in soft stone, and which became so prevalent in the succeeding Minoan Periods. On the clay sealing, Fig. 203, from this Deposit, is seen the im- 1 A. J. E., Knossos. Report, 1900 (B. 5. A., vi), p. 63. I T

THE PALACE OF MINOS, ETC.

Convoluted Bead-Seals.

Signets.

Signet Types.

pression of a more oval form of slightly bossed gem, showing a dog seizing a hind, executed in a naturalistic style, with a tree behind.

There seems also to have coexisted with the pure lentoid type another form, presenting, as in the former cases, two circular faces slightly bossed, but with flat edges, cut square (Fig. 204, a) a type which survives into the succeeding Period. 1 The rock-crystal specimen (-), 2 shows on one side a wild boar ( ), on the other (c) a hound seizing a wild goat; a banded agate of the same type, d, presents a group of three palms rising from rocks, also known, as we have seen, on the Palace jars here.

The presence of hieroglyphs of the advanced class (B) on many of the seal-stones themselves also enables us to assign certain types to this Period. Among those so authenticated is a graceful form of bead-seal with convoluted back (Fig. 204, e). s A seal of this form presented the remarkable decorative design shown inf, which may even have served as a portable pattern for a painted stucco ceiling, closely parallel with an Egyptian class. 4 In a somewhat allied variety of seal-stone the back is formed by two foreparts of lions in reversed positions. 5

The 'signet class of seal in a highly developed form is much in evidence, the stems of these being often elegantly cut and presenting decorative mouldings (Fig. 204, h-ni). On l-m appear two wild goats, browsing on a rocky knoll (tti) resembling that surmounted by palm-trees on d. A rudely executed, imp-like figure on a small signet from Mochlos " recalls the winged goblins on contemporary Melian vases and a demonic type of the Zakro sealings. A geometrical wingetl figure, evolved from a variant of the Egyptian waz symbol, 7 appears on the prism-seal, Fig. 207, c. The prism-seals 8 and q, the flattened cylinder s, and g supply characteristic examples of animal and bird types.

Scripta Minoa, i, p. 139, Fig. 81. For a better example see E. Babelon, Collection Pauvert de la Chapelle, No. 7 1 (PL VI and p. 2 8).

6 See below, p. 703, Fig. 526 (Seager, Mochlos, p. 58, x. b.

7 See below, p. 706, and Fig. 530.

8 Green jasper, East Central Crete. Faces 2 and 3, hieroglyphic groups. 4, Four feline heads.

FIG. 203. CLAY SEALING, FROM HIEROGLYPHIC DEPOSIT, KNOSSOS (f).

1 Often in connexion with designs representing the fronts of buildings.

2 From Siteia.

3 Scripta Alinoa, p. 140, Fig. 82, a.

4 See my Cretan Pictographs, c., p. 50 seqq. (J. H. S., xiv, p. 319 seqq.), and ib. Plate XII, where a ceiling pattern is restored with the aid of the gem.

FIG. 204. TYPES OF M. M. II SEALS AND GEMS (?); a, b, c, ROCK CRYSTAL; d, t, f, I, WHITE CORNELIAN; g, h, n, GREEN JASPER; , q, RED CORNELIAN; s, BANDED AGATE.

THE PALACE OF MINOS, ETC.

Prism seals.

Facing head and female costume.

Many circular seal-impressions were evidently taken from signets like Fig. 204, h, , and one at least of these with an elaborate decorative border, showing exceptional fineness of engraving (Fig. 205), J has the appearance of having been impressed by a metal matrix. One of the two hieroglyphs on this is of exceptional interest as representing an eight-stringed lyre. Other types of hieroglyphic signets of this class are shown in Fig. 207, 6, d.

Three- and four-sidedprism-seals were also evidently much in use, and the more elongated types of these now in vogue (Fig. 207, c, i) were specially adapted for containing hieroglyphic formulas. A cornelian seal of this class,

FIG. 205. IMPRESSION OF SIGNET-SEAL, M. M. II. (f) HIEROGLYPHIC DEPOSIT.

FIG. 206. IMPRESSIONS OF PRISM AND SIGNET ON M. M. II SEALING, (f) HIEROGLYPHIC DEPOSIT.

here for the first time reproduced, Fig. 207, c, presents features of great interest. The facing head here seen the counterpart of the winged symbolic figure of face i, above referred to with its locks flowing out on either side and terminating in coils, recalls that of Ishtar with her two side tresses and may be due to a suggestion from the Oriental side, where facing heads go back to the Sumerian Age. It shows prominent teeth and small globular ear-rings. The sex is clearly female and the two small hieroglyphs above may supply a name., on another prism-seal 2, presents a gowned figure with a peaked collar a survival of the female costume illustrated by the Petsofa figurines. Impressions of these prisms' often occur on clay sealings side by side with those of the 'signets' as, for instance, on that presenting the portrait, apparently, of one of the Knossian Priest-Kings (Fig. 20(5).

A perforated oblong seal with slightly rounded faces (Fig. 204, r-s), 3 1 Scripta Minoa, i, p. 161, P. 64 a (and cf. pp. 142, 146).

2 Three-sided. On face 2 hieroglyphs Nos. 13 (twice), 18,64; face 3, Nos. 5, 18, 64 of Signary, Fig. 214.

Cf. Scripta Minoa, i, PI. II, P. 41, and p. 147. The specimen shown in Fig. 204, r-s has two perforations, an unusual feature. From its style this intaglio may well be of M. M. II date.

more fully treated under M. M. Ill, also now appears, which may be described as a flattened cylinder.

The shape of the clay sealings found in the Hieroglyphic Deposit, on Three-which many impressions of seals of the above classes are seen, is more or less ciay three-sided. The sealings have one larger and two smaller faces, and show s

FIG. 207.   a, ROYAL BEAD-SEAL, CORNELIAN (f); 6, CHALCEDONY SIGNET, MOCHLOS (f); c, CORNELIAN, CENTRAL CRETE (f); ,, CORNELIAN (f); e,, k, GREEN JASPER, k, CANDIA

DISTRICT J A, SltEIA.

a perforation along the major axis containing carbonized remains of the string by which the merchandise or document was secured (e. g. Fig. 20li). The three-sided shape of these sealings is itself a natural one for pinched clay nodules to assume, which required more than one face for impressions and incised characters. It corresponds moreover with the prevailing three-sided type of the seals themselves.

THE PALACE OF MINOS, ETC.

Seals with Hieroglyphic Script.

The hieroglyphic script of Crete itself attains its highest point of development by the Second Middle Minoan Period. The sign-groups engraved on the seals are of more artistic execution, while at the same time a more linearized hieroglyphic script now makes its appearance for the first time on clay documents and sealings. Among the inscribed seals of this

Royal Seal.

FIG. 208. CLAY LABELS AND PERFORATED BARS WITH HIEROGLYPHIC SCRIPT (B).

FIG. 209.   CLAY TABLET FROM PHAESTOS. ( ) class the most beautiful example is a red cornelian prism which probably contains the name and titles of a Minoan prince whose personal badge was a cat (Fig. 207, a). 1 The, leg, and gate hieroglyphs round this badge answer to those associated with the portrait head of Fig. 206, and may, as suggested above, represent a recurring title. The scrolls that enclose the sign-group on face c show a close correspondence with those on some M. M. II polychrome vases. 2 Interlocked scrolls appear on the contemporary signet 1 Scripta Minoa, i, p. 153, P. 23, and pp. 270, 271. 2 See p. 246, Fig. 186, a.

SIGNS ON SEALS

ON CLAY DOCUMENTS

SIGNS ON O CLAY

SEALS DOCUMENTS lrics i

FIG. 210. SIGN-GROUPS ON SEALS COMPARED WITH LINEARIZED VERSIONS ON CLAY DOCUMENTS.

UNITS) OR ;)))))onu l OR HI =

HUNDREDS- THOUSANDS. 0

FRACTIONS V, PROBABLY=f; V- IDEAL EXAMPLE .

FIG. 211. NUMERALS OF HIEROGLYPHIC SYSTEM.

THE PALACE OF MINOS, ETC.

Tablet with Hieroglyphic Script (B).

Clay Inventories.

Independent Development of Minoan Script.

(Fig. 207, ti), 1 wich, from the ship sign that it presents, may have belonged to a naval officer.

Besides the three-sided clay sealings already described, the hieroglyphic inscriptions of the advanced class (B) are found on clay labels', perforated bars, and oblong tablets (Figs. 208, 209). 2 The first two varieties seem naturally to connect them-selves with the safeguarding of possessions. The ideographic elements on these seem, indeed, like most of those on the later tablets, to refer to property and stores of various kinds. The appearance, however, of the clay tablet without any perforation suggests wider possibilities, and the flat, oblong form is clearly due to oriental influence, which may have reached Crete from the Hittite side.

Both the clay tablet from the Hieroglyphic Deposit at Knossos and the speci-men found at Phaestos (Fig. 209), belonging doubtless to the earlier Palace, seem, however, to be simply inventories. Thus, the Phaestos tablet, 3 bears conventional representations of a saffron- flower, flowering grain, a palm-like spray, FIG. 212. and what seems to be a fig branch. The hieroglyphic inscriptions often show, as here, a curious boustrophedon arrangement. In many cases x or + marks the beginning of a sign-group.

The Table, Fig. 210, 4 gives some of the sign-groups on the seals set beside their linearized equivalents on the clay documents. An elaborate system of numerals, from a quarter of a unit to 1,000, had also been evolved by this Period. (Fig. 211).

As in so many departments of Minoan culture, there can be little doubt that sug-gestions from the Egyptian side contributed towards this great 1 Seager, Mochlos, p. 39, Fig. 14. The arrow (Pernier, Man. Ant., xii, Pl. VIII, Fig. 2, sign is here restored. pp. 96, 97; Halbherr, Mon. Ant., xiii, p. 26, 2 Scripta Minoa, i, p. 147, Fig. 95; p. 148, Fig. 1 1).

Fig. 96. For a fuller account of the Hiero- Scripta Minoa, i, p. 261, Table XIX. The glyphic script I must refer to that work. shoulder (g)=khopsh; and m wsy.

Op. dt., p. 179, P. 121, and pp. 254, 255 5 Op. fit., p. 256 seqq.
SOME EGYPTIAN PARALLELS TO MINOAN SIGNS.
advance in the Art of Writing. But these influences were at most of a formative kind. As a whole, the Minoan hieroglyphic signary is independent of the Egyptian, and a good deal of the parallelism it shows is the result of conditions that underlie all systems of developed picture-writing. The selection for this purpose of certain categories of objects such as of parts of the human body, simple implements and weapons, domestic utensils, plants and animals, or the celestial luminaries, is itself of universal usage.

Here and there, however, the influenceof the Egyptian hieroglyphic system resulted in isolated borrowings of a direct kind. The imitation of the men or draught-board sign, described above, is a conspicuous instance. Further examples are given in Fig. 212, including the ankh or life sign, the libation ewer with a handle added and, what is specially suggestive, the bee of the royal title, and the Palace sign in a simplified form.

The characters of the hieroglyphic signary, many of which retained an ideographic value, are themselves an epitome of Cretan culture as it existed in the culminating epoch of the Middle Minoan Age. A full conspectus of this Signary is given in Fig. 214. We see the tools used by masons, carpenters, and decorators of the great Palaces, the libation vases, sacral horns, and Double Axes of ritual usage; we mark the progress in musical invention evidenced by the eight-stringed lyre. Among the domestic animals we note both the cat and the Molossian hound, swine, a horned sheep and the appearance of the long-horned Urus breed of oxen side by side with the native shorthorns. Agriculture is illustrated by figs and olives, and by various kinds of cereals. Repeated representations of the saffron-flower sign (Fig. 215, A) suggest the important part played by the dye produced from it, and the recurrence of the bee (Fig. 215,) points to the bee-keeping industry, so widespread still in the island. Bees, according to the Cretan legend, fed the infant Zeus. The frequency of a branch or spray, which in its better delineations it seems possible to identify with that of an olive-tree, has a special significance (Fig. 215, c). 2 There can be no reasonable doubt that the capacious jars with which the Palace Magazines were at this time stocked were devoted 1 Sfripta Mtkoa, i, p. 240, Table XVI. Op. cit., i, p. 219, No. 101.

Facilitated by Kgyptian Suggestion.

Some Direct Borrowings.

Fu; 213. CLAY SEALING SHOWING TO. IMPRESSION OF SIGNET WITH SHIP AND OLIVE SPRAY

SlgNS-

Hieroglyphs an Epitome of Cretan Culture.

Olive

Spray

Sign.

Minoan

Wealth in Oil:

Probable

Export to Egypt.

ALIZ X. WA

SS m-inl

LYPH to the storage of oil, and much of the wealth of the Priest-Kings was probably drawn from the export of oil to Egypt. An impression on a sealing (Fig. 213) and an inscription on a perforated clay bar have thus a special significance, since in both cases the olive-spray sign is associated with a ship.

As has been shown above, 3 good illustrations of ships are already found on seals belonging to the close of the Early Minoan Age. They now become still more frequent and the recurrence of the ship sign in the

FIG. 215. VARIOUS FORMS OF HIEROGLYPHIC SIGNS: A, SAFFRON; B, BEE; c, OLIVE

SPRAY; D, SHIP.

hieroglyphic series (Fig. 215, D) is a speaking commentary on the maritime enterprise of Minoan Crete in the flourishing days of the Middle Minoan Age. The ships show a high stern, and the prow terminates either in a barbed point or a kind of open beak. The number of oars given on the intaglios varies from five to fifteen, 5 but steering oars may be included. On the seals 1 Scripta Minoa, p. 161, P. 63 a. the more primitive hieroglyphic class (A).

2 Ib., p. 170, P. 100 d. " On an early lentoid of black steatite in my 3 See pp. 118, 120, 121. Collection.

4 ;., p. 203, No. 57. Types aa a belong to

THE PALACE OF MINOS, ETC.

of this Period the ships are all single-masted, but two-masters appear on some Late Minoan gems.

But of all the evidences of transmarine enterprise the most remarkable is afforded by certain hieroglyphic signs and gem-types which, if my interpretation be correct, connect themselves with the culture of the Silphium plant, of which Cyrene was in Classical times the exclusive centre.

Among the most frequently repeated characters of the hieroglyphic series is a f-like type, which in its completer form shows a foliate stem and

FIG. 217. HEART-LIKE SIGNS OF MINOAN SIGNARV, PERHAPS THE SEED VESSELS orsii. pmuM.

Flg. 216.-LIKE SIGNS OF MlnOAN HIEROGLYPHIC SlgNARY: APPAR-ENTLY REPRESENTING SllPHIUM.

FIG. 218. COINS OF CYRENE WITH FIGURES OF SILPHIUM PLANT AND SEED.

FIG. 219. COMBINATION OF AND HEART-LIKE SIGNS ON

M. M. II CORNELIAN SEAL- what may be taken for a triple bunch of fruits or flowers above (see Fig. 216). Whatever may have been the plant here indicated, it is clear that it played an important part in Minoan economy, the. sign itself, indeed, frequently recurring in formulas that seem to represent official titles. But we have only to refer to the conventionalized figures that often stand for the Silphium plant on the Greek coins of Cyrene to see how very close is the parallel that they present. On the early tetradrachm, Fig. 218, a, 1 we see the plant drawn in a more or less naturalistic style, but in Fig. 218, b and c taken from the field of coins, where it is shown in a conventional and abbreviated 1 L. Muller, Numismatist de tafrique ancieiine, I, p. 9, No. 2.

manner, we see a very close approximation to certain forms of the Minoan sign. There is, moreover, another remarkable feature. To the left of the plant in Fig. 218, a appears a heart-shaped object, which in Fig. 218,, e, 1 is repeated by itself accompanied by grains, and which reproduces the seed vessel of the Silphium. But in this heart-shaped figure we recognize a close parallel to another sign of the hieroglyphic series, Fig. 217,, 6, c. containing grains or seeds in its interior space.

The heart-shaped figure recurs on a series of Minoan intaglio types, apparently of amuletic significance, and for the most part of somewhat later date. What, however, is especially significant is the occurrence of a version of this figure in which triple shoots with annular terminations, resembling those of Fig. 216, g-j, above, are seen proceeding from it. This combination may be regarded as a strong corroboration of the view that the heart-shaped objects of the hieroglyphic signary connect themselves with the vegetable forms seen in Fig. 216. At the same time the double comparison thus established lends additional probability to the identification of both with the Silphium plant and its seed vessels.

So far as is known the Silphium, of which the virtues were so highly prized in antiquity, is now extinct. It is clear that it was an umbelliferous plant, and the nearest available comparison seems to be supplied by Narthex of North Kashmir. The possibility suggests itself that the plant may have been actually introduced into Crete and cultivated there in Minoan days. The climate of Cyrene and of the Cretan highlands must closely approximate, and African species form to-day a notable ingredient in the Cretan flora. Of the manifold character of the Minoan intercourse with the North African shores much evidence has been already adduced. We see indeed that ostrich eggs actually at this time supplied the source of a whole series of Minoan libation vessels. 2 As will be more fully illustrated in the succeeding Section, the relations with the Nile Valley were at this time specially intimate. But, whereas the mouth of the Nile is some 320 miles distant from the nearest Cretan harbour, the port of Dibaki on the South Coast is only 180 miles distant from Derna on the coast of Cyrenaica, and the prevailing Mediterranean current on that side, as well as the alternating spells of prevailing winds from the North-West and the South-West, greatly facilitate this intercourse.

1 L. Miiller, Ntimismatique de rafrique ancienne, p. 12, Fig. 30.

2 See above, p. 170, and Vol. II.

f 14. M. M. II: (F) EGYPTIAN MONUMENT AND RELATIONS.

Diorite Egyptian Monument of User found in Palace Twelfth or early Thirteenth Dynasty date; Connected with Nome of Goddess

Wazet (Aphroditopolite); Minoan intercourse with Egypt, uninterrupted to c. 1760 approximate date of close of M. M. II; Cretan craftsmen employed for Pyramids of Illahun and Hawara; Egyptian religious influence OH Crete; Sea-communications discovery of submerged pre-Hel-lenic port of Isle of Pharos; Colossal construction of harbour ivorks; Estimate of Minoan and Egyptian factors in their execution; Port of Pharos visited by Menelaos; Qjiestion of Minoan ports of Crete; Considerable submergence on N. Coast; Andent harbour and port town of Knossos includes

Venetian port of Candia; Island of Dia; Minoan port of Hagia Pelagia; Catastrophe at end of M. M. II synchronous with break-tip of Egyptian unity; Perhaps symptomatic of wider movements in E. Mediterranean Basin.

Chrono- As noted above, the fine polychrome ware of the developed M. M. II

Equa 3. style (b) derives a special importance from the chronological equations tions with supplied by the discovery of similar pottery in Egyptian deposits of byn. approximately ascertained date, belonging to the latter part of the by P Egy d p- Twelfth Dynasty or the beginning of the Thirteenth.

tianfinds But the synchronisms thus established find a remarkable corrobora- Pottery. tion from a discovery made in the Palace of Knossos itself. In the Diorite North-West area of the Central Court, near the Antechamber of the Monu- later Room of the Throne, there was brought to light the lower part found in a seate d Egyptian figure of diorite of a late Middle Kingdom style and Palace. with hieroglyphic inscriptions on three sides of its base. The monument was found about 70 centimetres below the surface of the Court, at a point where the later limestone slabbing had been removed. As it lay clearly below the earliest Late Minoan level, it was from the first evident that the date of its deposit fell within the limits of the Middle Minoan Age. In neighbouring parts of the West Quarter of the Palace a well-marked M. M. Ill deposit occupied this position, 1 but as a matter of fact the Monument occurred in association with painted fragments of the M. M. II b polychrome style. 2 1 It was owing to this that in my Essai de 2 These fragments were vaguely referred to

Classification, c., 1906, p. 9, the Monument in my 1900 Report (p. 27) as Kamares', in was erroneously assigned to the M. M. Ill accordance with the nomenclature then in

Period. vogue.

In 1913, by raising strips of the slabbing of the paved area immediately adjoining the spot where the monument was discovered, it was possible to stratum arrive at an accurate knowledge of the underlying stratum and thus to supply? " ta a conclusive answer regarding the medium with which the monument was Monu-associated. Except on the borders of the adjoining Ante-room, whose Late ascer-Minoan foundations had cut into the earlier deposit, the evidence was Jj d singularly uniform. M. M. II.

It was proved to demonstration that the limestone pavement had simply taken the place of the floor level, of whatever materials, which had already existed here in the early part of M. M. III. Relics of this latter Period made complete default, and a Late Minoan stratum was directly superimposed on one containing typical polychrome and other sherds, as well as complete specimens of small plain vessels, all of M. M. II b fabric. In two directions this deposit was crossed by drains, one of terra-cotta, the other of stone, containing similar relics, the upper surface of these being struck at 50 and 70 centimetres respectively. That the diorite monument belonged to this widespread M. M. II stratum there can be no reasonable doubt.

The figure is that of a seated male personage who, as will be seen Figure of from Fig 220, is represented nude. His hands rest on his knees in a User-schematic attitude, and the square throne on which he is seated bears an inscription behind and on both sides, presenting considerable difficulties. 1 It reads as follows:

RIGHT SIDE (very ill engraved) = ( ) v- v J

LEFT SIDE: jj J 7 I 0 O ast s g n probably blundered 0).

wwvi- f ID X a V 1

Back: Devoted to the Great God, Lord of Heaven, heart of Gold, whom the Wazet-nome (?) produced (?), User, true of voice.

Sides: The Devoted heart of Gold, whom the Wazet-nome (?) produced (?), User, true of voice, born of the devoted Sat-Hathor, true of voice.

The collocation p) in r) 1 P s thets oratitle. perhaps of some high-priesthood =::: (or possibly father's or grandfather's name with the crux of the inscription. Mr. F. I. I. Griffith fi, iation gi omjued as m contemporary (Arch. Rep. E. E. F., 1900, p. 6) at first read it n as a strange compound name, but this he now h eratic). In his opinion V T looks most regards as hardly credible. The last element, Wazet, the name of the Xth Nome of Upper

User, is frequent as a proper name and he sug- Egypt (Aphroditopolite), though the serpent gests that the preceding groups represent epi- lacks the ostrich feather on its back.

THE PALACE OF MINOS, ETC.

FIG. 220. DIORITE MONUMENT OF AB-NUB-MES-WAZET-USER FOUND IN M. M. II l STRATUM OK CENTRAL COURT, KNOSSOS. (c.)

The serpent suggests a connexion with the Goddess Wazet or Buto, her- Born in self a double of Hathor. Her chief seat was in the Delta, where she had con- ph j od cealed her infant son Horns in the papyrus thicket a mythic episode which, Nome, at the hands of Semitic intruders, was to supply the origin of the story of Moses' mother hiding him among the bulrushes'. Her emblem was the serpent, of which she at times took the form, and the influence of her The cult at Knossos itself on the native Snake Goddess will receive illustra- Goddess tion below. The early adoption in Minoan Crete of her sacred waz or Wazet. papyrus symbol has been already noted. 1

The connexion between this Goddess and the User of the Egyptian. monument that had found its way to the Palace of Knossos has thus a special significance.

Mr. Griffith observes that the names are of Middle Kingdom style, Middle such as lasted to temp. Thothmes III, but it would be impossible to character find such a collocation of old names on an Eighteenth Dynasty monument. of Monu-The epithet m ' Jirw, "true of voice", (meaning, practically, " deceased "ft. excludes the period before the Eleventh Dynasty. The style of the statuette is also that of the Twelfth or the Thirteenth Dynasty.

This approximate chronology has been generally accepted by Egyptologists, and the diorite material itself affords a strong presumption against a later dating. The alternative reading Sebek 2 User would not in itself involve a date later than the latter part of the Twelfth Dynasty, since Sebek ' Wazet or Crocodile names (more characteristic, however, of the early part of the XHIth Dynasty) were already coming into vogue at that time. 8 But a distinctive feature visible in the hieroglyph above the Nome sign, as seen in the inset b. elow, can leave no reasonable doubt that it is the serpent with abruptly upraised head of the Goddess Wazet. 4 1 See above, p. 200 and cf. p. 291, below. sign the neck slopes up gradually forward from 8 This was the reading of Professor Petrie, the line of the body, accepted by Mr. H. R. Hall after a study of the while in the case of monument in the Candia Museum (P. S. B. A., Wazet the neck of the xxxi, 1909, p. 224). Asp rises erect. The 8 Thus Sebek-Khu appears as a famous sign is at best sum-commander of Amenemhat III, and the last marily executed, and ruler of the Twelfth Dynasty was Queen Sebek a slight flaw is visible Neferu. in the stone between 4 The inset here given (reversed) from a the upper bend of the squeeze taken from the best preserved example Asp and the fore-foot of the disputed sign will, however, I venture to of the Afes sign. But think, serve to settle the point at issue. The the Asp's neck clearly essential difference between the two hieroglyphs turns up at an abrupt is that in the case of the Sebek or Crocodile angle. The support is not appropriate to Sebek.

THE PALACE OF MINOS, ETC.

Evidence of Intercourse with Upper Egypt.

Chronology of Last Xllth Dyn. Epoch.

Cretan Craftsmen employed for Pyramids.

Continued Minoan Intercourse during Early Xlllth Dyn.

Long

Period of Intensive

Contact with

Egypt.

The connexion of the personage of the monument with the Tenth Aphroditopolite Nome must itself be taken to point to a time when intercourse between Minoan Crete and Upper Egypt had not been severed either through the internal disruption of the

Egyptian Monarchy or by the ensuing-occupation of the Delta by the Semitic, Hyksos tribes.

The Tenth Aphroditopolite Nome lay immediately North of the Thinite Nome in which was situated Abydos, where, within a closed tomb, the polychrome vase above described, belonging to the earlier phase of M. M. 116, was found in association with a cylinder of Amenemhat III (t 1801-1798 B. C.). The occurrence of User's monument in the Palace of Knossos may in fact be regarded as the natural correlative of the other discovery.

Thanks to the Kahun papyrus, which gives the place of the heliac rising of the planet Sothis in the seventh year of Senusert III, the chronology of the closing epoch of the Twelfth Dynasty is very precisely fixed, within a margin of three years either way. The Kahun materials themselves and others from neighbouring sites begin with Senusert (Sesostris) II, the builder of the neighbouring Pyramid of Illahun, 1 which stands at the Nile Gate of the Fayum. To his reign (1903-1885 u. c.) may be referred the earliest imported Minoan sherds from that site which, as already shown,- fall within the upper limits of the M. M. 11 a phase. But the evidence of the papyri found here shows that the town continued to flourish not only under Amenemhat 111 (c. 1846-1798 B. C.), who made it the entrepot for the works of his great Pyramid of Hawara, a little N. W. of Illahun, and of his son of the same name, but also throughout the reigns of the earlier kings of the Thirteenth Dynasty, Ra-sekhem-khu-taui and Sekhem-ka-ra, 3 or approximately to 1765 B. c. As the unity of Egypt was still preserved and Kahun still apparently a populous centre, it seems reasonable to suppose that some of the later polychrome sherds found here belonging to M. M. II b may come down even to a later date. It is clear, on the other hand, that the breaking off of the Egyptian connexion was followed after no long interval by the end of this ceramic phase, and we have good warrant therefore for bringing down the Second Middle Minoan Period to a date approaching the close of the Eighteenth Century B. c.

We are here confronted with the remarkable fact that not only the Delta but Middle and Upper Egypt throughout almost the whole duration of the Twelfth Dynasty as well as the earlier part of the Thirteenth, in

Cf. Petrie, Kahun, c., p. 21 seqq. See above, p. 266.

3 See Griffith, Illahtin, Kahun, and Gurob (The Hieratic Papyri), p. 50.

the great days, that is, of the early Palaces at Knossos and Phaestos including part of the First and the whole of the Second Middle Minoan Period stood in continuous relation with Minoan Crete.

It has, indeed, been shown, on irrefragable evidence, in the earlier The Sections of this work that the influence of the Nile Valley on Crete evidence goes back to the very beginnings of the Minoan Age. Imported stone fkgyp-vessels and imitative shapes, as well as other phenomena with which we Relation", have to deal, prove indeed that this influence goes back even beyond the proto-dynastic period of Egypt, and the deep impress left not only by forms but by ideas that seem to have taken their rise in that quarter is even suggestive of an actual immigration into Crete of some fragment of the old population of the Nile Valley. The new fact, of which we have evidence during the Twelfth and Thirteenth Dynasty Period above referred to, is the incipient reaction of Minoan culture on Egypt.

In view of the very early transmission of ideas as well as of objects from Minoan the Nile Valley to Crete it seems probable that existing opinions as to the Active naval equipment of ancient Egypt from the very beginnings of its history Agents, will require serious revision. On the other hand, during the Middle Kingdom Period with which we are now principally concerned it looks as if the Minoan Cretans had become the active agents in this intercourse. The immense stores of oil, of which the great pithoi in the Palace Magazines are a speaking witness, reveal a mainspring of this commerce. But. the Minoan sherds of Kahun seem to connect themselves with the actual presence of Cretan workmen in Middle Egypt, employed by the Pharaohs in their great architectural and engineering works. In this and the succeeding epoch we notice at Knossos and elsewhere an acquaintance with Egyptian religious ideas and artistic forms that seems hardly explicable except by the existence of a colonial Egyptian Minoan element on the soil of Egypt itself. The reflection of the cult influence of the Hippopotamus Goddess referred to above, 1 and of Wazet herself as on c seen in the Snake Goddess of the succeeding epoch- the appearance of her papyrus emblem or waz in the decoration of the Early Palace itself, 3 the imitation of Egyptian ceilings, the evolution of the Labyrinth in Art, and a score of subtle indications in various directions betray an acquaintance with Egyptian life and thought such as could only have been the result of personal intercourse on a considerable scale.

Had the Minoan lords some seaport at their own disposal in the Delta or its borders?
1 See p. 199. s See above, p. 201, and Coloured PI. I, K.
2 See below, p. 509.
THE PALACE OF MINOS, ETC.
Maritime Communications between Crete and
Egypt, and presumably inminoan Hands.
The early commerce between the pre-dynastic population of the Nile Valley and Crete seems to have passed through A-ur the Great Door or Port near the Canopic mouth. 1 As far as we can ascertain from the monuments of Dynastic Egypt, havens on the open sea were foreign to its tradition. The Egyptian shipping, though it seems to have at times frequented wider Mediterranean routes than has been hitherto suspected, found its harbours on the lower reaches of the Nile, the Canopic mouth being the station for the North-West. The early Greeks, indeed, followed the Egyptian lead in their station at Naukratis farther up that branch. But the navigation of the old inhabitants of practically riverless Crete began on the sea itself.

Discovery of Submerged Port of Pharos of pre-Hellenic Date.
FIG. 221. SKETCH-PLAN OF PRE-HELLENIC PORT OF PHAROS.
Their intercourse with Egypt was due to their seafaring enterprise, of which we have a record in the high-built ships of the native seal-stones. 2

The data on which the whole question rests have now received a new complexion owing to a remarkable series of discoveries clue to Monsieur Gaston Jondet, 3 establishing the existence in pre-Hellenic times of a vast system of harbour works based on the ancient island of Pharos. 4

When Alexander the Great, imitating his achievement at Tyre, linked the island to the mainland by his great causeway, the Heptastadion, and thus created the Eastern and Western havens of Alexandria, his engineers seem to have had no knowledge of these much more ancient works. By a 1 See P. E. New-berry, The Petty Kingdom of the Harpoon and Egypfs Earliest Mediterranean Port (Liv. Annals, c., vol. i), p. 17 seqq.

8 See above, p. 277, Fig. 207. b; p. 281, Fig. 213, and p. 283, Fig. 215, D.

3 Engineer in Chief of Egyptian Ports and Lighthouses.

1 Les forts submerges de rancienne lie de Pharos (Me"moires presented a 1Institut Egyptian, 1916).

process of submergence, apparently considerably advanced at that date, these are now almost entirely beneath sea-level. The plan of the pre-Hellenic port as now recovered is reproduced in the annexed sketch-plan, Fig. 1'1.

West of the point of the former island of Pharos, known to the Arabs as Ras-el-Tin, and between it and the rock of Abu-Bakar, extends a depression in the sea-bottom giving at present a depth of from about 6 to Its Colos-10 metres which was skilfully included in the great inner basin of the struction. harbour. Its entrance, by a deep channel of sea, is marked just off the point of Ras-el-Tin by a landing quay 14 metres wide, formed of great rough-hewn blocks, some of them 5 metres or over 16 feet in length; the surface of these being grooved into a remarkable pentagonal chequer-work. 1 A jetty running out from this abuts on the entrance passage on its E. side, and the harbour wall, starting again from the W. side of the opening, follows a submerged reef in an irregular course for about 700 metres to a point just beyond the rock of Abu-Bakar. The course of this part of the work, with its angular salients and returns and its roughly S. Wall of,.? J Harbour, horizontal construction, somewhat escarped externally, may tempt comparison with the primitive Cretan fortifications, as illustrated by the walls of Juktas. s We shall see that the character of the rough mosaic formed by the upper surface of the blocks is even more suggestive of Minoan methods.

By the rock of Abu-Bakar the pivot of the whole vast plan of Great 13re iic-construction the harbour wall takes a short turn North, backed by a second water, line, and then strikes due East facing the open sea and forming a great breakwater over 2,000 metres long.

The Western section of this formed a single wall of somewhat irregular course like that described, following a submerged line of reefs, but the Eastern part of the course, where such a solid base was lacking, exhibits a construction of a still more imposing kind. It was here prolonged by means of two escarped supporting walls of huge rough-hewn blocks, their upper surface 8 to 12 metres wide, slightly sloped towards the sea, 4 and with 1 The grooves are about 45 cm. deep, and J This, as M. Jondet shows (pp. fit., p. 19), in M. Jondet's opinion contained a wooden was an addition to the original plan. It is framework (pp. cit., p. 18 and Fig. 2). It may also of different construction, be suggested that this framework rose a little " See above, p. 155, Fig. 113 a.

above the surface of the blocks, and served to 4 The plan of their upper surface shows give security to a cement filling which would a rough mosaic arrangement similar to the wall otherwise have been swept away by the waves, on the South. A trench about i metre deep,

The pentagons themselves were 8 metres in for the implantation of some protective hairier, their longitudinal axes and about 4 metres ran along the centre of the outer wall (op. cit., broad. p. 26).

the intervening space of 40-50 metres filled with rubble material, so that the whole would have formed a platform about 60 metres in width. The great basin thus enclosed, 2,360 metres in length by about 300 in breadth, contains an area of about 150 acres, and might according to M. Jondet's calculation have sheltered 400 galleys or triremes of 30 metres length V But this was not all. Beyond the great basin, on the sea side, was a second harbour showing considerable remains of its outer breakwater at a greater depth than the former, 2 and enclosing a basin over half the size of the great inner harbour. A subsidiary outer port, called by M. Jondet the commercial harbour, is also visible, adjoining the principal constructions on the East. Seaport These stupendous works, the record of which has thus been recovered

"hole of from beneath the waters that had slowly engulfed them, represent an area Egypt- probably larger than the original surface of the Island of Pharos itself. What we have here in fact is a port devised with reference to the whole land of Egypt, watching the Nile mouths and controlling the main South-Eastern terminus of the Mediterranean Sea routes. Its colossal construction vies with the boldest undertakings of the great builders of Egypt, but neither the practice of the native Egyptians nor the general character of their shipping-are consistent with the idea of a port on the open sea. No Pharaonic record refers to the existence of such, and so far as the present discoveries extend they are not associated with any fragment of Egyptian sculpture. Was it of On the other hand, such a bold and elaborate system of harbour

Origin? construction as has here come to light could only have been conceived by the engineers of a seafaring people, schooled for generations in such work. As has been pointed out by M. Raymond VVeill, 4 we are almost inevitably led to look for its originators in the direction of Minoan Crete. This, as he shows by no means implies that the construction of the island port of Pharos was made without the sanction of some contemporary Egyptian king. Settlements of foreigners within the borders of Egypt, as in the case of Goshen, were at different times tolerated by the Pharaohs.

But so huge an undertaking could not have been carried out without something more than passive acquiescence on the Egyptian side. The 1 60 hectares. progressively as the works were farther from 2 Op. fit., p. 72. the original coast-line.

3 The remains of this are to be seen on calm Les ports antehelleniques de la Cote a days at a depth of 6-50 to 8-50 metres. M. Alexandrie et F Empire Cre'tois (Extrait du Jondet notes that the subsidence of the old Bulletin de 1Institut Fran9ais darcheologie harbour works, which is local in its character, orientale, T. xvi).

increases in proportion as they are farther out 5 Op. cif., p. 18 seqq. to sea. The process of submergence increased tion.

M. M. II: EGYPTIAN MONUMENT AND RELATIONS 295 magnitude of the task almost of necessity implies the material co-opera- Colossal tion of the Pharaonic power. The material itself was supplied by the vjjj limestone quarries of Mex and Dekhela on the neighbouring mainland Evidence coast. But the extraction and transport of the huge blocks, some of them tian Col-over six tons in weight, could hardly have been effected without the superintendence of architects acquainted with such mighty works as the Pyramids themselves. 1 Special massiveness of construction was here no doubt necessary to resist the force of the open sea, but the colossal scale of the work surpasses anything that we know of the Minoan builders' craft.

The narrow strip of land where the (marries were situated, between the sea and Lake Mariut, afforded a certain protection on the land side against a sudden attack, but it is difficult to believe that the neighbouring island port and arsenal could have come into existence or have long subsisted without some very solid understanding with the rulers of Egypt. It has already been remarked that as a seaport it was designed on such a scale that it must have had the whole of Egypt in view, and it would therefore seem probable that the Egyptian Government claimed a share in its actual control.

The further discovery of massive structures on the reefs and eyots Channels West. of Abu-Dakar, that guard the channels to the inner haven, 2 shows that p roa ch it was defensively organized against possible attacks from the high sea. In g" arded-a certain sense the port of pre-Hellenic Pharos was based on the Egyptian mainland. It must not be forgotten, however, that this mainland tract, West of the Delta, was occupied by men of the older Nilotic race, who here preserved to the last their Libyan speech and traditions. 3 Their rowing galleys, as we have seen, had already breasted the Nile in prehistoric days and had not improbably ventured into open Mediterranean waters.

It is difficult in constructions like those of these great harbour works, Com- consisting mainly of huge rough-hewn blocks, to fix on characteristic details j ve-" definite enough to possess a comparative value. It has been noted above " " ts s of that the Southern course of the harbour wall with its salients and returns with suggests Minoan parallels. Dut the paving of this and other sections of the M S noa e n. quays as well as of the great breakwater certainly displays a great con- 1 M. Jondet, op. at., p. 72, remarks: la masse quarries to the port of embarkation, des materiaux mis en oeuvre est colossale 2 These are marked on M. Jondet's plan (of.

comme dans tous les Edifices pharaoniques et fit., Pl. Ill) as the Passe des Corvettes, the Passe leur mise en place a present des difficultes de Boghaz, and the Grande Passe. For his plus considerables que l entassement des pierres more recent discoveries of the works on the employees a la construction des grandes Pyra- rocks and islands V. of Abu-Bakar see R. Veill mides. He observes that in the first place (Lesports anteiellenitues, C. p. 7). a road would have had to be built from the " Herodotus, ii. 18. Cf. pp. 17, 64, 83.

THE PALACE OF MINOS, ETC.

formity though on a larger scale with that seen in the Courts of the Early Palaces of Crete. Thus in Fig. 222 a, 1 showing part of the surface of the great breakwater, the paving slabs form a rough mosaic recalling on a larger scale the early pavements of Knossos, Fig. 222 b. In the case of these quays and moles the interstices between the blocks were packed with sand or small angular fragments of stone. In the Minoan pavements, on the other hand, it is clear that the interstices originally contained a cement filling, best seen in the finest representation of this class of work the mosaiko' pavements described above. 2 It is certain that the action of the

FIG. 222 a. PAVING OF GREAT BREAKWATER.
EDGE Of CAUSEWAY
FIG. 222 b. PAVING AT S. E. CORNER OF W. Cou: KNOSSOS.

waves would have removed this from the Pharian quays, but there is considerable probability that this feature, which gave a finish to the surface, also originally existed in their case too. 3 It is a noteworthy point in regard to these comparisons that they refer to the Middle rather than the Late Minoan stage of the Cretan Palaces. The characteristic examples of pavements with large irregular blocks, to 1 Fig. 222 a is from Jondet, op. cif., p. 26, Fig. 6. (Cf. too p. 21, Fig. 4; south wall of harbour.) M. Jondet notices a certain radial arrangement of the slabs, also occasionally visible in the Minoan pavements.

2 See p. 210, and p. 214, Fig. 158.

3 It has already been suggested above (p. 293, note i) that the deep pentagonal grooves of the landing quay formed the base of a framework enclosing a cement facing.

which the name kalderim has been applied, go back, as we have seen, to the close of the M. M. I Period. The fine mosaiko class, which is an outgrowth of this, belongs to the close of M. M. II. From the date of the last Middle Minoan Period onwards, including the Late Minoan Age, pavements with squared slabs were generally in vogue, the mosaiko' type only surviving for central panels, like those of the Throne Room system.

It will be seen that the period to which the above analogies lead us Cretan corresponds in a remarkable manner with the age of intimate contact between pa risons Minoan Crete and Twelfth and Thirteenth Dynasty Egypt, of which such "-xni remarkable evidence has come to light, not only at Knossos itself but on Dyn. Egyptian soil in connexion with the work of Senusert II and Amenemhat III at Kahun and neighbouring sites and even at Abydos in Upper Egypt.

The great harbour works of the Island of Pharos may indeed have Harbour continued to serve Minoan mariners at a later epoch, and, as the addition of perhaps the jetty to the landing quay shows, 1 they are not themselves all of the same " Latel date. The discovery of the alabastron lid with the name of the Hyksos Pharaoh Khyan, described below, points to a renewal of intercourse in his reign, referred here to the penultimate M. M. Ill phase. At no time, moreover, were relations between Crete and the Nile Valley more intimate than under the Eighteenth Dynasty, which largely corresponds with the First Late Minoan Period, and it is reasonable to believe that at this epoch the Minoan shipping continued to avail itself of the great facilities afforded by this insular port. Nay more, though Egyptian records are silent about the island harbour of Pharos which was to give its name to all lighthouses-it was not unknown to the Achaean Greeks, who took over so much of Minoan tradition. This was the island in the rough sea over against Egypt, and Known to a day's favourable sail from its river, having within it a haven with fair Greeks; moorings where Menelaos sheltered his vessel awhile and took in a water- f supply for his return voyage. 2 It was already the legendary haunt of Proteus, hostile Epic monster, otherwise identified by the Greeks with an Egyptian king.

The traces of the Minoan wharves and harbours in Crete itself remain Question to be investigated. On the North Coast the question is again complicated seaports by the very considerable subsidence that has taken place since Minoan times.?, n: a While the South Coast of the Island has risen, and the Greco-Roman port Great

Submer-1 See note 2, p. 293. lv 8 Ai jv tvopfios, ooiv T airo vijas civus gence on Homer, Od. iv. 354: ts irovrov SciaAowm, d wro-a iot exa C 7T ltf Tts COTl 7ToaliC VOTll fvL TTOVTtp Of.

7rpoirapoi0e ipov t i KIK IJ- The sea off the Alexandrian coast is particularly stormy.

THE PALACE OF MINOS, ETC.

Port of Knossos repre- thatof b Candia.

of Phalasarna on the extreme West has been left high and dry, 1 at Cherso-nesos, to the East of Candia, I observed the walls and floors of the ancient harbour town beneath the sea at depths which pointed to a subsidence

O f quite two metres since Roman times, l a measurement which, assuming .,,.

the rate of subsidence to have been approximately even, must be multiplied at l east two an d a na lf times for Middle Minoan remains. That the seaport o f the ancient Knossos is in part represented by the small Venetian port of Candia is highly probable. The Venetian wharves are themselves superposed on earlier moles, and whether actually in position or replaced, many Minoan blocks are visible in the harbour itself. But the point on which the Castle stands was anciently prolonged by a reef which runs for some distance East at a few fathoms' depth. It is the basis of existing plans for the extension of the port, and that this supported the foundations of a Minoan breakwater is highly probable, though the terrific storms caused by the prevailing N. W. gales in this windy gap of Crete can have left few remaining traces. That the Minoan harbour town extended along the opposite coast is at any rate clear from the existing remains of houses which are traceable for some distance East of the walls of Candia, 3 and a fair proportion of the pottery here found is of Middle Minoan and earlier date. The existence of similar traces show, moreover, that the settlement extended to the mouth of the little river Kaeratos, which was doubtless also utilized for the ancient island of shipping. Seawards, again, about six miles to the North, the desert island of Standia, the ancient Dia, traditionally connected with the Minoan Goddess under the name of Ariadne, offered secure protection to vessels against the prevailing wind. Her cult may indeed be said to have been perpetuated by the little shrine of the Panagia in the largest creek. In the bay of Hagios Georgios a little to the West of this are visible blocks of an early wall, close to the sea, and above this are some levelled areas and early cultivation terraces, where on different occasions I collected fragments of Minoan pottery of more than one Period. Dia, or Standia, has in a certain sense served the same 1 Spratt, Travels and Researches in Crete, ii, p. 232 seqq.

2 The remains of a basilica on the headland above show that Roman Chersonesos was still flourishing in the fifth and sixth centuries.

3 As I have pointed out elsewhere, Preh. Tombs of Knossos (Archaeologia, lix, p. 171), the important Late Minoan cemetery of Isopata, including the Royal Tomb, stands in connexion with the harbour town of ancient Knossos rather than with that about the Palace site.

4 I was detained three days in this bay in 1902 owing to a fierce N. W. gale which prevented my Greek steamer approaching Candia, and had an occasion to re-explore this and the neighbouring bays to the E. in 1907. In the Panagia valley is a torrent

bed with a well, that of H. Georgios, which is rather brackish. The island is at present a limestone wilderness, the purpose as Pharos to the overlying mainland. In the sheltered deep waters of its bays, the larger Venetian galleys, like those of the Saracens before them and of the Turks after them, found the accommodation which the shallow and confined harbour of Candia itself could not offer. 1

So far as my own investigations go, however, the best existing remains Minoan of a Minoan port are to be seen at Hagia Pelagia about 12 miles West of

Candia, where is a peninsular site of dark schistose formation, the low cliffs of which are capped with the remains of walls consisting of well-squared blocks of the same material, enclosing house-foundations with sherds going back to the earliest Minoan times. On either side of the promontory are sandy coves. 2 It is worth noting that the name of the Christian patroness of this now untenanted port only thinly veils the form of Isis Pelagia, inventress of the sail, whose Mediterranean cult survived the Age of Constantine and the principal scene of whose worship was still to the last the Isle of Pharos. 3

The close of the present Period as is shown by the evidence from Cbrono- . logical Kahun overlapped the early part of the Thirteenth Dynasty, while its clues to beginning, as we have seen, goes well back into the Twelfth Dynasty. As M-M11- already observed there seems to be good warrant for placing the approximate limits of M. M. II between 1900 and 1700 n. c.

It is clear that this stage of Minoan culture was cut short by a cata- M. M. II strophe, which from its widespread character may be thought to connect itself with a greater current of history, Ivintr outside the insular limits. put 8h? rt . by wide- It has been shown that a series of contemporary deposits, representing spread the last phase of M. M. II and resulting from a general overthrow of s, roph c. the earlier Palaces, is visible throughout a great part of the site both at Knossos and Phaestos. The ceramic remains found in this stratum on the Parallel two sites are, as we have seen, absolutely parallel. We recognize the same at advanced polychromy, while the forms of the vessels and the types of the 59 s and ordinary ware present the same similarities. The knobbed type of pitlios occurs in the Early Magazines of both Palaces. A typical minor indication is supplied by a common form of plain cup, often roughly made and with the walls abode of rabbits, Cretan wild goats iagrimia) tombs mostly L. M. Ill 6, but some earlier.

and peregrine falcons. Beyond aromatic scrub The site continued in occupation in Greek such as mastic, only wild fig-trees are to be times, and in a tank a little above the coast- found. Roman pottery is also fairly abundant. guard station was found the funeral stela with 1 See too the remarks of Admiral Spratt, a Cretan archer in relief described by Benndorf, Travels in Crete, i, p. 35. Jnhreshefte d. Oesterreichischen Arch. Inst.

2 On undulating hills S. W. of the site are 1903, PI. I.

extensive remains of a cemetery with tholos The Goddess was also known as Isis Pharia.

pared, which constantly recurs amidst the latest debris of the earlier Palaces on both sites. The latest ceramic remains found on the lower floors in the region of the Magazines and elsewhere at Phaestos, and those accumulated in the circular, walled rubbish-pit in connexion with the earlier West Court there, are in many cases indistinguishable from those from the Loom-Weight Deposit at Knossos, from the Early Magazines, and from the analogous stratum recently explored in the great halls of the Domestic Quarter and along the West border of the Central Court. They equally correspond with the pottery found in the early walled rubbish-pit which was partly covered by the later structures of the Theatral Area.

We have, in fact, abundant evidence of a contemporary disaster which befell both the great Palatial centres of Minoan Crete at the close of the Second Middle Minoan Period. Date of It will be seen that the date of this catastrophe, as indicated by the strophe evidence from Kahun, followed shortly on the close of the first, brilliant period Sne itb of tlle T mrteentn Dynasty. It thus synchronizes with the break-up of the Break-up unity of the Egyptian kingdom, of which advantage was to be shortly taken Egyptian by the roving Sheikhs of the Eastern Desert to overrun the Delta. It is Kingdom. c j ear t j iat fo t j le internal disruption of Egypt and the ensuing Hyksos encroachments must have put an end for a while to the intimate relations ntolof between Crete and the Nile Valley. On the other hand, there is no Hyksos warrant for invoking any direct agency from the Hyksos side to account for croach- the contemporary destruction that fell on the early Cretan Palaces and the Delta 8 m overt hi"ow of what we may perhaps call the old regime in the island. 1 The earlier Hyksos invasions were in fact rather in the nature of piece-meal and irregular settlements under numerous small chiefs than of organized Destruc- conquest, and their power was that of the desert, not of the sea. But the M. M. II tide which the breaking of the Pharaonic dam let loose may well have had perhaps reactions on the Mediterranean side about which we have no information, Symptom and the disaster that befell Minoan Crete at this time may be ultimately of Wider,.,.,

Move- shown to stand m connexion with wider historic movements which also affected the neighbouring Anatolian coastlands.

1 Dr. Eduard Meyer (Geschichte des Alter- destruction in the Palaces, on the other hand, turns, i 2, p. 716) brings the destruction of the is of earlier date, when Hyksos settlements in Minoan Palaces into connexion with Hyksos the Delta were only, at most, in an incipient conquests, and hints that the discovery of the stage and there can be no question of a con-alabaster lid of King Khyan may be an indica- quest of Crete. The Khyan relic is rather an tion of actual Hyksos dominion in the island, indication of a new peaceful relationship with But the lid (see p. 4i9seqq.) belongs to the re-united Egypt, penultimate epoch of M. M. III. The great

J 15- M. M. II: (G) THE TOWN MOSAIC.

Town Mosaic Circumstances of discovery in M. M. Ill filling material; rrobably heirloom from M. M. 7b Sanctuary; Ivory Draughtsmen in same deposit; Fragmentary remains of large Composition; Central feature towers and houses of fortified town; Associated features relating to land and sea; Warriors, ship and negroid figures; Facades of Town Houses; Modern impression four- and six-pancd windows; Architectural affinities ii. it h Terracotta Shrine and M. M. II construction; Sanctuary on Wall; The Warriors and their Arms; Figured representations more archaic than those of faience objects of Temple Repositories; Comparison with Chest of Kypselos; L ibyan element in Composition Comparison of negroid heads with Jeivel Relief; Plaques in shape of scales with Double Axe marks; Scales, Oriental Convention for rocks; Survivals on later Minoan rhytons' with Siege Scenes; Theme of the beleaguered City and Epic tradition.

TIIK evidence from the site of Knossos discussed in the preceding Discovery Sections that relate to the acme of the Early Palace civilization has been Mosaic." mainly concerned with the inner life and structural features of the Palace itself. But the remarkable remains of a faience mosaic found on the Northern border of the Loom-Weight Basements' has afforded an actual glimpse of a Minoan town of this epoch, situated, moreover, it would appear, in close proximity to the sea.

The stratigraphic conditions under which the discovery of the Town in filling Mosaic was made are not indeed, as has been already observed, by them-selves so conclusive as were those under which most of the other relics found in this area came to light, whether M. M. II or M. M. III. The ment. remains of the faience tablets were found in the interspace between the Loom-Weight Basement and the substructures of the N. E. Portico, dispersed through a layer of what seems to have been filling earth between 60 cm. and 2-10 metres throughout a space, that is, of a metre and a half beneath a clay and plaster pavement on which, as in the adjoining sections South, rested typical tripod pots belonging to the close of the M. M. Ill Period. Beneath this deposit again, from a depth of 2-75 metres beneath the upper floor, lay a clearly defined M. M. b stratum, on all fours with that of the Loom-Weight Basement immediately South of it, and containing indeed fragments of the same objects, such as parts of the terra-cotta shrine and of the gold-mounted faience vase, that occurred in that area and which had in both cases been derived from a M. M. II b chamber above.

Found in It will be seen that in the Section shown in Fig. 187 b, p. 250, the horizon flirtfilling f t ie f aie nce inlays to a certain extent corresponds with that in which the material. Spiral Fresco and other relics were deposited, belonging, as will be shown below, to the earlier M. M. Ill phase. But no remains of M. M. Ill fresco or painted stucco such as occurred so abundantly in the adjoining area came to light in association with these inlays. The deposit in which they were found was not, as in that case, the result of precipitation from an

Probably upper floor but was simply filling material which had found its way here during torn 00 " 1 the earlier phase of M. M. III. It is reasonable, therefore, to suppose that

M. M. II some objects included in it had been taken from an earlier M. M. II stratum.

It is in any case clear that the Town Mosaic itself must be placed in the same connexion as the Terra-cotta Shrine, and the inlaid chest to which these fragments probably belonged may well have originally formed part of the furniture of the same sanctuary chamber, belonging to the close of the

M. M. II Period. An alternative conclusion, taking into account the asso- ciations in which they were found, would be that the chest to which these faience inlays belonged, had been preserved for a while as an heirloom in the M. M. Ill Palace.

ivory The only other noteworthy objects found in the same deposit as the m 1 a, ughts " faience tablets were four ivory men obviously belonging to some kind of

Minoan draught-board. These objects are described below l as supplying a valuable illustration of the magnificent inlaid Gaming Board, which itself seems to have been the work of the closing M. M. 1 1 1 phase.

Frag- From the soft, perishable nature of the material, most of these inlays su of were in a very fragmentary state. The existing remains, striking as they many of are can only represent a small proportion of the original mosaic. It is clear Tablets, that many of them had been repeated from the same mould. Fortified The central feature, as already noted, consisted of the towers and houses

Surround- f a fortified town. There were, however, also abundant remains of inlays ings. of another class, trees and water, goats and oxen, marching warriors, Warriors: spearmen and archers, arms and equipments, the prow apparently of a ship, Negroid an d curious negroid figures. It is suggested below that we have here

Figures, g remains of a siege-scene analogous to that on the silver rhyton from Mycenae. 2 1 See p. 477 seqq., Fig. 342. 2 See Vol. II.

Unexpected as have been many of the revelations of this ancient Cretan culture the appearance of these house facades with their two and three stories and roof attics and their windows of four and even six panes of a date not later, probably, than the last half of the eighteenth century it. c. is perhaps the most astonishing. In view of the generally grandiose character Facades of the Palace itself, the indications in it of upper stories appear natural enough. But in the houses of the Mosaic we can hardly fail to recognize the dwellings of the ordinary Minoan citizens. That these should have already attained the tall proportions of a modern street-front points surely back to long generations of civic life. Some of the plaques representing house-fronts and towers have been tentatively placed together in the photographic view, Fig. 223. Window openings of somewhat later date have been recognized both in the inner Courts of the Palace and the outer walls, showing the dowel-holes for their wooden framework. Thus Suppl. Pl. VII shows the window in the South wall of the light-well of the Hall of Colonnades, which lighted the landing of the back-stairs, with the woodwork restored, 1 while another, in the light-well of the Double Axes, is given both as found and as restored (Figs. 253 a, 253 6). 2 The windows in question follow a conventional type, such as we see on the tablets B, D, G (Fig. 2 2(5), and others, in which their sills and lintels are continuous with the horizontal beams that traverse the masonry. But it is to be observed that another type, foreign it would seem to the later Minoan structural fashions, is well represented in the house fasades (A, C, H, and S seqq.) in which the framework of the windows is isolated in the masonry.

That windows with four or even six panes, containing some substitute for Great window glass, should have already existed at this time is itself only another O f proof of the extraordinary anticipation of modern civilized usage achieved in l t the great days of Minoan history an anticipation not less marked in their tecture. hydraulic and sanitary appliances. The house-fronts are clearly those of town houses, adapted to standing in rows.

Apart from the scarlet filling of the windows and window-panes, not always pre-served, the colouring of the tablets, though of somewhat more sombre tones, ap-proaches that of the faience objects to be described below from the Temple Reposito-ries. The ground is of a pale or greyish tint, the timbering and disks are brown with transitions to crimson and green. The analysis given below:! of the faience material of the relics of that distinctly later deposit is also applicable to the Town Mosaic.

1 See p. 353. See below, p. 352. See p. 486 seqq.

THE PALACE OF MINOS, ETC.

Restored drawings of characteristic types by Mr. Theodore Fyfe, based on my reconstruction of the faience tablets themselves, are given in Fig. 22i, 1 together with others of perfect specimens. Somewhat enlarged representations of two of the house-fronts, with keys to their colour scheme, are given here, Fig. 224, a, b. It will be seen that the attic on b has a decided slope, doubtless in order to shed the rain-water, and the inclination visible in the roof of the two wings of the house must have had a similar object. As a rule, however, the house roofs are represented level, as in a.

DARK GA. EY GROUND. WITH
CRIMSON STRIPES S WHDOW fmM S
UPPER WINDOWS OPEti RIGHT THROUGH
LOWER IJINDOM, SUNK, WITH SCARLET FILLING
ALL C. K. y 8, WHITE.
UHDOUS. 3UMK.
SECTOH
SCARJ. CT FILLING
FIG. 224. RESTORED DRAWINGS OF FAIENCE HOUSE-FRONTS. (i)

The architectural fa9ades on these tablets betray a distinct affinity in Architec- several details with similar features on the component parts of the n j t y w. j t,

Miniature Terra-cotta Shrine, belonging to the M. M. II b stratum of this Terracotta area. The elongated window openings, as in Fig. 22(, D, F though here Shrine: seen in pairs are closely analogous to those above the rectangular block of masonry represented in Fig. 225, a. The alternating dark horizontal bands and light bands with rows of disks shown in Fig. 225, b, absolutely correspond with a constantly recurring arrangement of the house-fronts 1 The plaques vary in size, the mean of the houses being about 4-50 cm. in height and 4 cm. in breadth.

THE PALACE OF MINOS, ETC.

on the plaques. What perhaps is a still more important point is the appearance in the case of the masonry reproduced in the Terra-cotta Shrine of distinct interstices between the blocks. The method of laying the limestone blocks on a bedding of clay mortar, which gives rise to these well-marked intervals, is itself, as illustrated above in the case of the South light-area of the Queen's Megaron, a characteristic feature of the earlier type of Middle Minoan architecture as compared with the finely compacted blocks of the fully developed M. M. Ill style. But this earlier form of construction is clearly reproduced in the isodomic masonry of the tower-houses seen in Fig. 226, S, T, U.

That some constructive features such as the wooden framework were to a certain, extent common to the developed M. M. Ill style is not surprising when we remember that masonry encased in wooden timbering is already illustrated by the Early Minoan buildings of Vasiliki. But the architectural forms displayed by the House Tablets really represent the traditions of the earlier part of the Middle Minoan Age. They cannot as a whole be taken to reflect the architectural fashions that emerge to view in the existing remains of the Domestic Quarter, which indeed were largely taken over by the Late Minoan builders. The Town Mosaic must in short be placed in the same M. M. 1 l context as the Terra-cotta Shrine. In spite, however, of their early elate and archaic tradition the effect produced by the fa9ades of these Minoan town-houses is on the whole surprisingly modern. Though in some cases details of the restoration are necessarily conjectural, the general accuracy of their presentment, as seen in Fig. 226, can hardly be contested. Of the types of building there shown,

FIG. 225. SPECIMENS OF STRUCTURES FROM-TERRA-COTTA SHRINE.

I,,; I (Wwwc ' """ r ""'1' r T 'T'

"II.:,,:,,.,.–,-'-M

T t r 1 ihir. T.–,-. tr–'- VV–i"t -.-.-I fer rtr 1 i—- millimetres, are in some cases given

A-G depict front views of houses showing considerable variety in structure. The elevations O-W seem, on the other hand, to be the backs of similar houses built for defence without lower windows, and probably ranged along the town wall. I-M are outer towers and gates K showing two double entrances. Of the towers, I is remarkable from the clear rendering of the upright posts of the gate recalling that on the silver vase from Mycenae with the siege scene, and Egyptian parallels. The small window here to the left of the entrance was evidently intended for observation on the part of the warder.

Of the exceptional fa ade, Fig. 22, N, two specimens occurred. Its curious incurved window-openings recall in outline the Minoan altar bases, and, as shown below, we may here recognize the back of a sanctuary building dedicated to the Minoan Goddess.

We are here, as already noted, outside the walls of the Palace itself. Neither can the house fa9ades before us be regarded as typical of the more spaciously planned mansions of its immediate surroundings. They display, on the contrary in an eminent degree the restricted frontage of houses shut in by city walls. Their defensively constructed backs, in fact, together with the towers and bastions, sufficiently show that we have here to do with a fortified City, though the details of the architecture, the timbering and panel work, the windows, the imitation of the round beam ends, and the isodomic masonry are still of Cretan type.

We see here, indeed beyond all hope recovered for us an actual presentment of the street fronts and outer borders of a fenced Minoan City as it existed at the close of the Second Middle Minoan Period.

Whether ve may locate the town in the immediate neighbourhood of the Palace itself or in Minoan territory abroad, the towers constructed of isodomic masonry, the gates and bastions here before us must be taken as evidence that the idea of fortification was still quite alive in the island at this time. Interesting parallels, moreover, are to be found in the castel- Castellated buildings that appear on some clay sealings, of slightly later date, Build-found at Zakro in East Crete (Fig. 227, a, 6). 1

That the castellated structures on these, the first of which (a) presents isodomic masonry, found a further source of strength in divine or heroic guardianship is shown by the associated emblems, best seen on b. The helmet with ear-pieces and the 8-shaped shields recur on ritual vessels, 2 and the object to the right seems to be a seated Sphinx.

1 Hogarth, Zakro Sealings, J. H. S., xxii, goblets of religious use from Tomb V at p. 88, and Pl. X, Nos. 130, 131. Isopata (Archaeologia, Ixv, 1914, p. 26 seqq.

2 They are seen together on polychrome and p. 27, Fig. 37, a, 6). See Vol. II. THE PALACE OF MINOS, ETC.

I he sealing c, 1 on the other hand, apparently represents a gateway, over which, as in the case of that of Mycenae, the lion supporters of the Great Minoan Goddess kept watch and ward. Here, too, as in the Lions' Gate, we see between the piers though not here as a support of the guardian animals themselves an altar base with incurving sides such as has Portals of been illustrated above by the Miniature Sanctuary of still earlier date. 2 Here, in fact, is the explanation of the buildings with similar incurved openings, an example of which is shown in Fig. 226, N, which seems to have stood on the wall line of the fenced city represented by the faience tablets. As will be shown elsewhere, a curious parallel to this is afforded by the besieged town of the silver rhyton of Minoan fabric from Mycenae, in

Sanctuaries.

Town Mosaic Part of Larger Composition.

Warriors.

FIG. 227, a, b, c.   SEAUNGS FROM ZAKRO SHOWING CASTELLATED BUILDING (a) AND FACADE AND PORTAL OF SHRINE (b, c). (f) which a shrine with the sacral horns is visible on an outer wall of distinctively Minoan construction. 3

From the numerous fragments found of these architectural plaques, it seems probable that they formed part of a mosaic representing a considerable town. This itself, moreover, appears to have stood in connexion with a larger composition, as may be gathered from the stray pieces given in Fig. 228, though the evidence for the completion of this is unfortunately of a very fragmentary nature.

We see Minoan men, most of them, it would seem, warriors with spears and bows (Fig. 228, p, t perhaps of both the European and Asiatic types-clad in short, close-fitting loin-cloths recalling the Cup-bearers of the Procession Fresco (Fig. 228, p. 4 On two fragments appear what seem to be curved and crested helmets (Fig. 228, m; Fig. 229, c), on another a conical head-piece (Fig. 228, ; 229, b while one (q) shows part of a bow. Some of the men are 1 Hogarth, op. tit., p. 87, Fig. 28 (No. 112).

2 See p. 220, Fig. 166, H.

3 See Vol. II. This interesting detail occurs on a newly discovered fragment, but has not been hitherto noted. 4 See Vol. II.

FIG. 228. REMAINS OF FAIENCE PLAQUES REPRESENTING; V RIOUS SUBJECTS FOUND WITH

HOUSE TABLETS. (-.)

Negroid Types.

THE PALACE OF MINOS, ETC.

marching; others, probably archers, are in a half-kneeling pose. In another case there is seen part of a prostrate figure (Fig. 228, r), or, perhaps, of two men grappling with one another.

The Minoan figures are tinted with a pale ochreous hue, but besides these are fragments of others of a more swarthy skin colour, while the steatopygous rump, abdominal prominence, and prognathism displayed by some of these are clearly negroid (Fig. 230, a, 6, c). Another of the

FIG. 229, a, b, c. FRAGMENTS OF FAIENCE PLAQUES (enlarged about 2 diams.

Animals, Trees, and Water.

FIG. 230, a, b, c. FRAGMENTS OF FAIENCE PLAQUES WITH NEGROID FORMS, (f. 2 diams.) dark-skinned figures is seen in a grotesque attitude squatting like a frog (Fig. 228, z), others are exceptionally small, and with their hands stretched out as if in the guise of suppliants.

Remains of more than one plaque (Fig. 228 c, d, e) depicting the Cretan wild goat or agrimi point to hunting scenes, but there was also the foot (6) of an ox or bull, which may have belonged to a pastoral or agricultural theme. Others show trees, some with ivylike foliage (jf). A very suggestive tablet is entirely covered with a waved design depicting water (gg) in riverless Crete, surely, the Stream of Ocean. It seems probable that the remarkable fragment Fig. 22!, i is part of the prow of a vessel with Prow of an eye painted on it as on the galleys of later Greece.

In examining the figured representations on these tablets we are at once struck, as in the case of the architectural features, with their archaic aspect as compared with the types in vogue at the close of the Middle Minoan Period or in the early part of the Late Minoan Age. Compare for instance the goat, Fig. 228 e, so stiffly rendered, and the head of the other, Fig. 228 c, with such a living presentment as that of the she-goat and young on the faience relief from the Temple Repositories illustrated below. 1

The variation in the size of many of these tablets would not in itself preclude their having formed parts of the same scene, if we may suppose that they had been set in the same plaster field. This indeed seems to have been the case with the component parts of the faience group described below which includes the flying fish. 2 But where, as in certain figures, we have to do with a difference of scale for instance in the archer (fl) and the spearman () we must naturally infer that they belonged to different zones. It seems probable indeed that the inlays had belonged to separate panels, forming part of the decoration, perhaps of a large wooden chest, 3 a true Scusaxea dpia like that of Dana. We may even venture to see in it Parallels the prototype of the Chest of Kypselos porcelain plaques here antici- chest of pating ivory. The varied character of the subjects themselves the city, an y d p the scenes of peace and war, of hunting, pastoral life and tilth, the waves Shields of 1 icniklt. s of ocean bring this into the cycle of great Minoan compositions in relief, and the tradition of which was to be handed down in Greek epic. 4

Like the faience material itself, the suggestion of the present mosaic may have come from Egypt, though the designs themselves are purely indigenous. We may infer at any rate that part of the scenes depicted lay on the further side of the Libyan Sea whose actual billows, it seems, were not Libyan omitted from the composition. The ship might suggest that we have here in c. ts the harbour town of broad Knossos, or it may be that we have a pictorial position, record tantalizingly incomplete of some actual Minoan expedition on the African side. In that case the fenced City here depicted may have represented some Minoan overseas foundation on the Libyan shores. There are, as will be seen, some reasons for supposing that the parallel subject, 1 Fig. 366, p. 510. a mass of carbonized cypress wood, apparently

See p 521. forming part of a small chest.

A number of faience plaques were found See Minoan and Mycenaean Elements in in the Room of the Throne, together with Hellenic Life, J. H. 5., xxxii, pp. 288, 289.

THE PALACE OF MINOS, ETC.

Painted Relief of Jewel with Negroid Heads.

Libyan Sources of Gold.

Plaques in Shape of Scales.

the siege scene on the Minoan silver rhyton from Mycenae, was laid outside Crete, in that case on the Anatolian side.

Another piece of contemporary evidence regarding connexions with the further coast of the Libyan Sea is, moreover, to be found in a fragment of a painted stucco relief, apparently belonging to the close of the succeeding Period, showing a man's hand coloured red according to the Minoan canon fingering a gold necklace with pendants in the form of heads of negroid affinity, with large triple earrings (Fig. 231). It looks as if the gold of the jewel itself may have come from Nubia or some other African source. Nor is it necessary to suppose that it came through an Egyptian medium. Caravans consisting of veiled representatives Tuatis and others of the old Libyan stock still bear gold-dust to the Tripoli markets from across Sahara. 2 It is noteworthy that though the heads of this necklace show certain negroid features such as the curly black hair, thick lips, snub noses, and large ears, their colour is a tawny yellow like the gold. It is true that the colour may be clue to the original material of the pendants having been of gold with inlays in other materials. It is possible, however, that we have here to do with members of some African race under negroid influence rather than with actual niggers.

Among the plaques of the Town Mosaic, which were otherwise of rectangular shapes, appears an exceptional and well-represented series moulded in the form of scales, Fig. 228 i, j and of a pale green hue. 3 The under sides of these were also abnormal in displaying on their lower surface a double axe in relief. The marking of the material thus with the

EZ3 VELLQW WM RED mm BLACK

FIG. 231. PENDANT OF NECKLACE IN FORM OF HEAD WITH NEGROID FEATURES (f).

1 The jewel se. ems to be attached to some article of dress of a blue colour. To the left of it is part of a lock of hair, presumably belonging to the wearer of the necklace. It is illustrated below, p. 526, Fig. 383, in connexion with the painted plaster reliefs of the M. M. Ill Period.

a I was a witness of this traffic at Tripoli itself in 1897. In this case the gold-dust was brought by inhabitants of the Oasis of Tuat, some of them veiled in the Tuareg fashion.

3 An inherent feature of this conventional pattern is the placing uppermost of the rounded surface in contrast to the true scale motive, as seen in armour, and the analogous feather ornament such as we find in Egypt (Petrie, Egyptian Decorative

Art, p. 50 seqq.), where the rounded border is, naturally, below. The position of these scale inlays is shown by the double axes on their lower surface.

consecrating emblem seems itself to indicate that the inlays had formed part of an object belonging to a sanctuary of the great Minoan Goddess. This conclusion, it will be seen, fits in with the parallelism already established with the Terra-cotta Sanctuary, and enhances the probability that the Chest which the Town Mosaic seems to have adorned had found a place in the same sanctuary chamber.

The scale inlays themselves should by no means be regarded as merely of decorative import, and seem indeed to form an integral part of the composition itself as a conventional representation of a rocky landscape. As an indication of a rocky or mountainous site this convention is of very early oriental usage. It was indeed already employed by the Sumerians at an epoch anterior to the Semitic domination and at least as early as the beginning of the Third Millennium B. C. (Fig. 232). 1 At a later date, on the well-known stela on which Hammurabi is seen receiving the law from Shamash, 2 the seated figure of the Sun God has his feet on a scaled base similar to that of earlier usage, which here stands for his Holy Mountain. So, too, at a later period the same convention in a more stylized form survives in Assyrian and Phoenician art. 3 The peak, moreover, on which the Minoan Goddess stands in the later sealings of the Central Palace shrine at Knossos shows the same scale-like formation. 4

Double Axe Mark on these: Sign of Consecration.

Scales old Oriental Convention for Rocks.

FIG. 232. SUMERIAN. PERFORATED PLAQUE SHOWING SCALES AS IN-DICATION OF ROCKY GROUND ON WHICH A MALE FIGURE POURS A LIBATION TO A GODDESS (c. 2900 B. C.; LOUVRK).

1 The Scale convention is here seen on a perforated plaque of about Eannatum's reign, c. 2900 B. c., representing a votary before a seated Goddess (L. Heuzey, Description des Monuments, 209; Louvre Catalogue, No. 11; L. W. King, History of Sumer and Akkad, p. 68, Fig. 20). On this subject see A. Reichel, Stitiiien zur kretisch-mykenischen Kunst (Jah-reshefte d. Oesterreichischen Arch. Inst., vol. xi (1908), p. 251 seqq.).

2 J. de Morgan, Mt moires de la Delegation en Perse, T. iv (1902), Deuxieme Sevie, Pl. 3.

5 Notable examples are supplied by the Cypro-Phoenician silver bowls.

4 Compare, too, the base of the faience relief with the goat and kids from the Temple Repositories, p. 510, Fig. 366, below. The same scale-like formation constantly appears as the equivalent of rocks on the borders of Minoan intaglios.

THE PALACE OF MINOS, ETC.

Scale Convention on Minoan Rhytons with Siege Scenes.

Theme of Beleaguered City and its Epic Survivals.

It is of special interest to note that this scale convention in a more decorative reticulated form appears as an indication of a rocky steep on an interesting fragment of a L. M. I rhyton, where an archer is seen in the act of mounting it. This fragment, as is shown in a later Section of this work, 1 undoubtedly belongs to a composition analogous to the Siege Scene on the silver vessel of the same class found at Mycenae. In the latter case not only the sea margent but the rocky surface of the shallows is indicated in the same manner, while on a painted clay rhyton from Pseira, where dolphins are surrounded by a similar reticulation, it may be taken to represent the sea itself.

The conventional rendering of a rocky background by means of scale inlays in the Town Mosaic affords another link of connexion with a later cycle of subjects such as the above, the central theme of which is a besieged city. There is good warrant indeed for concluding that we have here a version, coeval with the earliest Palace of Knossos, of epic scenes, the later transformations of which may be detected not only in the Minoan reliefs referred to, but in the shields of Herakles and Achilles, as described by Hesiod and Homer. The theme of the beleaguered city treated of in these Minoan compositions was as old in Egypt as the days of the Early Dynasties. More, however, will be said on the comparisons there supplied in considering the Minoan version on the silver rhyton found in the Mycenae Grave. At a later date it was to take immortal shape in the tale of Troy divine.

THE THIRD MIDDLE MINOAN PERIOD MIDDLE MINOAN III 16. M. M. Ill: (A) THE BEGINNING OK THE NEW ERA.

Epoch of Transition; Heralded by great catastrophe at end of M. M. II; Continuity of culture preserved but emergence of new elements; Possible Dynastic change; Neiv linearized Script, Class A; Partial dislocations at Knossos; Close of Period well marked by stratified deposits and great Remodelling; those of W. and E. wing contrasted; Great filling in on E. slope; Evidences of intermediate M. M. Ill phases; Line of delimitation between M. M. Ill and L. M. I more definite in pottery; Difficulties attending some of the greater naturalistic ivorks such as wall-paintings and reliefs; Such can only be referred to a great transitional epoch; Importance of Spiral Fresco Deposit; Magazine of Medallion Pithoi and Corridor of Bays.

THE epoch at which we have now arrived is pre-eminently one of Epoch of transition between Middle and Late Minoan traditions. A new Era in t j on fact begins which overlaps them both. It is heralded, as we have seen, by what appears to have been a widespread catastrophe both at Knossos and Phaestos, which seems for a time at least to have brought with it a real set-back to the Middle Minoan culture so brilliantly illustrated by the remains of its Second Period.

This overthrow, as has been shown above, seems to have followed at no Great long interval the interruption of direct relations with the Nile Valley which t hrowof was a natural consequence of the break-up of Egyptian unity at the close of I 1 6,,! M: the first brilliant era of the Thirteenth Dynasty. Its approximate date, which c. 1700 must be. taken as a term for the beginning of the present Period, has been set down at 1700 B. C. The local catastrophe seems to have been so general and thoroughgoing that the Palace sites both at Knossos and Phaestos may, partially at least, have remained for an appreciable time uninhabited and have existed as mere heaps of ruins.

Although the temporary set-back must in any case have been considerable and the new order of things was only gradually built up, this does not mean that the essential continuity of Minoan civilization was at this time broken off.

THE PALACE OF MINOS, ETC.

Appearance of Novel Features.

The Linearized Script.

Architectural Fashions.
Probable Dynastic Change but
Essential Continuity.
Partial Dislocations in Palace Area at Knossos.

Certain changes indeed of great significance are visible in the new order, such as the cessation of the traditional hieroglyphic form of script and its replacement by a more advanced and linearized type, which cannot be said to be its direct outgrowth. Side by side with this, too, is the appearance of new types of signet and new methods with regard to sealing. Novel architectural features also emerge, such as the compact masonry, the fondness for floor-cists or kaselles', and, towards the close of this Period, other new-fashioned constructive methods. As the art of M. M. Ill moreover grows to maturity we witness a remarkable manifestation of the naturalistic spirit.

That the overthrow at the close of M. M. II was accompanied by a dynastic change is extremely probable. The possibility can by no means be excluded that new ethnic ingredients had introduced themselves. Yet, with all this, the survival and evolution of the older elements of the earlier Cretan civilization is still so intensive in its quality that we cannot speak of any such break in the continuity of Minoan culture as would, we may suppose, have resulted from subjection to a foreign yoke. It is clear, for instance, that in the earlier M. M. Ill stage, a, much of the architectural traditions of the M. M. II b phase still survived.

Some discontinuity, however, in the architectural traditions of the Knossian Palace there undoubtedly was at this epoch. Many features indeed in the Palace plan as it at present exists go back no further than the Third Middle Minoan Period. This, it will be seen, is especially true of the interior of the Domestic Quarter, throughout a large part of which something like a clean sweep was made in order to carry out the new arrangements. In this case there seems to have been a good deal of deliberate demolition. Even here, however, the bases of several important walls survived, while in the neighbouring area of the Loom-Weights, the lower courses of the M. M. II walls were largely used as foundations for their M. M. Ill successors. A certain amount of dislocation, however, is in this case, too, visible in the plan.

This Loom-Weight area, as is demonstrated below, 1 proved as important for the history of the present Period as for the preceding. As will be seen from the section given in Fig. 187 b above, there were here two M. M. Ill floor-levels with characteristic contents, overlying that which marked the latest M. M. II phase.

The importance of the earlier M. M. Ill stratum here brought to light, illustrating the mature stage of what may be called M. M. Ilia, in its relation to the original structural core of the Domestic Quarter, will be pointed out below. 1 It is represented by the penultimate floor-level in the section of the Magazine of the Medallion Pit hoi given below in Fig. 2.":. and its place in the stratification there shows that it marks the result of a gradual revival after a long interval of stagnation which has left its record in the thick stratum above the late M. M. II pavement.

The deposits illustrating the closing phase of this Period here denned Stratified as M. M. Ill b are of very wide extent, and the story that they tell is not always the same. It is clear that throughout a large part of the Western Wing there must have been a considerable conflagration, probably accompanied by lawless plundering. In the case of the floor cists' of the w. wing Sanctuary Area and the adjoining West Magazines, as well as in the basements of the South-West, 2 a burnt M. M. Ill stratum underlies the Late Minoan structures. The cists themselves were filled in with carbonized debris, often, as in the case of the Temple Repositories', containing the remains of valuable possessions.

On the East Slope, however, the phenomena with which we have to Pheno-deal seem to be largely of a different order. There is little of this burnt M. M. Ill deposit, though it is clear that a wholesale remodelling took place over a large part of this region early in the Late Minoan Age, accompanied by the filling in of M. M. Ill Magazines or basements. In several Magazines the M. M. Ill vessels were here left on the floors, as antiquated or of little account, at the time when the new structures were built above them.

This filling in of walled spaces on what had been the upper terrace on Filling in this slope seems to have been part of a methodical architectural plan carried "n.,. out at the beginning of the Late Minoan Age for raising the level of struc- zines, c., tures along the Eastern border of the Central Court. This process is in fact slope, visible both South and North of the great Cutting on this side. To the South of this was a distinct insula presenting the remains of a compact aggregation of M. M. Ill buildings, including a small lustral basin and its dependencies and a group of Magazines. These Magazines, named after the Lily Vases in one of their compartments, 3 were at this time deliberately earthed under, with their contents intact, to afford a platform for a L. M. I step-way running up to the Central Court. So, too, in what may be termed the Northern quarter on this side, the N. E. Magazines with their stacks of plain M. M. Ill pottery and the adjoining N. E. Hall were covered in in the same manner.

1 See p. 325 seqq. 10, n, Figs. 3, 4). See pp. 554, 555. Fig.

"In one of these an inscribed M. M. Ill 416, b. jar was found (Knossos, Report, 1901, pp. See below, p. 575.

Immediately South of this again, along the N. border of the great Cutting, was a well-defined rectangular enclave representing, as will be shown below, the basements of a M. M. Ill East Hall, a little below the level of the Central Court. Here a similar filling in on a still larger scale seems to have taken place at the beginning of the First Late Minoan Period with the object of erecting a new East Hall the Portico of which should step up from the Central Court. The filling in of the Corridor of the Bays andthe connected Magazine of the Medallion Pithoi was part of this work.

On this side at any rate, there was no trace of violent conflagration, and there can be no doubt that in the Domestic Quarter a good deal of the M. M. Ill structures had survived to the last days of the Palace.

The catastrophe that undoubtedly befell the West Wing at this time Burnt accompanied as it seems to have been by the ransacking of the floor cists Cisttand mav account for their general filling in or conversion to superficial vats as well Reposi- as f or their eventual paving- over in the early part of the succeeding Late tories of.,. 1111 i 11 w. Wing. Minoan Age. It also implies some wholesale changes in the method of storage, rendered necessary by the closing of the old repositories. The traces, remaining in some of these in the region of the West Magazines, of gold foil, the bronze fittings of boxes, and inlays of crystal and faience, and the remains of the faience figures belonging to the Central Palace Shrine, may well represent the leavings of somewhat hasty pillagers.

In another direction the extension of the West Court at the beginning Rubbish of the Late Minoan Age entailed the filling in and paving over of the circular Cour t fw walled rubbish pit on that side, containing heaps of M. M. Ill sherds.

Thus in one way or another a large amount of stratified material was clearly marked off in various parts of the Knossian Palace at the close of the

Third Middle Minoan Period. In many cases, moreover, this deposit was separated from the Late Minoan level by actual paving slabs. It is due to the operation of these causes that this mass of material has been preserved, giving a collective picture of the fabrics of the M. M. Ill culture in its final

Definite phase. We have here, in fact, one of the most definite lines of stratigraphic graphic demarcation to be found at any stage of Minoan history, and, on the whole, it

Line in w ju be seen that certain characteristic products lie on one or the other side of

Pottery.

the chronological landmark thus supplied. The fine ceramic class, for instance, formerly associated with the term Mycenaean, distinguished by its prevailing dark decoration on a buff ground, its brilliant iron glaze, and its crisp consistency the result of improved technical processes is practically confined to the Late Minoan side of the boundary. It must at the same time be recognized that in the higher departments of naturalistic art, the endeavour to lay down any fixed lines of delimitation between the works of the mature M. M. Ill phase and those of the earlier part at least of

L. M. I is fraught with much greater difficulties. Much of the material, such as the frescoes and painted reliefs, is of a character that does not follow Natura- ordinary stratigraphic laws. It is true that, as conventionali-m becomes more orks perceptible and heraldic designs gain ground, we feel that ve are on the Late

Minoan side of the border. But some of the highest products of Minoan Transi- art can only be described as belonging to a great transitional epoch. Epoch.

It has been already noted that the remains found in the stratum beneath the later pavements and fillings in show the Middle Minoan style in its most developed phase. It follows from this that the data thus afforded naturally exhibit the maximum amount of differentiation from the characteristic products of the latest M. M. II stage, such as its advanced polychrome wares. They are separated from this M. M. II stage not only by an accumulation Inter-of deposit and new structural elements, but in many places by a succession stages of of intermediate floor-levels. It should therefore be constantly borne in mind M M- " that, though less abundantly forthcoming, there is distinct evidence of a series of transitional phases within the limits of M. M. Ill itself.

Even after the revival from the great catastrophe at the close of M. M. II was already well advanced, there is evidence of a series of partial destructions and renovations on the Palace site of Knossos. The important M- M.- in section Fig. 187(5 above, 1 giving the successive structures of the Loom- tion of Weight Area, shows the walls of a M. M. Ill building set above the earlier t remains. On the pavement of its latest floor-level, above its M. M. Ilia Area-deposits, were characteristic pots answering to types found in the series of deposits that mark the closing phase of M. M. III.

So, too, in the section of the pavement of the Queen's Megaron, illustrated in Fig. 155 above, 2 at least two floor-levels are visible between the mosaiko' pavement of the closing M. M. 11 phase and the gypsum slabbing of L. M. I date. Of great chronological importance, moreover, is the fact that there are, as will be shown below, conclusive reasons for referring the M. M. Ill stratum in which occurred the alabastron lid with Stratum the name of the Hyksos Pharaoh Khyan to a date anterior to that retaining presented by the latest floor-deposits of this Period. It will be seen that this important relic is here regarded not as an indication of an imaginary Hyksos Conquest of Crete, but rather as a token of the restoration of peaceful 1 See p. 248 seqq. See p. 210.

THE PALACE OF MINOS, ETC.

intercourse with Egypt at the time when it was again reunited into a single monarchy at the hands of this Egyptianked Hyksos dynast.

An interesting example of intermediate stratification was brought to light

M. IABJfrmEDALLION PltHOI ON THIS FLOOR

GYPSUM SLABS

VERY 5UKCK CARBONIZED EARTH WITH SHERDS

WHITE PLftsTER FLOOR

BLACKISH CARBONIZED-EARTH WITH SHERDS

WHITE PLASTER FLOOR

EARTH WITH SHERDS

LIMEitONi PAVEMENT ("MOSAIKO") WITH WHITE CEMENT IN INTERSTICES M.

NEOLITHIC ,30 3 CENTIMETRTS

FIG. 233. SECTION BENEATH M. M. 1116 PAVEMENT OF MAGAZINE OF MEDALLION PITHOI.

Section in the course of test excavations made in 1913 beneath the gypsum pavement zhie of a " of the Magazine of the Medallion pithoi (Fig. 233), which, together with

Medal- t j le ac lj o ining Corridor of the Bays, formed an annexe to the first floor of

Pithoi. the Domestic Quarter. A terminus a quo for this pavement was supplied by of a row of pitkoi found upon it, decorated with medallions' showing white rosettes, more fully described below, as typical products of the closing M. M. Ill phase. 1 The carbonizing process due to the oil which these originally contained had much blackened the gypsum slabbing, and this process had extended to two strata below. At a depth of 37 cm. beneath ents: this gypsum floor, immediately resting on the Neolithic clay, was a pave- M. M il.

Fi.;. I:)!. SECTION BENEATH M. M. 1116 PAVEMENT OF MAGAZINE OK. MEDALLION PITHOI, SHOWING INTERMEDIATE STRATA AND M. M. II MOSAIKO FLOOR BELOW, WITH PLASTER STAND FOR LARGE OIL JAR.

ment of the M. M. II b mosaiko' class, 2 consisting of polygonal slabs of very fine limestone, the interstices of which were filled with white plaster. In some pavements of this class the plaster is bright red.

In the overlying deposit above this mosaiko' floor lay shallow bowls, nter. small plain vessels and fragments, a few M. M. II, but mostly typical of the T J? 1

M. M. Ill class. At 17 cm. above it was a plaster floor over which was Floors, a carbonized layer, 5 cm. thick, with further M. M. 111 sherds. Then followed another plaster floor and a similar deposit, still more carbonized, imme- 1 See p. 562 seqq. and Fig. 409. See above, p. 210.

THE PALACE OF MINOS, ETC.

diately underlying the gypsum slabs of the M. M. Ill Magazine in its final form. We have here, therefore, the record of three successive floors between the close of M. M. II and that of M. M. 111 (see Section, Fig. 233). A further interesting circumstance was the discovery on the earlier mosaiko floor of a raised plaster circle 1-13 metre in diameter, adapted to hold a jar with a base of about 94 cm. (Fig. 234). It follows that the use of this space as a Magazine for oil storage goes back to a distinctly earlier date, when the floor level was lower. The large pithos base is in keeping with the M. M. II tradition. The Magazine itself was somewhat narrowed at a date slightly

FIG. 235. VIEW OF ENCLAVE CONTAINING MAGAZINE OF MEDALLION PITHOI AND THE CORRIDOR OF THE BAYS (THE ROYAL MAGAZINES). To LEFT is MIDDLE E. W. CORRIDOR.

anterior to the storage of the Medallion pithoi by the rebuilding of its E. wall on a broader scale.

In the adjoining Corridor of the Ba)s (Fig. 236) were found remarkable hoards of contemporary vessels of culinary and probably also of ritual usage 2, and this with the contiguous Magazine, built on an upper terrace-level of the East Slope, together formed an isolated enclave in connexion with the adjoining first floor of the Domestic Quarter.

There can be no doubt that the primary function of the massive piers of masonry that divided the Corridor into separate bays for storage was to act as supports for the pillars of what seems to have been the great East Hall of the Palace, which, in its M. M. Ill shape, was somewhat below the 1 The flat border of the plaster circle was 9-5 cm. in diameter.

2 See below, p. 565 and Fig. 412.

Magazine ofmedallion Pithoi and Corridor of Bays.

Piers supports of Great East Hall above.

level of the Central Court. As will be more fully demonstrated below, the general plan of this is very clearly suggested by the existing substructures in this area. That an important upper Hall was in existence here before the close of the M. M. Ill Period results from a variety of evidence, and it will be shown that the stone drain-heads found on the same terrace-level must be brought into connexion with the drainage of its roofs and light-court. In relation to this may be also placed the early column bases, the Spiral Fresco, and the painted stucco low-reliefs found, as we shall see, in the M. M. Ill

ROYAL MAGAZINES
CORR-OF BAY5 MAC OF MEDj, PITHOl

Kic. 236. PLAN OK ROYAL MAGAZINES SHOWING ENCLAVE OFF LAND-ING OF GRAND STAIRCASK. (THE RECTANGLE SHOWS WHERE PAVEMENT WAS RAISED.) stratum of the Loom-Weight Area. Later on, at the beginning of the L. M. I Period, it appears to have been succeeded by another Hall on a higher level but following much the same lines. To this seem to have belonged the magnificent high-reliefs of painted stucco representing agonistic scenes.

The Magazine of the Medallion Pithoi, however, together with the The Corridor of the Bays, had no connexion with this upper Hall. They constitute an enclave, built, as already said, oft" the first floor of the Domestic Quarter zincs and designed for its convenience. From the stately character of the store jars themselves, some of them stamped with official seals, the group of structures may be fitly described as par excellence 'the Royal Magazines'.

GRAND
STAIRCASE,
FIG. 237. SECOND AND PART OF FIRST FLIGHT OF GRAND STAIRCASE. (SKETCHED, IN COURSE OF EXCAVATION AND BEFORE RE-SUPPORTING OF UPPER FLIGHTS, BY THEODORE FYFE.)

Dramatic development of (he Excavation discovery of Grand Staircase and Residential Quarter in great East Cutting; The "Domestic Quarter; Preservation of Upper Stories; ork of Restoration; Halls of Colonnades and Double Axes; Queens Mcgaron; Court of Distaffs; Alteration of Drainage System; Service Quarter and Staircase; Room of Stone Bench and Upper Hall of Double Axes; System above Queens Megaron Bedrooms, Bath-rooms, and Latrines; Treasury of Shrine; The Grand Staircase of five flights, approached from Central Court; Tapering wooden columns their origin in primitive stone pillars; Lmu column bases; Use of Cypress wood; Evidence of fluted columns; M. M. Ill Construction; Timber framework of walls and windows; Important architectural equations supplied by area of Spiral Fresco; Chronological data structural core of Domestic Quarter M. M. HI a Existing superficial features mainly M. M. Ill b and Late Minoan; Passage East of Domestic Quarter Marbled and Labyrinth frescoes; Egyptian Meander as House Plan; The Labyrinth and Minotaur at Knossos.

IT was in working South from the last section of the Corridor of the Bays, Dramatic and thus through a blocked doorway to a threshold beyond, that the course memo of excavation on the Palace site of Knossos took its most dramatic turn. 1 lhe. 1 xca"

vation: Immediately in front of the doorway appeared the ascending steps of a flight Discovery of stairs, flanked by a stone parapet with the socketed bases of carbonized stair wooden columns. A couple of paces to the right, on the other hand, the Casepaved surface hitherto regarded as the ground-level of this part of the building suddenly began to step down, and turned out to be the landing of a descending flight of twelve steps. This led to another landing, stepping down to a third, from which, at right angles to the left, the head of a lower flight came into view.

A sketch of the first results of this exploratory work by Mr. Theodore Fyfe is given in Fig. 237, showing the void caused by the crumbling away of a carbonized wooden column that had supported the landing block between two upper flights. Another landing block for a fifth flight of stairs, grooved for the great beam ends, is seen in situ at the further end of the middle wall.

This part of the excavation proved to be altogether miner's work owing 1 See Knossos, Report, 1901, p. 102 seqq.

THE PALACE OF MINOS, ETC.
Miner's Work.

to the risk of bringing down the stairway above, and necessitated a constant succession of wooden props. It was therefore a happy circumstance that two of the workmen had worked in the Laurion mines. Eight days of dangerous tunnelling brought us beyond the second landing, down another flight of twelve steps, to what, after long additional excavation, proved to be a columnar court lighting the successive flights of the Grand Staircase.

FIG. 233. VIEW OF LOWER FLIGHTS OF GRAND STAIRCASE AND SURROUNDING REGION OF DOMESTIC QUARTER, AS PROVISIONALLY SUPPORTED; FROM LOOK-OUT STATION ON CENTRAL COURT.

A sketch of this light-court, known as the Hall of the Colonnades', taken by Mr. Fyfe at the time of the excavation and before the interval between the first and third flight of stairs had been opened out, is given in Suppl. Pl. V. The wooden columns both of the Hall itself and of the stair-case balustrades were here as elsewhere subsequently restored in stonework with a plaster coating. The photographic view, Fig. 238, taken from a look-out station on the terrace of the Central Court immediately above, also gives a general view of the Staircase, the adjoining section of the Middle Mast-West Corridor, also now brought to light, and of part of the Hall of the Colonnades below as seen before its restoration.

The sudden stepped descent to the right on emerging from the Residen-Corridor of the Bays was the first intimation of the existence of the great Q, artcr Cutting in the East slope of the Palace site, the execution of which has in. re; lt been referred in Section 9 above to the M. M. II Period. 1 Of the earlier ting: constructions within it, the light-area to the South, and the containing walls to West and North have already received illustration. The drainage system i ts in its original form also belongs to this epoch, and some M. M. II door- jambs were found in position opening from the Corridor of the Painted mostly Pithos' into an early chamber with a kalderim pavement. Beyond a ted. this, however, and the earlier pavements beneath the Queen's Megaron little remains within the Cutting that can be certainly referred to this earlier period of construction, though it is clear that some stepped descent must have preceded the Grand Staircase as it at present exists.

The M. M. I II architects in constructing here the new residential The quarter evidently worked on some of the earlier existing lines. The j lan of supporting walls that enclosed the boundaries of the Cutting were naturally adhered to and to a certain extent earlier lines were doubtless followed in the interior divisions. A good instance of the superposition of the later walls on the original lines is indeed supplied by the section of the neighbouring Loom-Weight Area. The older drainage system was in the same way adapted to the new conditions, but the inner area of the Domestic Quarter must on the whole have been re-designed with great freedom. As will at once be seen from Figs. 2:59, 240, it forms a highly elaborate but brilliantly unitary plan.

It would seem that the debris due to the falling in of masses of sun- Upper dried bricks from the upper stories had infiltrated (partly owing to the "" es subsequent solution of the clay) into the covered part of the building ported by below, ami thus led to the formation of a compact filling which had held up Fallen the floors and terraces above. The wooden columns themselves seem to have for the most part survived awhile in an unburnt condition. Later on, however, when owing to the result of chemical action they had become carbonized, their function of supporting the incumbent structures above had i ied been taken up by this natural concretion of the fallen materials. Only in Columns the case of their wooden architraves and the transverse beams that traversed Beams.

1 See p. 204 seqq.

the walls the carbonizing process left a certain void, usually involving- a subsidence of the overlying structures to that extent.

Except for this slight lowering of level, however, almost the whole floor of the first story, including pavements and door-jambs, was found in situ throughout this Quarter, to a degree that seemed little short of miraculous. But to profit by this fortunate circumstance and to preserve the upper remains, hung thus as it were suspended, while at the same time to lay bare the lower halls and chambers involved a task such as never before probably has confronted excavators. It was necessary by provisional means to prop up the upper structures while substituting more permanent materials for the carbonized posts and columns. Simultaneously the great transverse beams, many of them 40 cm. thick, were replaced by girders embedded in concrete, and for this part of the work the collapsed masonry that they had supported, often weighing several tons, had to be carefully removed block by block and replaced at its original level. The result of Domestic part of this work as executed by Mr. Christian Doll in the case of the R Ua tored Grand Staircase and the neighbouring Halls of the Colonnades, of the Double Axes, and of the Distaffs, will be seen in the figures given below. Other views show some of the upper pavements and door-jambs. Throughout the greater part of this area, indeed, the evidence went far beyond the existence of a single upper story. It seems certain that in the inner bay of the Domestic Quarter, at any rate, there were at least three stories. In the case of the Grand Staircase it was possible actually to restore five flights, the uppermost rising above the level of the Central Court.

The scientific skill and harmonious disposition displayed by the structures of this Quarter, the felicitous compactness of their arrangement, centring as it were round the inner private staircase, represents a development of domestic architecture for which we may look in vain for a parallel in Egypt or Chaldaea or any other Oriental country. In many of its aspects, indeed, it is more modern than anything that has come down to us from ancient Greece or Rome.

Plan of A. good idea of these arrangements will be gathered from the revised Quarter: Plans of the ground floor and first story of the Domestic Quarter by Mr. fod! fica- Christian Doll given in Figs. 239, 240. It has been already shown that the tions. masonry of the South light-area of the Queen's Megaron and the lower courses at least of the containing walls of this Quarter were already in existence in M. M. II. Most elements in the fabric, however, date from the

M. M. Ill Period, though certain features in the principal Halls and some details of the Service Quarter behind it must be referred to the early part of the Late Minoan Age. A more important modification, however, to be noted in the plans is the blocking of the E. end of the Lower East-West Corridor, which originally seems to have afforded a direct outlet on this side, and the construction of a new flight of stairs leading down directly at this point from the Corridor above. This alteration, as will be shown in a later Section of this work, is of Late Minoan date.

It will be seen that the ground-floor Plan (Fig. 239), largely repeated on the first story (Fig. 240), included, besides the fine columnar court known as the Hall of the Colonnades', Fig. 248 below, which acted as a light-well for the Grand Staircase and adjoining Galleries, two large Halls evidently designed for receptions, an account of which in their final form is reserved for the second volume of this work. The first and larger of these, known as the Hall of the Double Axes from the signs on its blocks, is triply Hall of divided by lines of doorways, and is provided with porticoes and light-areas Axes. on three sides. Its traditional character as a Hall of State Receptions was preserved to the last, and was manifested by the remains of a wooden throne against the N. wall of its inmost section, probably repeated in the section adjoining. Its Central and Eastern sections are shown in Fig. 241, its W. light-court in Fig. 250.

There are good reasons for supposing that this Hall to a certain degree served as a model for the Great Megaron of the Little Palace, built on the hill to the West of the earlier building about the beginning of the Late Minoan Age. The similarity in construction, the successive sections Parallel with their lines of doorways and frontal and lateral colonnades all point to this IVreat conclusion. But the parallel almost necessarily leads us a step further. The Great Megaron of the Little Palace and the Peristyle and Hall of the stepped Palace. Doorways, to which it stands en suite, must undoubtedly be taken in connexion with an entrance system beyond. But there are many indications that an entrance, which at this time must have been of considerable importance, did in stands in ! r-r- i r, T.,-iii relationto met exist in the extreme S. E. angle of the Great Palace, and indeed, the most Entrance convenient access to the rich valley of the Kaeratos is opened at this point.

This corner of the Domestic Quarter, including a large part of the Southern and Eastern light-areas of the Hall of the Double Axes, has suffered a good deal of destruction. There are grounds for supposing that the East colonnade of this Hall formed part of a Peristyle Court with three columns on each side, bounded on the East by an outer wall line of which 1 A reused gypsum block visible on the tions that seem to have been originally intended Plan. Fig. 239, and in Fig. 241, in front of the for a column base at this point. N. Iolumn base on this side overlies founda- the foundations have been preserved. Such a Court, opening on an entrance system beyond, would have functionally corresponded with the Peristyle that fronts the Great Hall of the Little Palace.

The light-court opposite the Southern portico of the Hall of the Double Axes had been re-enclosed, perhaps on a dimished scale, by walls of Late Minoan date. It is clear that it was originally flanked by a portico on its W. side, separating it from the structural barrier at that end of the Queen's Megaron. 1 The existing wall on that side, as will be shown below, is also late, but was preceded by a broader construction with openings admitting free communication between the two areas.

A fuller account of the Hall of the Double Axes and its connected system is reserved for the Second Volume of this work and to a Section dealing with the First Late Minoan Period, to which its external decorative features in the state in which they were discovered seem mainly to belong. But the core of its original structure is, as will be shown, an inheritance from the earlier phase of the M. M. Ill Period. 2

From the Western section of the Hall of the Double Axes a passage, called from its crooked plan the Dog's-leg Corridor, 3 and well adapted for securing privacy, led to the secluded inner Chamber, known as the Queen's Queen's Megaron (Fig. 242), the low benches of which seem to be best in keeping with female occupants. The Dolphin Fresco found in connexion with this apartment is here attributed to the last M. M. Ill phase (see below, p. 542, Fig. 394), but other features in its decoration are certainly of L. M. I date, as also the East wall as it at present exists. Its full description, therefore, with an attempt at detailed restoration will be given in a Section of this book dealing with that Period. This Megaron, according to its existing plan, with its pillared. division a kind of interior window its secluded inner compartment, complete with portico and light-court of its own, and the little bath-room opening from its Western section, affords an interesting and varied piece of architectural design without rival among Minoan remains. 4 A surprising Private discovery in connexion with it was a second doorway, beside that opening leading to from the Dog's-leg Corridor, which led to a private stone staircase and thus uppei brought the Megaron and its dependencies into communication with a suite of similar spacious apartments above. There is evidence, however, that 1 According to the principles of Minoan 3 See Knossos, Report, 1902, p. 45. construction a covered space must intervene A restored view of this will be given in between two light-areas. Vol.11. For a photographic view of the remains 2 The remains of a limestone stylobate visible as excavated, see Suppl. Plate VI. in the E. Portico probably belong to that epoch.

rooms.

according to the original plan, the Queen's Megaron was not so entirely shut original off on its Eastern border from the Peristyle Court which ex lypolhesi fi"-, 0 formed the Southern approach to the Hall of the Double Axes. Both the Mcrarpn Walls of the E. light-well of this Megaron, which are of fine limestone masonry, end in two distinct anlae, and the wall that at present blocks the interval between these is of later construction. 1 A test excavation made by me in 1913 in the N. E. corner of the light-well brought out, at a depth of 45 centimetres beneath the surface of the cement floor, and separated by an interval of about 30 cm. from the base of the later wall, the broad foundations 2 of an earlier structural barrier running roughly along the same line. It seems clear that this earlier barrier had openings on the adjoining Peristyle Court. Thus, according to the original disposition of this suite, complete privacy was only attained on the upper story.

From the Queen's Megaron a back passage, known from a large L. M. I Back jar found at its entrance as the Corridor of the Painted Pithos, led to what a n" a seems to have been the Service Quarter. At the point where it makes Service a short turn to the North parts of a painted stucco dado with a spiral frieze were found still attached to the wall like similar remains in the adjoining bath-room. Entrance was thus obtained to a room containing in its South-West corner an oblong plaster dais which may have served as a couch. Room of Within the massive block of masonry that formed the South wall of this Couch. Chamber ran down two shafts connected with the roof drainage, and at the same time served two small latrines on the upper floor. As has already been pointed out the construction of this block, with its massive timber, framing separate piers of masonry, corresponds with that of a large part of the

Domestic Quarter and is clearly of the same M. M. Ilia date. It stands, moreover, in an organic relation with the remarkable latrine illustrated above, 3 and which must also unquestionably be attributed to the same epoch. This is clearly the period of the Palace history in which the sanitary arrangements reached their highest development.

On the Eastern side of the Room of the Plaster Couch was a square 1 The tests made in 1913 brought out full depth for doorways. The foundations I,. M. I sherds beneath this wall. Remains of stopped about 20 cm. short of the E. border of the Dolphin Fresco' were found on either the later wall-line. Below them, at a depth of side of this wall, but not beneath it. 95 cm. from the surface of the later cement

These foundations were broader than the floor of the light-well was early Kalderim later wall (t. i-40 m. as compared with 70 cm) paving with M. M. II pottery above it. and imply that the line of the structures above See p. 228, and Plan and Section, Fig. 172, them was the same thickness as the older and compare Knossos, Report,.1902, p. 65, and walls of the Megaron (e. 1-20 m.), allowing a Fig. 32.

THE PALACE OF MINOS, ETC.

Latrine, c.

slab with an aperture for a sink, and immediately behind this the entrance to the small latrine above referred to. The Room itself like all the chambers of this system lined with fine gypsum dadoes up to the level of the frieze wzmmvttmmm !!;. 243. VIEW IN COURT OF THE DISTAFFS, SHOWING EAST AND SOUTH WINDOWS RESTORED.

Court of the Distaffs'

Alteration Drain.

gave at one time access to a little Court or Light Area called the Court of the Distaffs' from certain signs on its blocks. 1 It had double windows-both on its South and East side; the masonry above these, which was found in a tumbled state owing to the decay of the woodwork, has been restored to its original position. (See Fig. 243.)

According to the original arrangement, as shown in the Plan, Fig. 171 a 1 See Knossos, Report, 1902, p. 64 seqq. and central division were visible in the stone ! The dowel-holes for the two side-posts sills.

above, a tributary duct carried off the surface waters of this Court directly into the main channel of the built drain. Apparently in the latest period of Course of the Palace, perhaps in order to avoid effluvia from the latrine, the whole J e r n sed arrangement was revolutionized and the waters of the little Court were carried off in the opposite direction, through the Hall of the Colonnades.

To effect this alteration the old drain was blocked on this section and a passage forcibly hewn for the new duct through two massive walls. 1

A doorway in the N. E. corner of the Room of the Plaster Couch gave access by a double turn, analogous to that of its S. E. entrance, to two further sections of passage way, by which the full circuit of the corridor system of this Quarter was completed. The first section of these, lit by the East window of the Court of the Distaffs, passed, immediately on the right, the The entrance of a small chamber which amongst all the rooms other than those of basements brought out by the excavation of the Palace site at Knossos was the most secluded. It was window-less from its very position, and except for artificial light must have been quite dark. It formed the centre of the somewhat labyrinthine system of the surrounding corridors, and was jocosely referred to during the excavation as the Lair.

The complete seclusion of this room only dated, however, from this Kurlier Period. Originally there had been a-series of door openings on its S. side, the remains of which were found under the later wall. To this earlier phase, too, belonged a massive kalderim pavement of stone slabs, found underlying the later floor-levels. 2 This room was also called the Treasury Deposit of from the discovery here of part of the Deposit of Ivories' belonging to what seems to have been the treasury of a shrine. But these precious relics seem to have been precipitated from the corresponding chamber above. 3

Beyond the entrance of the Lair the Corridor, by a bend N., gave Service access to another private staircase, affording the Service Quarters direct communication with the rooms above. This seems to have been entirely of woodwork (restored in the Plan), only the stone casing of which is preserved. At the foot of this staircase a doorway, controlled from within, gave access from the last section of the Corridor to the Hall of the Colonnades.

Of the marvellous preservation of the upper story the Room of the Upper Stone Bench, immediately above that of the Plaster Couch, will give a good. K Jf: idea (see Fig. 244 This room derives its name from a stone bench still Stone . Hench.

in situ against its back wall, and it has been possible to maintain in 1 See Vol. II.

1 This lay about 80 cm. below the top of the later door-jambs. See Vol. II.

THE PALACE OF MINOS, ETC.

position not only the gypsum jambs of its doorways and other architectural features, but much of the pavement. In its S. W. corner was another small latrine flushed by the roof-waters which were here conveyed to the main drain below by means of a stone shaft. A small closet seems to have been connected with the shaft immediately E. of this.

Above the Hall of the Double Axes, again, were brought out the remains
Upper Hall of Double Axes.
FIG. 244.   VIEW OF UPPER FLOORS IN S. W. CORNER OF DOMESTIC QUARTER, INCLUDING ROOM OF STONE BENCH. (THE OPENING IN PAVEMENT SHOWS POSITION OF DRAIN SHAFT.) of an Upper Hall of the same form, only slightly sunken beneath its original position. The containing walls with two lateral doorways are here visible, answering to those below, as well as the door-jambs between its first and second sections and parts of the pavement. Two jambs even remained in situ of the Southern line of the second section. In a later Section, dealing with the First Late Minoan Period, reasons will be given for believing that the remains of a fine painted stucco frieze, representing Minoan shields linked by a spiral band, belonged to this Upper Hall of the Double Axes. 1

The private staircase leading up from the Queen's Megaron, lighted: J P pcr on the first landing by a window of which the sides and the dowel-holes System: of the woodwork below were preserved, overlooking its E. light-well, gave access to an Upper Story system on that side similar in its general arrange- a "d bath- ment to that below. The bath-room and the two Western sections of the

Hall seem to have been repeated, but it ended East in this case in a columnar parapet overlooking the light-area. What we may suppose to have been a bedroom with a window looking on the S. light-well and perhaps a little bath-room attached, opened beyond. At the West end of this Southern light-area the double window of another bedroom has been restored in the

Plan, Fig. 240. Immediately West of this on the other side of an upper passage was a dark chamber, entered by a single doorway and answering to that jocosely called the Lair below. It was from this room, as we shall see, that the scattered Deposit of Ivories and other relics evidently belonging to a shrine had been precipitated, and heaps of more or less fragmentary seal Treasury impressions had also fallen from it into the underlying area. It may there- fore best be described as the Treasury of a Shrine. Like the Lair below it forms a kind of nodal point of this whole region.

The gypsum door-jambs and threshold slabs of the adjoining Corridor leading to the Service Stairs' and the Upper Hall of the Colonnades' were mostly preserved, and substantial remains were also found of the pavement of the Middle E.-W. Corridor with its columnar parapet, overlooking the light-well of the Hall of the Colonnades (see Fig. 238).

It is clear that throughout a large part of the area of the Domestic second Quarter there had been also at least a third story. stories of

The main approach to the Domestic Quarter, like that of the Royal Domestic Villa to be described in a later Section, was from above, by means of an entrance from the Central Court, which would have abutted on a landing of the Grand Staircase. The staircase itself must be regarded as the most Grand daring exhibition of Minoan architectural enterprise. Of this magnificent work three flights and part of a fourth were found still in position, while the landing-blocks of the fourth and fifth, fallen below, have been replaced. The Flights of two lower flights of the staircase, backed by the massive double wall that staircase, here encased the face of the clay cutting:, were laid themselves on solid main-

J tamed in 1 Near the base of the N. wall of the Upper remains of a fresco showing the foot of a bull position. Hall of the Double Axes, close to the entrance and belonging to the L. M. II remodelling on that side, were actually found adhering of this section.
T Z

RECONSTRUCTED ELEVATION OF GRPND STAIRCASE.
FLAT HOOP
FLKT ROOK
UPPERMOST LANDING i,. J =s= = BLOCK IN POSITION HERE- 55 EAST-WESfr-
CORROOfl 2 t "iinii r . ilil.:-.–:. f-
CHRISTAN C. TDOLL 20
FEET
SCALE Cf METRES Fir,. 247.

earth. Otherwise the flights rested on horizontal beams supported, tier above tier, by wooden columns, of which the carbonized remains were found, socketed in rising balustrades. That, in spite of the carbonization of the columns, the third flight of stairs and adjoining landings remained in position was, as already pointed out, due to the fallen debris, sun-dried bricks and clay from the upper stories which, under the influence of moisture, had been transformed into a compact mass. The wooden shafts, charred remains of which were found socketed in the balustrades, were replaced by stone columns with a stucco facing. Masked girders were substituted for the architraves above, which had been equally charred, and, under Mr. Doll s skilful direction, the great landing blocks that had sunken or fallen from their pristine levels were at the same time raised to their places.

One special task of considerable risk had to be faced in the course of this Novel ex-work. The middle staircase wall above the first flight was found to have a dangerous list outwards involving a continual risk to the remains of the whole fabric. In this emergency I had recourse to a novel expedient. Under the superintendence of our trusty overseer, Gregorios Antoniou, the wall was first harnessed and secured by planks and ropes, its base was then cut into along its whole length on either side, wedge-shaped stones and cement being held in readiness for insertion in the outer slit, and sixty men on the terrace above were then set to pull the ropes secured to the casing. The mighty mass was thus set in motion, and righted itself against the solid wooden framework prepared as a stop. This was then removed, the outer slit wedged and cemented, and the whole structure re-fixed in its upright position.

By these various means it has been possible to maintain the staircase and balustrade at their original levels, and thus to restore to the modern world the structural aspects of this great work which dates back some 3,600 years.

The restored elevation of the Grand Staircase by Mr. Christian Doll Restored given in Fig. 247, though the great cypress beams play so important a part ()f onuut in it, is not in this respect a matter of conjecture, but is based on their Staircase, carbonized remains as found in situ, often in a well-preserved state, at the moment of excavation. The elevation, indeed, for the greater part of which the evidence has been preserved in the marvellous manner described, may be regarded as unique among ancient buildings. It extends to the uppermost landing block of the fifth flight of stairs which it was possible to replace in its original position above its restored support. Fig. 24(j presents a general view taken from the gallery above the Hall of the Colonnades, while Fig. 248 shows the two lowermost flights, as seen from the N. E. corner of that Hall, the columns of which are here restored. A window here appears in the South

THE PALACE OF MINOS, ETC.

Downward Taper of Columns.

Prototypes in Primitive Stone Pillars.

Minorcan and

Maltese Analogies.

wall of the Hall (Suppl. Pl. VII), which gave light to the private staircase of the Service Quarter. Fig. 245 represents the fourth flight as restored, including three of the original steps, and the landing block of the fifth flight as raised and resupported.

It will be seen that this fifth flight rose above the level of the Central Court. Access from this Court was obtained, as may be inferred from the respective levels, by nine descending steps, necessary to reach the level of the landing of the fourth flight of the Grand Staircase and the uppermost of the East-West Corridors. The steps that thus led down from the East border of the Central Court almost exactly correspond with the entrance, also stepping down, of the Central Sanctuary area on the West of the Court. Immediately to the North of them a broader flight would have led to the portico of a great East Hall. This in turn, seems to have been faced on the opposite side of the Court by a Stepped Porch, of which we have the later representative.

The downward taper of the restored shafts as shown in the restored work answers to the shape of the columns, with inserted double axes, of a M. M. Ill sanctuary building as reproduced in a contemporarywall-painting, 2 and also to those of the little Palace Temple depicted in the Miniature Fresco belonging to the beginning of L. M. I. 3 This feature, as I have elsewhere pointed out, is inherent in the origin of certain primitive stone pillars which gradually widened in their upward course in order to support the capping stones of vaults constructed on the horizontal system. Good examples of this are afforded by the early megalithic structures of the West Mediterranean Basin of which two illustrative specimens are given in my work on Tree and Pillar Cult. One of these is a comparatively rough pillar from a Nau of Minorca. 4 The other, of more advanced shape, is from a cell of Hagiar Kim in Malta, one of a series of monuments belonging to the close of the local Neolithic age, the spiraliform decoration of which, however, both in its character and in its application to friezes and ceilings, presents such remarkable analogies with the Minoan. 5

The same tapering formation of the column is repeated in the case of a small ivory column from the Spata tomb 6 and that of the ivory frieze 1 As there is an element of doubt in the matter, the columns in Mr. Doll's elevation have been shown in each case with equal diameters throughout.

2 See p. 443, Fig. 319, below.

3 See Vol. II.

4 Cartailhac, Monuments primitifs des lies Baleares, PI. 46; Myc. Tree and Pillar Cult, p. 89, Fig. 61.

See above, p. 22 and p. 261.

6 Bulletin de correspondance helltnique, 1878, PL XIII, 8.

from Menicli. 1 On the other hand the columns of the early terra-cotta sanctuary show no taper, and the same holds of certain Late Minoan examples, including, at Knossos, the column in low relief of the Tomb of the Double Tapered Axes. 2 It is also clear that both the column of the Lions' Gate at Mycenae 3 0 f Knos and the half columns of the facade of the Treasury of Atreus must be re- ". moved from the category of those which dwindle gradually towards their base, and H. ot

But the consistent evidence of the contemporary copies in wall-painting, A " s e supported by later survivals in sculpture and intaglio, is surely sufficient to demonstrate that this downward taper was a characteristic feature of shafts in the M. M. Ill Palace. So far as could be judged by the carbonized remains themselves, a column of the Hall of the Double Axes, of which 2-60 metres out of a total length of about 3 metres was preserved, showed a decided taper. 4 Its lower end was 45 cm. in diameter, that of its gypsum base 65 cm., but, judging by Minoan practice, it is extremely probable that the wooden surface was covered by a coloured plaster coating. The vivid hues of the columns and capitals of the shrines of the fresco paintings could hardly have been otherwise achieved.

In the earlier M. M. Ill stage seen in the Spiral Fresco Deposit the Low-tradition survives of comparatively high column bases of variegated materials, Bases" 11 but, by the close of this Period, they are regularly of lower formation and of gypsum or limestone, as in Late Minoan times.   6 An interesting survival Class.   of the earlier practice is even traceable in the stockinged appearance of the columns in the contemporary frescoes, the lower part of the shaft being there marked off in a darker colour. 0 1 Das Kuppelgrab, Pl. VIII, Fig. 10. 4 See Knossos, Report, 1901, p. 114. This

Archafologia, vol. Ixv, p. 37, Fig. 49. was the Northern of the two columns in the See also Vol. II of this work. In the Lustral W. light court. The other was also well pre-

Area of the Little Palace the impressed flutings served. Both showed a slight South-Easterly of the columns present indeed the appearance inclination. It was found impossible to pre- of their dwindling below; and Mr. Fyfe's serve the carbonized shafts of these columns.

original measurements bear this out Mr. Doll's The charred mass published by Dr. Durm, observations, however, have led him to the op. tit., p. 58, Fig. 16, as part of one of these, conclusion that the diameter was the same at is in reality part of a massive beam from the top and bottom. N. E. corner of the Hall of the Colonnades.

Contrary to the received idea, based on Dr. Durm's objection that this very shapeless photographs of the Berlin cast, the column of mass shows no evidence of having belonged to the tympanum of the Lions' Gate has been a tapered column therefore falls to the ground.

shown by Professor Durm to be of the same Neither does he seem to have been aware of diameter throughout (Jahresfufte d. Oester- the analogy supplied by the primitive stone reichischen Arch. lust., p. 53 seqq.). For the pillars of the class referred to.

half column from the Treasury of Atreus' see 5 See below, p. 370.

op. fif., p. 47 seqq. See below, p. 443, Fig. 319.

THE PALACE OF MINOS, ETC.

Cypress
Wood.

The Cypress Grove of Rhea at Knossos.

Evidence of Fluted M inoan Columns.

M. M. Ill Stone Lamp in form of Spiral Column.

The material of the columns, as tested by expert examination of charred specimens, seems in all cases to have been cypress, 1 which also supplied the massive beams and framework. In the Palace of Odysseus, too, the door-posts were of cypress.- It is clear that the Minoan rulers must have had at hand abundant supplies of fine-grown trees of this species to draw upon. In classical times indeed Crete was regarded as its native home 3 and supplied materials for the temples and cult-statues of Mainland Greece. 4 Straggling clumps of cypress-trees are still to be seen in the glen below the Palace site last remaining relics, it may well be, of the ancient cypress grove which in Hellenic days surrounded the ruins of the House of Rhea at Knossos 5, perpetuating thus the sacred tradition of the spot.

The shafts of the columns have been reproduced with a plain surface. But there are strong indications that the originals were, in some cases at least, fluted, though this feature may have come in under Egyptian influence at the beginning of the Late Minoan Age. Instances of convex flutings of the Egyptian kind are afforded by the Lustral Area of the Little Palace; on the other hand concave fluting of the Doric class is exemplified by the little ivory column from Mycenae, 0 and the half columns of the Tomb of Clytemnestra. In the area of the Hall of the Colonnades, on the level of the floor of the Middle East-West Corridor, a little to the S. E. of it, was found part of the carbonized shaft of a small column, 7 which when first uncovered showed signs of fine fluting of this class. As far as I was able to reckon at the time of its discovery, the number of the flutings was twenty-four.

Our knowledge of a highly decorative type of fluted column belonging to the time of the M. M. Ill Restoration is due to the discovery of a columnar lamp of purple gypsum in the contemporary South-East House bordering the Domestic Quarter on that side. This magnificent object, as will be seen from the restored drawing shown in Fig. 249, presents a spirally fluted shaft supporting a capital adapted from that of an Egyptian palm-tree column. 8 The raised leaf-like pattern that winds up it also goes back to an 1 Cypressus Sempervirens.

"Od. xvii. 340.

"Plin. xvi. 141 hidepatria insiila Creta.

See Hehn, Kulturpflanzen, c. 2, p. 244 seqq.

5 Diodoros V. 66 ert KCII vvv Seiviirrai 0 Ata Peas oikcnrex xai KVirapitTiav dacros i. K Traxaiof Xporov d. vtij. fvor.

c Et. Ap X., 1888, Pl. viii. 8; Perrot-Chipiez, Histoire, vi, p. 525, Fig. 204.

7 The diameter of one end, which was fairly intact when found, was 35 cm. It seemed too small for the sockets of the adjoining parapet, which were 58 cm. in diameter, but it may be from an upper story. Unfortunately it was impossible to preserve the charred remains.

"A curious feature of this lamp is the perforation visible in the shaft. It was, perhaps, traversed by a bar from which some indis-

Egyptian source, being in fact a derivative of the sacred uaz or papyrus sceptre motive which in other directions had such a strong influence on Minoan Art, there too with a religious intention. The particular form in which this decoration appears here has, moreover, a very definite chronological association. It recurs in an identical shape on a bronze cup of the Vapheio type found by Mr. Seager in a M. M. 111 interment at Mochlos and illustrated in another connexion as an early example of this class ofvessel. 1 Thischronologi-cal datum is corrobated by the associations of the lamp itself. The history of the S. E. House where it was found apart from a brief and partial occupation by later squatters-lies, as we shall see, within the limits of the M. M. III Period.

Spirally fluted columns, as is clear from gem-types, survived well into the Late Minoan Age.

pensable objects such as trimmers wen-suspended (compare the chain attached to the bron. e lamp from Tomb 35 at Isopata, 7 if o Knossos, p. 39, Fig. 35, Only a fr. ig-nient of the capital was preserved, but enough

Ki;. 249 COLUMNAR LAMP OK PURPLK GYPSUM, trOM S. K. HOUSK. (FROM A DRAWING BY THEODORK FVKK.) to ensure its complete restoration. As is natural in the pedestal of a lamp the diameter of the shaft is even throughout.

1 See Vol. II, and Mofhos, p. 62, Fig. 31, XII.. With it was also found a jainted clay

THE PALACE OF MINOS, ETC.

Late

Minoan

Changes

Domestic

Quarter.

Floors beneath later

M. M. III.

Light-Well Construction.

A clay seal impression, found together with the remains of inscribed clay tablets with the Linear Script B, on the second landing of the Grand Staircase, shows a horned sheep in front of a column the shaft of which presents the indication of a compact spiral fluting, but is in this case surmounted by a double capital of a typical Minoan form. 1

Many internal decorative features in the Domestic Quarter certainly belong to the First Late Minoan Period, while the staircase descending East from the Upper East-West Corridor may be of still later date. A new style of painted stucco decoration, of which there are traces both in that Corridor and the adjoining Upper Hall of the Double Axes, can be shown, indeed, to be the work of the latest Palace epoch (L. M. II). The Queen's Megaron again was, as we have seen, more open to the East, where the existing wall of the light-court is not earlier than L. M. I. Of the wall decoration of this Hall, the Fish Fresco comes probably within the lower limits of the present Period, but on the whole the superficial features both of the Queen's Megaron 2 and bath-room in the state in which they were excavated are best included in the Late Minoan phase of the Palace history. 3

At the same time the characteristic elements of the fabric throughout this Quarter must undoubtedly be claimed for the present Period. The outward features are Late Minoan, but the inner anatomy is M. M. III.

The stratigraphic evidence is at any rate conclusive as to the posteriority of many of the constructions throughout the inner area of the Domestic Quarter to the M. M. II Period. The M. M. II floors whether kalderim or mosaiko lie well below those with which M. M. Ill pottery is associated and often, as is notably the case in the Queen's Megaron, do not stand in relation with the later wall lines. 4 On the other hand we have positive evidence at many points that enables us to connect certain characteristic structures with the present Period.

We are able thus to contrast the clearly compacted masonry of the M. M. Ill light-areas with similar remains of the M. M. II Period, such as cup with a double key-pattern motive somewhat recalling the Maze fresco, p. 357, Fig. 256, below.

1 Compare, too, the spiral columns on a cylinder from Mycenae (Myc. Tree and Pillar Cult, p. 43. Fig. 24).

Both in the Western and Eastern sections of the Queen's Megaron the exploratory excavations made in 1913 showed L. M. I sherds immediately below the gypsum pavement (tests 25, 27, 31, 32, 33, 34).

3 See Vol. II.

4 Thus in the N. W. corner of the W. section of this Megaron the mosaiko' pavement (here 14 cm beneath the L. M. I gypsum slabs) shows on its N. edge an earth border from which some earlier wall had been removed. On the other hand its E. margin fits on to the threshold of the private stairs, evidencing a certain degree of continuity.

the South area of the Queen's Megaron, Fig. 153 above, where the blocks show a distinct clay interval. A fine M. M. Ill example is presented by the light-court of the Hall of the Double Axes, Fig. 2r n.

The wall of this, the closely compacted blocks of which were incised with the Double Axes that have given it its name, is limestone masonry backed by rubble construction. The wooden beam above its fourth course was tied by rounded cross-pieces to another on the Western face of the wall just above the gypsum dado. 1 These beams with their round insets might naturally suggest a decorative mask or frieze of rosettes such as runs through this whole system. In the covered part of the Hall the practice, already known in Early Minoan times, of dividing the stonework of the interior walls into sections by the interposition of upright posts tied together by horizontal and transverse beams emerges once more into Timber prominence. This method offered advantages in dealing with the blocks W0 rkof derived from the ruins of earlier structures, as also in systematizing door and window frames and it came now generally into vogue in the interior of M. M. Palace walls. The lower part of the walls was at the same time masked by Fabric. a gypsum dado.

An excavation made into the base blocks of the interior of this light-well wall at its S. W. corner showed that the latest sherds it contained were M M. II b. It had therefore been built at a time when the remains of that Period were already stratified. But the organic connexion of the core of this structure, including its horizontal beam, with the Lower East- West Corridor enables us, as will be seen, to be still more definite. The characteristic panelled masonry of the adjoining South wall of this Hall moreover confirms the result of these comparisons.

Fig. 251 gives a view of a part of the South wall of the same s. Wall of Hall showing its construction as visible above the irregular edge of Double the gypsum dado, the upper part of which was here broken away. The Axes-intervals left by the upright and horizontal timbering are clearly marked, and when first opened out were largely filled with carbonized material. Attached to the masonry are seen in places patches of coarse plastering that had supplied a backing for the finer painted stucco, which seems to have formed its original decoration before it was covered with a gypsum dado. Above this runs a horizontal beam, the charred remains of which were partially preserved.

1 The tubular casings left by the decay of Report, 1901, p. 213) that the cross-pieces these in the interior of the wall showed the projected into the light-well so as to support daylight through in places. The idea(Amvflv, a gallery is unwarranted.

An interesting pendant to this is supplied by Ii-.!!. showing a part N. v.-ji of the inner Northern wall of the East-West Corridor. The lower wall E WC construction here is of the earlier Middle Minoan style, consisting of large Corridor.

1 i.;. 2i. IARI i S. WALL OK HALL OK DOUBI. K AXES MIOWIM; TIMBER FRAMEWORK. BROKEN EDGE OK GYPSUM WAINSCOTING BELOW.

rough blocks on a setting of clay and stones. Above this, in places over an intervening layer of smaller blocks, has been laid, apparently at the time when the earlier Palace structure was in ruins, a huge horizontal beam, 1 found in 1 The object of this supplementary layer of height of the wall below the horizontal timbering small blocks of masonry above the massive to the height of the gypsum dado (about earlier work is clear. It was to adjust the two metres, according to the M. M. Ill and

THE PALACE OF MINOS, ETC.

Timber a crushed and carbonized condition, which formed the starting-point for workof wa construction of the M. M. Ill type, consisting of upright and horizontal Walls. timbering, framing separate piers of stone-work. The horizontal line of

WALL OF LOWER E.-W. CORRIDOR SHOWING TIMBER FRAMEWORK AND INTERVENING PIERS, SUPERIMPOSED ON EARLIER MASONRY.

timbering here seen coincides with the lintel of the neighbouring doorway of the Corridor and is continued at the same level in the neighbouring Halls.

But the great importance of this later wall-construction lies in the fact that while on the one hand it is thus dovetailed as it were into the fabric of

L. M. I system), which ran immediately under the edge of the beam. This stratified wall construction, M. M. II below and M. M. Ill above, can be traced North from the East opening of the Lower East-West Corridor to the Western border of the Court of the Stone Spout. It here forms the Eastern wall-line of the Loom-Weight Basements. See above, p. 248 seqq.

the neighbouring part of the Domestic Quarter, on the other hand it is seen Chrono- to be part and parcel of the original M. M. III system that overlies the Loom- Evidence Weight Basement. The South wall of the Lower E.-W. Corridor and its s b u y PP ed Northern branch running towards the Court of the Stone Spout, which illus- spiral trates in a slightly varied way the same structural succession, form in fact two Area. of the outer walls of the enclave which contains the area of the Spiral Fresco belonging, as will be shown, to the earlier M. M. Ill phase. The M. M. Ill substructures of the inner part of that area repeat in fact the same story. They are in most cases actually superposed, at about the same level, on the Early stumps of the M. M. II walls. 1 In one case they immediately rest on the v a v) 1 ls"

deposit containing characteristic M. M. II fabrics. From these archaeological super- i-ii- i j posed on equations we can only draw one logical conclusion as to the connected M. M. n.

walling in the Hall of the Double Axes, and as to the Domestic Quarter generally. It too must have owed its original construction to the building activity of the earlier M. M. Ill phase.

But this inevitable architectural conclusion, that much of the inner core of the fabric of the Domestic Quarter goes back to the mature epoch of the earlier M. M. Ill phase (a), has to be reconciled with another aspect of the case. The external features of this

Quarter, as far as they have been pre- M. M. served to us, demonstrably belong to a later stage of Minoan architecture. features Certain items of this are due no doubt to Late Minoan changes, but in the f main the outer lines of this part of the building are undoubtedly the work of Quarter, the close of the present Period. In place of stucco floors 2 and painted dadoes such as were in vogue in the days to which the Spiral Fresco belongs we see gypsum pavements and dadoes generally in use. Instead of the comparatively high column bases of variegated stones such as those found in the area of the Spiral Fresco, which perpetuate the M. M. II tradition, and of which we have abundant evidence in the contemporary later Palace at Phaestos, we find everywhere the low column bases that continued to be in use in the Late Minoan Age. As a matter of fact the gypsum pavement Affinities of the Corridor of the Bays on which, as in the adjoining Magazine, M. M. III b Minoan pottery was found, was continuous, under the blocking of L. M. I date, with Style-that of the second landing of the Grand Staircase. The latest sherds under intact portions of the pavement of the Hall of the Double Axes were still 1 See Section, Fig. 187, b, and compare the the M. M. Ill b store-jars rested was of stucco. Plan, Fig. 187, a, p. 250, above. It was on this that remains of a smaller spiral 2 In the floor section of the Magazine of the fresco were found, contemporary in style with Medallion Pithoi (p. 320, Fig. 233, above) the the other. See p. 374, below.

floor underlying the gypsum slabbing on which -3D-

THE PALACE OF MINOS, ETC.

M. M. III. So, too, in the N. E. Hall and its dependencies, submerged at the end of the Middle Minoan Age, and on the floors of which M. M. 111 vessels were found in situ, the system of low limestone column bases and gypsum dadoes was already adopted. If, therefore, a good deal of the structural core of the Domestic Quarter must be referred to the earlier phase of M. M. Ill, we must at the same time recognize that there was a

FIG. 253 a. WINDOW N. OF V. LIGHT-AREA OF HAI. L OF DOUBLE AXES, AS FOUNH.

wholesale re-modelling towards the close of this Period. Its outward architectural features in fact better range themselves with the Late Minoan style.

Windows The evidences of the massive framework illustrated above were no-

Domestic where more conspicuous than in the case of the window openings. l

he Quarter. g reat beams and posts of these were boldly designed to support tons of superincumbent masonry, and the carbonization of the wooden material had resulted in a serious fall of the overlying blocks, which gave occasion for much difficult work of reconstitution. In Fig. 253 a is seen the window of the Lower East-West Corridor, looking on the W. Light-Area of the Hall of the

Double Axes, as it was uncovered, only a small space of the original opening being in this case maintained by the falling in of rubble stones. Fig. 253

FIG. 253 b. WINDOW NORTH OF W. LIGHT-AREA OF HALL, AS RE-STORED, WITH THE MASONRY ABOVE RAISED TO ITS ORIGINAL POSI-TION.

on the other hand shows the framework replaced by masked girders and the overlying blocks weighing at least 6 tons and one of the full length of three metres restored to their former level. Coping slabs of stone have here i A a

THE PALACE OF MINOS, ETC.

been placed above the lower sections of the window openings in accordance with a usual Minoan practice: in all cases the coping slabs of balustrades and

FIG. 254. LOWER E.-VV. CORRIDOR LOOKING TOWARDS HALI, OF COLONNADES AND FOOT OK GRAND STAIRCASE. (IMMEDIATELY TO LEFT OF THE FIGURE is VISIBLE PART OF THE ENTRANCE TO THE HALL OF THE DOUBLE AXES AND BEYOND is THE WINDOW OPENING ON ITS W. LIGHT-WELL.

REMAINS OF THE GYPSUM DADO SLABS ARE SEEN ON EITHER SIDE BELOW.) the piers of columns are laid on horizontal beams separating them from the masonry below. Above this window there had been at least two others opening on the successive stages of the upper Corridors. In the Court of windows L T-L- rr. i i L e j. and their the Distaffs the same phenomena recurred in the case of windows opening, in both the E. and S. walls, the first on a Corridor, the second on the s adjoining Room of the Plaster Couch. These again would have been repeated on the successive upper floors.

A similar falling in of the overlying masonry had taken place in the case of the window in the South wall of the Hall of the Colonnades that lighted the lower flight and landing of the Service Staircase on that side. In the case of this window, a view of which is given in Suppl. PI. VII, it was not possible to restore the full original thickness of the cross-beams. A similar window opening on the North side of the E. Light-Area of the Queen's Megaron lighted the private staircase connected with that hall. In all these cases we have to imagine further windows above those preserved, answering to the upper flights of their staircases, now no longer existent.

Where the woodwork had disappeared or been disintegrated the dowel-holes were visible in the masonry below by which it had been attached. From the position of these it appears that there had been always a central dividing shaft. The evidence of the house tablets' described above l indicates that already in the preceding epoch the windows often had cross-bars or transoms dividing them into four or even six openings, and the vermilion colouring of these suggests that they may have been fitted with the equivalent of later panes in the shape of brilliantly stained parchment.

The Lower East-West Corridor, Fig. 254, originally continued East Lower beyond the point where it was blocked in a late Palace epoch. In this direction it seems to have stepped down to another important passage-way on the terrace below, leading to a bastion and postern that clearly existed at Ap-the S. E. angle of the Palace, 2 affording thus the nearest access to the Kaeratos stream below. At this point it would appear to have been joined, sumed probably from the earliest times, by a step-way descending the slope imme- Gate at diately South of the Great Cutting. 3 Of the Water-gate itself some indications may be traced near the outlet of the united drainage-system of the East Slope.

The course of this lower passage-way, which seemed to have almost exactly answered in width to the E.-W. Corridor, can be traced within the second enceinte wall on this side, and here at a point a little East of the Hall 1 See p. 303. dependencies in the glen immediately below.

1 It is known that much masonry was This stepway in its L. M. I shape ascended removed from this angle of the building for directly to the Central Court, above the the construction of the Bey's house and its M. M. Ill Magazines of the Lily Vases.

THE PALACE OF MINOS, ETC.

Dis- of the Double Axes were found, fallen backwards from its inner wall, considerable remains of painted stucco decoration. The exceptionally fine technique and the somewhat sober style of colouring of these remains lead to the conclusion that they were executed about the close of the present Period. The painted fragments were in two groups, lying respectively N. and S. of each other, one belonging to a dado and the other evidently derived from the upper part of the same wall. They lay near the surface and above the earlier Palace wall-foundations.

and Labyrinth Fresco.

Painted Dado

FIG. 255. PAINTED STUCCO DADO WITH IMITATION MARBLING.

The dado (Fig. 255) 1 was divided by fine dark strips into panels imitating reproducing, though in more varied hues, the veins of fine gypsum or Gypsum. a a baster slabs. The veins were executed in reddish brown on a light yellow ground with bands of darker yellow and orange and some black lines. Beneath the slabs was a horizontal plinth imitating the grain of woodwork, a decorative feature already noted on Early Minoan pottery. 2 The Marbled Fresco' itself is of special importance as one of the earliest instances of the substitution of painted stucco decoration for variegated stonework;!, which became so usual in the Second Late Minoan Period. The The remains of the other fresco, which doubtless filled the wall space

Fresco nth above the dado, are of great interest as delineating a labyrinth pattern 1 See Fyfe, Painted Plaster,-f., p. 112, variegated stone-work are seen in the fresco Fig. 13. 2 See above, p. 59. depicting the M. M. Ill Pillar Shrine (p. 445 3 Good contemporary representations of and Fig. 321, below).

(Fig. 256). It represents in fact a series of mazes executed in the same dark reddish brown colour as appears in the veining of the dado, on Egyptian a yellowish ground. We see here a more elaborate development of the types of key and meander patterns that have been noted above on ivory and other J

FIG. 256. THE LABYRINTH FRESCO.

seals of the Third Early Minoan Period,- and which have been there brought into connexion with similar motives on Egyptian schist seals and plaques of the VIth Dynasty and immediately ensuing period. In a tomb 1 Seelooa'tiossos, Report, 1902, pp. 103,104, indication that we have not here to do with and Fig. 62. The fact that the remains of this ceiling decoration, fresco were found face upwards is a clear See above, p. 121, Fig. 90.

THE PALACE OF MINOS, ETC.

Ideographic elements in Meander patterns.

Egyptian Palace Sign.

of early XIIth Dynasty date two ceilings occur with such patterns, 1 affording thus a still nearer comparison with the Knossian wall-painting.

Meander patterns, sometimes very elaborate, are a natural outgrowth of textile decoration, and are widely diffused through both hemispheres. But they often incorporate ideographic elements. Thus the simple key pattern, as the angularization of a wave, was a water sign in Ancient Peru and Mexico, 2 giving a special significance to the frequent appearance of the meander on vases. The Greek fret at times repeats the same story. The Chinese meander 3 goes back to a coiled type, recalling the whirlwind sign of some North-American Indian tribes, and bears the name of Yiin-lei-wen or thunder-cloud pattern. 4 A recurring component element, moreover, in such meander patterns is the fylfot or Svastika which itself represents a kind of resting-point in ornamental development, reached by more than one turn. It occurs as a Minoan sacred symbol, 5 probably astral or solar.

It is not surprising then, in view of these analogies, to find that certain ideographic Egyptian signs which illustrate the key pattern in its simplest form have a precise signification as the plan of a Palace. One of these, Fig. 257, a, is of special interest in the present connexion since it represents a plan of a Palace courtyard with a two-storied tower-like building standing in its inmost angle. This building with battlements above, and the diagonal line probably representing a ladder, 0 also stands by itself as the Palace sign (aha, and is one of the Egyptian hieroglyphs that can be said to have been taken over into the Minoan signary. 7 the upper part is concerned it is reproduced almost totidcin with ladder and battlements, in the Minoan sign here

The Egyptian hieroglyph appears in a more compendious form as a simple key pattern (Fig. 257, b). This pattern itself may in turn be regarded as the nucleus of the somewhat more developed meander type, 257, c, which also appears on Cretan seals. 8 It does not seem an extravagant supposition that, just as the tower of the old Egyptian Palace sign was adopted as a Minoan hieroglyph, so the simplified figure of the whole building 1 Wilkinson, Ancient Egyptians, Pl. VIII, with the Knossian wall-painting.

Fr. Hirth, Maunder und Triqiietruin in der chinesischen und japanischen Ornamentik (Z. f. Ethnologic, Berlin, 1889, p. 489 seqq.).

5 See below, p. 515, and Fig. 372.

6 F. Ll. Griffith, Hieroglyphics, p. 36. In its certainly So far as line i s, 4, 20. (From Tomb of Hepsefa: temp. Senusert I.) 3 R. P. Grey, The Fret or Key Ornamentation in Mexico and Peru (Archaeologia, xlvii, 1882, p. 157 seqq.).

3 A specimen of a meander pattern in Old Chinese cloisonne enamel, there arranged diagonally (A. R. Hein, Maander, c., Vienna, 1891, p. 10, Fig. 3), shows a close parallelism fuller form it signifies the King's Palace (aha).

7 Scripta Minoa, I, p. 197, no. 41.

8 e. g. the Zakro seal-impression No. 133 (Hogarth,. H. S., xxii, Pl. X).

l-u. 259. MAN in i i. ON EARLY DYNASTIC Ikis. M SKAI. OF HLAI K STEATITE, FROM KAKNAK.

FIG. 258. a, b, f, MAZES AND MEANDERS ON EGYPTIAN SCHIST SEALS. SOME WITH HUMAN FIGURES; V! TH AND SUCCEEDING DYNASTIES.

FIG. 260. LABYRINTH AND MINOTAUR ON CRETAN SEALS AND COINS: a, 6, E. M. Ill SEALS, H. TRIAHA;-, SEALING, XAKRO; J, e, LENTOIDS, KNOS-SOS; i, i, g, COINS OF KNOSSOS.

should have been taken over to represent the Cretan Palace-Sanctuary, in other words, the Labyrinth. On the Egyptian seals that supplied the proto- Maze pat-types of a Cretan sphragistic series human figures repeatedly occur beside latyrin or in the middle of maze patterns that must be regarded as labyrinthine,", of plans of dwellings (Fig. 258 6, c). dwellings.

The labyrinth of Classical monuments is consistently rendered as a building, often indicated on Attic vases by a pillar with meander decoration. 1 In the daughter City of the Cretan Miletos the marble ceiling of an inner staircase in the Didymaeon is decorated with a huge meander and the staircase is described in an inscription as AABYPINOOC. 2

The comparative examples given in Fig. 260 3 suggest that the coin- Labyrinth types of Knossos, that kept alive the record both of the Labyrinth and of M the Minotaur, may have been largely based on the earlier seal-types, which on, c j;! in seem to have been specially rife in this Cretan district. The quadruple Seal-types meander that forms the essential nucleus of the seal b is closely akin to j OS r f I, where the central star reproduces a feature of the labyrinthine Egyptian ceilings cited above. The Minotaur on the reverse of the coin (a), being wholly human except for his bull's head, differs from the ordinary Late Minoan type d, c, but the Zakro seal-impression c shows human arms. It will be shown below that the Man-bull was himself only one of a series of composite monsters current in Minoan art, but the type (which may ultimately connect itself with Ea-bani) is of more primitive origin. 4 A rude proto-dynastic example from the Karnak prism is given in Fig. 259.

The appearance of the maze pattern on an entrance passage of the Minoan Palace is certainly a highly suggestive circumstance. That some of the painted stucco decoration clung to the walls of the building in comparatively exposed areas long after even its latest occupation by Minoan denizens is clear from the circumstances attending the discovery of the bull-grappling reliefs by the Northern Entrance. It is then quite within the bounds of reasonable possibility that the Labyrinth in Art, as seen on the walls of this Corridor of the Eastern Palace border, may have met the eyes and excited the wonder of Early Greek settlers.

1 See P. Wolters, Darstellungen des Laby- The lower part of Fig. 260 a is here completed.

rinthes (Sitzungsberichte d. Bayer. Akad., 1908, The lentoid gems Fig. 260, d, e, and the two 191 3). coins are in my own collection. (For the coins 3 Haussoullier, Rev. Philologique, 1905, cf. Svoronos, Num. de la Crete ancienne, p. 265, and Didyme. p. 93, c.; Wiegand, Abh. Pl. IV, 25, Pl. VI, 6.) A small gold plate with d. Berliner Akad., 1911, p. 49, and cf. 1908, a repousse maze pattern (contemporary with p. 35. See, too, Bosanquet, Recent Excavations the Knossian fresco) was found in the H.

in Miletus (Dublin Lecture). Triada Palace (unpublished).

3 For the Egyptian seals cf. p. 122 above. See above, p. 69.

EAST HALL

Northern Branch of Lower E.-W. Corridor; Columnar Lobby and Upper Story block; N. E. Room Sttbmergence of M. M. II Magazines of Great Knobbed Pit hoi; Court of Stone Spoilt and M. M. Ill Wall; Earlier gypsum fa fade line of a N. E. Insula, running E.-W.; Presumed Stepivay to E. Postern; Corridor Nortli blocked in M. AI. b and converted to Magazine; So-called School Room; Enclave including Loom-Weight Basement; Its later M. M. Ill stratification; M. M. Ill Walls superposed here on M. M. II; Important Deposit with Spiral Fresco, Column bases, and painted stucco bas-reliefs of bull-grappling scenes; Comparison of fresco bands ivith decoration of tank in biill-catching scene on gem; Remains derived from M. M. Ill East Hall above; Drainage system of its Court Vertical ducts, stone drain-heads, and Conduit; Stone spout and blind well choked with M. M. Ill sherds; Substructures shoiving Plan of great East Hall.

N. Branch FROM the point where the Eastern course of the E.-W. Corridor was f E-."- eventually cut short there started a Northern branch following the Eastern wall-line of the Loom-Weight area which must have originally brought the Domestic Quarter into connexion with a stepway leading directly down to the Eastern Bastion and Postern.

Columnar This Northern section of the Corridor passes first through a kind of lobby, stride known from its characteristic M. M. Ill framework, here very visible, as the and Room of the Wooden Posts. It had a good gypsum paving, thickly covered

Story with a deposit of lime, perhaps due to a work of restoring the stucco wall coating, which may have been on foot at the time of the final catastrophe. From this room light was secured for the passage-way by means of an open balustrade (Fig. 261). About 2 metres above the S. end of this balustrade was a worn gypsum block, which from the beginning of the excavation Land- had been noted as a landmark on the Eastern slope of the hill. It was found Hill-side. to re st on flat slabs, and these again on wooden beams, of which carbonized remains came to light. These were temporarily replaced, and, by means of the construction of a stone pillar below, the upper block was maintained exactly at the level which it had occupied on the hillside. This is shown in the photograph reproduced in Fig. 261, which has therefore a certain historic interest, though the analogies supplied by subsequent researches in the Domestic Quarter and elsewhere indicate that the base block at this end of the balustrade had in fact supported a wooden column. Owing to the disappearance of this, the sinking of the upper block has been considerable,

FIG. 261. BALUSTRADE, WITH SURFACE BLOCK ABOVE, IN POSITION AS FOUND; SEEN FROM ROOM OF WOODEN POSTS. DOORWAY TO LOWER E.-W. CORRIDOR VISIBLE TO LEFT. THE TOPMOST LANDING-BLOCK OF THE GRAND STAIRCASE is SEEN IN THE BACKGROUND.

and its original level, at present 3-10 metres above the pavement below, must have been just a metre higher on the same level, that is, as the floor of the first story of the Domestic Quarter.

The balustrade itself showed the usual gap for a woodwork framing, here restored, beneath its gypsum coping slabs. On the North side of

THE PALACE OF MINOS, ETC

N. E. Room.

Submergence of M. M. II Magazines.

its opening, in a line with the cross-wall, was a stone-work pier. The section of the Corridor beyond this (blocked and converted into a Magazine before the close of this Period M. M. Ill b) led to a fine oblong chamber the North-Eastroom-opening by acentral doorway on the little Court named from the Stone Spout projecting from its Western wall. Both the North-East chamber and the Court itself represented an entire remodelling in M. M. Ill a of an area occupied in the M. M. II Period by an extensive group of Magazines containing the huge Knobbed Pithoi described above. 1 A smaller

RUBBLE FILLING
N. E. Room.
MMM PL-ASTED FLOOR
FIG. 262. FRONT VIEW OF N. WALL OF N. E. ROOM SHOWING ALTERED DOOR OPENING AND UNDERLYING M. M. II FLOOR.

store jar of contemporary fabric was in fact found on an earlier floor, 90 centimetres below the later floor of the North-East Room, and the base of one of the great M. M. II pithoi came to light in situ, partly beneath the foundations of its North wall (Fig. 262). 2

This North-East Room was evidently a feature of some architectural importance in the early part of the present Period. Its North wall, formed of exceptionally fine, closely compacted limestone blocks, was symmetrically divided by a doorway, opening on the little Court beyond, on either side of which was, probably, a window. In the later part of this Period, when the Chamber itself was subdivided, the door opening was narrowed, being partly blocked by the partition wall, and the old threshold seems to have been raised and shortened (see Elevation, Fig. 262). This N. wall itself, as will be here seen, was laid on a rubble filling overlying a M. M. II 1 See p. 231 seqq. and Fig. 175.

- Excavations of 1913.

plaster floor, and, as above noted, was partially superposed on the base of one of the early Knobbed Pithoi.

The spout in the West wall of the little Court (see Fig. 2(ii3) was, as Court will be shown below, 1 the outlet of a contemporary drainage system connected spout." with what seems to have been a great Palace hall on the terrace above.

Kic. 263. COURT OF THE STONE SPOUT, SHOWING LOWER BLOCKS OF NORTH WALL OF NORTH-EAST ROOM AND OPENING OF CORRIDOR BEYOND. (THE STEPS ARE MODERN, BUT ON THE LINE OF THE OLD STEPWAV.)

The water from this, as will be seen from the Plan, Fig. 26H, p. 367 below, found its way by a small conduit to a circular blind-well in the Court itself, which was found choked with pottery belonging to both the earlier and the concluding phase of the M. M. Ill Period.

1 See p. 378 seqq.
THE PALACE OF MINOS, ETC.
M. M. Ill W. Wall of Light Court.

This connexion enables us to assign the well-built section of limestone walling from which the stone spout protrudes (Fig. 263) to the M. M. Ill a epoch. Both the compact structure of the masonry itself and the character of the incised signs seen upon the blocks of the latter are identical, moreover, with the work on the W. light-area of the Hall of the Double Axes, belonging, as already noted, to the earlier M. M. Ill phase. The blocks here show

FIG. 264.   GYPSUM ORTHOSTAT AND PLINTH OF EARLY INTERIOR FA9ADE LINE OF N. E.,! NSULA OF PALACE. (SEE PLAN, FIG. 266, TO RIGHT.) the trident sign, sometimes two on the same stone, and it is noteworthy that the same sign predominates on the North Bastion of the North Entrance Passage, which, like the other two Bastions, displays a great similarity in construction. Like the light-area of the Hall of the Double Axes, all these structures can be shown to belong to the earlier part of the M. M. Ill Period.

The N. end of this M. M. Ill light-court wall abutted on what seems Frontage, to have been the original facade line of a distinct Palace insula (see Plan, way dep 1 152 above), running Eastward down the slope. A partof the gypsum stone scending plinth of this, triangularly cut, supporting a fine orthostat of the same material, Postern, is still visible on the N. border of this little Court (Fig. 264). The plinth shows a rectangular cutting a little E. of the gypsum block, and here was certainly an opening in the frontage line which gave access to a gangway between it and a parallel inner line of walling. In this we may with great probability recognize a somewhat narrow stepway, running down to a postern gate and bastion on the East side. It has been since restored for the convenience of the site. 1

The greater part of the remaining structures of this Enst Bastion and the steps that descend from it are, as will be shown in a succeeding Section, of L. M. I date, but it is clear that there must have been some stepped approach on this side from the earliest days of the Palace, ascending the successive lower terraces of the East slope. It seems probable that this stairway, in some form or other, was the final goal of the E. line of Corridor that led from the Domestic Quarter to the Court of the Stone Spout.

It is evident that a good deal of the quarter of the building traversed Quarter by this Corridor came considerably down in the world about the close of t d o e the present Period. The North Section of the passage-way itself was, as bier uses already noted, blocked at this time and converted into a Magazine, which M. MAIL was found to contain ordinary jugs, tripod cooking-pots, ladles, and other vessels characteristic of M. M. Ill 6. 3 A group of these is given in Fig. 279 at the end of this Section. The once stately North-East Room beyond was divided into two compartments by a rubble wall. 4 In the Eastern of these a group of similar plain pots was found on a stone ledge S. of the doorway.

The Western compartment of the old chamber exhibited a curious disposition. Against its back wall was a stone bench with a rounded plaster-covered pillar at its W. end, the upper surface of which was hollowed out like a bowl (see Fig. 265). At the E. end of the stone ledge, moreover, was a lower, stucco-covered pillar with a similar cavity. Against the W. wall of this little room was a large raised block. Both on this and the opposite side, as well as against the outer wall, stone ledges were arranged in a double gradation, 8 those on the sides sloping inwards towards the S. wall so that the whole presented the appearance of a class room (see Plan, Fig. 2(5(5). Owing to this it received the name of School Room at the School 1 See Fig. 263 to right for some of the built, and one end of the original threshold restored steps on this line. slab broken off, in keeping with the nanower

See Vol. II. door. (See the Elevation, Fig. 262).

3 See below, p. 369, Fig. 266. Only the lower gradation was preserved 4 The door-way into the Court of the Stone on the W. side, but it seems probable that Spout was narrowed at the time that the party there had been an upper ledge here too, as in wall between the two later compartments was the case of the opposite wall.

THE PALACE OF MINOS, ETC.

Probably Workmen's Quarters.

Room of

Stone

Pier.

time of the Excavation. 1 The suggestion was even put forward that the cavities might havebeen used to prepare the clay for tablets and that instruction had actually been given in the Art of Writing which in that case would have been the Linear Script A.

But the room had been wholly cleared out at the time that it went out of use. However its disposition is to be explained, it seems to be most probable that this, with the adjoining area, was devoted to workmen's uses at the end of M. M. Ill perhaps during a transitional period when it had been already decided to fill in its rooms and passage-way as a platform for new upper structures. These upper structures, executed early in the Late Minoan Age, included the chamber to which the Taurea-dor Frescoes belonged and the neighbouring Lapidary's Workshop. It was doubtless with a view to give extra support to these upper rooms that, apparently about the close of this Period, a square stone pier was built up against the inner face of the early wall that limited this area on the East (see Plan, Fig. 266). This chamber is hence known as the Room of the Stone Pier.

The little chamber and adjoining closet at the back of the Room of the Stone Pier were carved out of it at the close of this Period, as is shown by the M. M. 111 adeposits beneath the party wall. 2 Thus the whole rectangular section 1 See Knossos, Report, 1901, p. 96 seqq. follows: (i) patchwork gypsum paving (in- ! These M. M. IIa deposits in turn over- eluding step of an old stair); (z) M. M. b

FIG. 265. STONE BENCH AND RAISED STUCCO-COVERED PILLAR WITH BOWL-LIKE CAVITY IN SCHOOL ROOM.

lay a M. M. II flooring of rough blocks (kalderim) 40 cm. beneath the base of the wall. Along the E. face of this wall (in the Room of the Stone Pier) the section was as deposit with shallow cups, showing spiraliform grooves internally but otherwise approaching L. M. I; (3) at 70 cm. down a floor of white beaten earth; (4) M. M. Ill a deposit: higher of the building, of which the Plan is given in Fig. 26(5, consisted, according to its original and finer plan, of the Corridor itself and three rooms which were afterwards divided up. It further appears that throughout the Central and Northern part of this area kalclerim paving of the M. M. I-II class underlay

ROOM OF STONE PIER

W7M7,

FIG. 266. PLAN OK N. E. BORDER SECTION SHOWING M. M. 1116 PARTI-TIONING.

the later floors at a depth varying from c. 70 cm. to 1-17111. There is every reason, moreover, to suppose that the massive limestone plinth that borders this area to the East and of which many of the base blocks are still in position is of early Palace date. One of them bears a large incised sign of the earlier class.

The branch of the lower E.-W. Corridor described above, that, Enclave turning North, brought the Domestic Quarter into connexion with the Court of the Stone Spout, follows on its Western border a rectangular turn of the cups, with similar spiral coil, due to rapid wheel, parts of dark-faced pots with white spots (see below, p. 414 and note i)and broad plain merit pans; (5) at 1-17 metre below the gypsum slabbing, a M. M. II kalderim floor of large blocks (Excavations of 1913).

THE PALACE OF MINOS, ETC.

same massive wall that flanked the former Corridor on its inner side. The Northern continuation of this wall repeats the structural succession already observed in the case of the section bordering the E.-W. Corridor its lower

FIG. 267. WEST WALL OF SCHOOL ROOM, BORDERING THE LOOM-WEIGHT AREA; THE LOWER COURSES HERE ARE M. M. II AND ABOVE THESE ARE SEEN THE SOCKETS FOR THE POSTS OF THE M. M. Ill STRUC-TURE: A GYPSUM DOOR-JAMB FROM ABOVE HAS FALLEN TO ONE.

M. M. II p ar t being of M. M. I I masonry, while, at the same level as in the other Elements section, about 2 metres, that is, above the floor level this construction dorwaii changes and we recognize the typical M. M. Ill feature of piers of stonework separated by upright wooden beams (Fig. 27).

There is, however, one noticeable difference, as will be seen from a comparison of Fig. 2(57 with Fig. 252 above. The upright posts in this case, of which the charred remains were visible at the time of excavation, did not rise from a horizontal beam, but rested directly on the topmost course of the earlier masonry. 1 The sockets which held the feet of these posts are clearly visible in Fig. 2(57: a gypsum door-jamb had fallen into the second socket from the right.

It has already been pointed out that these massive wall-lines on the Structural inner side of the Lower E.-W. Corridor and its Northern branch shut s. ucces-.

sion as in in an independent enclave of the building containing the Loom-Weight Loom-Basements', the contents of which have been shown to be of such primary Area. " importance in the history of all this Palace region. The structural succession, M. M. II below and M. M. Ill above, of these Corridor walls corresponds, as we have seen, with that of the Loom-Weight Basements and with the later system superimposed on them. It was also interesting to observe that in the Magazine formed by the blocked section of the Corridor, as also in the adjoining strip of the School Room, a M. M. II floor-level was struck at a depth roughly corresponding with that of the Loom-Weight Basement on the West side of the intervening wall. 2

On the floor of this Magazine, as already noted, M. M. III5 vessels occurred in situ (see Fig. 279 at end of Section) corresponding with the pots of a late floor-level found above the Spiral Fresco deposit in the adjoining area. Beneath this later floor there came to light here too a M. M. 111 a stratum.

If we now turn to the adjoining area West, primarily named from the Stratifica-Loom-Weights, and the lower deposits of which, containing the miniature Area of Terra-cotta Shrine and offertory vases, were so richly illustrative of the j" ts mature M. M. II phase, we shall see that its upper elements were equally andspiral important for the present Period.

The Plan and Section of the M. M. Ill walls and floor-levels, superposed on the earlier structures and remains, has been already given in Figs. 187 a, b, p. 250 above. The stratification there seen, especially in the case of the Area of the Spiral Fresco, overlying the more Northerly of the 1 In some cases, however, they may have This floor-level corresponds with that of been superposed in the sockets on the ends of a kalderim pavement brought to light on cross-beams. the E. borders of the School Room, and ; The depth at which this M. M. II floor was which underlay the fine S. wall of the Court now struck was here about 90 cm. below that of the Stone Spout. On this floor were on which lay the M. M. 1116 pots. On this found the remains of knobbed and corded earlier floor was found a small M. M. II pithos pithoi and polychrome pottery of the later with a triple line of handles and rope work. M. M. II class.

THE PALACE OF MINOS, ETC.

Polychrome feet for wooden shafts.

basement compartments, is of unique value in the light it throws on the evolution of the M. M. Ill culture.

The Spiral Fresco itself, the painted stucco reliefs and the column bases which found their way into this basement, evidently belonged to a chamber of exceptional size and importance, in which, as shown below, we must recognize a great East Hall of the Palace, afterwards, it would appear, to be restored in a Late Minoan guise. These remains were found irregularly disposed in a layer about 70 cm. thick, beginning about a metre below a later clay and plaster floor, on which rested plain tripod-pots of the usual M. M. Ill b type.

FIG. 268. BRECCIA COLUMN BASES, OF HIGH, EARLY FORM, FOUND IN AREA

OF SPIRAL FRESCO.

The lower deposit was thus clearly denned as belonging to an earlier M. M. Ill stage. It seems to have been thrown into the place in which it lay at the time when the clay floor above was made. 1 It has been already noted- that two column bases came to light in this deposit cut out of a black breccia with bright orange-red veins shot with crystalline white and identical with that still obtained from the quarries of the neighbouring Kakon Oros (Fig. 268).

Both the high form of these bases and their polychrome material are characteristic of the Earlier Middle Minoan architectural style and it is possible that these, together with another found in position in the East Portico near by, may have been taken over from the earlier building. 3 The small column bases of variegated stone beside the light-area of the South- 1 Fragments belonging to this deposit were " The base to the left in Fig. 268 seems to also found on the neighbouring pavement W. have had part of one side pared off to fit it for at a higher level. 2 See above, p. 212. a new position.

East House l attest, however, the actual survival of such into the present Period, and we see a contemporary reflection of this style in the painted representations of pillar shrines where the wooden shafts show stockinged feet. 2

FIG. 269. PAINTED STUCCO BAND WITH SPIRALIFORM DESIGN, FOUND WITH BULL RELIEFS IN AREA ABOVE LOOM-WEIGHT BASEMENT (-).

It must be supposed that these column bases had fallen into the area where they were found from the stylobate of an early M. M. Ill hall, the position of which is indicated by the massive line of wall bordering the area in which they lay to the West (see Plan, Fig. 278, p. 383 below).

1 See below, p. 425.

- See below, p. 443, Fig. 319.

THE PALACE OF MINOS, ETC.

Spiral

Fresco.

The painted stucco fragments with spiraliform patterns, amongst which these column bases were found embedded, occurred in great masses, sloping away from the West wall of this area. These formed part of decorative bands of distinctive design and colouring (Fig. 269).

The body colour of the wall was a dark Venetian red. The pattern of the band decoration consists of an interlaced double row of spirals',

FIG. 270. CORNER OK SPIRALIFORM PATTERN, RESTORED, d) springing from white disks. Its coils are of a deep ultramarine blue, with black outlines and spurs, the whole on a white ground. One of the larger fragments 2 showed a very remarkable arrangement, indicating that this was not a dado frieze in the ordinary sense. A part of the spiraliform band is there seen running off at an acute angle, leaving a black interspace.

1 Mr. Fyfe's earlier restoration (Vyte, Painted bands, executed for me in 1914 by Mr. J. P.

Plaster Decoration at Knossos: R. I. B. A. Droop (Fig. 269 made it clear that there were

Journ., x, 121, Fig. 45) showed a third line of only two rows, and this conclusion is adhered spirals, on which however he did not insist, to in the restoration given in Fig. 270. A reconstitution of a section of one of the 2 Fyfe, loc. cil., Fig. 46.

The angle thus formed is exactly 45, or half a right angle, and leads to the conclusion that these decorative bands had formed a square frame with two diagonals. The restoration of the corner piece of the design (Fig. 270) to which the above fragment belongs, executed, in accordance with my

FIG. 271. LATTICE-WORK PATTERN IN BAY OF NORTHERN ENTRANCE PASSAGE OK CENTRAL COURT OK PALACE, PHAESTOS.

suggestion, by Mr. Fyfe, illustrates a simple and harmonious method for effecting the junction of the diagonal bands with the rectangular frame. 1

There exist, indeed, two remarkable bits of evidence, relating to the immediately ensuing epoch, which show that this pattern of a rectagonal space with 1 The spiraliform bands forming the frame position) was bounded on the outer margin of the design were bounded internally by by a black followed by a white strip, to the a black field. Mr. Droop's restoration of part outer borders of which again were attached of one of the bands (presumably vertical in fragments of the red field of the wall (Fig. 269).

diagonals was in vogue about this time. Such a pattern in fact occurs as a motive of wall decoration in the case of the two bays on either side of the opening of the Northern entrance passage of the Central Court at Phaestos, belonging to the close of the Middle or the beginning of the Late Minoan Age (Fig. 271). 1 In that case the ornamentation consists of lattice work, and it is of great interest to note that its exact replica recurs as the decoration of a square tank that serves the purpose of a decoy in a bull-grappling scene on a fine Minoan gem of contemporary date (see Fig. 274, p. 377). Attention will be called below to the importance of this representation in this connexion.

To whatever decorative system the bands of the Spiral Fresco were adapted their simple geometrical scheme, combined with the deep body colours of the wall surface, must have been decidedly imposing. Its somewhat sombre aspect contrasts, moreover, with the colour effects of many Late Minoan frescoes in which the bright kyanos' or cobalt blue was so much employed. It is to be noted that the spur-like excrescences of the spirals fit in with certain shell-like motives that appear on contemporary pottery.

Ana- The investigations of the parallel stratum immediately underlying the
Fi S n ds S of M. M. Ill b pavement of the Magazine of the Medallion Pithoi, carried
M. M. out by me in 1913, brought to light fragments of another spiraliform band
Spiral repeating the same colour scheme of deep blue, black, and white. A
Frescoes. c h arac t e ristic feature of this pattern was the border of black dots following the inner spiral bands. Remains of an almost identical frieze with a similar detail was found among the fresco heaps on the North border of the Palace, thrown out apparently at the time of the L. M. II remodelling of that region.

As this was capable of fuller reconstitution it is here reproduced in Fig. 272. 2 Its triangular interspaces are alternately black and Venetian red.

The sympathy in tone and design between the Spiral Fresco of the basement deposit above described and that belonging to the stratum underlying the pavement of the Magazine of the Medallion Pithoi, which has been shown to belong to the closing phase b of M. M. Ill, affords a chronological equation of great value. The Spiral Fresco in the present stratification occupies in fact an analogous position beneath a floor-level on which were vessels representing this latest M. M. Ill stage. From the Section of the various floor-levels beneath that of the Medallion Pithoi given in Fig. 233, p. 320, above, we gain in fact a kind of chronological chart of the place occupied by both these spiral frescoes and the connected deposits in the history of M. M. Ill 1 Pernier, Man. Ant., vol. xii, p. 8r, Fig. 21. the same Deposit, showing the spirals springing a After the reconstruction by Mr. Droop from a white disk, is given by Mr. Fyfe, op. (1914). Another closely allied fragment from fit., p. 122, Fig. 48.

culture. The lower stratum in the section referred to, above the M. M. II b 1 mosaiko pavement, may be taken to represent the close of that Period and the ensuing epoch in which the site was perhaps temporarily left in its ruinous state. This layer is practically equal in thickness to the three M. M. Ill floors, two of them plaster and the topmost gypsum, seen above it. The stratum of the spiral frescoes overlies the middle of these and may be taken to represent the mature stage of the earlier M. M. 1 1 1 phase, a. It is with this stage that we have to do in the case of the present deposit.

Of great importance in relation to this mature M. M. Ill stage are the remains of painted stucco low reliefs brought to light with those of the

FIG. 272. FRESCO FRIEZE WITH SPIRALIFORM DESIGN FROM NORTH-WEST QUARTER OF PALACE, KNOSSOS M. M. Ilia, (i t.)

Spiral Fresco, and which point already to considerable progress in an art that had reached its acme by the beginning of the Late Minoan Age. 1 These from their very nature must have formed part of the decoration of –y—.

a spacious chamber. The most numerous were fragments of figures of bulls in somewhat lower relief than those discovered in the Northern Entrance Passage. They were mostly about life size, and among these were a left fore-shoulder, two hoofs, and several fragments of legs, including the knee of

Frag- stucco

Kellers:

Bull- 1 The proof here afforded of the existence at this time of painted stucco reliefs already in a highly developed stage received a further illustration from a discovery made during the investigations of 1913, beneath the later floor of the S. light area of the Hall of the Double Axes. A fragment was here found, representing part of the thigh and robe of a female figure in comparatively low relief. Already in 1901 fragments belonging to the relief figure of a bull were found underneath the Service stair S. of the Hall of the Colon-nades. It looks therefore as if these painted reliefs had formed part of the original decora-tion of the Domestic Quarter.

THE PALACE OF MINOS, ETC.

a hind-leg. One of them, Fig.273, shows, just above the fetlock, rounded black spots on a white ground which may stand in a derivative relation to a conventional Egyptian rendering of black spotted white oxen common in the time of the Middle Kingdom. There was also a tip of a horn, white on a red ground. With these, also in low relief, was part of a human leg or arm, though the colouring of the surface was too much worn away to give an indication as to the sex. It lay at the top of the deposit, about 70 cm. clown.

It is clear that we have to do with a Minoan bull-grappling or bull-catching scene of the usual kind. Several full-sized animals must have been represented, so that a large extent of wall-space would have been necessary. From the great masses of plain red-faced stucco found in this deposit we may infer that part of this had gone to form the background of these reliefs, as it did of one side of the framework of the Spiral Fresco. A fuller account of the class of scenes to which these fragments belong is given in connexion with the bull reliefs of the Northern Entrance Passage. On the other hand the clear indications supplied by the remarkable fragment referred to above, that the bands of the Spiral Fresco belong to a square frame with diagonals suggests that this decorative design may have had a real connexion with the subject of the reliefs.

It has been already noted that a similar pattern in lattice-work executed in painted plaster occurs on two bays of the Central Court at Phaestos

FIG. 273. PAINTED STUCCO Low RELIEI-(M. M. Ilia) SHOWING PART OF A BULLS FOOT. SPIRAL FRESCO DEPOSIT. (c.) (Fig. 271). But on the contemporary gem reproduced in Fig. 274 we encounter a still more remarkable parallel. Here the lattice-work border with its diagonal is applied to what seems to have been a tank that has given a Minoan cow-boy the opportunity of springing down from some coign of vantage and seizing the neck and fore-legs of a gigantic bull as he drinks. The hair of the acrobatic performer flies upwards as he springs, and his sinewy figure is rendered on a diminutive scale as compared with the beast. To the Minoan artist the bull was evidently of greater importance, and the skill and boldness of the engraving of this part of the design is almost unsurpassed in its own line, though the perspective of the left horn is

FIG. 274. MINOAN INTAGLIO SHOWING BULL CAPTURED WHILE DRINK-ING AT A TANK.

curiously rendered. The gem belongs to the culminating phase of Minoan art that marks the transition from the Middle to the Late Minoan Age.

It is not necesssary to suppose that this tour de force was actually performed in a Palace Court, though the Phaestian parallel might supply some warrant for such a supposition. But the feat itself evidently belonged to a recognized class in which the King of Minoan beasts was grappled in some specially prepared area rather than while ranging at large. It fits on in fact to the Circus scenes which, as will be shown below, were a special theme of the later wall-paintings on the Palace walls of Knossos. But

Tliis gem, a flattened cylinder of onyx, presented by the Phaestos wall pattern, be once in the Tyskiewicz Collection (Furtwangler, certainly regarded as of Cretan fabric. It was

Antike Gemmen, PI. VI, 9, and Vol. II, p. 26), said to have been found at Priene. The gem must, in view of the extraordinary parallel is at present in my own Collection.

these wall paintings in the flat were themselves the later outgrowth of painted reliefs of the preceding Palace stage.

Fra s- It looks as if these remains had originally fallen on to a somewhat fallen 5 higher level and had thence been dumped into the basement space by the Upper M. M. b workmen to whom was due the new plaster floor that covered Hall. it in and on which the tripod pots rested. An indication of this is supplied by the fact that a fragment of the leg of one of the bulls and pieces of the red-faced stucco and of the Spiral Fresco itself were found, at a higher level, at the East end of the cement-paved Corridor defined in the Plan, Fig. 278 below. The occurrence here of fragments of painted stucco decoration belonging to a considerable chamber is itself only compatible with the conclusion that they had fallen from a Hall above. In other words, the whole group of remains with which we are concerned, including the Spiral Fresco and the fragments of painted reliefs depicting bull-grappling scenes, together with the column bases, must have belonged to an Upper Hall, the pavement of which would have been approximately on a level with the fourth landing of the Grand Staircase and of the Uppermost E.-W. Corridor. This level is slightly below that of the Central Court.

It seems further probable that the fragments of painted spiraliform bands of contem-porary fabric embedded in the corresponding M. M. Ill stratum beneath the pavement of the Magazine of the Medallion Pithoi had found its way there, at the time of the same catastrophe, from an anterior section of the same M. M. Ill East Hall from a portico, that is, facing the Central Court.

Thestone There remains a still more cogent piece of evidence that an important
heads Palace Hall existed at that level in this Period. In the walled interspace mstaken
between the Royal Magazines' and what seems to have been another small

Presses, store-room immediately West of the Area of the Spiral Fresco came to light
two square stone receptacles connected with ducts, which, owing to wrong analogies,
were at first taken for olive-presses. A more intimate acquaintance, however, with the
drainage system of the Minoan light-courts has conclusively shown that they were in
fact drain-heads, 1 in this case in communication with vertical shafts by which they
carried off the water from the roofs and light-well of the open part of some large Hall
above.

There were here two stone drain-heads, a larger and a smaller, both of 1 To Mr.
Christian Doll belongs the credit the Room of the Olive Press' has in con-of having
first realized the true function of sequence of this received the name of the these basins.
The space formerly known as Area of the Stone Drain-heads.

limestone (see Fig. 275). The latter showed cement and terra-cotta frag- Vertical
ments adhering to its upper surface, which had evidently belonged to a draining
cement-cased vertical duct; a section, moreover, of a square-cut terra-cotta conduit,
forming an elbow, stood in connexion with this drain-head. A larger shaft must have
run up from the other stone drain-head and the basin of this below opened on a stone
conduit, of square section like the other but of larger capacity, the course of which, as
will be seen, it was possible to trace down two terraces to the East.

It is clear that the ducts running downwards to these drain-heads were
FIG. 275.   STONE DRAIN-HEAD AND CONDUIT. (! NSET, SMALLER
DRAIN-HEAD.) from the first surrounded, for their support as well as for the consolidation of the platform above, with filling earth; nothing, indeed, derived from the
upper story was found on the floor-level of this area.

The stone conduit which proceeded from the larger of the stone drain-heads turned
almost immediately East, and at the point where it approached the M. M. Ill North-
East Portico, described below, a passage had been cut for it through its S. E. angle.
The course of the stone channel through this 1 Of the original East wall of the area
that contained the drain-heads and near to which they stood, only the substructures
remained. This wall had originally formed a section of the upper terrace fa ade line.
The drain-heads themselves were set on the platform of the terrace, and thus occupied
a secure position.

Course of Conduit through E. Portico to Stone Spout and Blind well.

Portico is shown in Fig. 270 opposite. From its terrace it made its way, probably
by a descending duct, to a lower level and thus across the intervening space to a stone
spout (formerly called the Oil Spout), which here projects from the M. M. 111 wall
overlooking the little Court named after it (see Fig. 263 above and Plan, Fig. 2(50).

Hence, doubtless by means of a small descending shaft or pipe and a gullet below,
the water found its way into a short continuation of the stone conduit, the remains of
which were brought out by me in 1913 on the terrace level below, and thus, through
a rectangular basin, to a circular walled cavity or blind-well. It is clear, however, that
this blind-well would itself have overflowed after heavy rains, and we must suppose,
therefore, that there had originally existed some channel by which its surplus waters

reached a prolongation of the Eastern branch of the main drainage system described above. 1 M. M. ill This blind-well, which would thus have served as a kind of settling BJi" in tank, was found choked with pottery representing the earlier and the con- well- eluding phase of M. M. III. In the topmost layer and the entrance basin were also found some L. M. I sherds. The well contained fragments of hole-mouthed vases of an interesting type imitating inlaid stone vessels, and referred below to the penultimate phase of this Period, which were also found associated with the debris of the N. Lustral Area and with the deposit containing the alabaster lid inscribed with the name of the Hyksos Pharaoh, Khyan. On the other hand, some of the painted sherds resembled types found in the Magazine of the Lily Vases belonging to the closing epoch of the present Period. This ceramic evidence is of special value in fixing the date of the constructions to which the stone conduit belonged that had fed the blind-well. Many of the sherds found in the blind-well had doubtless been washed down by means of the descending ducts from the light Court of the great East Hall, the existence of which, as we have seen, is established by so many converging lines of evidence.

As noted above, the sherds found in the blind-well include not only the ceramic phase of the early M. M. Ill class which would represent the stage marked by the spiral fresco and reliefs, but also cover the concluding phase to which the Medallion Pithoi tripod pots and other vessels of the immediately overlying floor-levels belong. It looks then as if the M. M. Ill East Hall including the light-court from which the conduit started had in some restored form survived to the end of the present Period. As a matter of fact the Magazines below it, though renovated now and provided with gypsum paving and dadoes, continued still in use." Even when, at the close 1 See Plan, Fig. 171 a, facing p. 227.

PTERRA-COTTA HEAD AND STONE DRAIN ipn (HEAD
STOrjje CHANNEL
NORTH-EAST PORTICO
LOWER LEVEL L
SCALE OF
FEET
FIG. 276. PLAN OF DRAINAGE SYSTEM OF EARLY EAST HALL (M. M. III).
THE PALACE OF MINOS, ETC.

of this Period, these Magazines were filled in to provide a higher platform for what seems to have been a Late Minoan version of the same great Palace Hall, it looks as if the light-area of this had been connected up with the older drainage system and the presence of a certainproportion of L. M. I sherds in the topmost layer corroborates this conclusion. It would thus appear that this later Hall had substantially followed the same lines as its Middle Minoan predecessor. It is to this later Hall that I have ventured

FIG. 277. CORRIDOR OF BAYS SHOWING PIERS THAT ACTED AS SUP-PORTS FOR FRONTAL
PILLARS OF EAST HALL ABOVE.

to refer the fallen remains of the painted stucco high reliefs the crowning achievement of Minoan Art- and the Griffin Frieze, which had survived in situ in this area to
the last days of the Palace. 1

A glance at the M. M. Ill plan of this section of the building (Fig. 278) is itself
sufficient to suggest the stately lines of a great Upper Hall, with its entrance piers and
successive lines of basement walls and its middle space with M. M. ill the earth filling
adapted for the support of stvlobates and colonnades and of

East Hail.

1 See Vol. II.

Substructures showing Plan of Great

ROYAL MAGAZINES

CORR-OF BAY54 MAG OF MED; PITHOl

RITUAL VES5US

M. M. III. b.

MEDALLION PITHOI7

DRAIN 5HAFTS FROM LIGHT AREA ABOVE

FILLING EARTH

SUBSTRUCTURE OF EARLY FACADE

PAVED AREA MM. Ilia MAGAZINE FILLED in.

FILLING

EARTH

V V XX RATIVE

DEPOSITOR

SPIRAL

FPE6CO POTTLRY

M. M. III. al

AT HIGHER LEVEL. ON THIS AND ADJOINING SPACES. N.

FRESCO,

COLUMN BASES BULL RELIEFS (M. M. III. a)

HIGH RELIEFS AND GRIFFIN FPIEZE(LM-lo PRECIPITATED HERE

O STOR E. OOOM

X WITH M. M. lll. b. POTS.

00 w i i M n. rn. oooocco

FIG. 278. GROUND PLAN SUGGESTING THE ARRANGEMENT or A GREAT
M. M. Ill EAST HALL ABOVE.

THE PALACE OF MINOS, ETC.

the inner Court. The massive piers visible in the Corridor of the Bays (see Fig.
277), forming as we have seen part of the Royal Magazines, were clearly designed to
support the frontal pillars of an important building facing the Central Court.

That the original elements of this M. M. Ill East Hall had fitted on to those of a
great part of the Domestic Quarter is placed beyond doubt by the evidence already
supplied. The fabric of the lower part of its supporting walls to South and East forms,
as shown above, an integral part of the construction of the adjoining Lower E.-W.
Corridor and its Northern branch. The component elements of these, including the
timber framework and masonry panels, extend, as we have seen, into the neighbouring

Halls of the Colonnades and of the Double Axes, practically without a break. The interrelation thus established is indeed of primary importance in its bearing on the history of the Domestic Quarter.

FIG. 279. M. M. III POTS FROM MAGAZINE (FORMED BY BLOCKED SECTION OF EARLIER CORRIDOR)

Continuation North of Upper Terrace Fafade; The North-East Portico' through passage to Postern on the East; The Northern Quarter; Destritction due to Vicinity of Later Town; In M. M. Ill, probably Work-metis Quarter; Signs of improved Conditions in L. M. I; Discovery of Inlaid Draught-board; Fallen from Upper Floor connected with L. M. I East Hall, though probably M. M. HI heirloom; Ivory Draughtsmen from border area; Description of Gaming Board postponed to later Section; The Corridor of the Draught-board and Stepway to Central Court; North-Eastern Hall and connected Store-rooms four-columned Megaron; N. E. Magazines; North-E astern Entrance; Its system probably linked with that of Northern Entrance; Built drain running to main Cloaca of N. Entrance; The Northern Entrance Passage; Narrowed in M. M. Ill, with Bastions on either side; M. M. Ill Masonry and Signs; Eastern line of Bastions later removed; Portico above W. Bastions, subsequent to this removal; Sally Port and inner Gateway; Bastion and Tower dominating outer Gateway; Approached by Roadway from West and from Harbour Town the Sea Gate of the Palace; P ropy Ion and Guard-room; Extensive fortification of N. approach; Hall of Eleven Pillars probably Depot, with Loggia above; North Pillar Crypt M. Af. fjIa. Construction and Signs; Crypt of Columnar Sanctuary; Well of Greek Geometrical Period.

IT has been shown above that the original upper terrace fa9ade of the Continua-Early Palace, after being interrupted by the Great Cutting of the Domestic N "rth o Quarter, renewed its course along the E. borders of the section which P e includes the area of the Stone Drain. Beyond this section, where only its Facade, substructures are preserved, it took a short easterly bend, but its original gypsum construction reappears on the W. border of the N. E. Portico, and there is every reason to suppose that, as indicated in the Plan, Fig. 152 above, it continued its northerly course thence to the boundary wall of the Palace on that side. It would thus have formed the Eastern limit of a distinct Palace Quarter or Insula, bounded on the opposite side by the

The N. E. corner of the Central Court and by the Northern Entrance Passage. or t ie sa e distinction the general name of the Northern Quarter lias been given to this region, It was flanked on its Eastern border by another very distinct Quarter, described above as the North-East Insula. 1

The quasi-independent character of this region is well marked. It was approached from the North by a separate gate from which, as this area was at a higher level, flights of steps led up to it. From this N. E. Entrance, moreover, a special stone-built conduit conveyed its surplus waters to the main Northern drain. At the S. W. angle of this Quarter, a stone staircase, the original elements of which go back to the earliest age of the Palace, supplied an avenue of communication with the Central Court. Opposite the foot of these stairs, moreover, by means of an opening in the old Upper Terrace fa9ade and an adjoining Portico, this line of communication found its continuation down the slope to a postern on the Eastern Palace border.

The doorway that here opens in the remaining section of the old gypsum facade above referred to, was in fact of the greatest functional importance as holding the key to one of the principal through routes across the Palace on this side. The doorway itself, of which one jamb has been preserved, leads to a A-co imiiat loggia on the same terrace level, here described as the North-East Portico'. The passage through this of the stone drain on its way from the East Hall to the Court of the Stone Spout below has been already described in a previous Section 2 and is well illustrated in Fig. 280. Immediately above it to the left in the Figure appears a part of the gypsum facade, while to the right of the platform, resting on massive foundation blocks, is one of the column bases in position. 3 The great pains taken to secure the stability of these and the corresponding column at a higher level on the slope of the hill will be more fully realized from the view given in Suppl. PI. VIII. The column base that has been preserved is of the same breccia as those associated with the Spiral Fresco 4 and was originally of identical shape. It had, however, been readapted for a wooden column of smaller dimensions by a ledge cut round its upper circumference. In all probability these bases had once formed part of a great East Hall of the Early Palace.

The North-East Portico which was thus a radial point of this whole Palace region evidently gave access from the North end of its covered area to the upper landing of a stepway decending the slope to the East. The 1 See Diagrammatic Plan, Fig. 152 and part was found actually in place. The cavities p. 203 above. visible on its upper surface are not dowel- ," P. 379 and Plan, Fig. 276. holes but are of natural formation. 1 The base had been broken and only one 4 See above p. 370, Fig. 268.

course of this is shown by the parallel lines of walling on the Plan, Fig. 152. and it clearly found its outlet in an earlier predecessor of the Late Minoan postern gate on this side. It ran immediately within the preserved section of the gypsum South fa ade of the North-East Insula (see above p. 364, Fig. 24).

Like this N. E. Insula that borders it on the East, the Northern Destruc-Quarter seems to have suffered greatly from the vicinity of the Greek and t o Late Roman town and modern village. It is clear that most of the better lime- Bullders-stone masonry of this part of the slope was used as a quarry by later builders. This Northern Quarter, as we shall see, seems to have been flanked by a stately Corridor, but there is no evidence that important buildings of the present Period existed within its area. Its rubbish heaps contained masses Probably of plain clay cups and sherds of the latest M. M. Ill class, and the character ji of the buildings here found also points to its occupation at this time by Work-workmen or slaves. The finer relics found in this area seem rather to have Quarter. belonged to the beginning of the Late Minoan Age. A black steatite signs of tripod, once gold plated, and associated with an abundance of gold foil, that improved came to light on the borders of the North-East Magazines here situated ditions in themselves containing poor M. M. Ill b pottery belonged to an overlying L M I stratum with ceramic remains of a better class, characteristic of the early part of L. M. I. Similar L. M. la pottery, including a pithos, was also found above the floor in the region of the neighbouring North-East Hall, and its Dis-occurrence here has a special chronological value since, from the same level 17 of above the Corridor immediately East of this little Hall (see Fig. 281). there Draught-was brought out the inlaid Ivory Draught-board the most magnificent relic discovered in the whole course of the excavation.

This precious object lay, with the greater part of its framework bent indeed, but practically intact, somewhat irregularly disposed on an earth layer, accompanied by fallen fragments of stone, a few centimetres above the Fallen paving of a gangway, which, owing to its discovery, has been known as upper the Corridor of the Draught-board. There is every reason to believe that Floor it had fallen from an upper floor. It may, therefore, well have formed part Probably of the belongings of some annexe of the Great East Hall of the Palace, as it loom from existed at the beginning of the Late Minoan Age. On the other hand there are reasons for supposing that the Draught-board itself belonged to the latest M. M. Ill phase. It is certainly in accordance with the law of probability that this object stood in some kind of relation to the ivory draughtsmen brought to light on the North border of the Loom- Weight Area. 1 Even if we are hardly 1 See above, p. 30; and pp. 477, 47 8 below. CC 2 ivory justified in referring the Draught-board itself to so early a date as these, the men U of ts discovery of the ivory draughtsmen certainly indicates that some chamber Border j n tm s q uar t e r of the Palace was traditionally associated with the kind

Area.- i of gaming that it represents.

As this remarkable work is best considered in its relation to the more fragmentary remains, apparently of similar objects, among the treasures of the West Palace region, its full description and illustration is appended to the account of the contents of the W. Temple Repository. 1

Corri- The broad paved gangway, known from this discovery as the Corridor Draught- f the Draught-board, ran immediately within the old facade line of the b "c t e upper terrace of the East slope. Only its Southern section was preserved; way to and in this direction, at the S. E. corner of the North East Hall described Court below, are visible four low steps ascending West, and indications of a passage leading hence round the outer walls of the group of store-rooms attached to this Hall. Some five metres above the four steps that are preserved are traces of others turning North between passage walls of good limestone construction. About the same distance farther on, the same passage takes another turn West, past a massive Bastion, and thence by another angle seems to have found its way to a point near the upper opening of the Northern Entrance Way. Most of this work seems to belong to the Early Palace (see Plan, Fig. 152 above). In the angle between this winding step-way and the Corridor were situated the best-preserved remains brought to light in this region. N. E. These consisted of a porticoed chamber known as the N. E. Hall and Con- an d its dependencies, together with an annexe the N. E. Magazines connected taining great stores of plain pottery belonging to the latest phase, b, of this Rooms. Period (see Plan, Fig. 281). The Hall itself was entered from the Corridor of the Draught-board, and a double doorway on the opposite side led to a small interior chamber and magazine. The dimensions of the Hall are 8-45 by 5.35 metres, and it contained within it a square cement-paved light-area bounded N. and S. by a two-columned stylobate. 2 This little light-court was so disposed as to leave a comparatively deep covered section at the South end, while the corresponding space between the Northern 1 See below, p. 468 seqq., and Coloured 2 There are only indications of the Southern

Plate V. To raise these highly friable remains stybolate, but its position together with the from their irregular backing was a matter of extent of the area covered by the cement floor extraordinary difficulty. (See Knossos, Report, was clearly ascertained by Dr. Mackenzie in 1901, p. 77.) the supplementary explorations of 1907.

M. M. Ill: NORTH QUARTER AND ENTRANCE 389 stylobate and the wall l was only just wide enough to afford shelter to those passing from the outer to the inner door. This arrangement, showing a four-columned light-well, is unique at Knossos, but recurs in the Palace at Phaestos in the Megaron of the Women's Quarter, also described as the Family Meeting Room. 2 . CORRIDOR OF DRAUGHTBOARD

FIG. 281. PLAN OF NORTH-EAST HALL AND MAGAZINES.

The double inner doorway of the N. E. Hall is explained by the curious subdivision of the walled space into which it opens. The door on the right hand leads through a kind of vestibule to a passage-way beyond, passing on 1 The limestone column bases (70 cm. in Sola di convegni famigliari; No. 50 diameter) were only i-io metres from the N. in Dr. Pernier's Plan, Man. Ant., xiv. wall of the Megaron. op. fit., p. 374, Fig- 23; a" d P- 379. Fi 8- 2 7- the left the entrance of a small magazine. The left doorway, on the other hand, gave entrance to a small square chamber 1 divided from the more public space to the right by a thin gypsum partition such as occurs elsewhere in the case of the latrine in the Domestic Quarter, described above, as well as in certain Magazines of this Period. 2 Both the closet itself and the adjoining space were very well preserved, and the gypsum dado slabs that lined the walls, as well as the combination of the central door-jamb with the thin partition, together present a characteristic specimen of the late M. M. Ill architectural style, so similar in its general features to the earlier Late Minoan.

A terminus a quo for this whole group of structures is supplied by the pottery found in the little store-room behind the adjoining space. This was all of the same character as'that of the adjoining N. E. Pottery stores, ordinary ware, that is, belonging to the latest M. M. Ill b class.

This little magazine, moreover, contained two objects which threw a useful light on the furniture of the Hall itself. One was a low portable seat of hard white-faced stucco with a clay core, resembling the lower class of stone seats found in the Later Palace, which seem to have been used by the women. The other was a tripod hearth faced with the same white stucco resembling those, with the ashes still on them, found in Late Minoan tombs. 3 But the occurrence of this in connexion with this little Hall with its four-columned light-well, has a special interest in its bearing on the numerous fragments of similar stucco-hearths found with M. M. Ill sherds in the circular rubbish pit (Kouloura) beneath the later pavement of the West Court. The borders of some of these, as is pointed out below, 4 are in fact decorated with the same notched plume motive that recurs on the fixed hearth of the Megaron at Mycenae.

N. E. In the space outside this store-room were also found two plain pecles- talled lamps of grey steatite. Beyond the lobby where these occurred a small ascending passage gave access to the square building containing the group of M. M. Ill pottery stores known as the North-East Magazines (Fig. 281). A key plan of these with reference to the forms of vessels that they contained will be found below. 8 On the

West border of these, in the immediately overlying stratum, were rouleaux of typical L. M. I cups.

1 It was possibly a bath-room, or we may 2 As for instance in the North Lustral Area, have here to do with a latrine of a simple the S. E. House, and Royal Villa at Knossos.

kind, with movable utensils, such as is still s Prehistoric Tombs ofknossos(Archaeologia, common in parts of Southern Europe. The vol. lix), p. 36, Fig. 33.

dimensions of the closet were 2-50 by 2-70 4 See p. 550 metres. 5 See p. 569, Fig. 1H.

It may well be that the N. E. Hall and the rest of the building with which it was connected was the residence of a foreman or official overseer of the potters.

It is probable that the northward continuation of the Corridor of the N. E. Draught-board brought it, by a turn West, into connexion with the gate by Entrancc-which this Quarter was entered on that side.

This N. E. Entrance, as will be seen from the suggested restoration in Fig. 282, seems to have also given access, by a passage-way running directly Eastwards through an opening in the Upper Terrace Fa9ade, to the

ENTRANCE TO N E. MACAZ. INES

FIG. 282. RESTORED PLAN OK NORTH-EASTERN ENTRANCE, AS RE-MODELLED IN M. M. III.

region, otherwise much isolated from the rest of the building, described on the Diagrammatic Plan, Fig. 152 above, as the North-East Insula. The Royal Pottery Stores, indeed, that were situated on the upper level of this must have stood in constant need of some convenient access from the outside world, if only for the carrying in of the needful supplies of fine clay. The Entrance passage itself by which these passed was probably flanked by some kind of guard-room.

The main passage that leads South from the North-East Entrance and which served the Northern Quarter with which we are now dealing, after a course of about a dozen metres, turns Eastward at right angles up a flight of steps (see Fig. 283). a A smaller flight, however, continued South, thus giving direct access to the North-East Magazines of the contiguous area.

The W. wall of the entrance Gallery consists of fine limestone masonry, the inner section of which slightly projects in front of the other.

FIG. 283. VIEW OF N. E. ENTRANCE LOOKING S. STEPS TO LEFT LEADING TO MAIN CORRIDOR OF N. QUARTER; SMALLER STEPS TO RIGHT HEADING FOR N. E. MAGAZINES ON TERRACE ABOVE.

Both in this feature and the character of the blocks this wall closely resembles those of the Bastions of the Northern Entrance Passage belonging to the early part of M. M. Ill, but in this case the blocks showed no incised signs. Most of the wall on the left of the entrance passage, which was of the same fine construction as that opposite, has been torn away 1 The steps of this flight, of which four were preserved, are 1-50 metres wide, 15 cm. high, and 50 cm. deep.

by later builders: this, however, allows parts of the lower steps of the Eastern flight to be clearly seen.

The N. E. Entrance debouched externally on a gangway turning West, of which a small section of the original pavement has been preserved. It seems highly probable that this gangway brought the North-Eastern Entrance into direct connexion with the fortified approach from the North and West described below. It is possible that an actual passage existed. through the central avenue of the covered area described as the Hall of the Eleven Pillars, which immediately faced the outer gate on this side.

The organic connexion of these two Entrance systems receives indeed a further illustration from the convergence of their two main drainage channels. A built drain, to which attention has already been called, Built which must originally have served this Quarter, passed under a rectangular structure immediately W. of the N. E. Entrance, and can be followed thence from N. E. to the point where it entered the main Cloaca of the Northern Entrance to Main Passage. These drains belonged to the earlier elements of the building, (and there can be little doubt that the entrance of the Northern Quarter from which this affluent runs also goes back in its original form to the earliest days of the Palace.

The Northern Entrance Passage itself underwent a great transformation Northern in the present Period. It is probable that the upper part of this Passage had never been more than about two metres wide in its upper section. Here the E. border of the early Keep juts forward and a row of foundation slabs opposite this points to a symmetrical arrangement of wall line on the other side. The early built drain ran under this, and the interspace between the two walls was doubtless filled by an. ascending ramp or stairway that gave entrance to the Central Court.

But the space below the projecting angle of the Keep seems originally now nar-to have formed an open area some seven metres in width between two w j tn terrace walls, that to the West forming the border on this side of the North-West Portico and adjoining entrance. At the time, however, of the great side. M. M. Ill Restoration, to which so much in the Domestic Quarter was due, the lower part of this Entrance Passage was reduced to the same width as the upper section by the construction in front of the terrace walls on either side of three great Bastions, as shown in the Plan, Fig. 280. The back of the Western line of Bastions rested on the lower courses of the early wall that flanked the North Portico on the left.

The masonry of these Bastions and even, as we shall see, the character of their incised signs agree so closely with that of the light-well

THE PALACE OF MINOS, ETC.

M. M. Ill Masonry and Signs of Bastions.

Eastern line of Bastions later removed.

Portico above W. Bastions.

Sally Port at N. Entrance.

walls of the Court of the Stone Spout and of the Hall of the Double Axes, that the same chronological equations there arrived at must apply in the present case. In other words, the Bastions of the N. Entrance Passage belong to the earlier stage of the M. M. Ill Period. Here, too, we find the trident, the double axe, the branch, and the star, incised in the same manner that we see in the above structures and in other contemporary parts of the Domestic Quarter. It is perhaps not an accidental coincidence that the blocks of Bastion A, the Northernmost of its series, and immediately overlooking what was the Sea Gate of the Palace, are repeatedly and exclusively marked by the trident sign. The parallelism both in construction and in the incised marks is carried still further, moreover, on the still existing bases of the similar bastions, stepping up on the left-hand side of the entrance ramp. Not only does the general appearance of the masonry recall that of the base of the Grand Staircase in the Hall of the Colonnades, but its blocks bear the same broad arrow sign, which may have had a reference to analogous constructions.

Curiously enough, in the succeeding Late Minoan Period the Eastern half of the lower Entrance section was again widened out, so that the area recovered two-thirds of its original width. The upper part of the line of Bastions on this side, AA, BB, cc was removed, and what remained was now lost beneath the ascending roadway, the level of which gradually rose throughout succeeding stages of its history. The lower courses of the original Eastern line of the Bastions as at this time sub merged by the ascending roadway are shown in Fig. 284. Part of the sloped coping slabs of the great built drain as it descended the entrance passage are visible in the photographic view. It is obvious that the ramp in its original form ran on or somewhat above the level of these.

It is probable that the new road of approach continued at the same breadth through the upper section of the Entrance Passage. It is clear, moreover, that at the same time some stately Portico was constructed above the Bastions on the Western side of its lower section, which were left undisturbed. The splendid remains of painted stucco reliefs representing bull-catching scenes that here came to light, largely on the upper level of the roadway below, as well as a limestone column base, must have belonged to this Portico.

Immediately below the line of Bastions to the East of the Entrance Passage was a curious walled recess of elongated form that may have served as a Sally Port or Guard-room. Its outer wall, with its well-marked interstices filled with clay mortar, repeats the construction of the S. light-area of the Queen's Megaron, which has been cited as a typical example of M. M. 11 construction. It shows, moreover, a similar projecting coping above on its exterior face (see Fig. 287).

The opening of this Sally Port and a part of the contemporary Eastern terrace wall of the N. Entrance Passage, which is of the same construction, are shown in Fig. 285. It is evident that the actual gateway was some-
FIG. 284. VIEW UP NORTHERN ENTRANCE PASSAGE SHOWING THE REMAINS OF THE
EASTERN LINE OF BASTIONS.
where near this inlet, but only indications of it came to light. This, as will be seen, would have been the inner of two gateways on this side.

Below this point the avenue of access was shifted somewhat East by a Outer i- L i j Bastion massive projecting line of masonry which seems to have belonged to an ant j additional Bastion immediately dominating the approach to the inner gateway (see Fig. 286). A triple wall line is traceable behind it, and at a distance of about five metres North of it are visible the massive lower courses
THE PALACE OF MINOS, ETC.

of a small tower, which, it is to be noted, was provided with its own water supply by means of socketed terra-cotta pipes.

Guarding The Bastion on one side, and the Tower with its associated structures on

Gate- of the other, guard what seems to have been an outer gateway, opening West, Palace. t h e true g ea Q ate o f the Palace, on the principal road of access not only from

FIG. 285. VIEW OF EAST SIDE OF N. ENTRANCE PASSAGE, SHOWING SALLY PORT

AND EARLY TERRACE WALL.

that direction but from the harbour town, lying about four miles North Roadway of the Palace. That the roadway which opened immediately from the anct Northern Entrance Passage could not itself have had a straight Northern Harbour course is shown by the fact that at a distance of only about 45 metres from the Inner Gateway on this side, the access in that direction was blocked by the important building to which the Pillared Crypt described below belongs.

The existence of the outer Gateway facing West explains this arrangement. There are, in fact, visible in situ a series of gypsum blocks in the interval between the above-mentioned Bastion and Tower, which seem to mark the position of a double door-opening on this side, while another to Pro- the left of these may well belong to a guard-room within the bastion itself, d on flanking the entrance passage. It may be further assumed, as shown in the Guard- Plan, Fig. 286, that there was a similar double entrance in a line with the Western. face of these structures. We have here in fact a regular Propylon with a covered passage between its inner and outer gates.

It is evident from the existence of dependencies of the Palace, including the later Theatral Area, some forty metres West of this outer entrance, that the roadway on this side must have almost immediately taken a Northerly turn, in the direction that is of the Harbour Town. Extensive The main line of public access was thus guarded by a double barrier thro of " the Propylon, and, at right angles to it, the inner North Gate of the Palace A P- lying opposite the sally port. It seems probable, moreover, that the whole of the inner space to which the Propylon gave access, between the inner gateway that barred the Northern Entrance Passage and the Pillar Crypt facing it on the North, was securely fenced in. On every hand, indeed, we have indications that the Northern approach to the Palace the approach most liable to a piratical raid was strongly fortified. From the Bastions beside the entrance passage downwards, most of the work in its existing state seems to belong to the earlier part of the M. M. Ill Period.

Within the rectangular fortified space outside the Northern Entrance and imme- diately facing the outer Gate, was a structure of another character. Hall of Here were brought to light 1 the base slabs, and in several cases the lower Pillar blocks of massive gypsum pillars, cut square, 2 and evidently forming the supports of a consid- erable covered area somewhat over 19-20 metres in length. The pillars were eleven in number distributed in two rows, six in front and five in the second line, where the coping of the wall of the sally port served as the sixth support. The line of pillars fronting the roadway must have been open. Except on the South, the character of the walled enclosure on the other sides remains conjectural. A view showing the existing remains of eight of these Pillars and the monumental line of the Bastions, dominating the Northern Entrance Passage beyond, is given in Fig. 287.

It is reasonable to suppose that this spacious Pillar Hall standing just outside the Sea Gate at what seems to have been the converging point 1 Knossos, Report, 1902, pp. 5, 6. with slight variations. They were placed at - The blocks of the pillars were cs5 cm. x 85, intervals of 2-65 metres.

THE PALACE OF MINOS, ETC.

Perhaps o f access from the interior of the island on one side, and from the port with on the other, fulfilled the functions of a ddpot and perhaps a Custom House f r goods destined for Palace use. Analogy would suggest, moreover, that there had been here an upper story reached by some lateral staircase, in above.

FIG. 288. VIEW FROM UPPER PART OF N. ENTRANCE PASSAGE LOOKING NORTH TOWARDS PILLARED CRYPT. THE PILLARS OF THE HALL OF THE ELEVEN PILLARS ARE VISIBLE TO RIGHT.

Northern Pillar Crypt.

which columns were superposed on the pillars below. It would thus have formed a magnificent loggia in front of the entrance gate, witli which its central intercolumnia-tion exactly corresponds.

At this point, owing to the denudation of the slope, the dependencies in immediate conjunction with the Palace break off, as well as the traces of the continuation of the great built drain. At a distance of about 25 metres

North of the Pillar Hall, however, was found the pillared basement of an important building, clearly of contemporary construction. As will be seen from the view given in Fig. 288, taken from the upper part of the Northern Entrance Passage, this building must have been the principal feature that met the eye of those issuing from the Sea Gate. Its direct relation to the Palace is moreover brought out by another indication. A paved Causeway forming a branch of the line of access from the Little Palace on the West, and which starts immediately above the Theatral Area, 1 heads directly for the point where a prolongation of the Northern road would reach the Southern face of this edifice.

The part of its structure that has been preserved evidently lay beneath the original surface of the ground and consists of a pillared Crypt with passages and rooms in communication with it. Its main feature is an oblong chamber 7 80 metres long by 5-81 broad. It presents in its present state four limestone bases over the inner pair of which are two square gypsum pillars with bevelled angles. Both of these are monolithic, one attaining a height of about 2-10 metres (see Fig. 289). This area had suffered much from later devastations, and there is a reasonable presumption that thecrypt in its original shape had contained six pillars, symmetrically arranged as shown in Mr. Doll's Plan, Fig. 200. The walls of this chamber were composed of exceptionally long limestone blocks, one in the North Wall being 1-60 metre long by 0-64 m. high. Though carefully finished on the interior face of the walls, the blocks were more or less wedge-shaped behind and were left rough in the manner usual with terrace walls. They were obviously built against an earth cutting, and we have here therefore the remains of a subterranean pillar crypt of the class well illustrated by the Little Palace.

The character of the gypsum pillars with their square bases brings M. M. them into obvious relation with those of the Hall of the Eleven Pillars' IU "C n- struction.

above described. They undoubtedly are the work of the same epoch, and in this case a further clue is supplied by the fallen blocks found on the floor of the chamber, some of which presented the star and trident signs executed in the same manner as similar signs seen on Bastions A and B of the Northern Entrance, on the West wall of the Court of the Stone Spout, and elsewhere, and belonging, as already demonstrated, to the earlier part of the M. M. Ill Period.

Masses of carbonized wood were also found with the fallen blocks, but Crypt of nothing unfortunately was left in place of the upper structure of the building, which had been originally above ground. We are warranted in believing, tuary.

1 See Vol. II.

THE PALACE OF MINOS, ETC.

M. M. Ill: NORTH QUARTER AND ENTRANCE 403

PLAN

COLUMN BASt?

IN ONC ffcf OF CYPSUM 1-96 LONG

PLAN OF WEST PILLAR

JULY 1918

FfloBABLf LfvCL or UPPER FLOOR

SECTONA. A.

FIG. 290. FLAN AND RESTORED SECTION OF NORTH PILLAR CRYPT.

IN ONf PICCC or CYPSUM -55S

PLAN OF EAST PILLAR

CMRtsTIAH C T. DOLL however, that it consisted of a hall with six columns answering to the pillars below (see Section, Fig. 290).

The appearance of fine masonry in a covered area agrees with what is seen in the Pillar Room of the S. E. House and in that of the Royal Villa, and in these and other cases there is clear evidence, as shown below, that such pillared crypts fulfilled a religious function and stood in relation to a Columnar Shrine above. There can be little doubt that we have here the remains of an important sanctuary facing the inner Sea Gate of the Palace and forming a monumental dependency of it on that side. A striking feature of the Plan (see Fig. 290) is the appearance of the four openings at or near the corners of the pillared chamber leading to small rooms and passages beyond, which give the whole a curiously labyrinthine aspect.

Well of Such evidence as might have been obtained from minor relics has been

Geome- here obscured by the later intrusion on the spot not only of squatters of Period. tne me tne re-occupation of the Palace but of Greek inmates of the Geometrical Period, good ceramic remains of which were found in a later well sunk close to the original South wall of the Pillar Crypt. 1 This is the nearest point to the Palace site where clear evidence of Early Greek settlement came to light. On the line of the Minoan road and on the hill of Hellenika to the West, however, such evidence became frequent, and in the Little Palace especially the Minoan foundations were honeycombed in places by later wells, several of them going back to the Greek Geometrical Period.

1 The wooden roofing which it was necessary to place over this well for safety's sake appears in the foreground of Fig. 289.

N. W. Entrance System scene of initiatory rites; N. W. Bailey and Temenos of Lustral Area; The Lustral Basin; Its Store-house or Treasury; Stratified deposit within Basin; Earlier and Later stages of M. M. Ill represented; Ritiial vessels of Clay and Stone from Basin; Stone Ewers; Inlaid limestone bowls their painted clay imitations; White-dotted Ware and other contemporary types; Moulded ears of barley on small jug; Pedestalled Vases; Polychrome imitation of Egyptian A labastron type; hite-dotted Ware M. M. Ill a; Discovery in same Deposit of A labastron lid of Hyksos King, Khyan; Place of Khyan in Hyksos scries; Pharaonized Dynast re-unites all Egypt; Predecessor of the Apcpis; Chronological materials; Wide range of Khyaris Monuments; Approximate date of close of M. M. Ill a. Khyan s lid evidence of peaceful intercourse rather than of Conquest; Use of Alabastra iri connexion with Lustral Basins.

IN contrast with the Northern Entrance System, standing in relation to N. w. the main route of public access to the Palace both from the harbour town and system from the interior of the island, was the private and probably ceremonial line J " 0 " of approach by the terrace level immediately behind the triple group of Cha-Bastions on the West side of the Entrance Passage. This line of approach, as shown above, 1 was through an outer walled enclosure, the North-West Bailey of the Diagrammatic Plan (Fig. 152), and thence through the North-West Porch with its double system of doorways. The early Palace wall on which the E. border of the Porch and adjoining Piazza had rested was partly demolished early in M. M. Ill in order to support the Western Wall of Bastion A, but there is every reason to believe that the entrance itself continued in use till at least the close of that Period.

The interesting feature of this entrance system, as shown above, is its N. W. evident relation to an inner Temenos' within this N. W. Bailey. This Temenos enclosure is here defined as the Initiatory Area. Its centre point was r r usl a sunken basin approached by a descending staircase, and this seems to have been the scene of lustral functions performed by pilgrims or others approachincr the Palace Sanctuary for religious purposes. It is in fact the Pilgrim's ,,., i, ir Entrance.

most capacious existing example of a series of such lustral basins at Knossos and elsewhere, to which that of the Room of the Throne affords a later parallel. 2 1 See p. 215. See pp. 4, 5, above.

THE PALACE OF MINOS, ETC.

Lustral Basin.

It has been suggested above l that the original elements of this structure, especially its backing of comparatively small limestone blocks resting on thick layers of clay mortar, possibly go back to the earliest age of the Palace. But the external features, both of the gypsum-lined basin

DEPOSIT SIMILAR TO

PROBABLE EXIT VOTARIES 1 RUNNING BtnEATHLATff TWHL AND CON-TAINING AjaLABASTERlIID

WITH NAME KING KHYAN

LUSTRAL BASIN

FORE- HALL OF INITIATORY A A
OF VOTARIES
CONJIECTURAL STEPWAY
FIG, 291. PLAN OF LUSTRAL BASIN AND INITIATORY AREA.
itself and of its balustraded stairs, may certainly be claimed to belong to the early part of the present Period.

A view of this Lustral Basin from a sketch by Mr. Fyfe made at the time of excavation is given in Fig. 292 and a Plan and Sections looking East and West in Figs. 293, 294, A, B, the latter showing the earlier wall construction. A restored Plan is given in Fig. 291. The basin itself was almost exactly 2 m. deep and 2 square. 2 As will be seen, it was approached by two flights 1 P. 215.

2 The Lustral Basin found in the S. E. Palace Quarter was 2-20 m. X 2-0 m. in dimensions, those of Phaestos 2-25 m. X 2-25 m. The Ladies' Bath there and two of those to the

South-East were 2-20 m. X 2-0 m. Dr. Pernier, Mon. Ant., xiv, p. 388, note, has remarked on the approximate correspondence in the size of these basins. That of the Little Palace at Knossos is 2-50 m. X2-i8m.

M. M. Ill: NORTH-WEST BAILEY AND LUSTRAL AREA 407
THE PALACE OF MINOS, ETC.
of steps, flanked by a descending balustrade with four pillars, three of them for the support of columns, the base of the lowest column being fairly preserved.

The paving of gypsum slabs and the gypsum lining or dado which still
FIG. 293. PLAN OF LUSTRAI, BASIN.
to a great extent covers the walls are quite in keeping with the architectural fashion of the present Period a fashion that survives into the early part of the late Minoan Age. The pillars and descending balustrades of the flights of steps also suggest a comparison with the Grand Staircase of the 1n;. 294. SECTIONS OF NORTHERN LUSTRAL BASIN, LOOKING EAST (A) AND WEST (B).

Domestic Quarter. We note here, however, a more archaic touch. In this case the columns were not socketed into their pedestals, but rested on circular projections in one piece with the base, in conformity with the usage of the Early Palace.

indica- The fore-hall East of the Lustral Basin through which, ex hypothesi,
Sacristory votaries entering the Palace Sanctuary passed in order to perform certain or Store- initiatory and purificatory rites, was possibly provided with a throne and benches for sacerdotal use, like the later Room of the Throne and its Antechamber. West of the Basin the surface had been much denuded, but from the remains of vessels found both within the Basin itself and in the S. W. angle of the enclosure beyond we may infer that part of this area was occupied by some kind of Sacristry or Treasury serving for the storage of ritual vessels. As usual, the objects of precious metals had disappeared, but the remains of the decorative stone ewers and inlaid bowls here brought to light and notably the lid of the Royal Egyptian alabastron may supply at least some samples of its contents.

It is to be remarked that, here as in all other cases, the plaques of the walls and floors of the Lustral Basin were of gypsum, an unmistakable sign that they had been originally roofed over, probably by means of a clerestory. In the case of spaces open to the air, such as light-wells, the floors were invariably coated with cement. They were also provided with drains, of which there is no trace in any of these sunken areas.

Stratified It is probable that it is to the penultimate rather than the latest within M. M. Ill phase that we must refer the actual contents of the Lustral

Basin as excavated. Not only, as will be seen, the character of the objects found, but the stratigraphic evidence supplied by the overlying deposit point to this conclusion.

Above the deposit of carbonized materials with which the greater part of the basin was choked, and which represented the debris from upper structures belonging to the same system, were remains of walls dating from two distinct epochs. It would appear that already before the close of the M. M. Ill Period the site was cleared to the level of the top of the basin, and a new building of a different character erected in this area largely out of the earlier blocks, and partly following the old exterior lines. A wall of this, set somewhat back from the edge of the North wall of the staircase, is shown in Mr. Fyfe's drawing reproduced in Fig. 292, and a jamb remained of a later and narrower doorway on the East side. Two parallel walls belonging to this later building, with large blocks like that of the wall described, were also laid across the centre of the basin itself, and it is interesting to note that a piece of painted stucco showed a black ground with alternations of blue lines, a colour scheme which itself would lead us to place this later fabric still within the M. M. Ill limits. On the other hand, above this level and adhering to upper blocks on a later terrace wall, immediately South of the basin, were fragments of painted stucco exhibiting spiraliform decoration in brilliant colours, and of a style pointing to the early part of the Late Minoan Age.

The stratification with which we are here confronted, in fact substantially repeats the cultural succession revealed by that of the Spiral Fresco basement and adjoining area. We have evidence once more of a local catastrophe that supplies a line of demarcation between an earlier and a later M. M. Ill phase. The section presented by this deposit is indeed as important for our knowledge of the vessels of stone and pottery characteristic of the earlier part of the Third Middle Minoan Period as was the area of the Spiral Fresco for the decorative wall-paintings and stucco reliefs of that epoch. The floor of the basin was covered by a stratum containing remains of clay and stone vessels of forms which, as will be shown below, must be regarded as characteristic of M. M. Ilia. Fragments of painted stucco were also found with these, presenting a dark bluish green ground with Venetian red stripes, in the sombre style distinctive of that epoch. It is to be noted as perhaps having a direct relation to ceremonial functions performed in the sunken area, that there also occurred in this stratum quantities of remains of coarsely made vessels of grey clay, a good deal smoked in the conflagration, of the type shown in Fig. 295. These may well have contained oil or unguents for some ritual purpose. Fragments of similar vessels were found in the smaller Lustral Basin of the same kind brought to light in the S. E. Quarter of the Palace (Fig. 418).

Of great beauty were the stone ewers, of which abundant fragments also occurred in this layer. These were executed in limestone, generally grey or brown, but occasionally of white, close-grained material resembling

Earlier and Later Stages of M. M. Ill represented.

Ritual Vessels of Clay and Stone from Basin.

FIG. 295. CLAY VESSEL FROM N. LUSTRAL BASIN, (f)

Stone Ewers'.

THE PALACE OF MINOS, ETC.

Inlaid Limestone Bowls.

marble. A distinguishing feature of these vessels was the plait-work decoration covering their bodies, apparently imitated from leather-work. A restored specimen from this deposit, of brown limestone, is given in Fig. 296. As in the case of the other examples the neck is in a separate piece, showing a well-marked rim above the line where it was socketed into the body. The handles were riveted on after the insertion of the mouth-piece, which they helped to fasten on. This was further secured by a rivet on the side opposite to the handle. A fragment was also found of a more precious vessel of this type, executed in liparite, the mottled volcanic glass of the Aeolian Islands. Below the ring round the neck were grooved running spirals.

With the ewers were numerous remains of brown limestone bowls with bridged spouts and two side-handles thus recalling the typical M. M. II hole-mouthed class. They presented, however, the traditional Egyptian feature of a flat collar round the rim. Their distinctive feature, however, is the decoration of the central zone of the body by means of circular borings filled with white shell inlays (see Fig. 297). 1 At the same time the zone from which 1 A fragment of what seems to be a later stone bowl of this class without the inlays and with an inscribed handle was found in a house

EWER OF BROWN LIMESTONE

RESTORED. (-J f.) 296.

of the Akropolis at Mycenae (Tsuntas, p. 214, Figs. 2, 3; Ts. and M., p. 29, Figs.

M. M. III: NORTH-WEST BAILEY AND LUSTRAL AREA 413 the handles spring, and that above the base, presents a triple series of grooves identical with those seen beneath the handle of the ewer, Fig. 296. This class of stone bowls with their characteristic inlaid decoration

FIG. 297. SPOUTED Bowi. OF BROWN LIMESTONE WITH BORINGS FOR SHEI. I.

INLAYS. ((.) a (r.) b (i,-.) t

FIG. 298. a, LIMESTONE BOWL WITH SHELL INLAYS FROM ISOPATA; b, POTTERY IMITATION, KNOSSOS; c, PART OF SIMILAR VASE, KOULOURA.

are of special importance from the fact that they were imitated in painted clay by the contemporary potters. Fragments of these occurred both in the Lustral Basin itself and in other deposits, in some cases clearly

THE PALACE OF MINOS, ETC.

White-dotted Ware.

imitated marked as belonging to the earlier M. M. Ill phase. 1 A good illustrative day"" fragment from the circular walled rubbish pit or Kouloura beneath the later West Court Pavement is given in Fig. 298, c, and beside it a sketch of the most complete vessel of this class which was found in a deposit W. of the Palace (Fig. 298, 6). 2 In these cases both the flat collar of the original and the white-dotted zone of the body, here with a black ground, are clearly reproduced. The upright set of the handles is also characteristic, and the flat, relatively broad rim is covered with a white wash. Beneath it, too, are the triple grooves. A good example of an inlaid stone vessel of this class from Isopata, near Knossos, 3 with the shell inlays well preserved, is shown beside these in Fig. 298, a.

The vessels with which the bowl, Fig. 297, was associated form valuable
FIG. 299 a. SMALL JUG WITH MOULDED BARLEY-EARS, (f)
FIG. 299 b. BARLEY SPRAY ON SIMILAR VESSEL.
links of connexion with a whole ceramic class belonging to the same earlier M. M. Ill phase. They are distinguished by their black glazed bodies sprinkled with white dots, which in this case may be a reflexion of shell inlays like those of Figs. 297, 298 a. The dark ground of most of these vases is itself an early characteristic, the M. M. Ill b pottery having generally a paler, lilac ground.

1 Pieces occurred in the M. M. Ill a stratum Pottery in Crete (J. If. S., xxi), p.88, Fig. 14. of the Room of the Stone Pier. 3 See The Tomb of the Double Axes

The bowl, Fig. 298, l, and fragments of others of the same type was found, Other together with Fig. 299 a, amidst a heap of sherds outside a house to the W. of p0 rary the Palace at Knossos, excavated in igoo. 1 Among the vessels found, the! t s t 0 j small high spouted jug, Fig. 299, is of great interest as presenting on both sides Ware, a triple spray of ears of barley moulded in high relief. Fig. 299 b shows the barley spray itself. It was accompanied by raised decoration of a kind recalling Moulded some of the old barbotine work. Though the vessel is small we may perhaps Bariey on infer that the liquor for which the vases were intended was not unconnected? i " all with John Barleycorn. The ideographs coupling cereals with certain forms ofvessels seen on tablets of the Linearclass indicate that in Late. Minoan times, at all events, some kind of beer was brewed in Crete. Its usage seems to have preceded that of wine in the island. A portion of an identical vessel was found in the lower stratum of the blind well of the Court of the Stone Spout in a deposit belonging to the earlier M. M. Ill phase.

In the same heap West of the Palace with the above occurred the two Pede-remarkable high-footed vases, Fig. 300, a, b, upon the upper part of the bodies V a S e S O f of which are seen similar white dots on the black ground. The triple handles Whlt V of these are themselves an archaic feature inherited from a large M. M. I Ware. family of the barbotine class. 2 The cable border on a recurs on a remarkable ostrich egg rhyton of contemporary fabric as a polychrome feature; it represents a decorative tradition of the Third Early Minoan Age. On some associated remains of similar vases the raised ring at the base of the neck was painted red. In these cases both handles and neck are painted a creamy white, like the rim of the vase. Fig. 298, c, above.

Both this creamy white wash and the pedestalled character of these vessels Poly-bring them into a very close relation with a typical class of M. M. Ill vessels jj 6 with two upright handles, of which a specimen 4 is given in Fig. 301. Like tion of the above, this vessel also shows clear traces of a surviving polychrome Alabas-tradition, the body being covered with a maroon slip, while round the neck are zigzagging red lines. But the shape of the vase is of special interest in the present connexion from the evidence that it supplies of the presence 1 Hogarth, op. tit., p. 80 seqq. and Figs. 7, 8, L. Pernier, Mon. Ant. xii, p. 107, Fig. 39.

9. Here was also found a jug with a double axe This specimen is from the Palace at Phaestos.

in white, suspended on the dark ground (p. 86, The edge of a flat lid is visible. Others were

Fig. 10). found at H. Triada and fragmentary re- 3 Examples from the exterior cells of the mains at Knossos. The type seems to have

Early Tholos Ossuary of Hagia Triada are given persisted to the close of M. M. Ill, but in Fig. 129, p. i8r, above. the later examples show less trace of poly- 3 See below, p. 594 and Fig. 436 f. chromy.

THE PALACE OF MINOS, ETC.

of Egyptian alabaster models, of which a very important original is represented by the lid of Khyan to be presently described.

Except for the two upright handles a regular Minoan adjunct to

FIG. 300, a, b. M. M. Ilia, WHITK-DOTTED VASES (i f.).

borrowed Egyptian types the form is in fact obviously evolved from a well-known Middle Kingdom type of alabastron with a pointed end below socketed into a separate stand, often of clay (see Fig. 302). Like Egyptian alabastra, moreover, it was provided with a flat lid. In the Cretan version

M. M. III: NORTH-WEST BAILEY AND LUSTRAL AREA 417 the two component parts have grown together, but the once separate upper rim of the stand is still sharply profiled. It is interesting to note, moreover, that the same coalescence took place in a handleless Egyptian type from Buhen (Fig. 302 6). It had been covered with a pinkish slip.

FIG. 301. PEDESTALLED POLY-

FIG. 302 a. EGYPTIAN ALABASTER

FIG. 302 b. EGYPTIAN

CHROME VASE IMITATED FROM VASE AND BURNISHED CLAY STAND.

Cl. AY VASE (Buhetl, Pl. 48,

EGYPTIAN ALABASTRON."

TWELFTH DYNASTY.

s. xliii).

No specimens of vessels belonging to the white-dotted class White-described above seem to have occurred among the rich deposits of pottery pottery brought to light at Knossos in the Magazines and floor-cists belonging M. M. to the close of the present Period. There is good reason, therefore, for referring them to a somewhat earlier phase.

But this conclusion is of special interest in view of a further discovery which stands in inseparable connexion with the actual contents of the

THE PALACE OF MINOS, ETC.

D; s- Lustral Basin. On the upper level, about six metres West of its border on that side, a stratum containing a mass of carbonized wood and other remains, identical with those within the basin, was found to extend beneath the foundations of a rubble wall of a later chamber, and under an earth deposit about same Deposit of Ala-bastron Lid of Hyksos King, Khyan.

LEVEL OF TOP OF UPPER TERRACE WALL

CLAY PAVEMENT

EARTH I-IJ DEPOSITa

STRATUM CONTAINING CHARCOAL, LID OF ALABASTPON HYKSOS KINO KHYAN AND FRAGMENTS OF STONE VASE. S AND POTTERY 303.

SECTION SHOWING STRATUM CONTAINING ALABASTRON LID OF KHYAN BENEATH LATER WALL AND FLOOR.

a foot thick that underlay its clay and plaster floor (see Section, Fig. 30i5). The chamber itself showed the lower part of a painted stucco dado with horizontal blue and yellow bands, attached to the West face of its rubble wall. In the stratum referred to, immediately beneath the wall foundation, and in company with fragments of stone ewers with plait-work decoration like those described, inlaid pots, and similar sherds, was found an Egyptian alabastron lid inscribed with the cartouche of the Hyksos Pharaoh Khyan (Fig. 304 6). The lid evidently belonged to a vessel of the traditional

FIG. 304 a. TRADITIONAL MIDDLE KINGDOM TYPE OF AI. ARASTRON.

FIG. 304 b. ALABASTRON LID INSCRIBED WITH NAME AND TITLES OF HYKSOS KING, KHVAN (-J f.)

Middle Kingdom form shown with its lid in Fig. 304). The method by which the lids of these alabaster vessels were tied down and sealed is well illustrated by contemporary paintings of the tombs at Beni Hasan. 3 The inset shows one of these with the tie above the lid secured by a clay seal impression. The lid of the Egyptianizing Cretan vase, Fig. 301, was doubtless fastened in a similar way.

The cartouche on the alabastron lid from Knossos reads: Nlr nfr s.

1 Knossos, Report, 1901, p. 63 seqq. For the section of the wall, c., and underlying deposit, see p. 64, Fig. 20.

For Sixth Dynasty versions of the same type in alabaster and diorite and a Cretan imitation of one in the latter material, see above, p. 92, Figs. 60, 61.

3 Newberry, Scarabs, p. 16, Fig. 5 (lower-part restored).

THE PALACE OF MINOS, ETC.

Place of Khyan in Hyksos Series.

Pha- raonized

Dynast:

Reunites

Upper

Lower

Egypt.

Predecessor of Apepis.

Approximate Date.

Wide Range of Khyan's Monuments.

wsr-n-R s R Hyn The good God, Suserenra, son of the Sun, Khyan V

No discovery made in the whole course of the excavations at Knossos can rival in historic interest the finding of this record of the king who seems first to have united the whole of Egypt under the Hyksos dynastic sceptre. The appearance of this relic in the Minoan Palace is itself highly symptomatic of a renewal of the relations with the Nile Valley broken off by the process of internal disruption that had set in in Egypt during the Thirteenth Dynasty. 2

Thanks largely to the recent researches of Monsieur R. Weill 3 and to the evidence of scarabs, the place of Khyan in the Hyksos series is now fairly ascertained. The Hyksos invaders, unquestionably of Semitic stock, appear first, under the later Sebekhoteps of Egypt, as small Princes in the Delta region. Among these, Jakeb and Jakebher (or Jakeb-el) show an unmistakable affinity with the Tribe of Jacob. Khyan (whose name already appears among the later Sheikhs of this class) may have taken over the legitimist Egyptian claims of some native dynast of Tanis and reduced the whole country, including the Thebaid, to his sway, with the full Pharaonic titles. He was thus the predecessor of the Hyksos kings belonging to the Tanite Dynasty of the name of Apepi, one of whom survives under the form Apophis in the tale preserved in Manetho. He is there represented as the suzerain of the native dynast Skenen-ra, who appears, after an interval, at Thebes, and whose revolt heralds the final liberation under Kames and Aahmes and the advent of the Eighteenth Dynasty about 1580 is. c. Weill 5 places the disappearance of the last Sebekhotep from Thebes and the accession of Khyan about 1633 B- c-, ai "d if, as would seem to be a reasonable hypothesis, we may take the appearance of this inscribed alabastron among the Royal treasures of Knossos as a sign of official intercourse, its deposit may well have dated from shortly after the middle of the seventeenth century B. c. It is to be observed that the lid itself was in absolutely fresh condition.

The finished execution of the alabastron lid itself and the fine engraving of the inscription are remarkable. It is indeed evident that the Hyksos king who restored Egyptian unity, as well as his successors, had the command 1 F. LI. Griffith, Archaeological Report of the (Ib., 1915, Juillet-Aoilt); Complements (Il.,

Egyptian Exploration fund, 1900-1,9.37. 1917, Janvier-Fdvrier); Livre des Rois (Ib.,

See above, p. 300. I 9 r 7) Mars-Avril).

3 Monuments et Histoire de la Periode com- Cf. Weill, op. fit., Rec. des Memoires, T. iv, prise enre la fin de la xii e Dynastic et la 1914, p. 107.

Restauration thebaine (Joitrn. Asiatique: Re- 6 Op. cit., T. vi, 1915, p. 47. des Memoires, 1914); Synthese historique of the best that Egypt had to give in the way of Art. They built temples and erected monuments in the old style, and it cannot be doubted that their wide dominion was accompanied by a commercial revival.

The extent of Khyan's dominion in the Nile Valley is marked by the black granite block at Gebelen, South of Thebes, and by the base of his inscribed statue at Bubastis in the Delta. 1 Another monument of his, a lion weight of black basalt, found its way as far as Bagdad. 2 The Ka name of Khyan anq adebu embracing territories' and his further title ruler of foreign Peoples illustrate his imperial claims. In the latter title Hq-Iis-wt also borne by another Hyksos prince a plausible derivation for the wordtfo-wi itself has been found. 3

The position with regard to the Third Middle Minoan Period, now Approxi-better ascertained, in which this relic occurred, fits in very well with a date Date for not much later than the middle of the seventeenth century B. c. for the time, l0 01 of its deposit. It corresponds, as we have seen, with the mature stage lll. of the earlier phase, a, of the culture of that Period. On the other hand, the catastrophe to which the Period owed its close and to which was due at Knossos such a wholesale covering in of M. M. Ill remains belonging to its later phase, b, immediately preceded the earliest Late Minoan stage which runs parallel with the beginning of the New Empire in Egypt from about 1580 B. C., that is, onwards.

The intermediate chronological place with which the alabastron lid J!?. is thus associated by the archaeological evidence makes still less probable denceof the conjecture that it should be taken as actual evidence that Khyan's 1 dominions had included Minoan Crete. 4 It should rather be interpreted as Bourse a symptom of the renewal of peaceful intercourse between the Nile Valley than and Crete, for some time interrupted by the break-up of Egyptian unity and the interposition of hostile elements in the Delta. But although it cannot be taken as evidence of Hyksos sovereignty in the island, it may well be regarded as a token of personal relations between Khyan and the Minoan priest-kings. It is by no means improbable indeed that already at this time Cretan envoys to the Hyksos Court may have borne gifts interpreted as tribute similar to those borne by the Keftians and their fellows to the officers of Thothmes III. They may have taken back, too, royal presents such as this alabaster box of ointment of spikenard very precious and 1 Naville, Bubastis Pl. XII. 4 This is E. Meyer's view (Geschichte des

Now in the British Museum. Aliertums, second edition, p. 716): Es ist . Max Miiller; cf. Griffith, Archaeological sehr moglich, dass das ephemere Veltreich der Report, c., 1900-1, p. 37. Hyksos auch Kreta umfasst hat.

THE PALACE OF MINOS, ETC.

Use of Alabastra in connexion with Lustral Basins.

FORE-HALL OF INITIATORY AREA worthy of the highest Pontifical functions, to the Minoan Palace, where it found its place in the repository connected with the Lustral Basin.

An interesting parallel to this is indeed to be found in connexion with the similar lustral basin attached to the Room of the Throne constructed in the last Palace period (L. M. II) and compared above with the Hall of Initiation of Men Askaenos. 1 There upon the pavement, near the steps leading clown to the basin, were found three Late Minoan alabastra, and beside them an over-set oil-jar, evidently used for their filling, just as it was left in the moment of catastrophe. There is every reason to believe that these vessels served for some ceremony of anointing, probably the completing touch of a purificatory function.

The Lustralbasinand surrounding Initiatory Area formed, as has been already observed, a Temenos within the North Western Bailey which juts forward in front of the main Palace wall-line on this side.

RTH-WEST
MOSAIKO"
PAVING
FIG. 305. PLAN OF NORTH-WEST PORTICO.

Access to it, as shown above (see Plan, Fig. 291), was gained through the covered area of the North- West Portico, itself approached by a ramp or stepway, in connexion with a road-line from the West. This Portico, 2 of which the Plan is here repeated in Fig. 305, 3 is distinguished by its bi-columnar opening on a small light-area on its E. side, one of the column bases of which, of fine grey and white veined limestone, is the best example existing in situ of the high Middle Minoan class. 4 Considerable remains also exist both in the covered and open part of this area of the fine mosaiko pavement characteristic of M. M. II. That in its original form this Portico belonged to the Early Palace there can be little doubt. Its light-area was flanked by what seems to have been a Guard-Room and its inner section faced a double doorway giving entrance to an open passage-way leading up by a somewhat tortuous route to the Central Court.

See pp. 4, 5, and Fig. 1. See p. 216, Fig. 161.

See too, p. 217, Fig. 162. See above, p. 370.

Approach to Central Court from N. W. used by Votaries; Miniature Frescoes from Upper Samtitary on this side; W. Porch Royal or Official entrance; Porch and Corridor in existing shape Late Minoan; W. Palace Section Tripartite division; Sanctuary and Treasure-house; Pillar Rooms Crypts of Columnar Sanctuaries; Significance of Double Axe Marks; Evidence supplied by S. E. House of M. M. Ill date; Us Pillar Room and ritual table; Double Axe sign on pillar and pyramidal base of Axe; Vessels of offering and Sacra Knot of ivory; Sacra! Knots in Minoan cult; Minoan Tartan; Early Cave in corner of Pillar Crypt; Pillar with Double Axe sign in Palace of Malta; Discovery of Sanctuary of Niru Khani colossal Double Axe heads; Bases of Double Axes in Knossian Palace; Ritual from Sarcophagus of H. Triada; Evocation of the Dead; Tomb of Double Axes at Knossos; Columnar sancttiary above Pillar Room at Knossos; Bases of fallen Columns; Fragments of architectural frescoes found beneath later Cists; Facade of Columnar Sanctuary of Double Axes; Axes inserted in Columns; Comparison from Mycenae; Use of Variegated materials; Frescoes from Shrine above; Double Axe central feature in cult of Minoan Goddess; The Palace regarded as House of the Double Axes.

REASONS have been given for regarding the Lustral Basin of the Approach XT-ITI- i-i-r. f., tocentral

N. W. Bailey as belonging to a purificatory station for votaries entering the court

Palace Sanctuary. From the N. W. Portico, with its double doorway that gave entrance, as already noted, to the interior Quarter of the building on used by this side, a ramp winding round the N. W. angle of the Early Keep seems to have skirted the area originally occupied by this and have thence led up towards the N. W. Corner of the Central Court.

It is clear that the insula denned by the course of this gangway on Minia-one side and the Northern Entrance Passage on the other had shared co s'froni the specially religious character of the Western Palace region. Of the bril- Upp r liant decoration of its upper chambers a record has been preserved in the tuary on heaps of painted stucco fragments found beneath the floor of the modern 1 Its course is conjecturally given in the diagrammatic Plan, Fig. 152, facing p. 203 above.

Threshing Floor that overlay the remains of the N. W. Porch. 1 Most of these fragments seem to have been thrown out at the time of the great remodelling of this part of the building in the last Palace epoch, and some at least of the fragments may go back within the limits of the present Period. The more complete remains of the Miniature Frescoes and the Spiral Ceiling found on the basement floors themselves point to the conclusion that at the opening of the Late Minoan Age there had existed highly decorated sanctuary chambers at the angle between this end of the Central

Court and the West border of the N. Entrance Passage. But these remains seem to be better grouped with the earliest L. M. I elements of the Palace.

w. Porch, The N. W. Portico and adjoining purificatory area may well be regarded Official as tne natural avenues of approach for pilgrims and devotees visiting the Entrance, religious centres of the building. On the other hand, the Western Porch and Corridor, if we may judge by their later associations, present every appearance of having been the chosen avenues of royal and official approach.

w. Porch This porch, as already shown, represents an amplified version of an rifo m' on g ma l pl an characteristic of the earlier part of the Middle Minoan Age, existing and of which good examples exist at Phaestos. 2 Its fundamental lines possibly ijte 6 belong to the present Period, but the existing external remains such as the wall Mmoan. decoration and pavement are clearly Late Minoan.: i The same is true of the

Corridor on which it opens, and beneath the pavement of which characteristic M. M. 1116 sherds occurred. Much of this fine entrance system on the West, including the Propylaeum to which it led above the Southern Terrace and the stepped approach beyond, seems, in its original shape, to have gone back to this and, in part at least, to a still earlier epoch. The details, however, that have been preserved, such as the remains of the stately

Procession Fresco, mostly fit on to the later architectural history of the Palace, and are best dealt with in that connexion.

w. Palace is clear indeed that a good deal of the basement plan of the West Section: Section of the Palace goes back to its earliest stage. With some superficial tripartite!

division, remodelling indeed it survived to its latest days, except where, as in the Throne Room region, it was displaced by entirely new constructions. The existing remains in this region rest for the most part on the tabula rasa of Neolithic clay left by the levelling away of the original hill top, though here and there were pockets in this, like the Vat Room Deposit, illustrating the incipient phase of M. M. I and which may have belonged to a still earlier Palace Sanctuary. Exclusive of the Magazines, which form a separate zone, 1 Knossos, Report, 1900, p. 46. The main 2 See above, p. 214, Figs. 159, 160. heap lay above the east line of the porch. 3 See Vol. II.

this Western Palace Section, as will be seen in the Plan Fig. 152 above, presents a curiously symmetrical, tripartite arrangement. This consists of a middle block containing the two Pillar Rooms and their surroundings, and two others of almost exactly equal dimensions which may be distinguished respectively as the West Central insula North, later occupied by the Throne Room system, and the West Central insulasouth.

Together with the Magazines themselves, this region maintained to the last a double character. On the one hand it was the scene of the principal Sane Palace Sanctuary, of which the Pillar Crypts continued in use throughout. On the other hand it was the chief repository of the treasures of its Priest- house Kings, whether in the shape of precious metals or of the oil contained in the huge store-jars of its Magazines.

Among the remains, moreover, of this Western Palace region we are able to detect certain characteristic elements which are specially connected with the present Period.

These include both religious features of the building and the methods employed for the storage of its precious contents.

It is clear that the massive gypsum pillars of the two small chambers in the centre of this region (see Suppl. Pl. X) belong to the original Palace structure. The deeply incised double-axe signs on their blocks are themselves characteristic of the earlier class.

The view, set forth in my Report of 1900 dealing with the first discovery of these pillars, that the double-axe signs, repeated twenty-nine times on their blocks, had a direct religious significance, 1 has since received ample corroboration. A series of discoveries of similar Pillar Crypts was Crypts of made in the adjacent houses and Little Palace at Knossos, in which they sanc-were actually associated with ritual objects, some of them specifically l concerned with the Minoan cult of the Double Axe symbol. One of these Pillar Rooms in the South-East House is of special importance in the present connexion, since that house presents certain early characteristics not traceable Evidence in any other building of the area surrounding the Palace. Chief among up g d these are the somewhat high column bases of polychrome materials visible House.

1 See Knossos, Report, 1900, p. 32 seqq. and in a similar way on three sides of every block.

Fig. 6. Each pillar consisted of four blocks Of the general consecrating character of the with dowel holes for beams on the upper sur- double-axe signs in the sanctuary regions of face of the topmost blocks. Their height was the Palace and on exterior features of the 1-75 1-78111. On the West Pillar the double building see p. 134 above. In a larger sense a c is repeated on every side of every block, the Palace itself was the House of the Double imd on the upper face of the topmost block Axe, in all 17 times. The E. pillar is marked

THE PALACE OF MINOS, ETC.

its in the little Court in front of its Megaron, and which clearly represent the fa m earlier M. M. Ill phase. 1 The remains of wall-paintings found in this house, such as the olive sprays and the beautiful lily group and spikes of

FIG. 306. PLAN OF SOUTH-EAST HOUSE. F i. EARLY PERISTYLE WITH COLUMN BASES OF POLYCHROME MATERIALS: H i. APPARENTLY EAR-LIER LIGHT-WELL WITH FINE ASHLAR MASONRY, LATER ROOFED OVER: K i. SMALL MEGARON (f, f, f, RAISED DAIS): L i. INNER ROOM USED AS SHRINE IN REOCCUPATION PERIOD (g, SACRAL HORNS L. M III): A i. PAS-SAGE (1,1, LILY AND OLIVE FRESCOES): C i. PILLAR ROOM (a, PILLAR: b, b, STANDS FOR RITUAL VESSELS: A, SACRAL KNOT OF IVORY: k, COLUM-NAR LAMP): D i. MAGAZINE OPENING OFF CRYPT (d, PLASTER STAND.) reeds illustrated below, 2 rank among the finest specimens of naturalistic plant designs found on the site of Knossos, and may also be placed within the limits of the present Period.

1 The curiously splayed door-jambs W. of 2 See below, p. 537, Fig. 390, and Coloured the Court are also noteworthy. Plate VI.

A plan of the South-East House is given in Fig. 30(5 showing its three-columned Court on the left and the Pillar chamber on the right, backed by two flights of stairs. 1 A view of this Pillar Crypt is shown in Fig. 307, including Pillar part of the outer house-wall on this side, which exhibits the interesting struc- Q E. tural feature of a somewhat projecting lower course of limestone blocks House-surmounted by three of gypsum, succeeded in turn by two limestone courses. On a block of the limestone plinth is seen a curious stand of painted plaster with six feet and a raised square enclosing an oval aperture with a collar like that surrounding the cups of contemporary libation tables. Its coloured Ritual decoration deep red with zones of creamy white rosettes suggests a very Table near relation to the miniature Sanctuary found in the Loom-Weight Area, and it seems to have been a ritual table belonging to the earliest furniture of the Crypt, in the ante-room of which it came to light.

The pillar, of six blocks 2 resting on a larger slab below, derives Double a special interest from the fact that a double axe sign is finely engraved on an upper block. In this case, moreover, the base of the cult object itself was and pyra in position in the shape of a truncated pyramidal block of gypsum set close base of to the foot of the pillar on its North side. This pyramidal block showed Axe-a socket above, and it is now clear from many other analogies that it formed the actual base of the sacred Double Axe. Such bases, as a rule, show distinct steps, as in the case of the fine example from the Western region of the Palace itself given below in Fig. 314. A small stepped base of steatite was found together with the actual blades of Double Axes, of corresponding dimensions, in the votive deposit of the Psychro Cave, 3 and the fragment of another occurred in company with the magnificent bull's head rhyton in the shrine in the Little Palace at Knossos. 4 In the well-known design of the Sarcophagus of Hagia Triada, where the actual pouring of libations before the sacred symbols is depicted, the Double Axes, of which a pair is there shown, rise from bases with a double gradation and painted according to the usual Late Minoan convention for representing the polychrome veins of some decorative stone. 6 The socketed base by the pillar in the South-East House had been doubtless originally coated with painted plaster displaying some similar imitation of the grain of variegated stone.

1 I have given a full description of this See below, p. 438, Fig. 315.

house in Kiossos. Report, 1903, p. 4 seqq. 4 See Vol. II. Another stepped base found

The Room marked i,, had been converted into at Palaikastro was rightly recognized by Pro- a shrineinthereoccupationperiod(L. M. Ill;). fessor Bosanquet as having served a similar 2 The five upper blocks are of limestone, function (B. S. A., viii, p. 300). the sixth is of gypsum, and the base block, 5 See below, p. 440, Fig. 317. again, limestone.

From the foot of the pillar here a rough foundation runs to the North wall of the room. Along this wall were ranged a series of flat stone bases, circular and oblong, that had served as stands for vessels, doubtless containing food and drink offerings. Remains of the pottery itself were found showing a dark ground, and of a typically M. M. Ill character. In the South wall was a niche or loculus.

This Pillar Crypt was associated with a curious natural phenomenon. Early Cave in A block at its South-West corner was found to close an aperture leading corner of into what seems to have been a natural swallow hole, 1 which lower down, apparently in the Neolithic Age, had been enlarged into a small artificial cave cut out of the soft rock. It was largely filled with earth, which seems to have filtered into it by aqueous action, and in which some Neolithic and Late Minoan sherds occurred. There was no sign of any cult usage during the period to which the South-East House belonged, but it is conceivable that its existence had given some special sanctity to the spot where the Pillar Room was built. Except for such half light as may have penetrated through the doorway, leading to an entrance lobby, this Pillar Crypt (as seems to have been usual in such constructions) was entirely dark.-

Very interesting evidence as to its artificial means of illumination was Columnar supplied by the discovery of the shaft and part of the basin of a beautifully Lamp. sculptured lamp of purple gypsum. 3 This magnificent object, which must be taken to represent the model of an architectural original, has already been described in connexion with the (lutings visible on the carbonized columns found in the Domestic Quarter. 4 The spirally arranged decoration of its shaft derived from the sacred waz or papyrus sceptre of the Egyptian Delta Goddess may, as in other similar cases, have still possessed a sacral significance in its Minoan shape. It is shown above that the waz decoration, in the particular form in which it appears on this pedestal, recurs on a bronze cup of Vapheio type from a M. M. Ill interment, a valuable indication of date. 5

Near the exterior of the North Wall, apparently fallen from the columnar 1 Two other swallow holes ending in small s The upper part of this lamp had in some natural caves were found lower down the East mysterious manner found its way to the neigh- Slope, in each case with a built drain running bouring village, where it was recognied by one into them. That of the S. E. House was not of our workmen.

utilized in this way. 4 See above, p. 344 and Fig. 24! t.

2 The suggestion made in the original See loc. cit. and Seager, Mocklos, p. 62, Report that there was a window in the North and Fig. 31.

Wall does not seem to have been warranted.

THE PALACE OF MINOS, ETC.

Sacral Knot of Ivory.

Minoan Tartan chamber of a sanctuary character, such as in all cases seems to have been superposed on the pillar crypts, lay an ivory object, the associations of which throw a further interesting light on the cult with which we are concerned.

This was in the form of a kind of knot with a loop above and two fringed ends hanging down below (Fig. 308). It shows a diaper pattern, and looks as if it were copied from some kind of scarf. It is interesting to note that objects of similar form in faience, which there is good reason to believe belong to the Palace fabric of Knossos, were found in the Fourth Shaft Grave, the early elements of which belong to the Third Middle Minoan Period. Three pairs of such Sacral Knots' were here brought to light, each of them divided into two pieces, namely, the looped knot and the fringed ends (Fig. 309). All the pieces had perforations that had been used for nails, doubtless to fasten them to a woodwork frame (see Fig. 309,), and theyseemto have been connected with the Draught-board found in the same grave, probably as an indication of its sacral character. 1 The loop of the knot was in these cases bent forward, as shown from above in Fig. 309, d. The ground colouris a greenish brown, decorated, as in the case of the ivory example, with cross lines in a lighter tone. A noteworthy feature of the fringe is the knotting together of its threads into tassels with what in the original may have been gold wire. Altogether these KNOT are remarkable reproductions of textile material. HOUSE, (f).

The check pattern of these knots here set diagonally is itself very characteristic of primitive loom work. It is, indeed, a true tartan design, the double or quadruple lines, in a lighter tone here enclosing dark green squares being suggestive of that of the Grahams or Macalpines. Otherwise the whole might be taken as a model of a fashionable scarf.

The significance of these knots generally seen in pairs in their con- 1 The photographs from which Fig. 309 shows three indented lines like those on the was taken were kindly sent me by Dr. Karo, back of the faience medallions of the board FIG. 308. SACRAL for whom they were executed with Dr. Staes' permission. Dr. Karo offers the suggestion that they were connected with the faience draught-board found in this Grave (see below, p. 482), and the fact that the loop of which the back is shown in Fig. 347, p. 484 below, corroborates this view. Dr. Staes Collection Mycenienne, and ed., p. 58) has suggested that the knots formed part of the inlays of a wooden coffin. Schliemann, Mycenae, p. 252, Fig. 235, illustrates one of the knots, but describes it as Alabaster.

nexion with Minoan ritual usage is illustrated by a series of examples on signets and seal impressions. 1

On a gold signet ring from a tomb of the Lower Town of Mycenae Sacral a pair of these objects are seen suspended from the entablature on either side of the capital of a Sacred Column, to which are chained two lion guardians (Fig. 310, b). On a clay impression of a seal-stone of amygdaloid form found in a M. M. Ill stratum in the Court of the Stone Spout at Knossos, a similar figure hangs on either side of a palm-tree, evidently as an indication of its FIG. 309 a, , c. SACRAL KNOTS IN FAIENCE FROM FOURTH SHAFT GRAVE, MYCENAE.

d. LOOP OF ONE CURVING FORWARDS. (c.).

sanctity. On another Minoan signet-ring 2 (Fig. 310, a) two well-defined knots of the same fringed kind recur again, in front of a charging bull. It depicts an episode of the favourite Minoan sport, and the cowboy who had endeavoured to seize the bull's horns has here been badly thrown. From the appearance of a rock border round the field above, the scene is evidently laid in some natural glen, but the Sacral Knots here certainly indicate that the sport was as much under the patronage of the Minoan Goddess as the acrobatic feats of a similar nature that in other cases were carried out in arenas actually overlooked by her shrine.

1 See my Mycenaean Tree and Pillar Cult, p. 61, Fig. 39, and p. 62.

"Acquired at Smyrna, but probably brought from Crete by one of the numerous Moslem emigrants after 1898. The core of the ring is of bronze originally, no doubt covered by gold plating, since replaced by gilding. This signet-ring is in my own Collection.

THE PALACE OF MINOS, ETC.

The religious significance of this knot in connexion with Minoan cult is further brought out by the signet type shown in Fig. 310, c. The central theme of this design is a scene of divine communion, where a female figure, probably a votary, partakes of the fruit of a sacred tree, which inspires her with ecstatic frenzy. To the right is a Minoan shield itself, like

FIG. 310. MINOAN SIGNET RINGS SHOWING PAIRS OF SACRAL KNOTS, (f). a. SMYRNA (PROBABLY FROM CRETE), b, c. MYCENAE, d. PALAIKAS-TRO. e. GOURNIA (Pl. IX. 12).

the Ancilia, a medium of religious possession with an object attached to it in which we must certainly recognize a version of the sacral knot. The loop is clearly seen above, and a part of the fringe of the second end of the scarf is traceable in front of the lower part of the shield. 1 1 In my Mycenean Tree and Pillar Cult (p. 78 seqq.) I had at first taken the object for a rudely executed design of a small female figure. Otherwise the object had been identi- fied as an insect (Tsuntas, E. Ap, 1890, p. 170) and as a helmet with a high crest (Max Meyer, Jahrbuch d. Arch. List., 1892, p. 189).

A remarkable comparison supplied by a small ivory relief from Palai-kastro, Fig. 310, d? shows that the little figure in the field above must be taken to represent the sacred Double Axe in a combination similar to that of the shield. The usual pair of knots here coalesce, with a single, plaited loop above, and three fringed appendages below, that in the middle longer than the others. The Knot itself may be supposed in this case to be inside the socket of the axe, the ritual adjunct being here substituted for the shaft. This symbolic arrangement became the prototype for a decorative device of the later L. M. I ceramic style (Fig. 310,).

It further appears that Sacral such sacral knots were worthy actually worn by Minoan Votar v-votaries. Near the North-West Palace angle, together with an architectural frieze and other fragments apparently belonging to a small Pillar Shrine of the last epoch of the building, were found remainsof fresco panels depicting figures of votaries of both sexes seated on camp-stools, and in some cases holding goblets of precious metals. One of these, a girl, distinguished by her large eye and cherry lips, is wearing what is shown from other analogies to be a short-sleeved garment. Behind her neck is seen a loop, which at first was regarded as a part of the robe itself, bunched up behind (Fig. 311). 2 There can be no reasonable doubt, however, in view of the above examples, that this is in fact a Sacral

FIG. 311. BUST OF FEMALE VOTARY WEARING SACRAL KNOT ON HER SHOULDER.

1 Mentioned in B. S. A., xi, p. 284, as having been found in Room 10 of House, p. 182, Fig. 3, with a large bronze double axe. The plaque (probably of M. M. 111 date) had been cut down and re-used in L. M. I. Prof. Dawkins (Joe. fit.) noted the resemblance to the symbol on the Mycenae ring. The relief is here reproduced through his kindness from a drawing in possession of the British School.- Knossos, Report, 1901, p. 56 (see Knossian Atlas, I).

THE PALACE OF MINOS, ETC.

Egyptian Parallels.

Analogous flounced Object of Minoan Cult.

Connected with Double Axe Cult

Knot, and we may further infer that one, or more probably a pair, of these was fastened to the collar of her dress as some kind of ceremonial badge. 1

On the magical virtues connected with knots in primitive belief, it is not necessary here to enlarge. The nodus Herculeus affords a good classical example. But the attachment of the Minoan knots to sacred trees and pillars, of which illustrations have been given above, suggests a near parallel to the association of an Egyptian Ankh or Girdle-tie with the (el or tree-pillar of I sis. 1 A still nearer Egyptian parallel, however, is presented by the aper, consisting of looped pendants worn behind the shoulders. 2

The ivory knot from the South-East House may possibly have formed part of the inlaid decoration of a chest deposited in the upper columnar sanctuary, which we know from other evidence to have existed above the pillar crypts. It seems, moreover, highly probable that in this and other cases looped knots, in some textile material were hung on either side of the sacred column of this upper shrine, from the roof beam that it supported as depicted on the Mycenae signet, Fig. 310, 6, above.

The relation of the Sacral Knots to the central Palace cult is paralleled by a closely analogous object of which a remarkable illustration also presented itself on the site. In a M. M. Ill stratum in the Court of the Stone Spout was found a steatite intaglio, Fig. 312, a, in a rough contemporary style, on which the Goddess is seen holding her Double Axe on one arm and with the other a peculiar object with a double flounce below and reticulated above, which it seems necessary to regard as some article of ritual apparel. On a Zakro sealing, 3 again, of contemporary date, where two male figures occur in the typical bagged garment then in vogue, that to the left is seen adoring the Double Axe, while the votary in front of him carries a similar flounced object on his shoulder. So too, on an onyx lentoid from the site of the Argive Heraion (Fig. 312, r), 4 belonging to the early part of the Late Minoan Age, this object 5 recurs on either side of a bull's head, above which the Double Axe appears in a reversed position. It is clear that in these cases we have to do with a larger article than the

A similar object appears by itself on another 1 Professor Newberry kindly called my attention to this parallel. As the trunk of the tree had concealed the coffin of Osiris, it had a special funereal significance, and the (el and knot appear together on the panels of wooden sarcophagi.

2 M. A. Murray, Ancient Egypt, 1921, Pt. II, pp. 36, 37.

3 Hogarth, J. H. S., xxii, PI. VI, 6.

4 Furtwangler, Antike Gemmcn, PI. II, 42 (cf. Schliemann, Mycenae, p. 362, Fig. 541).

gem from this site (V. Vollgraf, Bull, de Corr. Hell., 1904, pp. 388, 389 and Fig. 32): it was there conjecturally regarded as a young palm and placed upside down.

5 A curious detail is perceptible in the figure as it appears on this gem. The band above the flounces, which borders the lower part of the baggy part above, shows a decorative chain-work often found in Minoan jewellery.

Sacral Knot, possibly the skirt of some ceremonial robe. That it was intimately connected with the worship of the Double Axe may be inferred from all these representations.

Of the dedication of articles of apparel we have direct evidence in the Suspcn-votive robes for suspension found among the faience relics of the Temple votive Repositories of Knossos. 2 To attach a part of the dress round the baetylic (iar- i 11 i i c i -. merits.

object or actually to tie it round it is a regular part 01 the rite of sleeping in, or incubation, in sanctuaries. I have had a personal experience of this practice in a primitive pillar shrine, 3 such as are to this day connected with Saints' Graves throughout the Islamic World.

It will be seen that the remains of the South-East House supplement

Cult.

(!) MS)!)

Fit;. 312. a, STEATITE LENTOID, KNOSSOS (M. M. Ill); b, CLAY SEALING, ZAKRO; c, ONYX LENTOID, ARGOS.

in more than one respect our knowledge of the Central Palace cult as it s. E. existed in the closing Middle Minoan phase. The tradition of its specially relation religious character seems to have clung to it indeed in later days. When, J 61 towards the close of the Minoan Age, a part of the house, like some of the Palace adjoining Palace region, was re-occupied by poorer denizens, the inner room, L. i, on the Plan, Fig. 306, was converted into a shrine, where, at a somewhat higher level, horns of Consecration were found resting on a pebble flooring. To the original importance of the building from the religious point of view the artistic skill lavished on the decoration and the presence of such a magnificent accessory of cult as the sculptured lamp bear sufficient witness. It seems probable that it was occupied by some priestly functionary.

1 An analogy is suggested by the cuirass', See below, p. 506, Fig. 364. with its reticulated body and pleated flounce, Mycenaean Tree and Pillar Cuf, p. lozseqq.

At Tekekioi in North Macedonia. It was necessary to tie an under-garment round the holy pillar and to lie down for the night within sight of it.

worn by the rustic leader of the harvesters on the H. Triada rhyton (Savignoni, Man. Ant., xiii. Pl. Ill, and cf. sealing, p. 42, Fig. 9).

THE PALACE OF MINOS, ETC.

The engraving of the Sacred Double Axe on a block of the pillar here, in addition to placing its actual base before it, has now received a new and striking illustration.

In the Middle Minoan Palace, lately discovered by Dr. Hatzidakis at Malia, some 20 miles East of Candia on the same Northern Coast, an M c a e i ia analogous Pillar Crypt was brought to light with a pillar of the exceptional

Pillar Crypt of Early Palace

FIG. 313. HUGE RITUAL DOUBLE AXE FROM SANCTUARY OF NIROU KHANI,

NEAR KNOSSOS, 1-20 METRE IN D1AM.

dimensions of a metre on every side. Here, too, on one of the blocks, was a Double Axe symbol, in this case deeply incised. 1 In face of such striking analogies there can no longer be any hesitation in accepting the view that the Double Axe signs on the pillars- of the two basement chambers of the Palace have a direct relation to that form of Minoan cult of which, at a later date, the scene on the Sarcophagus of Hagia Triada affords such a graphic illustration.

had not been excavated.

2 The object in these cases seems to have been the consecration of the material. The incised signs themselves were doubtless often covered with plaster. But the question of their actual visibility does not affect the religious intention.

Eft)fj. fpi;, Oct. "5, 1919. Dr.

Hatzidakis has kindly supplied me with a photograph of the pillar, of which two layers of massive blocks are preserved. The Double Axe sign is on one of the lower of these, and in the sharp character of its incision resembles that of the Knossian pillars. The room itself

Of the importance of the Double Axe cult in the neighbourhood of Knossos new and very important evidence has been recently brought out by the Ephor, Dr. Stephanos Xanthudides in the course of his excavation of a large

Minoan building at a spot called Nirou Khani, 1 a little East of the promontory of Kakon Oros that dominates the old harbour town of Knossos on that side. The building itself, which occupies about i,000 square metres and contains some forty rooms, seems from the character of the pottery found within it to date from the beginning of the Ltite Minoan Age. 2 Its principal chamber was entirely devoted to cult purposes. It contained a number of tripods faced with painted plaster like the usual Minoan hearths,:) but in this case probably altars of offering, closely stacked together in piles of five. Besides these there were stone lamps, some with high pedestals, and clay chafing pans or censers. But the most remarkable objects were four huge bronze Double Axes of the sacral kind, with flat blades rivetted to their sockets. The dimensions of these far exceeded any known examples. One of them measured 1-20 metre 45 inches in width, and 60 cm. in height (Fig. 313).

The analogy of the early column bases and the tradition preserved in the veined decoration of the plaster as seen on the Hagia Triada sarcophagus makes it probable that the original bases of the sacred symbol in the Pillar Crypts of the Knossian Palace were of variegated stone. A good example of a stepped base of gypsum, doubtless originally coated with painted 1 KpTtkt; E r;uep(, Aug. 5, 1919. been kindly supplied me by Dr. Xanthudides.

2 Photographs of the objects found in this The pottery is L. M. I. chamber, including the Double Axes, have See above, p. 390.

Discovery of Sanctuary at Niron Khani.

Colossal Double Axe heads.

FIG. 314. STEPPED PYRAMIDAL SOCKET FOR DOUBLE AXE; LONG CORRIDOR OF PALACE.

Bases of Double Axes in Palace.

THE PALACE OF MINOS, ETC.

Ritual performed before Double

Axes from painted Hagia Triada Sarcophagus.

plaster imitation of such polychrome graining, was found in the adjoining Long Corridor of the Magazines (Fig. 314), and may either have been placed there as an earnest of divine guardianship or have reached its present position from some sanctuary above. It probably belongs to the early part of the Late Minoan Age.

Part of a stepped socket of black steatite, originally, no doubt, coated with gold foil, was found with the Bull's head rhyton of the same material and other relics in a deposit belonging to a columnar sanctuary of the Little Palace at Knossos. A small example of a similar stepped socket from the Psychro Cave, of the same soft stone, is shown in Fig. 315, together with a bronze double axe of the thin ritual type, found in the same deposit. The upper step here shows a perforation for the rivet by which the shaft of the Double Axe was attached. 1

Of the actual ritual of the worship of this sacred symbol we have now a complete illustration in the sacrificial scenes on the Sarcophagus found in a chamber tomb at Hagia Triada. 2 On one side we see the blood of the sacrificed ox received in a vessel below, while a votary clacl in the skin of a victim officiates before an altar, above which appears a basket of fruit, indicative of offerings of another kind. Here, too, there is a double object of cult a sacred tree within a small shrine, above which rise the sacral horns, and a double axe on a trunk-like shaft resting on an oblong base. The other side of the Sarcophagus is partly occupied by a scene of offering, including a votive boat or ship, to a personage, who had evidently been a Sea Captain. 3 This Minoan 1 The shaft is here restored. These objects 2 I need only here refer to the original publi-were due to excavations made by me in 1894 cation, with coloured plates, by Paribeni, Man.

FIG. 315. BRONZE RITUAL DOUBLE AXE ANP SOCKET OF BLACK STEATITE. PSYCHRO CAVE.

in a stratum parallel with that in which the inscribed Libation Table subsequently came to light (see below, p. 625, and Figs. 465, 466). The axe-blade and socket are now in the Ashmolean Museum.

Ant., xix, pp. 5-86, Pis. I-III.

3 In a tomb of the Zafer Papoura Cemetery a small ivory boat was found with a similar high prow. (Preh. Tombs of Knossos, Archaeo-logia, lix, p. 27, Fig. 22.) mariner, summoned back awhile to the land of the living, 1 stands in front Double of his heroon, behind a stepped altar and a sacred tree (Fig. 316). In applied to the field to the left of this are two female votaries, one long-robed and J JK wearing the crested crown of Minoan sphinxes, who bears two vessels of deceased hero.

FIG. 316. DKCEASED BEFORE HIS HEROON AND OFFERING OK SHIP. PAINTED SARCOPHAGUS OF H. TRIADA. (For Colour Key see Fig. 317.) of-fering, while the other clad in a sacrificial skin pours the red libation into a large two-handled bowl. This rests on the upper steps of the bases of two Double Axes, the shafts of which are in this case clad with foliage, perhaps of palm-trees (Fig. 317).

Two significant features in both groups remain to be described, intimately bound up with the inner spirit of this aniconic cult. In both cases the divinity is charmed down into its material resting-place, not only by the sacrifice itself, but with the aid of music and ritual chants. Behind the sacrificed ox in the first scene a man, draped to just below the knee, 1 This figure, with open eyes and clearly Rodenwaldt (Mitth. d. Inst., 1912, p. I38seqq.) representing the resurrected dead, has been has seen in it the vivified cult-image of a God. sometimes strangely described as a mummy.

is seen playing the double pipes. In the fellow group a male minstrel, in a robe reaching to his ankles, sounds a seven-stringed lyre an instrument which, as we know from its occurrence as a hieroglyph, already existed in M. M. II. In both cases the sign of the visible presence of the Godhead, thus charmed down into the sacred symbol, is shown in the raven-like birds 111 RED IPCREEN SlsivELLOW

FIG. 317. LIBATIONS OFFERED TO DOUBLE AXES; FROM PAINTED SAR-COPHAGUS,

HAGIA TRIADA.

perched upon the Axe blades. It is the exact equivalent of the doves perched upon the columns of the miniature sanctuary described above, 2 and represents a constantly recurring idea of primitive religion.

The culminating result of the whole ceremonial machinery as depicted on the Sarcophagus is the calling back of the departed to the upper air for some brief communion with those by whom his memory was cherished. For

Mr. Warde Fowler (Von Duhn, Archivfilr head and beak that is peculiar to the raven. Religionswissenschaft, xii, p. 167, note 2) ob- 2 See p. 222 and Fig. 166, F. serves that the birds have all the outline of this, as in the case of Laoclameia, a higher sanction was required, and the divine possession of the fetish form of the divinity in the shape of the Double Axes had first to be secured. On the intimate connexion of the great Minoan Goddess with the cult of the dead, much light was shed by the discovery of the Tomb of the Double Axes' near Knossos. There the sepulchral Tomb of chamber was itself a columnar shrine with ritual double axes and vases for A libations, and the rock-cut grave was actually hewn into the outline of the Knossos. sacred symbol. 1

An interesting feature in connexion with the Eastern Pillar of the Palace was the appearance in the pavement on either side of it of two shallow stone vats. 2 These recur in other similar cases, and their use is more than suggested by the vessels for food offerings and libations, by which at times they are replaced or supplemented.

It should be borne in mind that the ground floor chambers in which in Bases of all cases such pillars stood were themselves only the Crypts of a columnar columns sanctuary above. These Pillars of the House formed in fact the direct support of the stone bases and wooden shafts of overlying columns, only Hall. separated by the intervening beam of the upper floor. The evidence of the Pillar Rooms of the Palace is indeed of special value in this connexion, since in this case the bases of two upper columns were actually found, precipitated into the entrance lobby that borders the E. Pillar Crypt on this side (Fig. 318). They are of plain gypsum 3 in place of the variegated materials of which the original column bases in this position were, according to all analogy, composed. They do not show the high proportions of the earlier M. M. Ill class. 4 At the same time the traces of the ledge round their lower circumference distinguishes them from the ordinary flat, drum-like, Late Minoan type, and recalls one of the bases found with the Spiral Fresco and ascribed above to the early part of M. M. III. It is probable that they belong to some work of restoration that took place in the later stage of the present Period. On that to the left, part of the imprint of the carbonized wooden shaft is clearly traceable.

The plan of the Upper Columnar hall 5 which seems to have formed the 1 See my account of this tomb, Tomb oj the is about 0-72 m.

Double Axes, c. (Arfhaeotogia, Ixv), p. 33 See above, p. 370, and Kig. 268.

seqq. This tomb belonged to the latest 6 Relics connected with the Treasury that

Palace Period (L. M. II). seems to have adjoined this upper Columnar 2 Both of these are 25 cm. deep. One is Sanctuary were found on and above the floor 80 cm. K.-W. by 47 N., the other 80 cm. by of the basement Room of the Stone Vases'. 53- A description of these, however, is reserved for

The upper diameter of these column bases a Section dealing with the Late Minoan Period.

THE PALACE OF MINOS, ETC.

centre of worship in its public aspect, together with its connected system, will be found conjecturally restored in a Section dealing with the later Palace. Thanks, however, to the discovery in a well-defined deposit of a remarkable group of painted plaster fragments, it is possible to obtain a glimpse of a part at least of these sanctuary structures devoted to the cult of the Double Axes, as it existed about the close of the Third Middle Minoan Period.

Floor-cists or Ka-selles'.

FIG. 318. GYPSUM BASES OF COLUMNS FALLEN FROM SANCTUARY ABOVE PILLAR ROOMS.

It will be shown in the succeeding Section that the floor-cists or Kaselles', that form such a characteristic feature in the M. M. Ill storage system, reveal in several of the Magazines two distinct phases in their history. These had been originally constructed with a depth of about 1-30 metre. But at a time of architectural remodelling which seems to have taken place early in the Late Minoan Age they were blocked by shallower and more superficial receptacles. In the lower part of the original cists and beneath their later floors were found rubble materials, pottery, and other relics dating from the close of M. M. Ill, and amongst these, in the case of the Kaselles' opened in the Ninth and Thirteenth Magazines, were some fresco fragments of great importance in their bearing on the architectural history Frag- ,. ments of of this epoch. architec-

These painted plaster remains had been evidently derived from upper tural fres- ., i. i coes found chambers in this Palace region. Amongst the fresco fragments found in the beneath lower receptacles of some cists of the Thirteenth Magazine, 1 together with parts of a small frieze with triglyphs and half rosettes closely approaching

FIG. 319. FRESCO SHOWING PILI. AR SHRINE WITH DOUBLE AXES STUCK INTO

COLUMNS. (t.) the L. M. I class. 2 were parts of architectural designs showing the facade of Facade of , i i v Columnar a Columnar Sanctuary executed in a somewhat earlier style, and which may Sanc. be safely placed at least within the lower limit of the present Period. Double

We see here parts of the facades of buildings with openings, in which, Axes, in one case, are set three wooden columns and, beside them, the familiar horns of consecration (Fig. 319).;! These columns, moreover, present an interesting feature, supplying a further connexion with the prevailing cult.

1 Nos. 2, 3, and 4 from the West End of the Magazine.

: The rosettes, however, were not of- the purely architectonic type seen in the miniature

Temple Fresco'. See Vol. II.

Below this architectural design is a rosette border. For a coloured illustration see B. S. A., x, PI. ii.

Axes inserted in Columns.

444 THE PALACE OF MINOS, ETC.

On each side of the capital appear pairs of white objects with curved ends, which, though sketchily indicated, in the fluid style of this fresco technique, unquestionably represent the double axes of Minoan worship, stuck into the woodwork of the sacred columns. This recalls a curious cult practice noted in the Dictaean Cave. In the inmost cavern shrine explored by Dr. Hogarth, votive bronze axes and other implements had been inserted in the crevices of the natural pillars of stalagmite.

FIG. 320. WINDOW OPENINGS OF SANCTUARY BUILDING WITH DOUBLE AXES INSERTED IN POSTS ON A FRAGMENT OF PAINTED STUCCO FOUND AT MYCENAE.

What, however, is of special interest in connexion with the double axes embedded in the wooden columns of the Palace Sanctuary is the recurrence of this ritual arrangement on a painted plaster fragment belonging to the earliest painted decoration of the Palace at Mycenae and clearly the work of

Compaii- a more or less contemporary Cretan artist. Fat female figures are seen

Mycenae, looking out from what appear to be the openings of a double window, on both sides of the upright middle bar of which, and on the inner side of the left post are visible, just under the cross-beam, double axes stuck in the same way into the woodwork (Fig. 320.) 1 The festoons, of beads and pendants, attached to the Double Axe blades, are a characteristic feature of Minoan shrines. 2 The character of the spectacle that absorbs the attention of the ladies in this loggia is well indicated by a companion fragment showing the hand of an acrobatic figure performing a somersault above the back of the bull. The sport in this case must have taken place within sight of the Palace windows.

The facades of the buildings with which the Columnar openings on the Use of fresco fragments from the Thirteenth Magazine are associated (see Figs. 319, gated 321) afford an interesting illustration, both of the division of the walls matena 's- into panels and compartments by upright and horizontal beams, and of the Middle Minoan architectural tradition as regards the use of variegated stonework. Among the panels depicted, some with black, green, and white spots seem to be taken from porphyry or Spartan basalt the lapis Lacedaemonius, of which a considerable store in rough pieces for working up was found in the Domestic Quarter. Its use would imply direct commercial relations with the Peloponnese, but this is quite in keeping with the view supported now by a mass of evidence that the beginning at least of the Minoan settlements on the Mainland side goes back to the present Period. It is probable that the small panels on this fresco rather reproduce imitative stucco panels on the M. M. Ill Palace walls than actual stone plaques. The wainscoting with variegated stone materials seems itself, as already suggested, 1 to have been more a feature of the early part of the Middle Minoan Age.

The Thirteenth Magazine, into which the remains of these architectural Frescoes frescoes had fallen, forms part of a square block at the N. W. Angle of the shrine Palace, including the whole group of Magazines from n to 16. (See above Plan, Fig. 322, p. 449 below.) This block juts forward into the West Court and constitutes a separate section of the facade on that side, while both its Northern and Southern walls are of abnormal thickness. There can be little doubt that it answered to a structural unit above, the sanctuary nature of which may be inferred from the character of the designs on the fallen fragments. It is not impossible indeed that they may be taken to give us an 1 From a coloured photographic proof looking out of a window on a Knossian frag-kindly supplied by Dr. Karo. See Roden- ment of that class (Knossian Atlas, PI. IV, waldt, Ath. Mitth., xxxvi (1911), PI. ix (with Fig. 15). The Mycenae fragments were found the acrobatic fragment). Rodenwaldt rightly in the area of the Grave Circle and were, recognized the double axes. He regards the curiously enough, put on one sidebyschliemann work as a copy of a Cretan original (up. tit., as Greek of early Fifth Century B. C. p. 228). He compares the style of the Minia-: See below, p. 494, and Fig. 353. ture Frescoes; three women, in fact, are seen See above, p. 214.

THE PALACE OF MINOS, ETC.

actual idea of the Palace facade on this section as shown in its upper story, about the close of the present Period. In the early part of the Late Minoan

FIG. 321. FRESCO OF I-ART OK PILLAR SHRINE WITH IMITATION STONE INLAYS. (f.)

Age a small shrine seems to have existed in the N. E. angle of this area of which parts of the stone frieze and other architectural fragments were found in a space below, together with considerable remains of painted amphoras in the later Palace Style, on some of which Double Axes form a principal part of the decoration. 1

A windowed structure with these sacred emblems served in the Mycenae Asso- wall-paintings described above as a kind of royal box for lady spectators Frag- of circus sports with trained bulls and acrobats. Among the fragments associated with those showing the Knossian pillar shrine was one depicting Bull-grap-dense crowds of spectators in a walled enclosure 2 and with it, on a larger show. scale, the head of a swarthy bull and parts of the flowing locks of an acrobatic figure. 3 We have here new proofs of the near connexion between the cult of the Minoan Goddess of which the Double Axes are the outward symbols and the bull-grappling sports.

The animal forms of the Minoan Goddess were manifold. Her visible central presence is often indicated by perched doves, as in the early Columnar eat " f of Sanctuary. On the painted Sarcophagus they are replaced by birds of raven- Minoan like appearance. Lions and pards are also seen in close association, and, as t e we know from the contents of the Temple Repositories described below, u uble spotted snakes were her peculiar emblem in her chthonic aspect as Lady of the Underworld.

But, taken in connexion with the traces of Minoan religion in its prevailing aspect, not at Knossos alone, but throughout the length and breadth of Crete, it is clear that the special aniconic form of the supreme Minoan divinity, as of her male satellite, was the Double Axe. The Palace Sanctuary itself was pre-eminently the House of the Double Axe, 4 The and the sacred symbol formed the centre of domestic cult in countless O f h e e smaller dwellings. Even in the days of the last Minoan decadence, when Double the ruins of Knossos were in part made use of by humbler occupants, the cult of the Lady of the Double Axe was perpetuated on the spot, and the sacral weapons themselves found a place in her little shrine brought to light in the South-East quarter of the site. 5 The scene on the Sarcophagus of Hagia Triada, however, in which, by ritual offerings before the sacred symbols, the deceased hero is restored awhile to the upper air, may incline us to believe that the cult of deceased and heroized members of the line of Minoan priest-kings was associated with that of their divine Mistress in the Palace Sanctuary of Knossos.

1 See Vol. II. place of the Labrys', see above, p. 6.

3 See below, p. 527, Fig. 384. See Knossos, Report, 1902, p. 93 seqq. and See below, p. 529, Fig. 385. Fig. 55.

4 For the Carian parallel I abranda = 'the

Disuse ot part of W. Magazines.

Separate enclosure of Magazines in M. M. III.

The En. clave of the Ka- selles.

Separate enclosure of section of West. Magazines; Enclave of tlie Kaselles' or Floor-Cists; Those of tlie Long Gallery; Remains of precioiis contents; Some Cists used as Vats; Original Cists; Closed at end of M. M. Ill; Stratigraphic evidence of Cists beneth Stepped Por-ch; Kaselles of Eighth Magazine; Superficial recipients, of later constriction; M. M. Ill relics in filling beneath these; Traces nf later se as Oil Vats; Mostly paved over by close of L. M. 1; Three Epochs traceable in West Magazines three Stages in construction of their Entrances.

THE Western Palace Section, as already observed, seems to have served two. main purposes. On the one hand it included the buildings that were the central scenes of the Palace cult. On the other it guarded the principal repositories of stores and precious objects belonging to these sanctuaries.

According to the original arrangement, the whole West frontage of the Palace seems to have been occupied by an uninterrupted series of Magazines, some twenty-two in number. At a comparatively late date the Southernmost of these (A, B, c, in the Plan, Fig. 152 above) were remodelled and converted to other uses. It is further clear that some time in the Third Middle Minoan Period a wholly new system of arrangement was adopted in the case of the central group of Magazines that extend from No. 4 to No. 13, inclusive. While Nos. i, 2, and 3 were apparently left in their original condition, as well as the separate enclave formed by Magazines 14-18, this central group was now shut off from the rest to form a section apart (see Fig. 322), and a new system of storage by means of remarkably constructed floor-cists, known to the Cretan workmen as Kaselles' (B"ao- AAaty), was carried out throughout its extent.

In order to secure the enclave containing these floor-cists, the original Long Gallery of the West Magazines was again cut short by a cross wall (see Fig. 323) overlapping a part of the N. wall of the Third Magazine, and provided with a central doorway 98 cm. wide the gypsum jambs of which were incorporated in the Late Minoan pavement when this barrier itself was subsequently removed. This doorway, it will be seen, was con- 1 See Knossos, Report, 1904, pp. 36-9, and Fig. 12

M. M. III. FLOOR-CISTS OF W. PALACE REGION 449 trolled from the South. Immediately within, to the right on entering, opened a passage-way leading to the Pillar Rooms and associated system. On the other hand access to this section of the Magazines was apparently confined on the North to the staircase at that end, the insula formed

WEST COURT
AREA

REMODELLED IN LAST PERIOD OF THE PALACE AND OCCUPIED BY
THRONE-ROOM SYSTEM
VAT ROOM DEPOSIT rpoM TREASubv
QF PRE-PALATIAL SHRINE
ENTRANCE TO
ENCLAVE OF
KASELLES 9A Kftbrcb
WALL X DOORW
PYRAMIDAL5OCKC1 Op Pf3. SYMBOL
FACADE or LATCR
CENTRAL COURT
FIG. 322. PART OF WEST SECTION OF PALACE, SHOWING ENCLAVE
OF KASELLES AND REPOSITORIES NEAR PILLAR CRYPTS OF CENTRAL
SHRINE.

by Magazines 14-18 being cut off by another smaller cross wall barring the The
narrow passage West of the staircase. This Enclave of the Kaselles' was thus converted
at this time into a kind of Palace Treasury, shut in in such under a way that it could
be kept under careful custody. That it was specially dlvl "f. placed under religious
guardianship is shown, not only by the recurrence of ship, i Gg

THE PALACE OF MINOS, ETC.
Earlier Storage in Walled Pits.
The floor-cists or Ka-selles'.
In Long Gallery.

the sacred symbol on the jambs of the Magazines a phenomenon which itself dates
from the days of the earlier Palace but by the discovery, above the later floor of
the Long Gallery, near the jamb dividing Magazines 8 and 9, of one of the stepped
pyramidal sockets in which the heft of the Double Axe had been originally inserted
(see above, p. 437, Fig. 314).

It has been pointed out that the practice of storage in pits of which the deep-walled
cells of the

Keep seem to afford 3"" MAGAZM. the most conspicuous instance goes back to
the earliest Palace Period both at Knossos and Phaestos. But the final development
of this system the sunken stone cist or kasella is' in a special way associated with
the Third Middle Minoan stage. It may be that, in some cases, these kaselles' were
themselves fitted into walled receptacles of earlier masonry belonging to the First
Palace.

It having been decided, owing to the appearance of floor-cists in the West Magazines, to raise some slabs of the adjoining Long Gallery, the surprising discovery
was made that the whole extent of this, from the opening of the Fourth to the South
door-jamb of the Fourteenth Magazine, was underlaid by a series of twenty-seven
cists. The Plan and longitudinal Section of these is given in Fig. 325, A, u, c, D.
They belong, as will be seen, to two sets, A and B, which are essentially different in
formation. The cists of type A, of which there was only a single series of seven, as
compared with four groups of five each in the case of the others, were very elaborately
constructed. They are formed of four thin gypsum plaques, the

LONG GALLERY

FIG. 323.

PLAN OF CROSS WALL AND DOORWAY MADE TO SECURE ENCLAVE OF KASELLES.

two shorter fixed in grooves cut out of the longer, and all socketed into a base-block of soft limestone. Apparently for the sake of dryness, the intervals that separated them from the retaining masonry and from the slabs dividing one kasella from another were filled with a fine red potter's earth resembling

FIG. 324. FAIENCE INLAYS FROM SIXTH KASELLA OF LONG GALLERY, SOME COATED WITH GOLD-FOIL.

that used for the clay tablets (see Fig. 325, c). Remains of a lead lining was also found within the cists themselves.

Various indications went to show that this group of kaselles' had Remains contained precious relics. 1 In their interior were found inlays of various materials, remains of gold-foil and masses of carbonized wood. The best evidence was produced by the sixth cist, opposite the door of Magazine 6.

1 See Knossos, Report, 1903, p. 31 seqq. Gg 2

Here was found a heap of carbonized wood, apparently belonging to a chest in other cases bronze hinges of such occurred and numerous plaques of crystal and native faience with which it had been encrusted. The crystal Faience had been much splintered by the action of fire. The faience plaques, of which specimens are given in Fig. 324, were of a deep purplish colour some border pieces however (D) showing stripes of this colour on a pale green ground. The most abundant type was a kind of trefoil (A-A) with triple projections and incurved sides roughly arranged in a pattern in the Fig. and the fact that some of these projections had been abruptly truncated (as x-x) shows that they had been fitted into a rectangular frame. The parallelism between the faience inlays and those from the Temple Repositories described below bespeaks absolute contemporaneity. The pointed type c is interesting, since crystal examples of the same form were found not only in the Western Repository, but also in the Shaft Graves of Mycenae, and it Gold foil i s clear that in all these cases they represent the petals of a rosette pattern, covering, arranged around a central disk. One interesting feature observable on many of the plaques was that they still showed the remains of the gold-foil, in some cases carefully wrapped round them, 2 with which apparently all the faience inlays had been originally coated. This system of decoration is very characteristic of the times.

A large looped handle of bronze was found belonging to a wooden chest which these inlays had decorated. But of the precious vessels, the jewellery, and the other valuable objects that it may have contained nothing has been preserved to us. Of the character of these our only available evidence is supplied by the imported masterpieces of the Minoan goldsmith's Art found in the Shaft Graves of Mycenae, the early elements in which apart from some still more ancient heirlooms are contemporary with the closing phase of the Third Middle Minoan Period. 3 Had any of these, it may well be asked, found an earlier resting-place in the kaselles' and Repositories of the great Cretan Palace?

Floor- The more numerously represented series, B, of the floor-cists in the

Group B: Long Gallery, consisting of four groups of five each, are of a different used as construction, and were clearly designed to perform functions of another kind (see Fig. 325, D). They are of squarer plan, deeper and more capacious 1 Quatrefoil plaques of faience also occurred from the loin-cloth of the Cup-bearer Fresco, in the Palace, of contemporary fabric (an excep- " In other cases the inlays were covered by tionally large one near the N. E. border) This minute globules of melted gold, a further type of inlay was imitated in the Minoan em- evidence of a conflagration, broidery in the later Palace Epoch, as is seen 3 See Vol. II.

yj:-'"-"–" r.-.,-,;. y

FIG. 325. A, B, c D CISTS o LONG GALLERY- PLAN A SECTION of OSTB AND THEIR LATER CONVERSION INTO SUPERFICIAL VATS.

than the others. Though externally surrounded by the same dry medium of red earth, this was set, not against the masonry of a walled pit, but directly against a cutting in the Neolithic clay. They were lined, moreover, with a hard white plaster, like that of the interior of cisterns and drains, in place of the lead sheeting of series A. The slabs of the cists were here of limestone, and were placed round the base-block instead of being inserted in grooves of its upper surface. They were, however, compacted together by means of the same form of dovetailing that is illustrated in the case of the East Temple Repository described below. 2 The base-blocks themselves presented a significant feature. Square cavities, about 6 cm. deep, were sunk into their upper surface, which were apparently designed to receive the dregs and deposit of liquid contents such as oil.

This conclusion, that the! cists were in fact vats, probably for oil storage, explains the different character of the contents. The carbonized remains and inlays of treasure cists such as those of series A were here conspicuous by their absence. The contents of these cists consisted in fact of rubble material and limy earth heaped in to fill the void at the time of some restoration of this part of the building.

Among the debris swept into the cists at this time were several plain clay cist of bowls with a pale smooth slip, some of them filled with lime of a characteristic oxd at type identical with specimens used as lids for store jars with a purplish brown t? cl v? f ii surface and white bands that is of a definite M. M. Ill b class in the small Magazines of that date adjoining the School Room on the East slope. 3 The discovery of these vessels affords strong evidence that the cists of class B like the A series were covered in at the close of M. M. III. There is, however, a significant feature observable in connexion with all the cists of the Long Gallery, which reappears in the case of the contemporary cists (c) to be described below, North of the Temple Repositories', and the latest contents of which were also M. M. Ill b. In that case, as in the other, the gypsum slabbing with which the floor above was eventually paved was not immediately superimposed on the top of the cists, but was separated from them by a clay layer, 5 centimetres thick. This layer presents the full average thickness of the clay floors found in the Palace but in this case was probably laid down as a bedding for the gypsum pavement slabs. Later in both cases, the gypsum pavement underwent repairs, and it was 1 This is brought out in the Plan, 3 A specimen of such a bowl is given in Fig. 325, D Fig. 279, D, p. 384 above. The handled bowl 2 See p. 466, Fig. 334. E is of the same ware.

THE PALACE OF MINOS, ETC.

doubtless in the course of this work that some later painted sherds found their way into the superficial earth below. 1

Cists of These conclusions, as already noted, are strongly corroborated by the Group c. ana j 0 gy supplied by a group of three cists, c on Plan, Fig. 322, found in what

VESTIBULE OF STEPPED PORTICO (L. M. II)

REMAINS OF GREEN SCHIST PAVEMENT wmwmrymrwrwM RpbLE', i rfuwn-cys IUVM

SOME M. M. III POTTERY BELOW
STEPS TO FLOOR
OF PORTICO (L. M. II.)
DATUM LINE
PAVEMENT OF CE. NTRAL COURT (L-M- II) AMOVED
MIDDLE. MINOAN STRATUM
METRES

A. LIMESTONE. CI5T WITH M. M. III POTTERY FAIENCE

B. CORRIDOR OR MAGAZIN E. WITH GYPSUM SLABBING 3f DADOES FILLED IN c. REMAINS OF L. M. I. PITHOS: FOUND IN CORRIDOR

D. REMAINS OF BORDERS OF 5 SUCCESSIVE. PLA5TER FLOORS

FIG. 326. SECTION UNDER STEPPED PORCH (L. M. II) SHOWING L. M. I MAGAZINE

SUPERPOSED ON M. M. Ill ClsT.

had been a Magazine of this Period, immediately N. of the larger cist of the same class known as the Eastern Temple Repository.- These cists, which answered to the latter in construction, contained in their filling materials, though much more sparsely, relics and pottery similar to that from the 1 Some fragments of ordinary pithoi, perhaps L. M. I, were found, for instance in the superficial stratum of the Sixth Cist of Series A, the contents of which are described above So, too, beneath the pavement above cists of Class B, there occurred one or two painted sherds of a Late Minoan type. These are described in the original Report for 1903 as of the Latest Palace Period (p. 35), but this must be taken in connexion with the accompanying description of the M. M. Ill contents of the kaselles' as belonging to what was then called the First Period of the Iater Palace. The two cists of Class is neaiest the stairs at the N. end of the Long Gallery were found open and contained pottery belonging to the Period of Re-occupation (L. M. Ill 6). 2 See below, p. 468.

neighbouring Repositories, which afford the best evidence for the style in vogue at the very close of M. M. III. Here again, as in the other case, was a clay layer above the cists, intended as a bedding for a gypsum pavement, belonging to a later system. In connexion with this pavement were upright gypsum slabs along its border, forming a narrow corridor deter-containing remains of L. M. I Pithoi. 1 But the evidence did not end here. J nmed b x This Corridor was in turn cut short in the last Palace Period (L. M. II) by stratifica-a wall belonging to the Ante-Room of the Throne Room system, while the remaining section of it that above the cists was at the same time filled in to support the threshold of the Stepped Porch erected on that side at the same epoch. (See

Diagrammatic Section, Fig. 32G.) We have here, therefore, a well-clefined quadruple stratification 2, of great value as a clear indication that the cists violated at the close of M. M. Ill were covered over successively by a clay flooring and a gypsum pavement between that date and the concluding phase of L. M. II to which the Room of the Throne and its antechamber belong.

The size and arrangement of the kaselles' in the Magazines bordering the section of the Long Gallery that contained the floor-cists of types A and u varied a good deal, as can be seen from the Plan, Fig. 322.

The original method of construction seems here to have conformed with that of series A of the cists of the Long Gallery. But in nearly all cases there is evidence of a change in the original system, in virtue of Jyj gi which the receptacles were rendered more shallow by the insertion of Magazine a new bottom slab, about half a metre above that with which they were at first provided.

The best example of this dual arrangement is supplied by the Eighth Magazine, though the middle compartments had unfortunately been much destroyed by treasure seekers. The Plan and longitudinal Section of this is given in Fig. 325, E, F, 3 and a view of it in Fig. 327, which, owing to the above-mentioned destruction, shows a good deal of its anatomy. The cists are included in larger compartments of solid ashlar masonry, piers of which separate them into six sections. The original

See Knossos, Report, 1904, p. 30 seqq.; intermediate floor levels, perhaps belonging to

Figs. 9, 10, and Pl. I. small cist-like compartments. (See Knossos, 8 Attaching to a block underlying the N. E. Report, 1904, p. 33.) The bearing of these is corner of the vestibule of the Stepped Porch obscure, however, and they are omitted in the were fragments of painted wall stucco and diagrammatic Section, Fig. 326 plaster pavements pointing to the existence of By Mr. Theodore Fyfe.

THE PALACE OF MINOS, ETC.

gypsum wall-slabs of the cists themselves descend about 1-15 metres, fitting below into the groves of a massive base-block like those of series A above described. They were set in the same red earth and lined in the same way with lead sheeting. But, at some time after the removal of their earlier contents of a valuable kind probably themselves deposited in treasure chests Shallower cas kets the

Cists su- perposed OI the Old packed with on earlier.

and inlaid lower part cists was filling material to a height of from about 45 to 60 centimetres above their original floors, and new bottom slabs were let down on the surface of this. Shallower receptacles were in this way superposed on the earlier kaselles', the sides of these in places showing the original lead lining but in other cases being coated with hard plaster.

Asthebottomsof the new superficial cists were made to fit as closely as possible and their edges further cemented, the task of raising them in order to explore the intervening space between them and the original floors was one of considerable difficulty, involving careful mason's work.

FIG. 327. VIEW SHOWING STRUCTURES OF KASELLES BENEATH LATER PAVEMENT OF MAGAZINE 8, A PART OF THIS HAD BEEN PREVIOUSLY RUINED BY TREASURE-SEEKERS

M. M. III. FLOOR-CISTS OF W. PALACE REGION 457 In the case of the Eighth Magazine there was little but filling earth in either the upper or lower receptacle, stained green, apparently owing to the action of the lead sheeting. The upper receptacles indeed, both here and elsewhere, were largely empty, the paving slabs simply resting on the edges of the cists without the support of interior filling. The lower intervals of the cists, however, examined in other Magazines were found packed with rubble Relics material, including many odd slips of gypsum slabs and quantities of limy beneath earth, thus exactly reproducing the phenomena observed in cists B of the Long

FIG. 328. M. M. III POTTERY FOUND BENEATH FLOOR OF KASELLA IN THE FOURTH MAGAZINE.

Gallery. One gypsum fragment from the Thirteenth Magazine had been rudely scratched with lines, intended no doubt to be parallel, between which some scribe had practised engraving characters of the Linear Script A, Fig. 458.

The precious nature of the original contents of the kaselles' was evidenced by the discovery in their lower interspaces of not inconsiderable quantities of gold-foil, so largely used at this time for covering carved and inlaid materials.

In the fifth kasella from the West end of Magazine 5 quite a sheet of this was found crumpled up amidst the earth and rubble. In some cases there was a certain amount of pottery, all, as far as it presented distinctive M M U j features, of the M. M. III class. Among such remains the group shown Pottery in Fig. 328, found in the lower compartment of a kasella of Magazine 4, nafcfsts.

THE PALACE OF MINOS, ETC.

Later Cists of L. M. I construction.

Probably Vats.

Floor Cists mostly paved over by close of L. M. I.

Some still used as vats for oil.

includes a jar of bulging shape which seems to be typologically slightly earlier than similar vessels of taller proportions found in the Temple Repositories'. It may therefore be a survival from the earlier M. M. III phase. But, as a whole, the evidence of the remains found in the lower intervals of these kaselles' tends to show that they passed out of use at the same date as those of the adjoining Long Gallery and the Temple Repositories' themselves, at the close, that is, of the present Period. Some of the fragments of wall-painting already referred to as found in this position in the Thirteenth Magazine fit on, as has been observed, very closely to the earliest Late Minoan style.

The contents of these lower receptacles of the kaselles' opened in the Magazines differed in one important respect from those of the analogous group A of the Long Gallery. There were here no traces of burnt material; the remains of the easily detached gold foil being indeed the only clear record of their having been repositories of precious possessions. Possibly the conflagration that seems to have followed on the violation of the cists in the Long Gallery did not extend to the Magazines. In any case the original contents of their kaselles' seem to have been carefully withdrawn and no remains of burnt treasure chests were swept into them.

It would appear from the evidence given above that the construction of the upper and shallower cists was the work of the beginning of the Late Minoan Age, and their empty state when found would imply that they were used as vats rather than as receptacles for treasure. That the custom of constructing floor-cists was itself not wholly unknown in the new era is shown by the smaller superficial cists placed over the earlier Temple Repositories, apparently in the last Palace epoch. 1 It seems, however, to have been shortly realized that owing to the limited width of the Magazines and the size of many of the pithoi, floor space for these large jars was of more consequence than the vats. At a date, which from the evidence supplied by the stratification beneath the Vestibule of the Stepped Porch we may place at least within the lower limits of the First Late Minoan Period, they were for the most part paved over.

That in some cases, however, the new pavement was so laid down as to allow the use of the superficial cists as oil-vats appears from a piece of evidence supplied by the Sixth Magazine. The upper recipient seen in Fig. 329 shows the side flags of the pavement running even with the border, while one of its central slabs only projects as far as the original line of the 1 See below, p. 464 and Fig. 332.

cist end, since removed. Beside the open vat, pithoi were found in place, the nearest on the right being a fine example, probably early L. M. I, with palm-tree decoration, the others belonging to the last Palace Period. There is every reason to believe, therefore, that this arrangement represents that actually existing at the moment of the final catastrophe of the building,

FIG. 329. KASELI. A IN SIXTH MAGAZINE USED AS AN OIL VAT AND TRACES OK CONFLAGRATION.

and an interesting feature connected with it is the blackening of the pavement along the Northern margin of the vat, evidently produced by the combustion of the oil contained in it.

As the ragged edges of the broken pavements show, most of the subsequent uncovering of the cists was the ruthless work of treasure hunters. In some instances their slabs had been almost entirely removed, leaving little but the masonry of the walled pits in which they had been originally inserted,

THE PALACE OF MINOS, ETC.

as is illustrated by the view of the Fifth Magazine given in Fig. 330. 1 A good deal of this process of destructive research after treasure no doubt goes back to the time of the final catastrophe of the Palace.

FIG. 330. STRUCTURE IN WHICH KASELLES OF MAGAZINE 5 WERE ORIGINALLY ENCASED.

From the section of the Eighth Magazine, which illustrates the successive arrangements in the completest manner (see Fig. 325, F), we obtain the evidence 1 The remains of the ragged edges of the order to make the structural arrangement more pavement slabs have been here removed in clearly visible.

of three distant epochs in the history of the Palace store-houses. In the first Three or Early Palace stage the arrangements were evidently for storage in bulk. 0 f P vvv That great knobbed pithoi like those to the N. E. of the Palace site were at this time placed within these Magazines may be inferred, though the catastrophe of the close of M. M. 1 1 and the extensive reconstruction that took place in the succeeding Period, marked by the quantities of re-used and broken blocks visible in the walls, had entirely removed the remains of these

FIG. 331. PLAN OF ENTRANCE TO EIGHTH MAGAZINE SHOWING SUCCESSIVE CHANGES.

earlier jars. In the second or M. M. III stage we are confronted with the elaborate framework of the new kaselles', which, from their construction and relatively small capacity, seem to have been made for the reception of more valuable contents. Finally, the Late Minoan arrangement shows the cists at first reduced to superficial vats, and finally paved over in order to supply a wider platform for the great oil jars. It is specially interesting to observe, moreover, that the careful exploration of the entrance to this Magazine and others has brought to light three successive stages answering to the respective arrangements found within.

In the first stage, that of the Earlier Palace, we see a broad opening with massive limestone antae consisting of two high blocks, one over the other, with a continuous reveal to catch a wooden framework. There was

THE PALACE OF MINOS, ETC.

Three Stages of Magazine Entrance.

here, therefore, a doorway capable of being secured, but giving when open a wide passage. In the next Period, answering to that of the kaselles with more valuable contents, it was thought advisable to narrow the opening, and a new doorway was made inside the earlier one on the new plan of merely providing a gypsum footing for the wooden doorposts. This was the Period when the adjoining section of the Long Gallery was isolated from the rest as described above, and the whole enclave thus formed became a Palace Treasury. The narrower doorways constructed at this epoch were at the same time of sufficient breadth to admit the passage of the new class of pithoi with less bulky proportions that at this time makes its appearance.

Finally, in the third stage, answering to the First Late Minoan, the narrower doorways were removed, the low gypsum jambs paved over, and the whole width of the original structure opened out so as to admit the freer use of the interior of the Magazines for the purposes of oil storage. These successive changes are well illustrated by the entrance of the Eighth Magazine (Fig. 331).

Clearly, the main source of the wealth of the Priest Kings of Knossos consisted, from the earliest days of the Palace, in the oil for which Egypt seems to have supplied the principal market. In the closing phase of the Middle Period we may trace the results of this commerce in the accumulated treasure for which new receptacles were devised in the shape of the kaselles'. But after the great catastrophe and consequent plundering that befell the West Wing at the close of that Period the storage of the oil itself became again the chief end in view.

DRAUGHT-BOARD.

Treasury Quarter of Palace; Survival of pre-Palace Cult Centre; Superficial Cists of Later Shrine; Discovery of earlier Temple Repositories beneath them; Their Contents; M, M. III Pottery; Precious relics below; The Western Repository; Broken Stone Hammers; Remains of Treasure Chests; Gold foil and inlays; Comparison of inlays with Royal Draughtboard; Its description; Crystal plaques with Silver and Kyanos backing; Argonauts and Marguerites; Plan and Character of Game; The Citadel; Compared with

Greek Palis; Discovery of ivory men compared with Predynastic Egyptian type; Solar symbol on base of one of these; Connected with Minoan Goddess on mould and fresco; Reconstruction of part of Draught-board from J cmple Repository; Parallel remains from Fourth Shaft Grave at Mycenae; Small ivory disks with Minoan Craftsmen s marks; Faience inlays of Mycenae Board, of Knossian Palace fabric; Sacral Knots of faience associated with Board; Deposit of Gaming Boards in Tombs: Egyptian practice; Minoan Boards dedicated to Goddess and a special property of Dead.

IT is clear from the indications of the original contents of the kaselles Treasury described above that the enclave in which they were constructed, and which of Palace. was secured by special doors and barriers sometime in the third Middle Minoan Period, had formed a kind of Treasury Quarter of the Palace. It would further appear that the Central Palace Shrine, situated in the contiguous area to the East, and of which we may regard the two Pillar Rooms as the Crypt, had possessed a special Reliquary of its own.

The discovery, beneath the entrance to the Vat Room and on the Survival borders of the East Pillar Room, of a deposit belonging to some shrine p that had already existed in the period that preceded the foundation of the Cult existing Palace, shows how persistent had been the traditional sanctity of this region.

This religious character, as the Double Axe marks on the pillars and the jamb blocks of the Magazine entrances show, was taken over by the new Palace Quarter that rose on this area. That it clung to it, moreover, to the last is evidenced by the existence of what seems to have 1 See above, p. 165 seqq. The position of this Deposit is marked A on the Plan, Fig. 322.

THE PALACE OF MINOS, ETC.

Superficial Cists of later Shrine.

been a small columnar shrine facing the Central Court, in connexion with which, moreover, a series of seal impressions was discovered showing the Minoan Goddess on her lion-guarded peak. 1 It was in a small chamber immediately behind this later shrine and connected by a short passage-way with the E. Pillar Room that the most remarkable evidence of the Early Palace Cult came to light. The position of this little room is given in the Plan, Fig. 322 above. Here, in the Late Minoan floor, had been found, at the time of the first excavation, two superficial cists (Fig. 332), which from their shallow construction

FIG. 332. LATE MINOAN SUPERFICIAL CISTS IN PAVEMENT ABOVE THE TEMPLE REPOSITORIES.

present an obvious parallel to the Vats constructed above the lower part of the original kaselles' of the Magazines, ex hypotkesi in the First Late Minoan Period. The two small superficial cists in question, however, differed from the others in one important respect, their upper borders being here cut out so as better to secure a lid, of which in the case of the Vats of the Magazines there was no trace. They may, therefore, have followed the older usage and have acted as receptacles for solid objects, probably of ritual use. When considered in relation to the discovery of the more important cists below, it becomes evident, indeed, that they represented a religious survival. Two years after the first excavation, noticing a slight sagging in the pavement of the room containing the two superficial cists, I had some slabs raised, and it was then discovered that the floor here rested, not as elsewhere in this region, immediately on the Neolithic stratum, but on comparatively 1 See Vol. II, and Knossos, Report, 1901, pp. 28, 29, and Fig. 9.

JUG. 333. EXCAVATION OK TEMPLE REPOSITORIES, SHOWING SOME OF THE POTTERY. IN THE INTERVAL BETWEEN THEM IS SEEN ONE OF THE SUPERFICIAL ClsTS.

THE PALACE OF MINOS, ETC.

Dis-

Earlier 0 Temple

R. CDOS1- tories.

loose earth. On exploring this it was found that these cists were set in a pavement overlying earlier stone repositories of much greater capacity (Ficr. 333), the contents of which afforded what can only be described as a new revelation, both of Minoan Art and of the character of the Palace Cult. The stratification of both Repositories was practically identical, though the Eastern cist contained the richer contents. Immediately beneath the later pavement was a clay layer on which it had been set, in this case of a reddish terra-cotta hue. Below this the earth was darker, with an

FIG. 334. Two DIAGRAMMATIC VIEWS OF EAST CIST OF REPOSITORIES (M. M. Ill) SHOWING INTERLOCKING JOINTS OF SLABS.

Contents intermixture of debris and charred wood, together with some fragments of gold foil. In this deposit, from the surface downwards to a depth of i-io metres, there lay closely packed together a quantity of clay vessels, which, with the exception of a series of imported Melian bird-vases' to be described below, 1 were almost exclusively two-handled amphoras and pitchers, with a dark purple-brown ground, mostly with broad white spiral and simple vegetable decoration answering to the latest M. M. Ill style, as illustrated by the Magazine of the Lily Jars 2 and other contemporary deposits. A few, however, were in a late polychrome style A fuller account of these is reserved for succeeding Sections dealing with the pottery of this Period. 4

See p. 559 seqq. 2 See p. 578.

3 See Coloured Plate VII.

4 See p. 552 seqq., and Fig. 404.

From i-io metres down a change took place in the character of the Precious deposit. The pottery ceased and the earth grew fatter and more compact.

PLAN

FIG. 335 A. PLAN OF TEMPLE REPOSITORIES.

WEST CIST EAST CIST

SECTION ON LINE Avv FIG. 335 B. SECTION OF TEMPLE REPOSITORIES.

Throughout this stratum to the floor of the Repositories precious relics in various materials were heaped together.

The two Repositories differed radically in structure (see Figs. 334, While that on the Western side of the chamber was formed of massive masonry, that to the East was constructed of slabs dove-tailed together in the style of the Northern Series (B) of the Kaselles' of the Long Gallery and of the cists described above, 1 which were subsequently found immediately N. of these Repositories. It was composed of hard grey limestone slabs, 16 centimetres thick, and was 1-52 metres deep, 1-9 long, and 1-43 in breadth the dimensions being slightly greater than those of the other Repository.

Faience Here, in the fatty deposit beneath the stratum containing the pottery,

Eastern came to light a marvellous series of relics in the native faience, a large proportion of which, though mostly found in a fragmentary condition, it was possible eventually to put together.

These elegant faience objects, with others representing the actual fittings of the shrine, were almost exclusively contained in the Eastern Repository. That to the West of it, both as regards construction and contents, presents a striking contrast to it and was clearly designed for a different purpose- the actual safeguarding of treasure in precious metals.

Western This Western Repository was not constructed cist fashion like the tory S other, but was built of solid blocks of masonry, some 42 centimetres in thickness (see Fig. 335). With the exception of the uppermost course of the South wall which has two blocks, a single block goes the whole length of a side in every case. This masonry is in three courses, which rest all round on a lower course in a single piece with the bottom of the cist. As will be seen from the Plans and Sections the interior capacity of this cist is slightly less than the other. It has an inner width and breadth of 176 and 1-37 metres, and is 1-50 metres deep. A remarkable feature is presented by the dowel-holes which are worked both in the sides and floor. Such dowel-holes in the masonry point in other cases to a wooden framework, but it seems possible that there was here also a metal casing. Broken That the breaking into the vault or of chests contained in it was a work hammers ser ous difficulty is shown by a dramatic touch supplied by two objects left by those who had rifled it. Two stone hammers were in fact found within in a fractured and much battered condition. A view of half of one of these, finely executed in red and black breccia, is given in Fig. 336. It will be seen that, in addition to the main breakage, the edges of the butts at both ends have been completely chipped away by hard usage. The stone hammers are of a type of which perfect specimens of more or less contemporary date have been found at Hagia Triacla and elsewhere. It will be seen that, in 1 See p. 454.

contrast with the neolithic stone hammers given in Fig. 15 a above, the perforation shows a straight section and does not expand towards the mouth. Except for beads and inlays and one important fragment the middle part of the principal figure of the Snake Goddess the faience relics were contained in the Eastern cist. On the other hand, greater masses of Contents gold-foil were brought out of the Western receptacle than from any other spot R epos j on the site. There was also found here a bronze looped handle (Fig. 337, B) tor y-15 centimetres in width, and another of less dimensions apparently belonging to a smaller box. The bronze object (Fig. 337, A) with rivet-holes at its smaller end is possibly part of a clamp belonging to a larger coffer. With these were the carbonized remains of what must evidently have been

FIG. 336. BROKEN HAMMER OF BRECCIA FROM W. REPOSITORY.

a treasure-chest, together with quantities of inlays, many of them of crystal. But, as usual, the massive objects of goldsmith's work had been removed by plunderers. Once more we have to face the fact that for the vessels or other objects in precious metals belonging to this brilliant stage of the Palace history we have still to look to the imported treasures brought to light in the Shaft Graves of Mycenae. We are even tempted to believe that some of these had actually found their way there from this treasury of the Palace Shrine at Knossos. That the fluted types of gold cups found in the Fourth Shaft Grave at Mycenae, as well as the goblets with the Vapheio handles, go back at Knossos as far as the Second Middle Minoan Period has been demonstrated above. 1

A good deal of the gold-foil found in this Repository showed signs of having been cut out to be applied to inlays. Some pieces exhibited 1 See p. 243 and Fig. 183.

Remains of

Treasury Chests.

Gold-foil and Crystal Inlays.

THE PALACE OF MINOS, ETC.

a petal-like form resembling that of many of the crystal plaques, while others presented a ribbed surface, also characteristic of some crystal fragments. 1

The crystal petals, of which over a score came to light (Fig. 337), were, slightly hollowed out above, like natural petals, and in some cases they

FIG. 337. FRAGMENTARY RELICS FROM W. REPOSITORY: A. BRONZE CLAMP; B, c. BRONZE HANDI D. GOLD-FOIL FROM RIBBED CRYSTAL BARS; E, F, GOLD-FOIL FOR VARIOUS INLAYS; G. CRYSTAL DISK SILVER BACKING; H. CRYSTAL PETALS OF MARGUERITE PATTERN.

were partly enveloped with gold-leaf. The under-side of one or two of them was coated with closely adhering silver-foil recalling the backing of many of the crystal inlays of the Royal Gaming Board described below. In one 1 A part of a ribbed crystal bar is shown on Fig. 337, between the petals and the large crystal disk.

instance there was further attached to this a casing of gold-leaf, laid behind the silver-foil apparently to preserve it from oxidization, to which immediate contact with wood or ivory might have rendered it liable. The crystal petals, which were 3-4 centimetres in length, seem to have formed part of Marguerite flowers, like those seen on the borders of the Gaming Board. Their larger scale, however, in the present case, which points on the above analogy to their having surrounded the cloisons of disks slightly more than their length in diameter, leads to the conclusion that they occupied a more central position in the composition to which they belonged. They are thus shown in the restoration given below. 1 From the number of the petals it is clear that they had formed part of more than one medallion.

In addition to these there was found a large crystal disk 10-8 centimetres (over 4 inches) in diameter, slightly convex above and backed below in the same way with silver-foil. It seems probable that it had formed part of the inlays to which the medallions containing the crystal petals belonged. It is a noteworthy fact that a crystal disk, also somewhat convex above, was found, together with smaller bossed disks of the same material, in a deposit attributed to the third stage of the Second City at Hissarlik. 2

As to the character of the object of which these formed part considerable light is thrown by other relics from this Repository in the shape of plaques for inlaying, composed of the native faience, some of them with incurved edges that had evidently been adapted to the circumference of medallions such as the above. These, as will be shown below, present a remarkable conformity both in shape and even in the details of the painted decoration of the native porcelain with similar inlays found in the Fourth Shaft Grave at Mycenae. In that case too the faience plaques inlays were associated with others of rock crystal, and a portion that it has been possible to put together 3 receives its true explanation from the still more of Royal magnificent work of the kind, the Royal Draught-board, to which board. reference has already been made. 4 Its discovery, described above, stands in relation to the remains of an important Hall on the Eastern borders of the Central Court, but it has been thought desirable to reserve its 1 See below, p. 481, Fig. 344. I lion. Faience beads and a curious object

Now in the Museum fur Volkerkunde at in a similar glazed paste (pp. tit., p. 391, Figs.

Berlin. One of the smaller bosses is attached 374, 375) were found in the same deposit.

to a copper backing. Professor Hubert 3 See below, p. 482, and Fig. 346.

Schmidt kindly drew my attention to these 4 See above, p. 386 seqq.

objects, which are not described in Troja und description for this place since it illustrates in its most perfect and sumptuous aspect a class of object that had also formed a "special feature in the Treasury of the Priest Kings, as represented by the contents of the Temple Repositories. The correspondences in detail will be fully illustrated by the restoration attempted below of parts of similar objects from the Repository itself and from the Fourth Shaft Grave.

From the close parallelism presented between the Royal Draughtboard and these other remains it is clear that its fabric must date from the same epoch the closing phase, that is, of M. M. III. At the same time the worn state of the gold plating that had originally covered so much of its surface may be taken as an indication that it had been for many years in Crystal use. As already stated, moreover, the position in which it was found points from 5 to the conclusion that this magnificent object may have survived as an

Room of heirloom in the great Hall of the Late Minoan Palace. The same con- Throne.

elusion may also apply to some crystal inlays found in the lustral basin that flanks the Room of the Throne, and which clearly formed part of the intarsia work of a similar board. One of the plaques here found was made so as to fit the angle between two medallions about 1 1 centimetres in diameter, while another petal-shaped piece not only reproduces the form of those that border the upper medallions of the Royal Draught-board, but showed traces of a similar eye of Egyptian Blue having been applied to its lower surface. 1 Owing to the very careful methods adopted in raising and securing the Royal Gaming Board 2 it has been possible, in spite of the friable nature of the framework, to preserve the original arrangement in all essential details.

Rctal Some idea of this magnificent work is given in Coloured Plate V 3

Draught- which shows its present condition. The larger fragments here are given in a darker tone, but a great deal of the remaining part of its superficies existed actually, in a more or less disintegrated condition. The pale brown here represents ivory, and the yellow, gold, but there were also considerable further remains of thin gold plating. Many ragged edges of this overlapped the ivory inlays, and it had once entirely coated them over. The grey colour shows the crystal plaques where they were backed by silver plates, and the white the same restored. Similarly, the darker and lighter tones mark the crystal where still, or originally, backed by a cobalt paste formed of pounded kyanos. 4 1 See below, p. 473, and Fig. 338. Both this and the silver plates were 3 See above, p. 387. backed by white plaster.

3 From Mr. Fyfe's drawing.

PLATI V INLAID;. MIM; HOARD

The board as completed is 0-965 metre in length and 0-553 wide, and it is to be noted that several of the component parts are exact multiples of the whole. Thus the diameter of the larger medallions answers to I of the length, that of the smaller medallions to-, that of the marguerites

The framework of the board is compacted of ivory pieces, and it is probable that there was originally a wooden panel supporting those below. Some pieces of ivory reliefs, including small argonauts, for which there is no place on the surface of the. board, point to the probability of there having been ornamental sides below. The analogy, moreover, of Egyptian draughtboards and of the Mycenaean specimen found at Enkomi in Cyprus suggests that the board itself may have also served as the top of a box that once contained the pieces of the game.

The daisies or marguerites of the outer border had central bosses Character consisting of convex disks of rock crystal, set perhaps on a gold back- tars j a ground. Within this border, round the central and lower part of the board work-was a second band of plaster coated with blue paste or kyanos, some Mar-sections of which were preserved in position. There can be little doubt fnd Ar that these had been covered with crystal plaques that had fallen off. gonauts.

Beginning now at the top of the board, the left-hand corner of which is reproduced in Fig. 338, the angles formed by the beautiful argonaut reliefs T were set round with crystal plaques, one of which was found with traces of and Silver its original kyanos backing. Like the marguerites, the argonauts had also been adorned with a central boss of crystal. There next follows a very beautiful group of four large medallions inserted among crystal bars backed with silver plates. The curving cloisons of these medallions are formed of ribbed ivory, to the surface of which the original coating of thin gold plate was still partly adhering. The sockets thus formed are set with petal-shaped plaques of crystal, the outer row entirely lined with silver plates, the inner with blue eyes of kyanos, inserted in the silver. The inner circle of these medallions encloses a rosette pattern which, as already shown, goes back in Cretan intarsia work at least to the beginning of the Middle Minoan Age. 1 The vesicae piscis here are of ivory, doubtless originally gold plated, and they surround a central plate of silver-lined crystal with incurving sides.

These four upper medallions stand within a framework that might suggest the plan of a four-towered stronghold. Three disks in a kind of outer ward, 1 See above p. 170, and Fig. 120, and compare p. 268.

THE PALACE OF MINOS, ETC.

one projecting beyond the others, form a triple bastion, while a fourth fenced squarely round may be looked on as the inner keep. Below, six ribbed bars

FIG. 338. LEFT-HAND UPPER CORNER OF ROYAL DRAUGHT-BOARD.

of crystal backed by silver plates, alternating with five of gold-plated ivory, 1 separate what we may regard as the citadel from another enclosure, with a broad bastion in front and two wings, the flat ivory plaques of which 1 The crystal bars are flat, the ivory are rounded above. The ivory bars were still largely covered with their thin gold plating.

enclose the opening of ten smaller medallions, restored in the coloured Plate. 1 On either side of this bastion were four similar ribbed bars of crystal on silver, with bossed ivory partitions like the wider bars above. Between the two wings of the lower enclosure there were eight flat crystal bars separated by similar bands of ivory.

The essential core of the Plan and ,,. Character arrangement, stripped of its more 0 fgame. purely decorative elements, is shown in the diagrammatic plan Fig. 339. The citadel above, with its four disks fenced round by its outer ward and keep, is obviously the goal of the game. It is completely separated off from the enclosure below with its two wings and bastioned front, which presents ten disks of somewhat lesser diameter. It looks as if the game proper had been played on this, one player starting on each wing and the successive occupation of the squares of the citadel being dependent on the results obtained below. The victory in each case may have been marked by placing a piece on one of the upper disks, two wins on either side making of course a drawn game.

It is possible that the horizontal bars were used for marking the scores. The flat crystal bars, whether with a ribbed or plain surface, are set between the bossed ivory divisions in such a way that any small pencil-like

FIG. 339. ARRANGEMENT OF DRAUGHTBOARD, D1AGRAMMATICALLY SHOWN.

1 The remains of silver oxide in the centre of one of these indicate that these too were of crystal, silver-lined like the medallions above, and surrounded by similar vesicaepiscis.

These are here restored as consisting of crystal plaques backed with kyanos. They may, however, have been of gold-plated ivory.

THE PALACE OF MINOS, ETC.

Compared with C. reek Polis.

B BBMB MHMHMMpp rod placed on them would keep its position (see Fig. 340). Taking in the short bars on the sides, the total number of points that could thus be recorded with a short marker laid on the bars would be 10, a number corresponding with the disks below. The remaining four bars on either side, distin-guished by a plain surface, correspond with the number of the upper disks. The comparison that has suggested itself of the upper enclosure with a four-towered citadel calls up an interesting analogy with the Greek game of polls or city, and the underlying idea of an assault on a fortified city is no doubt common to both, as to the kindred Roman game of latrunculi. But the resemblance is only of a very general kind. The classical gaming boards seem to have been entirely divided into squares. The name ofdogs' (ewes), applied to the pieces used in the game of pois, 1 points to a derivation from those of similar Egyptian boards in the shape of jackals. 2 The arrangement of the Cypro-Minoan board found at Enkomi, 3 a triple group of four squares from the central set of which proceeds a file of eight others, is directly taken over from an Egyptian type. In the present case we have a highly differentiated variety and no close parallel to the Knossian Gaming Board has as yet been supplied either by Egypt or the Classical World.

The very simple character of the grouping of the disks in what seems to have been the compartment of the Board reserved for the actual play makes it clear that variety and interest was here supplied by the inclusion of an element of chance. What we have before us would in that case not iiimiiimii

MMMMM lillljlkuiifl

FIG. 340. SECTION OF BOARD SHOWING RIBBED CRYSTAL BARS, ALTERNATELY BOSSED

AND FLAT.- 1 Pollux, Onom. ix. 98, c. The name sometimes appears as TIo as, e. g. Plato, Republ. iv (p. 423) and the Scholiast on the passage. For an acute commentary on this see Ridgeway, J. H. S., xvi, p. 288 seqq.

Hatasu's Draught-board the pieces have lions' heads.

3 B. M. Excavations in Cyprus, p. 12, Fig. 19, and Ridgeway, loc. fit. On the Assyrian and Hittite characteristics of the hunting scenes on the side of the box see my Mycenaean 2 See Ridgeway, op. at., p. 289. On Queen Cyprus. J. Atithr. hist., xxx (1900), p. 210 seqq.

be a pure game of skill, like chess, but something analogous to backgammon, where recourse was had to dice-throwing or some other simple form of sortilege. Sections of split reeds, having thus a convex and a concave face, are in fact thrown against a wall by the Fellaheen to determine the moves in a modern game of draughts 1 as in our heads and tails'. An illustration of such, side by side with the draughtsmen themselves, already occurs in a Third Dynasty Tomb. 2 Dice were also used in Ancient Egypt and it seems possible that certain forms of prism beads showing circles and globules on their faces served as such. 3 A M. M. II specimen of agate is given in Fig. 341 from Papouda near Lyttos. Such dice might be conveniently strung round the wrist.

Supposing then that in the present case each player had four pieces distinguished perhaps like the Egyptian by their red and white hues these would have been set on the board and their moves regulated in some such manner.

On the form of the pieces used in this game a remarkable light has been thrown by the discovery in a neighbouring deposit bordering on the Loom-Weight Basement and the later area of the Spiral Fresco', of four ivory objects which were at once recognized as some form of draughts-men. Two of these presenting engraved bases 4 are given in Fig. 342, a, b. They were found in filling earth, which, as shown above, 5 must have been thrown in previous to the laying down of a plaster floor belonging to the latest stage of the M. M. Ill Period. It follows that they can hardly be brought down to this latest M. M. 111 phase, to which ex hypothesi the original fabric of the Gaming Board itself may be referred, though the discrepancy in date may have been small. The ivory men were themselves found on the borders of an area, which, as indicated by the heaps of loom-weights, was originally the quarters of women. The close vicinity of the two finds points to this area as having heen a traditional scene of such pastimes.

Dice probably used for game.

FIG. 341. PKRFORATKD AGATE PRISM (PAPOUDA)

Discovery ot Ivory men.

Ivory Draughtsmen.

1 Mr. P. E. Newberry has called my attention to these.

2 Quibell, Tomb of ffcsy, PI. X (Service des Antiquites, 1911-12). Ivory examples exist, cf. . Fine Arts Club Cat., 1921, p. 112, T. 10.

; i Dice formed part of the Egyptian form of the Game of the Sacred Way (see E. Falkener, Games Andent and Modern, p. 97).

4 The other piece had a plain base. It was approximately of the same as the others.

8 See p. 249.

THE PALACE OF MINOS, ETC.

Pre-

Dynastic Egyptian comparisons.

The diameter of the pieces given in Fig. 342 (8 centimetres) so closely corresponds with that of the disks of the Gaming Board that we may fairly conclude that they had belonged to a board or boards of a very similar kind.

The ivory objects are more or less conical in shape, and of more solid proportions than the usual Egyptian pieces. It is, however, interesting to note that their form closely approaches that of the prehistoric clay

FIG. 342 a, b. IVORY MEN WITH ENGRAVED BASES.

found, together with a gaming table of the same Nile mud, in a pre-dynastic grave of the Cemetery of El Mahasna. 1 Once more our Cretan comparisons with Egypt are carried back beyond the Dynasties.

So early in fact was the Egyptian game taken over in the island, that, as has been shown above, 2 not only is a draught-player depicted on an Early 1 E. B. Ayrton and W. L. S. Loat, Pre-dynastic Cemetery of El Mahasna, PI, XVII and p. 30. The surface of the mud table was divided into 18 squares, in three lines of 6.

Nine smaller and two larger pieces were found.

2 See p. 124 and Figs. 93 A, a 2, 93 c, a.

Minoan prism seal but the draught-board sign, men, under its primitive pre-dynastic form is actually imitated on another contemporary signet. Shell medallions with quatrefoil inlays, possibly from an earlier draught-board, occurred in the proto-Palatial (M. M. I a) Vat-Room Deposit. 1

The upper surface of the specimen Fig. 342, a shows eight flutings, like the petals of a rosette folded backwards 2, and on its base, answering to these, are eight incised circles arranged round the border the number perhaps corresponding with that of the men used in the game.

The piece reproduced in Fig. 342 b is of special interest since the radiated design incised on its base can hardly be regarded otherwise than as having a religious significance. The rayed circle surrounding an inner circle is one of a series of astral types belonging to the Cretan hieroglyphic signary which have been recognized as stellar or rayed solar symbols. 3 Elsewhere we see the outer rayed circle become a wheel, the four spokes of which intersect the inner circle, and this form of the symbol has a special interest since it forms part of a series of moulds on a stone matrix found in Siteia 4 in association with another showing the Minoan Goddess holding aloft two

Double Axes, and with others of Double Axes by themselves and of the Horns of Consecration.

Another even more remarkable parallel is supplied by a fragment of a fresco, approaching in scale the miniature class, completed in Fig. 343. 5

Rayed Solar symbol on base of Ivory Man.

IP BLUE MIRED. FIG. 343.

. YELLOW I BLACK

PART OF FRIEZE ON FRESCO FRAGMENT FROM IJTH MAGAZINE.

Solar

Symbol of Minoan

Goddess on Mould

Fresco.

1 See above, p. 170 and Fig. 120.

2 An Egyptian piece may be compared, showing a lotus petal decoration (Falkener, op. cit., p. 20). It is, however, of elongated form and with the usual knobbed top.

See Serif to. Ainoa, i, p. 221. No. 1073.

See below, Fig. 371, and Xanthudides,

Mijtpai apxauu IK STTCIOS TT Kptns, E. Ap., 1900, Plates 3, 4, and p. 25 seqq.

5 A coloured illustration of this fragment is given by Fyfe, Painted Plaster Decoration,-t., Pl. II, 4.

This fresco depicts the lower part of the front of a Minoan shrine, beneath its central columnar opening, and its central feature is a medallion enclosing a rayed circle within which appears a smaller disk. The symbolic figure here resembles that of the ivory piece even to the number of the rays, which are in each case sixteen.

Rayed At the side of this rayed emblem appears a triglyph of a decorative olivary f rm ar d the whole design is less conventional and freer from a direct piece architectural influence than in the case of analogous subjects belonging to religious the early part of the Late Minoan Age. In the miniature Temple Fresco' for instance, as in other examples x of that class, the frieze has taken its stereotyped form of triglyphs of structural formation between the usual elongated half rosettes. But the above fragment belongs to the category of those found beneath the late superficial cists of the 13th Magazine, showing a freer treatment, and which certainly came within the limits of M. M. III.

There need be little discrepancy in date between the ivory piece and the frieze to which this parallel design belongs, while on the other hand, as part of the decoration of the front of a Minoan shrine, it corroborates the religious significance of this rayed symbol.

That a form of game on which such luxurious fittings were lavished should have been associated in some way with the cult of the Minoan Goddess is itself a probable conclusion. It may be noted, moreover, in this connexion that the Egyptian chess-men with the heads of the lion of Basht or Sekhet, and of the jackal of Anubis, also stand in a religious association. The God Thoth was said to have been the inventor of the game.

In its original condition, with its ivory bands and reliefs still plated with gold, and its crystal plaques and bosses intensifying the glint and glow of the silver-foil and cerulean paste beneath them, the Gaming Board itself must have been of truly royal magnificence.

Recon- The comparative material supplied by this object makes it clear that o'rmrtof var i us remains of inlays, both of crystal and of native faience, as well as Draught- much of the coating of gold-foil found in the Western Temple Repository, from w. had belonged to a similar Draught-board. Certain fragments of faience tory. S plaques showing light green horizontal stripes on a dark greenish brown ground, indicate, as will be seen from the restored drawing, Fig. 344, that they formed part of the framework of medallions, approximately 11 centimetres in diameter. These dimensions as a matter of fact fit in well with the size of the large crystal disk, and would also harmonize with an arrange- 1 See Vol. II.

ment of the crystal petals round a smaller disk as shown in the drawing. Parts of the lateral arrangement, including the ribbed crystal bars, are also represented, Fig. 344 b, i, and sections of what appears to have been a moulded faience frame (3). An incurved lozenge-shaped fragment of banded faience belonging to a central inlay between larger disks is also reproduced (4).

iiiiiiiiimiiiiiiiiiii
HWfmfwWHWIHWl!
Ill IllllllllllllltIlll -Crystal

FIG. 344. a. RESTORATION OF PART OF INLAID GAMING BOARD FROM W. TEMPLE REPOSITORY b. ASSOCIATED INLAYS OF FAIENCE AND CRYS-TAL.

In the restored drawing inner markings have been added to the crystal petals, a large number of which were preserved, on the analogy of those shown within the faience disks of what appears to have been a similar board from Mycenae, Fig. 346, below. The suggestion that the petals of the Knossos board were adorned in a similar manner by the application of a coloured foliation on the back of the crystal is itself fully warranted by the crystal eyes' on the back of the plaques contained in the larger medallions i i i

THE PALACE OF MINOS, ETC.

Remains of Parallel Board from IVth Shaft Grave.

of the Royal Draught-board. This completion of the rosettes, moreover, receives a strong confirmation from a nearer source in direct dependence on Knossos. At the neighbouring site of Tylissos in a more or less contemporary deposit was found the remains of a lid of an ivory box inlaid with faience disks, probably from the Palace fabric, decorated with rosettes, the petals of which present similar inner foliations, here outlined in a lighter tone against the dark calix borders (Fig. 345). 1

The remains of the similar board found in the Fourth Shaft Grave at Mycenae, of which a restored drawing is given in Fig. 346, 2 present, as will

FIG. 345. LID OF IVORY Box FROM TYLISSOS INLAID WITH FAIENCE ROSETTES.

be seen by a comparison with Fig. 344, a very close parallel to those from the Temple Repository. The rosette patterns of the medallions, here executed in faience, may well be regarded as copies, in that material, of cloisoned crystal work such as that of the Knossian example. The central plaque of incurved lozenge-shaped form that filled the space between the medallions is of the same faience as the remains of similar plaques from the Temple Repository, 3 and its decoration of horizontal bars, alternately of 1 J. Hatzidakis, Tua rros Muwtxr; (Apx- E., 1912), pp. 223, 224, and Fig. 32.

2 The drawing reproduced in Fig. 346 was executed for me by M. E. Gillieyon, fils, with the kind permission of the Ephor, Dr. V. Stais.

3 Fig. 344, b 4 shows part of a larger lozenge-shaped plaque of similar material, belonging to a disk about 15 cm. in diameter, also found in the W. Repository.

dark brown and pale green, also corresponds. The Sacral Knots', moreover, found with the remains of the draught-board in the Fourth Shaft Grave which are of the same faience material, present a tartan pattern identical with that of the ivory knot from Knossos. It is clear in fact that these faience objects must be regarded as actual products of the Palace fabric of Knossos, about which more will be said below.

FIG. 346. FAIENCE MEDALLION INLAYS FROM DRAUGHT-BOARD. SHAFT GRAVE, MYCENAE.

FOURTH

That the Sacral Knots' in this case were directly connected with Sacral the draught-board found in the same Shaft Grave is further shown by connected a significant correspondence in makers' marks. On the back of the upper with part of the knot reproduced in Fig. 347 A are seen three indented strokes, board, evidently the number of a series, which also occurred on the back of the

THE PALACE OF MINOS, ETC.

Small Ivory Disks.

faience medallions, Fig. 347 B. 1 Groups of similar indented strokes are also characteristic of contemporary inlays in various materials found at Knossos and on other Cretan sites.

With these faience relics there were also found in the same Shaft

Minoan Craftsmen's Marks' on Inlays

FIG. 347 A, B. CRAFTSMENS MARKS ON BACK OF FAIENCE DISKS, AND UPPER PART OF SACRAL KNOT. FOURTH SHAFT GRAVE, MYCENAE.

Grave numerous flat crystal bars, some with square ends like those of the Knossian Draught-board, others with their ends cut diagonally, as Fig. 348. a It is clear that in this case, as in the remains of the draught-board from the Temple Repository, intarsia work in crystal and other materials was. combined with faience inlays.

A set of six small pieces with signs and groups of dots on their lower face found in the same grave have been regarded as men belonging to the board, but their small size alone must preclude this idea. To judge from Knossian pieces illustrated above, these must have been proportioned to the size of the medallions. The signs and numbers on these ivory disks cannot indeed be separated from similar marks on a very large category of Minoan objects, 1 Complete remains of these only existed on also occurs at Knossos) and eleven of the one medallion, but parts of similar strokes are rectangular, besides broken specimens. For seen on two others. On the edge of the these and other details I am much indebted to.

central lozenge-shaped piece were four strokes. Mr. A. J. B. Wace.

1 There were fifteen of this form (which

FIG. 348. INLAYING.

SPECIMEN OF CRYSTAL BAR FOR FOURTH SHAFT GRAVE, MYCENAE.

and it seems to be clear that in all cases these signs had to do with the fabric itself. 1 They are either found on the bottom of inlays or in places where they would be concealed from the spectator's eye. Thus the T-shaped sign here seen is frequent, with or without accompanying dots, on the under sides of the faience roundels for inlaying found in the Room of the Throne at Knossos, and, again, in the same position, on the bone inlays in the shape of vesicae piscis that presented such a variety of marks and numbers from a drain-shaft of the Domestic Quarter. 3 A more probable hypothesis would be that these disks, coated with gold-foil, had been set in the centre of rosettes forming a border to the Mycenae draught-board like those of the Royal board of Knossos.

The conformity of signs and numbers here seen with the Cretan Equa- Craftsmen's Marks itself supplies a new link of connexion. The equations between presented between these relics from the Fourth Shaft Grave with those cp u th of the Temple Repository at Knossos are also of great value as a chrono- Grave logical datum for the early elements of the Mainland interment. positories.

The Sacral Knots in connexion with the Mycenae draught-board themselves reveal a dedicatory intention such as that which led to the deposit of its counterpart in the Reliquary of the Knossian shrine.

The practice of depositing p-aming- boards in tombs was of great Custom . r,. of placing antiquity in Egypt, going back there, as is shown by the clay example Draught- from El Mahasna-, to the Pre-dynastic Period, and finds its most splendid To bs," illustration in the ivory draught-board and men found in the Tomb of Queen Egyp- tian. Hatasu. In historic tombs the deceased himself is at times represented in the act of playing a game. To the Minoan princes who founded the great dynasty Sacred to of Mycenae, a draught-board was, too, such an indispensable possession that Goddess it followed them to the grave. 4 Nor are the signs of consecration without their a p d special significance. The game itself was sacred to their patron divinity, of Dead, whose realm included the Nether as well as the Upper World, and in the halls of the Great Goddess it might still be played.

1 I hope to deal with these Craftsmen's belonging to a similar board, in Tomb A at Marks' in the second volume of my Scripta Kakovatos (L. M. 1 1). See Ath. Mitlh., xxxiv, Minoa. PI. xiv, 14, 15. The draught-board found in 2 Knossos, Report, 1900, p. 42. the tomb at Old Paphos (Enkomi) shows that Ib. 1901, pp. 118, 119. the practice continued to the latest Minoan 4 There were remains of inlays, perhaps Period.

Faience fabrics from IVth Shaft Grave identical with those of Temple Repositories at Knossos; Evidences of early development of native faience in Crete; Its Egyptian origin; Moulds found at Knossos; Analysis ofknossian faience (Researches of Church and Hea(oii); Mettod of manufacture; TJie Palace fabric of Knossos; The faience beads imitations of Egyptian types; History of the segmented variety; Diffusion of faience bead types by Minoan Commerce; Occurrence of segmented and other imported forms in S. E. Spain and British Isles; Chronological bearing on Western Bronze Age; Gemral indications of Minoan connexions with West Mediterranean Basin; Festoons, apparently of beads and pendants, between Columns of Minoan shrines.

Faience ATTENTION has been called at the end of the last Section to the absolute
fromtvth correspondence, not only in the form, but in the texture of the material, the
Shaft hue and even the details of the decoration visible in the remains of the identical
faience inlays of the two draught-boards one from the Western Temple of Temple
Repository at Knossos, the other from the Fourth Shaft Grave at Mycenae. Reposi-
The phenomenon itself has a double value from the archaeological point of tones.
view. Since the identical relics from the Repository were found in association with
pottery of the M. M. Ill b class, we have a definite clue to the elate of those found in
the mainland interment. Both, moreover, were clearly the products of the same fabric,
and the overwhelming balance of the evidence shows that the place of origin in both
cases was a faience factory at Knossos, in connexion with the Great Palace. Like the
Sacral Knots' of the same material displaying the Minoan tartan, found together with
the inlays in the Shaft Grave, the whole group of faience relics there discovered must
be regarded as of Cretan importation.

Evidence This exquisite Minoan glazed ware, the most extraordinary revelation
Develop- f which was afforded by the group of the Snake Goddess and her votaries
ment of found in the Eastern Repository, brings us face to face with what towards
Faience the close of the Middle Minoan Age maybe regarded as perhaps the highest
: te- technical accomplishment of the indigenous art. This native fabric, not only of
beads but of actual vessels, has been shown to go back to the Second
Early Minoan Period. In the proto-Palatial deposit, again, of M. M. I a date,
beneath the Vat-Room, besides beads showing a VIth Dynasty tradition, inlays of this
material already occurred, forming part of medallions and perhaps indeed belonging
to an earlier draught-board.

FIG. 349. BLACK STEATITE MATRICES FOR MOULDING FAIENCE OB-
JECTS, WITH MOULDINGS

BESIDE IT. (f f.)

Elaborate products of the same artistic industry, dating from the close of M. M. I I
have already received illustration in the case of the Town

THE PALACE OF MINOS, ETC.

Egyptian Origins of Cretan Faience.

Moulds

Faience

Objects found at

Knossos.

SIDE.

Mosaic V The extraordinary proficiency attained in the fabric of this beautiful
glazed ware as seen in the relics from the Temple Repositories is itself indeed a
sufficient indication of a long independent development of the art on Cretan soil.

The art itself had been beyond all doubt implanted there, together with many other
technical acquirements, through that early contact with Egypt to which in the course
of this survey we lllicfsnr ltl have had such frequent j G j3M occasion to refer. The l
i"

parallelism of the marks 2 found on some of the

Knossian inlays itself affords an indication of a continued relation of the Egyptian and Cretan craftsmen down to Late

Minoan times.

It is impossible to doubt that these wares were actually made on the site of Knossos, and indeed a black steatite mould for objects of this class, probably belonging to the epoch immediately succeeding that of the Temple Repositories, 3 was actually found in a dependency to the North-West of the Palace. 4 One side of this presents matrices (Fig. 349, c) of trochus and trumpet shells, 6 a segment of a spiral bracelet, a rosette, and semilunar plaque. The other side of the stone shows a mould for a clenched human hand, probably an amulet, b, and a very elegant kind of bracket, 0, developed in Fig. 1350. Faience specimens of such objects, 1 See above, p. 301 seqq. The small gold- On the faience inlays from the Temple Remounted vase of blue faience from the Loom-Weight basement belongs to the same epoch (see p. 252, Fig. 189 a, above).

2 See A. J. E., Knossos, Report, 1900, p. 42. The marks on the faience roundels found in the Room of the Throne are there compared to

PUA. M ON TOP

FIG. 350. DEVELOPMENT OF BRACKET BASED ON SECTION GIVEN BY MOULD, FIG. 349, a.

those of Tell-el-Yahudiyeh, but they are of an earlier date. Similar signs were found on faience plaques at Phaestos and H. Triada.

positories with the exception of the double axe there are only notches and dots.

3 Cf. the slightly later L. M. I b example from the Messenian Pylos (p. 489, note i).

4 The North-West Building (see Vol. II).

5 Apparently copied from a fossil form, e. g. Ptychoceras gaultinus, a cretaceous species.

6 On a smaller side of the stone is a mould for a larger console of the same class.

though not so elegantly formed, have been found both at Knossos and in Mainland Greece. 1 They all show a horizontal perforation through the rolled projection above and, usually, two rivet holes, one above the other, in the sunken disk below. The exact application of these objects remains uncertain, but it seems clear that they served as brackets or supports. 2

The very careful examination and analyses of various specimens of Analysis this glazed ware 3 by Professor A. H. Church and Mr. Noel Heaton show f a n that they represent a true faience technique. The material is almost pure Faience-sand and clay, and was moulded into shape. The true character of the 1 A plain example in the native faience was found near the South Propylaeum at Knossos. The nearest parallel to the Repository type, though already somewhat degenerate, occurred in the tholos tomb of the Messenian Pylos dated by the pottery as L. M. I l (Ap. E. 1914, p. 103, Fig. 5). Such objects are frequent in Mycenaean Graves of late date (e. g. Mycenae, Et. Ap X. 1887, Pl. xiii, 18; Spata, Bull, de Corr. Hell. 1878, Pl. xiv, 5). These latter show reduplicated folds in decreasing order, and are very degraded copies of the fine foliate form given by the mould. A stone mould for a similar object was found at Mycenae (Schlie-mann, Mycenae, p. 107, Fig. 162) and part of another, op. cit., p. 109, Fig. 163.

2 The architectonic aspect of the object as seen in Fig. 350 is enhanced by the disks below, so characteristic of Minoan facades. The central feature with its rolled projection has been compared by Mr. Edward Bell Hellenic Architecture, its Genesis and Growth, p. 29) with the Corinthian modillion.

Professor Church observes: Besides silica, the glaze contained lime, a little magnesia, some soda, and a larger amount of potash. The friable and rather porous " body " or paste of this glazed material contains (in the state in which it was analysed): (a) moisture and other matters, 1-22 per cent.; (6) matters soluble in strong hydrochloric acid, 2-22 per cent.; (t) quartzite sand with traces of mica, felspar, and clay, 96-56 per cent. (= 100). (l) consists chiefly of lime and the oxides of iron, alumina, and copper, (c) consists of 97-01 per cent, of silica, 1-33 per cent, of alumina, and 0-17 per cent, of lime, with traces of lime, magnesia, copper, and alkalies. The paste when dry has received a coating of glaze, and has been fixed at a moderate heat, just sufficient to fuse the latter without softening the body. Professor Church considers that the glaze owes its colouring mainly to copper and that it is probably nearly related to Egyptian Blue. The dark browns and black, however, are referred by him to a ferruginous origin. These results have been confirmed by the preliminary researches of Mr. Noel Heaton. To account for the plasticity of the composition he suggested that 'the sand was mixed with a resinous material in order to give it sufficient plasticity to keep it in shape when pressed into moulds. It was then removed from the mould, dried, and painted with a mixture of metallic oxide and alkali the metal varying according to the colour desired and fired at a moderate temperature for a considerable time. Mr. Heaton thinks that the view that the manufacture took place in the Palace precincts is confirmed by a fragment of a re-used stone found by Mr. Doll in the upper part of a Late Minoan wall of the Domestic Quarter. This fragment is covered with glaze and corresponds with stones found in connexion with ancient furnaces, as in the case of the Roman potterykilns recently investigated near Chester. The stone may, however, have been used in a Palace pottery kiln.

THE PALACE OF MINOS, ETC.

Method of Fabric: True Faience.

Palace Fabric of Faience.

Faience Beads.

Imitation of

Egyptian Types.

manufacture appears from the fact that at times not only the surface but the whole composition of the objects consisted of vitreous paste. In that case they were intermediate between mere glazed ware and the moulded glass beads and plaques that came into vogue in Late Minoan and Mycenaean times.

The prevailing ground colour of this fabric, as produced in the nourishing days of its manufacture at Knossos, is pale green or bluish white, at times giving place to a pure white or to a yellowish or lilac tinge, more rarely taking a livelier tone of emerald green or turquoise blue. The patterns and designs are laid upon this field in a purplish or pure brown, deepening into black, and sometimes assume a pure lilac hue. The refined colouring and delicate nuances of tone lend a peculiar charm to this Cretan fabric.

It hardly needed the discovery of actual moulds to show that the Minoan Priest-Kings had anticipated the practice of many later rulers in establishing a fabric of artistic wares in connexion with the royal residence. The Palace manufactory of Knossos is the remote predecessor of that of Vincennes and Sevres, of Medicean Florence, of Urbino or Capodimonte, of Meissen, and other princely establishments of the same kind, whether the actual material was faience, porcelain, or majolica.

Among the objects from the Temple Repositories for which the earlier faience fabrics supply obvious comparisons, are the beads, of which great quantities were found (see Fig. 351). As in the case of the earlier examples their associations are clearly Egyptian. Here we notice the globular type represented already in the Vat Room Deposit of the early part of M. M. I. 1 The globular beads in this case, however, show a much smaller, sometimes quite a minute perforation. In their wide perforation the Vat Room specimens followed the Early Dynastic Egyptian tradition, while, in the present case, we see the reflection of that form of globular bead which was in vogue during the Middle Kingdom. In accordance with the same

FIG. 351.

FAIENCE BEADS FROM TEMPLE REPOSITORY (SLIGHTLY REDUCED).

1 The pear-shaped type which already occurs in E. M. II (see p. 85, Fig. 53 above) is no longer found. In Egypt itself it had developed into a larger and much more elongated variety.

law the paler tones of the earlier Egyptian tradition are here, as a rule, superseded by a much deeper, bluish green hue, though some of the beads were almost white, or parti-coloured white and green. The more oval type (6) reproduces a contemporary Egyptian form, and the same is true of the segmented beads (a).

This 'segmented type has an exceptional archaeological importance. History of It clearly originated in the Early Egyptian practice of threading together men'tecp"

Variety.

1 0-HID H I ID" CROUP OF SEPARATE BEADS UALE. BLUE)

ABVD05, PROTODVNASTIC, AISO SUCCEEDING PERIODS 2 MAHASNA XI 1-" DYN DEEP BLUE GREEN 7. XIX T H DYN BLUE GREEN c 1300 3. XVIII DVN 4. XVIII DVN 5. TEU-EL-AMARNA G. TEll-EL-AMARNA FABRIC 3 4. BLUE GREEN SURFACE TURQUOISE AND, CEZE. R

VER VITREOUS C. I5OO BC-4 PALE ULTRAMARINE C. 137.5 BC 8.9. CREMATION DEPOSIT GUROB IO. AINSHEMi II. I2TELL DEFENNEH

SE. TY II GI2M-1209 C. I2OO-IIOO XXVliB OVN C6OO. B. C 8. YELLOW-PASTE 9. BLUE GREEN BURNT PALE BLUE CREEK VERY PALE GLAZE

QDDDQD DOffieD 13 w TEMPLE REPOSITORIES

KNO5505 C-IGOO B. C. PALE BLUE GREEN

FUENTE ALAMO SPAIN BLUISH GREEN WHITE 5. E.5PAIN.

EGYPT 15-MACE BEARERS TOMB KNOSSOS L. M. III. a CMOOB-C- (VERY PALE. BLUE GREEN) MINOAN 16 PHAE. ST05 PALE BLUE C-KOO 17. CYPRO-MINOAN ENKOMI C 1350-1250 BC 18 LIOIR-LEDRAE

L. M. III. 6.

BLOXWORTH

OOWM, DORSET VERY PALE

BARROW. KING6TON PtvERELL WILTS
LAKE WIL. T5 BRITISH I5LES EARLY BRONZE AGE BAPPOWS.
IG. 352. SEGMENTED TYPES OF FAIENCE BEADS.
5TEVEN5TON separately short flat beads so as to form small groups, which led to the more convenient device of moulding them in one, as long single beads, the sections of their original subdivisions surviving as grooves. Traces of this practice appear already under the Xlth Dynasty, 1 but the ordinary segmented form of bead does not appear in Egypt, so far as the existing evidence goes, till

That it was current, however, at after the close of the Middle Kingdom. 2 1 Beads belonging to the latest elements in the cemetery of Mahasna (Ashmolean Museum) present the twisted type, No. 2.

2 A bulged version of the segmented type appears to go back to the Xllth Dynasty.

THE PALACE OF MINOS, ETC.

Diffusion of Faience Bead Types by Minoan Commerce. To Spain and British Isles.

least by the XVIIth Dynasty may be gathered from the appearance of the derivative Minoan type both in the Temple Repositories and in the IVth Shaft Grave at Mycenae. 1 It becomes frequent during the XVII Ith and Xlxth Dynasties, after which date it seems to be less abundant. In Crete the type continued to the Third Late Minoan Period. 2 (See Fig. 352.) But it is the far Western diffusion of these segmented paste beads that gives them such a special interest. Beads of the same form and material recur in tombs belonging to the mature Early Bronze Age in the cemeteries representing the Argar Culture of the rich silver-bearing district of Almeria in S. E. Spain where they were also imitated in bone,:! and it is a significant fact that these bone imitations, at least, recur in the Early Bronze Age deposits of the Maltese Islands. 4 They are found, moreover, still further afield in the Early Bronze Age barrows of Southern Britain, from Cornwall to Sussex, 5 the part of our country most open to direct intercourse with the Iberic world (see Fig. 352). At the same time, doubtless in the wake of this commerce, they made their way through Ireland, and following the ancient gold routes from that Western Eldorado, to Scotland. 0 1 In an exceptionally elongated form (Schlie- 5 In my remarks with reference to the mann, Mycenae, p. 153, No. 228). Bronze Age Chronology of Montelius, Proc.

1 Examples were found, for instance, in the Soc. Ant., 1907, p. 123 seqq., where I first called attention to the Minoan parallels, I did not take count of the Spanish evidence, which is conclusive as showing that this bead commerce with the West ante-dates the period of Phoenician intercourse. This tends to raise the dating of the British Bronze Age remains with which these imports were associated.

It should, however, at the same time be borne in mind that in the Spanish tombs, such as those of Fuente Alamo, these beads were found in company with bronze swords of fully developed form. An interesting discovery in association with segmented beads was made

Mace-bearer's Tomb L. M. Ill a (Fig. 352, No. 15; Prehistoric Tombs of Knossos, i, p. 18, Fig. 26). Others occurred in the Phaestos Cemetery (Fig. 352, No. 16; Savignoni, Man. Ant., xiv, 1904, pp. 632, 633, Fig. 102, c).

8 e. g. Siret, Les Premiers Ages de Metal dans le Sud-Est de FEspagne, Atlas, Pl. 65, 8, and Pl. 68 (Cemetery of Fuente Alamo). Cf. Text, p. 205. Fragmentary beads of the same vitreous paste seem also to have occurred in the cemetery of Argar (pp. fit., p. 209). Bone imitations of these segmented beads were of frequent occurrence in that and other cemeteries. The vitreous paste of the Spanish beads varied in hue from a pale whitish hue to a bluish green. The same was the case with the beads from the British barrows, though their surface is often entirely corroded. The alternation of white and green characterizes many of the beads of the Temple Repositories.

4 Hal Ta. Txien(Arcaaeohgia, Ixvii, Fig. 3, 2). The faience originals do not seem to have occurred in the Maltese Islands.

in a Bronze Age barrow at Aldbourne, Wilts. It contained a kind of incense vessel with a dark, burnished surface and with incised and punctuated chevrons and vandykings, Mediterranean in their affinities. (Prof. Sof. Ant., 1879, PP- 176, r?7-) 6 For Scotland, see L. Mcl. Mann, Proc. Sof. Ant. Scot., xl, 1905-6, p. 387 and p. 396 seqq.; and Abercrombie, Anthr. Journ., xxxv (1905), p. 256 seqq. With regard to Ireland In their diffusion through the British Isles they are associated with star-shaped beads which, in Egypt at least, have a very ancient origin. 1 These have their parallels not only among the faience fabrics of Akhenaten's Palace factory at Tel-el-Amarna where they merge with the then fashionable marguerite motive 2 but find analogies in certain radiated Late Minoan and Mycenaean types. 3 Both the segmented and the radiated forms are well represented among the Cypro-Minoan faience beads from Enkomi. 4 It is evident that the associations in which faience beads were found in the Spanish cemeteries of Alamo and Argar carry the date of their importation beyond the phase of Phoenician intercourse. Since Egypt itself had no maritime commerce of its own, there remains, therefore, a high probability that their diffusion, at least as far as the West Mediterranean basin, may have been due to Minoan enterprise. When, however, it is remembered that in addition to their native fabrics the Minoans and Mycenaeans themselves imported scarabs and other faience objects from Egypt it becomes by no means improbable that the beads with which they traded in the West may have been in part at least of Egyptian manufacture. 6

The chronological limits of this intercourse would lie between the begin- chrono- ning of the sixteenth century B. C., the date of the Temple Repositories at

Knossos, and the close of the Minoan era proper, about 1200 B. C. The later on intercourse, however, during the L. M. 1 1 1 Period, was probably the work rather Bronze of the Mainland Mycenaean branch than of traders from Minoan Crete. It Age may be, of course, that there were intermediate centres of manufacture in Sicily or even in Spain. The possibility indeed cannot be altogether excluded that some of the faience beads found in the British Isles were of local fabric. 8 the evidence, though certain, is at present not 4 Specimens of both types occurred in adequately forthcoming. Quoit-shaped faience Tomb 60 (B. M. Excavations in Cyprus, pendants of the type associated with the beads Pl. ix, 305).

in England and Scotland have been found B It may be remarked that the star-shaped there. beads and the bulging segmented type, the 1 Notched types with a green glaze, show- diameterof which increases towards the middle, ing cog-like projections, occurs already in the both found in our British barrows, and repre-proto-dynastic epoch. This seems to be the senting derivatives of Egyptian prototypes, ancestor of the Star shape found at Tel-el- do not seem to have been as yet found in Amarna, Petrie, Pl. xviii, 402. Minoan or Mycenaean deposits.

2 Compare the beads and moulds in Pl. Mr. Ludovic Mcl. Mann upholds the xviii of Petrie, Tel-el-Amarna, e. g. Nos. 354, theory that the glazed beads found in Britain 355, 402, 403, 404, and 426, c. were of indigenous fabric (Glasgow Herald, Jan.

3 Compare the star-flower bead of faience 31, 1920, and cf. Proc. Soc. Ant. Scot.,, 1906, from the Spata tomb, Bull, de Corr. Hell., p. 396 seqq.). He bases his opinion on the fact 1878, Pl. xv, 8. that the British beads are coloured in the in-

THE PALACE OF MINOS, ETC.

General indications of Minoan connexion with West Mediterranean Basin.

FIG. 353. FESTOONS BETWEEN COLUMNS OF SHRINE ON FRAGMENT OF PAINTED POTTERY.

Of the Westward extension of Minoan enterprise something has already been said, and the use of imported liparite from the Aeolian islands bears early witness of its importance. In a sealing from the Temple Repository, described below, 1 we may even trace an allusion to the myth of Scylla. There are indications of a colonial settlement in Sicily which may go back to the beginning of the Late Minoan Age, and a remarkable series of bronzes from Minorca and Spain itself points to a direct intercourse with the Iberic West about the same epoch, the reflex of which is shown in the appearance of the bronze halberd type of that region in a Mycenae Shaft Grave. It is at least in accordance with sane methods of archaeological deduction to infer that the Minoans were at the same time instrumental in introducing a kind of bead currency among the primitive populations of the Iberic Peninsula, which thence found its way by inter-tribal barter and native seafaring enterprise to the British Isles. The natural reflex of this would be the trade in tin.

From the analogy supplied by the dotted festoons seen between the pillars of small shrines such as that shown on a signet-ring from Mycenae, 2 it seems probable that the beads found in the Temple Repository had served a similar purpose. A festoon of the kind is given in the restored design of a fragment of a vessel found in the Domestic Quarter 3 (Fig. 353). It is there suspended between two slender columns above the sacral horns.

Similar festoons are seen between the posts of the Sanctuary windows on the fresco fragment reproduced above (p. 444, Fig. 320). On a seal impression and an ivory from Hagia Triada they hung between the legs of altar tables supporting Sacral Horns. 4 terior as well as the surface, and show a greater tendency to vitrification. But many of the specimens of Minoan faience exhibit the same characteristics.

At the same time, we must bear in mind the great skill shown by British artificers in other departments, such as metallurgy. The beads themselves are of three classes: (i) those of East Mediterranean shape and aspect, (2) those derived from such models, (3) those, like the quoit-shaped beads, the origin of which is obscure. The Ancient Britons copied the 'segmented type in tin (Hoare, Ancient Wilts, i, p. 103).

1 See p. 697, and Fig. 520.

2 See above p. 161, Fig. 116.

! This fragment was found by the S. Portico of the Hall of the Double Axes in 1902, and is of unique character, apparently of L. M. II fabric. It was sketched by me at the time of excavation.

4 Halbherr, Man. Ant., xiii (1903), p. 42, Fig. 36. For the ivory see Oest. Jahreshefte, x, p. 79, Fig. 27.

Contents of West Temple Repository inscribed tablets, seal-impressions; Bone and ivory relics; Sacrificial element Libation tables; Faience relics from Eastern Repository; Votive bowls and ewer; Rose-leaf Chalice; Fruits and flowers; The Snake Goddess; Her Votary or Double fashionable dress; Lioness crest of Votary; Lions, concomitants of Goddess; Votive robes and girdles of faience; Priestesses as Snake Charmers; Survival of Cult of Snake Goddess Chryselephantine figure from Knossos; Herin bronze figure with triple coil of snakes Cretan, L. M. I; Later shrines at Gournia and Prinias; Snakes emblem of Chthonic divinity; Snake as domestic genius; Wazet, Snake Goddess of Western Delta; Her papyrus symbol adopted in Crete; Her Uraeus suggests serpent crest of Minoan Goddess; Faience reliefs of Cow and Calf reflect Cult of I sis and Hathor Parallel group of Goat and Kids; Cruciform star symbols of Hathoric Cow, adopted by Minoan Cult; Cross, primitive pictograph of Star; Cruciform symbols on Sealings from W. Repository Cross as sole type; Cruciform inlay and faience; Marble Cross of Orthodox shape from Repository; Painted sea shells pebbles onfioors of Minoan Shrines; Flying fish panel and moulded marine subjects in clay; Compared with Fish Frescoes of Knossos and Phylakopi.

WHILE the more Easterly of the two Temple Repositories contained Contents the most detailed evidence as to the character and attributes of the Minoan Reposi-Goddess to whose Treasury they belonged, the Western Cist produced l a variety of objects connected with her worship, including a symbolic marble cross of primary interest, to be described below. The contents of the two Repositories, indeed, to a certain extent overlapped one another, and though the beautiful faience figurines and reliefs that form the most attractive element of these discoveries were almost exclusively found in the Eastern Cist, by a curious chance, the upper part of the figure of the Snake Goddess itself occurred in the other recipient.

In addition to the remains of the Draught-board, the bronze handles and clamp of small chests and quantities of gold-foil that had served as

THE PALACE OF MINOS, ETC.

Inscribed Tablets. Clay and Seal-impressions.

Bone and Ivory

Relics.

Sacrificial Element.

a coating for these and other objects, the Western Repository contained a variety of important relics. A clay tablet and three disks presenting inscriptions of the Linear Script A, l as well as a hoard of 1 50 clay seal-impressions, some, as will be seen, with religious emblems, were clearly derived from the archives of the sanctuary to which the Repositories belonged. Some account of these will be given below in connexion with other objects belonging to the same categories. 2

Various relics of ivory and bone were also found in this Repository. Among the bone inlays the most elaborate were in the shape alternately of flowers and buds, suggested by those of a pomegranate Flg 354rt BonE INLAYS IN FORM (Fig. 354 a). The under-sides of these OF POMEGRANATE BUDS.

pieces showed incised marks in the shape of a broad H, accompanied by a varying number of dots, a mark which is also traceable in relief on a silver dump found on the East Slope representing the transitional stage towards coined money. 3 A fragment of another piece for inlaying presented an Incised, a frequently recurring mark. An ivory inlay (Fig. 354 6) was also found of a crescent-shaped outline similar to others of faience and crystal that have occurred elsewhere in the Palace. Among other bone relics the arrow plumes with their curiously notched feathers will be seen to have a special relation to a decorative motive much in vogue at this time. 4 As votive objects, moreover, they have an intimate bearing on the cult of the Minoan Diktynna. The elegant ivory plate of a knife handle here brought to light (Fig. 354 6) may well have belonged to a sacrificial instrument. To the sacrificial element, perhaps represented by the knife handle, may be added the discovery of the cores of horns of Roe-deer, and the greasiness of the deposit, which attained its maximum immediately above

FIG. 354 b. IVORY HANDLE
OF INSTRUMENT, AND INLAY: TEMPLE
REPOSITORY.

1 See below, pp. 618, 620.

2 See below, p. 617 seqq.

3 See my Minoan Weights and Currency (in Corolla Niimismatica, 1906), p. 363, Fig. 15.

4 See below, p. 547 seqq., and Figs. 399-402.

6 For a drawing of both sides of this and section see Knossos, Report, 1903, p. 61, Fig. 39.

the floor, was also possibly due to the presence of animal matter. The burnt corn also found in some abundance may have also had an offertory character.

In the same stratum of this Repository there came to light a series of Libation steatite Libation Tables (see Fig. 355, upper row). These receptacles, which taper gradually to a small base below, show on their square upper face a shallow cup-like hollow with a raised rim. They exactly resemble the Libation Tables with a single cup found in the votive deposit of the Dictaean Cave. 1 This type represents a simpler variety of that with three receptacles, exhibiting the early linear inscription, found beneath the same

FIG. 355. LIBATION TABLES OF STEATITE AND OTHER MATERIALS; W. REPOSITORY.

Cave deposit. A good example of one of these is seen in the centre of the group in Fig. 377. 2 Together with these typical forms of libation vessels there occurred a series of more or less cylindrical objects, the material of which seemed to be identical with the gritty paste that forms the core of the faience ware. These were hollowed out above into shallow basins showing that they had also served for libations.

As already noted, the actual cult objects and fittings of the Shrine had Faience been mostly swept into the Eastern Repository. The relics there found fo E. included a wholly unique collection of objets dart, executed with extra- Reposi-ordinary skill in this indigenous kind of porcelain, the fabric, but not the 1 A similar steatite libation table was Others occurred at Palaikastro and elsewhere, obtained by me from a sanctuary at Arvi, on a This libation vessel appears in the figure the S. E. coast of Crete (. H. S., xvii, p. 357). in a somewhat disproportionate scale. I K k

THE PALACE OF MINOS, ETC.

Small

Faience

Bowls

Ewers.

forms of which, must have been learnt from Egypt. These faience objects included figures of a Snake Goddess and votaries, their votive robes and girdles, cups and vases with painted designs, flowers, fruit, foliage, and shells in the round, small reliefs of cows and calves and wild goats with their kids, a variety of plaques for inlaying, quantities of beads, and heaps of painted sea-shells, which had apparently served to adorn the floor and ledges on which the cult objects rested.

FIG. 356. FAIENCE VESSELS AND PENDANT; TEMPLE REPOSITORIES It is a significant circumstance that miniature vessels of polychrome pottery in the earlier shrines, such as the M. M. II examples from the Loom-Weight Area, are here replaced by small bowls and ewers of the local faience. Specimens of these are given in Fig. 356. One of the bowls is adorned with a border of cockles, another with Minoan shields. The small jug with its spiraliform decoration is clearly taken from a prototype in precious metals recalling a gold ewer from the Fourth Shaft Grave at Mycenae 1 and a plain silver example belonging to the beginning of the Late Minoan Age 1 Schliemann, Mycenae, p. 232, Fig. 341.

from the South House at Knossos. 1 This fine glazed ware was no doubt to a certain extent used, like the earlier egg-shell pottery with metallic lustre, as a substitute for plate.

But of all the small faience vessels that here came to light the most exquisitely designed were chalices (Fig. 357, a, b, c) with fern-like decoration on their sides, one with a rose-leaf spray in relief, flung, as it were, across its inner margin.

An elegant faience pendant, included in Fig. 356, presents a conventionalized floral motive, in the outer sprays of which we may recognize two

FIG. 357. FAIENCE CHALICES, a WITH ROSE-LEAF SPRAY IN RELIEF (f).

lilies, with their characteristic recurved petals and central cluster of stamens. It affords a good illustration of the Minoan faculty of adapting natural forms to symmetrical designs such as was so often exemplified by the Egyptians in their treatment of the lotus and papyrus.

Other relics found showed attempts, of which the rose spray of the Faience chalice must be regarded as a successful example, to imitate plant forms in j " ' a naturalistic manner. On Fig. 358 is seen a group of saffron flowers in and relief, and a fruit (perhaps a plum). Still more remarkable is part of a brown coloured trunk in high relief an offshoot of which is seen in the shape of a stem with striped curving leaves and the calix of a lily-like flower. 2 1 See Vol. II. bluish green with purplish streaks, are con- 2 The colours of the leaves and flower, a pale ditioned by the ingredients of the glaze.

THE PALACE OF MINOS, ETC.

Snake
Goddess.

The leaves and petals are actually reproduced in full, as it might be in delicate porcelain a transference to another material of an artistic tradition which in goldsmiths' work had been handed down from the Early Minoan Age. The best parallel, indeed, to this tour de force of faience work is to be seen in the golden lilies, 1 from the Mycenaean tholos tombs at Dimini and Volo. There can be little doubt that the fruits and flowers illustrated by these faience relics themselves had religious associations.

The central figure of the shrine was a Goddess apparently the Under-World form of the great Minoan Goddess with a triple group of spotted snakes twined about her. Her figure, as reconstituted, is 34-2 centimetres (i3 inches) in height (see Coloured Frontispiece). She wears a high tiara of a purplish-brown colour with a white border, a necklace, and a dress to be more fully described below, consisting of a richly embroidered bodice with a laced corsage, and a skirt FIG. 358. FAIENCE FRUIT AND FLOWERS (f-.).

with a kind of short double apron. Her hair, cut square in a fringe above her forehead, falls behind her neck and on to her shoulders; her eyes are black, as also her eyebrows, which are given in relief, and her ears, partly owing to the snaky coils that surround them, appear to be of abnormal size. Her breasts, which are almost entirely bare, are of matronly proportions. The ground colour of the whole, including the flesh tint, is generally a milky white, the various details being laid on in purple, purplish-brown, or black.

1 See p. 96, Fig. 68.

About the Goddess are coiled three snakes with greenish bodies spotted with purple-brown. The head of one of these she holds out in her right hand, its body follows the arm upwards, then descends behind the shoulders, and ascends again to the left arm, which held the tail. 1 Round the hips of the Goddess, below the waist, and forming her girdle, two other snakes are interlaced. One of these, whose head appears in the centre of this serpentine girdle, is continued in a festoon down the front of the apron, and, thence ascending along the edge of the bodice to the neck, coils its tail round the Goddess's right ear. Finally, a third snake, whose tail-end forms part of the plaitwork about the hips, runs up along the left fringe of the bodice over the left ear and coils up round the tiara, from the summit of which its head (here restored) originally projected.

A back view of the figure, showing Her the richly-embroidered bodicewithits spirali-form decoration, is given in Fig. 359. With the Goddess were remains of two other figures. Of these the best preserved was at first set up as shown in Figs. 3(50, 3(il in a headless state. It is somewhat smaller than the other, 2 and it seems probable from her attitude that she should rather be regarded as a priestess or votary.

The hair, longer than that of the other figure, falls down behind her to her hips. Though she is altogether slimmer than the Goddess, her breasts, which are bare, are prominent, and her fine torso

FAIENCE.

is well shown in profile view in Fig. 360, a.

She wears a bracelet round the wrist of her right arm which holds out a small snake, tail upwards. The left forearm is wanting, but doubtless also held out a snake in a similar 1 The 1. fore-arm with the tail is restored.- Height to neck 20 centimetres.

Fio. 359. BACK VIEW OF FIGURE OF SNAKE GODDESS, (c.

THE PALACE OF MINOS, ETC.

FIG. 360, a, b. FAIENCE FIGURE OF VOTARY (OR DOUBLE) OF SNAKE GODDESS, (c. f) position. The skin here is pure white, the bodice a dark orange with purplish-brown bands, and the rest of the dress shows designs of the same purplish-brown on a pale ground.

These representations, including the back view shown in Fig. 361, give a good idea of the costume. The Votary wears a skirt Her of many flounces over which a IC is the same double apron tress. and the sleeved bodice, cut away so as to expose the bosom and laced in front. Round her waist in place of the snakes is what appears to be a tight-fitting metal belt into which the lower border of the bodice is tucked. The lines adopted are those considered ideal by the modern corset-maker rather than the sculptor, and the effect is that of a fashionable Court lady.

The double apron, which in fact represents a primitive garb common to both sexes, may perhaps be regarded as a ritual survival. But the costume on the whole must be that of the epoch to which these works belong. Two features that mark Late Minoan fashions are here absent the chemise, the upper border of which is seen beneath the neck, and the V-shaped arrangement of the flounces in itself suggestive of a divided skirt.

This votary, or double of the Goddess, shown in Figs. 360, 361 in its headless state, was eventually found capable of complete restoration. Part 1 For a detailed account of the original discoveries see Anossos, Report, 1903 (B. S. A., ix, 62 seqq.). " Lady Evans, B. S. A., ix, p. 81.

FIG. 361. BACK VIEW OF VOTARY OR DOUBLE OF SNAKE GODDESS, (c.)

THE PALACE OF MINOS, ETC.

of a headpiece had already been brought into connexion with it, showing a series of raised medallions, forming perhaps a conventional rendering of an original crown of roses. A small circular rivet hole on the flat upper

FIG. 362, a, b, c, d. UPPER PART OF FAIENCE FIGURE WITH HEAD RE-STORED (a, b); f, d SHOW LOWER PART OF SEATED ANIMAL AND TIARA WITH RIVET HOLES, (f)

Her surface of this (see Fig. 362, d was further found to answer to a similar Crest. feature on the base of a miniature lioness or spotted pard from the same Repository (c, suggesting the almost certain restoration seen in Fig. 302, a and b. The spots taken over, perhaps through analogy with the snakes, 1 This observation was first made by the artist, Mr. Halvor Bagge, to whom the restored drawing in Fig. 362 is due.

need hardly stand in the way of the identification of the animal with the lioness, sacrecl, as we know from other pieces of evidence, to the Great Minoan Goddess, later identified with Rhea. 1

This connexion is further borne out by two seal impressions belonging Lions to the large hoard from the Western Repository. On one of these (Fig. ta n"s 0 ot" 363 a) a female figure, presumably the Goddess herself, and wearing Goddess, a peaked tiara, is seen holding in one hand what seems to be the shaft of a spear and laying the other on the hind-quarters of a lion who looks up at her. On another sealing ( ) a warrior wearing a peaked cap and holding a spear and shield of a known Minoan class marches beside a lioness or pard.

FIG. 363. SEALINGS a, b FROM TEMPLE REPOSITORIES, c HAGIA TRI-ADA. (f)

A supplement to these is afforded by a seal type from Hagia Triada 2 where a warrior with similar peaked head-gear, but holding a horn-bow, stands beside a lion. His loin cloth is remarkable as exhibiting a double flounce.

Remains of a third faience statuette, of which the upper part of the body is wanting, showed a skirt and apron exactly resembling those of the Goddess. Of the skirt enough remained to admit of its full restoration, and the parts above, including the apron, metal girdle, and a piece of the jacket and laced bodice were well preserved. The girdle presented the same spiral decoration as the borders of the apron. As in the case of the last figure, her hair fell down in long tresses to the hips. We have here, 1 The connexion with the lion recalls the Egyptian representations of Semitic Goddesses assimilated to Hathor. The Moon Goddess, Qetesh, stands on a lioness. Ashtoreth has a lion's head. As the great Goddess of Den- dera, Hathor assumes the form of a lioness with an uraeus on her head (cf. Budge, Gods of the Egyptians, i, p. 429).

- Man. Ant., xiii, p. 44, Fig. 40.

THE PALACE OF MINOS, ETC.

too, to deal with a Votary or attendant rather than with an actual Goddess. The lower part of this figure as restored is given in Fig. 382 at the end of the Section. It also appears on the right in the collective group, Fig. 377 below. Votive robes and girdles for suspension, of faience, were also found (Fig. 364, a, b, c, rt, showing rich decoration. On the front of two of

FIG. 364, a, l, c, d. VOTIVE ROBES AND GIRDLES OF FAIENCE, FOR SUSPENSION. FROM

TEMPLE REPOSITORIES. ( ) the skirts appears a kind of Watteau panel with a group of the sacred and saffron-flowers, in which the influence of Egyptian lotus clumps is clearly ? aien e ce. f traceabl e The votive articles of attire find an analogy in the Sacral Knot described above.

These figures have been sometimes referred to as Snake charmers' but the whole associations in which they were found show that they were Pricst-of a religious character, and formed in fact the central objects of a shrine, snake So far, indeed, as the attendants or votaries of the Goddess here worshipped are concerned this is really a distinction without a difference, for the practice of snake-charming would clearly have been part of their priestly functions.

Accumulating evidences are now before us of the survival of the cult of Survival a Snake Goddess at Knossos itself and in other parts of Crete. There are, indeed, good reasons for believing that the beautiful crowned female figure of Cult.

FIG. 365. UPPER PART OF MINOAN BRONZE FIGURE, SHOWING TRIPLE COIL OF SNAKES (BERLIN Mus.).

of ivory holding out two golden snakes in the Boston Museum, and described in a later Section of this work referring to the First Late Minoan Period, had belonged to the same Palace reliquary of the Domestic Quarter at Knossos as the ivory figure of the Leaping Boy.

Since the discovery of the Shrine of the Snake Goddess and her votaries, moreover, more than one archaeologist has recognized the fact that the bronze female figure in the Berlin Museum, the provenance of which was once doubtfully referred to Troy, belongs to the same class. 2 1 L. D. Caskey, Museum of Fine Arts- Furtwangler referred to it in conversation Bulletin, vol. xii (1914), p. 52 seqq. as a Schlangenfrau. Caskey, in the Mus. of

Chryselephantine Figure from Knossos.

Berlin

Bronze

Figure with

Triple

Coil of

Snakes

THE PALACE OF MINOS, ETC.

Later

Snakes emblem

Chthonic

Divinity.

Owing to certain characteristics of the dress it is ascribed below to the beginning of the Late Minoan Age, and from the occurrence of bronze female figures in a very similar style from Cretan sites, there can be little remaining doubt as to the place of origin. Careful drawings executed for me to show the arrangement of the snakes on the upper part of this statuette are given in Fig. 365. 1 It will be seen that here, as in the case of the principal figure of the Knossian Shrine, the serpents formed a triple group, plaited together behind her neck and with their tails reaching to her girdle. A coiling lock of hair, easily distinguishable, falls down to the right of these. As in the case of our Snake Goddess the head of one serpent seems to have been placed, uraeus-like, above the front of the figure's head. The position of the heads of the other snakes is uncertain. In order to seize hold of one of the reptiles the figure reaches her left hand to her right shoulder. Her other forearm is raised in front of her forehead, and her head is slightly inclined indications these that we may have here to do with a priestess or votary rather than with the divinity itself.

Of the latest Minoan epoch is the little Shrine found at Gournia, which contained a rude female idol rising from a cylinder below, with a serpent coiling about her waist and over one of her raised arms. With this, together with other cult objects, are bases, tapering upwards and set with Sacral Horns, above which other serpents raise their heads. Parallel with these relics and clearly contemporary with them are the remains of similar clay objects found at Prinias, where the female figures have snakes trailing along their forearms like the faience Goddess of the Palace Shrine. The Gournia group is of special interest, since there the relics dedicated to the snake cult are associated with small clay figures of doves and a relief showing the Double Axe.

These conjunctions are singularly illuminating since they reveal the fact that the Snake Goddess herself represents only another aspect of the Minoan Lady of the Dove, while the Double Axe itself was connected with both. Just as the celestial inspiration descends in bird form either on the image of the divinity itself or on that of its votary, or in other cases, as we have seen, upon its aniconic columnar shape, so the spirit of the Nether World, in serpent form, makes its ascent to a similar position from the earth itself. Nor need this manifestation of the chthonic side of the divinity be invested with any malignant significance. It has on the contrary a friendly and domestic aspect with which those acquainted with primitive ideas as they fine Arts Bulletin, loc. cit., regards it as given in Vol. II under L. M. I. The drawings a figure of a snake-charming lady. were made by Mr. E. J. Lambert from the 1 Full representations of this figure will be excellent cast in the British Museum.

still exist on European soil must be very familiar. In many peasant Snake as dwellings the snake, with his love of warmth which leads him to find Genius, some cranny near the hearth, is regarded, as of old, as a kind of good genius. To my own knowledge in Heraegovina and the Serbian lands, East of the Adriatic, it was not an uncommon thing for snakes, who had sought such human hospitality, to be fed with milk and treated as domestic pets. Such a household snake is known, indeed, as domachitsa or housemother.

In its homely origin, from the religious tending of the household snake, Snake the cult itself may be supposed to be of old indigenous tradition. At the western same time the exceptional prominence of a similar cult in the Western Delta. Delta can hardly be left out of account. That there was at any rate a reaction of this Nilotic cult on that of the Minoan chthonic Goddess as its Re-finally evolved is clear from more than one feature in her attributes and Crete! symbolism.

The snake raising its head above the tiara of the Goddess of the Knossian Shrine itself curiously recalls the uraeus in similar positions on the head of Hathor and other Egyptian Goddesses. The Delta Goddess Wazet: Wazet, in many respects the double of Hathor, the mother of Horus, and Goddes identified in later times with Isis, could herself take the form of a serpent, Her Waz and an uraeus snake is seen entwined about her papyrus sceptre. The a d j t d latter symbol of the Goddess, moreover, the waz, in its simpler form b y.

., 1,1 e i M moans.

a papyrus stem, has been already shown by a curious catena of evidence to have played a special part among the borrowed materials of Cretan decorative art. Early in the Middle Minoan Age we have seen the waz symbol and associated canopy taken over as a type of Cretan signets, not, we may imagine, without some sense of religious sanction. In derivative shapes it continues to fulfil these sphragistic functions to the borders of the Late Minoan Age and is interwoven with a series of fantastic seal-types of the Zakro class. 1 As incorporated in a decorative band we meet it again on Was the pedestal of a columnar lamp 2 from the pillar Crypt of the S. E. House at Knossos, and it inspires a whole series of ornamental designs in Late Minoan Art. frescoes and vase paintings. An influence productive of such continuous results cannot be lightly set aside. Considering the very ancient and intimate relations of Crete with the Nile Valley going back to the Pre-dynastic Age, and not improbably marked by the actual settlement in the island of Egypto-Libyan elements 3 it was natural that the great Delta Goddess, whose 1 See below, pp. 704-6, and Fig. 528. See above, p. 345, Fig. 249.

3 See above, p. 79 seqq.

THE PALACE OF MINOS, ETC.

chosen haunt was the papyrus thickets of Buto, should have impressed herself in an exceptional degree on the Minoan religious imagination.

How much of the spiritual being of the Egyptian Mother Goddess may not have been absorbed by her Minoan sister? How much indeed of the of Egyp- later traditions of Rhea and the infant Zeus may not go back to a far earlier acclimatization of the legends and the cult of Isis and Horus?

A curious sympathy with the cycle of the Egyptian Mother Goddess

Far- tian

Mother

Goddess.

Wild Goat and Young.

FIG. 366. FAIENCE PANEL, GOAT AND KIDS: TEMPLE REPOSITORIES (f:.).

was in fact afforded by the subject of certain animal reliefs found in the Temple Repository.

Amongst all the faience relics that had formed part of the furniture of the shrine, the highest artistic level was reached by a series of panels with reliefs showing groups consisting of a goat and kids or of a cow and calf. The most beautiful of these, of which the remains of several panels ocurred, was that with the Cretan wild goat or Agrimi and two kids reproduced in Fig. 366. The goat is here seen in a rocky field suckling a kid, while another stands before her, bleating for her turn. Not only is the modelling of the animal forms here most successfully achieved, but the grouping is of a very skilful kind. The artist has seized the right moment of an idyllic scene, every detail of which he has thoroughly visualized.

The Wild Goat and young naturally associate themselves with the Cretan Goddess in her capacity of divine Huntress a character which

FIG. 367. FAIENCE PLAQUE, Cow AND CALF: TEMPLE REPOSITORIES (-.) clung to her to a much later day under her indigenous names of Diktynna and Britomartis. This aspect of the cult is indeed further illustrated by the votive arrow plumes of bone found in the Western Repository. 1

We are led, however, in a very different direction by the companion piece supplied by another series of reliefs, the parts of which were of varying dimensions, showing a cow suckling a calf (Fig. 367). In this case we see an architectural basis with a striped border as in painted stucco imitations 1 See below, p. 548, Fig. 399, a.

of banded stones. An interesting fragment, Fig. 368, shows a similar band forming part of a faience bracket or console, stepping back below in the Minoan fashion. In this connexion it is important to note that a base with the same stonework imitation occurred in painted stucco beneath the Griffin

Frieze belonging to the great East Hall of the Palace, to be described under L. M. I. 1 With it was also found a console in the same material, analogous to the miniature example in faience. These parallels may be taken to indicate that the faience panels were set in like fashion against the back wall of the little shrines to which these remains belonged.

A very natural figure of another suckling calf, from a faience panel of somewhat smaller dimensions, is given in Fig. 369. The forelegs are here shown in a kneeling position, and the loose, angular limbed frame of the young animal is very skilfully brought out.

FIG. 368. FAIENCE BRACKET OR CONSOLE. Cow and Calf.

FIG. 369. CALF SUCKLED BY Cow ON PART OF FAIENCE PANEL.

The group of the Cow and Calf is a familiar subject of Egyptian art in connexion with the cult of Hathor, and was afterwards, as is well known, taken over into Phoenician and Classical art. But the close observation of nature, especially in the attitude of the calves, places these works in a very different category from the Egyptian prototypes. These parallels, however, 1 See Vol. II. The faience console will be also illustrated there for comparison with the painted stucco example.

may serve to remind us that both this and the she-goat and young had Hathoric probably; i religious intention in connexion with the Cretan Mother Goddess, Religious though in this case as assimilated to her Egyptian sister. intention

". of Reliefs.

The group of the Cow and Calf of the Egyptian Mother Goddess, enlisted here in the cult of the analogous Cretan divinity, leads us to another

Fie. 370. A, c. CRUCIFORM STAR SYMBOLS ON HATHORIC Cow: B, D. MINOAN ADAPTATIONS.

interesting comparison of a symbolic character. The Egyptian Goddess, as Lady of Heaven, appears as the Cow of the Underworld, the body of which, in place of natural spots, shows asterisk marks or simple crosses, symbolizing the starry firmament of Night, as on the animal shown in Fig. 370 A. 1 By a convention, moreover, which shows a kind of compromise with Nature, these symbolic crosses are often rendered by quatrefoil spots, 1 Naville, Xllh Dvtiasfr Temple of Z V el-Bahari, Part III, Pl. XXX. On a votive cloth. T I. 1

Cruciform Star Symbols of Hathoric Cow adopted by Minoan Cult.

as in the case of the great painted figure of XVIIIth Dynasty date found in the Hathor Shrine at Deir el-Bahari (Fig. 370 c). 1 It is a remarkable fact that both the plain cross and the derivative quatrefoil are taken over, as religious marks, in substitution for the natural spots in Minoan representations. 2 On a late Cypro-Minoan vase we see the body, in this case of a bull, with four simple cruciform marks and a series of trefoils, a simplification of the quatrefoil seen on the Egyptian Cow of Hathor (Fig. 370 B). In the quatrefoil shape the same marks appear on Minoan bull's-head rhytons as is well illustrated by the inlays on a ritual vessel of that kind found in the Tomb of the Double Axes, near Knossos (Fig. 370 D). In the hunting scene of the Tiryns fresco the cruciform spots are transferred to

Cross Primitive Picto-graph of Star.

FIG. 371. RAYED SOLAR SYMBOL WITH SPOKES FROM SITEIA MOULD.

deer It does not need the star-markings of the Hathoric Cow to explain the early significance of the cruciform figure. Not only among the primitive population of the Old World till quite recently even in the pictography of the Lapp troll-drums but among widely remote peoples, such as the North American Indian tribes, an equal-limbed cross has a currency as the simplest form of the star sign. In a derivative sense, as is well known, it thus came to be, as in Babylonia and elsewhere, a general indication of divinity. 4 Sometimes, as the day-star, it coalesces with the rayed disk of the sun, as in the case of the symbol, already referred to above, from the Siteia mould Fig. 371." A smaller disk on the same mould held up by a little figure, apparently a votary, shows this star-sign in its simple cruciform shape within a dotted circle above the lunar crescent. On the fellow mould the Minoan Goddess holds aloft two Double Axes. The smaller symbolic disk, as contrasted with that of the rayed solar emblem, must be taken as symbolic of the Goddess as Queen of the Under- 1 Naville, op. cit., Pt. I, Frontispiece.

2 Most of these figures were probably of bulls rather than cows, but the bovine heads of the rhytons may have belonged to either sex.

3 Tiryns, ii, Pl. XV. They also appear on the lions of a Mycenae dagger-blade.

4 For the cross as a sign of divinity see L. Miiller, Rehgwse Symboler af Stierne-, Kors-, og Cirkel-Form, c., p. 7 seqq. As specifically a star sign, a cross appears above the heads of the Dioscuri, e. g. on a bronze coin of Caracalla, struck at Tripolis in Syria (pp. cit., p. 8, a; B. M. Cat: Phoenicia (G. F. Hill), Pl. XXVII, 18, and p 218. 0 See above, p. 479.

1900, Pl. 3, above.

world and of the starry vault of Night. Associated with the cre. ent the cross on the mould might be taken specifically to represent the Evening Star.

Cruciform symbols of more than one kind appear on several relics from Cruci- the Temple Repositories. The Swastika, or Crux Gammata, is seen on symbols a clay seal impression of which eighteen examples occurred (Fig. 372). It is? n s al there placed over a horned sheep exactly resembling the animal seen on a seal- N. Retype found in the Pictographic deposit of the Palace, in that case performing

FIG. 372. CLAY SEAL IMPRESSION FROM TEMPLE REPOSITORY. SWASTIKA AND HORNED SHEEP (J).

FIG. 373. CLAY SEAL IMPRESSION WITH INFANT AND HORNED SHEEP. (HIEROGLYPHIC DEPOSIT.) (I)

FIG. 374. CLAY SEAL IMPRESSION WITH CRUCIFORM TYPE.

FIG. 375. FAIENCE INLAY. KNOSSOS.

the functions of the goat Amaltheia to an infant beneath it (see Fig. 373). If this latter design covers, as may well be inferred, an allusion to an alternative form of the legend of the nurture of the infant Zeus, 1 the appearance of this religious symbol above the same animal on the seal impressions from this Temple Treasury has a high significance. The animal in any case may be naturally taken to stand in a close relation to the primitive Mother Goddess, whose cult is otherwise so well illustrated by this deposit. Another type, of repeated occurrence in the hoard of sealings found in the

Western Repository, presents a Cross as its sole type (Fig. 374). It 1 Sie my remarks, Kttossos, Report, 1903, pp. 88, 89. 1,1 2

THE PALACE OF MINOS, ETC.

is to be noted that this symbol in the somewhat elongated form here seen is a regular character of the Linear Scripts both A and E at Knossos. In its earlier phase this sign shows equal limbs. In the script it possessed not only a (presumably) phonetic value, but could be used by itself as an ideograph. It is found, in its equal-limbed form, among Cypro-Minoan characters, 1 and in the Cypriote Syllabary has the equivalence of lo. The equal-limbed

FIG. 376. MARBLE CROSS FROM V. REPOSITORY.

type also occurs on a faience inlay from Knossos 2 (Fig. 375), and a small gold cross of similar form was found in the Third Shaft Grave at Mycenae. 3 In the case, however, of such small inlays, as of certain painted stucco patterns, the natural evolution of the cross as an element in various decorative designs, often of textile origin, must be always borne in mind.

The occurrence of the cruciform stellar sign as a symbol of the Great 1 Scripta Minoa, i, p. 70, Fig. 39, Table III. a pale ground.

- The inner cross is of a purplish brown on 3 Schliemann, Mycenae, p. 194, Fig. 294.

Minoan Goddess under her Chthonic aspect, in the shape of amulets and small inlays, or as the type of signets, is itself in accordance with widespread parallels. But the discovery in the Western Repository of a marble cross of the equal-limbed Orthodox Greek shape, and belonging to a class that can only be described as monumental, is certainly a unique phenomenon. The cross is of fine grained marble of white and dark grey tones. Its width, about 22-2 centimetres (8- inches), and its thickness is very slight, only 1-2 centimetres, or somewhat less than half an inch. The face was finely polished, but the under side is less finished, and there are visible on it incised lines running parallel to the ends of the limbs at somewhat uneven distances from them. A part of one limb had been broken off, but it seems to have finished off like the others, as restored in Fig. 376. It is evident from the comparatively rough back that the cross was set in some other material, possibly belonging to a large intarsia design.

No Minoan votary could have regarded it with greater veneration than did the orthodox Greek pope whose parish included the remains of the Palace-Sanctuary, and it did much to confirm the views of his flock that the fresco figures found were icons of Saints of old.

Its special religious significance can hardly be a subject of doubt, though whether it may have been fixed to the wall or embedded in the floor of the shrine must remain uncertain. In Fig. 377, where I have grouped the principal relics in a manner suggested by the altar ledge of the late Shrine of the Double Axes found in the S. E. Palace region, the marble cross is tentatively placed in the middle as an actual object of cult.

A curious feature of the remains found in the Repositories was the abundance of painted sea-shells, of which some are shown in Fig. 377 in front of the other relics in various materials. It is noteworthy, moreover, that in several Minoan sanctuaries the idols and cult objects were placed on rounded pebbles that may have been picked up on the sea shore or even of water-worn sherds. 2 We have here evidently a refined and very beautiful substitute for this practice. The shells from the Repository (see Fig. 378) 3,

As in the case of the later shrine of the Mactra stiiltorum, Tellina (worn), tube of Double Axes in the S. E. Palace Quarter. Serf uiid worm, and piece of an Echinid. The In the late (L. M. Ill b) shrine in the names were kindly supplied me by the late Prof.

South-East House. W. F. R. Weldon, F. R. S., from some specimens s Among them were the following species: submitted to him. The worn state of the valves

Dolium galea, Trochus lincatiis, Cardiiim edule, in the case of one or two examples made it

Pectunculus gfycimeris, Spondylus gaederopiis, difficult to attach the specific name. Venus vernicosa, Venus muuihimellata(T), bushels of which were taken out, were the ordinary sea-shells of the neighbouring coast, many varieties being included, though cockles were the most abundant. But they had been streaked and banded with brilliant artificial tints crimson, venetian-red, orange, brown, green, and black tastefully applied in unison with the natural lines and hues. The Minoans, in their taste for brilliant colour effects, would hardly have hesitated to gild refined

FIG. 378. PAINTED SEA-SHELLS FROM FLOOR OF SHRINK.

gold or paint the lily, but in this case, at any rate, the process was harmonized with Nature.

This custom of strewing the floors and altar ledges of their little shrines with sea-shells and pebbles clearly marks the religion of a people long accustomed to look towards the sea as a principal source of livelihood. It appears indeed to go back in Crete to a very remote epoch. As already noted, 1 a primitive clay female idol was found in a Neolithic deposit at 1 See above p. 37, and cf. Mun. Ant., xix, 'squatting type (cf. p. 48, above, Fig. 13, 3). 1908, p. 151 seqq. The clay image (p. 152, A fcclunailus shell had been flattened at the Fig. 8) seems to have belonged to the early bottom to be used as a miniature cup (Fig. n).

Fhaestos in company with miniature cups of clay and numerous pcctuiuulns shells. The refined practice of lining the floor and altar of our Palace Shrine with delicately painted shells may itself have been handed down from a time when these fruits of the sea formed an important part of the diet of the inhabitants and would thus result from conditions analogous to those of the Kitchenmidden folk of Northern strands.

The marine aspect of the cult also comes out among the contents of Flying the Temple Repositories in a series of very beautiful faience objects in

FIG. 380. MOULDED TERRA-COTTA RELIEFS OK CRABS AND MARINE OBJECTS WITH TRACES OF PAINTED DECORATION (f c.).

relief or in the round, representing flying fish, rocks and shells, and other sea creatures.

The most exquisite of these relics are the argonaut shells of various sizes, modelled in the round, and lustrous with a pearl-like sheen. These may have been placed upon the altar ledge beside the other votive objects as a more sumptuous substitute for the sea-shells themselves. Most of these marine forms, however, were in the shape of isolated reliefs with flat backs, and it is clear that they must have been applied to some kind of plaster backing. They doubtless belonged to a series of picturesque panels analogous to those exhibiting the animal groups. A group of these with two flying fish in the centre had been tentatively put together in Fig. 379, the argonauts in the round being here placed with the other objects. The ramifying border seems to represent some kind of coralline or other zoophytic growth.

Fish Sea pieces like the above at once suggest striking parallels with two of res Minoan wall-paintings the flying-fish panel of Phylakopi l and the dolphin

Phyla- fresco found in the Queen's Megaron at Knossos, described below. 2 A

Knossos. contemporary parallel to the reliefs of marine objects in faience is moreover afforded by some interesting, though as yet unpublished, ceramic remains of this Period. Isolated reliefs of whorl shells or cockles have been found

FIG. 381. FRAGMENT OF SIDE OF CLAY BASIN WITH TRITON SHELL IN RELIEF (f).

on vase fragments, some of them showing the dark black glaze of M. M. II tradition. The most striking comparison, however, is supplied by a series of moulded pieces in terra-cotta, which seem to have formed part of a large marine piece found in the circular walled rubbish pit of the West Court in company with heaps of characteristic M. M. Ill sherds. On these appear pectens, tritons, or, perhaps, purple shells, limpets and barnacles on a rock-like surface, and small crabs of singularly natural appearance (Fig. 380). Indeed, when the first fragments came to light it was hard to believe that one had not to do with fossil shells and Crustacea resembling those of our Coralline Crag! It seems clear that the moulds for some of these reliefs were formed on the natural objects themselves. Traces appeared of white painted decoration. 3 1 See below, p. 541, Fig. 393. 3 Some parallel reliefs representing rock-work

See below, p. 542. Fig. 394. showed traces of both white and blue.

A parallel fragment, in this case belonging to a flat-bottomed basin, Clay showing rock-work and a triton shell in relief, is given in Fig. 381. Vessels of this latter type, decorated with subjects of this nature, reproducing the familiar forms of the sea-shore and its rocky pools may have been actually Perhaps used as dishes to serve friitta di mare fresh for the delectation of the Palace gourmets. The whole class of terra-cotta vessels with marine reliefs belonging to the last Middle Minoan Period, coupled with similar reliefs on steatite vessels, has a very important bearing on the ceramic repertory of the succeeding L. M. I Period in which the reproduction of similar designs of sea creatures amidst rocks are executed on the flat in the familiar brown on buff technique.

Fir,. 382. LOWER PART OK FAIENCE FIGURINE, KROM TEMPLE REPOS-ITORY. a. FRONT VIEW; b. BACK VIEW.

Painted Plaster Reliefs imitated in those of faience; Dating of the mural reliefs; The Jewel Relief fragment part of a life-size toilet scene; Probably derived from Columnar Hall above Pillar Crypts; M. M. Ill frescoes on the flat; Scenes of Bull Ring; The Minoan Fresco process; Early Minoan plaster partly striictui al; Advanced Middle Minoan technique; Stucco layers thinner on Gypsum; Stucco Reliefs; Analysis of material Subterranean Quarry whence obtained; Labyrinth of Gortyna compared; Early Minoan Red facing; Pigments used in later frescoes the Egyptian Blue; True fresco process on wet plaster; Pure caustic lime plaster, a lost Art; Artistic Shorthand of Miniature Frescoes; M. M. Ill Frescoes of S. E. House; The Lily Fresco; Olive sprays; Spikelets of Reeds-masterpieces of Naturalistic Art. Parallels from H. Triada;

The Cat and Pheasant fresco parallels at Knossos; Free adaptation of Nilotic Scenes; Flying Fish Fresco, Phylakopi work of Knossian School; Dolphin Fresco of Queens Megaron M. M. Ill; Conntxions of Fish Frescoes; Fine fresco designs of female forms by Knossian hand in Melos; The Ladies in Blue; Notched plume decoration on votive arrows; On wings of Sphinxes and Griffins; Combined with asterisk a stellar symbol; Asterisks on stucco face of Sphinx; Notched plume motive on skirts of Goddess; Degenerations of notched plunte motive; Its occurrence on hearths at Knossos and Mycenae.

Painted THE beautiful relief panels of the Palace faience, such as those described

Plaster j n e p rece di n g Section, must be regarded as the correlatives of contemporary , compositions of monumental character executed in painted plaster. It inthoseof has indeed been already noted that the group of the Cow and Calf shown in ce Fig. 3(57 above is placed over an architectonic base, the alternating light and dark bands of which reproduce a usual convention of variegated stonework.

In Fig. 368 again is given a faience console, with similar bands, that had clearly acted as a support for a relief panel like the other. We shall see that such supports were actually found with the remains of the Griffin

Frieze, described below in connexion with the L. M. I East Hall of the

Palace. 1 1 See Vol. II.

Of contemporary reliefs of this character we have abundant though Fainted unfortunately very fragmentary remains from the Area of the Spiral Fresco, O f spiral belonging to bull-grappling episodes. These remains, as shown above, 1 were derived from what seems to have been the M. M. Ilia predecessor of this great Palace Hall. Reasons have been given, moreover, for regarding the Spiral Fresco itself, found with these reliefs and consisting of a frame and diagonals, as having formed part of the design illustrating one of these performances. The combination of painted reliefs with subsidiary subjects executed in the flat was indeed a constantly recurring device of the Minoan artists.

The tendency of all works executed in the very hard material that Dating was the Minoan equivalent for gesso duro to persist on the Palace walls Mural makes it often difficult in dealing with this part of the subject to attain to Reliefs, absolute chronological precision. It is clear, however, that the analogous bull-grappling scenes found with the high reliefs of human subjects in an adjacent area belonged to a later structure than that from which the Spiral Fresco remains were derived. These later reliefs had reached the position in which they were found at the time of the final castrophe of the Palace, and there is every reason for assigning them to the East Hall as, ex hypothesi, reconstructed at the beginning of the Late Minoan Age.

In a Section devoted to that epoch it has also been thought preferable to include the noble relief of the bull's head and other associated fragments found in the Northern Entrance Passage, and which seem to form part of the same cycle as that illustrated by the Vapheio Gold Cups. It is by no means impossible that these works slightly overlap the last M. M. Ill phase, but the circumstances of their discovery bring them into the closest connexion with the history of the later phase of the Minoan Palace, while, from the superficial position of the deposit in which some of the fragments lay, it is probable that a part at least of these reliefs had still clung to the walls in days when an Achaean Knossos was already rising on the neighbouring slope.

For the present Period, on the other hand, may certainlybe claimed a fine The Jewel painted plaster relief fragment found at a low level in a basement West of prag. the later Stepped Portico. A man's fingers are here seen holding the end inent of a gold necklace to which is tied some article of attire of a deep blue colour, and chequered in a manner recalling the tartan of the Sacral Knots' already described. 2 The necklace itself consists of globular beads and pendant heads of a negroid type, which have been illustrated in detail above. 3 1 See p. 375 seqq. " See p. 430 seqq. See p. 312, and Fig. 231.

THE PALACE OF MINOS, ETC.

The dull orange colour of the beads and the faces of the pendants shows that the material was of gold. A raven lock, evidently belonging to the wearer of the jewel, partly shuts out the left of the two pendants. It looks as if we had here a fragment of a toilet scene, sacral probably in its relations, where a necklace attached behind the neck to a piece of stuff was fitted above its owner's bosom. That the wearer was of the female sex is a natural supposition, and its fitting on by a male hand might seem appropriate to Marriage, some wedding ceremony perhaps a Upos yaioy. In other respects the

Part of a Life-size Toilet Scene.
Perhaps from
Sacral
Probably derived from
Columnar
Hall above
Pillar
Crypts.
Flg. 383.

FRAGMENT OF PAINTED STUCCO RELIEF OF MANS HAND HOLDING CORNER OF ROBE AND JEWEL (-J-).

subject suggests a close analogy with the Ladies in Blue described below, one of whom is depicted as fingering a necklace of round beads.

Small as it is, this fragment gives a key to a figure group of life size-forming part perhaps of an extensive frieze that had adorned some upper chamber in the immediate neighbourhood of the Central Palace Shrine. From the position indeed in which it lay it may well have found a place in the Columnar Hall above the Pillar Crypts, to which the large column bases belonged that have been illustrated above. 1 The exquisite finish of this work is unsurpassed by any Minoan painted relief of which remains have been preserved, and the careful rendering of the smallest details may be compared with that of the best Miniature Frescoes' of the succeeding 1 p. 442, Fig. 318.

epoch. The colours are exceptionally well preserved. The ground is a milky white, the fingers Venetian red, the beads and the faces of the negroid heads are a rich yellow, indicating the golden material; their hair is black and the earrings and the details of the features are of a bright red. 1 The knotted end of the piece of stuff is of a deep blue not of the Egyptian cobalt tint and the tartan pattern visible on it is marked out with black lines.

The best dated deposit of painted stucco belonging to the close of the Third Middle Minoan Period was that, already described in another con-

FIG. 384. PAINTED STUCCO FRAGMENT ILLUSTRATING FRESCO SHORT-HAND: FROM BELOW KASELLA FLOOR OF XIIItH MAGAZINE ( ).

nexion, 2 found between the Kasella floors of the Thirteenth Magazine. The facades of columnar buildings there seen (Figs. 319, 321) are of special interest as supplying, on a somewhat larger scale, the immediate forerunners of the designs on the so-called Miniature Frescoes', belonging, as is shown by other evidence, to the beginning of the First Late Minoan Period. With these architectural frescoes there were, moreover, fragments, designed on a corresponding scale (Fig. 384), showing, above traces of a line of wall, dense crowds of spectators, 3 like those associated with the miniature 1 See the enlarged reproduction, p. 312, See Knossian Atlas, i, PI. VI, Fig. 12. Fig. 231, with the colour scale. The group of spectators seen on the principal 2 See above, pp. 443, 445, and cf. Knossos, fragment are backed by waved zones of yellow Report, 1904, p. 4oseqq. and sky-blue.

THE PALACE OF MINOS, ETC.

Hull Ring.

panels. These too were hastily sketched in what may be called a pictorial shorthand due to the necessities of the fresco process, and except for their somewhat larger size and rougher execution, very closely approach the later Scenes of series. 1 A clue to the character of the spectacle is probably supplied by another painted fragment from the deposit, derived, however, from a panel on a larger scale, depicting a fine bull's head, together with the ends of the flying locks of some acrobatic figure (Fig. 385). This fragment evidently belonged to a circus scene, resembling those of the later wall-paintings found in the East Quarter of the Knossian Palace. The bull's head in this case, however, is executed in a superior style, and may best compare with the head of one of the finest painted stucco reliefs from the Northern Entrance Passage. 2 The religious features in the columnar buildings seen on the painted fragment with which the bull's head was associated, make it probable that, as in other cases, these sports of the Palace arena were held in honour of the Great Minoan Goddess.

It will be seen from the above examples that, by the Third Middle Minoan Period, the art of wall-painting had attained its full maturity of technique and design. The researches and minute analysis of specimens of this painted stucco, carried out by Mr. Noel Heaton, have now conclusively shown that, though occasionally supplemented by some slight recourse to tempera, this was a true fresco process, in its execution akin to the biion fresco of the Italians." Its remarkable characteristic is that it seems to have been carried out in pure lime plaster. This at least is the conclusion to which all tests hitherto applied to it have led. The first crude beginnings of this lime plaster can be traced back almost to Neolithic times. It began with a definite utilitarian object, the protection, namely, of the surface of loose rubble and sun-dried brick, of which the early walls were constructed, and we see it already well illustrated on those of the E. M. II and E. M. Ill buildings at Vasiliki. In this case the plaster contained about 40 per cent, of carbonate of lime, the remainder being made up mainly of silica and alumina, with a backing of pebbles, fragments of pottery, and chopped straw. A typical section 4 shows about 5 centimetres thickness of this plaster with a well-marked line of cleavage indicating that there was an upper coat, about one and a half centimetres thick, of somewhat

The Minoan Fresco Technique.

Utilitarian origin 1 See Vol. II 2 See Vol. II.

(1911), p. 697 seqq.; and On the Nature and Method of execution of specimens of painted 3 The Mitral Paintings of Knossos, Journ. plaster from the Palace of Tiryns (in Tiryns II; R. Society of Arts, 1910; Minoan Lime Plaster Die Freshen des Palastes, Athens, 1912). and Fresco Painting, R. I. B. A. Journ., xviii 4 R. I, B. A. Journ., xviii, p. 698, Fig. i.,

THK PALACE OF MINOS, ETC. This plaster was of a dirty yellow colour and very hard finer texture, and tenacious.

Advance In the Middle Minoan Age a greater proportion of lime was used, and

Minoan 6 we note a progressive refinement in the stucco material till the surface layer becomes practically pure and beautifully white in section, though this was generally applied to a coarser backing. By the close of the Middle and the early part of the Late Minoan Age the technique attained its highest per-

Tech-nique. Stucco Layers.

FIG. 386. SECTION OF TYPICAL PAINTED PLASTER ( ).

fection. 1 A section taken by Mr. Heaton from a fragment of painted plaster belonging to the last Palace Period is given in Fig. 380, showing part of the coarser backing and two layers of fine plaster above.

Thinner Where there was a gypsum backing the finer stucco could be applied

St a ucco d directly and the plaster layer was therefore appreciably thinner, or at times, Layers on a s in the case of the staircase of the Royal Villa to the N. E. of the Palace, -1111 i a mere wash. 2 It seems possible that the comparative thinness 01 the Gypsum.

1 According to my own observations (mainly due to the test explorations of 1913), some very pure stucco occurs occasionally in M. M. II deposits, and the Saffron-gatherer Fresco must be taken as an illustration of this. But the bulk of the plaster still contained an admixture of clay and grit down to M. M. III. It is at this time that painted stucco generally assumes the fine white texture which continues to character-ize it throughout the Late Minoan Age.

2 About one-sixteenth of an inch (Heaton, R. I. B. A. Journ. xviii, p. 702). The plaster was usually about half an inch thick when directly applied to gypsum walls. In the case of the Marbled Fresco' it was less than this. The view is expressed elsewhere that the gypsum dadoes were generally decorated with a painted stucco wash.

plaster layer of the fragments on which the Marbled Fresco described above was painted may be due to the fact that it had been applied to gypsum slabs. Its fine alabaster veining would thus have a direct bearing on its place on the walls.

In the case of the stucco reliefs as is well shown by the remains stucco of 'two female breasts (Fig. 387) belonging to the series of the High

FIG. 387. PARTS OF HIGH RELIEF OF PAINTED STUCCO REPRESENTING FEMALE BREASTS AND SHOWING THE FlnE SURFACE COATING OVER-LAID ON THE SCORED MOULDING BELOW.

Reliefs (L. M. I) the finer coating was overlaid on a roughly modelled surface of more clayey composition, scored with incised lines to give a hold to the surface layer (Fig. 387). It further appears that this modelling was sometimes added after the flat surface had been already prepared, and in one case even treated to a thin wash of red. 2 The labour was thus in this case divided between the ordinary house-painter and the skilled artist.

1 These high reliefs in painted stucco are fully illustrated in a Section of Vok II. Heaton, R. I. B. A. Journ., xviii, p. 710.

Analysis The material of this fine plaster proves, from the analysis of a number Material typ 1 samples by Mr. Heaton, to have consisted of practically pure chalk lime. 1 As he points out, 2 by using this material for the plaster of the walls something was lost of the hardness and tenacity which the admixture of alumina silicates had given to the earlier class. But the main object now was, not so much the structural reinforcement of the walls, as to provide a perfectly smooth surface for their painted decoration.

FIG. 388. ENTRANCK HALL OF SUBTERRANEAN QUARRY, KNOSSOS, WITH SQUARE-HEWN PILLAR SUPPORTING ROOF.

Pure The analysis of various specimens of this fine plaster brought out the Placer interesting fact that the limestone, by the burning of which this material was obtained, corresponded with that of the great subterranean quarry, the cave-like mouth of which opens on the hill-side, at Hagia Irini, about 2 miles above the site of the Palace. 3 This quarry, with many branches and Sub- labyrinthine turns and with vaults at intervals, supported by huge square cut Quarry?" P ars (see Fig- 388), honeycombs the neighbouring range and finds another whence ex jt j n a defile beyond. Its vast scale shows the persistence with which the obtained.

1 The content of carbonate of lime was:! Heaton, R. I. B. A. Journ., xviii, p. 700, found to vary from 90 to 94 per cent. Fig. 3, reproduced here as Fig. 388. He

R. I. B. A, Journ., xviii, p. 699. remarks that the composition of the plaster ,"s too closely similar to be accidenta.

Early

M. M. Ill: MINOAN FRKSCO: WALL PAINTINGS, ETC. 533 finest layers of the rock were sought, no doubt mainly for structural purposes, from a very early time. Some blocks half sawn out are of a Minoan character and the laminations of the stone answer to those visible on many of the Palace blocks. A similar subterranean quarry above Gortyna, long known to travellers, has been described as the Labyrinth. 1 It is clear, however, that classical tradition connected the name of the Labyrinth at Knossos with the remains of an actual building, the portico of which is shown on vases representing the slaughter of the Minotaur. 2 There can be little doubt. that it was the great Palace itself.

In Early Minoan times only a single colour seems to have been applied to the plaster-surface, a red ochre which was afterwards burnished by hand. This red-faced plaster was applied indiscriminately to walls and pavements. 3 But by the close of the

First Middle Minoan Period, as is shown by the remarkable fragment of painted stucco from the Early Palace reproduced in Coloured Plate I above, a considerable advance both in colour and in the decorative method had been already achieved. We note here the presence of three colours, red, white, and black, and can trace not only the skilful imitation of the barbotine decoration of the contemporary Facing. polychrome pottery, but the use of some mechanical appliance for printing the curvilinear pattern. There can be little doubt that the complicated spiraliform designs of the Middle Minoan Age were produced as in this case with the aid of a stencil or of a template, and it has even been possible, with the help of an engraved figure of the latter object on a craft-man's signet of M. M. II date, to reconstruct the pattern of a contemporary ceiling. 4

Of the colours mainly used in the wall-paintings at the time of the full 1 nents perfection of the Art in the Knossian Palace, Mr. Heaton 5 considers that Later the white was composed of calcium carbonate, probably employed in the 1 Spratt (Travels and Researches in Crete, rinths (Sitzungsberifhte d. K. Bayer. Akad., i, p. 65), who knew of the Labyrinth of 1907, p. 113 seqq.).

Gortyna, did not advance beyond the con- 3 A good example of this Early Minoan jecture that there might have been a similar red-faced plaster was found near the N E.

subterranean quarry or labyrinth in the heart Magazines at Knossos. The wall plaster was of the adjacent hills that surround the site here indistinguishable from that of the floor of the Capital of Minos'. The mouth of the and both were hand polished. For the use of

Knossian quarry is much concealed, which this red-faced plaster at Vasilild, see above, may account for the fact that its existence had p. 72.

escaped the observation of himself and other See Cretan Pictographs, erv.(. N. S., xiv) travellers. Pl. XII and p. 50 seqq., and cf. p. 274, above.

- See P. Volters, Darstelliingen des Laby- " A. . B. A. Journ., xviii, pp. 4, 5.
THE PALACE OF MINOS, ETC.
Egyptian Blue.
True Fresco Process on Wet Plaster.
pressed lines for guidance.
form of hydrate of lime, as used in modern and mediaeval times. The black seems to have been of the nature of a carbonaceous shale or slate like the Italian chalks described by Cennino Cennini. 1 The red and yellow colours presented all the characteristics of iron earths. The yellow answers to yellow ochre and this on calcination produces a light red. The deep red which was largely employed from the earliest times- is a purer form of oxide of iron, probably prepared from haematite. 3 In the earlier part of the Middle Minoan Age a deep natural blue was in use. Somewhat later, however, a blue of brilliant cobalt hue, a crystalline silicate of copper, 4 begins to take its place, and by the beginning of the Late Minoan Age the predominance of this splendid pigment was fully established. It is clear that this is identical with the blue pigment early in use in Egypt and may be regarded as an Egyptian product. Its frequent use in Crete from the closing phase of. the Middle Minoan Period onwards is one of the many indications of close corhmercial relations with the Nile Valley. This material is the classical kyanos' and mediaeval smalt V The green that occurs in the case of foliage was prepared by mixing blue and yellow; it is only later, as at Tiryns that a pure green pigment was

employed, probably obtained by grinding malachite. 6 The use of a pigment of this character goes back, however, to prehistoric times in Egypt.

It is impossible to doubt that the painted stucco was the result of a true fresco process. Everywhere we find indications that the pigments were applied when the stucco was still moist. Sometimes outlines are sketched by means of a blunt point passed over the soft surface. In the architectural pieces the artist's brush was guided by horizontal lines at close intervals, and these were also produced by means of taut string. In the case 1 In Tiryns, ii, p. 215, Mr. Heaton speaks of the black pigment there used as an impure form of carbon containing a large amount of mineral matter, probably prepared by charring bones'.

2 Mr. Heaton quotes Professor Flinders Petrie (Abydos, ii, p. 38) for the statement that this pigment was imported into Egypt from Crete in Early Dynastic days. The cups, however, referred to as containing red ochre cannot be regarded as of Cretan fabric.

3 Heaton, Tiryns, ii, p. 215.

4 F. Fouque, Bull. Soc. des Mines de France, vol. xii, p. 36, and Comptes Rtndus, c., vol. 108, p. 325. Fouque s results were con- firmed and amplified by Dr. A. P. Laurie (Prof. R. S., 1914 (No. A. 612), p. 418 seqq.). The blue he states (p. 421) was prepared from copper carbonate quartz and fusion mixture alone or from the same ingredients with the addition of calcium carbonate. The material is of the same composition as that used from Prehistoric times in Egypt for glazing objects of sandstone (pp. cit., p. 428).

5 This is not, as Mr. Heaton points out. Mural Paintings of Knossos, p. 5, note, identical with the modern 'smalt, which is a potash glass coloured with cobalt.

"Heaton, in Tiryns, ii, p. 216.

of elaborate decorative designs the parts of the surface that they occupy were habitually divided up into small squares by lines arranged horizontally and vertically in reference to the pattern. A good example of this procedure will be seen in the patterns of the sleeves in the fresco given below representing the Ladies in Blue. 1 These guiding lines were only drawn in the places where they were actually required and were not continuous over the whole field.

Owing to the wet process we also constantly find the pigments interfused with the stucco coating to an appreciable extent beneath the surface. The upper washes of colour have also a tendency to penetrate the lower and even at times to enter the stucco below. The durability of the colours is marvellous, and pieces of the painted stucco that have been exposed to the elements for over ten years since the excavation are to-day even brighter than when they were exhumed. That the colours were so exceptionally fixed seems to stand in relation to the abnormally thick stucco coating on which they were laid, the lime solution, or calcium hydrate, that supplied the fixing material finding its way to the surface from a greater collecting area.

All the analyses and microscopic observations carried out by Mr. Heaton lead to the conclusion that the plaster was essentially composed of pure Pure caustic lime, without the admixture of inert material such as the L ime. C marble dust used at Pompeii or in mediaeval frescoes.- But how this magnificent lime plaster was prepared by the

Minoan craftsmen remains A Lost a matter of conjecture. The traditions of their craft have vanished with them. 3

The depth of the stucco coating itself afforded special facilities for the Artistic e f j I u J Short- fresco painters, since the plaster surface remained longer moist, but rapid han i O f execution was still a prime necessity. Thus in the more detailed work, such j as the Miniature Frescoes with their crowded groups like Fig. 384 above,; 1 See below, p. 545, Fig. 397. examined this possibility, informs me that it 2 The Mural Paintings oXnossos, R. Society is inconsistent with the actual phenomena. of Arts Journ, 1910, pp. 5, 6. Colours laid on either a moist or dry stucco 3 It is, as Mr. Heaton points out. contrary surface by this process are neatly superposed to the unanimous opinion of those who have on one another, and a section shows clean flat had practical experience of plaster that pure layers. But the pigments of the Minoan frescoes lime could produce the magnificent stucco that were constantly interfused and also often we have before us. J. A. Schneider-Franken spread beneath the wet stucco surface. Mr. (Ath. Mitti., xxxviii, 1913, p. 187 seqq.) has Heaton admits the possibility that lime-water suggested that the colours were simply fixed may have been mixed with the colours, but by mixing lime water (Kalchmilch) with the this at most would have been a supplementary pigments. But Mr. Heaton, who had himself device.

THE PALACE OF MINOS, ETC.

Frescoes ofs. E.

House.

we have constant evidence of a kind of artistic shorthand. 1 In the smaller compositions such as these and the Taureador Frescoes' the process was assisted by the subdivision of the fields into comparatively small panels the remainder of the wall space being covered by a flat wash of white, or more frequently red. In some cases, notably in the Flying

Fish fresco' from Melos, itself clearly the work of a Knossian artist the edges of the plaster have a smooth flat surface as though the picture had been enclosed in a wooden frame V 1 Mere horizontal bands, and borders of mechanical design might be executed by the ordinary-workmen, the more elaborate panels being filled in by artists of a higher grade working with a rapidity and certainty born of constant practice and long established tradition. Although, as the modelling of the

FIG. 389. FRESCO FROM BASEMENT BY STEPPED PORTICO, s t ucco reliefs shows they SHOWING FLOWERING OLIVE SPRAY (f-.).

were fully aware of the value of such features, the artists limited themselves to outline and wash in two dimensions. 4

Apart from the fragments with the architectural and other designs from the Kaselles fl and the Spiral Fresco and reliefs derived from the M. M. Ill East Hall," the best stratigraphic evidence as to the wall-paintings of the present Period is supplied by the South-East House, to the importance of which in relation to the Central Palace cult attention has been already called. 7

See my remarks, Knossos, Report, 1900, p. 47.

? See Vol. II, and Knossian Atlas.

3 Professor R. C. Bosanquet,) i jj, p.7i.

In the case of the Griffin Fresco, however, found in the Room of the Throne and belong- ing to the latest Palace epoch (L. M. II), shading is shown by means of cross-hatching.

5 See above, p. 443 seqq., and Figs. 319, 321; and p. 527 seqq., Figs. 384, 385.

c See above, p. 371 seqq.

7 See above, p. 425 seqq.

PLATE VI

The remains of frescoes that here came to light seem, from the position in which they were found, to have been mainly derived from a columnar hall above the Pillar Crypt of this house, the latest elements of which, as shown by the pottery, belong to the concluding phase of M. M. III. The wall-paintings here are of special value from the illustration that they afford of the high level by this time attained in the naturalistic rendering of plant forms.

The most striking of the fragments of wall-painting here brought to Lily light, derived apparently from this columnar hall, was a group of white

FIG. 390. FRESCO DESIGN WITH REEDS: SOUTH-EAST HOUSE, KNOS-SOS (f.)- lilies with orange anthers and green foliage on a dark red ground (see Coloured Plate VI). 1 Some of the petals of one of the lower flowers seem to have been detached by the passing breeze; a natural touch which goes beyond mere decorative art. This detail is so surprising that we might be tempted to ascribe it to accident rather than design, but trees swayed by the wind are seen on a seal impression of this Period. 2

The lilies themselves bear a certain affinity to those of the lily vases' Fresco to be described below, but in a freer style. Near this group were found ments other fresco remains showing graceful olive foliage. Another painted stucco sp e j et of Reed 1 PI. VI is from the drawing by Mr. H. Bagge Candia Museum and is now a botch-work. an d Oli of the fragments as originally reconstituted. It 2 See p. 697, Fig. 519, from the Temple Sprays, was broken up in the course of transport to the Repositories.

THE PALACE OF MINOS, ETC.

fragment (Fig. 389) depicts a flowering olive spray, already cited 2 as supplying a more naturalistic parallel to the conventional olive foliage with alter-

FIG. 391. FRESCO DESIGN OK CAT STALKING PHEASANT. HAGIA TRI-ADA (".).

nating red and white leaves seen on a fragment of a M. M. II polychrome vase. In the present case the seasonal variations in the tints of the leaves are indicated by dark ruddy brown and ivory white.:; 1 From a basement W. of the Stepped 3 A coloured illustration of this will be given Portico on the Central Court. in my Knossian Atlas, i, PI. D. 2.

2 See above, p. 263.

Even more exquisite in its natural inspiration is a small piece (Fig. from the S. E. House, showing spikelets of reeds or grasses, round one of which is coiled the tail of what appears to be a small harvest mouse.

This fragmentary design, sketched by a master hand, may at least give Master-some idea of the free spirit that pervaded the panel to which it belonged. 3". Were it the only record of such work belonging to this Age at Knossos, we tic Art. should be entitled to believe that a similar naturalistic school existed here to that which produced the much more fully preserved frescoes found by Professor Halbherr in a room of the Palace of Hagia Triada. The reconstructions Parallel of the remains of these by Dr. Stefani show that there was here a series of scenes of animals amidst ivy-covered rocks and various kinds of plants and flowers. A part of one of these wall-paintings here given for comparison, Fig. 391, 2 shows a cat stalking a pheasant-like bird, which, as will be Hagia seen, finds a near parallel at Knossos 3. The characteristic contour-lines of Frescoes: the rocks on these frescoes also bear a close resemblance to the alabaster- p? tan like graining of the Marbled Dado from the South-East borders of the Knossian Palace, ascribed above to this Period. 4

Among the unpublished fragments from Hagia Triada a portion of a kneeling female figure, apparently gathering crocuses, seems to be a somewhat later variant of the Saffron-gatherer fresco. The crocus-flowers here are arranged in tufts resembling those on the votive faience robes from the Temple Repositories. These like the clumps of lilies belonging to the same fresco, reproduced in Fig. 445 below recall examples on M. M. Ill pots and jars.

These comparisons enforce the conclusion that the Hagia Triada frescoes fit on to the other artistic works that mark the culminating phase of the M. M. Ill Period.

The tufts of flowers seen in these Hagia Triada frescoes suggest some Hybrid-slight reflection of the lotus and papyrus clumps of Egyptian Nile-pieces. p " n s A certain hybridism, as Professor Halbherr has observed, 5 is noticeable j". H; . Triada in the flowers and foliage leaves of Liliaceae being combined with flowers of Frescoes. Compositae. Flowers like white violets have leaves of a more bramble-like character.

That the cat and pheasant fresco of Hagia Triada had its analogy at 1 For a coloured illustration see Knotsian: 1 For the bird compare also a fragment

Atlas, i, PI. I), i. of a fresco from Phylakopi (Phyakopi, p. 77,

Halbherr, M, i. Inf. xiii, PI. VIII and Fig. 65).

p. 58; compare Rizzo, Sloria delf Arte Greca, See p. 356, Fig. 255.

. 101, Fig. 34. s Man. Ant., xiii, p. 57.

THE PALACE OF MINOS, ETC.

Knossian Knossos is shown by two painted stucco fragments found closely juxta- posed

Calami 0 n one tne h ea P s on tne North border of the Palace. One of these

Pheasant (Fig. 392 B) gives the upper part of the head of a cat, though of a different type from the animal of the Hagia Triada design (inset). The ears are more rounded, the yellow ground of the side of the face is covered with white spots, and the pupil of the eye is blue. For some of these details the

KEY TO COLOURS of A B

RED fi YELLOW i? BLUE '"'

FIG. 392. A, B. FRESCO FRAGMENTS SHOWING PARTS OF BIRD AND CATS HEAD, KNOSSOS; HEAD OF CAT, HAGIA TRIADA (INSET).

artist may have drawn on his fancy, at the same time the white patch round the eye is a feature characteristic of the wild-cat, a common Cretan species. The other fragment (Fig. 392 A) displays a section of the tail and outspread wings of a bird of brilliant plumage. The tail feathers indicate an elongated form and seem to have been banded with dark stripes, but their colours are not as well preserved as those of the wings. These show an outer row of red- 1 Miss Dorothea Bate remarks, a wild cat (Felts agnus) is not uncommon in the island, and seems to resemble most closely specimens from Sardinia (The Mammals of Crete, in Aubyn Trevor-Battye, Camping in Crete! 255)- tipped orange plumes and a double row within of blue feathers with darker tips. It may be observed that the colours of these Knossian fragments are much better preserved than those of the Hagia Triacla painting, which have suffered from fire. Certainly in this case the brilliant plumage seems best compatible with some kind of pheasant, but the analogy supplied by the cat's head does not lead us to expect accuracy in the colouring.

FIG. 393. FLYING-FISH FRESCO FROM PHYLAKOPI: KNOSSIAN SCHOOL ((.)

The cat's head and bird are here again turned in the same direction, which agrees with the supposition that the animal was in pursuit of its prey.

An obvious comparison with these scenes is supplied by the well- Free known Nile-pieces in which cats are seen pursuing water-fowl amidst fj on p 0 f papyrus thickets. The cat and land-bird amidst ivy covered rocks in fact Tllotlc represent the translation of the Egyptian river-side motive into indigenous terms. It is characteristic indeed of the independent spirit of this epoch that these Nile scenes were not as yet taken over literally, as they undoubtedly were early in the succeeding Late Minoan phase. 1 1 See Vol. II.

THE PALACE OF MINOS, ETC.

It has already been noted that the faience reliefs from the Temple Repositories, exhibiting flying-fish and other marine creatures amidst rock-work, bear an extraordinary resemblance to the well-known painted stucco panel from Phylakppi presenting similar subjects (Fig. 39J5). 1 That this is the work of a contemporary Knossian artist can hardly be gainsaid. The

FIG. 394. PART OK THE DOLPHIN FRESCO FROM QUEENS MEGARON, KNOSSOS.

picture, as already noted, seems to have been enclosed in a wooden frame, and the suggestion has even been made that the painted panel was exported ready-made from Knossos. 2 But this conclusion is hardly necessary.

Executed with the rapid touch of the fresco painters' art, this design 1 Excavations at Phylakopi, PI. Ill (from ings, however, with human figures, equally a drawing by M. Gillieron), and see Prof. R. C. Knossian in character (see below p. 544),

Bosanquet, op. cit., pp. 70-2. must certainly have been executed on the

Bosanquet, op. fit., p. 71. The wall-paint- spot.

is an unsurpassed rendering of the lively and varied motions of these Swallows of the Sea. Their alternate course in air and water is here exquisitely rendered by the play of the wings, now open for flight, now thrown back for diving beneath the surface of the waves, and all amidst a swirl of spray and bubbles.

This composition, though more vivacious in character, shows a close The parallelism in style and subject with the much larger fresco of dolphins Fre'sco' and other fish found in the Queen's Megaron at Knossos (Fig. 1394). Knossos-This Dolphin Fresco seems to have been cleared from the walls on the occasion of the great remodelling that had set in during the last epoch of the Palace,- and its remains were found in too fragmentary a condition for it to be possible to reconstruct the composition in its original form. It had Dolphin evidently occupied a consider- Knossos. able wall-space, but the most that could be done was to place the figured pieces together in a certain relation to one another according to a tentative scheme of my own. Fig. 3514, photographed from the original fresco, reproduces a part of this for the better illustration of the details and technique.

The body colour of the upper part of the dolphins and of their fins and tail is a deep blue of the older class, more ultramarine than cobalt in tone, with black outlines. A double band of orange yellow runs along their sides and their bellies are of a creamy white. The smaller fish by which they are surrounded show variations of the same colour scheme. Some remains of a border were also found, of which a fragment is shown in Fig. 395. It is of a dark bistre hue and presents an irregular edge with prickly projections, perhaps intended to depict coralline-covered rocks, and according to analogy, shells, sponges, or other marine growths would have been coupled with this.

1 Xeaisofoiapo. were found among the latest elements of the 2 The fragments mostly occurred along the stratum in which they occurred.

line of the comparatively late wall, which The panel containing this fresco in the formed the liastern border of the E. light-area. Candia Museum was put together by Mr.

of this Megaron according to the existing Theodore Fyfe in accordance with this arrangement. Some sherds of L. M. II pottery scheme.

RED BAND

Fit;. 395. FRAC. MENT OF CORALLINE BORDER
BELONGING TO DOLPHIN FRESCO.
THE PALACE OF MINOS, ETC.
Representations of Sea-spray.
M. M. Ill Connexions of Fish Frescoes.
more

Beneath the rock border were remains of a Venetian red band, presumably belonging to a dado. A suggestion of the original place on the walls of this marine painting will be seen in the restored view of the Queen's Megaron, to be included in the Second Volume of this work.

As noted above, this work, though of finer technique and careful execution, presents singular points of comparison with the instantaneous sketches preserved to us in the Flying Fish panel. The resemblance extends to minute details such as the sea-spray and bubbles, which here fly off from the fins and tails of the fishes in azure wreaths and coils dotted on the white ground, and impart a marvellous sense of motion to the whole design. Both paintings are works of the same Knossian school, and the marine, like the floral style of these frescoes, was reflected in M. M. Ill ceramic designs. 1

The connexion between these marine designs and those of the faience reliefs of marine subjects is so clear that it seems safe to refer them to the same approximate date. The Phylakopi wall-painting was found on the floor of the Pillar Crypt of the early Palace in association with sherds of a Melian class, parallel with the M. M. Ill phase in Crete and belonging to the last epoch of the Second City of Phylakopi. 2

With the flying-fish fresco at Phylakopi, and, like it, presumably fallen from a columnar hall above, 3 were found remains, evidently executed on the spot by a Knossian artist, of larger pictures showing parts of two female

FIG. 396. FRESCO DESIGN OF PART OF A WOMAN. PHYLAKOPI (.

1 See especially the sepulchral urns from Pachyammos, pp. 608, 610 below.

2 My information as to the pottery is due to Dr. Mackenzie, who excavated the room. Pottery parallel with L. M. I was found on a higher and later floor level.

3 A column base (Phylakopi, p. 6r, Fig. 56) belonging to this was actually found in the same area as the fresco fragments. It shows a square footing from which rises a circular base for the shaft and thus answers to a type of ledged column-base that seems to have been in vogue by the beginning of M. M. Ill (see above, p. 213).

. y—wx i-os

Fine figures, the limbs of which, according to the regular convention, are outlined Fresco on a w hit; e ground. One of these wears a robe, embroidered, just below the

Desifirns of Female girdle, with two swallows flying in opposite directions, and holds up a skein-

Knots S ian y like object which she fingers with the other hand. 1 The other is seen in hand in a stooping position with both arms held down in front (Fig. 396).- The drawing here is of singular purity and beauty, suggesting a figure on a white

FIG. 398. HAND SLIGHTLY UNDER LifE SIZE, FROM LADIES IN BLUE FRESCO

Athenian lekythos some twelve centuries later in date. It is in perfect harmony with a series of fragments, also delineating female figures, found, much smoke-stained, in a deposit outside the North wall of the Royal Magazines' at Knossos. From the locality in which they were unearthed it is probable that these had formed part of the decorations of the great East Hall of the Palace as it existed about the close of this Period.

Sparse and fragmentary as are these remains, a careful 3 study has 1 Phylakopi, p. 73, Fig. 61. new links of evidence. On the basis of these 2 Op. tit., p. 74, Fig. 62. Monsieur Gillieron has executed the brilliant 3 Supplementary researches made for me restored sketch seen in Fig. 397. The heads by Mr. Droop in 1914 brought out some of the ladies are his own addition, and the resulted in the reconstruction of the upper part of what was clearly a group of Restored seated ladies (Fig.:!)"). They are of natural size, and anticipate in their pose m P and expressive gestures those of the Miniature Frescoes to be described in Knossos: a succeeding Section. Their bosoms are open and they wear blue short-sleeved Ladies bodices with rich embroidery. Their wrists, necks, and tresses are bejewelled, " and the action of one of the hands, shown nearly life size in Fig. 398, which is seen fingering the beads of a necklace, and of another, apparently about to grasp the border of her neighbour's dress, sufficiently suggests the subject of their conversation. The Jewel Fresco', illustrated in Fig. 383 above, showing a man's fingers adjusting a lady's necklace, is a variant of the same theme. The fine outlines of the arms and hands on these frescoes seen against the white ground again curiously recall the beautiful designs on white Athenian lekytkoi.

The Ladies in Blue convey the impression of a nobler and less mannered execution than that seen in the case of the Miniature groups, and, inferentially, may be taken to belong to a somewhat earlier artistic phase.

These works, which so far as the human form is concerned, must be regarded as the most exquisite products of the Knossian limner's art, are shown by the examples executed for the small Early Palace of Phylakopi strati-to be of the same date as the fish frescoes. Works of this school f j,. had already made their appearance at Melos at some time anterior to the of date catastrophe of the building in which they were found, which itself, as the lakopi. vessels found on its original floor-level demonstrate, must have taken place at the end of M. M. III.

Vases showing L. M. I influence were in fact found in a higher and later stratum above the floors of the Pillar Crypts on which these frescoes lay. 1 We have here an exceptionally precise clue to the date of this whole allied group of wall-paintings.

An interesting feature both in the border decoration of the dresses in this group of frescoes, and in the contemporary designs from Phylakopi, details of the coiffures are conjectural, but they The date of the final catastrophe of the are here reproduced as giving unity to the com- Pillar Rooms at Phylakopi is ceramically equated position. Another set of fragments put together with the bird-vases' described below (p. 557), by Mr. Droop show part of the bosom, jacket, and contemporary with the imported cxam- and right forearm of another female figure be- pies found in the Temple Repositories at longing to a similar group. In contrast to the Knossos (See Mackenzie, Phylakopi, p. 262).

Ladies in Blue, the prevailing colour of the This would imply that the date of the struc- dress was here yellow, turned to a deep ruddy tures themselves and of their painted stucco hue by severe burning. The original decoration decoration goes back to the earlier phase of in this case was red on the yellow ground. M. M. III.

THE PALACE OF MINOS, ETC.

Wave or is the recurrence of a wave-like motive, the origins of which, however, do Plume hed not Belong to textile industry.

decora- The same ornament is seen in its true connexion on two votive arrow-

Votive plumes of bone found with other relics of the Shrine of the Snake Goddess Arrows.; n t h e y Temple Repository (Fig. 399,).

FIG. 399. a, BONE ARROW PLUME AND b, FRESCO FRAGMENT, APPARENTLY OF LARGE GRIFFINS WING, SHOWING NOTCHF. D PLUME DECORATION.

Votive The associations in which these objects were found may be taken to Minoan f m ply that they were dedicated to the Minoan Goddess in her quality of Artemis. Lady of the Chase, so prominent in her later impersonation as Diktynna or Britomartis, identified by the Greeks with Artemis. On a cornelian lentoid from Crete, indeed, the Goddess, here of very matronly proportions, is seen in the act of drawing a bow. 2

Both specimens of these plumes are smooth below, with two rivet-holes, by means of which they seem to have been attached to a plate of metal.

1 See, too, Anossos, Report, 1903, p. 61.

- Furuvangler, Antike Gemmen, P. ii, 24; Berlin, Katalog, No. 2.

Their lower ends, too, are sawn off as if for attachment by means of a collar to a metal shaft. 1 The stem of the arrow is ornamented with grooves, in some of which is a red inlaying material and traces of this are also seen between the plumes. These are artificially cut in a series of crested waves, outlined in relief against the red background.

The curious method of notching the plumes that we see on these votive arrows seems to have had a wider religious association in Minoan Art. It is also applied to the wings of Sphinxes and Griffins. It occurs, for example, on the wings of a Griffin (Fig. 400) 2 in the minature style that took its rise in the transitional epoch, about the close of the Middle or the beginning of the Late Minoan Age. In these cases it is often coupled with an asterisk mark itself a stellar symbol which also appears in place of the simple star-cross on the Cow of Hathor. A part of a wing, belonging apparently to a large figure of a Sphinx or Griffin found in the fresco heap to the North of the Palace at Knossos is given in Fig. 399, b 3 with this asterisk mark between the notched plumage, and here we see a common variant of this design in which wavelets appear between the wave-like notches of the plumes. On a remarkable Sphinx's head found at Mycenae, executed in the round in painted stucco, 4 similar asterisks, in this case of a ruddy hue, appear on the chin, cheeks, and forehead. It is quite possible that the same symbolic figure was depicted on the surface of the red inlay of which only traces now remain between the notches of the votive arrow-plumes of the Knossian Shrine.

Perhaps the best indication of the religious character of the notched plume motive is supplied by its adoption as a recognized ornament of the skirts of the Goddess herself or of her votaries. Thus it is seen in a simple form on the flounces of the bronze figurine described above, 5 and on the

Notched Plume Decoration.

Wings of Sphinxes and Griffins.

Combined with Asterisk a Stellar Symbol.

FIG. 400. FRAGMENT OF MINIATURE FRESCO, KNOSSOS, SHOWING GRIFFIN WITH NOTCHED PLUMES.

Asterisk on Stucco Face of Sphinx.

Notched Plume Motive on Skirts of Goddess.

1 See Knossos, Report, 1903, p. 61, Fig. 40. From the fresco heaps above the N. W. Portico at Knossos.

3 Probably of Early L. M. I date.

4 Tsuntas, Ef. Ap., 1902, p. i seqq., and Pl. i.

5 See p. 507. To be more fully illustrated in Vol. II."

THE PALACE OF MINOS, ETC.

golden borders of those of the remarkable chryselephantine statuette of the Snake Goddess, to be described in a later Section dealing with the Deposit of Ivories. 1

As a decorative motive, but still no doubt retaining its sacral associations in the same way as the waz already described it gained a more general currency. It appears on the swallow's wings that formed part of the embroidery of the dress of one of the Phylakopi figures belonging to the same connexion as Fig. 396 above. 2 As a textile motive it is still frequent

Degenerations of Notched Plume Motive.

FIG. 401 A. PAINTED STUCCO DECORATION HEARTH OF MEGARON, MYCENAE (T V)-

FIG. 401 B. FRAGMENT OF WALL-PAINTING (KNOSSOS), SHOWING SPIRAL AND NOTCHED PLUME ORNAMENT ( ).

in Late Minoan frescoes, as for instance on the borders of the Cup-bearer's dress, and the motive under its original aspect forms part of the ceramic repertory of the later Palace Style. 3

Already, however, in the L. M. I Period this design begins to fall away from its originally elegant outlines, suggestive of the crests of breaking waves with stars between, and degenerates into a mere zigzag with dotted intervals. It is thus seen, for instance, on the borders of the dancing lady's dress in the fresco from the Queen's Megaron, attributed to the succeeding Period 4 and, as pointed out in a later Section of this work, its appearance, in a decadent stage approaching this, on the wings of the Griffin on the axe of Queen Aah-hotep, Fig. 402 5 with the name of her son Aahmes c. 1587-1562 B. C. is a point both of religious and chronological importance.

1 See Vol. II. 4 Vol. II.

"See p. 546, and Phylakopi, p. 73, Fig. 61. 5 From an enlarged photograph kindly pro- 3 e. g. Preh. Tombs of Knossos, p. 157, cured for me by Mr. C. C. Edgar of the Cairo

Fig. 142 b. Museum.

Of great interest, moreover, in this connexion, was the discovery in the Notched circular walled pit of the West Court at Knossos paved over at the close of the Third Middle Minoan Period of fragments of movable clay hearths on MOV-coated with painted plaster with decorative zones, among which appeared Hearths this notched plume motive. We have thus the antecedent of the fixed Knossos.

FIG. 402. GRIFFIN ON AXE-BLADE FROM QUEEN AAH-HOTEPS COFFIN WITH NAME OF KING AAHMES, SHOWING DEGENERATED NOTCHED PLUME MOTIVE.

hearth of the Megaron at Mycenae, which shows a similar decoration Taken (Fig. 401 A),! coupled in this case with a running spiral zone. On the o"i "d painted stucco fragment from Knossos (Fig. 401 n) we see the notched Hea h plume and spiral ornament placed in juxtaposition in the same way as Mycenae, on the hearth at Mycenae. In the earlier period at least, the decorators of the Palace at Mycenae were craftsmen from the great insular seat of the Minoan civilization, and their acclimatized successors, as in this instance, faithfully preserved its tradition.

1 Schuchhardt, Schlianiinn's Excavations (Ed. Sellers), p. 289, Fig. 286 a. The drawing by Dr. Dorpfeld (cf. UpakTuca, 1886) is described as representing the third of five painted plaster layers. Miss Winifred Lamb, however, of the British School at Athens, who, in 1921, carefully re-examined the hearth, in- forms me that it is the eighth layer (out of 10) though it much resembles the fifth. The earliest shows the simple notched plume without the stars. Some of the intervening layers present mere horizontal bands, indicative of make-shift restoration. But there is a constant reversion to the sacral prototype.

Abundant material supplied by Palace deposits; Falling off of ceramic fabric consequent on Catastrophe of M. M. II; Quick wheel, too, fatal to egg-shell and embossed wares; Symptoms of recovery; Reaction on pottery of revival of Stone Vase-making; Naturalistic mouldings on Clay vessels; Palatial Store-jars; Influence of naturalistic Wall-paintings; M. M. Ill Pottery Stores and deposits of Palace; S. W. Basement-fish-bones in kitchen tilensil. inscribed jar; The Temple Repositories imported Melian vessels; Bird on Melian Vases derived from Minoan Griffin; Incised signs on handles, etc.; Royal Magazines Medallion pithoi; Pithos with signet impressions; Signets with architectural facades; Store of culinary and other pots knobbed decoration; Probable ritual destination; N. E. Magazines; M. M. I II layer above Royal Pottery Stores; Area E. of these; The S. E. Insula its sanctuary character and Initiatory Area; Ointment pots from S. E. Lustral Basin; Residential Section ofs. E. Insula; Magazine of the Lily Jars Candlestick of Egyptian type; S. E. Bathroom and painted clay Bath; Domestic Shrine; Magazine of False-spouted J ars; Their evolution symptomatic of improved conditions; Quadruple Axe motive; Brtrial Jar with stellar symbol; Urn burials and clay coffins; Deposit with Ink-inscribed Crips; Forms of MM. Ill Clips; Signs of quick wheel spiral Convolutions and string-cut bases.

Abun- THE M. M. Ill pottery, great quantities of which were found, much of it
O f the intact, in the Palace store-rooms and repositories submerged by the Late
Material. Mmoan strata, not only in itself offers rich materials for study but suggests some interesting problems in connexion with the history of the building and of the whole epoch to which it belongs.

Falling In many respects it presents a remarkable contrast to the artistic
Fabric at P roc lucts that distinguish this phase of culture in other departments.

T M n reat ea l f it s coarse. ill-made, with a badly finished surface, inferior in its glazing to that of the preceding and succeeding Age. There is a great falling off in polychromy, which tends to disappear entirely.

Prejudi- This ceramic decadence is so abrupt that it is impossible not to cial Effect.
1 1 i t T ofcata- recognize in it a result of the great catastrophe that befell both Knossos
M r M he i f ancl Pnaest s at the end of the Second Middle Minoan Period. It looks as Palace if the same destructive forces that were at work in the overthrow of the actual mic Art. buildings had been at the same time fatal to some of the artistic craftsmen who in the preceding Age had produced the masterpieces of ceramic fabric within its walls. The exquisite egg-shell wares had no successors.

That, when the first effects of this destruction had been overcome and a period of renewed prosperity and of architectural restoration had set in, the pottery still remained for the most part at a comparatively low level may be partly explained by the substitution for it of other materials at the board of the Minoan lords. With the new era of wealth now reached, Diversion vessels in precious metals doubtless came into larger use. At the same time the skill of the potters themselves may have been to a great extent diverted Fabrics at to a new channel the production, namely, of the beautiful fabrics in the Revival. native faience. Under these circumstances earthenware would for the most part have been relegated to the cellars and store-rooms or to the use of slaves and others of low degree. It is nevertheless clear that by the symp-mature stage of this Period a certain ceramic revival had set in and the j v M. M. Ill potters were finding new means of artistic expression adapted to the new conditions.

It is not surprising that the wealth in precious metals should not receive Metal adequate illustration from the actual contents of the buildings. In periods la y s of catastrophe such objects are laboriously sought out either by their to seek. actual owners or by subsequent plunderers. It is obvious that at Knossos even the floor chests were thoroughly ransacked. Our only chance of recovering any sufficient evidence as to contemporary vessels in gold and silver would be the discovery of rich tombs. As it is, we have to turn to the Shaft-Graves of Mycenae.

The general use of the quick wheel for all except the largest vessels was Quick itself fatal to the production of the delicate egg-shell and embossed wares, f at j e to imitative of metallic forms, such as excite our admiration in the M. M. II Eg s. he vases brought to light in the Royal Pottery Stores. Neither was the later bossed technique capable of imparting to their surface the brilliant metallic sheen that distinguishes many of these. A falling off in these respects had indeed been very perceptible in the later ceramic phase of the preceding Period (M. M. 116) and with it a decline in polychromy.

On the other hand a revival in the art of stone vase-making, that seems Revival of btone to have taken place in M. M. 1 1 1, together with the renewed import of alabaster Vase-vessels consequent on the reopening of trade relations with Egypt certainly reacted on the contemporary pottery forms. Examples of this have been given above in connexion with the remains found in the N. W. Lustral Basin and the adjoining area where King Khyan's lid was found. 1 In particular, 1 See above, p. 415 seqq.

THE PALACE OF MINOS, ETC.
Naturalistic Mouldings on Clay Vessels.
Palatial Store-jars.
Influence of
Naturalistic Wall-paintings on
Ceramic Designs.
M. M. Ill Pottery-Deposit of Palace.
Pottery Store in S. W. Hase-ment.

stone bowls with shell inlays were, as we have seen, imitated in a class of vessels the dark surface of which is dotted with white, while another common form is copied from a typical Middle Kingdom alabastron. as set on its stand. The relief style that now begins on steatite vessels also had its influence.

In the case of certain large clay basins, in the fabric of which the method of quick rotation did not enter, we have seen that beautiful marine reliefs were executed quite on a par with those of the contemporary faience and implying a similar artistic training on the potter's part. The applied ears of barley on a smaller class of vases also afford evidence of considerable skill in naturalistic moulding.

A truly palatial element is at the same time visible in the stately store-jars or Medallion pithoi, to be described below, that were found in the Royal Magazines, and which mark the latest phase of the present Period. The great revolution in vase forms that characterizes this epoch, accompanied by a general tendency to raise and elongate the vessels, was productive moreover of many fine profiles which often recall those of choice oriental jars. Finally, towards the close of this Period the influence of the naturalistic style then prevalent in the frescoes on the Palace walls began to reflect itself in the monochrome designs of the vase-painters, and helped to compensate for the almost total disappearance of the earlier polychrpmy.

Owing to a fortunate conjunction of circumstances, the Palace of Knossos proved to be extraordinarily rich in deposits of the pottery of this Period. Apart from the more fragmentary remains, though themselves of considerable importance, found in the N. W. Lustral Area and its borders, and the masses of M. M. 111 sherds from the Kouloura or walled rubbish pit beneath the later West Court pavement, a whole series of stores of M. M. Ill vessels in a practically perfect condition were found, buried not only by catastrophic causes but by a deliberate process of filling in throughout the Palace site. From the point of view of the present work a summary account of the principal deposits is here given in connexion with the magazines and repositories in which they occurred.

S. W. Basement.

Some remains of vases of this Period were found, as already described, 1 among the early elements of the Kaselles' of the West Magazines, including the group shown in Fig. 328 above. In a basement South of the Magazines near the S. W. angle of the Palace there came to light a set of complete vessels of a kitchen type, some of which are shown in Fig. 403.- They 1 See p. 457. found over 2 metres below the upper floor level 2 Knossos, Report, 1901, p. 10. They were in a stratum of carbonized wood.

M. M. Ill THE PALACE POTTERY STORES 555 show a light clay-coloured surface, except that A is broadly decorated with a triple spray of reddish brown. With them were plain barrel-shaped pots Iot with with tripod bases, 1 one of which contained a grey deposit with fish's ebmc vertebrae an interesting contribution to our knowledge of the Minoan dietary. A contemporary intaglio 2 found North of the site shows a fisher-

FIG 403. GROUP OF VESSELS FROM S. W. BASEMENT. (t.) man holding a cuttle-fish and a very plump fish, probably the much-esteemed Cretan Skaros'. Fish-bones are easily missed in an excavation, but the 1 Similar pots were found in the N. E. A sardonyx of the flattened cylinder

Magazines. See below, Fig. 414. form much in vogue in this Period. See p. 677, Fig. 497, below.

theory, built formerly on negative grounds, that the Mycenaeans', as they were then called, abstained from fish l must definitely go by the board. 2 jar with The most remarkable vessel found in the deposit was a tall two-handled tion of jar, resembling that shown in Fig. 403, p,, of the elongated class very character-Ciass r A st c f th 8 Period, which bore upon its shoulders a graffito inscription of five characters, belonging to the Linear Class A, 3 incised when the clay was still wet (see Fig. 453). The vessel itself, which except for its handles presents a curiously Chinese contour, is reproduced in Fig. 410, b.

It is interesting to note that all the graffito inscriptions on pottery found on the Palace site, including single signs as well as groups, presented characters of this earlier linearized Class and belonged to M. M. Ill vessels. 4 The chronological value of this phenomenon is evident.

The Temple Repositories.

Pottery of It has already been noticed that the Temple Repositories contained

Reposi- a l ar g e store f vessels belonging to the latest M. M. Ill phase. These tories. vessels were found in an upper layer, over a metre thick, above the shallower, fatty stratum containing the objects of art and cult. Some of these have been already illustrated in the photographic Fig. 333 as they were set on the pavement above at the time of excavation. Another representative series is given here in Fig. 404 and two interesting specimens showing. a survival of polychromy will be illustrated in the succeeding Section. 5 Of the vases given in Fig. 404, a reproduces a jar resembling a specimen which presents incised on its rim an inscription of Class A, c while b is important as showing the favourite grass motive of this epoch, white on a lilac brown ground, and as illustrating the division into light and dark panels which is already seen as a characteristic feature of some of the finest M. M. II vessels. The exceptional vase, g, supplies an example of dark decorative patterns on a light ground. The surface, however, unlike that of the typical L. M. I vases, is dull. It is of special interest to note that this Minoan type as well as fragments of ewers like f with their broad white spirals on the dark ground the most numerously represented of all the types found in the 1 Tsuntas and Manatt, Mycenaean Age, not arrived at a definite classification of the two pp. 69 and 334. phases of the Linear Script, but it was at once - With this, too, must go the comparisons apparent that the characters on this jar showed made loc, cit. with the supposed aversion of variations from those of the ordinary clay tablets the so-called Graeco-Italic stock including of Class B. See Knossos, Report, 1901, p. 10. the Homeric Achaeans to a fish diet. On 4 See p. 616 seqq. this subject see Keramopoullos, Mvo raika, 5 See below, p. 593 seqq., and Coloured
Aexriw, 1918, p. 88 seqq.). Plate VII. When this discovery was made in 1901, Iliad See below, p. 617.

Repositories recur among the earliest elements of the Shaft Graves at Mycenae.

A similar community with the Shaft-Graves (see Fig. 4or,,-) is shown

FIG. 404. POTTERY FROM TEMPLE REPOSITORIES (h, MELIAN VESSEL) (c.).

by the occurrence of the remains of at least a dozen vessels of a well-known imported Melian type (Figs. 404, 405,), presenting figures of flying birds. Flying bircls of the same kind appear on a series of vessels of this and other forms found at Phylakopi in Melos in a stratum the Third Middle Evi- Cycladic which also contained fragments recalling the Cretan lily jars. ohnter- The recurved neck of Fig. 405, d must be regarded as a survival from primi- course t; ve s m vesse ls, which in Melos and in the Middle Aegean area generally, between.,.

Crete and greatly influenced the shapes of pottery. In Crete, on the other hand, this influence seems to have been at a minimum, but the reaction of early stone types on pottery is there very much more manifest than in the Cycladic area. The key to the birds on these vases is supplied by a small representation seen on both sides of the upper part of the body of a high-beaked ewer, with its neck only slightly drawn back, Fig. 405, a, b, found in a stratum at Phylakopi answering to the earliest phase of the Third Middle Cycladic Period and corresponding with the beginning of M. M. III.

influence This design, Fig. 405, c, is a misunderstood copy of a winged griffin as on lehan seen ln tne characteristic action of the Minoan flying gallop 5 an action, Types. it is to be observed, never associated with Egyptian animal forms, either natural or fantastic, during the Middle Kingdom. The Melian artist not understanding the winged quadruped in this position has in fact converted the hind-legs into the long tail feathers of a pheasant-like bird the tail itself being apparently interpreted as a curving plume. This metamorphosis is itself of great chronological value as throwing back the winged griffin type of the Minoan model at least to the beginning of the M. M. Ill Period. Type The exceptionally minute scale of this design at once strikes the eye.

frontseai n t le ater typ 68 as illustrated by the Repository Vase, Fig. 405 d, the bird impres- derivatives have assumed normal dimensions. The ceramic assimilation is here complete, but the fact that throughout the great days of Minoan art animal forms were tabooed by the vase-painters 3 forbids us to suppose that the galloping griffin that supplied the prototype of the earlier hybrid figure was of ceramic origin. On the other hand its surprising small dimensions suggest that it may represent an attempt to copy a current type of seal impression such as the officials of the Minoan Priest-Kings used for the security of their possessions and doubtless also in the case of exports. Such clay sealings, as we know from the contents of the Hieroglyphic Deposit, were attached to the strings and bands that bound up bales and packages,

The vase is represented, Phylakopi, PI. with imported fragments of polychrome M. M.

XIV, 2. Fig. 405 c is my own enlargement II pottery. The influence of the griffin type from this. This type of ewer is the immediate was noted by Mr. C. C. Edgar, op. cit., p. 109. successor of those with the winged goblins' See below, p. 711. about which Dr. Mackenzie (see below, p. 704) 3 See p. 605. has noted that they were found in association sions.

FIG. 407. CAPPADOCIAN VASE FRAGMENT.

and the clay stoppers of vessels with liquid contents may have been directly impressed. The griffin as a guardian of treasure was naturally adapted for use on such official signets l and various representations of the monster are in fact found among the seal impressions of this epoch. 2 Another obvious sacral type was the Double Axe, and evidence will be given below that a specially sphragistic form of this, exemplified by the hieroglyphic sealings of Knossos, did in fact give origin to a curious class of winged goblins that appear on Melian ewers of the immediately preceding epoch.:1 A parallel griffin type from the same source with a less outstretched action made its way about the same epoch across the Aegean, in this case too, doubtless, through Cycladic adaptations. In the secondary aspect of this, which alone has been preserved to us, the hind as well as the fore legs of the prototype are still traceable but the wings have been interpreted as antlers. Two vessels showing variations of this type and probably of Mainland fabric were found in the Shaft Graves of Mycenae, Fig. 406, a and 6, the latter only recently put together by Mr. Wace from Schliemann's fragments. 4 The antler-like excrescences from the back of the heads recall suggestive parallels presented by the figures of stags on vases of a widely diffused Anatolian class of painted pottery of which a fragmentary specimen from Kara Euyuk in Cappadocia 6 is given for comparison in Fig. 407. Both the matt black 1 On a Late Minoan lentoid seal to be described in a later Section, two guardian griffins stand on either side of a

Cereal sign which recurs on a series of clay inventories of the Linear Class B referring to the grain stores of the Later Palace at Knossos.

2 See below, p. 712.

5 See below, p. 704 and Fig. 527.

1 I am greatly indebted to Mr. Wace for supplying me with this comparison. One sherd was given in F. u. L., Myk. Vasen., p. 55, Fig. 32.

5 Chantre, Mission en Cappadoce, Pl. XI, I. For the geometrical decoration of the Anatolian class Dr. Mackenzie, in an as yet unpublished monograph proposes the term Hither-Asiatic Metope Style. This ceramic class extends

Sphragistic origin of Melian winged goblins.

Antlered monsters on parallel Helladic Class of

Anatolian parallels.

through Syria to Canaan, where it survived to form the base of the later Philistine wares in which it blended with Minoan elements (cf. Mackenzie, in Memoires, Delegation en Jerse, xiii, p. 79, n. 7). It also presents unquestionable affinities with the Second Style of Elam. (See E. Pettier, Delegation en Perse, xiii, p. 67 seqq.) For the Anatolian province, see Myres, The Early Pot Fabrics of Asia Minor (Journ. Anthr. us., xxxiii, p. 377 seqq.). This matt paint style which has such very early roots in Elam and extends to the Anau oasis in Turkestan, some 300 miles east of the Caspian (Pumpelly, Expl. in Turkestan, 1904; Prehistoric Civ. of Anau, 2 vols., 1908), is circum-Pontic in its distribution.

and red colouring of this class and its geometrical designs, divided into panels, show a decided sympathy with the Helladic group to which F g. 400, a, b belong, the inclusion of the purplish red bands within black borders affording a specially significant point of comparison. Some cross suggestion from the Eastern shores of the Aegean may perhaps be ultimately recognized in the case of these antlered griffins of Helladic art.

Bird type The high-beaked ewer, Fig. 405 a, b, supplies the typological antecedent Solved f a S rou P f Melian pots including the Repository type d and belonging to in Melos. the succeeding phase of the Third Middle Cycladic Period, answering to the latter part of M. M. Ill, in which the neck is pulled further back and the body is more full-bellied. On these vessels, which belong to more than one class, and on a parallel series of cups, jugs, and bowls from Melos, 1 the metamorphosis into the bird type is completed, the hooked beak and the coils about the neck, however, still preserving reminiscences of the griffin and, more remotely, of the head of the Sacred Hawk of Egypt. 2 In the Repository examples (see Fig. 405 a) these bird-griffin features are grouped round large red to brown disks, recalling those of this class of Melian ware, 15 and are apparently derived from the characteristic disks of M. M. I pottery. This bird-type with the long tail feathers is found at Phylakopi itself 4 and on one of the varieties of the bird-vases from the Shaft Graves (Fig. 405 b. 6 In the other variety, better represented in those Graves (Fig. 405 c 6), the tail assumes a different shape, and seems to imitate the conventional outline of fishes' tails as seen on somewhat earlier Melian pottery. 7 1 Phylakopi, Pl. XVI, 4, 20. found according to Dr. Mackenzie, who took 2 See below, p. 709 and Fig. 533. part in its excavation, in a mature Middle : 1 The technique differs somewhat in the case Cycladic III stratum

answering to the later of the Repository specimens. The disks are not phase of M. M.
III.

hand polished red as those from Phylakopi and s The pheasant tail has been added,
as the Shaft Graves. At the same time they show a fragment with that feature was
ascribed by the darker circle round the central disk. Furtwangler to this vase. (F. u.
I,., Myk.

In Dr. Mackenzie's opinion, however, they Thongef., p. 8, Pl. X, 45, 45 a.) This
Shaft are undoubtedly of Melian fabric and of the Grave type of bird differs from that
of the same period as the similar vessels presenting Repository vases in the indication
of a fore wing, the true black and red style. 6 The bird vases' from the Shaft Graves
4 Phylakopi, Pl. XXI, 5,10, c. A fragment differ in clay and fabric from those of
Phylakopi, of a jar of the Repository type is shown in but must in any case stand in
the closest

Fig. 12. In 10 we see the characteristic relation with Melos. Another variety of
bird pheasant tail and the large ruddy disk on the vase with a more fantastic tail was
found at side as seen on the Shaft Grave vases. A Thera (Dumont et Chaplain, Les
Ceramiques specimen of a large jug of the spherical, Shaft de hi Grece propre, Vol. I,
Fig. 33.

Grave type, now set up in the Museum at Edgar, Phylakopi, Pl. XVIII, 5, and

Athens (see Edgar, op. tit., p. 159, n. 2) was p. 117. This earlier Melian class is
referred by

These bird vases' were from their particular shape well adapted for the safe carriage
of liquid contents, and may have held some welcome offerings to the Priest-Kings in
the shape of Melian wine. The volcanic soil of the island is in fact specially favourable
to the cultivation of the vine, which may have begun here relatively early. To-day
the wine of Melos, like that of Santorin, has a special renown for its potency in the
Aegean world. One remarkable feature of these vessels was that they presented a
series of signs incised, after baking, on the handles. Specimens of these are given in
Fig. 408, and it will be seen that they may be practically regarded as excerpted from
the Minoan signary of Class A, 1 though with some slight differentiations. It would
appear, therefore, that they were the marks of Minoan donors, nor is this circumstance
surprising in view of other evidence of the existence at this time in Melos of Cretan
merchants and craftsmen. 2 Two Minoan characters, indeed, also belonging to Class
A, and representing a personal name that recurs in Crete, were found engraved on the
base of a vessel of Melian fabric found at Phylakopi. 3 As will be shown below, a
sherd from the neighbouring Cycladic island of Thera (Santorin) also presents signs
of this class.

The occurrence in the case of these handles of single characters only makes it
unlikely that they represented personal names. It appears, however, that single characters in both advanced linearized scripts had an ideographic as well as a syllabic or
alphabetic value. Single signs were also found cut on the handles and shoulders of
contemporary jugs of indigenous Minoan fabric, fragments of which were found in a
large rubbish heap to the South East of the site. These included two simple forms T
and H, but were also of special interest as showing a double-axe sign and its linearized
derivative. 4 Incised Signs on Handles of Melian Vases.

Their
Minoan
Aspect.
FIG. 408 INSCRIBED SIGNS ON MELIAN POTS COMPARED WITH SPECI-
MENS OF MINOAN LINEAR SCRIPT A.
Single Signs on Knossian M. M. Ill Vessels.
Mackenzie to the beginning of the Third Middle Cycladic Period.

1 The triangle sign is found in the Hieroglyphic Signary and in the Late Mycenaean
Signary, as illustrated by the stirrup vase from Orchomenos (see Scripta Minoa, i, p.
5 7, Figs. 31, 32). It also occurs on an early signet with characteristic signs of the
Linear Class A. 3 See above, p. 542.
3 Scripta Minoa, i, p. 35, Fig. 16. See below
P- 637- 4 See Table, Fig. 477 below.
The Royal Magazines.
It is not surprising, considering the solidity of the great store jars, to find that some
specimens that may probably be referred to the closing phase of
M. M. 111 were found on the floors of the West Magazines, having survived to the
last days of the Palace through all the alterations that these had under-
Medal- gone in the interval. The chief repository, however, of the most imposing
Pithoi f these, the pithoi presenting medallions with white rosettes on the dark of
Royal p Ur ph s h brown ground, were the Royal Magazines' described above, as zin
a e g s a " forming an annexe to the first floor of the Domestic Quarter opening to the
North from the second landing of the Grand Staircase. The entrance to this annexe,
as has been shown, was blocked and the Royal Magazines' themselves filled in at
the close of the present Period, but the remains of a series of the Medallion pithoi
themselves, several of them capable of complete restoration, were left in situ on the
floor of the inner compartment, though, owing probably to. their nearness to the
surface of the denuded slope of the hill, their upper portions had been a good deal
broken. The
Strati- section beneath the pavement on which these stood has been given above, 1
Portion ar d clearly brings out the fact that it forms the last of a series of clay and
of Pithoi. plaster floors representing the earlier M. M. Ill phases and superposed on a
fine Mosaiko pavement characteristic of the latest stage of M. M. II.
On the gypsum slabs of this latter pavement, moreover, was the plaster support of a
pithosof the huge early class. From all this it will be seen that these Medallion pithoi
occupy a very definite place in the ceramic series of the Palace.
These stately jars, only found at Knossos and well worthy of their place in the Royal
Magazines, are in many respects divergent from the Early Palace Class ofknobbed
pithoi. 2 Had we not even the evidence of the successive strata that intervene between
the floor on which these later pithoi rested and the latest pavement of M. M. II, we
should be compelled to infer that a very considerable period of time had elapsed
between the two classes. The form is more graceful and elongated and in most typical
examples shows, in place of the ropework pattern, flat strips with a succession of
impressed rings. But the most interesting development with which we are confronted
is the transmutation of the low bosses, which replace the knobs' on some of the M. M.

II jars, into slightly convex medallions' presenting rosettes, laid on in a chalky white medium on the lilac brown glaze

See above, p. 320, Fig. 233 and Fig. 234.- See above, p. 232, Figs. 174, 175.

THE PALACE OF MINOS, ETC.

Pithos net h lmg " pressions.

ground and surrounded with raised rings. A good illustration of a Medallion pithos of this type is given in Fig. 409. l The small raised disks, slightly cupped, of the upper zone are also very characteristic, while the waved black and white decoration of the rim, also frequent on vases of this Period, is an inheritance from the earlier Middle Minoan polychrome tradition. 2 In the Magazine of the Medallion pithoi were also found remains a var iant type of store jar showing diminutive impressed rings, within which, in place of the painted rosettes of the typical Medallion pithoi appear a series of seal impressions. As will be seen from Fig. 410 these reproduce the same outline, and are evidently formed, not by a signet pressed askew on the damp clay, but rather by a broken seal-stone.

There can be little hesitation in recognizing in the panelled pattern, of which we have here a fragment, a variant of a class of designs very frequent on Cretan seals of this and the preceding period, and which in fact are conventionalized representations of architectural facades. In Fig.411, c, i, 2, a crystal intaglio of the flat-edged type, which had its greatest vogue in M. M. II, 3 from the Knossos district, and in the red jasper lentoid, d, we see complete designs of the same class, and the fragmentary sealings from the W. Temple Repository, a and d, must be assigned to a similar category. One of the circular inscribed clay disks from the same deposit was impressed round its margin by a similar signet.

These conventional representations of the fronts of buildings belong to an early tradition which continued to run parallel with the more realistic architectural subjects such as the castellated structure on the Zakro

FIG. 410.

PITHOS WITH IMPRESSIONS OF BROKEN SIGNET.

l This specimen was found in the Xth W. Magazine (from a drawing by Mr. H. Bagge). Those of the Royal Magazines were not so perfectly preserved.

2 It goes back as early as the M. M. I poly- chrome vases with fish decoration (see Excavs. at Vasilik't, Penn. Trans., vol. ii, Ft. 2, PI. XXX, l, and above, pp. 180, 182).

3 See above, pp. 274, 275, Fig. 204, a, l,; d sealing, reproduced above. l In the present case a parallel example is seen on the contemporary seal impression, just referred to, from the W. Temple Repository, Fig. 411, a, where squares of masonry are shown on one side, and on the other the upper part of a doorway a feature very characteristic of these designs. The potter's seal had no doubt broken in the course of signing a long series of similar store jars, but the fact that its type had consisted of a conventional fa ade of a building may well suggest a reference to the Palace itself. We may have here in fact the cachet 2 of" a master-potter who executed his craft by official appointment. It emphasizes, indeed, the palatial style of these fine store jars.

FIG. 411. a, HALF SKAL IMPRESSION FROM TEMPLE REPOSITORY SHOWING PART OF DOOR AND SQUARES OF MASONRY; l, FRAGMEN-TARY SEAL IMPRESSION FROM Do.; c, CRYSTAL INTAGLIO WITH CON-

VENTIONAL FA9ADE OF BUILDING, KNOSSOS DISTRICT; d, RED JASPER Do., CENTRAL CRETE, (f c.)

Partly in the Middle Bay of the first Section of the Royal Magazines, and Store of partly in a small niche or loculus' near the entrance of its adjoining Corridor, 3 a, ldotlier and on a level with its pavement, there came to light a series of vessels of Pots-quite a unique character, of which typical specimens are shown in Fig. 412. 4 These vessels were often of plain clay, at times smoke-stained, but in many cases there was evidence that their surface had been covered with the purplish brown glaze medium usual at this time. Great elaboration is observable in some of their forms (Fig. 412).

The small high-necked jugs and the cups, some of them handled, some 1 See p. 308, Fig. 227, a. glyphic signature of Class B, has been given 3 An example of an earlier cachet of a potter above, p. 242, Fig. 182, c. who made fine vessels of metallic type, on See Plan, Fig. 236, p. 323, above. a goblet from lalaikastro, presenting a hiero- Compare KHOSSOS, Report, 1901, pp. 85, 86.

FIG. 412. KNOUBKD AND OTHER VESSELS FROM MAGAZINE AND CORRIDOR OK THE BAYS:

ROYAL MAGAZINE. (J- r.) of the common handle-less class, 1 plainly connect themselves with drinkables, while the three-legged pipkins with perforated covers would stand in a culinary connexion. The small ewers with the raised rings or collars where the neck joins the body, and the teat-like knobs that decorate their walls and handles betray the influence of metallic models. 2 The knobs are evidently a decorative imitation of rivet heads, while in metal vases of kindred forms the joint of the separate plates that compose the neck and body is often masked by a raised ring. On a faience libation vessel of the last Palace Period both the neck-ring and the studs round the shoulders in that case, however, more slightly bossed are similarly taken over from an original in metalwork. 11 The insistence on this feature with the teat-like form of the knobs, however, on the present series suggests the question whether, in whatever way they originated, they may not have had some religious association in connexion with the Mother Goddess. The best parallel, indeed, is afforded by a later clay image (Fig. 413), certainly representing a TToxvfiaatos form of divinity recalling the Ephesian Artemis, found in the pillar-room of an early house at Hagia Triada. 4

The archaic features visible in these ewers, as well as their unique character, are themselves a reason for suspecting that they may have had a ritual destination. The survival of a Middle Minoan tradition is further brought out by the raised decoration of one of the vessels " which is reminiscent of the barbotine style. The presumption of a religious usage, moreover, is borne out by some of the associated forms. The double pots set at the two ends of a flat base, 0 and with their upper rims again connected, do not suggest any

Decoration.

Comparison with many-breasted Figure.

Fu;. 413. CLAY FIGURK OF FEMALE DIVINITY OF MANY- BREASTED TYPE. H. TRIADA (-J- f.).

lrobable Ritual Use of Pots.

1 These present the sharp-cut base characteristic of cups of this type belonging to the transitional M. M. III-L. M. I epoch.

: There seems to be here no direct relationship to the knobbed decoration of the M. M. I-II pithoi, though knobs in a modified shape appear on some smaller vessels of the early part of the Middle Minoan Age.

3 See Vol. II. The raised ring round the neck is also frequent, for the same reason, on composite stone vases, e. g. p. 412, Fig. 296.

4 Paribeni, Man. Ant., xiv, p. 725, Fig. 24. The house had been later used as a tomb, and the image itself is certainly of L. M. Ill date.

5 The seventh in order in Fig. 412.

0 The flat base of a similar object, with the two pans above it broken off and showing only kind of form of ordinary domestic use. Apart from the fact that they were thus connected above as well as below, they recall the proto-Egyptian double vases, especially the goblets on a common base, 1 which had certainly a religious destination. Like the pipkins and the pans to be described below, they were covered with perforated conical lids.

Censers The most remarkable of the vessels found in this deposit, however,

Chafin- were th e single pans of the same form as the last, and provided with similar pans. perforated lids but with a double interior. Within the outer wall of-these vessels, as is well shown by Fig. 412, 2nd row, and separated from it by a narrow interspace, is a second recipient, sometimes rising only half-way to the level of the outer rim. This inner receptacle has perforations both on its sides and base, and in many but not in all cases there were also borings opposite these in the outer walls. These perforations, repeated in the lid which in some cases was blackened, show that the inner pan was devised for the combustion of some material. Whether, however, the vessels were intended to be simple chafing-pans or for the burning of incense it is difficult to decide. For either purpose, the interspace between the outer and inner walls may have been intended to keep the exterior of the pan at a temperature not too high for them to be conveniently grasped by the hands.

We have here a parallel form to a class of clay fire-boxes which, under variant shapes, can be traced back in Crete to the beginning of the Middle Minoan Age. 2 Their principal feature is a perforated cavity rising to a boss above, and with an orifice at its base (or sometimes at the side) through which the burning charcoal was introduced and which was afterwards plugged.

The North-East Magazines.

The same process of deliberate filling in at the close of the Middle Minoan Age of which we have evidence in the Royal Magazines was carried out in the area immediately North that included the North-East Hall and adjoining Magazines.

Pottery The North-East Magazines contained a plentiful store of the ordinary of N. E. pottery of this Period, and their contents differ in character from those of

Magazines, their bases, was found at Phaestos among the: e. g. Petrie, Naqada and Ballas, PI. XXIX, later elements of the Palace (note made on So, 84, 86.

the spot). These examples seem to be the 2 A plain specimen, unfortunately broken ancestors of a L. M. Ill type of double pan round the rim, was found inside a polychrome found in Crete (one obtained by me from M. M. la jar under the floor of the Third

Kedria, near Girapetra; in Candia Museum; Magazine at Knossos (Knossos, Report, 1900, cf. too Gournia, Pl. X, 6). p. 21).

the other Palace store-rooms and repositories of this Period, since they do not represent vessels already in use in various departments but the assorted stock of a fabric. The pots were of domestic kinds, presenting a plain clay surface (see Figs. 414, 415), and they were evidently made to supply the needs of what seems at this time to have been a quarter of the Palace occupied

L. M. ICOPS

HERE. OH

HIGHER L. EVSI-. go oo

FIG. 414. SKETCH-PLAN OF THE NORTH-EAST MAGAZINES AND CON-TENTS by workmen or slaves. It is noteworthy, indeed, that in the area immediately East of this, where were the Royal Pottery Stores so rich in the exquisitely tinted egg-shell ware of the M. M. II Period, a higher stratum came to light on which lay stacks of ordinary vessels like those found in the present case. No contrast could be more complete.

A plan of these North-East Magazines, as conjecturally completed, has been already given in connexion with the North-East Hall. 1 That portion of it within which the vessels were preserved (Sketch-plan, Fig. 414) forms a rectangular enclosure within which the store rooms are grouped on either side of a gangway, 2 an arrangement that finds a parallel at Phaestos and which in Egypt can be traced back to the days of the earliest Dynasties.

FIG. 415. GROUP OF VESSELS FROM THE N. E. MAGAZINES Q- ".).

Owing to the denudation of the slope of the hill, the later structures that had been constructed when the Magazines were filled in had almost entirely disappeared, and the stacks of pottery began to appear almost immediately beneath the surface. 3 Some remains, however, pointing to 1 See above, p. 389, Fig. 281. of the Magazines, which had a depth of from 2 This gangway was only 90 cm. wide. 1-50 to 1-40 m. on their Western borders, lay 3 Owing to the slope of the hill the floors only 80-70 cm. down at their East ends.

an improvement in the conditions of this area in the ensuing L. M. I Period occurred in the superficial stratum. Among these was an elegant tripod stand of dark steatite (see Fig. 414) found in the upper level of Chamber 5. Its palmette-shaped legs were embedded in a stratum of carbonized wood with quantities of gold-foil such as was used as a decorative coating for various materials. The date of these later deposits was further indicated by stores of L. M. I tortoise-shell ripple cups found on the same level, outside the W. wall of Chamber 4. Of great interest, moreover, was the discovery at the same level of a man's arm in painted stucco relief.

Some idea of the manner in which the pottery was stored is given by my Sketch-plan (Fig. 414) made during the course of the excavation. The pots, as will be seen, were methodical!) distributed in rows and piles of the interior compartments as indicated in Fig. 415. The bowls were Arrange-so cketed into one another, and the cups stacked in rouleaux (see Fig. 415, A pottery and D). Many of the larger pots showed the trickle decoration, and some " vessels bore traces of white on a brownish lilac ground. Otherwise the pottery found here presented a dull clay surface.

A private stock of similar vessels was found in the little store-room behind the N. E. Hall and, near by, a stucco seat and tripod hearth. 1 These structures communicated with the N. E. Magazines by a small passage-way behind, and may have formed part, as suggested above, of the residence of the master-potter.

M. M. Ill Layer above Royal Pottery Stores.

So extensive now was the fabric of rustic ware throughout this M. M. ill Palace region that the use of the old Royal Pottery Stores that lay beyond ove the terrace wall East of the N. E. Magazines was now revived to afford al rottery additional accommodation for these cheap products. In a stratum, separated Stores. by layers of clay and burnt materials from that containing the fine egg-shell cups and bowls of the earlier fabric, lay piles of these comparatively rough vessels, many of them plain wide-mouthed pots with trickle ornament, like those of the N. E. Magazines, Fig. 416, c, but some with a lilac brown ground and white bands, of the form reproduced in Fig. 410, a.

These vases, like b, the inscribed jar from the S. W. Basement, and Elonga-c, belonging to a series abundantly forthcoming in the N. E. Magazines, afford good illustrations of that elongation of shape which is a very characteristic feature of this epoch. The type illustrated in Fig. 416, c, as Mr. Seager 1 See above, p. 390, and Fig. 281.

points out, seems to go back to a form of breccia vase, with a spout, two suspension handles, and a knob behind, found in an Early Minoan tomb at Mochlos. 1 It is shown here for comparison in Fig. 417.

FIG. 416. EXAMPLES OF ELONGATED M. M. Ill VASES, a, ABOVE ROYAL POTTERY STORES; ;, INSCRIBED JAR, S. W. BASEMENT; c, N. E. MAGAZINES. (c.)

Area E. of Royal Magazines.

M. M. in East of the Royal Magazines and above the area of the Spiral Fresco C the same filling-in process was carried out at the close of M. M. Ill,

Maga- Explorations in the Island of Mochlos, in which the vase was found appears to belong zine s. p. 79 (Fig. 46 and PI. III). The tomb (XXIII) to the E. M. II and E. M. Ill Periods.

the object being in this case to form a platform so as to be able to construct a new East Hall more on a level with the Central Court. Tripod vases, like those of the N. E. Magazines, were found on the floor of a compartment in this area, while the School Room and the adjoining M. M. Ill storerooms were simultaneously earthed under in the same manner. A group of contemporary vessels from one of these the Magazine formed out of the

Section of the earlier Corridor has been illustrated above. 1

Area South of Domestic Quarter South-East Insula.

On the upper terrace level im- The mediately South of the Domestic K t Quarter is an area enclosed between Insul; i the original enceinte wall and what seems to have been a ramp leading to the Central Court from the South. This region, the interior of which is marked on the Diagrammatic Plan of the Earlier Palace, Fig. 152 above, as a blank, presents a whole system of buildings belonging to the M. M. Ill Period. Here, too, at the close of that Period, we find further traces of the consistent endeavour, already noticed in the area North of the Domestic Quarter, to raise the ground level. In the North-Western parts of the area, especially where this raising process had to be carried out to a greater height, this operation resulted, as in the former case, in a considerable earthing under of the pottery stores of the M. M. Ill Magazines.

The Plan of the M. M. Ill structures in this South-East Insula as it existed on the original terrace level is shown in Fig. 418. What seems to have been the residential portion, on the Northern borders of the region, is well preserved and its essential lines, like those of the Domestic Quarter, go back to the beginning of this Period, including

FIG. 417. BRECCIA VASE, MOCHLOS 1 See above, p. 384, Fig. 279.

THE PALACE OF MINOS, ETC.

probably, as there, elements taken over from the Early Palace arrangement.

The Insula itself will be seen to be divided into a Southern and

MAG. OF FAISE-
SPOUTED PITHOI
PAVED PANEL Of CHAMBER.
1OO CENT " METRE
"Fie. 418. PLAN OF M. M. Ill STRUCTURES IN S. E. INSULA OF PALACE.

Sane- a Northern Section. The Southern part was clearly of a Sanctuary nature, character though the square patch of Mosaiko' paving that is visible there must now of s-. be regarded not as an altar base but as the central pavement of a chamber

Section.

or lobby belonging to the early Palace. In the area immediately West of S E-this came to light a Lustral Basin approached by steps and resembling on Basin and a smaller scale that discovered outside the N. W. Portico of the Palace. This

PRESUMED LEDG. POK
MAGA2HE. OF FAtsf JPftHOI
FIG. 419. PLAN OF CONSTRUCTIONS IN N W. ANGLE OF S. E. INSULA,

little Quarter, having a specially sacral character, seems indeed to have P nfm possessed a small Initiatory Area of its own, in relation to an entrance from the South. Here, too were remains of clay vessels of the same peculiar

THE PALACE OF MINOS, ETC.

Later Shrine of Double Axes.

Domestic Arrangement of N. Section of S. E. Insuia.

shape as those found in the larger Lustral Basin 1 and doubtless used here too to contain the oil for ritual anointing. Near this was a small chamber which, if we may believe in religious tradition, was designed for purposes of worship.

In the Re-occupation Period it was used as a shrine, with vessels of offering on its later floor, and an altar ledge with clay figures of the Dove

Goddess and her votaries and double axes set in the Sacral

Horns. 2

The Northern Section of this group of structures has a decidedly domestic appearance, and may have been the residence of a priestly functionary. This part of the S. E. Insuia was more especially affected by the process of filling in, and many of the contents of its domestic buildings were thus preserved in sihe. in the same way as those of the Magazines North of the Domestic Quarter.

A Plan of the small chambers and Magazines here unearthed is given in Fig. 419, and it will be seen that it was divided into two parallel groups, each approached by a narrow passage.

That to the left ran straight to the aperture of a narrow closet or small store-room filled with vessels, including the lily jars, and at this point turned South at right angles into a small paved chamber which, as will be shown, served as a bath-room.

FIG. 420. CLAY AND PLASTER CLOSET OR SMALL MAGAZINE CONTAINING THE LILY JARS AS EXCAVATED.

See above, p. 411, and Fig. 295. 2 Knossos, Report, 1902 (H. S. A., viii), p. 93 ff., Fig. 55.

THE PALACE OF MINOS, ETC.

Magazine of the Lily Jars.

Magazine The little Magazine or closet, which proved to contain pottery of great Lily Jan. interest, was enclosed on its Western and Northern side by a clay partition, only 12 centimetres (or 4 inches) thick and faced on both sides with red plaster. 1 The general arrangement of the pottery in this little store closet

FIG. 422. M. M. Ill CANDLESTICK FROM MAGAZINE OF LILY VASES (c.).

appears in the Plan, Fig. 419, and a view of it as first brought to light is shown in Fig. 420. At the further end were piles of jars with a beautiful decoration of clumps of lilies, white on the lilac brown glaze ground (Fig. 421, 7, 10), specimens of which are more fully illustrated in Fig. 444 below. About the

FIG. 423 a. EGYPTIAN CLAY CANDLESTICK, FOURTH DYNASTY (ASHMOLEAN MUSEUM) (-).

FIG. 423 b. EARLY MINOAN CANDLESTICK, SIVA NEAR PHAESTOS.

middle of the closet stood a large full-bellied jar with two handles to its rim and two smaller on its shoulders, the dark brown glaze medium of which was decorated by broad white spiral bands recalling those of the pitchers so abundantly represented in the Temple Repositories.

i cm. thick.

In Fig. 421 there are shown some other types of vessels found in this small Magazine, including a miniature form (4) of the hole-mouthed class of jugs typical of the earlier phases of the Middle Minoan Age, a vase with a quatrefoil contour (5), and a series of cups, one (i) showing a somewhat late derivative of the 'tortoise shell, another (3) with a red lack-lustre glaze spiral ornament on the buff ground. The vessel, of which the lower side is seen in No. 2, showing white spirals on the dark brown ground, is of an interesting candlestick form, more fully illustrated in Fig. 422.

The type is identical with Egyptian clay candlesticks' of Fourth Candle- sticks' Dynasty date (Fig. 423 a). Its prototype, however, had been already of Early introduced into Crete in the Early Minoan Age with other proto-dynastic elements. An E. M. II example from a Tholos Ossuary at Siva, 1 near Phaestos, is given in Fig. 423.

South-East Bath-room.

This utensil, which may have held some kind of torch, was probably S. E. useful in connexion with the small and apparently dark chamber into which r0 om the entrance passage opened on the left (Fig. 419). From its square shape and its good gypsum paving and dado this little chamber was from its first discovery regarded as a bath-room.

But this conclusion subsequently received a strong confirmation due to the piecing together, in the course of a gradual work of restoration, of some large pottery fragments derived from this particular area. These proved to M M-be parts of a bath of elegant shape, tapering from the shoulders to the foot, which it was possible to reconstitute almost in its entirety (Fig. 424). It shows a ribbed moulding above with triple streaks at intervals, and its sides are divided into panels. Within these, on a warm buff ground, were found traces of brown glaze decoration in the shape of sprays of reeds or grasses such as frequently occur in the painted designs of this and the ensuing Period.

The bath has been placed in the Plan in its probable position within the bath-room: its length is 1-45 metre, and its greatest height 50 centimetres. From the panelling of its surface it would seem to have been copied from a woodwork original. Its taper form and the raised outline towards the head give it a curiously modern appearance. In this latter particular it differs from the known Late Minoan baths, the level profile of which enabled them to be fitted with lids and thus made use of either as chests or coffins.

1 R. Paribeni, Ausonia, viii, col. 22, Fig. 10. P p 2

THE PALACE OF MINOS, ETC.

Larnakes' or clay sarcophagi of this form are not infrequent in Late Minoan Crete 1 and recur in Mycenaean Greece. 2

Separated from the passage leading to the little bath-room by a wall was another narrow gangway leading to the second group of chambers of the system shown in Fig. 419. This entrance way, which formed the only access on that side, was filled in at the close of M. M. Ill, and a small interior staircase of which seven gypsum steps were preserved was built directly over it

FIG. 424. PAINTED CLAY BATH FROM ROOM ADJOINING MAGAZINE OF LILY VASES.

as a means of approach to a new building of which part of the pavement (visible to the left in Fig. 425) was preserved at a higher level.

Domestic Shrine.

Supposed The original entrance passage on this side gave access to a kind

Sh rine St " f P ave d lobby, against the Northern wall of which was a stone ledge or dais, which is a constant feature in Minoan shrines. That there was here in fact a small domestic shrine with its altar ledge is made probable by the 1 For instance, the elegant painted example found at Milatos on the North Coast E. of Candia (Orsi, Urne Funebri Cretesi, Mon. Ant., 1890, Tav. II and p. n). The swimming fishes painted in the interior of this are appropriate to the idea of a bath. The usual holes made in the base of the ordinary clay coffins for the drainage of moisture were wanting. There was, however, one horizontal perforation at the base. A second plain specimen was found in the same rock chamber.

- Remains of a clay sarcophagus of bath shape were found in Tomb 3 of the Ismenion at Thebes (Keramopoullos, Ap. Aeariw, 1917, p. 92, Fig. 66). Another bath-shaped coffin has recently come to light at Mycenae (see Illustrated London News, Dec. 4, 1920, p. 936).

occurrence close to it of a triton-shell, 1 a usual concomitant of these sanctuaries. Such conch-shells were in fact used as trumpets in Minoan cult for calling down the divinity to altars of offering, as is shown on a crystal lentoid already illustrated which was found in the Idaean Cave. In the S. E. an 1e of this chamber were found a steatite pyxis', a cup, with dull

MAOAHNE Of LILY JARS

FIG. 425. VIEW OF ENTRANCE TO MAGAZINE OF FALSE-SPOUTED JARS, SHOWING CLAY PARTITION.

red spirals on a pale buff ground, and other small vessels, but the objects of worship had been removed.

Magazine of the False-spouted Jars.

This lobby led on the left to two inner store-rooms divided by a clay and plaster partition like that described in the case of the Magazine of the Lily Jars'. 2 The clay core of this was in places cooked red, showing that a In Knossos, Report, 1902, p. 2, the conch- large jars. The sanctuary character of the shell and pyxis are erroneously described as lobby was also missed, having been found in the Maga. ine with the 2 See above, p. 576, Fig. 420.

THE PALACE OF MINOS, ETC.

Magazine of the False-spouted Store-jars.

Their

Evolution from

Smaller

Jugs.

conflagration had here preceded the filling in. The more Western of these Magazines formed an elongated compartment along which the gypsum pavement was continued. This compartment contained two or three small vessels; the more roomy Magazine on the left, however, had three fine jars ranged against its S. wall, and in front of these, together with other smaller vessels an elegant one-handled jug. This vase, which was 43 centimetres in height, showed besides its white bands some traces of flowers and foliage on its purplish brown ground.

The large jars themselves, which repeat the same colour scheme, in two cases presented the peculiarity, very characteristic of this epoch, of showing a false or atrophied spout, that to the right in Fig. 426 a mere knob. In other words, these jars bear in their conformation the evidence that they were originally derived from mere handled jugs with a spout for pouring and

FIG. 426. RIMS OF JARS, SHOWING ATROPHIED OR FALSE SPOUTS.

easily raised by the hand. They have been heightened and enlarged and provided with a stout collar like those of the early pithoi, and the spout has been either blocked or reduced to a mere rudimentary excrescence. 1 This conversion of small portable jugs into jars which were intended as fixtures for storage itself affords an interesting commentary on the gradual recovery that succeeded on the great catastrophe at the close of M. M. II, and which seems to have marked the earlier course of the present Period. Pithoi of the old capacious type had mostly disappeared. Only gradually,

Sympto- part passu with the increase in wealth in such commodities as oil, did a new improved class of store-jar evolve itself out of humbler vessels. This is not, indeed, to say that amoncr the Minoan lords a more direct tradition did not survive of the earlier corded pithoi. The evidence of this is supplied by the Medallion pithoi.

The finest of the jars discovered in the above Magazine, which was i-io metre in height, is reproduced in Fig. 427 a. It shows the atrophied ditions.

1 In the case of the lily jars', described below, and others of the class, we see a mere knob or raised disk in place of the spout of the prototype.

spout on the left and is interesting as presenting in white on the purplish brown ground four axe-like spokes radiating from a central ring with sprays

FIG. 427 a. PAINTED M. M. Ill STORE-JAR, KNOSSOS (c.

FIG. 427. MINIATURE BLADE OF STEERING OAR, XIItH DYNASTY.

between them like triple blades of grass, which also appear beneath the Quad- handles. A kindred axe motive has already been noted on M. M. II poly- Motive chrome pottery, 1 and it has been shown to be a Minoan adaptation of on J ar- 1 Compare fine polychrome cup, p. 241, p. 262, Fig. 194, b, where the Egyptian jewel Fig. 181, above, and for the quadruple form, type is also given.

a quadruple combination of lilies such as was known to jewellers of the Egyptian Egyptian Middle Kingdom. A similar comparison is suggested in the Affinities. p resent ns tance by the design on a miniature Egyptian steering oar of Twelfth Dynasty date (Fig. 427 fr). The Egyptian figure clearly represents a cruciform arrangement of the double bow symbol 1 of Neith, the Goddess of the Western Delta. That the quadruple motive of the jar had a reference to the Double Axe of the Minoan Goddess is equally clear, and the symbolic parallelism is remarkable. The appearance of the sacred weapon on a vessel of a store-room connected with a domestic shrine is natural enough.

Store-jars used for Burials.

Burial jar A contemporary type of M. M. Ill store-jar, of which numerous frag- Knossos merits were found in the M. M. Ill deposits of the East Slope, is best illustrated by the perfect example of a similar vessel and evidently of the same Knossian fabric (Fig. 428) found by the Ghazi stream a few miles West of the site where it had been used as an ossuary. 2 With it was found a plain M. M. Ill handled cup, 3 like Fig. 434 below. The jar shows a white decorative motive in the form of a six-rayed star surrounded by its Stellar a CLls p ec i border. 4 The stellar sign with its central disk recalls the clearly religious symbol already referred to in connexion with ivory draughtsmen and the fresco fragment depicting part of the facade of a shrine. 5 It is Axes on possible, therefore, that here too, as in the case of the axe-shaped spokes of Burial pjg 4.-27 j we ma y trace a symbolic meaning. On the shoulders of a contemporary burial jar from Mochlos, 0 containing the skeleton of a child, were impressed a series of double axes, with white, dotted outlines. On a burial jar described below, we see a lily plant with flowers terminating like axe-blades. 7 1 Miss M. A. Murray, Ancient Egypt, 1921, 4 The cusped circle itself stands in a natural Pt. II, pp. 35-7, points out that the symbol of relation to the ordinary rosette patterns. The Neith is not a shuttle but two bows of early central design may in fact be regarded as a large Nilotic type in a case. dark rosette, the petals of which are traversed 2 Hatzidakis, Miwixoi ra oi lv Kpifn; (Ap. by the white rays. The cusped arrangement, Aeariw, 1918, p. 61, and Pl. VI). Its height either as a complete circle or a canopy, detaches is 1-04 metre, and the breadth of the mouth itself from the rosette and becomes an indepen-0-60 metre. The vessel lay with its mouth to dent feature of Minoan decorative art. As the West. The head of the skeleton was at a canopy we see it on the votive skirts of the bottom, and the knees were drawn up faience (Fig. 364, l, above) and, again, above level with the mouth. A similar burial jar the conventional floral design of the polychrome in the same position was found at Anopolis, vessel on Coloured Plate VII.

E. of Knossos. Both heads were set to the 5 See above, p. 478, and Figs. 342, b, 343. East. 6 Seager, Mochlos, p. 88, Fig. 51.

3 Hatzidakis, loc. c: t., p. 58, Fig. 5. 7 See below, p. 610, Fig. 448.

The use of M. M. Ill store-jars like the above as ossuaries was first Ossuary brought into notice during the 1902 campaign at Knossos by an accidental circumstance. On the other side of the stream, E. of the Palace, a cow put its foot through the bottom of a jar, quite plain but otherwise resembling those of the Magazine described above, and also provided with a false spout, 1 containing the remains of a child's skeleton and a few small rustic pots. It had been placed upside down the usual arrangement with these ossuaries in a round hole just large enough to hold it. The search for further tombs in the vicinity proved unavailing, but whole cemeteries containing similar jar-burials have since come to light, notably at Pachyammos andsphungaras, and this system of interment is now seen to go back to the lower borders of the Early Minoan Age. The practice seems to have died out in L. M. I. The bodies must have been trussed either before death, like those of the ancient Libyan tribe described by Herodotus, 2 or at any rate before the rigor mortis had set in. It is clear that the ordi-

FIG. 428.
BURIAL JAR FROM NEAR KNOSSOS (HEIGHT 73 CM.).

nary store-jars were used for this sepulchral purpose, though those with certain sacral or symbolic designs seem to have been occasionally selected by preference as in the above cases. Part pas. su with the jar-burials, clay cists or coffers continued to serve for holding the contracted skeletons and this practice, unlike the other, survived to the close of the Minoan 1 Knossos, Report, 1902, pp. 88, 89, and Fig. 49. It has what appears to be an ordinary mouth with protruding lips, but the aperture in the wall is blocked. 5 iv. 190. See above, p. 126.

THE PALACE OF MINOS, ETC.

Age. A clay coffin or larnax of this class from Pachyammos, apparently of M. M. Ill date, with handles for the attachment of the lid is given Fig. 429, c. 1 The tendency, as we see from the succeeding Late

Minoan class, was to substitute a purely angular for the earlier more or less rounded types. A small urn of oval form, probably dating from E. M. Ill, is given in Fig. 429, u, 2 and the approximation of this type of ossuary to

FIG. 420. c. CLAY COFFIN (LARNAX) OF M. M. Ill DATE (A AND B PROBABLY

M. M. I); PACHYAMMOS. (c.) a characteristic Nilotic type going back to the pre-dynastic period has already been noted. 3

A curious feature of the burial chest c is the appearance in vertical order between the two handles, and again to the right, of marks, clearly shown in the photograph, which closely resemble written characters of one or other of the Linear Scripts. It will be seen from an interesting discovery made on the East Slope that characters of Class A, in that case ink-written, are inscribed on two cups of this Period.

1 From a photograph kindly supplied me by Mr. Seager (cf. Pachyammos, Pl. XII, x, a, and p. 20). The coffin had been placed upside down, resting on its lid. Mr. Seager inclined to attribute it to M. M. Ill, and its rectangular shape and square-cut rim bear out this conclusion.

2 Ib. xvii, c, and p. 28. It bears a drip pattern in yellowish white paint, characteristic of thee. M. Ill Period.

3 See above, p. 126.

Deposit above Early Monolithic Crypt: Jar and Inscribed Cups.

These cups were found with a large jar and other vessels on a higher Deposit floor above the early Basement of the Monolithic Pillars, itself, as already Inscribed pointed out, the crypt of a sanctuary among the early elements of which Cu P s-

FIG. 430. M. M. Ill JAR FOUND WITH CUPS PRESENTING INK-WRITTEN INSCRIPTIONS OF CLASS A.

was the dove-shaped vase suggestive of the cult of the Minoan Goddess. The stratigraphic portion of this deposit was well defined, since it was itself surmounted by a L. M. I layer. Here came to light the two cups presenting the ink-written inscriptions of the Linear Class A to be reproduced in the succeeding Section. 1 The fine jar, Fig. 430, which stood on the same floor with them must therefore also be considered as somewhat earlier than the fabrics of the various Magazines above described, which were covered in at the close of this Period. The profile of the rim is very characteristic of M. M. Ill jars, and it will be seen from its associations that the vessel belongs to the earlier part of this Period.

The high build of the inscribed cups (Fig. 131, a and 6) is in fact conclusive in this respect, the contour of a, indeed, recalling cups of the latest M. M. II

FIG. 431. M. M. Ill a CUPS WITH INK-WRITTEN INSCRIPTIONS ( ).

M. M. in phase. The gradual modification of the contour was well illustrated by the and b. resu ts f supplementary excavations made in 1913 beneath the pavement of the Room of the Stone Pier as well as in the adjoining area by a blind well. Two distinct strata were there brought to light separated by a floor of white beaten clay. 2 In the lower of these, answering to the M. M. Ill a stage, were plain clay cups with the typical profiles shown in Fig. 432, a. a. a.–In the upper layer extending to 70 centimetres beneath the pavement the cups were decidedly lower and broader in their proportions (Fig. 432 6,6) closely approaching indeed the L. M. I Class.

1 See Fig. 431 a, 6, and below, p. 613 seqq., their greater diameter 9-3 to 8 cm.

Figs. 450-2. 2 See above, p. 366, note 2. The height of the cups (b, b was from 3 The height of the cups of the earlier 5-5 to 4-5 cm., their greatest breadth 11-5 to stratum (a, a, a varied from about 6-5 to 5-8 cm., 10 cm.

Very characteristic of the cups of this Period are the spiral convo- Spiral lutions visible in the interior. This feature also marks in a special degree fionsof 1 " certain flat circular bowls (Fig. 433) of which numerous specimens were Cu P sand IJuwis.

FIG. 432. OUTLINES OF PLAIN CLAY CUPS FROM LOWKR (a, a, a) AND UPPER (l,) STRATUM UNDER PAVEMENT OF Rcxm OF STONE PIER; M. M. Ill a AND b ( ).

found in the M. M. Ill stratum referred to above containing the earlier class of cups. The spiral fluting in these cases is due to pressure of a finger on the revolving clay. It seems almost to have been regarded as an element of decoration.

FIG. 433. M. M. Ill BOWLS WITH SPIRAL FLUTING IN THE INTERIOR ( ).

Such a result could only have been produced by the rapid revolution of Signs ot the potter's wheel, a further symptom of which is the appearance of a sue- wheel, cession of elliptical curves on the bottoms of vessels due to severing them, while in quick rotation, from the base by tightening a noose of string- ,., i, ji j c cut Bases.

string. 1 A good example of this on the base of a typical handled cup 01 1 This procedure was first explained by Mr. in relation to the Kamares pottery, he notes

R. M. 1 a vkins in relation to the early group that these string-markings do not appear on of Zakro vases (M. M. Ill); J. H. S. xxiii, the Early M. M. II pottery from Palaikastro p. 249, and Fig. 2. In returning to the subject (B. S. A. xix, pp. 21,22, and n. 3). It is clear,

THE PALACE OF MINOS, ETC.

early M. M. Ill fabric, the clay surface of which is tinted with a red wash, is seen in Fig. 434, b. This cup was found with a nest of others of similar form fabric on a M. M. Ill floor of a house to the North-West of the Palace.

FIG. 434. a, CUP, SHOWING SPIRAL FLUTING; b, BASF. OF CUP WITH STRING MARKS, (f f.)

Spiral fluting both inside and out was produced in the case of these cups by the pressure of a slender finger-tip winding upwards from the bottom, accompanied by counter-pressure on the exterior (Fig. 434, a). Signs of the quick wheel are very generally present on all but the largest vessels of this Period.

however, that these markings are not infrequent on the later class of M. M. II ware. Several instances occurred, for instance, on the base of vessels from the Late M. M. II floor of the Area of the Loom-Weights. The procedure is well known to modern potters from Japan to Britain. Monsieur M. L. Franchet (who systematically ignores previous researches) makes the same observation with regard to these elliptical striations Rapport sur line Mission en Crete et en Egypte, p. 39; Nouv. Arch, des Missions scientifiques, xxii (1917).

The suggestion made in Boyd Hawes, Gournia, p. 42, PI. VIII, 32, 33, that certain stone disks were potters' tables, but there left open, is made his own by M. Franchet (op, cit. p. 43 seqq., and cf. Pis. I and II) and sup- ported by fresh specimens from Crete as well as by Hindu and other analogies. These stone disks are often roughened below, and show traces of the cement by which they were probably attached to wooden supports. Their weight gave momentum to the rotatory movement. The specimen (Knossos, 72), however, is in fact part of a tripod stand, for the legs of which triple pairs of rivet holes are seen below. A clay example from Tylissos is given by Dr. J. Hatzidakis, "Apx- "Ec., 1912, pp. 230, 231, and Fig. 39 (below). These disks seem to be mostly Late Minoan. For useful comparative material on this and other questions connected with the primitive potters craft see Franchet, Ceramique primitive, Paris, 1911.

OF NATURALISM.

Dated deposits of close of M. M. Ill; Contrasts ivith M. M. II result of Catastrophe; Monochrome decoration again general; Tortoise-shell rippled ware, anticipation of new style; Survivals of true polychromy; Polychrome Rhyton of Oslrich Shell type zvith group of decorative Palm-trees; Vessels from Well, Gypsddes; Polychrome jars from Repositories; Imitations of conglomerate and breccia; Basin with coloured imitation of granulated rock-work; Minoan wash-basins prototypes of Melian Class; Coiled sprays, M. M. Ill feature on painted sherds from Mycenae Shaft Graves; Shaft Grave sherds paralleled by jars from Temple Repositories; Influence of Naturalistic Wall-painting on pottery; The Lily jars' compared with H. Triada fresco; Vetches, Tulips, and Reeds or Grasses on Vases; Exclusion of Human and Animal figures from pottery contrast with wall-paintings; Fish, however, represented; Reflection of Dolphin Fresco on M. M. III jars; Class of small reliefs of marine subjects; Axe plants' onm. M. Ill jar, anticipation of late Palace Style; Tangential loops on M. M. Ill Vases link with early L. M. I decoration.

WE have seen that, owing to a local catastrophe followed by a far- Dated reaching restoration at the beginning of the Late Minoan Age, the Palace "seof was peculiarly rich in a series of dated deposits of pottery, all illustrating M. M. ill. the closing phase of M. M. III.

This series of deposits extends to both wings of the building, including on the one side such characteristic groups of vessels as those of the Temple Repositories and on the other those of the Royal Magazines, the N. E. Magazines and of the closet containing the lily jars as well as the other store-rooms of the same S. E. system. It is only here and there as ex hypothesi in the case of the N. W. Lustral Basin and adjoining area and in certain stratified floor deposits of the East Slope that we obtain, in a more fragmentary form, some glimpses of the earlier M. M. Ill stages.

The result of this, as already observed, while multiplying examples Contrast belonging to the latest ceramic phase of this Period, is to enhance the M"M. II; contrast with the style of pottery in vogue at the close of M. M. II. It is Effects of clear, indeed, that this closing M. M. Ill phase began with a great set-back strophe.

THE PALACE OF MINOS, ETC.

Monochrome decoration again general.

Tortoise-shell Rippled Ware.

Anticipation of new Style.

Examples of M. M. IlandIll Tortoise-shell Ware.

and impoverishment, clue to the widespread disaster that marks what may well have been the end of an earlier Minoan Dynasty. We are struck from the beginning with the prevalence of a much rougher class of ware, the fabric of which is accompanied not only by the general disappearance of polychromy but by the great diminution of the lustre of the old black glaze medium, owing to the roughness of the surface, and its survival in the form of a brownish lilac wash on which the decorative designs are laid on in powdery white. Finally, towards the end of the Period, we note an increasing tendency to return to the plain buff ground with brown decoration, which itself represents a very old Minoan tradition that had never quite died out.

The clay bath, Fig. 424, with its tufts of grasses, has already supplied an example of this, and specimens depicting plants and dolphins are given below. This dark on light method may itself be regarded as an approach towards the almost universal Late Minoan practice, though the surface of the vessels is still somewhat rough and dull-

One particular class, however, presents, so far as glaze and fabric are concerned, a real anticipation of the later style. The class in question, which already makes its appearance in the Second Middle Minoan Period, 1 maybe described as 'tortoise-shell rippled ware (Fig. 435). We already see here the finely levigated surface with its pale buff slip, now often highly polished, and accompanied, as on Late Minoan vases, by a lustrous glaze decoration of deeper hue. This takes the form of upright striations artistically varied by the greater or lesser pressure of the brush, so that they shade off from dark brown through intermediate tones of bright orange to the buff background. A curious effect of fine tortoise-shell is thus produced.

Specimens of this ware are given in Fig. 435. The lower fragment from a M. M. II deposit at Knossos, shows the decoration carried over the bottom of a bowl, the striations radiating from the centre. 2 The cup above is to be referred to M. M. III.

The other colours are also generally accompanied by one or more horizontal bands of imperfectly fixed and often evanescent white. We have 1 Specimens occurred at Knossos in a pure M. M. II stratum in the Basement of the Loom-Weights on the East slope.

1 The early occurrence of this variety of the tortoise-shell ripple ornament is confirmed by Mr. Dawkins's observations on specimens of this ware from Palaikastro (. S. A., 210-11). He describes a Vapheio Cup with similar radial stripes on its base as having been found in company with a bowl of egg-shell fabric. It would therefore go back at least to the middle of M. M. II.

here polychromy indeed, but with a different colour scale, as adapted to a new method of laying on the glaze slip.

The ripple ornament on these vessels is curiously reminiscent in form of a Neolithic class, but it was probably immediately derived from the vertical and slanting barbotine ridge ornament of the preceding Age. In a somewhat decadent form it survives, as we have seen, into the Late Minoan Age, and the new form of polychromy that it represents essentially corresponds with that of a well-marked L. M. I class, which, in addition to the brown on buff and traces of the imperfectly fixed white, is enlivened by a brilliant orange red, recalling, though under a variant aspect, the bright scarlet hues of the older Middle Minoan tradition.

Elements of true polychromy survived in a modified form to the latest phase of the present Period, as we shall see from certain vases found in the Temple Repositories. We are almost bound to suppose, therefore, that polychrome vessels of the earlier class described above existed inm. M. Illrt. It seems probable indeed that certain fragments of cups and bowls found FIG. 435. TORTOISE-SHELL RIPPLED WARE: M. M. Ill j n t j ie ower deposit of the CUP AND M. M. II FRAGMENT BELOW.

Kouloura or Walled Rubbish-Pit of the West Court belonged to this category. On these appear finely foliated designs and friezes of disks in a style reminiscent of some of the vessels found in the Loom-Weight Area and belonging to the close of M. M. 11. But, while the old red colour medium was still employed in the decoration, the ground shows a pale brownish, almost matt lilac, in place of the lustrous black glaze of the earlier class. A mug with a similar style of i Q q

Tortoise-shell Kippled Ornament.

Survivals of true Polychromy.

THE PALACE OF MINOS, ETC.

Polychrome Rhyton ofostrich-Eggtype.

Ostrich-Egg Rhyton from Mycenae.

Decorative palm-trees traditional ele ments.

Influence ofgraffito technique.

foliated ornamentation in white on a reddish-brown glaze ground appears among the later ceramic remains of the Kamares Cave. 1

Some remarkable fragments of a vessel, restored in Fig. 436, c, which came to light in a M. M. Ill stratum of the Kafavtiov rubbish-heap S. E. of the site introduce us to a more distinctive style of polychromy. We have here a Minoan rhyton or libation vessel representing a clay copy of a type the body of which was formed by an ostrich egg. Actual remains of such a rhyton (Fig. 436, B 2), which hitherto have escaped recognition, were found in the IVth Shaft Grave at Mycenae, the mouthpiece being composed of Knossian faience, and a perforated gold plate applied to the lower end of the egg-shell. Fragmentary evidence has indeed been already noted 3 which shows that ceramic imitations of such ostrich-egg rhytons were already executed in the developed M. M. II polychrome style (see Fig. 436 A).

From the rough finish of the orifice it would appear that in the case of the present example a mouthpiece of precious metal had been fitted to it. The painted designs themselves are full of minute decorative details but the whole reflects palatial models. The three palm-trees depicted on the circumference of the vase recall the triple groups on the fine M. M. II jar from the Loom-Weight Basement illustrated above 4 and in this case too the inflorescence of the palms is shown. The sloping position here adopted is in accordance with a device that goes back to the beginning of the Middle Minoan Age to give the full development of plant forms within a comparatively low field. The cable decoration as applied to their trunks recalls a parallel device on a fine M. M. II b jar from Phaestos illustrated above 5 and the knobbed sprays introduced into the field are familiar ceramic appendages from M. M. I onwards. As a motive for an ostrich-egg type of vessel the palm-trees are specially appropriate and the incised lines with which they are emphasized a quite exceptional technique on Minoan painted pottery may well have been taken over from the engraved decoration natural 1 Dawkins, B. S. A., xix, PI. XII (above) and

Part of the faience mouthpiece of this vessel (found in the IVth Shaft Grave) was published by Schliemann (Mycenae, p. 256, Fig. 375) as a fragment of an alabaster vase. Its connexion with the ostrich eggs of the tombs was first brought out by Dr. Stais in itself a great step in advance. He regarded, however, what is really the mouthpiece as the pedestal of a cup and the gold plate at the base as a cover (Collection Mycenienne, 1915, p. 71, No. 828). He connected these fittings with the egg from Tomb V showing applied faience dolphins, but in Dr. Karo's view they belonged to one of the plain ostrich eggs from Tomb IV. It had, in fact, a central perforation. A fuller account of the evolution of Minoan rhyton-types of this class is reserved for Vol. II.

3 See above, p. 254, Fig. 190, and cf. Vol. II.

4 See above, p. 260, Fig. 193.

5 P. 260, Fig. 193.

.-:::.

to the egg-shell prototypes1 On the other hand, the cable band below the mouthpiece and the fellow to it restored round the lower circumference are suggestive of the decorative metal rings that surround the ostrich egg-cups of a well-known Mediaeval and Renaissance class.

The smaller scrolls of Fig. 436, c, as well as the cable bands, lead us to a characteristic style of decoration presented by a group of polychrome vessels brought out in 1913 during the excavation of a Minoan well on the

FIG. 437. CUP AND FRAGMENTS OF BOWLS FROM WELL, SHOWING M. M. Ill SURVIVALS OF POLYCHROMY (FROM MINOAN WELL, GYPSADES).

slope of Gypsades facing the Palace on the South. The great bulk of the pottery here found represented the earliest Late Minoan phase (L. M. la). M. M. ill Immediately beneath this deposit, however, was a layer clearly belonging c h r ome to the later stage of M. M. Ill, since it contained remains of vessels showing essels white lilies on a lilac-brown ground, resembling those from the Palace Well, Magazine described above. But the most remarkable feature of these 1 A somewhat variant parallel may be re- flying camels, from the Grotta diside at called in the engraved ostrich-shell cup, with Yulcii.

THE PALACE OF MINOS, ETC.

Polychrome Vessels from Temple Repositories.

Polychrome imitations of discoveries was the occurrence, in the stratum containing the remains of the lily jars, of fragments of cups and bowls belonging to a unique class of late polychrome ware, specimens of which are shown in Fig. 437.

The patterns here are of a finicking kind, and are executed in a dull madder red, picked out with white, on the brownish glaze ground. On the fragment shown in d, a white twisted chain runs along the border, succeeded by a reddish band, and below again by a running pattern of somewhat lace-like character. The portion of a cup, c, presents analogous features and the twisted white band or guilloche is a feature in several cases.

The circumstances of their discovery show that the remarkable class that these fragments represent belongs to the concluding phase of M. M. Ill and the same conclusion applies to certain large polychrome jars from the Temple Repositories, specimens of which are given in the Coloured Plate VII.

The vessel to the left, the top part of which is seen from above in the middle of the Plate, is a very characteristic type of M. M. Ill pitcherwithoval mouth. Thecoloured design on it, which had been concealed by a calcareous incrustation, only came out in the course of its FIG 438. SMALL JAR FROM GOURNIA, constitution. We see here, on 0 " REPRODUCTION the brown ground, a highly conventional representation of a plant with white foliage and pointed petals and disk-shaped buds of yellow ochre, also white bordered. The cuspecl canopy above, curiously Gothic in aspect, recurs over the crocus clumps painted on the votive robes of faience found in the Temple Repository, The complete cusped circle, as we have seen, is very characteristic of a group of contemporary jars with white on dark decoration, of which an example is given in Fig. 428 above.

It must be said that both the technique and polychromy of the vessels shown on Plate VII fall far below the fine M. M. II standard.

The vessel was reconstructed from fragments in the Ashmolean Museum.

Line cor the left.

rownis,

PLATK VII

The surface is rough, the lustre of the glaze medium hardly perceptible, and Con- ,,,. j glomerate the colours broadly applied. and

The jug to the right of the Plate is decorated with a symmetrical imitation of conglomerate, in which the pebbles are reduced to round disks, some of them washed with ochreous red, while the intermediate veins are dotted with white dashes on the brown ground. This imitation of stonework recalls what has been already said as to the early M. M. Ill class of dotted vessels', derived in that case from inlaid stone bowls. 1 An interesting parallel to this jug is supplied by a small jar from Gournia, given here in Fig. 438, also representing a polychrome tradition in which conglomerate stone-work is reproduced in a still more literal manner. The black rounded pebbles with their white striations are here surrounded by orange margins. 2

The handled cup on Plate VII is from Palaikastro, but is given here as another good example of late polychromy in connexion with rock-work graining. It is of a typical M. M. Ill b shape and shows both red and white decoration on the dark ground. The granulated pattern on an irregular border seen here above the bands is of special significance, since it is taken from a fuller design of a purely pictorial class. It represents, in fact, a part of the rocky foreground such as appears in wall-paintings like the Saffron Gatherer or Fish Fresco, and which finds an analogy in the undulating lower zone of the Dolphin jar illustrated below (Fig. 447 a). The granulations, by a curious convention, may be taken to indicate the rock itself in section.

A further specimen of granulated rock-work in the M. M. Ill poly- p y-chrome style is afforded by the interior of a remarkable flat-bottomed basin Basin. (Fig. 439), of which the larger part was preserved, found immediately North of the Palace at Knossos. The ground here agrees with the earlier Middle Minoan tradition in its blackish glaze; the foliate coils and dotted decoration are creamy white, as is the inner veining. The broader veins, however, which separate what are evidently intended for the pebbles of an original surface of cut breccia are of a bright orange red.

1 See above, p. 413, and Fig. 298. dark ground clearly stand in another context.

- Boyd Hawes, Gournw, PI. IX, Fig. 23, and The ridged base of Fig. 438 is of early tradition, p. 44. The jar, which is 27-3 cm. high, was and recalls some Pachyammos jars described found in a cellar with two cups of late M. M. Ill by Seager as Transitional Style M. M. Ill-character with white decoration on a dark L. M. I Periods' (e. g. Pachyammos, PI. X). ground. In the same cellar were also found For the M. M. I tradition compare op. at., three L. M. I a vessels, but the group with the PI. I (i-a).

THE PALACE OF MINOS, ETC.

Melian The basin itself is two handled and of oval shape, 55 cm. (c. 2i in.) in its greatest width, while its flat base is 23 cm. in its maximum

FIG. 439. M. M. Ill POLYCHROME BASIN, KNOSSOS. c. (A).

diameter. Its profile is shown in the inset. It was probably used as a washbasin and seems to supply the prototype of a class of flat-bottomed oval vessels, numerous specimens of which were brought to light at Phylakopi in Melos in a stratum answering to the early part of L. M. I. These vessels were recognized by the excavators as baths and wash-basins, their sizes varying from something over a metre to somewhat under a third. Like Minoan baths, they showed interior designs of reeds and swimming fishes, while their margins were decorated with spiral patterns affording an analogy with the coiled sprays seen on the Knossian specimen. 1

These coiled sprays have a special importance in connexion with the painted sherds from the Fourth Shaft Grave at Mycenae. They 1 Phylakopi, p. 140, Figs. 112, 113.

recur, as will be seen, in c and c, representing parts of a large jar, grouped Coiled with some polychrome fragments from the same Grave in Fig. 440. The sherds of decoration in this case was white on the dark ground; the other fragments Mycc-n Grave.

FIG. 440. a-f. M. M. Ill SHERDS FROM FOURTH SHAFT GRAVK AT MYCF. NAF.

here represented show crimson or reddish purple patterns on the characteristic M. M. 1 1 1 lilac-brown ground.

The rim of this jar and the handle and part of the rim of the polychrome shaft ewer, Fig. 440, , are entirely in keeping with forms from the Temple Reposi- tories, while in Grave V were found the remains of one or more jugs with paralleled broad white spiral bands on the rough dark-glazed ground, the most frequently positories.

1 From Furtwangler, Myktnische Thongefiisse, PI. VI.

THE PALACE OF MINOS, ETC.

recurring decorative feature of the vessels from this Palace store. 1 In

Grave VI, again, together with a fragment of 'tortoise-shell ripple ware of the fine Middle Minoan class, 2 was found the peculiar type of two-handled jar (Fig. 441), 3 both in shape and in the rippled band 4 round the shoulders approaching a unique Repository vessel, which, however, has three short feet' It has matt red bands.

As to the individual sources of the pottery of the Third Middle Minoan style found at Mycenae, Tiryns, Orchomenos, and other sites of Mainland

Greece it is often premature to judge.

Some of it points to local centres of

Cretan manufactures as yet uexplored.

On the other hand, the close comparisons that it is possible to establish with certain types from the Temple Repositories and other Palace deposits makes it legitimate to infer that, as in the case of the faience inlays and other imported objects, a certain prportion of the

M. M. III pottery found in connexion with the Shaft Graves was actually of Knossian origin.

The imitations of cut breccia and conglomerate such as we see in the

Knossian washing basin, Fig. 438, and the Repository jar, Plate VII, bring mic C po! y- home to us once more the interesting chromy f act that t ie attem p t to re p ro duce the effects of variegated stone-ware had been a main inspirer of the rise of

Variegated Stoneware main inspirer of

FIG. 441. FAINTED JAR FROM GRAVE VI.

1 Furtwangler, Myk. Thongeftisse, PI. VII, 41. His description, p. 7, applies word for word to the corresponding vases of the Repository type (Fig. 404 p. 557 above). Der Thon ist sehr grob und inwendig rot gebrannt. Das Schwarz des Grundes ist fast ohne Glanz, das Weiss sehr diinn aufgetragen.

2 Not later probably than the early part of M. M. III. It shows this decoration in a much purer form than that of Fig. 441.

5 Furtwangler, Mykenischethongefasse. XI and p. 8. It has a pale ground and yellowish- brown glaze bands, over which is dull white and red decoration.

4 The rippled ornament on both these jars is of the lale degenerate type that characterizes the close of M. M. III and the earliest phase of L. M. I.

5 See above, Fig. 404. The footless form recurs as an early L. M. I type at Pseira (Seager, Pseira, p. 22, Fig. 6). Here the tortoise-shell band is lowered and plants spring from its upper border.

ceramic polychromy at the beginning of the Middle Minoan Age. 1 Thus the stamp of its origin still marks the latest products of this class. At the same time the taste for brilliant colours on vases of which we here find the surviving traces recalls the much more remote historical connexion in which the beautiful stone-ware vessels of Early Minoan Crete have been themselves shown to stand. That they must, in fact, be regarded as the

FIG. 442. PART OF JAR WITH BRANCHED VEINED DECORATION FILLED WITH BARBOTINE.

reflection and in part as the direct copies of a pre-dynastic Egyptian class of variegated stone vases has been shown in detail in an earlier Section influence of this work. At the same time, the extraordinary vogue and perfection of Nilotic e this fabric among the old inhabitants of the Nile valley was itself due to the accessibility, through river traffic or by other means of transport, of natural stores of these gay materials.

Abundant deposits of a very brilliant kind of breccia occur in different 1 See above, p. 177.

ware.

THE PALACE OF MINOS, ETC.

Origin of White Borders of Polychrome Details.

Branched Veining on M. M. II Cups.

Imitated in M. M. III.

parts of Crete, such as those from the Coast region of Mirabello from which the material of the E. M. Vases of Mochlos and other sites was derived. Those of the promontory of Kakon Oros immediately to the N. E. of Knossos supplied the Palace with many of its early column-bases but, as the stone vessels of the Early Minoan tholos tombs show, a finer kind must have existed to the South, on the borders of Messara. It is clear that the fabric of vessels of this material, notably the small bird's-nest bowls with knobbed covers, 1 continued into the First Middle Minoan Period. It is a noteworthy phenomenon, moreover, that one particular feature of the breccia, of the Messara and Mirabello type, as seen on these, the white band surrounding the interior fragments itself due to chemical causes consequent on the igneous origin of the rock was first literally taken over into the painted clay imitations of this material and afterwards survived as a border of interior details in general.

The branched veining itself as a leading decorative feature occurs on some very beautiful M. M. II cups, of which a specimen is given in Fig. 178 above, 2 accompanied as in other cases with a fine stippling of the interior spaces. That this traditional stone-work motive survived into the present Period is shown by some remarkable fragments of a large jar, Fig. 442, found near the Deposit of the ink-inscribed cups, and probably, like them, belonging to the earlier M. M. Ill phase. It can hardly be doubted that the branched band with antler-like prongs, of which we here see a portion, represents on a larger scale the same kind of veining seen in Fig. 442. It will be observed that it is accompanied by the characteristic white border line.

The remains of the jar in question are of the usual M. M. Ill fabric with a somewhat rough surface and white decoration on a brown ground. The interior of the branched motive presents, however, an interesting feature. The surface here, which is painted white, affords a good example of the survival of the old barbotine style, and is worked up in the same way as 1 See above, p. 177, and Figs. 126, 127 a.

2 Dr. Einar Lexow, Bergerfs Museums Aarbok, 1918-19, pp. 1-14, Figs. 6, 7, has called attention to the close comparison presented between the antlered veining of a similar cup and the characteristic horned curvilinear patterns that appear in the shape of graffiti on pottery or of the raised ornaments of friezes in the prehistoric sanctuaries of the Maltese Islands. These comparisons, as I have shown on pp. 267 3, above, find a still wider field in the decorative repertory of Crete during the culminating phase of M. M. II. The stage with which they are associated at Hal Tarxien and elsewhere is, as Dr. Zammit has shown, the latest Neolithic of the Islands. But there are good reasons for bringing down its date to an epoch compatible with M. M. II influence.

p; irts of the rock-work surface of the large flat-bottomed dish with marine reliefs, a part of which is illustrated in Fig. 381 above.

FIG. 443. JARS WITH WHITE LILIES FROM MAGAZINE OK LILY VASES (:.).

The influence on vases of the naturalistic style of wall-painting now in vogue attains its maximum during the closing M. M. Ill phase. So far as plant designs are concerned, the beginnings of this influence have been

THE PALACE OF MINOS, ETC.

influence of Natu- ralistic painting on Vases.

already illustrated among the latest works of M. M. II by the close analogy that the flowers on the polychrome bowl, Fig. 197 above, 1 present to those of the Saffron Gatherer.

Another polychrome jug of the same date shows a lily spray, 2 which may also have been excerpted from some parallel composition on the Palace walls. The monochrome successors of such floral subjects that now appear make up for the deficiency of colouring by greater picturesqueness of treatment, and in this way present a nearer relation to their prototypes in the greater Art.

The fondness of the M. M. Ill vase painters for groups of lilies recalls the beautiful fragment of painted stucco from the South-East House belonging apparently to the early

The Lily Jars.

part of the present Period. The white

FIG. 444. LILY GROUP FROM FRESCO; HAGIA TRIADA (FROM A SKETCH).

Madonna lilies on a purplish ground seen on the jars of the little 1 See above, p. 264. 2 See above, p. 264, Fig. 196.

Magazine described above, which must be reckoned among the most beautiful products of M. M. Ill ceramic Art, are reproduced on a larger scale in Fig. 443. These closely resemble some clumps of the same flower that Com-appear in the foreground of a naturalistic wall-painting, representing the th d n closing phase of M. M. Ill, found in the little Palace of Hagia Triada. Triada A lily group from this fresco design is given in black and white for comparison in Fig. 444. 1

Other plant motives which appear in dark on light and in the new technique on the pottery of the beginning of the first Late Minoan Period had already made their appearance in white on dark at the present epoch. In this style, too, the saffron flower is a favourite motive. The exquisite vetch designs of the L. M. I pottery of Knossos also occur on M. M. Ill Vetches sherds from this site, but the best existing illustrations in the old style are supplied by the two jugs, Fig. 445, a, 6, found by the British excavators at Palaikastro. The jar, Fig. 44(i, from the Temple Repositories set beside these shows a group of flowers, in bud or only partly opened, apparently tulips, which still grow wild in the glens of Juktas. They are executed in a rough effective style somewhat suggestive of Dutch crockery.

On the pottery of this epoch from the same Repositories and other Reeds or sources, both in the case of cups and of larger vessels, tufts of grasses are very frequent and this motive is exceptionally prominent on the succeeding L. M. I a class. 2 These in their original shape rather represent reeds or sedges and take us back to the exquisite spikelets seen on the fragment of what had clearly been a wall-painting executed on a considerable scale (see above, P- 537. Fig 390).

It must nevertheless be noticed in comparing naturalistic designs of Exclusion the M. M. Ill vase painters with the larger compositions on the walls from and which they were excerpted that we are met by a remarkable lacuna. The plant designs of the frescoes are in their essence simply accessories to the fro n main subjects presented, which are human or animal figures. On the Contrast pottery, however, this essential feature is omitted, and only the vegetable. details are selected for reproduction. This is the more noteworthy since paintings. on a group of small steatite vessels, chiefly rhytons, the fabric of which 1 The wall-painting to which this fragment Remains of quantities of L. M. I a vessels belongs does not as yet appear to have re- with grass decoration were found for instance ceived illustration. It represents, apparently, in the well of Gypsades above the M. M. Ill a later subject of the same nature as the Saffron stratum. Gatherer.

THE PALACE OF MINOS, ETC.

certainly overlaps the close of this Period, human and animal figures take up the most prominent place.

FIG. 445 a, b.   WHITE ON BLACK DECORATION. SHOWING PEAS OR VETCHES: PALAIKASTRO, a (c.);

FIG. 446. M. M. Ill JAR WITH TULIP DESIGNS, WHITE ON BLACK; KNOS-SOS (c.

Why then should such representations have been excluded from the contemporary repertory of the vase painters? Tradition was to a certain extent in favour of their insertion, since attempts to depict the human form, executed it is true in a grotesque style, are already found in the earliest

M. M. III: SURVIVALS OF CERAMIC POLYCHROMY 607 stage of M. M. I polychromy. 1 They must have been tolerably frequent in that and probably also in the succeeding epoch, since such figures recur in imitative forms on pots of Melian fabric.- Yet from the time of these early essays to the latest Minoan days attempts to reproduce scenes involving human action were definitely abandoned on vases.

Was it perhaps that the figured representations of the frescoes, even such as recorded the sports of the arena, stood in a certain religious connexion and that there was some kind of taboo against the use of such material on vessels of ordinary domestic use? Or was it simply some fine sense of artistic reserve, which withheld from the potters subjects that were yet thought appropriate for other contemporary craftsmen, goldsmiths, and lapidaries, as well as artists who adorned the walls?

An exception was indeed made in favour of all forms of marine life, and Fish, the fish bones found in a Palace pot may suggest the explanation that it was the edible nature of various sea creatures that led to the admission of Dented on

Pottery.

this class of subjects into the vase painter's repertory. Fish and sepias had formed a feature in the earlier stages of Middle Minoan polychromy. 3 It seems clear, however, that at this time the sea-pieces on the Palace walls, especially those depicting dolphins, exercised a direct influence on certain monochrome designs of such subjects that were now executed on the pottery.

Figures of animals were also eliminated, though in this field, again, examples of Cretan wild goats have been cited above on vases of M. M." I 4 and even E. M. Ill date. 0 Yet it can hardly be doubted that the ceramic artists who produced such exquisite sprays of flowers and foliage could have attained some proficiency at least in depicting animals.

Even throughout the early part of the Late Minoan Age, to which Contrast must be assigned the finest of the stucco reliefs and the Miniature Frescoes (jr with their lively groups, we mark the same self-imposed abstention from " such subjects on the part of the Minoan vase painter. What the Greek vase painter most sought, designs involving the human form, he sedulously 1 For a specimen from the Kamares Cave, light example. The recurrence of these imi-see J. L. Myres, Proe. Soc. Ants., 1895, PI. II, tative types in Melos points to a greater cur-12 and p. 4, and L. Mariani, Man. Ant., vi, rency of these human designs on the M. M. I PI. IX, 10 and p. 337. pottery than might have been supposed from 2 Phylakopi, PI. XIII, Figs. 17, 18; white the existing Cretan evidence. The Fishermen on dark with lustrous surface. The rude male Vase (of L. M. I. date) is quite exceptional. figures here with upraised hands, one with 3 See above, for example, p. 182, Fig. 131. a dagger worn in the Petsofa manner and 4 See above, p. 183, Fig. 132.

naked to the waist, are clearly taken from See above, p. 113, Fig. 80 A, S. Cretan originals. Fig. 14 shows a dark on

THE PALACE OF MINOS, ETC.

avoided. Arms might be reproduced but not the man, symbolic shapes but not the divinity. Only on painted clay sarcophagi of the later phase of L. M. Ill do such subjects begin to appear in a sepulchral relation.

The lively representations of dolphins that now make their appearance on some fine M. M. Ill jars, are neither taken from the old convention nor

FIG. 447 a. JAR WITH DOLPHINS, ROCKS, AND PEBBLY BEACH, LIGHT ON DARK, PACHYAMMOS.

FIG. 447 JAR WITH DOLPHINS, DARK ON LIGHT, PACHYAMMOS.

They

Dolphins from a class of small marine reliefs, to which reference will be made. Ill Jan; breathe a larger spirit and we now catch a direct reflection of the picturesque of e wall n S rou P of wall-paintings to which the Dolphin Fresco belongs. The influence paintings, of the higher art on the vase painter is clearly recognizable in the very spirited design of dolphins on the jar from Pachyammos (Fig. 447 a) 1 The 1 R. B. Seager, Pachyammos, Pl. XIV and p. 23 (Fig. 447a was executed with Mr. Seager's kind permission from his original drawing). Mr. Seager explains the stippled white effect of the upper border as the tossing surface of the sea, with clouds of spray blown about by the wind. But analogy with low reliefs of the marine class tends to show that the outline above is dolphins are here shown as if leaping out of the waters, in a waved space that opens between spray-wreathed rocks above and a lower zone with white dots, here perhaps representing a pebbly beach.

The pendant to this is supplied by another jar from the same cemetery (Fig. 447 6), 1 also representing a school of leaping dolphins, in this case, however, depicted, without the rocks and pebbles, in dark paint, edged with white, on a warm buff ground. Another Pachyammos jar in the same early dark on light style shows a cuttle-fish with six tentacles in a style less purely decorative and geometrical than that reproduced above on a polychrome vase from the Kamares Cave. 2 These vases clearly belong to the later, transitional phase of M. M. Ill, in which we already have a foretaste of the prevailing ceramic fashion of the beginning of the Late Minoan Age.

Parallel with these monochrome designs of marine subjects on M. M. Ill Class of jars, which reflect the greater art of wall-painting, is another group executed in small relief, of which an example has already been given in the marine piece with its life-like reproductions of shells and barnacles 3 The counterpart of these, as already noted, is to be found in the faience representations of the Flying Fish panel. 4 Shells in relief seem already to have adorned certain vessels in the M. M. II Period.

Reliefs of this class, often very finely executed in steatite, had, as will be shown, a great influence on the vase paintings of the finest L. M. I style. But, as pointed out above, it seems to have been the greater works on the Palace walls that mainly influenced the marine designs on the M. M. Ill jars.

Amongst the remains of jars belonging, like the last mentioned, to the latest **M. M. Ill** stage there occurred at Knossos several specimens of broad handles terminating below in scalloped borders and some of them coated with milky white enamel-like paint. A fuller illustration of the class of vessel to which these handles belonged is supplied by a jar from the Cemetery of Pachyammos, showing two scalloped handles of the same kind (Fig. 448)." The designs on this, dark brown on pale buff, as well as the meant for rocks. The idea that the rocks were Seager, Pachyammos, Pl. IX and p. 19.

washed by spray and that this came into the 2 See above, p. 246, Fig. 186, artist's mind may still hold good, since, both See above, p. 521, Figs. 380.

in the Dolphin Fresco and that of the Flying See above, p. 520, Fig. 379.

Fish, spray is actually represented. The white " Op. fit., Pl. XVII and p. 25. The body of stippling, however, here seen seems, as Dr. the handle appears white in the figure owing

Mackenzie points out, to have originated from to the plaster restoration. As the remains of the harbotine imitation of rocks as seen on its scalloped borders show, however, it had the fragment of a large M. M. Ill vase illustrated originally a dark ground.

above, Fig. 442.

THE PALACE OF MINOS, ETC.

Axe-plants' on M. M. Ill Jar.

Anticipation of late Palace Style.

subject that it presents, afford a specially valuable illustration of this transitional style. As in the case of the jar with the dolphins, Fig. 447 a, the dark part of the designs is bordered and ornamented with fine white lines and dots. The central feature here is a kind of plant with lily-like stems bearing strange curved objects in place of the natural flowers. Bladder-shaped sprays, apparently buds, coil up from their bases. We have here a combination of natural vegetable forms with purely conventional excrescences curiously anticipatory of the later Palace Style of Knossos (L. M. II). But what makes this comparison the more suggestive is that the appendages, here added to the stems, are in fact borrowed from the blades of axes and recall in their ornamental zones a recurring feature of the sacral Double Axe blades on a parallel class of jars of the same late Palace Style.

The incorporation of this Minoan religious element in the design may perhaps account for the fact that this comparatively narrow-mouthed pitcher was used for the same

FIG 448. JAR WITH SCALLOPED HANDLES AND DOUBLE AXE PLANT, PACHYAMMOS.

Tangential Loops on M. M. Ill Vases.

sepulchral purpose as the jars and clay chests. As already noted, a series of complete double-axes surrounds the shoulders of a M. M. Ill burial jar from a grave at Mochlos.

The lobes or bladder-like offshoots of this mystic plant stand in a close relation to a geometrical pattern consisting of a disk with tangential loops, which also supplies

a transitional element of great value. In one shape or another this decorative unit constantly recurs throughout a large part of the Middle Minoan Age. In its simplest form, as a disk with two loops springing from it in reversed directions, inlaid examples of this pattern ornament the upper margin of a stone bowl from the Sacellum of the Early Palace at Phaestos. 1 A triple version is seen on a jug of the white on black style from Gournia, Fig. 449, a, probably belonging to the earlier phase of M. M III, while Fig.-149,, a jug from Zakro, shows a more elaborate rendering of this type. It will be seen at once that the fine embroidered white decoration of the triple sprays on this vase harmonizes in a remarkable manner with that depicted on the axe-blades' of the jar illustrated in Fig. 448." Both vessels which already present on their bodies the buff ground of the succeeding fashion are of absolutely contemporary date and
Decoration.

FIG. 449, a, b. M. M. Ill VASES, SHOWING TRIPLE TANGENTIAL MOTIVE.
must be included among the latest elements that can be placed on the M. M. Ill side of the border.

Their tangential lobes themselves supply an interesting link of transition Lin with to some of the finest works that illustrate the early phase of the First L. M. I Late Minoan style. On these the same dark bladder-like excrescences? recur, springing either in pairs or triplets from the central disk, in some cases, as on a fine amphora from Pseira, 2 picked out with a very similar embroidered work, at times, as on a beautiful clay rhyton from Zakro, 3 enclosing white lily sprays. But a novelty in technique in the former design, the use of the new red, shows that the frontiers of L. M. I have already been crossed.

1 See Man. Ant., xiv, p. 479, Fig. 87, p. 445, Fig. 60, 3.

2 See Excavations at Pseira, Crete, p. 33, Fig. 14.

3 See J. H. S., xxii, PI. XII, 3.

Hieroglyphic system superseded by advanced Linear Script A; Palace documents of M. M. Ill date; C lps with ink-written Inscriptions from Sanctuary site; Graffiti on Palace pottery of M. M. Ill date; Clay documents of Temple Repositories; Early form of tablets; Tablets from S. E. Insula 'talent and drachm signs; Ihisiness documents ivith numerals inventories; Clay roundels, inscribed and sealed; Gypsum chip used as trial piece, from Kasella; Lapidary inscriptions of religious character; Inscribed votive stone Ladles from Mountain Sanctuaries of Knossos; Clay Votive Ladle from Early Minoan deposit at Knossos; Specimens from votive stations on peak of Juktas and on foot-hill at Trillion; Recurring dedicatory formula on Trullos Ladle associatedwith Throne and Sceptre Sign; Similar formula on Libation Table from Psychro Cave; On Libation Table and Stone Clip from Palaikastro; Inscribed votive tablet of bronze from Psychro Cave; Name of Votary inscribed in characters of Class A parallel phenomenon on Votive Figurine from Tylissos; Ritual interpretation of signs on tablet oaoauy?? Triple aspect of Cult of Minoan Goddess; Dedicatory formula connected with Cradle, Temple, and Tomb of Cretan Zeus; Official adoption of neiv Script due to hieratic influences; General knowledge of Art of Writing Graffiti on Walls; Diffusion of script for commercial purposes to Melos, c.; Earlier anticipations of advanced Linear Script on Seal Stones; Systematization by Central Authority in M. M. Ill; Synopsis of Class

A; Comparisons between Linear and Hieroglyphic signaries; Compound and barred signs and Numeration; Relations of Linear Classes A and B evidences of overlapping.

Appear- THE series of inscribed vessels from the Palace stores and deposits, to Advanced which attention has been called in the Section relating to the pottery, brings us f ace to ace with a phenomenon of double import that makes itself apparent at this epoch. It is not only the increased use of the Art of Writing for the purposes of ordinary life that now strikes us, but the evidence of the introduction of an advanced linearized script, so divergent from the preceding Disuse of hieroglyphic system, that it is only in about a third of the signs that we are Hiero- able to trace a direct relation to it. The use of the Hieroglyphic class seems System, in fact to have ceased abruptly with the catastrophe of the close of M. M. 11- the Phaestos Disk, of which some account will be given below, 1 being extraneous to the systems in vogue in Minoan Crete.

The form of writing that now appears has been classified by me as Class A of the advanced Linear Script. As regards half its characters it essentially differs from Class B, which was current in the Knossian Palace in the epoch that preceded its fall at the close of L. M. II. The evidence of clay tablets brought to light at Hagia Triada and elsewhere tends to show that the Linear Script A was still generally current in Crete during the First

Palace

FIG. 450. M. M. Ill CUP WITH INK-WRITTEN INSCRIPTION. SLIGHTLY REDUCED.

Late Minoan Period. The inscribed material from Knossos has, on the other hand, a special value since it enables us, from the associations in which they were found, to ascribe a series of documents in this form of script to the Third Middle Minoan Period.

Of special value in this connexion are the two cups illustrated above in Cups with Fig. 4.31, with their inscriptions written on their inner clay in a kind of w n r j t ten dark ink, like sepia. The profile and make of these, as above noted, points inscrip-

Larger 1 See Section 30, p. 647 seqq. below. Cup.

THE PALACE OF MINOS, ETC.

to the earlier part of M. M. II I as the date of their fabric, and shows that by that time this form of script was already fully developed. A view of the interior of the larger cup is given in Fig. 450. Since we may assume that the inscription was made to read continuously, and that it breaks off after running round about two-thirds of the outer margin of the cup, it seems best

FIG. 451. a, INSCRIPTION INSIDE LARGER CUP; , REDUCED TO NORMAL LETTERS OF CLASS A.

to assume that the three signs at the bottom represent its initial group. On this assumption is based the reproduction given in Fig. 451, a, where the characters are arranged according to their successive zones in three horizontal lines.

The difficulty of writing by means of a brush or, if we may judge from the execution of some of the characters, with a soft reed pen on a concave surface accounts for a certain amount of irregularity in the signs. As reduced to more or less normal types of this system they are therefore repeated in Fig. 451, 6. 1

According to the universal rule in both classes of the advanced linear inscrip-script, the characters run from left to right like later writing. In both the uf Linear Scripts A and B, moreover, contrary to the arrangement in vogue R 8 ht in the Minoan Hieroglyphic system as well as in the Egyptian, Babylonian, and Hittite, the animate forms are not set in the direction of the beginning of each group, facing as it were the spectator, but follow the course of the

FIG. 452. a, INK-WRITTEN INSCRIPTION INSIDE SMALLER M. M. Ill CUP. KNOSSOS. b, INSCRIPTION RENDERED IN NORMAL FORMS OF LINEAR CLASS A.

inscription. Thus in the above example we see the flying bird sign turned to the right in every case. The same is true of the two-legged figure in the final group of the other cup. The Phaestos Disk, on the other hand, of which a short account is given in the succeeding Section, 2 follows the older, Oriental and Egyptian tradition, and both the human and animal figures face counter to the direction of the writing.

The inscription in the shallower cup is literally reproduced, as arranged inscrip- ir e - i A TT A KO tion on horizontally in Fig.452, rt, andis repeated in normal formsof Class A in hig.452,0, shallower 1 Sign 3, which is clearly misshapen, is 22 does not seem to correspond with any (known sign. There are initial or dividing marks before 4, 6, and n. The dividing marks of line 3 seem to have been abraded, but we may assume that it consisted of more than one sign-group.

2 See below, p. 647 seqq.

restored as a variant of a type otherwise known in Class A and which often recurs in Class B; possibly a derivation from a pictographofalily,

Ylt "V 20, if rightly restored, is in a reversed position. 2 1 may be a repetition of i. THE PALACE OF MINOS, ETC.

though it will be seen that the nearest comparisons to characters 5 and 6 supplied by the tablets show considerable variation. The three larger signs to the right are a good deal abraded, but there can be little doubt that the first of these must be identified with a remarkable sign showing two human legs with an axe-like appendage, which recurs on some of the Hagia Triada tablets. It is there at times accompanied by a parallel figure with the same axe-like appendage below the neck, which gives it the appearance of wings, but with the outlines of a flounced skirt below. 1 We must regard the present sign therefore as the male form of a pair of symbolical figures. (See Table, Fig. 476, Nos. 89, 90.)

These signs may certainly be regarded as having a sacral character, and in this connexion the position in which the cups were found has a Site? 1 Y certain relevance. They had been placed with other vessels on a later clay Inscribed Cups found on Graffiti on Palace Pots; M. M. Ill date.

FIG. 453. GRAFFITO INSCRIPTION ON M. M. JAR.

floor above the early Crypt with the monolithic pillars described above. 2 It was on the early floor of this Crypt, which we may regard as the basement of a pillar sanctuary, that the M. M. I polychrome vase in the form of a dove was discovered, 3 that has been brought above into a ritual connexion with the cult of the Minoan Goddess. That the inscriptions on these cups had a religious character, perhaps of a dedicatory nature, is very probable. We may also, by way of analogy, recall the modern Arabic bowls within which are inscribed extracts from the Koran, imparting a talismanic virtue to their contents.

The numerous graffiti inscriptions of the same class brought to light on pottery within the Palace precincts were almost without exception clearly 1 On a remarkable tablet from Hagia Triada the male form, followed by numerals = 60, is associated with the prow of a ship followed by numerals = 30, while the flounced type has the appearance of holding out a bar terminating in a curved line (the lower part incomplete). Taken in connexion with the ship sign, this may naturally be interpreted as an anchor. If this identification be correct, it would seem that the fully developed metal anchor was already in use on Minoan ships. In Homer we still find the primitive usage of letting down heavy stones (. i. 436, iv. 77; Od. i. 137, xv. 498). This figure is followed by numerals = 18. The decimal signs on this tablet are of the later form.

2 See above, p. 146, and Fig. 100.

3 See above, p. 146, Fig. 107.

dated by the circumstances of their discovery to the latest M. M. Ill phase. The first clue to the existence of this earlier type of advanced linear script was in fact supplied by the graffito inscription on a very characteristic M. M. Ill b jar from the S. W. Basement, exhibiting features divergent from those normally presented by tablets belonging to the last period of the Palace (Class B), which afforded the only material at that time available (Fig. 453).

On a fragment of a large store jar found with quantities of M. M. Ill sherds in the S. E. Rubbish Heap was a graffito inscription which is not complete, but contains two characters that recur in a similar graffito inscription beneath the rim of a pithos that stood in a later Magazine at Phaestos. 2 In the same heap occurred handles and fragments with single signs, analogous to those already given in connexion with the Melian bird-vases from the Temple Repositories. 3 Among the large clay jugs of Cretan fabric found in these was one presenting a graffito inscription on the upper part of its rim. The inscription was poorly preserved, but three upright strokes beneath the terminal sign ' J may be taken to be an indication of its contents or capacity.

As already mentioned the Repositories also contained clay documents of Clay various forms. These consisted of an oblong tablet, Fig. 454, labels, and men ts in disks with seal-impressions round their exterior margin. The large hoard Ke p os-of clay sealings, some of the types of which are given below, was also found with these, and may have been originally attached to documents on perishable materials, relating to the sanctuary to which the whole deposit belonged.

The clay tablet, Fig. 454, is a typical example of the earlier and simpler Early form of those presenting the Linear Script A. As contrasted with the bulk-fabletof of the later specimens of this class may be noted its better baking, small size,: near A its well-squared outline and section (Fig. 454, c), and the brevity of the inscription. Among the numerals too, a pellet here stands for the decimal sign, as in the Hieroglyphic series. On the great majority of the tablets of the present class, this is replaced by-, universally employed for 10 in the 1 See Jfftossos, Report, 1901, pp. 10, n. The The Knossian fragment, with other epigraphic fourth and fifth characters, however, are there remains of the advanced linear classes, will not quite rightly reproduced. 4

seems to be appear in the second volume of my Scripta a variant of No. 3 of Table, Fig. 476; 5 perhaps Minoa.

a variant of No. 2 of the Table. See above, p. 561, Fig. 408.

2 Pernier, Man. Ant., 1902, p. 98, Fig. 32.

THE PALACE OF MINOS, ETC.

Linear Class B. Otherwise the hundreds, represented by circles, and the units by short upright lines, conform to the system prevalent in both the later classes. The total sum given on 0 = 95 J, that on b = 240. Con- The tablet form of inscription, which was undoubtedly due to Syrian or with Later Anatolian influence, had already existed, as we have seen, in the days of Types.

Tablets from S. E. Insula.

Hieroglyphic Script, 2 but the shape is wider in proportion to its height. The later tablets of the Linear Class A, such as those from Hagia Triada, though preserving as a rule the same form as Fig. 454, are usually larger and often contain much fuller inscriptions. We shall also have occasion to note in this connexion that a clay tablet of Class A, found

Fig. 454. CLAY TABLET FROM TEMPLE REPOSITORY ( ).

in association with the Phaestos Disk and M. M. Ill pottery, 3 closely corresponds in type with that from the Temple Repository. The tablets of Class B, on the other hand, peculiar so far to the later Palace at Knossos, show a greater variety of shape and a more considerable range in size. The great mass of them are wide in proportion to their height, and nearly all of them seem to have been simply dried in the sun.

Remains of two tablets of the same early class and form as that from the Temple Repository occurred in a small gallery flanking the Sanctuary area of the S. E. Insula (see Plan, Fig. 418 above). These were found on the pavement, answering to the neighbouring M. III b floors of the bordering structures, and must therefore be also referred to the present

The copy of this inscription given in Knossos, Report. 1903 (B. S. A., ix, p. 52) is inaccurate in some particulars.

2 See above, p. 278, Fig. 209, and Scripta

Minoa, I, PI. X, p. 120 (Knossos), and PI. XI, p. 121 (Phaestos).

3 See below, p. 648, Fig. 480.

Period. One of these is shown in Fig. 455, a. It appears to have been of the typical square shape, and the inscription is perfect with the exception of the initial sign. It is interesting from the occurrence here for the first time of the balance, so well represented on the tablets of Class B, belonging to the later Palace, where it is repeatedly associated with the ingot sign. 1 It is also found on the later tablets of Class A at Hagia Triada. The balance is here accompanied by vertical strokes = 3 and a compound sign followed by numerals = 5. This compound sign consists of- reversed, coupled with another in the shape of a fore-arm and open hand. The- 2 accompanied by numbers also occurs on a Knossian tablet of the later class above the ingot sign, 3 and had therefore some relation to weight

FIG. 455, a, b i, l 2. TABLETS FROM CORRIDOR BY S. E. INSULA.

or value. But, in such a relation, the hand sign with which it is linked may naturally be interpreted as having a fractional signification parallel to that indicated by the Greek

Spaxw or handful. That the Minoans possessed Talent a system of weights in which the balance or 'talent the Greek rdxavrov formed a higher unit is clear. From this tablet we may infer that there was signs, also a Minoan drachm.

With this was found part of another tablet inscribed on both sides and apparently of similar form (Fig. 455, b i, b 2). The hand and arm here recurs in ligature in the penultimate sign of b 2: it is probable the four small marks repeated here after the final character represent tens. On the third line of b i we see the same sign that terminates the inscription of the Repository jar already referred to, associated, as there, with three upright strokes 1 See on this my Minoan Ueights and Currency Corolla Numismatica, p. 361 seqq.

2 This is the Cypriote syllabic sign for fa.

3 Of. fit., p. 356, Fig. ii, 2.

THE PALACE OF MINOS, ETC.

Business Documents with Numerals.

signifying units. As in that case the amount clearly referred to the contents, we must assume a similar reference to quantity in the present instance.

The numerals that appear on all the clay tablets of the above series show that we have to do with business documents recording the amounts of divers possessions, and the same conclusion holds good of the later tablets of Class A brought to light in considerable abundance at Hagia Triada. There, moreover, we occasionally find pictorial figures such as ships, chariots, the saffron flower, looms, talents, tripods, and vases that enable us to identify the character of the property referred to on these documents. In the case of the tablets of Class B found in the later Palace these graphic illustrations of their contents become still more frequent.

Clay Roundels', Inscribed and Sealed.

FIG. 456, a, b, c. SEALED CLAY ROUNDELS FROM TEMPLE REPOSITORY.

With the square tablet in the Temple Repository were also found specimens of another smaller class of document to which the name of clay roundel may be applied containing solitary signs or single groups, the circumference of which, originally of a more or less circular form, is impressed with a series of seal impressions (Fig. 45(5, a, b, c). 1 Thus t, the sign on which does not seem to recur elsewhere, bears round its edges nine impressions of a signet showing an Agrimi or Cretan wild goat, couchant with its head turned back, a, the first sign of which is imperfect, presents on the part of the border that is preserved impressions of three seal-stones. One of these is a seated bull; the others, of which two impressions are seen in each case, are of special interest from their associations. One is the cruciform sign +, which also occurs as the sole type of a series of clay sealings 1 The first sign on a is completed in dotted lines. The impressed edges of this had been a good deal broken away.

from the Repositories. 1 The other roundel c, showing five rectangular prominences, 2 affords an example of the same signet type as that of which impressions were found on the store jar described above 3 found in the Magazine of the Medallion Pithoi, and which represents the conventionalized fa ade of a building. Similar clay roundels' sealed in the same way have been found, at times in a slightly later, L. M. I association at Gournia, Zakro, Hagia Triada and elsewhere, some with somewhat fuller graffito inscriptions and occasionally with numbers. Thus Fig. 457, a, b, from

Gournia given here for comparison, which is inscribed on both sides, bears on its reverse numbers = 5. It has five impressions round its border representing the hind part of an animal, apparently a bull.

FIG. 457, a, b. INSCRIBED CLAY ROUNDEL FROM GOURNIA WITH SEAL IMPRESSIONS.

It seems probable that these sealed roundels' represented obligations of some sort undertaken by the person or persons whose signet impressions they bore.

A curious inscribed object of which mention has already been made, Gypsum brought out amidst the rubble remains beneath the later floor of a Kasella of as Trial the Thirteenth Magazine, brings us face to face with a very important class of J lapidary inscriptions, associated here and elsewhere with M. M. Ill deposits. This was a fragment of a gypsum slab that had been used in a casual way by some Minoan workman as a kind of trial piece on which to practise the engraving of characters in the contemporary linear script. For this purpose he had, as a guide, very irregularly scratched what were evidently intended to be three horizontal lines within which to incise the characters (Fig. 458).

1 See above, p. 515, Fig. 374. " The sign on this to the right is No. 60 of the Table, Fig. 476 below. The other character is probably the 'throne and sceptre, No. 52, but turned to the right as in Class B.

See above, Fig. 410, and compare Fig. 411.

Deducting accidental scratches and the guiding lines, the inscription seems to have been much as shown in Fig. 459. As might be expected, it presents anomalous features, thus the third sign of the upper row which otherwise resembles a common linear character of Class A, is here differentiated by horns. The hand sign appears to recur twice in ligature. 1

FIG. 458. TRIAL PIECE OF GYPSUM WITH INSCRIBED CHARACTERS FROM KASELLA OF THIRTEENTH MAGAZINE.

FIG. 459. TRANSCRIPTION OF SIGNS ON FIG. 458.

Lapidary Such lapidary inscriptions had a special vogue in connexion with vessels tiontof of a ritual ancl votive character. Good illustrations of this are supplied

Religious by a particular class associated with the High Places of Knossos. Already racter. in the course of preliminary explorations of the rugged steep within the temenos and the actual precincts of what has proved to be the Peak

Sanctuary of Minoan Knossos, carried out in 1896, I had found fragments of 1 In the lower line it may be compounded with reversed. Compare the terminal sign of Fig. 455, a.

limestone vessels of a peculiar type. These vessels, which have a pointed inscribed spade-like outline with a shallow basin within (see below, Fig. 401) and are stone about 10 centimetres by 8 in dimensions, have the appearance of ladles J es the handles of which have become atrophied by their use for votive Sane-purposes. Clay ladles, some with comparatively short handles, are of frequent occurrence in the Neolithic deposits of Knossos and they appear amongst other vessels of ritual usage besides the primitive clay horns of consecration in the Early Minoan votive deposit of Mochlos.

1

Recent supplementary-excavations in the Loom-Weight Area at Knossos 2 Votive revealed, beneath a plaster floor of M. M. la date, a stratum, probably of the le last Early Minoan Period, in which together with remains of cups and other f m pottery of that date 3 was found the remarkable clay vessel, Fig. 40. Although brought out in a friable condition and somewhat distorted, its spade-like shape is clearly preserved and it unquestionably supplies the immediate prototype of the stone laohes' associatedavith the High Places of Knossos, and which, as will be sncnvn, belong to j l. M. III. That this clay vessel had also a religious destination may be inferred. We are tempted to recall the sacramental spoons used in the Oriental Catholic rites.

In 1909, as noticed above, I imjdejfcqjjk the excavatiof jtthe structure on the summit ridge 4 at the spot which later traditipn field to be fhe Holy Sepulchre of the Cretan Zeus. It provg in fact to be a Casa Santa of the Minoan Goddess. Here, in the" red stratum, amongst votive objects of the M. M. 111 Period, was brought out a fragmentary specimen of a similar limestowe-velssel much injured by fire, upon which were decipherable two linear characters 5 and traces of a third (Fig. 461).

But a much fuller inscription occurred on a votive stone ladle of similar form and material that was brought to light, in this case, too, amidst M. M. Ill pottery, in a lower sanctuary of the same cult, situated on a foothill at Trullos near Arkhanes, an important Minoan centre with a small Palace of its own, 6 and a natural starting-place for pilgrimages to the Peak 1 See Seager, Mochlos, p. 82, and above 4 See above, p. 154 seqq.

P- 57 Fig. 16, a, b. 5 The first character, which is of constant : Executed for me by Dr. Mackenzie in Sep- recurrence, is certainly derived from thedouble- temberiqzo. Dr. Mackenzie regards the early axe sign (Table, Fig. 476, below, No. 29). The deposit that contained the ladle as consisting second is found on the H. Triada tablets of of filling material. Class A, and also on Knossian tablets of Class B.

The cups had two bands round the rim and (Table, No. 28, variant.) The third seems to answeredtothee. M. Ill version of the Knossian be No. 67 of the Table.

type reproduced above on p. 73, Fig. 40. (The The orthostatic limestone facade of this cup in the top row and the first of the second) building underlies the house-fronts of a main.

THE PALACE OF MINOS, ETC.

inscribed Sanctuary of Juktas, as is the modern town to its Christian successor on the height, the Chapel of Avthentes Christas. A view of the ladle, showing the inscription round the margin, is seen in Fig. 462. The vessel, otherwise rounded, was flattened in the centre below so as to enable it to stand easily. A copy of the inscription in two horizontal lines with one or two of the characters completed in dotted outlines is given in Fig. 463.

from Trullos.

FIG. 460.   VOTIVE CLAY LADLE FROM EARLY MINOAN DEPOSIT BE-NEATH LOOM WEIGHT AREA, KNOSSOS. (c.)

FIG. 461.   BURNT FRAGMENT OF VOTIVE LIMESTONE LADLE, WITH TRACES OF LINEAR INSCRIPTION, PEAK SANCTUARY OF JUKTAS.

It seems originally to have consisted of twenty-four signs, and marks of division are visible after 6 and 10. Several of the characters, e. g. 3, 4, 6, 10, 12, 13, 14, and

22 show forms typical of Class A. 21, which is uncertain, may be a flower sign. 7 at the beginning of a group of four has a special Throne interest since it is, with one decadent exception, 1 the only example in an Sceptre mscn P t on of this class placed here in a reversed position of a character Sign. very prominent among the tablets of Class B found in the later Palace street of Arkhanes. This discovery is due to Hagia Triada. What appears to be a variant the acute observation of my overseer, Em- type of throne sign without the crook is manuel Akumianakis. common on tablets of Class A (see Table, 1 Another example occurs on a tablet from Fig. 476, No. 53).

at Knossos, which I have ventured to identify with a throne and crook or sceptre, seen in profile. A comparative series of these showing successive degradations from the original type is given in Fig. 464. The final degeneration might be taken for the letters Ti!

This comparison ma- be taken to show that the hill shrine of Trullos stood in a special relation to the Palace. The sign-group 11-14 is of still greaterimportance from the fact that it recurs totidetn litter is in a prominent position on the most interesting of all Minoan cult objects, the black steatite Libation Table from the Cave Sanctuary of Psychro on Mount Lasithi, a few hours from the site of Karnessos, 1 as Lyktos was known to the in-FIG. 462. LADLE-SHAPED VESSEL OF LIMESTONE FROM TRULLOS,,-;,, nr. llc cr 4r Tf ic WITH INSCRIPTION OF LINEAR CLASS A (indeed difficult to doubt that it must be identified with the reputed Birth Cave of the Cretan Zeus according to the Lyktian tradition preserved by Hesiod. 2 The large fragments of the Libation Table, of which a restored representation is given in Fig. 4(i5, was obtained by me in 1896 3 from the base of the Votive deposit.

to the Eastern promontory of the island. The Psychro Cave was, par excellence, the Mountain Cave Sanctuary of the Lyktos district.

3 See Further Discoveries of Cretan, erv. Script, J. H. S., xvii, p. 350 seqq.; Myc. Tree and Pillar Cult, p. 14 seqq. (J. H. S., xxi, p. 112

Recurring Dedicatory Formula.

Appearance of Identical Sign-group on Psychro Libation Table.

- Theogonia, 11. 477 seqq. The cave to which Rhea is made to speed with the infant Zeus is placed Atyaiu) iv "pei (1. 484), a name unknown to later geographers, but it is also described as in Dikta, which in historical times was confined

THE PALACE OF MINOS, ETC.

It consists of the remains of a three-cupped altar slab of black steatite, originally supported on four legs, with a central projecting disk below

FIG. 4(53- INSCRIPTION OF VOTIVE LADLE FROM TRULLOS, HORIZON-TALLY ARRANGED.

to rest upon the sacred stone or omphalos in other words the fiairvxos of the divinity, in this case, possibly, one of the stalagmitic cones from the

FIG. 464. THRONE AND SCEPTRE SIGN OF CLASS B AND SUCCESSIVE DEGENERATIONS.

cavern floor itself. Parts of the inscription, in the Linear Class A, remain and afforded the first monumental evidence of the developed Cretan script. 1 seqq.), where the survival of this baetylic altar form is shown in that of the later KOINON KPHTON. See, too, Scripta Minoa, i,

PP- I3-I5-

The discovery by shepherds in this cave of various votive relics, such as human and animal figures of bronze and clay, miniature bronze double-axe blades, and other weapons, led to its preliminary investigation by Prof. F. Halbherrand Dr. Hatzidakis in 1886 (Mitseo di Ant. Classifa, ii, p. 217 seqq. and PI. XIII). From 1894 onwards I visited the cave on repeated occasions and, apart from the result of my partial excavation of 1896, obtained from the peasants a considerable series of objects, now in the Ashmolean Museum. But the circumstances of the island rendered methodical excavation impossible till 1900, when Dr. Hogarth (working for the British School at Athens and the Cretan Exploration Fund) removed a vast superincumbent mass of fallen rocks and carried out a thorough exploration of the remains, not only in the entrance hall of the cave, but in the deep-lying lower grot withits stalagmitic pillars and subterranean pool. (The Dictaean Cave, B. S. A., vi, p. 94 seqq.) 1 See my Further Discoveries of Cretan, 6-v. Script, J. H. S., xvii, p. 350 seqq.

This remarkable relic was found in the Western bay of the great Libation entrance hall or Upper Grot, about two metres down, on the original floor of, ab I 1,, the Cave. It lay at the bottom of a votive or sacrificial deposit consisting Sacrificial of earth much blackened with carbonized materials, ashes, the bones of oxen,

FIG. 465. THE PSYCHRO LIBATION TABLE, RESTORED. (J (.) swine, and goats, together with the horn of an Agrimi or Cretan wild goat a foot and half in length. In this deposit, which proved to have a considerable extension, were also found quantities of pottery and other relics, including the votive double-axe blade and the stepped base, executed in the same black steatite as the Libation Table, which have been illustrated in

THE PALACE OF MINOS, ETC.

Fig. 315 above. It is to be observed that the lowest stratum, beneath which the fragment of the Table lay, contained M. M. Ill painted sherds, some with plant designs white on dark.

In the immediately adjoining area to the East, explored by Mr. Hogarth in the course of his methodical excavation of the Cave in 1900, there came to

FIG. 466. REMAINING PART OF INSCRIBED LIBATION TABLE OF BLACK STEATITE. ( ) light an altar-like structure of roughly squared stones, about which were remains of a series of smaller libation vessels, the earlier also of black steatite and with single cups surrounded by a raised rim, exactly resembling those of the Temple Repository. One of these presents three linear signs. 1 1 Hogarth, op, tit., p. 114, Fig. 50. Two of the characters are of abnormal form.

The triple receptacle indicated by the remains of the larger Table Triple corresponds with the triple aspect of the cult of this Cave Sanctuary, as cie for to which remarkable evidence is supplied by a votive bronze plate de- Libations, scribed below. The custom of offering threefold libation itself goes back to the earliest religious stratum of Greece. 1 According to the old Arcadian rite recorded in the Odyssey the dead before the falls of Styx were appeased by a triple libation:

TTXora fjKXlkptJTQ), i T 7T lta Sf rjsfi OlvO t

TO rpirov avo vsart.-

The chthonic aspects of the Minoan cult, to which attention has already been called, tend to strengthen these comparisons, and the offering of the
U.-i
FIG. 467. INSCRIPTION ON PSYCHRO LIBATION TABLE.
fj. f tkprjra would have been specially appropriate in the Cave where, according to the legend, the infant Zeus was fed by the Nymphs with mingled milk and honey. 3
A small fragment showing traces of three characters brought to light in inscrip-the same sacrificial deposit by Monsieur J. Demargne of the French School Libation at Athens in 1897, at a spot a little South of that in which the larger part of Table-the Libation Table occurred, and a cast of it kindly supplied by the finder, shows that it fitted on to its upper margin, with which it is incorporated in the photographic Figure 466. It appears, therefore, that there were originally two lines of inscription, both running from left to right, and arranged from the same point of view, possibly an indication that the table was set against the Cavern wall. The characters in their essential forms are reproduced in Fig. 467. i, 6, and 7 of the lower line can be completed with sufficient certainty. The smaller sign 8 above 7 is abnormal, and 2 which is 1 See my Further Discoveries of Cretan, t.
. ff. S., ii, p. 358.- Od. 519; xi. 27. 3 Diod. v. 70. For the ritual presentation of the miraculous nurture of the infant by she-goat and bee Amalthea and Melissa cf. Lactantius, De Falsa Jteligione, i. 21, 22.
THE PALACE OF MINOS, ETC.
Further Recurrence of
Palai-kastro Table.
unique bears a certain resemblance to the Egyptian festival sign. Of special interest in connexion with the Mountain cult of Knossos, however, is the second group YY2i w hich corresponds with that presented by the group of signs 11-14 on the votive stone ladle from Trullos. The first two characters of this group appear in an inscription, also of the Linear Class A, incised on a black steatite libation table with a single, rimmed cup and stepped base found in a cave near Palaikastro. 1 Eighteen signs are visible on the upper surface of this table of which face n, as shown in my copy,
FIG. 468. INSCRIPTION OF LINEAR CLASS A ON STEATITE LIBATION TABLE FROM CAVE, PALAIKASTRO.
Fig- 468, begins with the first two signs of this group M f, though unfortunately the narrow part of the margin which should have contained its completion is broken away. The Palaikastro cave stands in a near relation to the later site of the Dictaean Temple of the Cretan Zeus, and it is interesting to note that a good specimen of a mottled steatite table of similar type, though apparently uninscribed, was obtained by me in 1894 from the Knoll of Tartar! in the striking cleft of Arvi on the South Coast, 2 where in 1 B. S. A., xii, p. 2. The remains of the table were found by Mr. C. T. Currelly. The cave was later used for L. M. Ill larnax burials, but the inscribed libation table is clearly of the same date as that of Psychro which in turn is equated with those of the Temple Repository of Knossos (M. M. Ill b).
Near Viano. The libation table is now in the Ashmolean Museum.

later times was a sanctuary of the indigenous God under the name of Zeus Arbios.
1 The steatite libation tables found in the Temple Repository and elsewhere in the
Palace Sanctuary of Knossos were of the same class.

It is also a remarkable coincidence that a fragment of a steatite cup," Also on
found at Palaikastro itself in the course of the excavations by the British cup." School,
presents an incised inscription of four characters (Fig. 469), three of which correspond
with those of the MX A I, except that the last sign is shown in a reverse position. The
first sign of this, which here replaces the

FIG. 469. SIGN-GROUP ON STEATITE CUP, PALAIKASTRO.

, is derived below (Fig. 477 D) from the double-axe symbol. That the cup belonged
to a votive class seems highly probable.

In all these cases we seem to have to do with dedicatory inscriptions, These and it
may well be asked if the recurring sign-group f 1 A A I and the last tory mentioned
formula which so largely repeats it may not contain an actual reference to the Minoan
divinity with whom the cult was associated. with Cult f.,.-.,.,, ofminoan

A comparison oi the relics found alike in the Cave Sanctuary or on the Goddess.
crags of Juktas, and it may be added in the Palace of Knossos itself, points in fact to a
fundamental identity of worship. In the Cave, indeed, the votive clay figurines of the
peak-shrine are largely replaced by bronze, and 1 Steph. Byz., s. v. at Palaikastro.
The inscription has been pub-

The fragment seems to have belonged to lished in connexion with ihe Trullos vessel
by a specimen of a class of single-handled steatite Dr. S. Xanthudides in E. "Ap.,
1909, p. 192, cups with a spout opposite the handle, common Fig. 6.

THE PALACE OF MINOS, ETC.

Bronze
Votive
Tablet from
Psychro
Cave.

the single limbs and pathological specimens of the Petsofa class are wanting. On the
other hand, a votive male figure of bronze found with female images of faience by the
South Propylaeum at Knossos, and, in a grander way, the contents of the Repositories
themselves point, like the miniature axes of its shrines, to a votive cult within the
walls of the Palace very similar to that of Psychro. The double axes and other votive
weapons discovered by Mr. Hogarth in the lower vault of the Cave wedged into the
natural pillars of stalagmite find, as already noticed, 1 a ritual parallel in the double
axes

FIG. 470. BRONZE VOTIVE TABLET FROM PSYCHRO CAVE.

stuck into the shafts of the Knossian shrine seen in the early wall-painting a feature
taken over by Mycenae.

Interesting information as to the character of the worship with which the Psychro
Libation Table was associated is supplied by a small bronze tablet found some years
back in the votive deposit of the Cave and reproduced for the first time 2 in Fig. 470. It
is a thin oblong plate with rude designs executed in repouss outlines. Its double border
of short bars a pattern in its origin of textile derivation offers a distinct parallelism

with that of the well-known painted stucco tablet of L. M. I date 3 presenting a scene of worship from the Acropolis of Mycenae, itself of a votive character.

1 See above, p. 444.

2 This object, with other relics obtained by me during my early visits to Psychro, is now in the Ashmolean Museum.

3 See G. Rodenwaldt, Votivpinax aus Mykenai (Mitt, d. k. d. Arch. Inst., 1912, p. 129 seqq.).

From a small rivet-hole preserved in its upper left-hand corner, the bronze tablet had been evidently fastened to some object, probably of wood.

We see here a triple group of sacral horns, that in the middle larger than the others, with sprays rising behind them, while beneath the central of these is what appears to be an altar of oblong shape standing before a tree, the branches of which bend downwards. To the left 1 of this is a fish, and perched on the top of the spray that springs from the horns on that side is-a bird of disproportionate size, and in which from its outline we must recognize a dove. The clearly marked collar round its neck enables us, indeed, to go further and identify it with a ring-dove or wood-pigeon (Colnmba balumbus. Immediately below its beak is an oval object with a

FIG. 471. SIGNS ON BRONZE TABLET COMPARED WITH FORMS OF LINEAR CLASS A AND HIEROGLYPHS.

central dot. Above the dove in the upper corner of the tablet is the rayed symbol of the sun, and in the opposite corner the crescent moon.

To the right below, as seen in Fig. 470, is a rude male figure, naked s K of except for his girdle, who seems to be engaged in an ecstatic dance, with his an d right arm flung backwards and his left raised, open-handed, as if in the harac- 1 attitude of adoration. What is specially remarkable is that beneath his right ters of hand two linear signs are clearly incised, a, b of Fig. 471. The first of these, as shown in the comparative Table, Fig. 47G (32), is an offshoot of the Serpent sign of the Hieroglyphic signary, 2 which occasionally occurs in a similar shape in the Linear Script A. The second is a degradation, also not unexampled, of a sign common to the two linear scripts which would appear to be derived from a dolphin's head. 3 In the signs thus grouped we may with great probability recognize the Votive personal name of the votary. That, to ensure, as it were, the. recognition of i gure the votive image by the divinity, it was thought well to inscribe his name-fyiissos, with name 1 For the sake of convenience the direction clearer. On the face it is naturally reversed.? in-is given, as seen in Fig. 470, taken from the Scripia Minoa, p. 211, No. 84. back of the plate, where the outlines show See Table, p. 642, Fig. 476, No. 42.

THE PALACE OF MINOS, ETC.

Flying Bird Sign repeated on Psychro Tablet.

Suggested Ritual Interpretation.

Triple Symbols of Cult on Tablet; either on it or in close association with it, is a religious phenomenon constantly illustrated by Greek avaqr iara, and there also exists a contemporary Minoan parallel to this practice. A clay male figurine of the votive class found at Tylissos near Knossos (Fig. 472) bears upon it two incised characters, also of the Linear Class A, in which we are entitled by widespread analogies also to recognize a personal name. It recalls in fact the numerous bronze votive figurines found at Dodona inscribed with the names of the persons who dedicated them.

The use of the script here, as in later times, to fix the identity of the votary is in this case, however, supplemented by a still more remarkable phenomenon. Above the central horns, and on either side of the spray proceeding from them, appears another character, the flying bird, here set in an upward direction, which is of constant recurrence in the advanced linear scripts, but here most nearly corresponds with the simplified forms of Class A. 1 May we not in the repetition of this sign recognize some actual formula of devotion or adoration? The characters themselves are directed upwards in an abnormal way. The iteration, indeed, suggests the ritual orgiastic cry OXoxv-yrj or A a d of the old Anatolian cult 2 to which that of Minoan Crete was so closely allied, and the ritual of which was taken over by the local Rhea from its older Goddess.

This comparison may even give a hint as to the phonetic value of the sign that is here repeated. 2 In the present case, the central object of cult, emphasized by the disproportionate scale on which it is drawn, and saluted by the votary, is the

FIG. 472. INSCRIBED CLAY FIGURE OF VOTARY FROM TYLISSOS.

1 The flying bird of the linear signaries is certainly an eagle, the flying eagle being a constantly recurring symbol, probably of an amuletic nature, on a class of lentoid gems common throughout Central and Eastern Crete about the close of M. M. Ill and in the immediately succeeding Late Minoan Period. In this connexion, too, it is interesting to note that it survived on the early coinage of Lyktos (Svoronos, Numismatique de la Crete andenne, PI. Ill, 4 seqq.) as the special symbol of the native Zeus.

2 See on this, C. Theander, OXoxvyr; tinda, Eranus, xv, p. 99 seqq.

dove perched on the symbolic tree. This is of the greatest religious Tree, moment. It is the ritual equivalent of the birds perched on the leafy shafts owe. 1 of the sacred Double Axes on the Hagia Triada Sarcophagus, 1 of the doves resting on the capitals of the miniature pillar shrine, and of those which in the case of the gold relics from the Mycenae Shaft Grave poise, not only on the altar horns, but on the actual votary. 2 In all these instances, as pointed out above, we must recognize by the light of primitive religious ideas the visible sign of possession by the divinity, who, on the tablet and the pillar shrines is no other than the Great Minoan Goddess in her aspect as Lady of the Dove, while the fish brings in her marine attribution. 3 The celestial signs above help to complete her attributes.

The prominence here of the tree-cult illustrated by the sprays rising between the horns, and the central tree behind the altar apparently a pine-is noteworthy. It points to a time when the forest growth of Finns maritima that still clothes part of the Lasethi uplands had stretched about the Cave Sanctuary itself and supplied the Goddess with a sacred Grove.

The tree, dove, and fish, which here appear as the vehicles of divine possession, aptly symbolize her dominion of earth, air, and sea. The triple group of sacral horns further emphasize the threefold aspect of the cult which also explains the triple basin of the Libation Table. So, too, we see the pillar shrines of the Goddess like that of the Knossian wall-painting, regularly divided into three compartments.

At Knossos, indeed, the idea of the old religious relationship was never Dedica-entirely lost, and the name of the House of Rhea clung to the last to muia the ruined foundations amidst her Cypress Grove, 4 which we can hardly fail thus con- . nected to identify with the Great Palace. Elsewhere, however, and notably on the with neighbouring peak, the intrusive Greek element seems to have been instrumental in transferring the old holy places to her son, imperfectly assimilated as the mortal Zeus of Crete. It is certainly a significant coinci-dence that ritual vessels bearing this dedicatory formula should have been thus unearthed on sites associated by the Hellenic tradition with his temple, his cradle, and his tomb, but we must seek its interpretation in the light of the earlier, matriarchal aspect of Minoan religion.

1 See above, p. 440, Fig. 317. 4 Diod. Hist. lib. v. 66 TOVTOVS Bi (Tmiras) 2 See above, p. 220, Fig. 166, r; p. 224, r js K PUG-UK xapa X ta ""I 0 7? rtl oirovirtp in Fig. 1G9. (cat vw Scucrvrat 0ci Aia Peas oivojrcsa"

: l It is not necessary here to enlarge on the Kvirapimav oao-os IK iraxaiov XP VOV avfij. cvor.

interesting comparisons on the Syrian side On the fresco panel found in the Palace, suggested by this combination of the fish and depicting the sacred grove and dance, the trees the dove. seem to be olives.

THE PALACE OF MINOS, ETC.

Widespread use of Script A for Religious Dedications.

Suggests that

Hieratic Agencies promoted its Adoption for Official and

Business Purposes.

General Knowledge of Writing shown by Recurring Graffiti on Domestic Pots.

Graffito Inscriptions on Walls.

Example from H. Triada.

Other inscribed libation tables of steatite and veined limestone have occurred in East Crete, one with a high base, from the votive site of Petsoflt, and a second example from Palaikastro. The latter contained inscriptions on four sides of the rim, of which some thirty-two signs are fairly preserved. Enough in fact has already been brought to light to show that the new script was copiously used for dedicatory inscriptions on votive and religious vessels. At Knossos we see ink-written formulas on the cups found above the early pillar shrine. In the neighbouring settlement at Tylissos, besides tablets, we have seen that a votive male figure of terra-cotta came to light with four incised signs of this Class.

The extensive use of this script for religious objects suggests that its introduction as an official medium may have been due to some new hieratic current. That it was widely employed for purposes of business is clear, however, from the numerous clay documents relating to various classes of possessions such as those referred to above, and the accounts attached to these. Such documents have been discovered at a series of sites throughout Central and Eastern Crete, l and about a hundred clay tablets of this class at Hagia Triada, in particular, were brought to light, though these elate mostly from the succeeding L. M. I Period.

But the occurrence of so many vessels belonging to ordinary household stores with graffito inscriptions certainly points to there having been already before the close of M. M. Ill, a considerable diffusion of knowledge of writing amongst men in a comparatively humble walk of life, as well as among professional scribes. The incised gypsum slip from the Kasella suggests a picture of a stone-cutter practising the art of epigraphy in his leisure moments. Nothing perhaps gives a more vivid idea of the general acquaintance with the art of writing than the fact that in the little Palace of Hagia Triada several graffito inscriptions were found scratched in the painted stucco faces of the walls, which strangely call to mind the very numerous graffiti mostly of a personal nature scratched in the same way on the walls of Pompeii. A specimen of one of the Hagia Triada graffiti is reproduced through the kindness of Professor Halbherr in Fig. 473 a. This, like the others, is in the Linear Class A 2; in Fig. 473 b some of the characters are transcribed. The three last signs are repeated in the same position on another graffito.

Among places where such clay documents have come to light may be mentioned, besides Knossos, Palaikastro, Zakro, Gournia, Papoura on the northern pass of Lasethi, Phaestos,

Hagia Triada, and Tylissos.

In Scripta Minoa, i, p. 51, Fig. 27, I have reproduced a small graffito from the Palace of Knossos which seems to be of Class B.

Inscriptions painted on the walls, such as those of Pompeii, do not indica-occur, but some fragmentary evidence is forthcoming at Knossos of the use a"

of writing for descriptive or other purposes by the fresco painters. Scr P l at . e e. Knossos

The most convincing proof of this is supplied by a fragment in the by Fresco finest style of painted plaster technique showing sign No. 26 of the Table, Fig. 47(5 below. The sign in question, however, is common to the Linear Class B, and as the fragment was found in the same area as the remains of

FIG. 473 a. GRAFFITO INSCRIPTION ON WALL, HAGIA TRIADA.

FIG. 473 . TRANSCRIPTION OF GRAFFITO.

the Taureador Frescoes, it may be more appropriately referred to a date when this latter form of script was already coming into vogue.

That the linear Class A gained a wide commercial vogue is clear, Com-and an interesting indication of this is seen in the fact that two characters of this class are inscribed on the base of a bowl of indigenous fabric found in

Melos. The sign-group there exhibited, W C3. recurs on the later linear tablets of Knossos, and there are reasons for supposing it to be a personal name. 1 There is evidence, moreover, that the Linear Script A was also current in Thera. 2 1 See Scripta Minoa, i, p. 35, and Excava- tions in Santorin, found a fragment of the tions at Phylakopi, p. lyjseqq. rim of an indigenous pot with mat painting - Dr. R. Zahn, in the course of his excava- presenting two graffito characters and a part of

Clayseal- At the same time the occurrence of ink-written inscriptions in the cups

Docii- m P ens a wide perspective of much more numerous documents that may have ments in existed on perishable materials, such as parchment or even of papyrus able imported from Egypt. According to the curious tradition preserved by

Materials. Dj oc i orosj who drew on Eteocretan sources, the ancient Cretans had made use of palm-leaves for writing. The masses of clay sealings originally attached to such documents found in the Knossian Palace and elsewhere are unfortunately our only direct evidence of their former existence.

Advanced It seems probable that the use of pens and ink may have largely Script contributed to the evolution of this linearized script. It certainly did return to no t grow up in a night, but the signs show a considerable advance towards Tradition, more alphabetic types as compared even with the great majority of the Contrast graffito forms of the hieroglyphic script which, as we have seen, was in ihiero- official use in the Palace to the last days of M. M. II. Only about a quarter glyphic o f the known types of the latter, even including those summarily copied from the signet types on the clay surface of the tablets, have any claim to be regarded as alphabetiform. Taking it as a whole the glyptic stamp is still impressed on the hieroglyphic signary to the last. At the same time the pictorial shape in which its signs appear, coupled as it often is with linearized graffiti on the clay sealings, supplies a useful record of the origin of many characters belonging to the advanced Linear Scripts. We shall see, indeed, that these latter betray a considerable indebtedness to the hieroglyphic signary.

Earlier This signary itself is a conventionalized selection from what must have tionstof 1 been a much larger pictographic repertory going back to very early times, of

Advanced wm c h however, we have only a very imperfect record. Such early picto-

Script. graphs of their nature were largely linear and belonged to what may be called the primitive slate pencil style. The clothing of such skeleton forms, as it were, with flesh and blood by the artistic engravers of the hieroglyphic signets really acted as a setback to the alphabetiform tendencies already visible.

That the use of linear sign-groups, possibly of syllabic values, attaining a certain vogue by the close of the Early Minoan Age, and notably during the first phase of M. M. I, is attested both by inscriptions on seal-stones and by a series of graffiti on vases.

second seems to be a variant of a barn a third. Of these characters, of which he has kindly supplied me with a sketch (inset), thefirst is a recurring type of Class A (No. 69 of the Table, Fig. 476) to which it is peculiar. The

There exist, indeed, one or two examples of linear inscriptions on M. M. I pots, apparently of a votive character, which carry back our record of certain types of the present category considerably. Thus a of the comparative series in Fig. 474, which appears on a fragment of a pithos from the M. M. I a oval house of Chamaezi 1 reappears in the well-established form, of the linear Script A. 2 It may be taken to represent a house facade, and is followed by what looks like apian of a building. A contemporary vase 3 of a type that also recurs among the vessels from the Chamaezi house supplies another instance of a well-defined sign-group (Fig. 474, b, c, (f). Of these b, which seems to be the linearized equivalent of a human trunk with

FIG. 474. LINEAR SIGNS ON M. M. la POTTERY COMPARED WITH TYPES OF CLASS A.

two hands held sideways, may supply the fuller form of a more abbreviated sign of Class A 4 of which a variant is shown in . Whether k stands in a derivative relation to c is quite uncertain. The cross d is repeated after a window sign, and followed by . on a cup of a provincial M. M. I a type from near Goulas. 6

Several examples of linear sign-groups on early seals and whorls have been given in my first works on Cretan pictography and script.

To these may be added the evidence of a remarkable archaic seal-stone of black steatite, and almost certainly of Cretan origin (Fig. 475). From stone its unconventional form it would be naturally placed amongst the earlier class r a cters of seal-stones, but the spiral coil somewhat angularly drawn on the side b can- 1 Xanthudides, Ef. Apx- 1906, p. 152, with similar distinguishing marks.

Fig. 7. For the house and the associated Obtained by me in 1894 from Prodromes remains see above, p. 147 seqq. Botsano in E. Crete. See Cretan Pictographs, 2 This'form occurs on a libation table from.,. ff. S., 1894, p. 279 and Fig. 5. Palaikastro, and may probably be recognized See Table, Fig. 476, n a. This leads us to in Sign 5 of the Trullos ladle. On a Hagia the Phoenician 0.

Triada tablet it is closely associated with the Op. fit., p. 278, Fig. 4.

two characters indicated beside it in Fig. 47-J. 6 It was purchased by me at Athens, as

This sign recurs in the Linear Class B often coming from an Aegean source, probably Crete.

THE PALACE OF MINOS, ETC.

not be earlier than E. M. III. The N before this occurs on an early whorl, but the figures on side a are not found in any of the regular signaries. 1

What is extremely remarkable, however, is that the three characters that are perfectly preserved on the base (6) of the seal itself are exact anticipations of regular signs of the Linear Script A which, as we have seen, first comes into vogue in the Knossian Palace in M. M. III. The wheel-sign itself is common to both Linear Scripts. The terminal character is a broad example of the hand sign of Class A with two dashes above, such as are also seen above some mason's marks on early Palace blocks, at both Knossos and

FIG. 475. EARLY SEAL-STONE OF BLACK STEATITE PRESENTING SIGNS RESEMBLING LINEAR CLASS A.

Phaestos, and which probably have a diacritical value. The intervening sign like a B reversed followed by two dots is of special interest since it must with great probability be identified with one of the most distinctive characters of the origin of which, as will be shown below, finds its best illustration from a manacle sign that appears on the Phaestos Disk. As transcribed into characters of Class A the signs would take the parallel forms 2 1 The first sign on face a is a kind of swastika in a circle, No. 2 presents a curious resemblance to the later Greek Omega. The groove on one side of this seal seems to be the result of sharpening some tool on it.

2 The initial sign of the group is certainly the triangle, with the apex only wanting. This sign appears as No. 130 of the Hieroglyphic

The conventionalized hieroglyphic type of the Minoan script is, as Linear we have seen, essentially a calligraphic system better adapted for official emerges signets than for everyday purposes of script. The new type of advanced Linear fu "x r i-i i- 1- i. developed

Script that now emerges simultaneously mtsfcs w over a large area of Minoan in M. M. Crete has its roots in a still remoter stageof the insular culture. It rises into view, moreover, already fully systematized and reduced to certain fixed tizaiionby rules by some central authority. The official grammarian has been at work.

A fuller account of the advanced Linear Script A must be reserved for another occasion, but a provisional synopsis of the signary is given in The the Table, Fig. 476. It includes types taken from the whole of the material illustrative of this form of Script, and in this connexion it must be borne in CIass A-mind that the most numerous series of its clay documents with which we are able to deal date from the First Late Minoan Period. As however is clearly seen from the inscriptions found in the deposits of the Knossian Palace, and from the very important contemporary group on the Libation Tables and other ritual vessels such as the Trullos ladle, the signary had already taken its characteristic shape in M. M. III.

Some ninety characters are here put together, several of a clearly pictographic character being omitted, such as those which always appear in a solitary position before numbers on the tablets and are indicative of various possessions.

That there was a real community between the Hieroglyphic Signary com-and both the advanced Linear Scripts is clearly shown by the Comparative J,"" Table, Fig. 477. l In some cases we may have to do with parallel develop- Hiero- f i-i i i i i gyphic ments from common prototypes. In others, as in the prow and dolphins signary. head signs, the principle of the part for the whole is applied in the later script. But many coincidences in type are of such a nature as to enable us to recognize the substantial identity of the characters K P, M, W, Y, Z, A 2, and B- may be taken as supplying crucial examples. For some identifications, such as that of the lyre sign (J), nothing more than a strong presumption can be claimed. If, as seems probable, in the case of I the tablet for suspension of the earlier series is represented by No. 84 of Class A, the small sign contained within it may convey a hint of an original use of this form of tablet as a vehicle for script.

series, and again in a compound form in the Some other comparisons, such as the crook Linear Class B. It also occurs in the Minoan sign, T, common to the earlier and the later sign-group on a stirrup vase from Orchomenos, class, may be added to this list. On a recently with another character peculiar to Class A. discovered Hieroglyphic signet a form of the Inferentially we may assume that it belonged wheel sign (9) occurs, to some local signary of the A class.

THE PALACE OF MINOS, ETC.

.3-.

HIEROGLYPHS LINEAR CL A LINEAR CL. B. HIEROGLYPHS LINEAR CL A. LINEAR CL. B

FIG. 477. COMPARATIVK TAIU. K. OF SIGNS OF THK HIEROGLYPHIC AND LINEAR SCRIPTS ftcC

The linear reduction of the single axe sign given under D affords a very interesting parallel to the evolution of the linearized representatives of the Double-Axe sign (E), and strongly corroborates the view already expressed as to their origin.

Ideo- It is evident that, apart from those characters, already referred to, which

Element on b appear before numbers, and which represent material possessions, there in new was st; u a l ar g e ideographic element in the new linearized script. As in the System, case of the parallel Class B, almost any sign of the Linear Class A can on occasion stand alone, and must thus have been capable of expressing a single word or idea. But the combinations of the signs in groups afford at the same time sufficient indication that they were also used with a purely phonetic value as syllables or possibly even in individual cases as letters. That a certain proportion of the characters put together in the Tables possessed exclusively a pictorial signification is a fair conclusion. If, however, we may deduct a score of types as belonging to this category we should still have left some seventy signs which might well have been susceptible of a syllabic usage. In that case we should have to deal with a syllabary slightly larger than the later Cypriote.

It must also be borne in mind that in the case of personal names which at any rate on the clay documents of Class B seem to play such a conspicuous role signs of a pictorial character may often take their place in groups otherwise syllabic in their nature. The ship sign, No. 8j, for instance, which appears occasionally in such a position, may well, among a maritime people, have formed part of a name such as Navxpar or Nava-tkXfjs, of a kind so common in the later nomenclature of Greece.

Fre- A characteristic feature of the inscriptions of this class is the frequent of Com- occurrence of compound signs. This practice was, in fact, of very old pound inheritance in Crete, and is illustrated by the conjunctions of masons' marks, on the Early Palace blocks.

An example, in which the hand sign forms a part, has already been given in the case of a Knossian tablet l and on many of the later clay documents. These combinations are very methodically applied, especially in connexion with the hand and arm sign. It will be seen that it is linked thirteen times with other characters among the examples given in Fig. 478. Barred Another interestingf feature even more marked in the Linear Class B is the differentiation of certain signs by means of one or more cross bars. Examples of these will be seen in No. lod, Fig. 476.

A certain connexion with the older system of numeration 2 is traceable 1 See above, p. 619, Fig. 455, a. 2 See above, p. 279, Fig. 211.

in the forms used for tens and units as also the fractional signs of Class A as System of represented by documents belonging to its M. M. Ill phase. In the case of t the higher numbers, however, the change is of a radical kind, the old lozenge-shaped figure used for thousands, as well as the sloping line indicative of a hundred, being now replaced by the numerals shown in Fig. 47!).

The dot or pellet as the equivalent for 10, which was at first taken over from the older system, has a distinct chronological value in connexion with the linear script. It seems still to be universal in the early inscriptions of Class A, such as those belonging to the M. M. Ill Period found in the Palace of Knossos. On the tablets of the succeeding L. M. I Period it passes, however, by a gradual transition into a horizontal line, and it is under this form that the decimal figure appears in the script of Class B, the

R S TUVW X Y Z A?

FIG. 478. COMPOUND FORMS OF CLASS A WITH HAND AND ARM SIGN.

numeral signs of which are otherwise identical with those of Class A. This itself may be taken as an interesting piece of evidence as to the relatively late date of the existing tablets of Class B.

Otherwise the comparative examples of characters of this latter series given in Fig. 477 point to an origin in many respects as early as those of Class A. The parallelism between the two signaries is itself considerable, and of the types of Class A given in the Table, Fig. 47(5, many are identical or closely similar in the other script. It is interesting to observe, moreover, in this connexion, that some of the characters of B present features nearer to their presumed prototypes than the equivalents in series A.

More will be said as to the character and relationships of Class B in Relation a Section dealing with the clay archives of the Later Palace at Knossos. classes A It is an undoubted fact that it first emerges in a fully systematized shape at and B a date not long anterior at least to the beginning of L. M. II. As unquestionably, however, it contains independent elements which, as in the case of the common types shown in Fig. 477, are drawn from sources at least equal in antiquity with those of the rival script. On occasion, indeed, as already noticed, the forms of its characters are somewhat nearer the pictorial originals than the corresponding types of Class A. There is a certain presumption, moreover, that the use of Class B at Knossos as an official

UNITS- i = in = 5; c

TENS-

HUNDREDS- O = IOO. = 500; c

THOUSANDS- 1000, ' 4000,

FRACTIONAL SIGNS L OR L AFTER UNITS j 7

EXAMPLE X E E E j = 2496

FIG. 479. NUMERALS OF LINEAR SCRIPT, CLASS A.

system may have somewhat overlapped that of Class A it) other parts of the island. It may even at times have reacted on elements of the other signary. It is clear, for instance, that a variety of a group of quasi-pictorial signs that appear on the later clay documents of Knossos, in reference to swine, gives the key to an otherwise enigmatic character, No. 87 of Class A (see Table, Fig. 47(5) which is seen on a tablet from Hagia Triada.

3- THE PHAESTOS DISK IN ITS MINOAN RELATIONS.

Tablet of Class A found with imprinted Disk at Ihaestos: In Cist with M. M. III pottery; Non-Minoan character of Disk; Hieroglyphs stamped by novel method; Order of Sign-Groups on Disk; The Signary small common clement wili Minoan Scripts; The Manacles sign; Artistic execution of Signs compared with Minoan; At date of Disk Hieroglyphs superseded by linear signs in Crete; Indications of connexion with S. W. Anatolia; Plumed cap and round shield of later Sea-rovers; Arrow sign on Ship; Anatolian religious element Symbols of Goddess Ma; Pagoda-like building- Lykian parallels; Specialized character of signs on Disk; Pictographs not of ancient derivation but drawn from contemporary life; Phonographic elements dual Groups; Preponderant idcography; Simple mnemonic eltment; Division into Sections terminal dashes; Symmetrical arrangement of two faces; Recurrent sets of sign-groups suggesting refrains; Metrical character of Composition; Record of Sea raid connected with S. W. Region of Asia Minor; Comparison of later Egyptian Sea raids of Lykians and Confederates; Pylon of Medinet Flabu; Religious connexion of Disk a Te Deum of Victory; Cretan Philistines among later Sea-Raiders; But Disk not a record of Philistines in Minoan Crete; Non-Minoan accoutrements of warriors on Disk; Keftians true Minoan representatives; Disk a foreshadowing of later ethnic relations; An Evidence of M. M. III connexion between Crete and S. H. Anatolia; An unique record.

THE cumulative evidence as to the general use of the advanced Linear Tablet of Class

Script A at Knossos during the closing phase of M. M. 111, at a date, that is, f ou nd round about 1600 B. C., finds its counterpart in the recurrence of a typical p " tablet of this class (Fig. 480) with identical ceramic associations in the Palace Disk at v 5 Phaestos.

of rhaestos.

Its occurrence in that case, however, was accompanied by the still more remarkable discovery of the well-known Disk of baked clay imprinted on both sides with hiero-glyphic characters of a class hitherto unexampled in Crete or elsewhere (Fig. 482). At the same time it raises questions so intimately connected with the course of Minoan history as to demand careful consideration here.

The linear tablet, as will be seen from Fig. 480, presents the same abbreviated type of inscription, and is of the same, almost square, shape as the contemporary examples from Knossos, and belongs therefore to the earlier elements

THE PALACE OF MINOS, ETC.

in Cist of Class A. 1 It was found, a few centimetres from the Disk, in a built cist M! M. III analogous to the Kaselles' at Knossos which was situated in an annexe to pottery, the North-Eastern region of the Palace at Phaestos. In Dr. Pernier's opinion

FIG. 480 a, b. TABLET WITH INSCRIPTION OF LINEAR CLASS A, FOUND WITH DISK.

FIG. 481. BRIDGE-SPOUTED CLAY JAR FOUND WITH DISK SHOWING YELLOWISH WASH.

both these clay documents had found their way into this repository from an upper floor, and the same is true of the great hoards of tablets found in the later Palace at Knossos. The associated pottery was uniformly of the M. M. III b class, presenting for the most part the typical purplish brown

The tablet seems to be perfect except for a small border strip. On a the collocation of the third and fourth signs ofl. i (Nos. 47, 48 of the Table, Fig. 476) is frequent in inscriptions of this class. The bent spray seen in both lines supplies a link with the hieroglyphic tablet from Phaestos, p. 278, Fig. 209 above. The intermediate sign between the two lines is possibly No. 66 of the Table, Fig. 470. The penultimate sign of 1. 2 is uncertain On side I the first character of 1. 2 is incomplete. The penultimate sign is No. 66 of the Table.

THIC IHAKSTOS DISK

Around and white decoration and forms of vessels in some cases identical with those of the Temple Repositories. 1 There were also found fragments of a typical class of vessel with a bridge-spout and three handles (Fig. 481), further degenerations of which occur in L. M. I deposits. 2 This evidence would bring down the elate of the Disk to an advanced stage of M. M. III. 3 In default of the strongest evidence to the contrary, the inference would be almost obligatory that the clay Disk, found thus on a Cretan site and in purely Minoan associations, was itself an indigenous product. But there are serious objections of a negative character to this conclusion as well as positive indications pointing to a geographical area outside Crete.

The Disk itself, of which Face A is reproduced in Fig. 482, presents on either side a spiraliform inscription in hieroglyphic characters, each of which is separately impressed by means of a punch, a remarkable and novel feature in connexion with early script. It might, a priori, have been supposed 4 that

Non-

M mi M 11 character of Disk.

H iero-glyphs stamped by novel method.

1 Compare especially the pitcher with typical M. M. Ill b spiraliform ornament. Ausonia iii, p. 261, Fig. 3, and the fragments, p. 263, Fig. 6.

This type of vessel was found at Gournia with pure L. M. I decoration (Boyd Hawes, Gournia, PI. VIII, 21, 22). A L. M. I vase, showing a still further degeneration, was found in a private house at Hagia Triada.

3 For an account of the discovery of the Disk, and a detailed description, see Dr. L. Pernier, Ausonia, 1909, p. 255 seqq. Researches of my own on the subject have appeared in Scripta Minoa, i, p. 2 2 seqq., and Part III, The Phaestos Disk, p. 273 seqq. An acute study of the Disk was published contemporaneously by Dr. A. Delia Seta (Disco di Phaestos: Rendiconti della r. Accad. dei Lincei, 1909, Seduta di Maggio), whose views as to the order of the inscriptions I have felt bound to adopt. Almost simultaneously appeared Der Disktis von Phaestos unddie Philister-ton Kreta by Prof. Eduard Meyer (Sitzungsbe rithted. k. Akad., Berlin, 1909, p. 1022 seqq.), who lays stress on the Philistine element. Monsieur A. J. Reinach's article, Le Disque de Phaestos et les Peuples de la Mer (Rev. Arch., 1910, pp. 1-65), is mainly an ethnographic investigation on the same lines as the pre- ceding. In 1911 Dr. A. Cuny published a careful study of the Disk in the Rer. des Eludes anciennes (p. 296 seqq., and cf. too ib., 1912, pp. 95, 96). Prof. A. Sundwall (Der Ursprung der kretisthen Schrift (Acta Academiae Aboensis, 1920) labours to derive the signs on the Disk from Egyptian hieroglyphs. Prof. R. A. S. Macalister, Proc. R. I. Acad., xxx (1913), Sect. C, p. 342 seqq., without attempting to transliterate the document, has compared its arrangement with that of a contract tablet with a list of witnesses; Mr. F. W. Read (Quarterly Statement Pal. Ext. Fund, Jan., 1921, p. 29 seqq.) regards it as'the oldest music in the world.

4 This was at first my own view, but the technical arguments advanced by Dr. Delia Seta, loc. fit., have convinced me that the alternative view held from the first by Dr. Pernier was correct and that the inscriptions run inwards. Several cogent arguments for this view are advanced by Dr. Delia Seta (op. at., p. 12 seqq.). Such are (a) the abrupt widening of the outer column at the end of Section XII of Face A, and the somewhat strangled beginning of Section XIV. () The fact that on both faces there are slight superpositions of one sign by another, showing that in each case the sign to the right was the first impressed

THE PALACE OF MINOS, ETC f-ty;

Fig. 482. PHAESTOS DISK; FACE A.

the signs of the inscriptions had run outwards from the centre to the periphery, m which case the human and animate figures would have faced to the right (e. g. A. xvn. 3, 4; xxvi. i, 2; xxix. 2, 3, 4; by the grouping of the signs in Section XIX. B. xxx i, 2). (f) The evidences of crowd- In A, v, there has been a cancelling and ing towards the centre of A, specially shown correction.

with the other signs, as is the case with both the Cretan linear scripts.

But a more detailed examination of the Disk must remove all doubt that the contrary was the case, and that the inscription in fact starts in the Order of outer circle running from right to left, and so winds round to the centre. Groups

The animate signs are thus set facing the beginning of each group, which is on Dlsk- in fact the arrangement adopted in the Minoan hieroglyphic system as well as in the Hittite, Babylonian, and the Egyptian. On each side the beginning of the inscription is indicated by a vertical line with four knobs in the case of

Face A and five in Face B.

The habit, indeed, of mechanically reproducing hieroglyphic inscriptions Antkipa- was already known in Crete in the earlier part of the Middle Minoan Age, movable as is shown by the clay sealings. The signs were here impressed either type-singly or in groups, and by means of some of the long four-sided bead-seals it would have been possible to impress four successive lines, constituting an inscription of some length. This process, it will be seen, has some analogy with the mediaeval block-printing, but the method adopted on the Phaestos Disk of using separate punches for each sign is itself a real anticipation of the use of movable type.

The inscriptions on the two sides of the Disk include forty-five different signs on signs, a conspectus of which is given in Fig. 483. The signs are divided into categories resembling those of the Minoan and other hieroglyphic systems; but there is here, as will be pointed out below, 2 a greater specialization in many of the subjects. We have not to do with man or woman, for instance, in genere, but with particular ethnic representatives.

1 Reproduced from my Table, Scripta. Minoa, in profile). 18. Carpenter's angle. 19. Perhaps i, p. 276. The signs, following the order given, a plane. 20. Handled vase. 21. Double are: i. Marching or running man. 2. Male comb or rake, of unknown use. 22. Uncer-head with plumed crest. 3. Bare male head tain. 23. Square-headed mallet or beetle (P. with a double circle, perhaps earrings rather and I). S., column). 24. Pagoda-like build-than tattoo marks (not a female head, as ing (see below, p. 658). 25. Ship with arrow Delia Seta). 4. Captive. 5. Infant. 6. Woman on prow. 26. Ox-horn. 27. Hide or skin of in short gown and skirt. 7. Woman's breast, animal. 28. Ox's foot. 29. Felinehead(P., dog's 8. Fist wound round with cestus. 9. Tiara (see head). 30. Head of horned sheep. 31. Flying below, p. 657). 10. Arrow, n. Horn bow. eagle holding serpent (Sfripia Minoa, p. 279). 12. Round shield with bosses. 13. Knobbed 32. Seated bird, probably dove. 33. Fish, pro-club (according to Pernier and Delia Seta, bably tunny. 34. Moth with closed wings (less a 'stylized tree). 14. Manacles (more pro- probably bee, as Scripta Minoa, p. 279). 35. bably than yoke (D. S.); certainly not, as P., Plant, perhapsvine. 36. Probably olive-tree (see mountains'or territorial sign). 15. Amazonian below). 37. Plant, perhaps Styrax. 38.

Star axe. 16. Form of knife. 17. Unknown instru- flower. 39. Saffron flower. 40-45. Uncertain, ment (P., seal in profile; 1). S., round shield 2 See below, pp. 658, 659.
THE PALACE OF MINOS, ETC.
FIG. 483. SYNOPSIS OF SIGNS ON PHAESTOS DISK. Small common element with hieroglyphic signary, and it would be difficult to find parallels for it there in
Scripts, more than at most half a dozen cases. Nor do general resemblances, like the In this and other respects the series stands apart from the Minoan
THE PHAESTOS DISK fish, No. 33, the tree, No. 36, or the flower, No. 39, in themselves count for much.

Neither is it possible, except in one or two cases, to establish any close comparison between the characters on the Disk and what may be supposed to have been the root-forms of signs of the Linear Script, prototypes of which are discernible among the Minoan hieroglyphics. The flying bird, No. 31, bears an analogy indeed with Cretan types, but it either shows very prominent talons, wanting in these, or is holding a serpent in its claws. The hide (No. 27) recurs on a M. M. II hieroglyphic seal. 1 Of special interest, moreover, is the resemblance presented between No. 14 of the characters on the Disk (here set on end), which I have elsewhere compared with manacles', Fig. 484 a; and No. 62 of the Linear Signaryof which Fig. 4S4 b seems to be the earlier form. A very early comparison with this sign is supplied, however, as pointed out above, 3 by a seal-stone of a primitive class.

The fist wound round with a Cestus, No. 8, also receives illustration from a feature of Minoan sports. So, too, No. 16, so far as its general outline goes, recalls the Minoan hieroglyph, No. 25, representing a saw, but the most distinctive feature of this the teeth preserved to the last in its linear derivatives are wanting in the implement shown on the Disk. It must rather be regarded as a knife or chopper.

Certain resemblances in artistic execution between the figures on the Disk and Minoan works may also here be noted. The feline head, No. 29, bears much the same character as the cat's head of the Hagia Triada fresco. The ram's head, No. 30, also evidences a sympathetic natural treatment worthy of a Minoan gem-engraver. Close comparisons may also be found in the foliage of No. 35. But the parallelism shown in these cases is not more than might have been expected in the productions of some field of culture in close touch with the Minoan world.

It is clear that at the time when this Disk was deposited in the Palace archives at Phaestos, side by side with a clay tablet of the advanced linear script, the indigenous hieroglyphic system had long fallen into disuse in
Manacles'Sign.
Fir,. 484. MANACLES ON DISK
COMPARED WITH SlgN OK LINEAR
CLASS A.
Artistic execution of Signs compared with
Minoan.

At date of Disk Hieroglyphs 1 Seager collection: grouped with bull's head and hand.

2 Scripta Minoa, i. p. 277. The flat tops of manacles, the slots being for the attachment of thongs. Dr. Pernier's view, Ausonia, p. 287, that we have here a

version of the mountains of the two prominences in this figure as well as or regional sign can hardly be accepted. the slots in the base are characteristic features See above p. 640, Fig. 47. V

THE PALACE OF MINOS, ETC.

superseded by Linear Signs in Crete.

Crete itself. Neither have we here to deal, as might perhaps be suggested, with a survival of the old hieroglyphic script of Crete in some religious connexion. As already observed, there is hardly anything in common between the two systems, and the most frequent signs on the Disk are conspicuous by their absence among the Minoan hieroglyphs.

The indications as a whole must betaken to point to some neighbouring area where a quasi-pictorial form of script was in use at a later period than in Crete. That in the Hittite regions, at any rate, of Anatolia a hieroglyphic survival did take place to a considerably later date than this

FIG. 485.

SELECTED SIGNS FROM DISK.

indica- is a well-ascertained fact. It is clear indeed that the signary of the Phaestos connexion Disk is radically different from the Hittite system. But there are, as will e seen man y reasons for ascribing it to the intermediate region embracing the Sou th-Western angle of Asia Minor. Within this area no inscriptions of the Hittite class have been hitherto discovered, but a parallel hieroglyphic system may well have flourished there.

In view of the non-existence of comparative materials from that area the evidence is partly of a negative kind. The human figures, for instance, reproduced among some selected signs in Fig. 485, 1 are as markedly non-Minoan as- they are non-Hittite. The male figure a, performing the goose-step, is of different build from the Minoan, and his belt and short tunic 1 From Dr. Stefani's drawings in Pernier, Disco di Phaestos.

shows a certain affinity with the Hittite dress. It is, at any rate, distinctively non-Semitic. The woman (Fig. 485, d) is marked not only by a different costume with an under-skirt, but by a breadth of body in curious contrast to the usually pinched-in waist of the Minoan ladies. 1 Woman.

In b, again, we see an infant in a short shirt, equally unparalleled among infant. Cretan representations, c is obviously a captive, and e may be the head of Captive, another, apparently with double-ringed ear-rings, like the Negroid heads of the jewel depicted in Fig. 231 above. 2 In close connexion with the two preceding signs must be taken the object seen in Fig. 484, a, which seems, Mana-as already noted, to be a typical representation of manacles.

Of still greater interest is the head,", clad apparently in a close-fitting Plumed cap with plumes. This headgear at once recalls the plumed caps of the O f a ia ter Viking swarms from the North and the Great Green Sea, who ravaged Sea

Rovers.

the Delta from the Eighteenth to the Twenty-Third Dynasties. The general trend of the evidence points, as we shall see, to the South-West Coast of Asia Minor 3 as the original home of these peoples, and this connexion is borne out by the appearance, more or less contemporary with these Viking raids, among the reliefs of the ivory

Mycenaean casket from Enkomi or Old Salamis of a warrior in a short tunic, holding an axe and wearing a similar crested cap on his head. 4 The round shield (Fig. 483, 12) Round takes us into the same field of comparisons. Like the plumed cap it is non-Minoan, but it is worn by a warrior on another ivory relief 5 from the same Cypriote cemetery, and is characteristic of the same group of seafaring peoples. The belt and short tunic is also their usual attire, in strong contrast to the long gaberdines of Syrian fashion.

The composite horn bow of Asiatic origin, seen in i, is also very Asiatic characteristic of the Southern and Western Anatolian area, and the horned bow unstrung is a common Hittite sign. Both this and the simple Euro- 1 Pernier and others (e. g. Hall, J. H. S., where the parallel between the pagoda-like 1911, p. 119) have compared the small gold building and Lykian forms was first suggested, figure of a woman from a Mycenae Shaft A. S. Murray, Excavations in Cyprus, Pl. I Grave (Schliemann, p. 182, Fig. 273), which and p. 12, Fig. 19, and cf. p. 31. The tomb, is exceptionally broadly rendered. But the No. 58, in which this casket was found con- V-shaped flounces that she wears are those of tained two iron knives with ivory handles, and the usual Late Minoan fashions, without under- belong, therefore, to the beginning of the skirt. The contemporary M. M. III modes do Cypriote Iron Age.

not even present this amount of resemblance 6 On an ivory mirror-handle; op. fit., Pl. II, (see below, p. 680, Fig. 500). and cf. pp. 31,32. It was from the purely Bronze 2 See p. 312. Age Tomb No. 17 (Late Mycenaean). Cf. my See Sfripta Minoa, i, pp. 24, 25, and 287, Cyprus f. in Anthr. Inst. Journ., xxx, p. 212.

THE PALACE OF MINOS, ETC
Arrow Sign on Ship.
Anatolian religious elements Symbols of Goddess Ma.

pean or African form seem to have been early known in Crete, though they were mainly, it would appear, made use of for the chase the spear and sword being the usual weapons of Minoan warriors. It is to be noted that the arrow shown in k is without a barb, in this respect differing from Minoan types, though resembling an Egyptian class. 1 It looks very much as if the cross-bar projecting in front of the vessel with a pendant in front was made in the shape of the arrow sign, 2 and in that case it might be taken as a kind of symbolic attestation of the important part played by the bow in the maritime enterprise of the people to whom the Disk was due. The bark itself, unlike the Minoan hieroglyphic types, is without a mast, 3 a peculiarity which might be explained if the primary function of such vessels was the navigation of rivers or land-locked coasts. The prominence of this war-galley among the pictorial signs of the Disk is in any case a suggestive indication.

The Amazonian Axe, Fig. 483, No. i 5, is Anatolian in its associations. The knobbed club (A), resembling that of Hercules, is a primitive weapon, of which there are traces both on the Asiatic and the European side. In the region with which we are concerned it specially survived in the cult of Selge and that of the Carian island of Cos, but, what is still more significant, it is seen at Comana in the hands of the great Anatolian Goddess Ma. 4 The female breast itself, as a sign coming ex kypothesi from an Asianic quarter, is specially suggestive from its known associations with this Mother Goddess and her sister forms. In Cyprus it is found as a votive form of the

Paphian Aphrodite. Its connexion again with the allied cult of the Minoan Goddess is shown by the occurrence of mammiform types of sacral vessels. On the other hand the feline head which alternates with the breast on the Disk may be equally interpreted as having a special relation to one or other form of time. On another bronze coin of Comana, of Nerva's time, the club appears as the sole type (Babelon, Rev. Num., 1886, p. 444). These and other coins of the same class (77. M. Cat., Pontus, c., Pl. V, 6, and pp. 28, 29) are attributed to the lontic rather than the Cappadocian Comana. But the worship of both was devoted to the same Great Goddess, Ma, translated as Enyo by the Greeks (cf. Strabo, lib. xii, c. 2, 3 and c. 3, 32). On a relief at Malatia a knobbed club is seen in the hands of a Hittite God (Garstang, Liverpool Anns, of Arch. f., i. Pl. V).

1 Chabas, op. at., p. 85.

In Scripa Minoa, i, p. 278, I have called attention to the parallel afforded by the prehistoric Nilotic barges as seen on the early pottery of Naqada, c. On these, weapons, such as a double harpoon or the crossed arrows of the Libyan Goddess Neith, with appendages attached, are seen fixed to poles rising from small towers on the prows of the vessels.

3 A sign of the Linear Class A, however, shows the prow of a vessel without a mast. It has also at times a kind of bar across the prow.

Millingen, Ancient Coins of Greek Cities, Pl. V, 4, and p. 67, on a bronze coin of Severus's the same Mother Goddess. It is sufficient to recall the lion guardians of the Minoan Rhea and her Anatolian doubles, and the pardlike animal on the head of the Snake Goddess.

If, as seems probable, the object shown in m should be identified with some kind of peaked tiara, 1 we are once more led into the same circle of comparisons, though a form of this was shared, as we have seen, by the Minoan Goddess. In the Anatolian regions alike among the earlier Hittite rulers and the later Persian the tiara is a characteristic form of headgear. Two Hittite examples are given in Fig. 486, a, b? the latter of which evidently represents an early form of the Persian milra,

The most significant figure, however, among the signs on the Disk is Pagoda-the pagoda-like building shown in. 3 Here the in- j u uding tenor supports of the apex do not converge towards L f n. the centre of the roof as they would if it were the cupola of a round building, but seem to support the curving sides of a gable. From this we may conclude that we have to do with the facade v of a rectangular building provided with a carinated hull-shaped roof, in other words, with the architectural type preserved by the tombs and rock-carvings of Lykia. 4 The framework of the original structure was certainly of wood, and the projecting eaves and platform curiously recall the stone copies of wooden constructions that meet us in the Lykian rock tombs like that of Myra (Fig. 487), 5 and in certain prominent buildings which are seen rising above the town-walls in the Pinara reliefs. We have no evidence of similar buildings in Crete. 6 It will be seen from the above analysis that there is a very real distinc- 1 See Scripta Minoa, i, p. 277. 4 This comparison was pointed out in

Fig. a is from Hamath (Messerschmidt, Scripta Minoa, i, p. 26.

Corpus Inscript. Hettit., t. iv); b from Jerabis 6 Texier, Description de IAsie Afineurt, III, (., t. xi). Cf. Scripta Minoa, i, p. 277, Pl. ccxxvii, Fig. 3; Perrot et Chipiez, t. v,

Fig. 127. p. 377, Fig. 264.

3 Prof. J. Sundwall, op. fit., p. 7, in search 6 At the same time it must be observed for Egyptian hieroglyphic prototypes, identifies that built rectangular tombs have been found the figure with a bird-cage (Vagtlkfif?), in Crete belonging to the early part of the

Mr. V. LI. Griffith, however, who has made the I ate Minoan Age, with a hull-shaped vaulting, origins of Egyptian hieroglyphs a special study, The Royaltomb at Knossos(rfaisfartftamfis, informs me that no sign belonging to that c. p. 136 seqq.) and a smaller built tomb system bears any resemblance to the figure on more recently discovered, Archaeologia, Ixv, the Disk. There is no bird-cage hieroglyph, p. 6 seqq. are examples of this. There may,

Pictorial figures of bird-traps' indeed are therefore, have been a sepulchral tradition of known, but of quite a different character. some similar form of wooden dwelling.

THE PALACE OF MINOS, ETC.

Specia- tion between the character of many of the pictorial signs that appear on the character Disk and that of the Cretan hieroglyphs. This is specially apparent in the of Signs I lum an subjects. In the latter case we see a man as such, standing- or seated, on DISK.

and various parts of the body such as the eye, leg, hands, and arms in different poses, and elements of this kind are universal, ingredients of primitive pictographic signaries. On the Disk, however, this generic class is replaced by a specialized group, created, as it were, ad hoc.

As already remarked, the head with a plumed crest cannot be regarded as represent-ing a man's head in general, but has a distinct ethnic application. It is at least doubtful whether the marching or running figure, No. i, can be regarded as an ordinary man sign. The round shield with which it is coupled emphasizes this limitation. In the same way the head, No. 3, with the 8-shaped marks on his cheeks obviously illustrates a fashion of some particular tribe or race. So too in the woman sign, No. 6, we see a female form of specific character and costume. The captive seen in No. 4 may be reasonably referred to this special and topical class, and with it the manacles', No. 14, may be interpreted in an ideographic sense. The fist with the cestus thong, No. 8, may be directly connected, as in Minoan Crete, with a specific class of agonistic contests held in honour of the Great Goddess. The 'tiara, again, No. 9, must also in all probability be taken to refer to some contemporary sacerdotal office. The 'ship sign, No. 25, with the arrow on the prow, would also seem to have a definite application. In other words, in the case of the most important group of signs found on the Disk, we have not to do with conventionalized pictographs of ancient derivation but with graphic figures reproducing contemporary costumes and accoutrement. It follows from this that we must

FIG. 487. FACADE OF ROCK TOMB, MVRA.

regard the whole composition as a record of quite recent events. The picto- Picto-graphic method here exhibited is in fact a much simpler matter than that P g f s with which we are confronted in the more elaborate hieroglyphic systems, ancient where the phonographic element is clearly discernible beside the ideographic, tion, but On the Disk, indeed, the purely pictorial element is very marked.

The way in which many of the picture signs on the Disk succeed tem-one another with a complementary meaning as when the warrior's Rfj. ar5 head and shield are followed by a captive itself suggests very direct interpretation. In such cases the groups of signs can hardly, as is so largely the case in advanced hieroglyphic systems, represent mere phonograms or syllables.

That there was a distinct phonographic element in the inscription may, Phono-indeed, be fairly assumed. A great number of dual groups' are perceptible on Elements: the Disk, and from the incongruous character often perceptible in the pictorial dual signs thus coupled it is possible that here at Jeast we have to deal with words or parts of words phonographically expressed by means of signs representing syllables open or closed. Sometimes a two-sign group of this incongruous nature stands alone, such as the saffron-flower and bow (A. 18) or the ox's foot and marching figure (A. 15), sometimes it is preceded or succeeded by a single sign, sometimes it is followed by another dual group. Even in these cases, however, it must be constantly borne in mind that a fuller knowledge of the meaning of the signs might show that they were not really incongruous but that they supplement one another in the expression of a single idea.

On the other hand we must realize that we are dealing with a system Prepon-of writing much simpler in its composition than that of Egypt, and id e e nt where the relative importance of ideographic characters strikes the eye. graphy. There is reason for believing that the individual sign-groups themselves ought not to be rigorously interpreted as representing single words, but rather in many cases as concepts of somewhat wider extension.

It will be found, indeed, that in the case of some seventeen signs, or over strong a third of the total number represented on the Disk, a strong presumption phir arises of an exclusively ideographic application. These signs occupy no less Element, than 123 out of 244 places in the inscription, or over half the total number, occurring as initials, medians, and terminals. There is every reason to 1 This feature of the inscription has been due segni. To this nucleus may be added, qualified by Dr. Delia Seta (of. fit., p. 67) as as he points out, a monosematic prefix or disematism: I A scrittura del disco ha a sua suffix, or it can be united to other disematic base il disematismo, cioe il nucleo essenziale di groups.

THE PALACE OF MINOS, ETC.

Mnemonic elements

Division of Disk into Sections.

Terminal Dashes.

suppose, moreover, that some of the other characters, the forms of which it is at present impossible to interpret, belong to the same category.

The preponderant ideography of the Disk and the probability that some, at least, of the signs employed stood for entire concepts rather than single words may be taken as indications that the script here illustrated is on the whole more primitive in its method than the Cretan hieroglyphic system. It looks as if many of the characters may have had a simple mnemonic function, calling up to the contemporary reader's mind a fuller descriptive record. Advanced elements, such as we find in a syllabary, recede into the background, and the attempts to translate the inscriptions into a known language, such as Greek, which have already produced such strange results, seem to be based on a fundamentally wrong conception of the material. 1

Face A of this Disk (Fig. 482) is distributed into thirty-one sections, divided by upright lines, each containing groups of signs varying in number from two to seven. The total number of characters on this face is 122. Face B shows thirty similar sections with from two to five signs and 119 characters in all.

A remarkable feature of the inscriptions on both sides are the strokes, generally sloping to the right, but sometimes vertical, which recur at intervals under certain terminal signs of sections. 2 These marks are done with some pointed tool after the stamping of the letters, when the clay was still soft. They appear at the end of certain sections, but the sections themselves, which probably represent individual words or concepts, are in each case separated by horizontal lines, and these strokes must therefore have some other 1 It is hardly necessary to remind the curious that Prof. G. Hempl, of Stanford University, California, (Harper'smagazine, Jan. 1910, p. 187 seqq., c.) has read off the inscriptions into a species of Greek. Of this it need only be remarked that, while it does not correspond with classical forms, it has still less claim to represent a prehistoric stage of the language (Harper's Magazine, January, 1911.) Miss F. Melian Stawell, of Newnham College, Cambridge (Burlington Magazine, vol. xix, p. 23 seqq.), who has endeavoured to follow Hempl's lead, is by no means more convincing. Both attempts are based on a manipulation of syllables or letters representing the initial letters of the supposed equivalents of the signs in Greek. Invocations to divinities of an ecstatic nature are thus elicited. As a sample of the language and method the following extract from Miss Stawell's translation may suffice: Ta, Mare, da Behold Warrior Goddess! I(a a, Kla-ta-(n)-k K hail! ho! clang. Ti-o, Kro-ra-to I honour (thee) Mighty one. An-gu-nao-ta Queen of the Ways. The unsatisfying character (to say the least of it) of these interpretations, must not, however, be taken to exclude the possibility that the language is Greek.

2 Their distribution is as follows: Under the Marching Figure (No. r); twice; under the Male Child (No. 5), once; under the Female Breast (No. 7), three times; the Fist and Cestus (No. 8), three or four times; the Carpenter's Angle (No. 18), once; the Ox-horn (No. 26), signification. Those whose work has lain among advanced systems of writing have shown a tendency to regard these marks as indicating some subtle grammatical modification of the terminal syllable or letter. 1 But, when we consider the primitive stage of hieroglyphic expression to which this document seems to belong, a simpler explanation becomes more probable.

The view here suggested is that these dashes mark the end 2 of a connected Division., into Sen- series of sign-groups, each of which, as already suggested, represents an tences.

individual word or concept. In other words they mark off separate sentences, though occasionally these embrace only a single sign-group.

The inscription on Face A would thus fall into ten subdivisions, and Sym-that on B into nine. 3 If, however, we may believe that the first sign-group arrange-of A is a kind of exordium, there would then be exactly thirty sections on J either side of the Disk, divided in each case into nine groups. 4 In the Faces. subdivision of these groups, moreover, the number three or its multiples preponderates.

These evidences of a symmetric scheme of arrangement may help to explain how it was feasible to adapt the length of the winding inscription on both faces to the size of the Disk. They suggest the further conclusion that the inscriptions A and B represent successive portions of a metrical composition. It follows the laws of primitive music, 5 and, as we shall see, may well represent a chaunt of Victory.

In several places in fact we note recurrent sets of sign-groups suggestive Recur- of some kind of refrain. This is well exemplified by the subjoined com- of

Groups: three times; the Tree (No. 35), once; the though there is no place in it for the sign).

Rosette (No. 38), once; the Triangle (No. 43), In B the numbers are: 3, 3, 6, 6, 2, i, 3, 2, 4.

once. It is noteworthy that, in a total of nineteen 1 Meyer, for instance (op. cit., p. 1024), subdivisions, five contain three groups; two, regards this mark as the equivalent of the six; and one, nine; so that 3 or its multiples similar Sanskrit mark the virtima used as occur in eight cases.

an indication of the vowellessness of a charac- 4 Dr. Cuny (Rev. des Etudes Anciennes, 1911, ter. Delia Seta (op. tit., p. 23) also inclines to p. 307), who shares the view that the dashes see in it phonetic modifications of the last sign or virgules' mark the ends of the successive of a group. Cuny (op. tit., pp. 306, 307) agrees sections of the inscriptions, also lays stress on with me in interpreting the virgule as a mark their symmetric arrangement. I cannot follow of punctuation. him, however, in correcting the punctuation of In Scripta Minoa, i, pp. 288, 289, owing the ancient scribe.

to my original misconception of the direction 5 My suggestion to this effect (Scripta Minoa, of the inscriptions, I had regarded these dashes i, p. 291) is taken by Mr. F. W. Read (Pal.

as marking the beginning of such sections. Expl. Fund Quarterly Statement, Jan. 1921, 3 The numbers of sign-groups in the sue- p. 29 seqq.) as the starting-point for his theory cessive subdivisions of A would be i, 2, 9, 3, i, that the Disk contains not words to be sung 3, 2, i, 5, and 4 (regarding 31 as a terminal, to Music, but music itself.

THE PALACE OF MINOS, ETC.

suggesting refrains.

Metrical character of composition.

parison of groups A. 14, 15, i6, and A. 20, 21, 22 1 (Fig. 488,). A considerable parallelism is also shown between the series A. 16, 17, 18, 19 and A. 28, 29, 30, 31 (Fig. 488,J);

These balanced repetitions of sign-groups, the curious symmetrypresentecl by the two sides, perhaps even the circular form of the document itself weigh in favour of this metrical character. It seems possible, moreover, that it formed part of a larger composition. It can hardly be supposed that

Record of sea raid.

FIG. 488, a, b. REPETITIONS OF SIGN-GROUPS ON THE DISK, INDICATIVE OF REFRAINS.

such beautiful type as that here imprinted was executed for the two sides of this Disk alone. It is possible that it is but one of a series containing further staves of a longer metrical composition. It may even be that the number of knobs on the initial lines four in the case of Face A and five on B shows its place in such a series.

The ideographic element in the inscription is so patent that its principal theme can hardly be a matter of doubt. The preponderance of pictorial characters belonging to a certain group of allied subjects strongly suggests that it is mainly concerned with some maritime expedition, probably of a warlike kind, in which case we may see its material results in 1 It is to be observed, however, that, a further sign-group (13, the saffron-flower and whereas A. 20 and 21 form a complete section, bow) is included in the same section as 14, 15.

the form of spoils, captives, as well as the manacles with which they were secured. The plumed head recurs nineteen times, in fourteen cases followed by the round shield, 1 which itself appears in seventeen places; the ship with its armed prow is found seven times, the fish, which at least has a marine significance, six, the arrow four times. It seems probable that the marching figure, which occurs eleven times, should be taken in the same connexion. It will be found that this small but homogeneous group of pictographic signs makes up about a quarter of the total number of separate hieroglyphs contained by the two sides of the Disk, namely 58 out of 244.

A definite geographical indication is supplied by the architectural figure, Conner-No. 24, so reminiscent of the timbered dwellings of Lykia. At the same time, s. w? as has been already noted, the crested headpiece of the warrior and the Anatolia, round shield are characteristic of a group of peoples from the Southern coastlands of Asia Minor whose descents on the Nile-mouth are illustrated by later Egyptian monuments. The ship with the arrow at its prow suggests that we have here, in part at least, the celebration of a similar sea raid.

In view of the architectural parallel it is interesting to note that the Compari-pioneers among the sea rovers from the North, referred to by the Egyptian fa, er "I. records, were the Luku or Lykians, who already in the days of Amenhotep 111 P. a " and his son early, that is, in the fourteenth century u. c. had extended their sea raids descents from the shores of Alashia, 2 South of the lower bend of the Orontes, to the mouths of the Nile. In these and other similar piratic enterprises we see them associated with tribes like the Dardeny, 1 identified with the later Dardanians, and the Pidasa, whose name suggests a transcription of that of the Pisidians. In this latter name and in other cases, as in that of the Snikalasha and Akaitiasta, we note the typically Asianic name-ending, which in Lykian takes the form of-dzi and in Greek-asts,-assos. The first of these names 1 It is interesting to observe that in A. 5 the by Mr. G. A. Wainwright (Klio. xiv, 1914, plumed head and shield had been originally pp. 1-36.) See, too, Hall, P. S. B. A., xxx, omitted and afterwards inserted for the sake of 1909, p. 228.

clearness, the necessary space for this being The identification of the Dardeny with gained by erasing the original boundary line the Dardanians has been generally accepted, at the beginning of the section and carrying it VV. Max Miller suggests that

Pidasa is back within the space at first allotted to A. 4. a transcription of the name of the Pisidians.

See on this Delia Seta, op. at., pp. 17, 18, and He also cites n xo-o? on the Satnioeis (. xxi.

30,31. 87) and the Carian IltSao-cfs. The Karakisha 2 Tell el Amarna Letters, 28, from the King who appear with these he identifies with the of Alashia. The mainland location of Alashia, Kilikians.

as opposed to its identification with Cyprus, Kretschmer, Einleitung in die Geschichte has now been re-affirmed, with new arguments, der grieehischen Sprache, p. 311 seqq.

has suggested a connexion with Sagalassos, 1 the second seems to be the Achaians, with the Asianic suffix. 2 With these are the Shardina and Tnirsha, whose later associations have been sought in Sardinia and the Tyrrhene shores, and the Yevana, in whom we cannot fail to recognize the Ionians.

A group of these warlike sons of Southern and Western Asia Minor, among whom the Luku are mentioned, already appear among the reliefs recording Rameses II's victory over the Hittites and their allies at Kadesh, c. 1296 B. C. 3 They wear the characteristic plumed cap and the short tunic, which clearly distinguishes them from the gaberdined Syrian types with which they are intermingled. One of these warriors, it will be seen, holds a shield with incurved sides, also of use among the Hittites and which is of great interest as supplying the prototype of the Dipxlon or Early Iron Age form in Greece.

Pylon of B u t the fullest monumental record of these Northern invaders is afforded Habu. by the triumphal reliefs of Rameses III on the second pylon of Medinet Habu, 4 recording their double defeat by land and sea, c. 1 200 B. c. The ox-wagons with women and children captured in the struggle on the land side show that it was in some sort a migration of peoples and that the process had already begun which was to convert the coast of Canaan into Palestine. It is, moreover, a significant symptom that the Pulasati, identified with the later Philistines, and the kindred Tzakkaras now come to the fore. In the group shown in Fig. 439 6 some of these, distinguished by their plumed caps and short tunics, are seen fighting Egyptian warriors and a Shardina mercenary, who wears the national horned helmet. The appearance of the Asianic confederates, among whom are mentioned the Shakalashas, recalls in various features the figures on the Disk. They hold round shields, but their arms are the sword and spear, and not the bow, the Egyptian archery indeed being the determining factor in their overthrow.

The Lykians are not named among this later swarm of invaders, but they seem to have preserved the characteristic headgear to a considerably later date, since Herodotus records that the Lykians of Xerxes' army wore

H. R. Hall, op. cit., p. 17;,. 4 Rosellini, Monumenti dew Egitto e della 2 W. Max Miiller, Asien und Europa, p. 371. Nubia, i, PI. 128, 129, 131. Cf., too, Chabas, 3 Rosellini, Monumenti dell Egitto e della Etudes sur fantiquite historique dapres les Nubia,, PI. CIV Cf. Max Miiller, Asien sources egyptiennes, p. 246 seqq. and PI. I: und Europa, p. 361. Together with the Luku, Breasted, History of Egypt, p. 479 seqq.; the Pidasa, Dardeny, and Masa are here men- W. Max Miiller, Asien und Europa, p. tioned. See Petrie, Hist of Egypt, Xlxth to 359 seqq.

XXXth Dynasties, p. 49. From Rosellini, PI. 128.

THE PHAESTOS DISK c; ips with feathered crowns. 1 With them, at least, the horn-bow continued to be the characteristic weapon. 2

The evidence already given can leave little doubt as to the strong I ii. 489. PUI. ASATI (PHILISTINES) AND TSAKKARAS: ON PYLON OK MEDINET HABU.

religious connexion into which the warlike elements on the Disk are brought. Religious In the female breast, and other recurring signs, allusions have been traced nexion of of an Anatolian Mother Goddess. Thus the document bears every mark of l)K a Te Deum, and we see indeed the very symbol of Victory the flying eagle Deum ot

Victory.

irep TTTI 1 Herod, vii. 92 AIKIOI tl ov K ja yri iriaovs impoia

W. Max M tiller, op. tit., p. 362, and cf. H. R. Hall. The Oldest Civilization of Greece, p. 180, and clJ. H. S. xxxiii (1911), p. I2oseqq. The Assyrian mercenaries from Asia Minor(Layard, Nineveh, II, 44) wore a combination of the

Greek helmet and feather crown. In the Persian Satrapy Lists of Naksh-i-Rustam Darius I speaks of the Ionian mercenaries as wearing crowns (W. Max Miiller, loc. fit., who cites Takabare, Spiegel (Ed. i) 197). The Assyrian word translated crowns' is magidttta. 1 Herod., loc. cit.

THE PALACE OF MINOS, ETC.

Cretan Philistines among later sea raiders:

But Disk not a record of Philistines in M. M. Ill Crete.

bearing a serpent in its talons repeated on Face A in company with the horn of sacrifice and dedication. It may, as suggested, have formed part of a still fuller triumphal ode in honour of the native Goddess, herself so closely akin to the Minoan. Such a votive record may well have found its way from some cult centre of a kindred population on the Anatolian side 1 to the great Palace Sanctuary of the Southern Coast of Crete.

It is at the same time necessary to observe that the ethnographic comparisons suggested by the figures on the Disk, combined with the prominence given to the unquestionably Philistine tribes, the Pulasati and Tzakkaras, in the great record of the invasion of Egypt by the Northern invaders about 1200, on the Pylon at Medinet Habu, has led to a faulty method of deduction. The traditions connecting the Philistines in a special way with Crete are well known. It is only necessary to mention the existence of the Philistine tribe of the Cherethim the Kyxijres of thelXX and the persistent cult of the Cretan Zeus at Minoan Gaza. When, then, on this clay document, found on Cretan soil, we recognize features in costume corresponding with those of Philistine tribes of Rameses Ill's time it is at first sight natural to see in it a record of Philistines in their original home. 2

The matter indeed would be simple if the typical culture revealed by the Disk in any way belonged to Minoan Crete. But the detailed examination of the figures given above will have sufficiently demonstrated that this is not the case. On the other hand, as appears from the considerably earlier relief representing the battle of Kadesh at the beginning of the thirteenth century B. c., where similar costumes are shown, though the names of the Luku, Pidasa, and Dardeny are represented, those of the Pulasati and Tzakkaras are conspicuous by their absence. These costumes, indeed, seem to have been the common property of a large group of peoples inhabiting South-Western Asia Minor, and cannot by any means be confined to the Philistine tribes. It is fairly certain that they extended, in later times at least, to the intrusive Ionian and Achaean elements as well as to the Carians and their kin. It is evident indeed that in certain features, such as the Asianic and Hittite shield with incurved sider,, 3 and, later, 1 I observe that Dr. Cuny (Rev. des Etudes

Aniiennes, 1911, p. 312) suggests that the Disk may have been an amulet from some sanctuary of Asia Minor, and that the signs represent a cryptographic magico-religieuse. The execution of the fine 'type is in his view accounted for by the need of printing a number of similar examples.

2 Dr. Eduard Meyer, who has independently insisted on the comparisons with later costume of the Pulusati and their fellows afforded by the Disk (Der Diskus von Phaestos unddie Philister von Kreta, Sit, ungsb. d. Berliner Akad., 1909, p. 1022 seqq.), was carried away by this idea.

: 1 Mr. H. R. Hall, Early Age of Greece, p. 180, n. 2, suggests that the crested head- the round shield, these usages reacted on those of Greece in the Early Iron Age.

But the wearers of the plumed helmets and the owners of the round N (. in-shields seen on the Phaestos Disk, judged by all contemporary comparisons, accoutre are distinctively non-Minoan. When, in the course of the First Late Minoan " f Period we find repeated illustrations of the Keftians or other related n i'sk-peoples on Egyptian monuments, who have a true claim to represent the contemporary Cretan culture, we recognize the figures made familiar to us by Minoan the Procession Fresco at Knossos and, in their offerings, the artistic vases of the Minoan craftsmen. At the date when the Disk was executed not later, as we learn from the associated pottery of the Repositories type, than the beginning of the sixteenth century B. C. such attire as we see on the Disk was altogether foreign to Crete. It cannot indeed be supposed that at that time any part of the Anatolian mainland was in a position to impose its fashions on the centres of Minoan civilization. The exact contrary indeed is the case. In the next Age, the Egyptian sources above refer red to give us the strongest warrant for concluding that the Minoan emissaries for the most part reached Egypt from colonial centres already implanted in the North-Eastern angle of the Mediterranean basin.

The appearance of the Disk on Cretan soil and stored together with a document in the native linear script among the Palace muniments at Phaestos is none the less a phenomenon of far-reaching import.

In a certain sense it may no doubt be taken as a remote foreshadowing Disk of much later events. It is not an improbable supposition, indeed, that in the dark days that followed the break-up of the Minoan civilization in Crete, in g o(some part of the inhabitants (perhaps to an appreciable degree already ethnic Hellenized) threw in their lot with Viking bands of kindred stock from the relatlons Southern fiords of Asia Minor, represented by the Pulasati and Tzakkaras. that they assimilated their external characteristics, and under the name of Cherethites or Cretans took their place as a leading Philistine tribe in the new settlements on the borders of Juclah. 1 But such an interpretation of the phenomena before us is widely different from that which would see in the figures on the Disk the evidence of a Philistine community on Cretan soil in the early part of the sixteenth century before our era.

The Disk, however, must in any case be taken as evidence at that date of direct relations between Crete and the South- Western littoral of Asia dress worn by a warrior on a geometric vase blance is hardly sufficient. fragment, probably from Mycenae (Wide, Jahrb. For the stratigraphic place of the Philistine d. Arch. lust., 1899, p. 85, Fig. 44), may repre- remains in Palestine see above, p. 1 1, note i.

sent a similar plumed cap. But the resem- It is distinctly post-Minoan.

Evidence Minor with its insular dependencies an area corresponding with the old MM in Lykian region. 1 The manifestation of this intercourse that it supplies comes con; at a moment, moreover, when the tide of Cretan maritime enterprise is between setting to the North-West and at Mycenae, Tiryns, and elsewhere new centres sw 6 f Mm an culture are rising into view in what was afterwards Continental Anatolia. Greece.

It would seem indeed that the silver rhyton from the Fourth Shaft Grave of Mycenae a practically contemporary Minoan work of which some fresh fragments have been recently put together may throw additional light on the intimate relations at this time existing between Crete and the South-West Anatolian coastlands. A fuller consideration of this historic relic must be reserved for a later Section of this work. 2 The central theme of its reliefs is the attack and relief of a walled town, and it will be seen that certain structural features and religious objects, traceable on one of the new fragments, 3 support the view, suggested by the general appearance of the walls and towers, 4 that we have here to do with a Minoan fortified settlement in partibus infidelium. The ethnic elements, according to the view set out below, apart from some female figures on the walls and a Minoan relief party arriving by sea, divide themselves into friendly and hostile natives, mostly stark naked. Their weapons lances, slings, and horn-bows on the one side, and throw-sticks, stones, and simple clubs on the other seem to point in an Asianic direction. But this view would receive the strongest confirmation, if we may accept the acute suggestion of Dr. H. R. Hall, 5 that what have been taken for bristly shocks of hair on the heads of the friendlies are in truth reminiscences of the feather crest such as we see it on the Disk. In many cases the details are very sketchily executed, but the head of a man on a tower on one of the fragments recently set up enlarged in the inset certainly favours this comparison.

An As a written document the Phaestos Disk still stands out as an unique unique record, but its potential value must be constantly placed to a suspense account in any study of the contemporary Minoan culture.

1 The Lykian name probably originally in- 3 The sacral horns of Minoan cult seem eluded a much larger area. W. Max Miiller, to me to be clearly visible, as well as the op. cit, p. 363, adduces the name of Lykaonia characteristic 'superposed pillars'. (See in favour of this wider signification, and also Vol. II.) the apparently collective name of Liiku for all See above, p. 308.

the Asiaminor tribes in the Merenptah text. ' A Note on the Pimentos Disk. J. H. S., 2 See Vol. II. xxxi, 1911, p. ngseqq.

GREATER ART.

Change in Signet types no longer present inscriptions; Survivals of hieroglyphic prism seals; Lcnloid and amygdaloid bead-seals; Signet rings as those of IVth Shaft Grave impressions of such; Gems of Sphungaras Urns Talismanic Class; Milk Stones'; Architectural, pillared and Cabled, class-Rustic Shrines; Intaglios on Flattened Cylinders; Plated Steatite example and parallel supplied by rhyton fragment; Fisherman and Skaros' fish; Repository Hoard of Clay Seal-impressions unijite chronological value; Contemporary Hoards of Zakro and Hagia Triada; Specimens of Costume and armour on Sealings of these Hoards; Male types with lowing apron-illustrated by votive Jigtirine; The Ritual Cuirass'; Other contemporary finds of Sealings at Knossos; Use of Sieves in Excavation; Religious types from Repository; Honied sheep a nurse of infant God; Architectonic setting; Triple gradation beneath Bull-hunting scenes taken from supports of friezes; Triply graduated supports of Palace Reliefs; Illustrations from Steatite rhytons; Columns between agonistic groups pugilist and column on Scaling; Column equivalent of Grand Stand or Theatre; Fragment of Knossian rhyton; The fallen champion of Boxing Ring; Gladiatorial Sane on Sealing; Wounded champion supported on one arm; Scene of Combatants on Mycenae Signet adapted from agonistic episodes; Ultimate influence of Minoan Thealral episodes on Epic imagery; Episodes of Bull ring on signets taken over from frescoes and reliefs; Excerpts from Cattle Pieces; Various types of Repository Sealings; Instantaneous impressions of Nature; Prototype of Scylla Sca monster on Mycenae rhyton; Comparisons with Zakro seal-types; Middle Minoan and Early Egyptian Elements.

TOGETHER with the coming in of the new system of writing there makes itself apparent a revolutionary change in the fashions of signets. With the Types, cessation of the hieroglyphic form of script the custom of engraving single hieroglyphs or groups of signs on seals was also given up. The pictorial character of the earlier signs, enhanced as it was by decorative flourishes, in itself afforded quite elegant signet types. But the new linear class had not such aesthetic qualities. Seal-stones with linear inscriptions are practically unknown at this Period, though a single example, a green steatite bead of

THE PALACE OF MINOS, ETC.

No longer Inscriptions on Seals.

Graffiti, however, on Clay-Sealings.

Hieroglyphic sign-groups imitated as amulets.

almond shape, engraved with characters of Class A, was found on the site of the Little Palace at Knossos (Fig. 490). This, however, must be regarded as quite an exceptional phenomenon though, occasionally, single linear characters appear in the field of lentoid gems of the pictorial class. The rule was now, where inscriptions were necessary, for the writing to be incised on the clay of the sealing itself while still soft. In the last Age of the Palace, when the linear Script B was prevalent, this practice was much in vogue, and, as we shall see, not only were the pinched clay nodules endorsed on two sides, but the seal impression showing the pictorial type was itself often countermarked with one or more linear signs.

A class of seal-stones and signets makes its appearance indeed about this time which has a false hieroglyphic aspect. This class generally exhibits

FIG. 490. GREEN STEATITE AMYGDALOID FROM LITTLE PALACE, KNOS-SOS, WITH INSCRIPTION OF LINEAR CLASS A. (f).

FIG. 491. LATE OUT-GROWTH OF PRISM-SEAL.

heads of various animals grouped together, most of them taken over without method from earlier signets. Thus on a seal impression from Hagia Triada 2 we see the heads of a bull, a wolf, and a dog, and two other carni- 1 The characters of the uppei line answer to regular types of the Linear Class A. The first of 1. 2 is common to the Hieroglyphs (No. 25), but also finds an analogy in Class A. The second of 1. 2 resembles Hieroglyph No. 33. The transitional aspects of this part of the inscription incline us to place it very early in the M. M. Ill series.

Man. Ant., xiii (1903), p. 35, Fig. 26. My own interpretation of the figures is somewhat different from that there suggested.

vorous animals, while an agate lentoid from Mycenae of clearly cpntemporary fabric shows the facing head of a lion, part of the fore-part of another, a goat's head, a water-fowl, and the running figure of an animal. Seals with such groups must be referred to the amuletic class described below.

Just as certain signs of the earlier hieroglyphic type can be shown to survive with a talismanic value, so too we see the old prism. form of seal three-itself occasionally preserved in a modified aspect. A specimen of a three- a! sided cornelian of this class with cordiform and other motives is given in sp ais. Fig. 4 (,)1. The pattern on face c of this has a special interest since we see here an adaptation of a common M. M. II design, itself taken over from a Twelfth Dynasty scarab type, where the central circle stands as the hieroglyph of the Sun God, Ra. 2 It had, therefore, a traditional amuletic value. More globular versions of these three-sided types survived well on into the First Late Minoan Period.

Apart from such occasional survivals, however, the old three- or four-sided hieroglyphic prism seals and those shaped like a modern signet, come seemingly to an abrupt end at the close of M. M. II. Their place is taken by a pictorial class of perforated gems, usually worn as we know from later evidence of tombs and from the Cup-bearer fresco about the wrist. I n the Lentoid earlier phase the most frequent of these are the circular lentoids. Rudely engraved bead-seals of this type exist in black steatite, which go back, as the style of their designs and engraving shows, at least to the Second Early Minoan Period. In a somewhat separate category must be placed the thicker variety with square-cut edges which seems to have attained prominence in M. M. II and to have survived into the succeeding Periods. 3

By the close of M. M. II, as we learn from the sealings of the Hieroglyphic Deposit at Knossos, the engraved designs on these lentoids were already attaining a considerable degree of naturalistic perfection. Grotesque rock scenery was, as we have seen already, a favourite subject. The evidence Amygda of this Deposit also shows that, side by side with this round type, other seal-stones of elongated almond-shaped or amygdaloid form were also coming into vogue. This type, so usual in Late Minoan times, seems to have been ultimately derived from a proto-Dynastic Egyptian bead-form. It does not appear to have been used as a field for hieroglyphic sign-groups, but the impression of a seal-stone of this class, representing a dog chasing a wild 1 Furtwangler, An tike Gemmen, p. 52, who, F. LI. Griffith informs me, the sign of Jfa is however, speaks

of the signs as belonging to replaced by the amuletic nefer symbol = good, an actual
Bilderschrift. See above, p. 275, Fig. 204, a, and p. 565, 2 On other scarabs of this
class, as Mr. Fig. 411.

goat, appears already on a clay sealing from the Hieroglyphic Deposit. 1

Flat- Together with these the type of bead-seal or ring bezel, above described as

Cylinder resembling a flattened cylinder, 2 plays a prominent part. This was also
type- known in M. M. II, at times accompanied by hieroglyphic sign-groups, but it
seems to have attained its maximum vogue in M. M. Ill and the transitional epoch that
heralds the opening of the Late Minoan Age.

Signet The glyptic evidence that might have been derived from tombs of the
Fourth better class is wanting in Crete throughout the whole of the Middle Minoan
Shaft Age. For the close of M. M. I II, indeed, the Fourth Shaft Grave at
Grave.

Mycenae, which contains no imported pottery later than that time, supplied two
good examples of the signet rings now in vogue. These rings are of the usual Minoan
and Mycenaean form with elongated oval bezels, the major axis of which is set at right
angles to the hoop. Their subjects, which are illustrated below 3 in connexion with
the present materials, are in one case a scene of combat between warriors, in the other
two men in a chariot sions 6 of of primitive form hunting a fallow deer, a species that
does not seem

Signet- to have been indigenous in Mainland Greece. It will be seen that some of
Reposi- the oval impressions of the clay sealings from the Repository Hoard and
Hoard other contemporary deposits were clearly made by signet-rings of the same
type.

Gems In regard to one particular class of engraved stones belonging to the epoch
that marks the transition from M. M. Ill b to L. M. I, some direct evidence has been
afforded by the Urn burials of Sphunearas, 4 near Gournia.

Urns,.

M. M. III- The ossuary urns themselves in this case contained a series of intaglios
of

L M ' rough execution with stereotyped designs of a rustic class known to have been
in common use throughout the island, and indeed well represented in the immediate
neighbourhood of Knossos itself. Were it not for the very definite evidence afforded
by the Sphungaras specimens they might easily, from their rude style, be attributed to
a much later Minoan phase.

Tails- Since, however, the Sphungaras evidence points to their having over-
Cla'ss! lapped the early part of L. M. I, and in view of the fact that specimens
have been found in Melian tombs associated in some cases with imported pottery in
the later L. M. I style, it seems best to postpone a fuller consideration of this class of
seal-stones to a Section of this work dealing with that Period.

It will there be demonstrated that they largely served a talismanic or amu- 1 Scripta
Minoa, i, p. 22, Fig. na, and s See p. 691, Figs. 512, 513and Vol. II. PI. Ill, 73 a.
Edith H. Hall, Excavations in Eastern 2 See above, p. 275, Fig. 204, r-s, and Crete:
Sphoungaras (Philadelphia, 1912, pub-p. 276. lished by the University Museum).

letic purpose. Indeed, under the name of ya o Tpcui milk-stones many Modem of them are still worn for their special virtues by the Cretan women.

Among frequent motives represented are rough designs of fish and squids; plants, often associated with two-handled cups and spouted ewers, like those in the hands of the Genii who water vegetation, as seen on Late Minoan gems, 1 heart-shaped figures like Fig. 491, b, lions' masks, the Double Axe, and pillared structures. Though steatite is also used, the materials, as we see them at Sphudgaras, are mainly of hard stones such as jasper, cornelian, rock-crystal, and occasionally amethyst. It is noteworthy as showing that representatives of this class were already current throughout the whole of

FIG. 492, a, t, c, d, e. SUCCESSIVE DEGENERATIONS OF LIONS MASK SIGN ON GEMS USED

AS TALISMANS (f).

the Third Middle Minoan Period, that several of these types are in fact survivals of earlier hieroglyphs, which, it may be recalled, always retained an ideographic as well as a phonetic value. The lion's mask which occurs in sign-groups (Fig. 492, a) a and is often repeated has a specially prominent place among these later amuletic types. It first appears as the sole type on stones of the early round form, lentoids with the edge cut square. Fig. 492, 6, and passes, through intermediate stages such as c and d, to a series of almond-shaped bead-seals under a more or less conventionalized aspect, till, without a knowledge of the intervening links, the original meaning of the design would hardly be guessed (Fig. 492, e). 3 This latter type (e) doubtless possessed 1 See Myc. free and Pillar Cult, p. 3, Fig. t. 45; c, steatite, E. Crete; d, steatite, Knossos; See p. 643, Fig. 47", 74. e, cornelian, Siteia, and similar, haematite, 3 Fig. 492,, Agate, E. Apx., 1907, Pl. VII. Knossos district. A. E. Coll. I XX.

THE PALACE OF MINOS, ETC.

Conventional fagades of buildings.

Later class with pillars and gables.

Rustic shrines.

great strength-giving virtue: in an identical form it was very widely diffused throughout Crete.

In the case of these amuletic seal-stones a tendency may be observed to substitute, as in the instance given, an almond-shape for the lentoid form, which seems to have been the more usual Middle Minoan vehicle for the types they bear. This transition can be traced in the lion's mask series, and a characteristic example of it occurs in the case of certain types which stand in a near relation to the M. M. II-III specimens representing architectural fagacles illustrated above. 1 An interesting variant of this motive from the Knossos district is here shown in Fig. 493, a, from a green steatite lentoid of

FIG. 493. SEAL-STONES WITH FACADES OF GABLED BUILDINGS, M. M. III-L. M. I (f).

the early round shape with square-cut edges, traditional in this architectural class. Here we see the usual panelled front and central doorway, but with a gable above, curiously suggestive of a Greek temple pediment. In Fig. 493, b and c on the other hand, of amygdaloid shape, the gable surmounts a columnar front. Of these c from the

Pedeada district 2 East of Knossos, showing four columns, is engraved on a three-sided amuletic stone of the kind referred to above.

The three-columned type presented by b also recurs on one of the Sphungaras seal-stones. 3 It seems possible that some of these apparently gabled buildings were of circular construction with peaked roofs and would thus represent a form of round hut with posts under its eaves, such as that which in Ancient Rome supplied the prototype of the Temple of Vesta. A remarkable variety 1 See p. 565, Fig. 411. three-sided bead-seal with a high-spouted ewer 2 In the Candia Museum, bought at the and a two-handled chalice on the two other village of Geraki. See Xanthudides, E. Apx-, sides.

1907, PI. VII, Fig. 47 a, and p. 168, on a 3 E. H. Hall, op. tit., p. 70, Fig 45,0.
FIG. 494. RUSTIC SHRINE.
reproduced in Fig. 4J)4. 4 though it only shows a pillar on either side, is so cut by the engraver's wheel as to present a rounded contour. What certainly seems to be intended for serpents appear on either side. It looks indeed as if we had to do with a rustic shrine of the Snake Goddess.

Among the forms of intaglio represented at Sphungaras, in addition to intaglios the lentoid and amygdaloid types, is that which has been described above as e"ned Cy-the flattened cylinder, which seems to have played a specially prominent linders part in the Third Middle Minoan Period. A very fine example of this type,. showing a bull grappled by an acrobatic figure of a man, while drinking from a high tank, has been already illustrated, 1 and the correspondence between the decorative pattern there shown and painted plaster designs of the Phaestos Palace may be taken to bring its date at least within the lower limits of the present Period. Another secure chronological basis is afforded by the fact that inipressions of this rectangular type of intaglio were found amongst the hoard of sealings from the Temple Repositories, including the design of the male warrior beside a lioness, illustrated above. 2

A very interesting ex- Steatite ,,. e, example ample 01 this type of seal, p i a ted
FIG. 495. 7, STEATITE BEAD-SEAL OF FLATTENED.,, u:-li In its nki r anh with gold. CYLINDER TYPE COATED WITH GOLD PLATE; 6, SEEN FROM ABOVE (f). the free stjlc of its eiigrav- ing recalls the greater works of M. M. III art to which the Dolphin Fresco belongs, is reproduced in Fig. 495, a, b. It is of black steatite, but this material, in itself unattractive and easily worn, had been coated with a thin gold plating carefully impressed into the intaglio itself, which shows two dolphins swimming towards a rocky marge. As will be seen from the Figure, most of the gold plating has been preserved, and there are traces in the groove behind and beneath the edges of the gold of some adhesive material of a pinkish texture. The intaglio had evidently formed the bezel of a ring, the 1 A banded agate from East Crete. This use of seals of this type is also supplied by and Fig. 493, b, are in my own collection. more or less contemporary impressions on 2 See above, p. 377, Fig. 274. sealings from the hoards of Zakro and H.

3 See p. 505, Fig. 363, b. Evidence of the Triada referred to below, pp. 678-9.
THE PALACE OF MINOS, ETC.
metal hoop of which has worn a deep groove in the inner side of its

Relief of axial perforation. The coating of the black steatite intaglio with precious rlwtorf metal had at the time when I obtained it, in 1894, suggested the idea also gold- that the black steatite vessels with reliefs had been originally embellished in a like manner, and that this practice in fact supplied the antecedent stage to the later technique illustrated by the Vapheio Cups. 1 A discovery made on the same site during the excavations of the British School has since afforded a remarkable confirmation of this view. A fragment of a black steatite rh) ton was there found presenting in relief part of the figure of a charging boar in the finest naturalistic style of the present Period (Fig. 496) 2, and with a piece of the original gold plating attached to it. It will be shown that, from the Second Middle Minoan Period onwards, boars and boar-hunts were a familiar theme of Minoan Art. The more detailed representation of the sport on the Tirynthian fresco 3 doubtless had its forerunners on Cretan soil.

These flattened cylinders seem to have been specially in vogue during the present Period, though they were still in use in the earlier part of the Late Minoan Age. The gold beads of this form from the Third Shaft Grave at Mycenae 4 with the episodes of single combat, and of the lion-hunt in a highly advanced sensational style, may be referred like other elements of that tomb to L. M. I. Towards the close of that Period, however, this type of intaglio shows a tendency to die out 3 and survives later rather in the form of decorative beads.

FIG. 496. FRAGMENT OF STEATITE RHYTON FOUND WITH GOLD PLATE ATTACHING TO IT.

1 See Myc. Tree and Pillar Cult, pp. 3, 4: the intaglio was found at Palaikastro.

2 I owe the drawing from which this figure was reproduced to the kindness of Prof. Bosanquet and of the Committee of the British School at Athens.

3 See Rodenwaldt, Tiryns, ii, p. I25seqq.,

Fig. 55, PL XIII, and p. 126, n. 2.

4 Schliemann, Mycenae, p. 174, Figs. 253-5.

"A single example was found in the Cemetery of Phaestos (L. Savignoni, Mon. Ant., xiv, p. 625, Fig. 97 a, b. But none were found in the tombs of Knossos of L. M. II or early L. M. Ill date.

In Fig. 4J 7 is reproduced a specimen of an intaglio of this Class found to the North of the Palace Site at Knossos, which from its somewhat naively natural style must also with great probability be included within the limits of M. M. II I. It is executed in a beautiful mottled chalcedony and its Usher-subject corroborates the evidence supplied above by the fish-bones in the cooking-pot, 1 as to the part played by fish in the Minoan dietary. We see here. f a fisherman, draped about the loins, raising a cuttlefish with one hand and in

FIG. 498. CORNELIAN AMYGDALOID SHOWING SKAROS FISH, (f)

FIG. 499. CORNELIAN AMVGDA-LOID: FLYING FISH, ()

FIG. 497. MOTTLED CHALCEDONY INTAGLIO, KNOSSOS. (f) the other holding what appears to be the much prized Skaros fish 2 of Crete. Its characteristic features are more fully illustrated by a cornelian intaglio of the amygdaloid type 3 executed in a bold though somewhat summary manner and giving a curious perspective rendering of the fish swimming (Fig. 41)8). The Scarus Cretensis is a kind of parrot wrasse for which the Cretan waters were specially famous, and, under its ancient name is still considered by the Greeks to-day, as it was in Pliny's time, to be the first of fishes. 4 Its species is well marked by the sharp beak and it is surrounded by the sea-weeds 5 that supplied its food and the mastication of which gave the idea that it was a ruminant." An exquisite miniature reproduction of 1 Seep. 555. 4 Pliny, H. N. ix. 29 Nunc scaro datur 2 Compare the fisherman holding a fish, principals.

perhaps of the same species, on an elongated amygdaloid of haematite (probably Cretan), B. M. Cat., No. 80.

3 Acquired by me from near Lappa in 1895. Both this and the original of Fig. 497 are in my own collection.

Projecting ends of these are here confused with the posterior end of the fish.

Dr. Gunther quoted in R. Lydekker, F. R. S., Jf. Nat. Hist., v, p. 421. Pliny's words (H. N. loc. cit.) are Scarus. solus piscium dicitur ruminare herbisque vesci.

THE PALACE OF MINOS, ETC.

Repository

Hoard of Clay Sealings.

Unique chronological value for M. M. Ill types.

Contemporary Hoard of Zakro.

what appears to be the same fish will be illustrated in connexion with the Deposit of Ivories in the Domestic Quarter. 1 In Fig. 499 is seen a lively representation of a flying fish Xisovo- rapov in a style so closely approaching that of the faience reliefs of the Temple Repository and the Melian Fresco, that it is impossible not to regard it as a contemporary work, though the gem itself, a cornelian amygdaloid, was said to have been found on the Mainland side. 2

The most precise evidence for the dating of the intaglio types of this epoch is supplied by the hoard of clay seal-impressions found in the W. Temple Repository. Altogether over a hundred and sixty of these were discovered presenting some fifty varieties of designs. The clay nodules on which these were impressed showed the remains of carbonized strings or threads, which had run through them and by which they had originally been attached to documents on perishable materials perhaps parchment, or even papyrus. The associated clay tablets, belonging to the earliest phase of the Linear Class A, sufficiently inform us of the character of the script employed on these lost documents.

The designs here exhibited give us an invaluable insight into the seal-types current during the closing phase of M. M. Ill, though, as signets and engraved gems are of durable materials, it is always possible that one or other type may go back to a somewhat earlier time. The hieroglyphic class of seal of the earlier part of the Middle Minoan Age is, however, entirely unrepresented in this hoard.

The definite chronological limits, at least in the lower direction, here laid down afford a secure basis for classifying a considerable series of parallel types presented by the hoards of sealings found at Zakro and Hagia Triada under less strict chronological conditions.

The hoard of sealings discovered by Mr. Hogarth in a house excavated by him at Lower Zakro in Eastern Crete, consisted of some five hundred clay nodules bearing impressions of seals and signet rings. 3 These impressions, two or more of which sometimes occurred on the same nodule, included 144 varieties of type. The house itself (A), in which these sealings were found, contained some elements, such as a painted rhyton with marine subjects, 4 belonging to the fully developed L. M. I phase. But the great majority of the seal-types represented seem to go back beyond the limits of the Late Minoan Age.

1 See Vol. II.

It was purchased by me in Athens in 1896 and was said to have been found at Klitara in Arcadia.

3 Hogarth, The Zakro Sealings (. H. S., xxii, 1902, p. 76 seqq.).

4 Hogarth, Bronze Age Vases from Zakro (. H. S., xxii, Pl. XII. i, and p. 333).

Not only is their general character foreign to that revealed by Late Minoan seals from various sources, but the presence of certain specimens with hieroglyphic sign-groups shows that some of the clay nodules belong to the early part of the Middle Minoan Age. 1 The geometrical and decorative patterns on these sealings have also, as will be shown, early associations.

In form, moreover, some of the Zakro nodules closely approach those of the Hieroglyphic Deposit at Knossos, though others show a great resemblance to those of the Temple Repository. With them moreover occurred a-clay roundel of the same form as those there found with a graffito inscription of the linear Class A.

As in both the above cases, they bear the impress of very fine threads which seem to have fastened small documents, and at other times show a small perforation along their major axis, which had originally held the remains of string for securing various objects. Some of the types bear a transitional character, and it is difficult to say on which side of the border they individually belong. Few, however, can be classed with typical Late Minoan designs such as we meet with for instance on the intaglios found in the Vapheio Tomb, the lower limit of which as we know from the associated pottery, belongs to the later phase of L. M. I.

The hoard found in the Room of the Seals' at Hagia Triada Hagia numbered over 450 sealings, mostly counter-marked with signs of Class A. 2 Hoard. Many types of this hoard bear a strong similarity with those from the Temple Repository at Knossos, while others repeat compound or fantastic designs of the Zakro class. The sealings are of a roughly faced pyramidal form with seal impressions either on one side or on the base, and perforated at the apex for the string that suspended them to documents. A few showed traces of having been applied, as sealing-wax is still, to the bands or strings wrapped round packets. Traces of this practice also occurred among the Knossian speci-sealings. In other cases the clay nodule had been pressed round the knot ar c hajc that had tied the parcel. 0

A common feature in the seal-types presented by all three hoards is the j ngs of archaic character of the costume in the figured subjects. These generally occur on long oval fields which we may take to represent the bezels of signet 1 One of these nodules, No. 125 of Mr. prism-seal (op. fit., i, p. 151, P. 10, omitted

Hogarth's list, had been impressed by an ob- on Pl. I) belongs to Class A, and an unpub- ! ong bead-seal showing three hieroglyphs of the lished impression (No. 140 of Mr. Hogarth's advanced class (B), ascribed above to M. M. list) seems to be of the same class. II (Scrifta Minoa, i, p. 157, P. 45). Another J F. Halbherr, Scoperti ad

Hagtua Triada impression probably of a three-sided steatite (Man. Ant., xiii, p. 29, seqq.)

THE PALACE OF MINOS, ETC.

Shields helmets.

rings, and, as is usual in such cases, are for the most part of a religious nature. Some typical specimens excerpted from such types are given in Fig. 600. Of the female fashions, a, which shows the lion-holding type of the Repository sealing reproduced above, 1 and c are decidedly short-skirted, 2 a characteristic that disappears in the Late Minoan Age. In b we seem to see a shorter gown above the skirt as in some of the Petsof a costumes going back to M. M. I. 3 The elongated bell-shaped skirt, also well represented at

FIG. 500. CHARACTERISTIC TYPES OF DRESS ON SEAL-TYPES OF M. M. Ill DATE. (a, e, KNOSSOS; c, g, h, ZAKRO; b, d, , , HAGIA TRIADA.)

Petsofa, is illustrated by d, and shows a succession of horizontal flounces like those of the Snake Goddess and her votaries. It is to be noted that the later, V-shaped arrangement suggestive of a divided skirt, which in Late Minoan times is so generally in vogue, is here conspicuous by its absence.

Of the male costumes, e from the Repository Hoard, andfrom Hagia Triada, showing respectively a spearman and bowman associated with a lion and a pard, have already received illustration among the contemporary religious types. 4 The bow of is of the horned, Asiatic class, the shield of e is arched above like that held by the warrior on the contemporary 1 Sec p. 505, Fig. 363, a. represents the Minoan Goddess holding the 2 Another good example of this feature is to Double Axe and another sacred object.

be seen on the steatite signet from a M. M. III. deposit E. of the School Room at Knossos given above, p. 435, Fig. 312, a. It 3 Compare Myres, Sanctuary of Petsofo (B. S. A., ix), Pl. XI, 27.

4 See above, p. 505, Fig. 303, b, c.

signet from Mycenae illustrated below (Fig. 513), and is seen in its complete outline on the dagger-blade from Grave IV depicting the lion-hunt. 1 A similar shield is also seen in the hands of a spearman with a crested helm on a cornelian lentoid from East Crete, of rude execution, but further attesting the diffusion of this form in Minoan Crete. It may also be noted that the sole type of one of the H. Triada sealings is a crested helmet with cheek-pieces, like that worn by the protagonist on the Mycenae signet.

The double flounce of the loin-cloth in f is interesting as it represents Male a-process of development parallel with that which produced the flounced skirts of the women. In g and li, on the other hand, a kind of flowing apron apron, is added to the loin-cloth. This type, the essential features of which as seen on the seal-impressions, is here summarized in g and , recurs in a series of religious subjects, in several cases associated with the Sacred Double Axe. 3 It may therefore be regarded as a ritual garb which, as we see from one of the Zakro sealings, was used in ceremonial processions. This flowing apron, as is clearly shown by the Zakro seal-impression from which k is taken, was worn in front while behind him hangs a shorter piece of drapery not dissimilar from that of an ordinary loin-cloth. The best illustration of this Parallel costume, however, is supplied by a bronze votive figure obtained by me by "bronze from the same sacrificial stratum of the Psychro Cave that contained the JK ure inscribed Libation Table, and which may therefore be regarded as a contem- Votive porary relic of the cult. It is here for the first time reproduced in pj chjo'. Fig. 501. The figure is that of a youth with two curling locks of hair falling clown behind and stands on a base provided with a nail-like projection below to fix it to some sanctuary slab.

The personage from a Hagia Triada seal-impression, Fig. 500, i, shows The a flowing apron of this kind appearing beneath the ritual cuirass' like that worn by the rustic leader of the harvesters on the Hagia Triada rhyton, enabling us indeed to complete that figure. In this, and in other cases noted below, we see a very close correspondence between seal-types of this group 1 Schuchhardt, Schliemann's Excavations, there placed upside down.

p. 229, Fig. 227. Similar shields, also fully See above, p. 435, Fig. 312, b. Each of represented, are seen in the hands of two the two male attendants of this class seen on spearmen on another gold signet ring from either side of what seems to be a dancing

Mycenae, in the Ashmolean Museum. This figure of the Goddess on a seal-impression type of shield with its two angular shoulders from Hagia Triada (Man. Ant., xiii, p. 39, must be distinguished from the Egyptian class Fig. 33) holds aloft a double axe. (The blades with a fully rounded top. of these have since been recognized on one of 3 Man. Ant., xiii, p. 35, Fig. 27 and PI. V. the impressions, but are not shown in the

The object not having been recognized it is Figure.)

THE PALACE OF MINOS, ETC.

of deposits and the fuller scenes depicted on the reliefs of the steatite rhytons a correspondence of such a kind as to argue contemporaneity in date. This class of vessel will be more fully considered in a later Section of this work.

Certain other small hoards or isolated finds of clay seal-impressions at

Other contemporary finds of Seal-impressions Knossos, belonging to de- sos. posits of approximately the same date as the Temple Repository, help to supplement the evidence that it supplies. Among these may be mentioned sealings or fragments of such found in the Area of the Jewel Fresco, 1 and others which occurred by the blocked opening of the Corridor of the Bays and which must be brought into connexion with the knobbed ritual vessels found there and with the Medallion Pithoi of the adjoining Magazine, all belonging to the closing M. M. 111 phase. 2 Another group of sealings of distinctly early affinities some of them perhaps slightly overlapping the bounds of this Period came to light below the later Service Staircase of the Domestic Quarter. 3 Among these was the com-1 Among these impressions was a standing sealings clearly of a later style and associated

FIG. 501. VOTIVE BRONZE FIGURE FROM THE SACRIFICIAL STRATUM OF THE PSYCHRO CAVE.

figure of a bull, from an intaglio of the flattened cylinder type, a seated bull from a stone of amygdaloid form, and a fragmentary sealing showing part of an adorant against a plait-work background.

2 On the pavement of the Middle E.-W. Corridor was also found a scattered deposit of with clay tablets of the Linear Class B belonging to the last Palace Epoch.

3 See p. 713. In this deposit were found several designs showing lions seizing bulls or deer, and others representing grains of corn, a type of very early tradition.

pound type illustrated below (Fig. 536, c), showing two confronted griffins recalling Zakro types. More isolated finds of seal-impressions were made in M. M. Ill deposits by the Court of the Stone Spout, and in a rubbish heap on the South-Eastern border of the Palace. Some of the earliest seal-impressions from the site of the Little Palace may also have been made from intaglios that date from the close of this Period.

From the earliest days of the work at Knossos special efforts were made to recover this class of material, which, from the small size of the objects and their earthen aspect, it is most difficult to detect. For the first time, it may be claimed, in a great Excavation, sieves were constantly at work in dealing with all promising deposits. The great bulk, however, of the clay seal-impressions thus collected, with the exception of the Hoard in the Repository Cist, naturally belonged to the latest Age of the Palace, and the sealings were largely accompanied by contemporary tablets of Class B.

Examples of religious representations from the Repository Hoard have already been given, together with a parallel group from Hagia Triada. Another important contemporary example of this class came to light in the M. M. Ill rubbish heap, or so-called K. a(fti'tioi, on the South-Eastern border of the Palace (Fig. 502). Two female devotees are here seen wearing the peaked tiara which seems to have been a characteristic of the Palace Cult at this epoch. They wear skirts that do not show any trace of flounces, and are elegantly executed in symmetrically facing positions, holding up in both hands an object that has unfortunately been much obliterated, but which may with most probability be identified with a rhyton of the pointed shape. From the flatness and elongated shape of the field we may infer that the impression is from the bezel of a signet-ring. On No. 5 of the Zakro sealings a female votary robed as Fig. 500, c, above is seen with one hand raised before a figure, which is clearly an adaptation of an adoring Cynoce-phalus. 1 An adorant dog-ape, moreover, appears as the sole type of one of the sealings of the contemporary hoard from Hagia Triada.- Once more

Finds of sealings due to careful sifting of deposits.

Religious subjects.

FIG. 502. CLAY IMPRESSION OF SIGNET-RING, KNOSSOS (f).

1 Hogarth, Zakro Sealings (. H. S., xxii), p. 77 and p. 78, Fig. 4.

2 Halbherr, Man. Ant., xiii, p. 39, Fig. 32.

THE PALACE OF MINOS, ETC.

we have before us an unquestionable example of an Egyptian influence on Minoan religious imagery.

Infant God suckled by ewe.

Two symbols that are clearly of a sacral nature are found on the Repository sealings. In one case we see a plain cross used as the single type of a series of impressions. 1 In another case the Swastika appears above

FIG. 503. INTAGLIOS REPRESENTING HORNED SHEEP (f).

a horned sheep and manger (Fig. 518, K)? As noted above, the same animal is depicted on a fine seal-impression from the earlier, Hieroglyphic Deposit, with an infant below. These conjunctions, indeed, point to the conclusion that we have here early references to the infant God or hero suckled by an animal so repeatedly illustrated by the later mythology of the island.- 1

Num. Chron., 1896, PL II, 10 (now A. E.

1 See above, p. 515, Fig. 374.

2 See also above, p. 515, Fig. 372.

3 Coins of Praesos supply a variant of the Diktaean myth in which a cow is substituted for the she-goat (see Svoronos, Nutnisinat. que dela Crete ancienne, PI. XXVII, 2; H. Weber,

Coll.). Cf. too, A. B. Cook, Zeus, p. 660, Figs. 507, 508). On the coins of Kydonia we see the eponymic hero in the form of a child suckled by a bitch.

Amongst various sealings from the Repository presenting plant and Horned animal designs in a simple natural style shown in Fig. 518, a depicts another figure of the same horned sheep in a standing position, without accessories. The clay impression from which this was copied is somewhat blurred, but it leads us to a fuller contemporary portrayal of the same animal on a cornelian bead-seal of the flattened cylinder shape obtained by me on the site of Lyktos, Fig. 503, a, and to the similar type (b, on a chalcedony lentoid of the early flat-edged form 1 from Lasithi, in which, however, the animal stands on a stepped base as if forming part of an architectural frieze, and with a cornice and panelling above. The hatched decoration of this panelling corresponds in fact with those of the class of conventional fa9ades referred to above. fragmentary impressions of which, moreover, occurred among the clay sealings of the Repository Hoard. 2 To the importance of these architectonic features we shall have occasion to return.

On the red cornelian amygdaloid gem, Fig. 503, c, which also seems to be of relatively early fabric, the animal is seen in its wild state, lassoed by the hunter while engaged in suckling its young. The beast is here magnified, as is usual in such representations, and the Minoan artist had no more difficulty in depicting the ewe with long horns than he had with regard to the she-goat of the faience relief illustrated above. The animal itself is also of constant recurrence on Late Minoan intaglios, often shown in groups. The wild sheep depicted on these intaglios may be either the Armenian breed or the Cypriote variety. As a further illustration of its characteristic appearance the Late Minoan lentoid, d, is here inserted.

The manner in which this animal is shown on the early lentoid, Architec Fig. 503, b, as forming part of the frieze of an architectural faqade with a stepped base below, is of special interest. It stands in connexion with other similar phenomena illustrating the extent to which the Minoan gem-engraver's repertory was drawn from larger works of art, often, no doubt, through intermediary models supplied by the reliefs on vases of steatite or faience or from pyxides' of ivory. This figure is clearly taken from a frieze in which other animals are included, whether or not of the same species. A later parallel is indeed supplied by the ivory casket or pyxis from the beehive tomb of Menidi, the circumference of which is divided into two processional rows of horned sheep. 3 1 The shape of the stone (once in my posses- in the hoard, including those shown in Fig. 411, sion) resembles that shown in Fig. 493, a. above, a, b, above.

presenting a conventional facade. This type of Lolling, Das Kuppelgrab von Affniji, lentoid goes back, as we have seen, to M. M. II. Pl. VIII; Perrot histoire, vi, La Greet primi-5 Several fragments of such types were found tive, p. 827, Fig. 406.

THE PALACE OF MINOS, ETC.

Triple gradation beneath Bull-hunting Scenes.

But, apart from the clearly marked architectural setting reproduced in Fig. 503, 6, the double gradation that we see beneath the animal has a special value since it represents a recurring feature on a parallel series of gem-types, which reappears beneath the closely related reliefs on the zones of steatite rhytons and other vessels of transitional M. M. Ill L. M. I date. This base in its fuller form as indicated, for example, on two more or less

Evi- dence of their ap-

Walls.

FIG. 504.   BULL-HUNTING SCENES ON SEAL-IMPRESSIONS, a AND b SHOWING TRIPLE GRADATION BELOW, (a, l, c, ZAKRO HOARD; d, M. M. Ill b DEPOSIT, KNOSSOS) (f) contemporary sealings, Fig. 504, a and b, from the Zakro Hoard, shows a triple gradation, and the association in which this feature appears on tnese examples is of special importance since they belong to a series of types evidently taken from bull-hunting scenes that had already appeared on the Palace walls. Fig. 504, c, also from the same Hoard, which illustrates a similar episode, would doubtless have presented a similar graduated base had its lower part been preserved. 1 The same may be said of d, from the

The copies of the Zakro sealings, Fig. 504, a, , c, were specially executed for this work. The phototypes of them given in J. H. S., xxii, Pl. IX, 96, 97. and Pl. X, 123. do not bring out some of the details. Pl. X, 123, which answers to Fig. 504, a, is described in the

M. M. Ill b Depositof the Entrance to the Corridor of the Bays at Knossos, but which in style as well as subject so closely resembles the foregoing. With it was found another fragmentary seal-impression of the same class showing a fallen Cow-boy beneath the bull. 1 In both these cases the bulls display the flying gallop characteristic of Minoan Art. 2

The threefold stepping up of the base in these designs has a particular significance in this connexion. It answers in fact to a characteristic feature of the cornices and pilasters, which, in view of some surviving pieces of evidence we may assume to have regularly supported the friezes of painted stucco reliefs on the walls of the Knossian Palace. The bull-grappling scenes Triple on the sealings shown in Fig. 504 have taiter? " indeed a special relevance since the from s " p"

"ports of existing data show 3 that such sub- friezes, jects, anticipating the scenes on the Vapheio Cup, were already executed in plastic form during the earlier phase of M. M. III.

On the bezel of a gold plated ring Ring type from the Lower Town of Mycenae, architec-Fig. 505, we meet with a related f 01

FIG 505. RtnG BEZKL SHOWING CATTLE exhibiting two couchant oxen,

ON ARCHITECTONIC BASE (MYCENAE), (f) and the double graduated base that here appears supplies an additional feature of interest in the present connexion. We

see here the indication of vertical painted bands, reminiscent of variegated stonework such as those with which the architectonic base of the Cow and Calf Panel, Fig. 3(57 above, is decorated, and which reappear on the supports of the Griffin Relief. The alternating order, moreover, in which these are distributed corresponds with a recurring convention of the borders of fresco panels such as some of those of the Taureador Series.

A bracket or console stepping back below in three different planes has Triple been illustrated above in connexion with the faience plaques from the sup ports E. Repository presenting animal reliefs. 4 More detailed evidence, however. came out in association with the painted stucco reliefs of griffins, ex hypdthesi derived from the great East Hall of the Palace of L. M. I construction, and it looks as if in this case, besides pilasters, there were continuous graduated text as a Goat in Course, the arm of the aero- of a double base is seen below, batic figure being interpreted as a goat's horn. See below p. 713 seqq.

1 Compare the fallen figure on the ring bezel See above, p. 375. Fig. 310, a, p. 432. In that case the outline See above, p. 512, Fig. 368.

THE PALACE OF MINOS, ETC.

supports beneath the groups, of the same triple formation (see Fig. 506). The fullest evidence is supplied, however, by the reliefs on the steatite rhytons, of obviously architectonic origin, exhibiting both bull-grappling and pugilistic

FIG. 506. SUPPORT WITH THREE GRADATIONS FROM GRIFFIN RELIEF, KNOSSOS.

FIG. 507. FRAGMENT OF STEATITE RHYTON, KNOSSOS.

FIG. 508. SECTION OF STEATITE RHYTON FROM H. TRIADA.

illustra- scenes. A fragment of such a rhyton, of grey steatite, from Knossos, partly steatite 0 " 1 completed in outline is given in Fig. 507. Here, beneath the prostrate rhytons. bull, j s an o blong block of a peculiar class, which serves the purpose of a capital. But beyond this, doubtless, in either direction extended the triply

M. M. Ill: SEAL TYPES AND GREATER ART 689 graduated base, which on the more perfect vessel from Hagia Triadaacts as support of the bull-grappling scenes.

The capital shown in Fig. 507 reappears on the columns which on the Columns parallel rhyton from Hagia Triada, of which a section is given in Fig. 508, recur at intervals behind and between pugilistic scenes on the zone immecli-ately below that showing the bulls and cow-boys. We may therefore infer that there was a similar disposition of zones on the Knossian specimen.

FIG. 509. BOXING SCENE AND PILLAR ON REPOSITORY SEALING, KNOSSOS.

FIG. 510. FRAGMENT OF STEATITE RHYTON, KNOSSOS.

In this connexion the Repository sealing, Fig. 509, has a special interest. We see here a highly athletic figure of a pugilist who has just knocked out his opponent, while behind is a similar column with part of another immediately superposed on the oblong block above it. This, as will be shown in a later Section of this work, corresponds with the structural arrangement of the Grand Stands' on either side of the Shrine on the Temple Fresco of Knossos, where pillars of the same peculiar character are depicted.

The Grand Stands' there enabled crowds of spectators to look on at agonistic contests held, no doubt, in honour of the great Minoan i Y y

Pugilists and column on Seal-impressions.

Column equivalent of Grand Stand or Theatre.

THE PALACE OF MINOS, ETC.

Goddess. Their insertion in these epitomized versions of the subject as seen on the rhytons and the gem impressions has thus a definite meaning. They are the symbols of the Minoan Theatre itself as a religious institution, just as the Doric or Ionic columns on Greek painted vases represent abbreviated indications of the Temple or Stoa.

FIG. 511. DEVELOPMENT OF THE Two LOWER ZONES OF STEATITE RHVTON FROM HAC; IA TRIADA.

Fragment of Knos-sian rhyton.

The attitude of the pugilist on the seal-impression from the Repository is practically identical with that seen on a small steatite relief, Fig. 510,: belonging to a rhyton, found in the North-East Palace region, and the scenes on which the splendid example from Hagia Triada enables us to complete. There is a square break over the forehead which might suggest a helmet, but the youth's head seems in this case to have been uncovered like those of the boy boxers on the lower zone of the Hagia Triada rhyton (Fig. 51 1). On the sealing, as in the other cases, the pugilist holds out the left arm for defence while the right is drawn back as if about to deal a blow. Boxing gloves 1 Knossos, Report, 1901, p. 95, Fig. 31, and sec Vol. II.

were used and a cestus was bound round the wrist, of which traces can be seen in Fig. 51 o. 1

The bent knee of a fallen opponent visible on the vase fragment, The immediately in front of the victor's left leg, is in much the same position as champion that of one of the defeated champions seen in the lower zone of the Hagia of lioxing Triada rhyton (Fig. 511), 2 which seems to depict boy boxers, in contrast with the helmeted men of the zone above. The youth in that case has been sent flying, with one leg in the air, by a knock-out blow and saves himself from performing a somersault, as in another case, by means of his left arm.

Till. Si KM OF ARMED COMBAT IN ARENA, ON SEAL-IMPRESSION FROM 11 v; i TUIAUA ().

FIG. 513. SCENE OK COMBAT IN. MOUNTAIN GLEN, ON Goi. n SK. NKI KIN; FROM IVrn SHAFT GRAVE, MVCF. NAE (f).

Sealinj,.

The shoulder of the fallen champion seen to the left of the standing figure on the Repository seal-impression (Fig. 509) may indicate a similar action.

These episodes drawn from the boxing ring present obvious points of t. iadia-comparison with the subject of a remarkable seal-impression from the Hagia g " r Triada hoard (Fig. 512).: i Here, again, between the combatants we see traces H. Triada of a pillar, which may reasonably be supposed to indicate that, in this case too, we have to do with an agonistic contest of the arena, and, like the spectacle with which the Temple Fresco was connected, under the immediate auspices of the great Minoan Goddess. Here, too, we see pairs of combatants arrayed against each other, and have the results in part outlined for us. But the contest here depicted is of a more deadly nature. The gladiatorial 3 Mon, Ant. xiii, p. 45, Fig. 41 and Pl. VI (No. 15 in the series). Two hadly preserved seal-impressions from . akro, Nos. 12 and 13, show scenes of combat with traces of a column behind. It is uncertain, however, if the contest is of the pugilistic or the gladiatorial kind.

1 Compare the sign, No. 8, Fig. 483, of the Phaestos Disk.

: See Halbherr, Memorie dei r. Istituto Lombardo, xxi, Tav. 2, Fig. 3. The photograph from which Fig. 511 was made is due to the courtesy of Prof. Halbherr.

THE PALACE OF MINOS, ETC.

Wounded champion supporting himself on one arm.

Scene of Combatants on Mycenae signet adapted from agonistic types.

crested helmet, traces of which are visible on the head of the champion on the right, is in this case fully in place, for it is clearly an armed combat, and his right arm is drawn back in the act of thrusting a spear at his opponent, who seems indeed to be already stricken.

The parallelism with the boxing scenes is, moreover, carried further by the figure of the fallen champion behind, here, too, supporting himself on an arm and with his head bent downwards. The attitude is instinct with pathos and manifests an artistic mood comparable with that which in a much later age produced the Dying Gaul. We shall see that it was not in this episode alone that Minoan Art in its greatest days anticipated the Pergamene spirit.

The seal-impression itself, like the parallel example from the Repository, was obviously taken from the elongated oval bezel of a gold signet ring and, though both are imperfectly preserved, the details visible show that the engraving of the originals must have been of the finest quality. It is therefore of special interest to note the points of comparison presented between the Hagia Triada impression and the subject of the more or less contemporary gold signet-ring presenting a scene of combat found in the Fourth Shaft Grave at Mycenae 1 (Fig. 513). 2 In both cases we have to deal with two pairs of combatants. In both cases, too, we see a protagonist striking an already half-fallen adversary, while behind is the prostrate figure of the wounded champion raising himself on one arm. On the other hand the points of distinction are equally marked. Except apparently for the crested helmet, the figures on the sealing are entirely nude, while on the ring they wear belts and loin-clothing of the bathing-drawers kind. The warrior there on the left, moreover, is protected by a shield of the arched, square-shouldered form. Still more significant is the scene of the combat. The pillar, indicative of the Minoan arena, is here wanting, and instead we see the borders of the field set round with rocks which may be taken to show that the fight is supposed to have for its scene a wild mountain glen.

None the less it is clear that the essential mechanism of the composition is taken over from that older Cretan artistic cycle which depicted the sports, gladiatorial or otherwise, held in honour of the Minoan Goddess. The dual group of combatants, the central episode of the fallen warrior painfully raising his body, protected by the protagonist all is there. It seems legitimate to recognize the work of some engraver in the Conqueror's train at Mycenae, inspired by the new Berserker fury of combat, foreign to the older spirit of the insular art though the details, such as the crested helmet

1 Halbherr, Man. Ant., xiii, already noted 2 This Figure was specially drawn for me the resemblance to the signet-ring from the by Monsieur E. Gillieron. IVth Shaft Grave.

and arched shields, are still of typically Cretan form. The episode in fact has transferred itself from the arena to become an illustration of true epic.

Of the crowded spectators on the Grand Stands of the Palace arena at Knossos, we have already had a glimpse, and a fuller illustration will be given of them in connexion with the Miniature Frescoes of the ensuing epoch. Of the spectacles themselves the acrobatic performances with bulls illustrations have come down to us from many sides, and from the vase reliefs and intaglios we see something of the contests between man and man, not only with the fists but with actual weapons. To the excitement of the Spanish arena was added the even more poignant human thrills of the Roman amphitheatre, and in a Society wrapped up in such fierce sports it can easily be imagined how the ladies of Knossos, who occupied the front seats at these shows, leaned forward in suspense over the fate of wounded heroes of the ring or applauded the prowess of fellow champions, the Seconds in these well-matched groups of antagonists, who strove to defeat and avenge their fallen comrades.

In the Minoan world of that day the victors in such martial sports must have been at least as famous as the noted toreros of Spanish Corridas. Such scenes moreover being thus artificially grouped and separated off by this theatral arrangement of the duello it was comparatively easy to present an artistic record of these feats, which were by this means set in relief and brought home to thousands. But the mel e of actual war was very different, and Ultimate thus it seems to have come to pass that episodes already stereotyped in O f. linoan these spectacles of the arena were adapted to celebrate the prowess of l warrior chiefs, as on the Mycenae signet-ring. The characteristic feats of such on epic contests, perpetuated by these artistic records, were in due course reflected in the word-paintings of the bards, whose lays in turn preserved their tradition through the dark ages when their pictorial presentation was no longer possible. Thus when at a much later date these incidents of combat reappear, assimilated as to their essential outlines in the Homeric poems, we may haply trace exploits of heroes such as the Telamonian Ajax or Patroklos far back to the darlings of the Minoan arena. 1 1 I may refer to my remarks (J. H. S., xxxii, perpetuated in a Greek form, just as those ot 1912, p. 291 seqq.)on the illustrations of epic epi- the F. teocretans such as we know them from sodes supplied by Minoan and Mycenaean Art. Diodoros or from the recently discovered Dik-It is there assumed that on the Mainland side taean Hymn of the Kouretes (B. S. A. xv, there was a survival of the older ethnic element p. 340 seqq.) were transferred to the Greek-such as we know to have been the case in Crete, speaking population of Crete. Both as recorded This would have passed (like the other) through by Diodoros (v. 70-80) and as voiced in the a bilingual stage before becoming definitely Hymn, the traditional objects of the native Hellenized. In this way traditions and even religion, in the island, were Minoan in lays of the old stock would have been ultimately character.

THE PALACE OF MINOS, ETC.

FIG. 514. ACROBATIC SCENE OF BULL-RING FROM CLAY SEALING OF TEMPLE REPOSITORY (f).

may infer from the above seal-types and the parallel representations ring taken on the rhytons, that by the closing epoch at least of M. M. III the representa-frescoes llons of pugilistic and perhaps of armed gladiatorial contests were already or reliefs, executed in larger works of art parallel with those concerned with the hunting and grappling of wild or half-wild bulls. Another sealing from the

Repository indeed, Fig. 514, anticipates a thrilling episode of what should rather be regarded as a kind of Circus' scene of the latter class more fully illustrated by one of the Taureador Frescoes, which themselves are not earlier than the later phase of L. M. I. A youth is here seen, as on the wall-painting, turning a back somersault from behind the bull's neck to be caught behind by another figure, perhaps, as there, of the female sex.

That we have here the imitation of a slightly earlier example of one of these scenes such as were executed in the flat fresco technique seems highly probable. The influence of certain architectonic features connected with such panels is indeed unmistakable on some of the intaglio types of the ensuing Period. A good example of this is supplied by the gem-impressions visible on a series of clay nodules found in the Royal Tomb at Knossos, 1 where a bull appears above a frieze consisting of pairs of horizontal lines, which serve as the borders of a band presenting a succession of linked spirals (Fig. 515). This answers in fact to the typical L. M. I decoration of the Later Palace as seen in the Domestic Quarter, where a similar frieze containing linked spirals and rosettes runs above

FIG. 515. SEAL-IMPRESSION FROM ROYAL TOMB, KNOSSOS, WITH SPI-RAL DADO BELOW (f).

FIG. 516. CLAY SEAL-IMPRESSION, PALACE, KNOSSOS, WITH DADO (f).

1 Prehistoric Tombs of Knossos, pp. 154, 155, Fig. 138.

the plaques of the gypsum dadoes. In a basement near the Stepped Porch of the Central Court of the Palace was found the lower part of a clay seal-impression on which three warriors, with the Minoan 8-shaped shields, are depicted as if on the march above a similar dado band with the same spiral decoration, Fig. 51G. 1 We may here trace the reflection of a processional fresco of this kind on the Palace walls.

In the recumbent ox, Fig. 518, c, with his head turned away from the spectator, we have apparently an excerpt from a Cattle-piece which about this time seems from its constant repetition to have attained a considerable vogue. A fuller type is illustrated by the banded agate lentoid shown in Fig. 517; d in this a second ox is shown in front as if in the act of rising. It is interesting to note that two lentoid intaglios from the Vapheio tomb present almost exact replicas of this design, so much so that they may be regarded as coming from the same workshop. In all three cases, moreover, we see the same significant stepped base, here consisting of a double gradation. 4 The lower limits of the Vapheio tomb, as appears from the associated pottery, are L. M. I b, but the fragments of three sealings. in a fine large style, from the Bays Entrance Deposit at Knossos, enable us to carry back a variant of this type, in which the head of the animal behind is seen more in profile, to the closing phase of M. M. III.

Among other subjects of natural inspiration that appear on the clay sealings of the Repository Hoard, the fragmentary specimen, Fig. 518, d, shows part of a group of a goat and kid, very freely treated. It almost looks like a scene of parturition. In c we see the heads of dogs or wolves, and in f four owls probably of the small species Carine Noclua still so abundant in Crete the bird of Athena. The marine subjects, the crab, g, the conch-shells, i, and symmetrically grouped cockles, , recall the contemporary 1 Cf. ring from cemetery at Phaestos with similar design shown (upside down) Mon. Ant., xiv, P- 593. "ig- 55-

Purchased in Athens, but its associations pointed to a Cretan source.

3 Ef. Apx-, 1889, PI. X, 9, 10. One is described as a sardonyx, the other as cornelian. On an agate lentoid from the Lower Town

Excerpts from (a a It-pieces in vogue.

FIG. 51". AGATE LENTOID (J).

Various types of Repository Sea-ings.

of Mycenae the front animal turns his head back (pp. cit., 1888, PI. X, 20). Other variants on gems point to a larger group of animals.

4 On a three-sided agate from the Pelopon-nese (Furtwangler, Antike Gemmtn, PI. Ill, 19, and Berlin Cat., No. 49 a) the double gradation is repeated beneath a similar design.

THE PALACE OF MINOS, ETC.

FIG. 518. CLAY SEAL-IMPRESSIONS FROM WEST TEMPLE REPOSITORY (f).

moulded reliefs in faience and terra-cotta. In , a pallium-like figure is combined with three looped motives of early derivation, since they appear on a painted pithos from Phaestos belonging to the closing phase of M. M II. 1 , with a border resembling conventional rocks and horizontal bars above crescent stands, is wholly enigmatic.

The nodding, tulip-like flower, , with its wavy stem, which looks as if it were taken from a group, suggests some such instantaneous expression of the painter's art as has been illustrated above by the Lily Fresco. It leads us to the still more remarkable design reproduced in Fig. 519, in which three leafless stems are seen bending before the breeze beside what may be taken to be rippling water. The eminently pictorial character of the last mentioned designs strikes the eye.

But of all the types here exhibited the most interesting is that of a man standing in a light skiff and repelling whether with oar or spear is not clear a dog-headed sea-monster who raises her head from the waves that boil around (Fig. 520). The whole scene incidentally calls up to us the Homeric picture of Skylla's surging waters round Odysseus' bark, that seethed up from the depths like those of a cauldron on a mighty fire: cay (v nvpl TToaXS

FIG. 519. STEMS ISKNT IN THE WIND. GEM-IMPRKS-SION, KNOSSOS (i).

The dog's head, though in a multiple shape, is associated with Skylla in later art. In the Odyssey she has already six heads. But that there was an earlier and simpler form is made probable by the fact that down to late classical times a sea-monster with a single canine head, the so-called pistrix, was still believed to haunt her fabled abode, and was, indeed, placed on his coinage by Gelon, as a symbol of the great sea victory over the Etruscans that gave him the mastery of the Sicilian Straits. 3 It is belonging to the early part of the seventh century B. C. On a specimen from Epidauros Limera, in my collection (Furtwangler, Ant. Gemmen, i, PI. VI, 34), it appears bentath the prow of a vessel. Compare, too, the sea-monster, half dog, half fish, on an Italic dinos'

(Pettier, Vases antiques du Louvre, i, PL 40, E, 42), and that (labelled KVTOT) from 1 Man, Ant., xiv, PI. XXXIV a.

2 Od. xii. 237, 238; cf. Knossos, Report, 1903, p. 58, Fig. 36.

:1 Head, Coinage of Syracuse, p. 10, and cf. Holm, Geschichte Siciliens, i, p. 572, and my Contributions to Sicilian Numismatics (Num. Chron., 1894, p. 12). This pistrix type appears already on gems of the Melian class Instantaneous impressions of nature.

Prototype of Skylla.

Pistrix of Sicilian Straits.

THE PALACE OF MINOS, ETC.

noteworthy that on some recently reconstituted fragments of what is now Sea-Mon-recognized to be a silver rhyton of pointed shape, from the Fourth Shaft Mycenae Grave, 1 amongst the naked swimmers who seem to be endeavouring to reach the land from some wreck, a dog-like head is seen emerging from the rhyton.

FK;. 520. PROTOTYPE OF SKYLLA ON SEALING FROM TEMPLE REPOS-ITORY (f).

FIG. 5211. SWIMMERS IN DEEP WATER: SILVER RHYTON.

FIG. 521 a. DOG-HEADED MONSTER L., AND SWIMMERS ESCAPING TO LAND: ON SILVER RHYTON.

waters (Fig. 521 a), another indication that a sea-monster of this form was reckoned in Minoan times among the terrors of the sea.- The shallow, rock-floored sea is here indicated by conventional scale-work such as that surrounding dolphins on a painted rhyton from Pseira. On the borders of which Theseus rescues Andromeda on an early Corinthian amphora (Man. d. Insl., x, PI. 52).

1 On this rhyton see my remarks in Vol. II

The monster's head approaching two curved objects on a painted stucco fragment from Mycenae.(E. Ap X., 1887, PI. XI, i) has also been associated with Skylla by Studniczka,

Skylla in der Mykenischen Kunst (Ath. Mitth, 1906, p. 50). But the curved objects are clearly horns of a Cretan wild goat or Agrimi, and show the usual knobs, while behind them is part of its ear. The monster's head in this case (which shows a real reminiscence of Thueris) is undoubtedly that of one of the beneficent Genii, common in the early part of the Late Minoan Age, leading the wild goat, just as others are seen leading bulls, cows, and lions on Cretan gems of that time.

the shallows is visible part of the coast-line of a point of terra firma with indications on it of a tree. For comparison another fragment, Fig. 5 21 6, is here shown, with victims of the disaster in deep waters.

The whole context of the fragments from the silver rhyton, more fully illustrated in a later Section of this work suggest an incident from some Epic Cycle of Minoan antiquity. The scene on the Knossian seal-impression of the beginning, at latest, of the Sixteenth Century B. C. is, itself fundamentally the same as that of which the Odyssey has preserved a more elaborate tradition. 1 The myth, it appears, from the scene on the rhyton, already followed Minoan mariners beyond the coasts of their native island and was perhaps already localized in the Straits by this time. The Greek conception of Skylla would in that case go back to the days of far earlier, Minoan ventures into Tyrrhene waters.

The compound types, so common at Zakro, find Com-analogies among the Knossian seal-impressions of this t yp es. time. A specimen of the curious grouping together of elements often heterogeneous is seen in the Repository specimen Fig. 52'2, a, where beneath a barred arching band we see a pair of antlers, an enigmatic object with four projections, and a kind of cap or pileus' such as frequently enters into the composition of the Zakro designs. Another remarkable illustration of this tendency, in this case clearly of religious significance, is FIG. 522 a 6. COM- supplied by a clay seal-impression from the M. M. Ill b POUND TVIKS ON stratum of the Court of the Stone Spout, Fig. 52'2, 6, where by linking the horns of a bull's head with cross lines the outline of a double axe is obtained in the simplest manner. It will be seen that the style of the engraving here seen exactly corresponds with that of facing bulls' heads coupled with other adjuncts which recur among the Zakro sealings, such as Fig. 5 25, d, below.

The parallelism observable between these and other types of the Corn-Repository seal-impressions with those of the great Zakro hoard may

SEAL-IMPRESSIONS FROM KNOSSOS (f).

1 See my remarks, Knossos, Report, 1903, p. 58, note, and on the pre-Homeric illustrations of Homer in Minoan and Mycenaean Elements in Hellenic Life, J. H. S, xxxiii, 1912, p. 287 seqq. The analogies there suggested are admitted by Pfister, Skylla (Roscht s Lexikon, p. 1035).

Zakro

Seal types.

be taken to establish a general contemporaneity between the two deposits.

It will be seen from an analysis of some of the most characteristic of

Mmoan-.

and early these Zakro seal-types that they represent a combination of living forms with

Egyptian elements.

a FIG. 523.

SEALINGS FROM ZAKRO SHOWING DECORATIVE MOTIVES OF EARLY DERIVATION.

decorative motives drawn, like the examples, p. 201, Fig. 150, above, from an earlier sphragistic cycle which was itself essentially due to Egyptian influence. The inclusion in the Hoard of certain sealings presenting hieroglyphic groups shows that some of the signets used dated in fact from the first two Periods of the Middle Minoan Age. Other types are clearly of early tradition. Thus the meander or labyrinth, a specimen of which from this Hoard has been already given, 1 perpetuates a Fourth Dynasty tradition. The cordiform patterns visible on Fig. 523, a, 6, recur in company with lateral scrolls on sealings from the Temple Repository, Fig. 524. 1 hese in turn betray connexions with the Middle Kingdom motive of the canopied papyrus symbol (was) that appears already on M. M. I signets. 2 The cruciform pattern on c runs parallel with oval types of the same design on Egyptian papyrus sealings of Twelfth and early Thirteenth Dynasty date 1 It is interesting to note, moreover, as a chronological index, that this pattern occurs in the same circular form as c on one of the early grave stones of the Shaft Graves at Mycenae. 4

FIG. 524. CORDIFORM PATTERN ON SEALING FROM REPOSITORY.

1 See above, p. 359, Fig. 260.

See above, p. 201, Fig. 150.

3 Cf. Petrie, Kahun, PI. X. 20; Illahun, c., PI. X. 176; Griffith, Historical Papyri from in a later Section of this work. Kahun (ib.), pp. 47 seqq., and compare the M. M. II signet, Scripla Minoa, i, p. 141, Fig. Compare, too, Fig. 491, f, above.

4 Illustrated with other comparative material

Middle Minoan Elements of the Zakro Settlings; Fantastic types consant variation to baffle forgers; Fancy thus called into play rapid transformation of types; Humorous and Demonic creations; Horned Imp on Earlier signet Axe-winged Goblin on Melian pots; Underlying Egyptian motives talis-manic Value of Waz symbol; Bats and Butterflies wings winged symbol on M. M. II prism seal; Fantastic forms with birds' wings Creatures of Fancy rather than Religion; Did they become themes of Myth? Mythical accretions to ivinged figures of Minoan creation; Melian revival; Winged Types appropriate to Age of Daedalos; Winged forms in Crete and Xllth Dynasty Egypt; Prototypes of Griffin Hawk-headed Lions of Bcni-Hasan; Egyptian Seraphim and Cherubim; Early Egyptian Griffins with Hawk's head and Minoan derivations; Minoan Griffins in Flying Gallop; Crested Eagle-headed type; The Egypto-Minoan Griffin Peacock 's plumes of Late Minoan forms; Galloping Griffin type traced to M. M. II; The Flying Galop in Art introduced into Egypt from Crete; Examples on Queen Aah-hotep's Dagger-blade; Flying Gallop on M. M. Ill Sealings and Mycenae blades-parallel representations; The Flying Leap on Cretan Seals Recurrence on Hyksos Dagger-hilt; Engraved M. M. II dagger-blade illustrations of Flying Gallop; Fighting Bulls and Boar-hunt; The Boar-htint in Minoan Art; Converging evidence of Minoan character of Mycenae relics Arms and Goldsmith's Work.

THE evidence given in the preceding Section leads to the general Middle conclusion that the Zakro Deposit, though it contains elements belonging Elements to the early part of the Late Minoan Age, distinctly overlaps the Middle Minoan borders. Considerably over fifty per cent, of the Zakro types belong to a remarkable class which stands altogether apart from the Late Minoan Fantastic tradition. These designs, executed in a bold free style, exhibit a succession of fantastic and monstrous forms, one derived from another by a constant differentiation of details. The overlapping of types, shown by the occurrence in many cases of more than one on the same nodule, and the general similarity of style throughout, lead to the conclusion that we have not here a gradual evolution of forms of a more or less unconscious nature, accom-

THE PALACE OF MINOS, ETC.

Variation to Baffle Forgers.

plished in the course of a long period of years, such as we see, for instance, Constant in Celtic coin-types. Rather we have to do with the rapid and intentional variation of a limited number of types a variation born of the wish to baffle forgers of seals. 1 Of the existence of such forgeries, indeed, we have an actual proof from the Knossian Palace, where, in addition to a series of impressions apparently from a large gold signet ring, a baked clay matrix was found moulded on one of these. In this connexion, indeed, it is interesting to observe that No. 3 of the Zakro series is a replica of this Knossian signet.

Fancy thus called into Play.

Rapid Transformation of Types.

FIG. 525. FANTASTIC EVOLUTION OF TYPES ON ZAKRO SEALINGS (f).

The utilitarian impulse that seems to have been at work was very effective in bringing out the latent ingenuity of the engravers in evolving one type from another. The playful fancy here shown in calling to life mere decorative details, and the daring power of combination at times of the most incongruous elements afford illustrations of the individual spirit and changing moods of the Minoan artists as in no other department of his craft.

The types shift and transform themselves like the phantoms of a dream. A facing sphinx takes shape again as a winged cherub with lion's feet (1-ig. 525, a). 2 But, hey presto! the new impersonation in turn dissolves Cf. Hogarth,. H. S., xxii, p. 91. See, too, tail-piece of Section, p. 721.

itself. The wings remain, but the head is reduced to a mere loop, and the feathered breast converted (into a bucranium Next, the skull between the wings clothes itself with flesh and blood, and becomes the horned, facing head of a bull (c. But this undergoes a fresh transformation. The wings disappear; bestial heads grow from the horn-tips, and boar's tusks protrude from the steer's mouth (f). And so, on this and parallel lines, the metamorphoses proceed.

The incurved border of a butterfly's wing suggests the points of an antler; the antler naturally calls up a stag's, head, and to this are added human arms and a woman's breasts (Fig. 525, e). Sometimes we detect a grim humour, as where a Minotaur appears to be devouring his own hand (Fig. 525,), and there is quite a demoniac touch in the grinning head of a Minoan Puck Jooking out beneath a canopy formed of bat's or butterfly's wings (Fig. 525,-).

Already, on a chalcedony seal-stone of the early signet type, we find evidence of the same spirit in the appearance of a horned imp with upraised hands (Fig. 52(5). So, too, at Melos, which stood betimes in sympathetic relation with Cretan life we see on the same class of high-beaked vases that show the bird-like imitation of the Griffin in its earliest shape a series of grotesque creations, Fig. 527, c, d., mainly consisting of winged heads with goggle eyes, a grinning mouth, and high-set ears. 2 These cherubic goblins have, however, a small, tail-like body provided with clawed limbs. The wings themselves are suggested by the pairs of hatched triangles, joined at the apex, which form so prominent a feature in Early Minoan ceramic decoration and which in the succeeding Age are merged in the sacral type of the Double Axe. From a comparison of the winged motive shown in Fig. 527, 6, from a vase of the same Melian class with a form of the Double Axe symbol on a sealing from the Hieroglyphic Deposit at Knossos, Fig. 527, a, 4 the derivative character must in this case be placed

FIG. 526. HORNED IMP ON M. M. II SIGNET, MOCHI. OS.

Humorous and Demonic Creations.

Horned Imp on Earlier Signet.

Winged Goblins on Melian Tots.

Kvnlvcd from figures of Double Axes.

1 Seager, Mochlos, p. 58, Fig. 27, and cf. p. 274, above. From the mile character of the engraving and the simple form of the signet it is possible that it may come within the limits of M. M. I.

2 For c and d of Fig. 527 compare Jhyakopi, Pl. XIV, 6, 6c, and 9. The figures are here partly completed 1. wing and part of body of a; the evidence of 6 b and 6 c combined. A parallel to these goblins is seen in the winged serpentine figure (op. fit., p. 112, Fig. 8 4 X

Op. cit., Pl. XIV, 3. The lower eye is completed.

1 Scrifita Minoa, i, Pl. Ill, p. 70 A.

THE PALACE OF MINOS, ETC.

Underlying Egyptian Motives.

beyond a doubt. We see here the oval knob of the Axe and its forked base symmetrically converted into a pair of eyes, vertically set, which turned round-about have given the suggestion of the goggle-eyed faces. These goblin vessels were found associated on a house floor at Phylakopi with imported M. M. II polychrome ware 1 of the finest egg-shell fabric, and belong to an epoch of intensive intercourse between Minoan Crete and Melos. The anthropomorphization of the Double Axe that they illustrate is on all fours with the appearance of the bird griffin on similar vessels. An analysis of these seal-types emphasizes the fact, already noted, that certain Egyptian elements lie at the root of many recurring features in the

FIG. 527. EVOLUTION OF WINGED GOBLIN TYPE: a, DOUBLE AXE SYM-BOL, SEALING, KNOSSOS (M. M. II); b, MELIAN ADAPTATION; c, d, GOBLIN TYPES ON MELIAN VASES (M. M. II).

designs. Some geometrical types of Egyptian association occur, indeed in an unadulterated form, as in the case of the examples given in Fig. 523 above. Once more we find, among the elements from this source, a con-: spicuous place occupied by the waz (wz) or papyrus stem symbol, which,

Bu"o. as we have seen, had already made its appearance on Cretan seals of the First Middle Minoan Period. 2 The was itself, signifying green or flourishing, 3 was the special symbol of the Goddess Wazet (Buto), and is placed on scarabs, as already noted in connexion with the Snake Goddess, 4 Its Talis- with a definite amuletic intention. On the Cretan seals, where it is of very early appearance, 5 it may originally have been borrowed with some vague sense of its talismanic value. That the symbol of the Delta Goddess should find a ready currency in Zakro, indeed, is easily intelligible when its special geographical aspect is considered. Its harbour, to-day a favourite place of call for the Aegean sponge fishers in Libyan waters, would have manic Value.

D. Mackenzie, Phylakopi, p. 260. The

See F. LI. Griffith, Hieroglyphs, p. 28, information as to the character of the fabric Fig. 125. Under the New Kingdom waz is due to a subsequent communication from appears as a sign of the North Country.

Dr. Mackenzie.

2 See above, p. 201, Fig. 150.

4 See above, p. 509.

5 See above, p. 201, Fig. 150.

been a most convenient staple of traffic with the mouths of the Nile, and some kind of customs station may have been established here in Minoan times.

The diagrammatic sketches in Fig. 528 will give some insight into the manner in which the waz symbol, or conventionalized papyrus spray, as seen on Twelfth Dynasty scarabs coupled with a double scroll, became the starting-point for an elaborate series of types of the Zakro series in which eyed butterflies' wings play a part. In c, the suggestion of

Xll. h Dyn. Egyphan

Zakro N?72 Suggestion of Butttrf ty.

Zaire N l 89

FIG. 528. THE EGYPTIAN WAZ SYMBOL BETWEEN SCROLLS AND MINOAN DERIVATIVES.

abed FIG. 529. BATS AND EYED BUTTERFLIES WINGS ON SEAL TYPES (a-c. ZAKRO, d. KNOSSOS) (f).

butterflies' wings is already clear, though the scrolls themselves depict stellate flowers on curving stalks. In other frequent cases terminal circles formed by these twin scrolls are converted into women's breasts. Often, too, lotus or papyrus tufts turned upside down call up the idea of birds' tails, or are impressed into the design as wings.

That some of the wings represented are those of bats is made probable i by the curious design of the hindquarters of an animal seen in Pig. 529, a. flies More frequent are those of a butterfly with eyed and strongly cusped wings, x which plays a prominent part in the Minoan repertory of this and the succeeding Periods, and may well have had a religious significance. It takes a conventional and generalized form, but seems to be for the most i z z

THE PALACE OF MINOS, ETC.

Winged Symbol on M. M II Prism Seal.

Wings of Birds.

part based on the common peacock butterfly, though at times it suggests an eyed hawk moth. 1 In Fig. 529, b, wings of this class are combined with a boar's-mask. In c, however, they are gracefully associated with a type of sphinx, and perhaps convey a symbolic meaning. On a sealing from the Little Palace at Knossos (d four butterflies' wings with eyes perhaps suggested by the Eye of Horus- are combined into a decorative figure. It is clear, however, from the representations of eyed Icpidoptera on the gold plates from the Third Shaft Grave at Mycenae where they occurred in company with mature L. M. I vases that these butterfly types considerably overlap the early part of the Late Minoan Age. It has seemed preferable therefore to reserve the fuller consideration of this interesting motive, as well as of the Sacred Eye, to the Second Volume of this work.

In Fig. 530 is shown a remarkable decorative motive taken from a four-sided bead-seal recently discovered in Crete 3-and which stands in an obvious connexion with those given in Fig. 529, though it is here turned the other way up. The seal itself bears hieroglyphic groups of the advanced Class, B, and represents the acme of the M. M. II engraver's art. In the expanding object which forms its central feature must be recognized the upper part of the waz or papyrus wand more fully shown in Fig.

528, a and b, but here placed upside down. On each side of it we already see the twin stars of the butterfly tradition as illustrated by Fig. 528, c, and Fig. 529, b. Of special interest moreover are the two lateral appendages which spring on either side from the central stem and give the appearance of recurved wings of an upward flying bird, for which indeed the expanding stem below might supply the tail. 4 This example is of great importance as showing that the decorative antecedents of what in this case might be taken for birds' wings go back in Crete to the great days of the M. M. II Palace.

More than half of the wings of these fantastic creations are, in fact, those of birds. Their formation has nothing to do with the sacral scarab form of Egypt 0 At times they show an upward curve at their tips, but they are the natural wings of birds with long terminal quills.

FIG. 530. WINGED MOTIVE ON M. M. II HIEROGLYPHIC BEAD-SEAL.

1 See Vol. II.

2 Compare, too, the divine eye on a Minoan signet ring. See Vol. II, and The Tomb of the Double Axes (Archaeologia, Vol. Ixv), p. 10, Fig. 16.

3 See above, p. 277, Fig. 207, c. 1 Compare Fig. 531, d. 5 Cf. Hogarth, Zakro Settlings, J. H. S., xxii, PP- 92. 93-

The great majority of the winged figures illustrated on these seals do not stand in relation to any extraneous types of a religious character. The motives of security to which the perpetual variation of these seal-types was due make it unnecessary, with the exception of some special cases, to read into their origin a religious intention. The cherubs with lion-like hind legs, the winged goat-men and goat-women (Fig. 531, a, b, c), the crane with woman's breasts (rt 1), the winged bull (g) and the eagle with woman's creatures flounces () et hoc genus omne are pure monstrosities, and belong to of F " nc no cult. They are entirely creatures of fancy, and have not, like the ligion.

FIG. 531. WINGED CREATIONS ON ZAKRO SEALINGS (f).

daemons that appear on seals and other objects of the Late Minoan Age, an inherent sanctity in that case, it would seem, taken over, together with certain definite religious functions, from the Egyptian Hippopotamus Goddess.

It must not, however, be forgotten, that accidents of artistic invention Did they or of special technique have often produced types to which, later on, mythical c e s attributes have accreted themselves. Certain compound monsters common of Myth? to pre-dynastic Egypt and to a very early Cretan cycle have been already traced back to the crossed figures of early cylinders. The Minotaur himself makes his first appearance in their company. Were, then, the winged creations of the Minoan seal-engravers, such as we see them on the Zakro. nodules, an entirely sterile brood?

THE PALACE OF MINOS, ETC.

Mythical Accretions to Winged Figures.

in certain types

Melian Revival ofwinged Seal-Types.

Scarab Wings of Egyptian Origin.

Though the winged sphinx of Minoan creation perpetuated itself, its fellow type, the sphinx with butterfly wings, does not seem to have secured the permanence that its beauty certainly deserved. But the type with the wings and head of an eagle added to the body and skirt of a woman (Fig. 531,) continued to be repeated in Crete to the latest Minoan phase and some mythical accretion may well have accumulated round it. The kindred design in which the head of a bird of prey is coupled with women's breasts and a spreading tail (Fig. 531, e) might well stand mutatis mutandis for the prototype of the Classical Harpy.

That wings as an attribute of divinity survived to the end of the Minoan Age is shown by the existence of a L. M. Ill intaglio 1 in which the great Cretan Goddess is seen with what appear to be short wings proceeding from her shoulders, between two confronted griffins. The sphragistic revival that took place five centuries later, and in which Melian craftsmen played a principal part, is marked by the appearance of a variety of winged figures pegasi, winged goats, lions and sea-horses, Gorgons, and other daemonic or semi-divine forms.

That the winged goat type 2 was anticipated in Minoan times is shown by a remarkable agate lentoid found near Kydonia (Canea) and here reproduced in Fig. 532. 3 What appears to be a male divinity, nude except for his girdle, is here seen above the Sacral Horns. Behind him a Minoan Genius, of the Ta-urt family, holds an ewer for libation, while, in front of the sacred personage, a winged goat raises himself on his hind-legs, as a kind of supporter. Here we see this winged animal type in a clearly religious association. The gem itself may be referred to the close of the First Late Minoan Period.

How far other of these winged creations may be ultimately traced to Minoan sources would require a special investigation. But the upcurved ends

FIG. 532. GEM SHOWING MALE DIVINITY, WINGED GOAT AND MINOAN GENIUS.

1 On a haematite lentoid from W. Crete (Coll. A. E.).

2 Winged goat types, but with the lower part of the body both of male and female sex, with bathing drawers' and flounced skirt respec- tively, are seen on the Zakro sealings, op. at., Nos. 12 and 13.

3 Here for the first time illustrated, with the owner's kind permission.

of the wings, and traces of the wing covers of scarabaeiis sacer, visible in many of the Melian types, show at any rate that they are thoroughly transfused with Egyptianizing oriental influences.

The first appearance, at the epoch with which we are now concerned, 1 winged of a series-of winged types, the wings of which are of purely natural formation, is in any case a phenomenon of the greatest interest. There is, priatcto indeed, a curious felicity in the circumstance that at the epoch in which

Minoan arts and crafts attained their highest development the formative Age of the New Palaces, specially associated by later tradition with the activity of Daedalos the air, so to speak, should be full of wings!

The diffusion of winged forms on these Cretan seal-types must to inged a certain extent. be brought into relation with a tendency already visible in

Twelfth Dynasty Egypt. The motive from a M. M. II hieroglyphic signet Twelfth illustrated in Fig. 530 above shows winged appendages associated with an Egypt. outgrowth of the familiar papyrus wand. The winged Griffin, as we have seen, had already acclimatized itself in Minoan Crete at an epoch contemporary with the Middle Kingdom, and in the case of this monster the most important of all the bird-winged forms that appear on this contemporary group of sealings a direct indebtedness to Egyptian suggestion cannot be denied. Already, among the fantastic forms of monsters that haunted the Proto-desert wastes, such as they are depicted on the Twelfth Dynasty tomb-paintings of Beni-Hasan, we recognize the prototype of Griffins of both sexes. The male monster labelled Sere, Fig. 533, A, is in fact a lion with the head of a hawk, and with two wings symmetrically expanded on its back. The female form Saia (Fig. 533, B). also hawk-headed, had the body of a lioness, Hawk-and, being a female, threatened to produce other monsters as horrid as itself, with a facility unknown to ordinary hybrids'. 2 Its wings are folded at "eni-its side, its tail ends in a full-blown lotus, and it wears a collar with a long spike in front.

The suggestion has been made on more than one side that this winged Egyptian Egyptian monster, which guarded tombs, and appears on the spear of Kames pht and (Fig. 533, c) as the champion of the Pharaoh, betrays in its name Sere as well 9 hcru- as its attributes a relationship with the Hebrew Seraphim. 3 It is certainly a curious coincidence that the Sere should be associated on the walls of one 1 The winged goblin 'types on Melian vases Sir Gardner Wilkinson, The Ancient associated with M. M. II. sherds point to the Egyptians, vol. iii, p. 312 (isys ed.) Cf., too, existence in that island of fantastic winged types vol. i, p. 93, Fig. 358. 5. at least before the close of that Period. See Tompkins, cited by Cheyne, Encyclopaedia below, p. 711, Fig. 535 Bimica, s. v. Seraphim.

THE PALACE OF MINOS, ETC.

of the Beni-Hasan Tombs with another monster that presents an obvious parallel with the mysterious Cherubim of later tradition. This is represented in the form of a leopard, with spotted body and banded tail, exhibiting similarly set wings, between which rises a male head (Fig. 533, D). The head here is in profile, but the similarity of the conception to the Zakro sealing

Xll T f DYN BCNI-HAiaN.

EGYPTIAN CHERUB BENI HASAN

SACRED HAWK. E

X. IITI1 DYN.

GRIFFINS HEADS(F. G)

M ELIAN VERSIONS O K

M. M. III. PERIOD. MINIATURE FRESCO L-M-j

FOREPART OF MINOAN GRIFFIN, MYCENAE. M. M. Ill

FIG. 533. EGYPTIAN HAWK-HEADED GRIFFINS AND MINOAN DERIVA- TIVES.

showing the Cherubic facing head between bird's wings and with pard's 2 or lion's legs below, is in any case very remarkable. In this connexion the often repeated comparison between yaui and Kerub may well be recalled.

Early The fact that the earliest Griffin forms of Egypt have the head of

Griffin " a naw k: is of primary importance 1 The hawk there is the impersonation 1 This monster appears on Tomb III at Beni-Hasan. Fig. 533, D, is taken from Rosellini, Monumenti dellegitto, i, PL XXX.

1 The spots that appear on the Melian bird-griffin (Fig. 535) show that the pard as well as the lion entered at times into the composition of the Minoan Griffin.

3 Furtwangler, in his article Gryps', in J? oscher'slexikon, s'peak. s of the Egyptian Griffin as a lion with an eagle's head. Elements of the Sun, and hawks' wings are found attached to its sacred orb. The with species is supposed to be the sparrow-hawk, 1 and the arrangement and marking of feathers about its eyes suggested the lines that radiate from them in the sacral Egyptian versions (see Fig. 533, E). But, from the first, Minoan the Minoan artists in their adaptations of the Egyptian model converted

FIG. 534. GRIFFIN AT A FLYING GALLOP ON DAGGER-BLADE, MYCE-NAE.

FIG. 535. BIRD-GRIFFIN. ON MELIAN VASE OF EARLY MIDDLE CY-CLADIC III DATE.

these lines, which had some relation to natural features in their original form, into decorative coils that fall about the neck and spread along the lower part of the wings. The evidence supplied by the Melian ceramic design of the. beginning of the Third Cycladic Period, repeated in Fig. 533, i,.

., Griffins in clearly shows that these decorative coils were a characteristic of the Minoan Flying Griffin with the flying gallop that supplied its prototype, and which, as (already noted, is shown by the existence of this early derivative form to go up to within at least the lower limits of M. M. II. This elongated Griffin derived from the eagle became accreted to the Sacred Hawk later, but there is no trace of these in the earlier types.

1 F. Ll. Griffith, Bent-Hasan, iii (Hieroglyphs), p. 7.

THE PALACE OF MINOS, ETC.

Crested Eagle-headed Types.

type appears on a gold plate J and on a sword 2 and dagger-blade:! from Mycenae, and the latter example which must be regarded as more or less contemporary with the Melian vase motive, Fig. 535, is here set beside it. It seems probable that in the original design the Melian potter had before him a Griffin with a curlier tail. The spots on the body show, moreover, that the Minoan prototype in its reproduction of the foreign monster had combined something of the leopard with its leonine elements. A pard-like monster appears, as we have seen (Fig. 533, D), in the Egyptian series.

Seated Griffins of the same kind, in opposed positions, occur on one of the sealings from Hagia Triada. 4 These, however, show traces of crests, and in the Zakro type, Fig. 536, a, we see this feature, which characterizes all later forms of the monster, already fully developed. It seems to have been

FIG. 536. OPPOSED GRIFFINS ON CLAY SEAL-IMPRESSIONS (a, b, ZA-KRO; c, KNOSSOS).

suggested by some form of crested eagle and at the same time the appearance of the head and beak as thus portrayed in Minoan art is that of an eagle rather than a hawk. This aspect of the Griffin, it will be observed, as well as the crest, recurs with other Minoan characteristics the decorative coils and the notched plumes of the wings on the axe found in Queen Aah-hotep's coffin, bearing the name of her son King Aahmes, the first King of the Eighteenth Dynasty. 5 On the other hand the Griffin depicted in gold inlay on the two-handed sword c of his predecessor, King Kames, here for the first time illustrated in detail (Fig. 533, c), is of the severe hawk-lion type. The monster, impersonating Mentu, wears the White Crown, or Atef, of Osiris and Upper

Egypt, with horns as well as plumes, and, as 1 Schliemann, Mycenae, p. 182, Fig. 292.

Athens Museum, No. 748. Cf. Furt-wangler, art. Gryps', J? ost: her'sle. vion, p. 1745. The griffins are in relief.

3 Kumanudis, AOyvdiov 10, p. 316 and Plate.

4 Mon. Ant., xiii, Pl. V, No. 9.

6 See above, p. 551, Fig. 402.

c Described as a spear-head in Archaeo-logia, vol. liii, 1892, p. i seqq., and see Pl. I, Fig. 3 For its true character see P. E. New-berry in Burlington Fine Arts Club Cat., 1921, p. 99 (Q. 29). The original (from my Father's collection) is in my possession.

protector of its native dynast, beloved of Ra, he lays his left paw on the kneeling figure of the conquered Hyksos.

This substitution of the Eagle's head for the Hawk of solar cult, as much as the intrusion of the other Minoan elements such as the notched plumes', into the composition of the sacred monster on so important a relic The itself implies a reaction of Cretan influence on Egypt of the most profound Minoan" and intimate character in the early days of the New Empire. The Griffin Cmffin-type of King Aahmes can only be described as Egypto-Minoan.

Both in Crete and Egypt many later Griffins bear peacocks' plumes and Peacocks' such are already seen at Knossos in the fresco fragment in the Early L. M. I of" " miniature style, illustrated in Fig. 400 above. They appear, still more M noan clearly, issuing from the head of the couchant and wingless Griffin of the Room of the Throne, belonging to the latest period of the Palace. A softer spirit breathes indeed in these decorative types, and there is little left either of the hawk or the eagle.

On the Zakro seal-impression, Fig. 530, 6, we see a more decorative rendering of two fore-parts of Griffins, showing a protuberance above the beak which seems to be an anticipation of the knobbed projection in this position so characteristic of early Greek representations of this monster. 1 The clay impression, Fig. 536, c, from Knossos,2 supplies a variant of the scheme of two confronted griffins that we see in Fig. 536, a, b. In this case, however, the details of the design are imperfectly preserved.

The evidence, at once stratigraphic and typological, that enables us to assign the Melian jug with the fantastic bird griffin to the earliest phase of the Third Middle Cycladic is of the highest importance in relation to the artistic scheme represented by the Minoan design to which it stands in a derivative relation. It compels us in fact, as already noted, to project Galloping the Minoan motive of the galloping Griffin with his legs at full stretch Type" within the limits of M. M. II. The artistic convention for rapid motion t a ", d " which this design embodies, as illustrated by the Mycenae example. Fig. 534, is that distinguished by Monsieur Salomon Reinach as the flying gallop, The the chief distributing centre of which, as he has shown in the later pre-Gallop " historic phase, at least, of the East Mediterranean basin was Minoan Crete. m Art From this Aegean source it was diffused through a large part of the Ancient World passing to Egypt and from the Anatolian coast to Persia and ultimately reaching China and the Far East. 3 1 See Furtwangler, op. tit., p. 1759 seqq. Domestic Quarter.

; Found with other early seal-impressions La representation du galop dans 1art underneath the later Service staircase of the ancien et moderne (extract from Rei: Arch., Introduced to Egypt from Crete.

Queen Aah-hotep's Dagger-blade.

The evidence now before us, supported, as we shall see, by other recent discoveries, that figures like the flying Griffin of the dagger-blade, Fig. 534, were already known in the Second Middle Minoan Period, contemporary with Twelfth Dynasty Egypt, is of capital importance in demonstrating the indebtedness of Egypt to Crete in this matter. It shows that this free representation of the gallop was already known to the Minoan artists at a time when, as a glance at the reliefs of the Beni-Hasan Tombs would alone be sufficient to demonstrate, their Egyptian contemporaries proved themselves wholly unable to depict any rapid form of animal movement. The beasts there depicted walk or amble and, even in the attitude of cantering, their legs are never lifted from the ground. Very different is the action seen on the Eighteenth Dynasty Theban wall-paintings where the spirit of free movement, including the flying gallop, has fully taken hold of Egyptian art. In Minoan Crete, as we now know, the liberating process had declared itself at least two centuries earlier.

The artistic device, by which the galloping animal is gracefully elongated, was doubtless due to the recurring need of adapting designs to somewhat narrow bands. Thus it was well suited to the blades or median ribs of swords and daggers, and is nowhere so finely represented as on those of the Fourth Shaft Grave at Mycenae, which must be looked on as imported Minoan works belonging to this epoch. A good example of this has been already given in Fig. 534, showing a galloping Griffin executed in relief on a contemporary Mycenae blade. So too, when later transported to Egypt, 1900-1901). M. Reinach suggests that the later vogue of the galop volant in Persia and China may eventually be linked up with its earlier Aegean home through Greco-Persian art, on which it is already found in the fifth century H. c. He admits the difficulty, however, of its non-appearance in Ionian Art. But a very late Minoan example may be cited in the carved ivory draught-box from Enkomi (. M. Excavations from Cyprus, Pl. I), where this motive is copiously illustrated, which serves as a link with the mainland Hittite Art, and is itself of Syrian ivory. A lion springing on a gazelle, that appears on a Cypriote bronze bowl from Nineveh (Layard, Monuments, S. n, Pl. 60; P. and C. i r, p. 743, Fig. 407) with his hind-legs extended, also reproduces the Minoan motive. So do the horses of Assurbanipal and of his followers in the hunting scene on the bas-reliefs of his Palace. It would seem probable therefore that it was from an Assyrian source that the motive was taken over by Greco-Persian Art, and that its survival in Cyprus may supply the missing link.

M. Reinach is of opinion that the appearance of this peculiar motive in Minoan Crete and certain parallel phenomena in Denmark and Central Europe may be ultimately connected with its much earlier existence in Magdalenian art. But there is no hint of any such flowing designs in the stiff, linear representations of animals in the earlier Aegean phases. I have here suggested that it may have had an independent birth in Crete due to the effort to fit animal figures in rapid motion into narrow bands such as the ribs of weapons.

we see this motive in its natural place on the engraved rib of the dagger-blade of Queen Aah-hotep, Fig. 5: 7. 1 The episode, here illustrated, of a lion chasing a bull at a headlong gallop is in a purely Minoan setting. The rocks above, in an inverted position with their outer border and granulated

FIG. 537. PART OF ENGRAVED DAGGER OF QUEEN AAH-HOTEP, SHOW-ING FLYING GALLOP MOTIVE IN MINOAN SETTING.

inner section, are those of the Cretan frescoes and vase paintings of the Middle Minoan Age. The details as well as the spirit of the design are indeed so purely Minoan that it is difficult not to conclude that this part of the engraving, and with it probably the grasshoppers beyond, was the work of a Minoan craftsman.

FIG. 538. INLAID DAGGER FROM FOURTH SHAFT GRAVE, MYCENAE.

On a larger scale, no doubt, the flying gallop motive was equally adapted to friezes of painted stucco reliefs or of fresco on the flat. Of these indeed we may see a reflection in the bull-hunting scenes of the Vapheio cups as well as on the intaglio designs derived from the same cycle. To some of these, bearing traces of their architectonic inspiration in the triple base below, attention has been already called above. 2 It will be seen that 1 From a photograph of the dagger-blade, kindly supplied me by Mr. C. C. Edgar, of the Cairo Museum. z See p. 686.

Flying Gallop on M. M. Ill Sealings and Inlaid Blades of Mycenae.

THE PALACE OF MINOS, ETC.

the outstretched figures of this class of designs need an elongated oval field such as that on which the fine Knossian example, Fig. 504, d above, is exhibited. Impressions of this form were probably made by the bezels of gold signet rings.

The Mycenae dagger-blade reproduced in Fig. 538 is a good example j ityy–.-.–.".
,

FIG. 539. a, b, FLYING GALLOP ON M. M. Ill SEAL-IMPRESSIONS; c, FLYING LEAP ON M. M. II HIEROGLYPHIC BEAD-SEAL; d, VARIATION OF SAME ON SEALING, HAGIA TRIADA; AND e, PARALLEL ON MYCENAE DAGGER.

of the flying gallop as applied to a scene in engrailed metalwork. It shows three lions chasing one another amid rocks, conventionally rendered on the upper and lower border of the field, as on M. M. Ill frescoes. A striking counterpart to this, as adapted to an oval field is supplied by the Zakro seal-impression. Fig. 539, a, 1 where two lions are seen side by side in the same headlong course with a rock border below, and a palm tree above. Nearly related to this is the finely executed design of a lion springing on the neck of a lioness which is the subject of fragmentary sealings found at 1 This and Fig. 539, b and c, were drawn for me by Mr. E. J. Lambert.

Knossos in the area of the Jewel Fresco (Fig. 539, 6). In this case again a rocky ground appears below.

An interesting parallel to this subject is presented by another fine example of the flying gallop or leap on a contemporary impression found in the Room of the Seals at Hagia Triada, of which a reproduction is given in

Fig. 539, d. Here is depicted the rapid course of two wild goats, the male apparently trying to seize the female while in the act of leaping. But the scheme exhibited by this latter example of animal marriage by capture corresponds in a remarkable manner with that on another of the Mycenae dagger-blades of a different purport indeed, in which a lion is seen springing on a dappled deer the spots here being indicated by crosses as on the Cow of Hathor (Fig. 539 e). 1 The action of the pursued animal with his hind-legs flung upwards as if he were leaping down, his forelegs bent under him and his head bent round on his flank, is practically identical.

That in these cases, as in the design of the hunted bulls on the Vapheio Cups, the craftsman, working within the domain of the minor Arts, drew his ultimate inspiration from larger models such as painted reliefs on the Palace walls is probable enough. In the successive groups on the dagger-blades and the epitomized excerpts on the signets we may even at times trace the division of these larger continuous compositions into separate panels. But it certainly would appear that the engravers of the signet-rings in precious metals, with whom we have here to deal, stood in still closer connexion with those who executed the designs on the exquisitely engrailed blades, to which, owing to the conditions of space, the subjects showing the flying gallop were specially appropriate.

The design repeated above, of the hunted animal in the act of leaping clown with his legs thrown backwards at full stretch must be regarded as a variant version of the full flying gallop motive in which the fore-legs are equally extended. That this version of the leap with all four legs at full 1 See above, p. 513.

Parallel tions-

FIG. 540.   GOLD-PLATED HYKSOS DAGGER-HILT, SHOWING FLYING LKAP.

THE PALACE OF MINOS, ETC.

stretch was already in vogue by the close of M. M. II is shown by its appearance on an agate bead-seal of the flattened cylinder type represented in Fig: 539 c, on the other face of which are engraved characters of the Hieroglyphic Class B. Here a dog seizes the springing wild-goat below and conventional rocks are seen to the left of the lower field. In this connexion it is of interest to note that this characteristic motive of Minoan Art, which

FIG. 541. a, b, ENGRAVED BRONZE DAGGER-BLADE WITH BOAR-HUNT AND FIGHT BETWEEN BULLS, SHOWING FLYING LEAP AND GALLOP (M. M. II). 2 begins thus early in Crete and was later reflected on the Eighteenth Dynasty its Recur- wall-paintings, may be traced back in Egypt to the flourishing period of the Hyksot Hyksos dominion. As will be seen from Fig. 540, the motive of the flying Dagger- l eap appears in the embossed design of a gold-plated dagger-hilt of the Hyksos King Neb-Khepesh-Ra 3 whom an inscribed vase in the British

Museum enables us to identify with Apepi I or Apophis, the predecessor 1 Scripta Minoa,, p. 157, P. 41 (cf. PI. II).;1 Daressy, Annales de Service, vii, p. 115.

2 From photographs kindly supplied me by Mr. C. C. Edgar, of the Cairo Museum, kindly its possessor. (See, too, Journ. of Mus, of obtained for me the photograph from which Pennsylvania, 19:4.) Fig. 540 is taken.

of Khyan in Manetho's list. 1 The owner of the dagger, described upon it as Nhiman, is there seen spearing a lion, 2 engaged in the pursuit of an antelope, who springs above him with his hintllegs thrown out behind, much as in the Minoan scheme of the flying-leap illustrated above.

It has been already pointed out that the misunderstood copy of a Melian vase-painter had transformed a Griffin under his Minoan aspect as engaged in a flying gallop into a long-tailed bird, at a time corresponding with the earliest M. M. Ill phase. This derivative form makes it certain, as we have seen, that the Griffin, as he thus appears on an embossed plaque ffom the Third Shaft Grave, was already known in Crete before the close Kngraved of M. M. II. But this archaeological result confirmed by the hieroglyphic bead-seal, Fig. 53), c which would carry back the flying gallop motive in l)lade the island to an epoch contemporary with the Twelfth or Thirteenth Dynasty, Crete. has received a remarkable confirmation from the hunting scenes on an engraved bronze dagger-blade recently discovered in the Lasethi district, possibly in the Psychro Cave itself, Fig. 541, a, b.

The tang of this blade has been broken away, but its upper part, which is provided with three rivets, shows two short flanges on either shoulder to grip the edge of the wooden handle. The form itself is interesting, since. except that the shoulders are slightly more sloping, it exactly corresponds with a type of short sword found in the annexe of the smaller ossuary tholos at Hagia Triada 3 the tang being in that case so far preserved as to show another rivet-hole. This type, as pointed out above, is probably contemporary with the later class of polychrome pottery found in this annexe, which belongs to about the middle of M. M. II. The date of the Lasethi dagger can hardly be brought down lower than the close of that Period.

One side of the blade exhibits a fight between two bulls, both at a flying The gallop, that to the right with his hind-legs thrown upwards as if he were leaping down, and recalling the flying-leap of the wild-goat on the signet-impression, Fig. 53J), c. above, and of the gazelle on the Mycenae dagger-blade. it The off front leg of this animal is curiously contorted. The sprays marked against the bodies of the animals must be understood as issuing from the ground and indicate that the encounter takes place in a bushy country.

On the other side is a boar-hunt. The boar charges again at a flying and gallop and is encountered by the hunter with a spear-thrust at his forehead, hunt. A tuft of sprays indicates the thicket from which he has broken. The 1 See H. R. Hall, The Ancient History of- The object held in the hunter's left hand the Near East, p. 216 and n. 2. In Manetho's is undoubtedly a throwing stick. version the name is lannas'. 3 See above, pp. 194, 195, and Fig. 14-' ft

THE PALACE OF MINOS, ETC.
Comparison with
Mycenae Daggers.
The Boar-hunt in Minoan Art.
Converging evidence 3 ofminoan character of Mycenae Relics.
Broadswords and Rapiers.

man is bare-headed with a lock of hair curling over his forehead. He wears the usual Minoan gaiters, but his belt and the arrangement of his loin-cloth are abnormal. The waist-band shows vertical stripes, and its outline behind is for some reason doubled and appears to have a triple flounce. Two curving lines run out from the belt in front, perhaps the strings by which it was tied. The spear has a curious cross-piece below the head, which itself looks like a square shouldered dagger-blade.

There can be little doubt that to bring out the effect of the designs some conspicuous material was inserted into the lines of the engraving. There is a great probability indeed that the material with which they were filled was gold wire hammered in, as for instance in the case of the lines, less deeply incised, on the spear-head of the Egyptian King Kames. In the roughly drawn but vigorous engrailed work of this early dagger-blade we would thus see the direct forerunner of the varied inlays and far more elaborate technique of the blades found in the Fourth Shaft Grave at Mycenae, in associations that belong to a mature phase of M. M. III.

The fragment of the gold plated rhyton showing the fore-part of a charging boar illustrated in Fig. 490 may belong to some boar-hunting scene of the same kind as that on the dagger-blade. 1

The presence among the earlier remains of the Mycenae Shaft Graves of pottery and faience inlays identical with those of the Temple Repositories at Knossos is in keeping with the close parallels above established by the comparative materials drawn from the great contemporary hoards of seal-impressions. The marvellous inlaid designs of the Mycenae dagger-blades are now seen to go back to the earlier and simpler technique represented by the example from Lasethi. This last-named specimen moreover and a similar dagger-form from Hagia Triada supply the antecedent stage to the broad-bladed swords of the Mycenae graves with their tanged shoulders. At the same time the rapier type of thrusting sword so well represented in the same sepulchral armoury, can also be shown to be of Minoan derivation. 2 In its fully developed shape it came to light at Knossos in a deposit by the Isopata Cemetery, in company with an inlaid limestone vessel of a characteristic class of which fragmentary specimens were found with the Khyan alabastron lid. These have been above referred to the penultimate phase of M. M. III. 11 1 For a wild boar on an E. M. ivory seal see Mosso, La Preistoria, i, 192, Fig. 102, d. It recurs as a type on the M. M. II lentoid, p. 275, Fig. 204, b. The swine signs, Nos. 69 and 70 of the Hieroglyphic signary perhaps refer to domesticated animals since they are followed by the gate or fence (Scripta Minoa, i, p. 208).

See Vol. II. 3 See above, p. 413.

Of this evidence and the corroborative data supplied by the goldsmith's; 11-ornamentation, the vessels in precious metals and many other relics of the ofk, c. Mycenae Shaft Graves, including the earlier Stelae themselves, more will be said in the opening Chapters of the succeeding Volume of this book. Here it may be sufficient to remark that, among all the objects evincing a high degree of artistic culture and civilized life brought to light in those royal sepulchres, there are few indeed not directly imported from Minoan Crete, and there is scarcely a single specimen of which the antecedent stages cannot be traced back on Cretan soil by a continuous line of descent from an immemorial past. Many of these objects were in all probability derived from Knossos itself and are unmistakably the products of the artistic school that grew up round the great Palace.

The religion and cult forms of its Priest Kings were in the same way introduced at Mycenae by the founders of the new Mainland Empire. The Great Goddess of Minoan Crete is still supreme. Her sacred doves still al M-perch on pillar shrines and altars, and, as a visible sign of possession, on the votaries themselves. On two remarkable seal-stones brought to light by the recent excavations of the British School at Mycenae, her guardian lions stand beside her as on the Palace seals of Knossos and she bears above her here combined with the sacred weapon the snakes that symbolize her Underworld dominion. The Goddess presides over similar sports, held in the same arena and overlooked by similar theatral stands'. With her too the principal cult object of Minoan divinity, the Double Axe, makes its appearance both in its liturgic shape and as a celestial emblem in the new centres of worship now founded overseas.

KM) OK VUI. UMK 1

PRINTED IN ENGLAND

AT THK OXFORD UNIVKRSITV PRESS

BY FRKDKRICK. HAL,

SUPPLEMKNTARV IlmF I a. THORN-BOSSED POLYCHROME TAZZA, M. M. II. (See pp. 239, 240.) b, FLUTED TOP OF M. M II.-FKI 11 Sr i SHOWING IXKI. I i NIK OK METAL-WORK. (Seepp.242, 243.)

SUII'I KMIMAKV II. ATK IV

M. M. II. POLYCHROME VASK AND EGVPTIAN RELICS KROXI ABVDOS TOMB. (J-.) (Seep. 268.)

SUPPLEMENTARY PLATE V.

KNOSSOS : HALL OF THE, COLONNADES:

SKl. TCII MILWISC, PRESENT COM1IT1OS 1TK PEBR19 Cl. r. AKJI) WV(ASH 1ITKK CROSS V LL

KS, WZMCAKP.

HALL OF COLONNADES. SKETCH MADE PREVIOUS TO FULL EXCAVA-TION OK C. RANM SIAIKCAK AND BEFORE RESTORATION OF SUPPORT-ING COLUMNS OF BALUSTRADE, iiv THKODORK FYKE. (See p 326.)

OUITl. r. ME. il 1

Si II'I. KMKMAKV II. All. IX.

SUPHLKMKNTAKY Pi I I X

PIIIAR OF EAST PILLAR ROOM. Kxoos. INUH WITH CORNKR OF STONE VAT TO LEFT. (See pp. 218 and 441.)

SUPtl EMKNTAKY II. ATK XI.

LONG CORRIDOR 01 Visr MAGAZINKS, LOOKING SOUTH: RIIMJK AXH IKAK OK

JIKTAS BEYOND (p. 448).

Lightning Source UK Ltd.
Milton Keynes UK
UKOW03f2132190514

231960UK00001B/56/P